THE ARCHAEOLOGICAL GAZETTEER SER

Archaeology in the City of London, 1907–1991

A guide to records of excavations by the Museum of London and its predecessors

Museum of London Archaeological Gazetteer Series

1 Archaeology in the City of London, 1907–1991: a guide to records of excavations by the Museum of London and its predecessors, eds. John Schofield with Cath Maloney

ISBN 0 904818 81 0

2 Archaeology in Greater London, 1965–1990: a guide to records of excavations by the Museum of London, eds. Alan Thompson, Andrew Westman and Tony Dyson

ISBN 0 904818 80 2

3 Post-War Archaeology in the City of London, 1946–1972: a guide to records of excavations by Professor W F Grimes held by the Museum of London, ed. John Shepherd

ISBN 0 904818 82 9

THE ARCHAEOLOGICAL GAZETTEER SERIES, VOLUME I

Archaeology in the City of London 1907–1991

a guide to records of excavations by the Museum of London and its predecessors

Edited by John Schofield
with Cath Maloney

Museum of London 1998

First published in Great Britain in 1998 by the Museum of London, 150 London Wall, London EC2Y 5HN

Copyright © 1998 Museum of London

Maps reproduced from Ordnance Survey mapping with the permission of The Controller of HMSO© Crown Copyright Licence no MC 88194M

The rights of John Schofield and Cath Maloney to be identified as author of this work have been asserted by them in accordance with the Copyright, Designs and Patents Act, 1998

British Library Cataloguing in Data. A catalogue record for this book is available from the British Library

ISBN 0 904818 81 0

Project co-ordination: John Shepherd

Editorial: Monica Kendall, Mandi Gomez and Katie Frederick

Design: Tracy Wellman

Typesetting and layout: Jeannette van der Post

Index: David Lee

Printed and bound by Valente UK

A complete catalogue of Museum of London publications is available on request. This book is published to coincide with the opening of the Museum of London Archive.

Front cover: an early 13th-century waterfront excavated on the Billingsgate Market lorry park site in 1982, standing to a height of two metres.

CONTENTS

ACKNOWLEDGEMENTS

This *Guide* is the result of the work of many people. The excavation directors are named at the head of each site entry; the funding organisations are credited whenever they are known. Virtually all excavations between 1973 and about 1980 were funded by the Department of Environment. After 1980, the Department, and from 1984, English Heritage, funded only exceptionally significant excavations: notably Billingsgate lorry park (BIG82) and Leadenhall Court (LCT84). The major part of publication work on all sites in 1973 to 1991 was paid for by English Heritage, with additional funds from developers and from the City of London Archaeological Trust. Developers funded the production of archive reports on excavations from about 1980 in certain cases, and generally from 1984 onwards.

The text of this *Guide* draws on summaries made for the Guildhall Museum sites by Peter Marsden and Charlotte Harding; and for the DUA sites on the annual summaries compiled first by John Schofield, Charlotte Harding and Tony Dyson, and later by Andrew Westman and Cath Maloney. The bibliographical lists in the DUA entries are an extension of early work by Gillian Dunn and Natalie Tobert; much new information has been supplied by Cath Maloney and Deborah Hedgecock of MoLAS. The parts of the Guildhall Museum entries which deal with Roman remains also draw on the summaries produced by Ralph Merrifield for his gazetteer (1965). Information on SMR numbers has been updated from earlier work by Alison Woodcock of English Heritage. For comments incorporated into the Introduction, I am grateful to John Clark, Francis Grew, John Maloney, Peter Marsden, Nick Merriman and Angela Wardle. Special thanks go to Monica Kendall who has worked tirelessly on copy-editing all three volumes. The photographs in this volume are by: Jon Bailey, Andy Chopping, Maggie Cox, Trevor Hurst, ?Frank Lambert, Peter Marsden, Ralph Merrifield, Ivor Noël Hume and Jan Scrivener.

The publishers would like to acknowledge the generous grants made by English Heritage and the Corporation of London towards this volume.

ABBREVIATIONS

AML	Ancient Monuments Laboratory (English Heritage)
BMNH	British Museum (Natural History)
c	century or centuries
c	circa
CBA	Council for British Archaeology
DGLA	Department of Greater London Archaeology (of MoL)
DoE	Department of Environment (of UK government)
DUA	Department of Urban Archaeology (of MoL)
E	east
EDN	Excavation Day Notebook(s)
EH	English Heritage
EN	Excavation Notebook
ER	Excavation Register
ft	feet
GL	Guildhall Library
GLC	Greater London Council
GM	Guildhall Museum
GPO	General Post Office
HBMC	Historic Buildings and Monuments Commission (=English Heritage)
in.	inches
LAMAS	London and Middlesex Archaeological Society
m	metres
MoL	Museum of London
MoLAS	Museum of London Archaeology Service
MS	manuscript
N	north
NGR	National Grid Reference (Ordnance Survey)
OS	Ordnance Survey
PRG	'Post-Roman gazetteer of sites in the City of London' (MS in MoLAS archive by C Harding & P Marsden 1989)
RCHM	Royal Commission on the Historical Monuments (of England)
RMLEC	Roman and Mediaeval London Excavation Council
S	south
SMR	Sites and Monuments Record (English Heritage)
W	west

INTRODUCTION

Archaeological work in the City of London, 1907–1991

This *Guide* catalogues the records held in the Museum of London concerning archaeological excavations, observations and salvage work in the City of London from 1907 to 1991, and provides brief summaries of those excavations. The records of archaeological work in the City are in three originally separate archives, all now within the Museum of London (MoL), and this *Guide* is concerned with the first two: (i) sites of 1907 to 1973 excavated or observed by staff of the former Guildhall Museum (GM), which became part of MoL in 1975; (ii) sites of 1973 to 1991 excavated or observed by the Department of Urban Archaeology (DUA), initially of the Guildhall Museum, and therefore part of MoL from 1975. The DUA in turn became part of the new Museum of London Archaeology Service (MoLAS) in 1991, and records of excavations in the City of London after 1991 are not covered in this *Guide*. The third archive of excavations in the City before 1991 concerns those of W F Grimes for the Roman and Mediaeval London Excavation Council (RMLEC) between 1946 and 1972, which are the subject of a separate guide (Shepherd 1998b).

The Guildhall Museum was set up in 1826, as an adjunct to Guildhall Library (GL) which had been established only two years before. At first it comprised only a small room attached to the Library, which itself was only a narrow corridor. In 1874 the Museum transferred to new premises in Basinghall Street, which it was to occupy until 1939. After the Second World War the main gallery was subdivided with a mezzanine floor and furnished with metal racking for the Library, and this and adjacent rooms coincidentally became the home of the DUA from 1976 to 1981.

The history of the Guildhall Museum, and of the London Museum with which it was joined in 1975 to form the Museum of London, has been written by Francis Sheppard (1991); an outline of archaeological work in the City of London up to the 1960s forms part of the introduction by Ralph Merrifield to his *Roman city of London* in 1965. In the 19th century, under pressure from antiquaries such as Charles Roach Smith (1806–90), the Museum haphazardly acquired objects from building sites in the City. Many large construction schemes were digging up immense volumes of earth which comprised the strata of the Roman and later city: the formation of King William Street and the new London Bridge in 1829–35, for instance, or the trenches for the Underground railway from the 1860s. Some discoveries were reported in archaeological journals, though much material still lies unpublished (eg Fig 1). There were few archaeological excavations in the City in the 19th century; one of the earliest was by Colonel Lane-Fox, later known as General Pitt-Rivers, who recorded pile structures in the Walbrook Valley in 1866 without fully understanding them. The London and Middlesex Archaeological Society (LAMAS; founded 1855), led by J E Price, secured accurate measurements of the Bucklersbury Roman pavement which was unearthed in 1869, and contributed to the successful arguments for its preservation at the new Museum. In 1872–3 Price, then Museum Clerk for Guildhall Library, recovered a large quantity of Roman artefacts from the ancient Walbrook Valley during construction work of the National Safe Deposit Company building immediately west of Mansion House (Puleston & Price 1873; Merrifield 1995); these now form a substantial part of the Museum's considerable collection of Roman metal tools and other objects. In 1876 the Society conducted an excavation on the site of the Roman interval tower or bastion at Camomile Street (producing some of the earliest photographs of excavated remains from London), and this was the first experience of city archaeology for a young architect called Henry Hodge. He went on to make valuable watercolour drawings of many parts of the Roman basilica and medieval Leadenhall, uncovered at Leadenhall Street in the 1880s (used in redrawn form in the archaeological report on the forum and

Fig 1 An 'antique column' converted into a medieval pier base, found in a wall at Greyfriars in 1836, drawn by Alfred John Kempe (Society of Antiquaries, London Red Portfolio II, 30). Although a note of this remarkable discovery is in Archaeologia, 28, 1837, 410–12, the illustration was not included.

basilica by Marsden 1987), and of other masonry monuments: for instance, part of a wall of the 15th-century Ludgate prison, which had survived the Great Fire of 1666 and which probably still survives between buildings on Ludgate Hill (GM251). Most of these watercolours are in Guildhall Library. Although a small number of sites in this *Guide* were observed before 1907, their records formerly in the Guildhall Museum and now in the Museum of London only comprise a few photographs, and the start of archaeological work is taken as 1907, when Frank Lambert was appointed by the Guildhall Museum as the first qualified museum assistant with experience in archaeology.

Towards the end of the 19th century and in the first decade of the 20th century several observers, notably Philip Norman and Francis Reader, were recording remains on construction sites (eg Norman 1902, 1904; Norman & Reader 1906, 1912; not summarised in detail here except for photographs from one site, GM146); in addition Norman has left an enormous legacy of watercolours of vanished medieval and post-medieval buildings (there are collections in GL, MoL and the Victoria & Albert Museum). In 1914 Norman also successfully applied to the Goldsmiths' Company and to the Court of Common Council of the Corporation of London for funds to assist in recovery of artefacts from the large site opposite Goldsmiths' Hall, on the east side of St Martin's le Grand (GM318). It was to be another 64 years before a widespread policy of private (non-state) funding for archaeology in the City could be successfully pursued.

Lambert, who carried out the recording in 1914, was still in position after the First World War when building work recommenced (Lambert 1921). In 1912 the London Museum had been founded, and from then on until their union in 1975 both Museums had a part to play in City archaeology. For the Guildhall Museum, Lambert's successor in 1924 until his retirement in 1945 was Quintin Waddington, who recorded 19 sites which have records remaining (GM6, 8, 24, 35, 60, 62, 64, 89, 122, 138, 159, 266, 268, 276, 287, 292, 326–8). He also worked on some further sites and recovered unstratified material of significance, but these observations are not noted here as they have left no site records in the Museum. Some of these other sites up to 1928 are reported in the *Roman London* volume by the Royal Commission on Historical Monuments (England) of that year (RCHM 1928, 111, 134). This was one of a five-volume survey of monuments and buildings in central London up to the early 18th century by the Commission, as part of its national programme of recording chiefly standing structures. Another volume on *The City of London* (RCHM 1929) catalogued the medieval buildings and fragments then standing, and the churches built by Sir Christopher Wren and his associates after the Great Fire.

Under pressure from Mortimer Wheeler and others, the Society of Antiquaries funded a second post for an archaeologist to visit building sites: successively Eric Birley (1927–8; he observed only one site, the Midland Bank in Poultry, but this site is not in the present *Guide* as there are no records in the GM/MoL archive), Gerald Dunning (1928–34) (17 sites: GM46, 73, 104–5, 117, 121, 217–18, 221, 226, 243, 248, 252–5, 261) and Frank Cottrill (1934–7) (37 sites: GM9, 15, 18, 32, 34, 49, 51, 54, 59, 61, 68, 70–3, 79, 81, 85, 87, 97, 102–3, 114, 119, 125, 140, 164, 214, 220, 222, 224–5, 244, 246, 249, 257, 298). Their successes included the recording, albeit in summary form, of sumptuous Roman buildings at the Bank of England, parts of the Roman basilica and the city wall, along with many Roman buildings on other sites. There are also some observations of 1925–7, perhaps by Wheeler himself, in the RCHM's *Roman London* volume of 1928 (RCHM 1928, 116, 119, 134, 145; these are also not in the GM series of site records). After Cottrill's departure in 1937 no successor was appointed. In 1939–40 Adrian Oswald, for the Guildhall Museum, recorded remains of the Saxon and medieval church at All Hallows Lombard Street and other sites such as Roman Aldersgate (four sites: GM1, 5, 101, 215).

At the London Museum, meanwhile, Mortimer Wheeler was also producing catalogues of Saxon and Viking material, including finds from the City and from what we now know is the Saxon settlement of *Lundenwic* around the Strand. In 1940, J B Ward-Perkins produced the masterly *London Museum Medieval Catalogue,* largely of the London Museum but with some objects from Guildhall Museum, with a short but eloquent introduction which contains what may be one of the earliest discussions of 'medieval archaeology' as a concept and discipline (Ward-Perkins 1940). This *Catalogue,* long the standard work on medieval artefacts used by archaeologists all over Britain and over much of Europe, has never been replaced, and the work on the *Medieval finds from excavations in London* series by the DUA and now MoLAS (1978–, in progress) is an extension and refinement of Ward-Perkins's work.

During the Second World War, 50 of the City's 330 acres (20.2 out of 133.5ha) were destroyed by bombing (Fig 2). From 1944 the Society of Antiquaries had been proposing to the City that the opportunity should be taken for excavations before any future rebuilding. Wheeler's successor at the London Museum, W F Grimes, was made honorary director of the excavations. Between 1946 and

Fig 2 The view east from St Paul's Cathedral, c 1944 (GL).

1962 he conducted 63 excavations, all in difficult conditions and with very little funds; but (with the notable exception of the later stages of the Mithraeum site in Walbrook) they were not carried out under pressure of immediately impending redevelopment, and thus might be called research rather than rescue excavations. Grimes published two interim accounts (Grimes 1956, 1968) but no final reports except an account of his work at Charterhouse (Knowles & Grimes 1954); the most significant results are now being brought together for publication by the Museum (eg Milne 1997; Shepherd 1988a). Grimes's excavations are noted only incidentally in this *Guide,* and an archive catalogue of them is available separately from the Museum (Shepherd 1998b).

Work on sites actually being redeveloped was left to the Guildhall Museum, and to Ivor Noël Hume, in his own words 'a young unsuccessful playwright' who had spent the spring and summer of 1949 picking up artefacts on the Thames foreshore and bringing them for identification to Adrian Oswald at the Museum. From 1949, for eight years, Noël Hume was responsible for rescue archaeology in the City (Noël Hume 1978). He was supported at the Museum by Ralph Merrifield, who arrived in 1950, who served both the Guildhall Museum and the Museum of London until his retirement in 1978. Noël Hume was required to give all his considerable energies to excavation work, and publication was therefore secondary (several of his sites were later published by the DUA, with funds from the Department of Environment and English Heritage: Shepherd 1987; Wilmott 1982, 1984, 1991). Noël Hume excavated or conducted salvage work at many important sites: for instance the Cheapside and Billingsgate Roman bath-houses (GM37, 111); large sites of Roman buildings (GM144, 157); and Saxon and medieval churches (GM155, 160). His archaeological product tended to be isolated pit-groups and other contexts which are 'closed' (ie have little danger of intrusive later finds), with good related arrays of artefacts (particularly pottery), but with little external dating evidence.

Noël Hume left in 1957 to take up a post at Colonial Williamsburg, Virginia, and to become a leading figure in American historical archaeology. His successor in the watching of building sites was Eve Rutter (later Eve Harris), who carried out several observations and published a note describing one of them, the recording of a medieval undercroft near Mark Lane (GM172; Rutter 1958). Her colleague was a young amateur, Peter Marsden, who took over after her departure in 1959, and he provided nearly all the archaeological coverage on rescue sites in the City until 1973.

Marsden, aided by many unpaid volunteers throughout the 1960s, had many successes: the Huggin Hill and Billingsgate Roman bath-houses, the excavation on several sites of what he proposed as a palace of the Roman governor beneath Cannon Street station, work on several parish church sites, several substantial fragments of ships and boats, and in 1972 the excavation of the south part of the

15th-century Baynard's Castle, a noble mansion on the waterfront near Blackfriars rebuilt by Henry VII (main sites GM3–4, 7, 13, 19, 25, 29, 36, 55, 91, 95, 111, 123, 129, 131, 136, 152, 156, 181–3, 240; Baynard's Castle, GM152). At the same time there were difficulties and losses: in 1980 Marsden wrote that 'the years up to 1972 now seem like a bad dream, with missed opportunities and the ruthless destruction of large parts of Roman London' (Marsden 1980, 205). For instance, a large excavation adjacent to the north side of St Paul's Cathedral for the insertion underground of a cathedral works department was carried out by contractors in 1970 with no archaeological presence (see GM307). Marsden published many notes and small articles, but had to wait to be absorbed into the next organisation dealing with rescue archaeology, the Department of Urban Archaeology, before being able to write detailed and final reports. During this latter period of 1973 to 1993, he produced major publications on the Roman governor's palace (Marsden 1975), excavations on the site of the successive Roman fora up to 1985 (Marsden 1987), and two volumes describing all the significant finds of ships and boats in the London area dating from the Roman period to the 17th century (Marsden 1994, 1996). A small number of sites during this period were excavated or observed by others, for instance Brian Philp at the south-east corner of the forum in 1968–9 (Philp 1977); in 1972–3, as concern about urban archaeology in general grew, there were excavations or observations by Jeremy Haslam beneath the present Museum rotunda (Haslam 1973) and south of Thames Street (Haslam 1972), by Hugh Chapman at Aldgate (CASS72/GM191; Chapman & Johnson 1973), by Tim Tatton-Brown at Custom House in Thames Street (CUS73; Tatton-Brown 1974, 1975) and by Tony Johnson at Christchurch Greyfriars, in advance of the removal of the east end of the Wren (and medieval) church for road-widening (GF73; Johnson 1974). But it is largely Marsden's work which brings us to the end of the 'Guildhall Museum' (GM) sites in this *Guide*: from 1907 to 1972 (and including a small number of earlier findings for which photographs are kept in the archive), a total of 319 sites. One notable achievement of Marsden and Merrifield, working in the 1960s, was to find and bring together the records of previous excavations which form the basis of the Guildhall Museum part of this *Guide*.

In 1972, discussions in the Corporation of London, and well-publicised comment from organisations such as the newly formed archaeological pressure-group *Rescue*, resulted in the approval by the Court of Common Council of an outline strategy in a booklet called *Archaeology in the City of London: an opportunity*, compiled by Max Hebditch and the staff of the Guildhall Museum (Guildhall Museum 1972). This led to the creation of the Department of Urban Archaeology (DUA), and the appointment of Brian Hobley as its Chief Urban Archaeologist in December 1973. Hobley and a small team of managers were paid for by the Corporation, and all excavation and post-excavation work was funded by generous grants from the Department of Environment, requested annually. At last, in 1974, there was a reasonable and reasonably consistent source of funding for archaeological work.

For the first time, also, archaeologists in the City of London were working to an outline research agenda which addressed the whole City. This had been laid down in two documents: the report *Archaeology in the City of London: an opportunity* already mentioned, and the far more extensive *The future of London's past,* an ambitious review of the state of archaeological knowledge and needs in the City, including the mapping out of an organisational structure to deal with it, by Biddle and Hudson with Heighway (1973). The latter, published by *Rescue,* was important within European urban archaeology as a model for the management of urban archaeological resources, and was influential on the development of the discipline far outside London.

The *Archaeology in the City* document, being the first strategy to have the approval of the Corporation of London, was understandably cautious, politic and brief. It argued that 'while all the City is archaeologically important, some areas are more crucial than others' and outlined three levels or Categories of sites: Category I, where excavation in advance of redevelopment was desirable; II, where excavation of a small area or what became known as a 'watching brief' during construction works may be sufficient; and III, the rest of the city, which by implication did not need archaeological coverage. There were ten Category I areas: the city defences; parts of the waterfront; an area around Aldgate where a Roman camp had recently been suggested (on the GM191, CASS72 site); the Roman basilica and forum; the area of the Roman governor's palace; six medieval religious precincts (St Bartholomew's Priory, Greyfriars, Blackfriars, Austin Friars, St Helen's Priory and Holy Trinity Priory Aldgate); the area of the first Baynard's Castle; Bridewell Palace; the site of Leadenhall; and a 'central area' which comprised a number of blocks or areas where Roman and medieval streets and buildings would be found, in Cannon Street, Fenchurch Street and south of Cheapside.

This strategy with a certain emphasis on selectivity directed the courses of action in the first few years of the DUA's existence; even so the impressive number of first excavations was thought in some quarters to be too ambitious. In the first phase of DUA activity, to about 1980, the excavations were managed by David Browne (to 1975), Charles Hill (1975–7) and John Schofield (from 1977); the finds research was directed by Michael Rhodes; documentary history provided by Tony Dyson; and environmental archaeological services co-ordinated first by George Willcox (1974–7) and later Philip Armitage (from 1977), using facilities at the British Museum (Natural History). Modelling itself somewhat on previously established archaeological units, the DUA produced two interim reports which covered all its work (Hobley & Schofield 1977; Dyson & Schofield 1981). But after this the editors of archaeological journals turned against such reporting and there were no more. Annual summaries of excavations were provided in the magazine *London Archaeologist* and in period journals. A summary of the excavation results aimed at the wider public was produced with the financial assistance of Mobil Oil in 1980 (Schofield & Dyson 1980). Two annual lectures which made summaries of recent work were published in 1986 and 1989 (Hobley 1986; Dyson 1989); and in 1988 and 1989, annual reports of all the DUA's activities were produced (Spence 1988; Spence & Grew 1989).

In 1978 Hobley and Schofield began suggesting to every developer that they should pay for the necessary archaeological work on their redevelopment site. At first, the cost of writing an archive report and first study of the finds and environmental material was borne by the Department of Environment, but by 1980 developers were being asked to fund both excavation and post-excavation work. In 1982, while Schofield managed the large excavation at Billingsgate lorry park in Thames Street (supervised by S P Roskams), the job of excavations officer passed to John Maloney (briefly partnered by Dominic Perring, who left in 1983). From 1983, Schofield took on the direction of a major programme of post-excavation analysis and publication of the Department of Environment funded sites of 1973–83 which is summarised below, and in the period 1983–91 Maloney, aided by excavation officers Hal Bishop, Robert Ellis, Al Mackie, Marie Nally, Taryn Nixon, Eric Norton, Caroline Pathy-Barker and Simon O'Connor-Thompson, continued and expanded the policy of developer-funding. During this period the finds officer, Michael Rhodes, was assisted by gifted specialists as managers, the senior of whom were Francis Grew, Paul Tyers, Alan Vince and Angela Wardle. In 1984 the Historic Buildings and Monuments Commission, known now by its other name of English Heritage, took over government administration of archaeology in England from the Department of Environment. From 1982 the Department and then English Heritage funded only the most important excavations such as Billingsgate lorry park (BIG82) in 1982, and Leadenhall Court (LCT84) in 1984–6, though there were small further grants in exceptional circumstances. From 1984 to 1991, the principal beneficiary of English Heritage funding in the City was the publication programme (outlined in Schofield 1987a, 1993c). In 1991 the DUA, with the Department of Greater London Archaeology (DGLA) and the Environmental Archaeology Service, both also of the Museum, were restructured into the new Museum of London Archaeology Service (MoLAS). In the years 1972 (though the DUA took over excavation in late 1973, it applied codes retrospectively to a few sites) to 1991, 417 site codes had been issued for work in the City of London, and results obtained from all but a handful.

Since the editor of this *Guide* and writer of this introduction was a member of the DUA from 1974 until its disappearance in 1991, others must judge the successes and failures of the years 1973 to 1991 in the City's archaeology. The achievements are presented in the following paragraphs in the form of a summary of new and existing knowledge, as demonstrated in the publications which have been produced and by the reports and catalogues in the archive itself.

An outline of the archaeology of the City from the evidence in the archive

Before 1960, the archaeology of the City of London had been surveyed and summarised in ways that reflected current British archaeological interests: principally the remains and discoveries of the Roman period, and an antiquarian interest in standing medieval buildings. For the Roman and post-Roman periods to about 1700, the first half of the 20th century produced two substantial reviews of archaeological knowledge concerning the City of London and its environs: the first and only volume of the *Victoria County History* of London (*VCH*; ed Page 1909), and the five volumes comprising the survey of London by the Royal Commission on Historical Monuments (England) in 1925–30, of which volume III (1928), largely written by Mortimer Wheeler, dealt with the Roman city, and volume IV (1929) dealt with the medieval and post-medieval standing remains in the City. A third review of Roman London this century was made by Merrifield (1965), in a work which 30 years later stands as the basis for all topographical work. Further additions pertaining especially to the Roman, Saxon and medieval periods were made by Grimes in his survey of his work (1968).

In the following summary, which is largely of work in 1960–91, only the site codes of the principal sites which have contributed to a piece of research are mentioned. Study of the maps at the end of this

Guide will provide the references for other sites in the vicinity of the major discoveries.

Throughout this *Guide* the term *archive*, unless qualified otherwise, means both records (paper, computer files and photographs) and the finds and samples themselves.

In this survey only the City of London north of the Thames is considered, reflecting the organisation of its archaeology in the years covered by this *Guide;* where relevant work was undertaken on the borders of the city by the DGLA (especially on the sites of Roman cemeteries and of medieval religious houses), it is noted here. The archaeology of Southwark and Westminster, and other more outlying parts of London, is considered in a companion *Guide* (Thompson, Westman & Dyson 1998).

Prehistoric

Despite exhaustive searches, there is no evidence for any occupation within the city boundary in the immediate pre-Roman period. There is, however, evidence for small-scale occupation of this area of the Thames river terrace by prehistoric hunter-gatherers and farmers in the form of Mesolithic and Neolithic artefacts, Bronze Age smallfinds, and possible Bronze Age features such as pits (eg GPO75, BIP88, WES89, RAC90; flints from several sites, eg BOP82; Iron Age pottery from ORG86). This is only to be expected in a valley that saw occupation throughout the prehistoric period. The relative density of Later Bronze Age material seems to reflect the importance of the Thames Valley in this period, in contrast with the Iron Age when shifts of power to other areas are reflected in a sparser pattern of occupation.

The prehistoric period did not figure in the English Heritage-DUA publication programme of 1984–91, though reviews of prehistoric finds in the London area have appeared (Merriman 1987, 1990). The prehistoric material from the City will be reviewed in due course as part of wider surveys or studies. Current emphasis in research, in the new programme of publication by the Archaeology Service, is on rich prehistoric landscapes in west London, for instance in Uxbridge (Middlesex).

Roman London (AD50–410)

The advances in knowledge about the origin and early growth of London provided by archaeological discoveries in the period 1960–91 have been immense. The three most important have been: (i) the excavation of the Roman port, its revetments, buildings and the first bridge, with the wealth of finds in and around these structures (Milne 1985; Miller, Schofield & Rhodes 1986; Brigham 1990a); (ii) the excavation and elucidation on many sites of timber buildings, in a Roman city which was previously only known for stone buildings (see eg Merrifield's 1965 gazetteer); and (iii) several public monumental complexes, notably the elucidation of the forum and basilica (Marsden 1987; LCT84, WIV88, Milne 1992a), the complex of buildings beneath Cannon Street Railway Station which may be the Roman governor's palace (Marsden 1975), and a possible temple complex at Peter's Hill (PET81; Williams 1993). The Roman riverside city wall, excavated on several sites, was confirmed by the campaigns of the 1970s (Hill, Millett & Blagg 1980). Other investigations or studies of significance have been the development of dendrochronological frameworks for much of the period (reports in Miller, Schofield & Rhodes 1986; Williams 1993; C Maloney 1990) and the dating of pottery of AD50–150 to an extent which identifies the major pottery industries of the period in south-east England (Davies, Richardson & Tomber 1994; Fulford & Huddleston 1991).

Previous conclusions that London began as a military supply base in AD43 have been considerably modified. Pottery groups predating AD60 are notably uncommon; Claudian vessels are lacking in quantity. Ceramic and coin evidence suggests that settlement began around AD50; in Southwark roads converging on the bridgehead may date to c 50–65. A reassessment of the earliest London coinage also suggests a foundation date of c 50–5.

The more intensive work of 1973–91 provided evidence to refine earlier theories (for instance, by Dunning 1945) concerning the original centre of the settlement and to chart its growth. Civilian settlement, suggested by Tacitus, is now confirmed by several excavations. Widely scattered, though clearly planned, buildings and main roads were laid out by the time of the destruction attributed to the Boudican rebellion of AD60–1 (Marsden 1987 and Milne 1992a for the sites on Cornhill; Perring & Roskams 1991 for sites west of the Walbrook, principally GPO75, MLK76, WAT78). At Fenchurch Street, for instance, excavation in 1976 (FSE76) uncovered a range of timber, clay and brick buildings which may have been shops on the site of the later forum; one room contained a large deposit of burnt grain, probably a Mediterranean import and intended for sowing.

An examination of the upper Walbrook Valley in the prehistoric and Roman periods (OPT81; de Moulins in C Maloney 1990) suggests that prior to the Roman occupation the upper valley was marsh, the insect assemblages devoid of human influence. During the late 1st–early 2nd century streets and buildings were laid out; the environmental evidence suggests human disturbance of ground (perhaps fields nearby) and insect assemblages are those associated with human occupation. This study is encouraging in that it shows the spread of settlement may be charted by techniques of environmental analysis.

London's growing status in the late 1st century was emphasised by the construction of a first forum and what has been suggested as a provincial governor's palace (Marsden 1975), though other interpretations of this complex have been suggested (Perring 1991; Milne 1996). During the early 2nd century a fort was established at Cripplegate, on the north-western edge of the town, probably for the bodyguard and staff of the governor (Grimes 1968, 15–46); and the second forum, four times the size of the first, on the site of its predecessor (Marsden 1987; Milne 1992a; Brigham 1990b). Nearby civilian buildings had wall paintings of quality (FEN83; Rhodes 1987b). The civil zone was perhaps demarcated by a boundary or *pomerium* on the landward side (DUK77; J Maloney 1983). Such a boundary may have linked monumental arches on the roads to York, Colchester and Verulamium; their sites have been suggested (Bentley 1985 and in Perring & Roskams 1991), but none has yet been located.

Domestic buildings have been excavated on many sites, notably Milk Street, Watling Court and Newgate Street (MLK76, WAT78, GPO75), the last a suburban site until its inclusion within the city wall of c 200. The three main sites together suggest that the earliest Roman planning proposals, interrupted by the Boudican rebellion, were brought to fruition as a result of the massive expansion of the late 1st century, a process which continued in the 2nd century with development of the suburban area to the west, a new boundary being formalised by the building of the city wall (Perring & Roskams 1991). Several excavation reports, covering the Roman sequence of strata from the 1st to the 4th century, have dealt with other individual sites or groups of domestic sites (Wilmott 1982; Shepherd 1986, 1987; Williams in prep.).

At least one major and four minor bath complexes lay on the spring-line near the river. The largest, at Huggin Hill (Marsden 1976; GM240, DM188), was an elaborate suite of 2000sq m which flourished in the later 1st century and early 2nd; it may have been the grandest set of public baths for the city. The others were smaller domestic suites (of about 100sq m); those near Billingsgate (Marsden 1980; GM111, BIL75, BSA82, BBH87) and at Pudding Lane (Milne 1985; PDN81) continued in use into the 4th century.

Substantial timber-framed waterfronts have been traced for 300m above and below the site of London Bridge, and part of a pier of a late 1st-century wooden bridge was uncovered at the foot of Fish Street Hill, on the same alignment as the medieval bridge (PDN81). The construction techniques of the waterfronts developed as they advanced 35m into the river from the late 1st to the mid-3rd century, and many artefacts (especially imports) have been found in the silts around them (Miller, Schofield & Rhodes 1986 on NFW74; Milne & Bateman 1983 and Milne 1985 on PDN81; Brigham 1990a on BIG82 and general summary; for river levels, Milne *et al* 1983, and for some different conclusions, Marsden 1994, 174). For all the historic periods (Roman to post-medieval), London has also produced a notable range of fragments of boats and ships (Marsden 1994, 1996; main sites GM181–3).

An amphitheatre provisionally of late 1st-century date in timber and early 2nd-century date in masonry is now known to lie south-east of the fort in a position accessible to both the fort (which it evidently preceded in date) and the contemporary city (GAG87). The eastern access corridor flanked by chambers and parts of the arena wall have been identified, together with well-preserved timber-lined drains and other structures on its floor. The estimated dimensions of the arena are similar to that at Caerleon, with an area of 6000sq m (Bateman 1994a, 1994b, 1997).

Studies of Roman artefacts, further to their use for dating the excavated structures or suggesting functions, have been of pottery (Symonds & Tomber 1991; Davies, Richardson & Tomber 1994), woodworking including house construction (Goodburn 1991), jewellery-working (Henig 1984), ornamental stonework and statuary (Pritchard 1986; Blagg 1996; Henig 1996) and leatherworking (Rhodes 1987a). A major omission from the DUA programme, however, was any overview of Roman artefacts to match the series on medieval finds. It is to be hoped that this can be remedied in the future, in conjunction with analysis of Roman artefacts from sites in the Greater London area. The area south of the Thames in Southwark is being studied by MoLAS in a series of volumes which will analyse both buildings and finds (Cowan in prep.; Hammer in prep.; Yule in prep.).

Topics as yet unexplored in detail, from the excavations of the last 20 years, are the later Roman period (AD200–400) in general and the chronology of fortification in particular (Marsden 1985; Symonds & Tomber 1991; Williams in prep.). For the 3rd and 4th centuries evidence of settlement is contradictory. There are signs of continued prosperity and public munificence; built into the late Roman riverside wall were sculptured blocks from at least two monuments, a monumental arch and a Screen of Gods with six major deities on one side. The quality of decoration on both suggests a late 2nd- or early 3rd-century date (BC75; Hill, Millett & Blagg 1980). Also at about this time the city was enclosed with its first defences, a stone wall with six gates which however did not enclose the mile-long waterfront (Maloney 1983). A riverside wall in several phases followed from the late 3rd century; at the Tower, it was built or rebuilt in the late 4th century (Hill, Millett & Blagg 1980 (BC75); Williams 1993 (PET81, GM91); Parnell 1985). Within the city, the tightly packed buildings of the first two centuries are overlaid on a smaller number of sites by large courtyard buildings, widely spaced and well furnished with mosaics; and at least several temples, for instance that of Mithras, which was perhaps part of a private house (Grimes 1968, 92–117; Toynbee 1986; Shepherd 1998a). Between the secular and religious buildings, the 'dark earth' of the Saxon centuries (a term coined at the DUA in 1978) was beginning to form (Yule 1990). Outside the walls, one cemetery on the west side has been sampled (Bentley & Pritchard 1982) and several excavations of cemeteries on the east side of the city by the DGLA have been published or are in preparation (Whytehead 1980, 1986; Barber, Bowsher & Whittaker 1990; Barber & Bowsher in prep.). A survey of material from cemeteries in the Museum, the result of collecting and accepting material since the 19th century, lists records for burials from over 187 sites surrounding the Roman city, with evidence for at least 234 cremation burials and 1092 inhumations (Hall 1996; Werner 1998).

Since the 1960s, overall reviews of the development of the Roman city by Merrifield (1965; 1983), Marsden (1980), Perring (1991) and Milne (1995) have charted our changing understanding of the development of Roman London; Wacher (1995, 82–111) considers London within the Roman province and in comparison to other towns. One paper (Marsden & West 1992) has considered overall population changes, but this subject is not yet addressed in detail. The major topographical discoveries of 1973–80 were added to Merrifield's 1965 map and published by the Ordnance Survey in an excellent new map of Roman London in 1981. Fulford (1995) has also recently provided a brief review of the published output, and noted some outstanding questions (including new ones raised by recent investigations). He suggests that more work is necessary to clarify whether there was any conscious division of the city into different zones, beyond the obvious fort to the west and fora to the east. This zoning may also have changed over time, as the character and function of the city changed. Secondly, while London's role as a port for the distribution of imports has been impressively demonstrated, its potential role as a redistributive centre for British materials is, so far, less established. And thirdly, the largely unknown character of late Roman London, the provincial capital, remains a major objective.

Saxon London (AD410–1100)

Major reviews of Saxon London before about 1970, in comparison with those dealing with the Roman period, have been fewer in number and much thinner in bulk. In the *VCH* volume (1909), an essay by R A Smith dealt with 'Anglo-Saxon remains', largely chance finds of metalwork such as weapons and brooches, and understandably did not mention buildings since virtually nothing was known about them at that time. Wheeler's catalogue *London and the Vikings* (1927), after a historical introduction, is almost entirely a descriptive catalogue of objects; his later *London and the Saxons* (1935) has distribution maps, even though they had to wait until 1984 to be correctly interpreted.

The fate of London in the centuries following the collapse of the Roman administration in 410 is still uncertain. The substantial quays of the 240s had fallen into disuse by the third quarter of the same century; from coinage, the bridge itself was not used after c 300 (Rhodes 1991). It is now clear that by the 7th century London lay outside the walls of the old Roman town, on a site to the west in the area of the modern Aldwych (Biddle 1984; Vince 1984). This town, *Lundenwic,* was that described by Bede as 'a mart of many peoples coming by land and sea', and excavations since the early 1980s have found extensive evidence of buildings, pits, boundaries and lanes (Cowie 1988; Cowie & Whytehead 1988; Vince 1990, 1991). This has proved for the first time that a large population, manufactures, wealth, and participation in a trading network which focused on the Low Countries and their hinterland were characteristic of London from soon after the foundation of St Paul's, within the adjacent Roman city, in 604. While coin evidence suggests that 8th-century London was not at this time as significant as Southampton or eastern Kent, it was nevertheless a powerful attraction to kings and churchmen as a port and a place in which to do business (various essays in Blackburn 1989).

There is very little archaeological evidence of the 7th, 8th and early 9th centuries from the City itself, though St Paul's was founded within the walls in 604; documentary evidence for the period is rare, and it is now thought most of it refers to *Lundenwic* (Brooke & Keir 1975; Dyson 1980). In the late 9th century the area within the walls was resettled (for the written evidence, Dyson 1990) and the extramural settlement apparently abandoned.

Before 1973, with the exception of a small number of sunken-floored buildings excavated by Grimes (1968, 155–9), Saxo-Norman buildings were unknown in the City. Virtually nothing was known of the dating of Saxon pottery, let alone artefacts such as shoes or textiles. Dendrochronology, supported by fortuitous but welcome coin finds, has made it possible to outline several of the main topographical elements of the City, and provide typologies of pottery and many kinds of artefacts, including those in organic materials such as leather, wood and bone. This important work on the Saxon city is described in a series of three volumes on *Aspects of Saxo-Norman London* (1988–92). The first deals with street and building development (PEN76, MLK76, WAT78, PDN81; Horsman, Milne & Milne 1988). Archaeological and documentary evidence (Dyson 1978; Dyson & Schofield 1984) suggests that from the late 9th and 10th centuries a series of streets running north–south were laid out between the River Thames and Cheapside (Westcheap) in the western part of the city, and between Fenchurch Street and the river, centred on the bridge approach–Gracechurch Street (running north–south) and Cannon Street–Eastcheap (crossing it and running east–west) in the eastern part of the city. The remains of approximately 60 buildings have been recorded, the majority from near Billingsgate and around Cheapside. The second volume presents finds and environmental evidence from Saxon London: native and imported pottery, artefacts, coins, metallurgy, plant use and human parasites (Vince 1991; on textiles, Pritchard 1984). The third volume deals with the waterfront around the bridgehead and Billingsgate (both of which, it is argued, were established at about the same time, *c* 1000, as a single act of policy), describing the origins of St Botolph's Wharf and subsequent private reclamation into the river to *c* 1200 (NFW74, SH74, SWA81, BIG82; Steedman, Dyson & Schofield 1992). The main suggestion is that in London, as in Lübeck (Germany), economic stimulus came by boat, and topographical development was from the waterfront up into the City from the two main landing-places, Queenhithe (towards Cheapside) and St Botolph's Wharf–Billingsgate (towards Eastcheap); this has however been contested by Keene (1995).

The sites of several Saxon churches have been investigated: Grimes investigated St Alban Wood Street (Grimes 1968, 203–9) where the church may be the chapel adjoining the 8th-century palace of Offa probably within the Cripplegate fort; other churches recorded have been those of St Mildred Bread Street (MC73; Marsden, Dyson & Rhodes 1975), and St Nicholas Shambles (GPO75; Schofield in prep.), from the cemetery of which 234 skeletons dating to the 11th–12th centuries have been analysed (White 1988; Werner 1998). A review of all the excavations of parish church sites in the City (going back to 1818; detailed work at 51 churches and a dozen further smaller observations) shows that at least 27 churches have 11th-century or possibly in some cases 10th-century origins, and that this is probably the case for many of the 108 churches known to exist by 1300 (Schofield 1994).

Two overall reviews of the development of Saxon London, summarising and commenting on the recent advances, were published at the end of the 1980s (Biddle 1989; Vince 1990). In 1996, in the draft text of an assessment of all the archaeology in the Greater London area being discussed and prepared for publication by English Heritage and the Museum of London Archaeology Service, B Cowie points to some areas of study where future development would be fruitful. In the Early Saxon period (450–650), the Thames Valley was an important area of settlement, and the London area should produce many new sites. In the Middle Saxon period (650–850), *Lundenwic* needs much further work, and what was happening in the Roman city at this time, which is still largely unknown, must be tackled, perhaps by rethinking approaches to dark earth. For the Late Saxon period (850–1100), as excavations at Bull Wharf in the City (BUF90) have shown in 1990–5, the strata on waterfront sites have yet the potential to reveal the nature of the beach markets of Alfredian London, and the waterlogged conditions are our best chance of understanding the full variety of the capital's material remains.

Keene (1995) has recently considered the published output and some of the next questions. For *Lundenwic,* he suggests that the mid-Saxon settlement in its complexity and market orientation probably more closely resembled city commerce in the central and later Middle Ages than the model of a gift- and tribute-based economy proposed by Hodges (1982). By the 8th century London was becoming an increasingly important part of the kingdom or polity of Mercia which stretched from Chester to the Channel. By 1000 London's overseas trade, interrupted by the Vikings, was growing and the concomitant development of the bridge, wharves and Billingsgate was matched by timber buildings, some of innovative design, and the host of new churches (many private to begin with). The degree to which this growth was associated with London's new political connections to the Scandinavian world, or simply reflected wider European monetary and economic development, is a topic to be addressed.

Medieval London (1100–1500)

In the archaeological survey *The future of London's past* (Biddle, Hudson & Heighway 1973), which immediately preceded the establishment of the archaeological unit within the City, little hope was held out for recording substantial medieval remains in the centre of London, due to the damage caused by ubiquitous basements of the commercial capital; the top 3m of strata had been removed, largely unrecorded. But even this survey pointed to two potential growth areas: the fruitful comparison of archaeological with documentary evidence, and the waterfront, then an almost totally unknown entity.

Archaeological study of the medieval and post-medieval city can take advantage of a considerable wealth of largely unresearched documentary evidence from the mid-13th century (Keene & Harding 1985), and of cartographic evidence (including panoramas) from the mid-16th century (Prockter & Taylor 1979; Schofield 1995; Colvin & Foister 1996); many notable religious and secular buildings were later engraved or surveyed plans survive (Schofield 1987b). This documentary archive is being drawn upon by many historians, including those attached to the archaeological research programme (Dyson 1989; Taylor in Schofield, Allen & Taylor 1990; Dyson in Steedman, Dyson & Schofield 1992).

It is now known that the rising river reached its furthest point northwards in the Saxon period, and from the late 10th century, in areas around nodal points such as Dowgate and Billingsgate, wharves and narrow plots divided by fences pushed out into the river (NFW74, SWA81, BIG82). The fences became the basis of later property boundaries, and in some cases alleys, which ran down the side of plots up to 30m from the largely decayed Roman riverside wall, itself forming the south side of the new Thames Street. A succession of wooden revetments dated by dendrochronology to the period 1140–1480 have been found, surviving up to 2m high and with joints comparable to other examples of medieval carpentry; several suggestions can be made about the history of timber framing in buildings on land (SH74, TL74, SWA81, FRE78, BIG82, TEX88, VRY89, BUF90; Milne & Milne 1982; Milne 1992b). The dumps behind these revetments are tightly dated by dendrochronology and coins, and provide a long series of accurately dated artefacts of every kind. The waterfront sites have therefore formed the basis of ceramic typology for the City (Jenner & Vince 1983; Pearce, Vince & Jenner 1985; Vince 1985; Pearce & Vince 1988; Blackmore 1994; for Rhenish stoneware, Gaimster 1987) so that strata can now be dated to within 30 years in many cases. The ceramic phases (ie bands of time characterised by a specific mix of wares) thus created have been employed as the chronological basis of artefact catalogues based on the waterfront excavations (the *Medieval finds from excavations in London* series). So far volumes have appeared on knives and scabbards (Cowgill, de Neergaard & Griffiths 1987), shoes and pattens (Grew & de Neergaard 1988), dress accessories (Egan & Pritchard 1992), textiles and clothing (Crowfoot, Pritchard & Staniland 1992), the medieval horse and its equipment (Clark 1995) and objects illustrative of many aspects of home life (Egan 1998). A seventh volume in preparation is on pilgrim badges and secular souvenirs (Spencer in prep.). It is intended that future volumes will appear on coins and jettons, and on objects illustrative of manufacturing, beginning with the cloth-finishing trades.

During the compilation of the studies concerned with medieval artefacts, several waterfront sites were excavated both by archaeologists and during subsequent redevelopment by earth-moving machines. This meant that large volumes of earth used in the reclamation process, containing many finds, were taken out of the centre of London and used as landfill in suburban areas or downstream near the river. To deal with this, the DUA introduced metal detectors onto archaeological sites in 1981, and a relationship developed with the Society of Thames Mudlarks, the main group of detector users. This monitoring of organised spoil removal in the 1980s had an enormous effect on the numbers and range of metal artefacts, including coins, which were obtained. The later medieval finds volumes reflect these additions.

Expectations about the survival of medieval strata in general have been shown to be too pessimistic. Work on London's medieval public buildings has included reporting of investigations at Guildhall (GM145; Marsden 1981) and a notable study and reconstruction, from several types of evidence, of the 15th-century Leadenhall (LCT84; Samuel 1989). Medieval domestic buildings, frontages and plots have been excavated on many sites, notably in the Cheapside area (MLK76, WAT78, IRO80; Schofield, Allen & Taylor 1990) and on the waterfront; here the conjunction of archaeological and documentary evidence will result in extremely detailed reporting (SH74, NFW74, SWA81, BIG82: Schofield 1981b, 1990; Schofield & Dyson in prep.; LOV81: Gadd 1983). The Custom House of 1381 has been uncovered (CUS73; Tatton-Brown 1975) and a public access point to the river recorded at the East Watergate, later incorporated into Baynard's Castle, the noble waterfront residence rebuilt in 1428 (BC72/GM152).

Several medieval parish churches in the City have been excavated in recent years; publication is intended for the churches excavated by Grimes, and two excavated by the DUA in 1973–91, St Nicholas Shambles (GPO75; Schofield in prep.) and St Botolph Billingsgate (BIG82; Schofield & Dyson in prep.). A review of all parish church excavations in the City has also been made (Schofield 1994). London's many religious houses are the subject of a research project to publish the seven major monasteries comprehensively investigated archaeologically in the last two decades. In London, the rich survival of several types of evidence — documentary and cartographic records, later plans, and physical traces such as standing fragments of ancient architecture and moulded stones from the former precinct buildings reused as rubble — makes possible the reconstruction of several religious houses to a level of detail not available before. One, Holy Trinity Priory Aldgate (DUK77, HTP79, LEA84, MIR84, MIT86, LHN89; Schofield & Lea in prep.), was investigated by the DUA, the others by the DGLA as the sites lie in the boroughs around the City: St Mary Spital (Thomas, Sloane & Phillpotts 1997), St Mary Clerkenwell (Sloane in prep.), St John Clerkenwell (Sloane & Malcolm in prep.), Bermondsey Abbey, Merton Abbey and St Mary Graces. This series of monographs on religious houses in and around London will have common themes, such as the impact of each house on its local topography, the history of the individual precincts, the relationship of each house with its surrounding area and contrasting fates of the houses at the Dissolution. There has additionally been work on several friaries, but the present City-based programme has included only research on the garden of the Greyfriars; a study of microhabitats of small fauna in an abandoned well has been published and a report on subsidiary buildings of the friary in the garden, not known from existing records, is in preparation (POM79; Armitage & West 1985; Brown in prep.). Many cemeteries, at both parish churches and monastic sites, have been excavated and skeletal data recovered.

As with the Roman defences, there are no substantial studies of London's medieval (or post-medieval) defences in the recent publication programme, though the Tower Postern was excavated during its exposure and display as a monument (Whipp in prep.) and individual studies have also appeared (DUK77, HOU78; Maloney & Harding 1979). At the Tower of London, which did not fall within the Museum's responsibility, archaeological recording took place during restorations or ahead of improvements to visitor facilities (Parnell 1980, 1983, 1985; Hiller & Keevil 1994).

The ecology and environment of medieval London, including study of climate, plants and insect life, is in progress on several fronts, though little has yet been published. A first study of 14th-century pollution in the River Fleet, as revealed by ostracods and foraminifera, is promising (TUD78; Boyd 1981). Historians have meanwhile begun research into the documentary evidence for agriculture in the hinterland of medieval London (Galloway & Murphy 1991).

Two summaries of the development and character of medieval London, incorporating archaeological evidence but not giving a comprehensive coverage of archaeological work, have been made by the present author (Schofield 1993c, 1995, 6–26). There is currently no overall archaeological survey of medieval London to match those of Perring (1991) and Vince (1990) on the Roman and Saxon periods.

Post-medieval London (1500–1900)

Above ground, the great majority of the structures dating from this period which survived the Great Fire or were rebuilt after it have now disappeared. Below ground, continual redevelopment has ensured that the levels of this date have mostly been removed by the basements of later office blocks. In the City post-medieval deposits can be deep, especially along the borders of rivers; but in general they are shallow. Dug features such as wells and cesspits are however a frequent find, and they often contain good artefactual and environmental groups.

The source base of post-medieval archaeology comprises primary sources (strata, finds and structures) and secondary sources such as documentary records, maps and engravings. In comparison with earlier periods, both components of the source base are richer, in that the archaeological evidence has been decaying for a shorter period, and the documentary evidence is far fuller and more varied than before. The rich heritage of standing buildings in the City of London has been catalogued in many publications: the most recent comprehensive guide is the revision of the *Buildings of England* series volume, *London 1: the City of London* (Bradley & Pevsner 1997). Archaeological work on London in 1500–1900 has been on selected aspects of this rich period: royal palaces; the Dissolution; industries; the character of the East End; the Great Fire; and recording at Wren churches. In particular, studies of medieval waterfront tenements are taken up to 1666 and sometimes beyond, and some studies of secular sites provide detailed accounts of occupancies.

Baynard's Castle was rebuilt in 1501 by Henry VII as a royal residence; several excavations in

1972–84 uncovered the range on the riverfront and parts of the north range, including the gatehouse to Thames Street (BC72, BC75, BYD81). Henry VIII's Bridewell Palace (1515–23) was located in two excavations in 1978, and the plan of the whole palace has been reconstructed using them as a basis (BRI78, TUD78; Gadd & Dyson 1981).

Though the Great Fire of 1666 is a historical and archaeological turning-point, the study of post-medieval housing in London looks both before and after it. Four topics have recently been addressed: urban palaces carved out of the monastic precincts, 1530–70 (Schofield 1993b); the range of house types shown in the drawn surveys by Ralph Treswell, 1607–14 (Schofield 1987b, 1995); the archaeological evidence of the Great Fire itself (PEN79; Milne & Milne 1985; to be studied at NFW74 and BIG82, Schofield & Dyson in prep.); and the development of the suburbs, especially to the east, in the period 1500–1800 (AL74, Thompson, Grew & Schofield 1984; XWL79, Vince & Egan 1981). Since the mid-1970s there have also been some exercises in recording post-Fire houses in the City (Cherry 1975, 246; HIL84, MEN91) but the DUA sites have not yet been published.

The effect of the Dissolution on the religious precincts is a neglected subject, in London as in other cities and towns. Even more than for the medieval period, the 16th and later centuries in London are rich in evidence from standing buildings or fragments, archaeology, documents, maps and plans. The Dissolution forms an integral part of each of the monastic studies already described, and the City is represented in that series by Holy Trinity Priory Aldgate (DUK77, HTP79, LEA84, MIT86; Schofield & Lea in prep.). Such investigations do not concentrate only on the fate of the medieval religious house or on the Tudor mansions which grew out of them in the mid-16th century. These sites, suddenly made available for speculative development, soaked up many immigrant communities and new industries from the 1570s. Archaeological work has thrown light on production of delftware pottery by Jacob Jansen and others in the former Holy Trinity Priory by 1571 (HTP79). Other 16th- and 17th-century industries to be sought in the precincts include sugar refining, printing and shoemaking.

Heavy industries such as shipbuilding were being established downstream of the City. Industrial activity mixed with residential development in the expansion of the East End. Excavation at the PLA Warehouses, Cutler Street (CUT78; now Cutlers' Gardens) in 1978–9 found evidence (largely 1660–1700) of clay pipemaking, bell-founding, glassmaking, and ivory- and hornworking (Egan & Moir in prep.); one industry, as yet unidentified, involved the use of pits lined with cattle horn cores.

One of the main research programmes arising out of the recent excavations, for this period as for the previous ones, has been the creation of pottery typologies on which much future work depends. The post-medieval pottery of London has an importance far beyond the capital and its hinterland, for by 1800 London was the commercial centre of a worldwide empire. Thus the specification of date-ranges for the wealth of pottery types in use in London in this period is of importance both nationally and for colleagues studying this period in all Britain's former colonies. The first volume in this series is on Border wares from the Hampshire–Surrey border (Pearce 1992); other studies will follow on Redwares from Woolwich and Essex (Pearce in prep.), and a series on tin-glazed wares. In this third case the first volume (Edwards in prep.) will present a number of ceramic groups from the City itself as a place of consumption. Further studies, now being planned, will be of some of the many production sites of tin-glazed (delftware) fabrics in Southwark, Lambeth and other suburbs.

The character of the archive and the principles behind its formation

To explain the character of the archaeological archive at the Museum of London, and therefore to outline its potential for research and the advancement of knowledge about the past, it is necessary to describe briefly the main principles of rescue archaeology as applied by the Museum and its predecessors in the City of London.

As outlined above, the provision of archaeological coverage in the City of London has gone through three broad phases or stages of growth. Up to 1907, there was virtually no official interest, and the few sites which were recorded were the product of individual initiative by concerned antiquaries, who nevertheless deserve praise as being the first urban archaeologists in London. From 1907 to 1973, the City was covered by a succession of single archaeologists working largely in isolation from each other even when they did overlap in time. The recording system was as good as any of the day, but not developed by present-day standards for lack of time and resources. Urban archaeology as a discipline also had to grow from virtually nothing, and this it did mostly after 1945. The Excavation Register (ER) system used from 1951 came under considerable strain when large excavations were first undertaken in the mid- and late 1960s, as it was appropriate only for the salvage work and at best small excavations which had been the norm up until then.

The recording system developed after 1973, and the concomitant extraordinary rise in resources for archaeology which meant proper storage, conservation and study of the multitude of finds, is the basis of the present archive. The records and finds of 1973–91 represent perhaps 90 per cent by bulk of the archive itself. It is therefore appropriate to describe the records generated in 1973–91 as the core of the archive, and to treat the excavations and observations of 1907–73 as valuable but recorded to a less detailed level.

The archive is principally a collection of artefacts and environmental samples and associated observations. From this the archaeologists of the Museum have made summaries, described sites and made speculations which have been published; and the existence of the archive encourages other students to come to it and conduct their own research. It may help to explain briefly the principles shared by those who conducted the basic excavations and assessments of the finds. The basic philosophy and working practices of rescue archaeology in Britain in the 1970s and 1980s will not be described in detail here, as there are other national summaries (Heighway 1972; Rahtz 1974, especially one paper by Biddle on 'The future of the urban past'; Schofield & Leech 1987; Schofield & Vince 1994).

In 1975 the DUA developed a recording system to deal with the excavation of a variety of deposits on multi-period sites in rescue situations. It is important to stress the needs imposed by the circumstances: the system had to be (i) fast and if possible error-proof, since little if anything could be checked after the excavation; (ii) quickly learned by many people and applied consistently; (iii) designed so that, given the necessity for immediate action on construction sites, one archaeologist could smoothly pick up where a colleague had stopped, even in excavating the same layer. The evolution of the system and the principles behind it have been described by Spence (1993), and the present excavation site manual used by MoLAS is the most recent exposition of the recording system (Westman 1995).

The basic building-block of the recording system, which underlies all the records and the arrangement of the finds and samples in the archive, is the individual *context,* the item of archaeological interest. A context is usually a layer, but also can be a wall, a ditch or pit, a skeleton or a coffin. The context number, assigned in sequence as the excavation progresses, is the identity tag given to all the information about the layer, and to its finds. The way that contexts are grouped into broader phases to interpret the site and the activities carried out on it is described in the DUA's (now MoLAS's) *Post-excavation manual*, a series of internal procedures.

Levels of archive information: levels I to IV

DUA policy followed the division of archaeological records into *levels* made by S S Frere in his policy paper of 1975, which was widely accepted by archaeologists and which formed the basis of subsequent Department of Environment and English Heritage funding policy (Frere 1975) (see Table below). Site information can be viewed as being at four levels, from the physical evidence of the site — soil and finds — through basic factual recording to high-level conclusions and speculations. Level I is the physical object of the site, usually destroyed, and the actual finds retrieved from it. Level II records include the context sheets or site notebooks, drawings, plans and sections, and the Harris matrix (Harris 1975, 1979); the finds records at the same level include accession lists, photographs and X-rays.

Table: SUMMARY OF RECOMMENDED ARRANGEMENTS FOR STORAGE AND AVAILABILITY OF EXCAVATION DATA (Frere 1975)

Level	Site descriptions	Loose material	Availability
I	The site itself (destroyed)	Excavated finds	Storage in museums
II	Site notebooks, recording forms, drawings	Finds records, X-rays, photos, negatives, colour transparencies; samples	Available for inspection in museum or regional or national archive
III	Full illustration and descriptions of all structural and stratigraphic relationships	Classified finds lists and finds drawings, all specialist analyses	Publication as duplicates, microfiche, microfilm or computer print-out
IV	Synthesised descriptions with supporting data	Selected finds and specialist reports relevant to synthesis	Publication in journals or as required in multiple copies

The level III structural archive report is the most extensive description of the layer by layer history of the site. Computers are used in the writing of archive reports, which also enables the reports to be indexed by machine. Programs to help analyse and present the site information in the report were to be developed, and it was hoped that computer graphics programs could be used in the drawing of archive report and publication illustrations. Some sites, or parts of sites, would however only merit publication at level III, and in extreme cases, as when funds did not permit it, an ordered level II archive would have to suffice until more funds were available. The level III archive reports are the solid basis both of an archive and of the conventional level IV publication programme (articles, books and exhibitions). The published reports are seen as the publicly visible tip of a pyramid, supported by a much larger archive at one remove from outright publication, but available in the Museum for consultation (for accounts of the DUA archive system, see Schofield 1981a, 1987a).

Nearly every site excavated in this period appears in the annual summaries published in the magazine *London Archaeologist* (originally in the spring issue of the year following the excavation, but now a separate booklet appearing with the summer issue) and in the annual national summaries produced by the period journals *Britannia* (Roman period), *Medieval Archaeology* (Saxon and medieval periods) and *Post-Medieval Archaeology* (post-medieval period). These summaries, produced immediately after the excavation by the Site Supervisor and Finds Appraisal Supervisor, were the first interim statements, and the fuller level III archive reports, when written, should be preferred.

Assessment of site and finds records and level III archive reports

The concept of assessing all the archaeological material from a site soon after completion of the excavation — not only the finds and environmental samples, but the site records and even relevant documentary evidence — was developed in the late 1980s and promulgated as desirable national policy in English Heritage's document *The management of archaeological projects* (second edition, 1991). This concept arose partly from problems with the sheer volume of material from excavations, particularly from urban sites. It did not exist in 1974, though by 1989 the DUA was also beginning to address this issue. In 1974–91 it was the policy of the DUA to produce an illustrated level III (archive) report on every excavation. This was modified by practicalities and financial constraints, in that certain of the smaller, unproductive observations, or those which were only partly funded, remain in an ordered level II state. The contents of level III structural reports are standardised as far as possible to allow detailed comparison between sites.

The finds had to be assessed, if only for their immediate conservation needs. The assessment of finds material from current (ie newly excavated) sites, which was highly developed by 1982, involved several pieces of documentation: a Finds Appraisal Report; spot-dating lists; computerised phasing of the site (composed initially by the Site Supervisor); and level II catalogues and records (for the early development of the system, Tyers & Vince 1983).

The Finds Appraisal (available for most sites after 1981) comprised usually a brief assessment made shortly after the end of the excavation. Its main purpose was to summarise the potential for further work by drawing attention to important groups of finds and individual finds of merit, and by indicating how they may relate to the interpretation of the site. It also listed finds awaiting scientific analysis, photography, illustration and conservation; and included, when possible, a list of the cleaned and identified coins and of dendrochronological samples.

The initial assessment or spot-dating of the pottery, post-medieval glass and tobacco pipes for each site is carried out while the excavation is in progress or immediately after the completion of the finds processing. The basic spot-dating record for each context containing any of the above categories of finds consists of the following information: material type; size of the group; comment (usually a simple date code); earliest and latest date. This is followed by a list of types of pottery, glass and tobacco pipes present. All information is coded; expansions of the terms can be found in the DUA (now MoLAS) *Pottery archive users' manual*.

The purpose of the spot-dating assessment is to set date limits for those contexts bearing pottery, post-medieval glass and clay tobacco pipes, together with the coin list, in order to assist the Site Supervisor in the detailed phasing of the site and to provide data for subsequent, more detailed study of these and other finds. The spot dates themselves should be seen as initial or suggested dates, open to revision when further information is available; when looked at with stratigraphic information, they will refine the chronology, though the dating evidence from finds should never affect the original perception of which layer overlay which others. When interpreting the data it must be remembered that pottery can be residual in a later context so that in a group containing material of two or more periods it is not always possible, purely on the basis of the pottery, to distinguish the material that dates the group from the residual or the intrusive. Generally, also, the larger the group of pottery containing definitive types, the more likely it is that a good date can be given.

Pottery, post-medieval glass and tobacco pipes were (and are) the only categories of finds (apart from coins) to be spot-dated at present, largely because these are the only categories which can be accurately dated. On some sites, when resources permitted, the spot-dating extended to Roman glass, but the date-ranges obtained are broad. It is hoped that the dating of other types of finds will be improved over time so that they can also be used to offer reasonably accurate dates for the strata in which they are found.

Spot-dating lists in the above format exist for sites excavated since 1981. Prior to this, pottery data was recorded on record cards in such a way as to give only a broad date-range, stating the number of sherds of pottery, but without the details regarding forms and fabric which are available from current methods of recording.

Research on the finds in the period 1973–91 has been broadly divided into two categories: pottery and other finds. Whereas the Finds Appraisal Report acts as an initial assessment of the finds and outlines the potential for further research, the level III report is an exhaustive and detailed study of an individual or group of finds.

As it would be impractical to carry out a detailed study of all material recovered from an excavation, all finds were processed to level II and a selected number of objects or group of objects were treated in such a way as to provide more detailed information in a particular field of research. For example, the large amounts of building material collected were recorded to level II, but not all were analysed to the level III standard.

Environmental archaeology level III reports were written only for sites which had been selected to illustrate specific research projects of the Field or Finds Sections, or to investigate particular environmental questions.

Use of the archive for archaeological research in urban archaeology

The archaeological archive can and should be used as material for research both on the archaeology and history of London itself, and as a source of primary data with which to study the general evolution of towns and cities. Urban archives like the one catalogued here are being set up and maintained in other British cities such as Lincoln and York.

Archaeologists in many British towns have now reached a stage where a body of data has been gathered, and questions are being put to it. These questions concern both topography ('How did the town develop into its present shape?') and artefacts ('What equipment did the people use? What did the inside of their houses look like?'). Archaeologists should start with the topographical subjects where they can be most original and confident: street plans, building types and the distribution of debris (Carver 1987, 20). The debris will include evidence of manufacturing and trade, and the objects will represent a whole level of popular material culture which is representative of the life of the majority of people who do not appear in documents (and which have not figured in traditional museum collections). Spatial studies will be informed by dating of the layers which is provided by artefacts, coins and dendrochronology; and by careful use of the stratigraphic and dating evidence, typologies of individual forms of pottery or artefact — which type came first, and which later — can be constructed. These typologies, of which a pottery type series is the most important for the town, can then be used to date artefacts in less well-dated contexts, which are perforce the majority in both urban and rural excavations. As noted above, the framework of pottery dates developed for London in recent years, for instance, can date most groups of pottery in the capital from the 12th to the 15th century to 30-year bands (Vince 1985). This is soundly based on a framework of dendrochronological and coin dates.

From these basic sets of data concerning houses, streets, pots, brooches and human skeletons, we can proceed further. In towns, we find evidence of both long-distance and local trade, of exploitation of natural resources, of specialisation and of technological aspects of manufacturing, of social differentiation, of the means of political control, and of the religious and social aspirations of many different groups within the population. We can study what London meant as a town or a place of business, or refuge, or spiritual innovation, to different generations and to different peoples. And because the archive of excavations in the City of London recorded here is large, complicated and comparatively well ordered, those who have spent the last decades collecting the information hope that the London archive is useful for studying the development of towns generally, within Britain, within Europe and further afield. We watch with interest developments in the application of Geographic Information Systems (GIS) thinking to archaeological databases, including the possibility of the creation of 'search-engines' or forms of artificial intelligence which roam around the database, perhaps at night, looking for patterns in the evidence for the past which human observers have not yet seen (Openshaw 1994).

This *Guide*, concerned only with excavations in the City of London carried out by the Museum of London and its predecessors in the period 1907–91, is matched by two other archive guides: they are concerned with the excavations of W F Grimes in the City in the period 1946–72 (Shepherd 1998) and with excavations in the majority of the surrounding boroughs by the Museum's Department of Greater London Archaeology and its predecessor bodies (Thompson, Westman & Dyson 1998). The archaeological archive which is outlined in these guides is now being brought together and established in modern facilities (Fig 3) by the Museum. Students and scholars are welcome to visit this archive by appointment.

Fig 3 Interior view of the new Archaeological Archive at Eagle Wharf Road, N1.

Editorial method and conventions

The basic way into the archaeological archives is via the site code. The Guildhall Museum (GM) codes were allocated retrospectively in 1976–88 with a few additions in 1994–6. From 1973 (and retrospectively for a small number of 1972 sites) the DUA used a code of two or three letters for sites of 1974–5, standardised to three letters from 1977, followed by two digits representing the last two numbers of the year the excavation started: eg GPO75 (GPO Site, Newgate Street, where excavations began in 1975). Sometimes a site actually started in a later year but kept the original code. These site codes, which are intentionally unique within the Greater London area, are allocated when an excavation starts; this system continues today.

Each site entry comprises a summary of the findings on a specific excavation site, with bibliographic references concerning material from the site, and supporting information such as the site's OS grid reference and number in the EH Sites and Monuments Record (SMR). The great majority of the entries concern one excavation or series of observations, but in a small number of cases several observations over a period of time have been placed together. The summary is taken from existing literature, and reflects different degrees of discussion and reflection on the information recovered. This results in a certain uneven coverage of archaeological subjects, particularly reporting on the finds.

The entries dealing with GM sites list the archive records and finds groups for each site, because it was convenient to do so during compilation of this *Guide*. There are also lists of photographs which are kept at MoL. Archaeological sites and finds were recorded in several ways by the staff of the Guildhall Museum, and some of these forms of record overlap; some explanation is therefore necessary here. The main documentation for the GM excavations from 1924 to 1973 are:

- Excavation Notebook I (EN I): also known as 'Notes on excavations in the City, 1924–39'
- Excavation Notebook II (EN II): also known as 'Notes on excavations in the City, 1949–55'
- Excavation Day Notebooks I–XI (EDN I–XI), covering the years 1951, 1953–73.

From 1908 to 1951, finds were accessioned into the GM collections, and the GM accession numbers and the registers are the only documentation for finds recovered from sites in the City. Thereafter the bulk of the finds were kept in boxes under the ER number; and selected finds (for example coins, metalwork, early glass and complete or particularly significant ceramics) were extracted and accessioned into the main GM collections. This practice continued retrospectively after the establishment of the Museum of London in 1975, so that some ER material, even from early sites, may have Museum of London accession numbers (shown by the first two digits being '75' or a similar year number). The object's accession record should indicate the ER group of origin; the note on the ER group in the *Excavation Register* (explained below) should provide the link in the opposite direction to the accession numbers of extracted objects. The GM accession numbers have not been included in the present survey, except in a very few cases for notable objects.

The *Excavation Register (ER) numbering system* for finds groups began in 1951. ER Groups 1–52, 55–8, 61–62A were allocated by I Noël Hume on GM96, 41–51 Lime Street, in 1951. Thereafter, the ER groups are described in the EDN as follows:

- EDN I: ER groups 63–150 (March 1953–April 1954)
- EDN II: ER groups 151–266 (April 1954–February 1955)
- EDN III: ER groups 267–332c (April 1955–March 1956)
- EDN IV: ER groups 332c(a)–409 (March 1956–June 1958)
- EDN V: ER groups 411–489 (July 1958–June 1959)
- EDN VI: ER groups 491–608 (June 1959–July 1960)
- EDN VII: ER groups 609–693 (July 1960–March 1961)
- EDN VIII: ER groups 694–800 (March 1961–November 1962)
- EDN IX: ER groups 801–950 (November 1962–February 1965)
- EDN X: ER groups 951–1250 (1965–1967)
- EDN XI: ER groups 1251–1371 (1967–September 1973)

The ER groups were allocated and recorded in numerical order, so that notes on the provenance and often on the contents of individual ER groups can be found in the Excavation Day Notebooks quite easily. This could be useful as some ER groups have subsequently been subdivided or dispersed. Conversely, since the ER groups are nearly always noted under the site which generated them, the site notes in the Excavation Day Notebooks (given as a reference under each site description below) provide a check on the numbers of ER groups allocated.

It should also be borne in mind that an archaeologist from the Guildhall Museum might visit a particular site over several months, allocating ER numbers between contemporary sites as they were required. A single site may be reflected by one or more ER groups, not necessarily with consecutive numbers.

The ER groups were sometimes described in greater detail when the notes in the Excavation Day Notebooks were transcribed in the *Excavation Registers,* four bound volumes kept in the safe of the Museum Library. The first two deal with the GM sites up to 1973; the third and fourth were compiled by Michael Rhodes (DUA Finds Officer, 1974–91) when briefly following the ER accessioning practice in 1974–5. Thereafter the ER system was no longer used. The first two Excavation Registers contain occasional site plans which are usually copies of those in the EDN books. The Registers also contain accession numbers of individual finds which have been removed from ER groups (usually for display or special study). The ER groups are described in the Registers as follows: vol 1 (1952–9), ER 1–518; vol 2 (1959–72 and DUA 1973–4), ER 510–1371 for GM sites and ER 1372–464 for DUA sites of 1973–4; vol 3 (1974 DUA sites) ER 1465–628; vol 4 (1974–5 DUA sites) ER 4000–23. When finds have been removed from an ER group and given accession numbers, this should be noted in the Excavation Register (though coverage may not be complete). Brief notes on the contents of each ER group may be found on a card index held in the MoL archive.

The GM photographs have negative numbers such as 2156–50. This is a single number, not an elided series, and includes the dash. A continuous series of photo numbers is given as '58–50 to 67–50'. These photograph numbers are not cited in the present *Guide* except where the photos form the only record of the site in question. P Marsden's '1981 summary' refers to an internal file in the MoL archive.

In the reports of excavations up to 1973 the imperial system of measurement is used. One foot equals 0.305m.

Note that the name of the site (such as the name of a bank) is the name under which the site was known at the time of excavation. In some cases these names were changed during redevelopment or have been changed since. The maps at the back of this *Guide* are of the City in 1989.

References

Armitage, P, & West, B, 1985 'Faunal evidence from a late medieval garden well of the Greyfriars, London', *Trans London Middlesex Archaeol Soc*, 36, 107–36

Barber, B, & Bowsher, D, in prep. *The eastern cemetery of Roman London: excavations 1983–90*

Barber, B, Bowsher, D, & Whittaker, K, 1990 'Recent excavations of a cemetery of Londinium', *Britannia*, 21, 1–12

Bateman, N, 1994a 'Guildhall: beyond the amphitheatre', *London Archaeol*, 7, 258–62

Bateman, N, 1994b 'The London amphitheatre', *Current Archaeol*, 137, 164–71

Bateman, N, 1997 'The London amphitheatre: excavations 1987–1996', *Britannia*, 28, 51–86

Bentley, D, 1985 'Roman London: a first-century boundary', *London Archaeol*, 5, 124–9

Bentley, D, & Pritchard, F, 1982 'The Roman cemetery at St Bartholomew's Hospital', *Trans London Middlesex Archaeol Soc*, 33, 134–72

Biddle, M, 1984 'London on the Strand', *Popular Archaeol*, 6 (1), 23–7

Biddle, M, 1989 'A city in transition', in Lobel, M (ed), *The City of London from prehistoric times to c 1520*, British Atlas of Historic Towns vol 3, 20–9

Biddle, M, Hudson, D, & Heighway, C, 1973 *The future of London's past*

Bird, J, Hassall, M, & Sheldon, H (eds), 1996 *Interpreting Roman London: papers in memory of Hugh Chapman*

Blackburn, M S (ed), 1989 *Anglo-Saxon monetary history*

Blackmore, L, 1994 'Pottery, the port and the populace: the imported pottery of London 1300–1600 (Part 1)', *Medieval Ceramics*, 18, 29–44

Blagg, T F C, 1996 'Monumental architecture in Roman London', in Bird, J, Hassall, M, & Sheldon, H (eds), 43–8

Boyd, P, 1981 'The palaeoecology of estuarine deposits associated with archaeological sites, with particular reference to the City of London', in Brothwell, D, & Dimbelby, G (eds), *Environmental aspects of coasts and islands*, British Archaeol Reps International Series 94, 87–8

Bradley, S, & Pevsner, N, 1997 *London 1: the City of London*, Buildings of England

Brigham, T, 1990a 'The late Roman waterfront in London', *Britannia*, 21, 99–183

Brigham, T, 1990b 'A reassessment of the second basilica in London, AD 100–400: excavations at the Leadenhall Court site, 1984–6', *Britannia*, 21, 53–97

Brooke, C, & Keir, G, 1975 *London 800–1216: the shaping of a city*

Brown, G, in prep. 'Excavations in the Greyfriars' garden (POM79)'

Carver, M O H, 1987 'The nature of urban deposits', in Schofield, J, & Leech, R (eds), 1987 *Urban archaeology in Britain*, CBA Res Rep 61, 9–26

Chapman, H, & Johnson, T, 1973 'Excavations at Aldgate and Bush Lane House in the City of London, 1972', *Trans London Middlesex Archaeol Soc*, 24, 1–73

Cherry, J, 1975 'Post-medieval Britain in 1975', *Post-Medieval Archaeol*, 7, 240–60

Clark, J (ed), 1995 *The medieval horse and its equipment c 1150–c 1450*, Medieval finds from excavations in London 5

Colvin, H, & Foister, S (eds), 1996 *The panorama of London circa 1544 by Anthonis van den Wyngaerde*, London Topographical Soc Publication 151

Cowan, C, in prep. *Development of north-west Roman Southwark: excavations at Courage Brewery*

Cowgill, J, de Neergaard, M, & Griffiths, N, 1987 *Knives and scabbards*, Medieval finds from excavations in London 1

Cowie, R, 1988 'A gazetteer of Middle Saxon sites and finds in the Strand/Westminster area', *Trans London Middlesex Archaeol Soc*, 39, 37–46

Cowie, R, 1996 'Saxon period, draft text', for *London Assessment Document*, MoLAS

Cowie, R, & Whytehead, R, 1988 'Two Middle Saxon occupation sites: excavations at Jubilee Hall and 21–22 Maiden Lane', *Trans London Middlesex Archaeol Soc*, 39, 47–164

Crowfoot, E, Pritchard, F, & Staniland, K, 1992 *Textiles and clothing c 1150–c 1450*, Medieval finds from excavations in London 4

Davies, B, Richardson, B, & Tomber, R, 1994 *A dated corpus of early Roman pottery from the City of London*, The archaeology of Roman London 5, CBA Res Rep 98

Dunning, G, 1945 'Two fires of London', *Antiq J*, 25, 48–77

Dyson, T, 1978 'Two Saxon land grants for Queenhithe', in Bird, J, Chapman, H, & Clark, J (eds), *Collectanea Londiniensia*, London Middlesex Archaeol Soc Spec Pap 2

Dyson, T, 1980 'London and Southwark in the seventh century and later: a neglected reference', *Trans London Middlesex Archaeol Soc*, 31, 83–95

Dyson, T, 1989 *Documents and archaeology: the medieval London waterfront*, MoL

Dyson, T, 1990 'King Alfred and the restoration of London', *London J*, 15 (2), 99–110

Dyson, T, & Schofield, J, 1981 'Excavations in the City of London: second interim report, 1974–1978', *Trans London Middlesex Archaeol Soc*, 32, 24–81

Dyson, T, & Schofield, J, 1984 'Saxon London', in Haslam, J (ed), *Anglo-Saxon towns of southern England*, 285–314

Edwards, J, in prep. *Tin-glazed wares*, Post-medieval pottery from London 3

Egan, G, 1998 *The medieval household*, Medieval finds from excavations in London 6

Egan, G, & Moir, D, in prep. 'Post-medieval finds c 1450–c 1700: a selection from the City of London sites 1972–82'

Egan, G, & Pritchard, F, 1991 *Dress accessories c 1150–c 1450*, Medieval finds from excavations in London 3

English Heritage, 1991 *The management of archaeological projects (MAP2)*, 2nd edn

Frere, S, 1975 *Principles of publication in rescue archaeology*, DoE

Fulford, M, 1995 'Roman London', *London J*, 20 (2), 1–8

Fulford, M, & Huddleston, K, 1991 *The current state of Romano-British pottery studies*, EH Occ Pap 1

Gadd, D, 1983 'The London Inn of the abbots of Waltham: a revised reconstruction of a medieval town house in Lovat Lane', *Trans London Middlesex Archaeol Soc*, 34, 171–8

Gadd, D, & Dyson, T, 1981 'Bridewell Palace: excavations at 9–11 Bridewell Place and 1–3 Tudor Street, City of London, 1978', *Post-Medieval Archaeol*, 15, 1–79

Gaimster, D, 1987 'The supply of Rhenish stoneware to London, 1350–1600', *London Archaeol*, 5, 339–47

Galloway, J A, & Murphy, M, 1991 'Feeding the City: medieval London and its agrarian hinterland', *London J*, 16, 3–14

Goodburn, D M, 1991 'A Roman timber-framed building tradition', *Archaeol J*, 148, 182–204

Grew, F, & de Neergaard, M, 1988 *Shoes and pattens*, Medieval finds from excavations in London 2

Grimes, W F, 1956 'Excavations in the City of London', in Bruce-Mitford, R L S (ed), *Recent archaeological excavations in Britain*, 111–44

Grimes, W F, 1968 *The excavation of Roman and medieval London*

Guildhall Museum, 1972 *Archaeology in the City of London: an opportunity*

Hall, J, 1996 'The cemeteries of Roman London: a review', in Bird, J, Hassall, M, & Sheldon, H (eds), 57–84

Hammer, F, in prep. *Industry in north-west Roman Southwark: excavations at Courage Brewery*

Harris, E C, 1975 'The stratigraphic sequence: a question of time', *World Archaeol*, 7, 109–21

Harris, E C, 1979 *Principles of archaeological stratigraphy*

Haslam, J, 1972 'Medieval streets in London', *London Archaeol*, 2, 3–8

Haslam, J, 1973 'The excavation of a section across Aldersgate Street, City of London, 1972', *Trans London Middlesex Archaeol Soc*, 24, 74–84

Heighway, C, 1972 *The erosion of history*

Henig, M, 1984 'A cache of Roman intaglios from Eastcheap, City of London', *Trans London Middlesex Archaeol Soc*, 35, 11–15

Henig, M, 1996 'Sculptors from the west in Roman London', in Bird, J, Hassall, M, & Sheldon, H (eds), 97–104

Hill, C, Millett, M, & Blagg, T, 1980 *The Roman riverside wall and monumental arch in London*, London Middlesex Archaeol Soc Spec Pap 3

Hiller, J, & Keevil, G D, 1994 'Recent archaeological work at the Tower of London', *Trans London Middlesex Archaeol Soc*, 45, 147–82

Hobley, B, 1986 *Roman and Saxon London: a reappraisal*, MoL

Hobley, B, & Schofield, J, 1977 'Excavations in the City of London, 1974–5: first interim report', *Antiq J*, 57, 31–66

Hodges, R, 1982 *Dark Age economics*

Horsman, V, Milne, C, & Milne, G, 1988 *Aspects of Saxo-Norman London I: building and street development*, London Middlesex Archaeol Soc Spec Pap 11

Jenner, A, & Vince, A, 1983 'A late medieval Hertfordshire glazed ware', *Trans London Middlesex Archaeol Soc*, 34, 151–70

Johnson, T, 1974 'Excavations at Christ Church Newgate Street 1973', *Trans London Middlesex Archaeol Soc*, 25, 220–34

Keene, D, 1995 'London in the early Middle Ages 600–1300', *London J*, 20 (2), 9–21

Keene, D, & Harding, V, 1985 *A survey of the documentary sources for property holding in London before the Great Fire*, London Record Soc 22

Knowles, D, & Grimes, W F, 1954 *Charterhouse*

Lambert, F, 1921 'Some recent excavations in London', *Archaeologia*, 71, 55–112

Maloney, C, 1990 *The upper Walbrook Valley in the Roman period*, The archaeology of Roman London 1, CBA Res Rep 69

Maloney, J, 1983 'Recent work on London's defences', in Maloney, J, & Hobley, B (eds), *Roman urban defences in the west*, CBA Res Rep 51, 96–117

Maloney, J, & Harding, C, 1979 'Duke's Place and Houndsditch: the medieval defences', *London Archaeol*, 3, 347–54

Marsden, P, 1975 'The excavation of a Roman palace site in London, 1961–1972', *Trans London Middlesex Archaeol Soc*, 26, 1–102

Marsden, P, 1976 'Two Roman public baths in London', *Trans London Middlesex Archaeol Soc*, 27, 1–70

Marsden, P, 1980 *Roman London*

Marsden, P, 1981 'The pre-1411 Guildhall of London', *London Archaeol*, 4, 115–20

Marsden, P, 1985 'London in the 3rd and 4th centuries', in Grew, F, & Hobley, B (eds), *Roman urban topography in Britain and Western Europe*, CBA Res Rep 59, 99–108

Marsden, P, 1987 *The Roman forum site in London: discoveries before 1985*

Marsden, P, 1994 *Ships of the port of London: first to eleventh centuries* AD, EH Archaeol Rep 3

Marsden, P, 1996 *Ships of the port of London: twelfth to seventeenth centuries* AD, EH Archaeol Rep 5

Marsden, P, & West, B, 1992 'Population change in Roman London', *Britannia*, 23, 133–40

Marsden, P, Dyson, T, & Rhodes, M, 1975 'Excavations on the site of St Mildred's church, Bread Street, London, 1973–4', *Trans London Middlesex Archaeol Soc*, 26, 171–208

Merrifield, R, 1965 *The Roman city of London*

Merrifield, R, 1983 *London, city of the Romans*

Merrifield, R, 1995 'Roman metalwork from the Walbrook — rubbish, ritual or redundancy?', *Trans London Middlesex Archaeol Soc*, 46, 27–44

Merriman, N, 1987 'A prehistory for central London', *London Archaeol*, 5, 318–26

Merriman, N, 1990 *Prehistoric London*

Miller, L, Schofield, J, & Rhodes, M, 1986 *The Roman quay at St Magnus House, London*, London Middlesex Archaeol Soc Spec Pap 8

Milne, G, 1985 *The port of Roman London*

Milne, G, 1992a *From Roman basilica to medieval market: archaeology in action in the City of London*

Milne, G, 1992b *Timber building techniques in London, c 900–1400*, London Middlesex Archaeol Soc Spec Pap 15

Milne, G, 1995 *Roman London*

Milne, G, 1996 'A palace disproved: reassessing the provincial governor's presence in 1st-century London', in Bird, J, Hassall, M, & Sheldon, H (eds), 49–56

Milne, G, 1997 *St Bride's church London: archaeological research 1952–60 and 1992–5*, EH Archaeol Rep 11

Milne, G, & Bateman, N, 1983 'A Roman harbour in London', *Britannia*, 14, 207–26

Milne, G, & Milne, C, 1982 *Medieval waterfront development at Trig Lane*, London Middlesex Archaeol Soc Spec Pap 5

Milne, G, & Milne, C, 1985 'A building in Pudding Lane destroyed in the Great Fire of 1666: excavations on the Peninsular House site, 1979–80', *Trans London Middlesex Archaeol Soc*, 36, 169–82

Milne, G, Batterbee, R, Straker, V, & Yule, B, 1983 'The River Thames in London in the mid-first century AD', *Britannia*, 34, 19–30

Noël Hume, I, 1978 'Into the jaws of death ... walked one', in Bird, J, Chapman, H, & Clark, J (eds), *Collectanea Londiniensia*, London Middlesex Archaeol Soc Spec Pap 2, 7–22

Norman, P, 1902 'On the destroyed church of St Michael Wood Street in the City of London, with some notes on the church of St Michael Bassishaw', *Archaeologia*, 58, 189–216

Norman, P, 1904 'Roman and later remains found during excavations on the site of Newgate Prison, 1903–1904', *Archaeologia*, 59, 125–42

Norman, P, & Reader, F, 1906 'Recent discoveries in connexion with Roman London', *Archaeologia*, 60, 169–250

Norman, P, & Reader, F, 1912 'Further discoveries relating to Roman London, 1906–12', *Archaeologia*, 63, 257–341

Openshaw, S, 1994 'Two exploratory space-time-attribute pattern analysers relevant to GIS', in Fotheringham, S, & Rogerson, P (eds), *Spatial analysis and GIS*, 83–104

Parnell, G, 1980 'The Tower of London: the reconstruction of the Inmost Ward during the reign of Charles II', *Trans London Middlesex Archaeol Soc*, 31, 147–56

Parnell, G, 1983 'The western defences of the Inmost Ward, Tower of London', *Trans London Middlesex Archaeol Soc*, 34, 107–50

Parnell, G, 1985 'The Roman and medieval defences and later development of the Inmost Ward: excavations 1955–77', *Trans London Middlesex Archaeol Soc*, 36, 1–75

Pearce, J, 1992 *Border Wares*, Post-medieval pottery from London 1

Pearce, J, in prep. *Redwares*, Post-medieval pottery from London 2

Pearce, J, & Vince, A, 1988 *Surrey Whitewares*, London Middlesex Archaeol Soc Spec Pap 10

Pearce, J, Vince, A, & Jenner, A, 1985 *London-type ware*, London Middlesex Archaeol Soc Spec Pap 6

Perring, D, 1991 *Roman London*

Perring, D, & Roskams, S, with Allen, P, 1991 *The early development of Roman London west of the Walbrook*, The archaeology of Roman London 2, CBA Res Rep 70

Philp, B, 1977 'The forum of Roman London: excavations of 1968–9', *Britannia*, 8, 1–64

Pritchard, F, 1984 'Late Saxon textiles from the City of London', *Medieval Archaeol*, 28, 46–76

Pritchard, F, 1986 'Ornamental stonework from London', *Britannia*, 17, 169–89

Prockter, A, & Taylor, R (eds), 1979 *The A to Z of Elizabethan London*

Puleston, J H, & Price, J E, 1873 *Roman antiquities recently uncovered on the site of the National Safe Deposit Company's premises, Mansion House, London*

Rahtz, P (ed), 1974 *Rescue archaeology*

RCHM, 1928 *London III: Roman London*

RCHM, 1929 *London IV: The City of London*

Rhodes, M, 1987a 'Inscriptions on leather waste from Roman London', *Britannia*, 18, 173–81

Rhodes, M, 1987b 'Wall-paintings from Fenchurch Street, City of London', *Britannia*, 18, 169–72

Rhodes, M, 1991 'The Roman coinage from London Bridge and the development of the City and Southwark', *Britannia*, 2, 179–90

Rutter, E, 1958 'A medieval undercroft at 50 Mark Lane, London EC3', *Medieval Archaeol*, 2, 178–81

Samuel, M, 1989 'The fifteenth-century garner at Leadenhall, London', *Antiq J*, 69, 119–53

Schofield, J, 1981a 'Archive reports of archaeological excavations in the City of London', *Trans London Middlesex Archaeol Soc*, 32, 82–5

Schofield, J, 1981b 'Medieval waterfront buildings in the City of London', in Milne, G, & Hobley, B (eds), *Waterfront archaeology in Britain and northern Europe*, CBA Res Rep 41, 24–31

Schofield, J, 1987a 'Archaeology in the City of London: archive and publication', *Archaeol J*, 144, 424–33

Schofield, J (ed), 1987b *The London surveys of Ralph Treswell*, London Topographical Soc Publication 135

Schofield, J, 1990 'Medieval and Tudor domestic buildings in the City of London', in Grant, L (ed), *Medieval art, architecture and archaeology in London*, British Archaeol Assoc Conf for 1984, 16–28

Schofield, J, 1993a *The Building of London from the Conquest to the Great Fire*, rev edn

Schofield, J, 1993b 'Building in religious precincts in London at the Dissolution and after', in Gilchrist, R, & Mytum, H (eds), *Advances in monastic archaeology*, British Archaeol Reps 227, 29–42

Schofield, J, 1993c 'The capital rediscovered: archaeology in the City of London', *Urban History*, 20, 211–24

Schofield, J, 1994 'Saxon and medieval parish churches in the City of London: a review', *Trans London Middlesex Archaeol Soc*, 45, 23–146

Schofield, J, 1995 *Medieval London houses*

Schofield, J, in prep. 'Excavations on the site of St Nicholas Shambles, City of London, 1975–9', *Trans London Middlesex Archaeol Soc*

Schofield, J, & Dyson, T, 1980 *Archaeology of the City of London*

Schofield, J, & Dyson, T, in prep. *Medieval waterfront tenements*

Schofield, J, & Lea, R, in prep. *Holy Trinity Priory Aldgate*

Schofield, J, & Leech, R (eds), 1987 *Urban archaeology in Britain*, CBA Res Rep 61

Schofield, J, & Vince, A, 1994 *Medieval towns*

Schofield, J, Allen, P, & Taylor, C, 1990 'Medieval buildings and property development in the area of Cheapside', *Trans London Middlesex Archaeol Soc*, 41, 39–238

Shepherd, J, 1986 'The Roman features at Gateway House and Watling House, Watling Street, City of London (1954)', *Trans London Middlesex Archaeol Soc*, 37, 127–44

Shepherd, J, 1987 'The pre-urban and Roman topography in the King Street and Cheapside areas of the City of London', *Trans London Middlesex Archaeol Soc*, 38, 11–58

Shepherd, J, 1998a *The temple of Mithras in London: excavations by W F Grimes and A Williams at the Walbrook*

Shepherd, J (ed), 1998b *Post-War archaeology in the City of London, 1946–1972: a guide to records of excavations by Professor W F Grimes held by the Museum of London*

Sheppard, F, 1991 *The treasury of London's past*

Sloane, B, in prep. *Excavations at the nunnery of St Mary de Fonte Clericorum, Clerkenwell*

Sloane, B, & Malcolm, G, in prep. *Excavations at the Priory of the Order of the Hospital of St John of Jerusalem, Clerkenwell*

Smith, R A, 1909 'Anglo-Saxon remains', in *VCH*, i, 147–70

Spence, C (ed), 1989 *Digging in the City: the annual review 1988* (DUA, MoL)

Spence, C, 1993 'Recording the archaeology of London: the development and implementation of the DUA recording system', in Harris, E C, Marley Brown III, R, & Brown, G J (eds), *Practices of archaeological stratigraphy*, 23–46

Spence, C, & Grew, F (eds), 1990 *The annual review 1989* (DUA, MoL)

Spencer, B, in prep. *Pilgrim souvenirs and secular badges*, Medieval finds from excavations in London 7

Steedman, K, Dyson, T, & Schofield, J, 1992 *Aspects of Saxo-Norman London III: the bridgehead and Billingsgate to 1200*, London Middlesex Archaeol Soc Spec Pap 14

Symonds, R P, & Tomber, R S, with Lakin, D, & Richardson, B, 1991 'Late Roman London: an assessment of the ceramic evidence from the City of London', *Trans London Middlesex Archaeol Soc*, 42, 59–100

Tatton-Brown, T, 1974 'Excavations at the Custom House site City of London 1973', *Trans London Middlesex Archaeol Soc*, 25, 117–219

Tatton-Brown, T, 1975 'Excavations at Custom House — Part II', *Trans London Middlesex Archaeol Soc*, 26, 103–70

Thomas, C, Sloane, B, & Phillpotts, C, 1997 *Excavations at the Priory and Hospital of St Mary Spital, Bishopsgate*

Thompson, A, Grew, F, & Schofield, J, 1984 'Excavations at Aldgate, 1974', *Post-Medieval Archaeol*, 18, 1–148

Thompson, A, Westman, A, & Dyson, T (eds), 1998 *Archaeology in Greater London, 1965–1990: a guide to records of excavations by the Museum of London*

Toynbee, J, 1986 *The Roman art treasures from the Temple of Mithras*, London Middlesex Archaeol Soc Spec Pap 6

Tyers, P, & Vince, A, 1983 'Computing the DUA pottery', *London Archaeol*, 4, 299–305

VCH: Page, W (ed), 1909 *The Victoria [County] history of London*, i

Vince, A, 1984 'The Aldwych: Saxon London discovered', *Current Archaeol*, 93, 310–12

Vince, A, 1985 'Saxon and medieval pottery in London: a review', *Medieval Archaeol*, 29, 25–93

Vince, A, 1990 *Saxon London: an archaeological investigation*

Vince, A (ed), 1991 *Aspects of Saxo-Norman London II: finds and environmental evidence*, London Middlesex Archaeol Soc Spec Pap 12

Vince, A, & Egan, G, 1981 'The contents of a late eighteenth-century pit at Crosswall, City of London', *Trans London Middlesex Archaeol Soc*, 32, 159–81

Wacher, J, 1995 *The towns of Roman Britain*, rev edn

Ward-Perkins, J, 1940 *London Museum medieval catalogue*

Werner, A, comp., 1998 *London Bodies: the changing shape of Londoners from prehistoric times to the present day*

Westman, A (ed), 1995 *Archaeological site manual*, 3rd edn (MoLAS)

Wheeler, R E M, 1927 *London and the Vikings*

Wheeler, R E M, 1935 *London and the Saxons*

Whipp, D, in prep. 'Excavations at the Tower Postern'

White, W, 1988 *Skeletal remains from the cemetery of St Nicholas Shambles, City of London*, London Middlesex Archaeol Soc Spec Pap 9

Whytehead, R, 1980 'Excavations at Goodman's Yard, 1978', *Trans London Middlesex Archaeol Soc*, 31, 29–31

Whytehead, R, 1986 'The excavation of an area within a Roman cemetery at West Tenter Street, London, E1', *Trans London Middlesex Archaeol Soc*, 37, 23–126

Williams, T, 1993 *Public buildings in the south-west quarter of Roman London*, The archaeology of Roman London 3, CBA Res Rep 88

Williams, T, in prep. *The development of Roman London east of the Walbrook*, The archaeology of Roman London 4, CBA Res Rep

Wilmott, T, 1982 'Excavations at Queen Street, City of London, 1953 and 1960, and timber-lined wells in London', *Trans London Middlesex Archaeol Soc*, 33, 1–78

Wilmott, T, 1984 'Roman timber-lined wells in London: further examples', *Trans London Middlesex Archaeol Soc*, 35, 5–10

Wilmott, T, 1991 *Excavations in the middle Walbrook Valley, City of London, 1927–1960*, London Middlesex Archaeol Soc Spec Pap 13

Yule, B, 1990 'The "dark earth" and late Roman London', *Antiquity*, 64, 620–8

Yule, B, in prep. *Roman buildings on the Southwark waterfront: excavations at Winchester Palace, London, Part 1*

GUILDHALL MUSEUM SITE CODES BEFORE 1973

GM1	Post Office Court, 1–3 Abchurch Lane, EC4, 1939	30
GM2	Aldermanbury (junction with London Wall), EC2, 1961	30
GM3	Three Nun Court (formerly Church Alley), Aldermanbury, EC2, 1965–6	30
GM4	Guildhall Library (formerly Guildhall car park), Aldermanbury, EC2, 1965	31
GM5	Aldersgate, EC1, 1939	31
GM6	Aldersgate Street, EC1, 1924	32
GM7	Aldgate, junction with Duke's Place (east corner, site of Post Office), EC3, 1967	32
GM8	Opposite 78 Aldgate High Street, E1, 1925	32
GM9	52 Aldgate High Street, E1, 1938	33
GM10	St Botolph's churchyard / Botolph Street, EC3, 1965	33
GM11	Fore Street / 2 St Alphage Garden / St Alphage House (St Alphage churchyard), EC2, 1960 (=GM209)	33
GM12	Minster House, 12 Arthur Street / Laurence Pountney Lane, EC4, 1954–5	34
GM13	Guildhall offices formerly Bassishaw House (site of St Michael Bassishaw church), Basinghall Street, EC2, 1965	34
GM14	40 Basinghall Avenue (Route 11), EC2, 1962	34
GM15	19 Bevis Marks, EC3, 1935	35
GM16	St Mary Axe House, 56–60 St Mary Axe, 1–3 Goring Street, EC3, 1961	35
GM17	Billiter Street (sewer tunnel), EC3, 1953	35
GM18	19–21 Birchin Lane, EC3, 1935	35
GM19	Blackfriars Wreck 3, EC4, 1970 (=GM301)	36
GM20	Blossoms Inn, 3–4 Trump Street, EC2, 1956	36
GM21	Bow Bells House, 11 Bread Street, 46–55 Cheapside, EC4, 1958	37
GM22	Rear of 72 Upper Thames Street, EC4, 1961	37
GM23	Colchester House, Pepys Street, EC3, 1951	37
GM24	4 Bridewell Place, EC4, 1926	38
GM25	Site of Bush Lane, 152 Upper Thames Street, EC4, 1964–5	38
GM26	26–27 Byward Street (junction with Water Lane), EC3, 1968	38
GM27	4 Castle Court, EC3, 1976	39
GM28	25–29 (now 23–29) Camomile Street, EC3, 1958 (=GM299)	39
GM29	78–80 Cannon Street (site of Dyers' Arms), EC4, 1966	39
GM30	111 Cannon Street (site of St Swithun's church), EC4, 1961	40
GM31	Temple Court, 77 Cannon Street, Queen Victoria Street and 4 Budge Row, EC4, 1958 (probably=GM258)	40
GM32	106 Cannon Street, EC4, 1935	40
GM33	143–147 Cannon Street (Nicholas Lane site), EC4, 1961	41
GM34	67–69 Cheapside, 1–5 Queen Street, EC4, 1937–8	41
GM35	72–73 Cheapside, EC4, 1930	41
GM36	1–2 Bucklersbury, 76–80 Cheapside, 9–12 Pancras Lane (including site of St Pancras church), EC4, 1963 (including GM184)	42
GM37	110–116 Cheapside (Sun Life Assurance), EC2, 1955–6	43
GM38	137–144 Cheapside, EC2, 1957	44
GM39	Cheapside (opposite Milk Street), EC2, 1964	44
GM40	Cheapside (junction with New Change), EC4, 1963–4	44
GM41	5 Clark's Place, Bishopsgate, EC3, 1958	44
GM42	36–40 Coleman Street (site of St Stephen Coleman Street church), EC2, 1955–6	45
GM43	65–66 Coleman Street, EC2, 1953–4	45
GM44	8–10 Cooper's Row (and space at rear), EC3, 1962	46
GM45	5–7 Copthall Avenue, EC2, 1962 (=GM190)	46
GM46	52 Cornhill, EC3, 1930	46
GM47	69–73 Cornhill, EC3, 1959	47
GM48	Cousin Lane (north end), EC4, 1959	47
GM49	6 Crescent, EC3, 1938	47
GM50	28–32 King William Street (formerly Crooked Lane), EC4, 1961	47
GM51	2 Skinner's Lane, EC4, 1932	48
GM52	Suffolk House, Upper Thames Street (formerly 1–2 Ducksfoot Lane), EC4, 1966 (?=GM187)	48
GM53	Duke's Place (opposite nos 32–38), EC3, 1953	48
GM54	15–16 St Dunstan's Hill, EC3, 1937–8	49
GM55	Site of Bastion 6, Duke's Place, EC3, 1971	49
GM56	Noble Street (east side) / Falcon Square (south-east), EC2, 1956	49
GM57	125–135 Fenchurch Street, EC3, 1955	50
GM58	22 Fenchurch Street, EC3, 1964	50
GM59	31–34 Fenchurch Street, 23 Rood Lane and 4–8 Mincing Lane, EC3, 1935	50
GM60	112–114 Fenchurch Street, 17–18 Billiter Street, EC3, 1925–6	51
GM61	155 Fenchurch Street, EC3, 1934	51
GM62	154–161 Fleet Street, EC4, 1924–5	51
GM63	St Vedast House, 150 Cheapside / Foster Lane, EC2, 1962	51
GM64	16–45 Cheapside (formerly 5 Friday Street), EC4, 1925	52
GM65	8–10 Mansion House Place (formerly 13–14 George Street), EC4, 1961	52
GM66	St Alban's House, 124 Wood Street (formerly Goldsmith House, Goldsmith Street), EC2, 1961	52
GM67	Corbet Court, 3–6 Gracechurch Street (St Peter's Alley site), 53 Cornhill, EC3, 1964	53
GM68	17–19 Gracechurch Street, EC3, 1934	53
GM69	Midland Bank, 55–60 Gracechurch Street (site of St Benet Gracechurch), EC3, 1959	54
GM70	83–87 Gracechurch Street, EC3, 1934	54
GM71	11–16 Telegraph Street, EC2, 1934	54
GM72	London Wall Street (opposite Copthall Avenue), EC2, 1934	54
GM73	All Hallows Barking church, Great Tower Street, EC3, 1928–32, 1936 and 1951	55
GM74	Winchester House, Great Winchester Street, EC2, 1962–3 (=GM193)	56
GM75	2–12 Gresham Street (site of Waxchandlers' Hall), EC2, 1956–7	56
GM76	30 Gresham Street (formerly nos 20–38, and before that 26–27 King Street), EC2, 1960	57
GM77	Guildhall, EC2, 1951	57
GM78	8 Hart Street, EC2, 1950–1	58
GM79	28–30 Houndsditch, EC3, 1935	58
GM80	Huggin Hill (south-west corner), EC4, 1964	58
GM81	Sir John Cass College, 32–35 Jewry Street, EC3, 1933	59
GM82	9–12 King Street and Prudent Passage (Atlas Assurance site), EC2, 1963–4	59
GM83	13–14 King Street, EC2, 1956	59
GM84	26 King Street, EC2, 1960	60
GM85	33 King Street, 8–9 Lawrence Lane, EC2, 1938	60
GM86	34–35 King Street, 6–7 Lawrence Lane, EC2, 1955	60
GM87	39 King Street, EC2, 1935	60
GM88	1 King's Arms Yard (Bank of England Club), EC2, 1959	61
GM89	King William Street / Nicholas Lane, EC2, 1924	61
GM90	Old Change Court and Old Change House, Distaff Lane (rear of 128 Queen Victoria Street and formerly Knightrider Street), EC4, 1956 and 1961	61
GM91	101 Queen Victoria Street, Lambeth Hill (Salvation Army Headquarters), EC4, 1961 (=GM208)	62
GM92	Albion House, 34–35 Leadenhall Street, EC3, 1953	63
GM93	77 Leadenhall Street, EC3, 1968	63
GM94	139–144 Leadenhall Street, EC3, 1964	63
GM95	22–23 Lime Street, 160–170 Fenchurch Street (Barclay's Bank) (site of St Dionis Backchurch church), EC3, 1969	63
GM96	41–51 Lime Street / Billiter Street (Lloyd's site), EC3, 1951–2	64
GM97	15–18 Lime Street, EC3, 1932	64
GM98	15 Lombard Street (Coutt's Bank), EC3, 1958–9	65
GM99	30–32 Lombard Street, EC3, 1962	65
GM100	54–58 Lombard Street (Barclay's Bank), EC3, 1960–1 (=GM295)	65
GM101	54 Lombard Street (site of All Hallows Lombard Street church), EC3, 1939 and 1957	66
GM102	54 Lombard Street, EC3, 1933 (=GM296)	66
GM103	79 Lombard Street, EC3, 1933	67
GM104	Lombard Street (opposite St Clements Lane), EC3, 1937	67
GM105	Lombard Street / Nicholas Lane, EC3, 1937	67
GM106	Site of London Bridge, River Thames, 1967	67
GM107	150 London Wall (Museum of London), EC2 (formerly EC1), 1971–2	68
GM108	London Wall (opposite Coleman Street), EC2, 1961	68
GM109	London Wall (north-west of Aldermanbury), EC2, 1956–7 (=GM173)	68
GM110	Lothbury (opposite no. 5), EC2, 1963	69
GM111	Coal Exchange, 100 Lower Thames Street (Billingsgate Roman bath-house site), EC3, 1951 and 1968–71	69
GM112	Lower Thames Street (west side of Billingsgate Market), EC3, 1960	69
GM113	18–28 Ludgate Hill, EC4, 1960	70
GM114	26–28 Mark Lane, 28–29 Mincing Lane, EC3, 1935	70
GM115	43–51 St Mary Axe (site of St Mary Axe church), EC3, 1950–1	70

GM116   1 Masons Avenue (Butler's Head), EC2, 1955   70

GM117   St Michael's House, 1–2 St Michael's Alley, EC3, 1932   71

GM118   Opposite 140–150 London Wall (west gate of Roman fort), EC2, 1956   71

GM119   20–28 Moorgate, 1–4 Copthall Close, 10–11 Great Swan Alley, EC2, 1936   71

GM120   30 Moorgate, EC2, 1951   71

GM121   55–61 Moorgate, EC2, 1929   72

GM122   46–47 New Broad Street, EC2, 1925   72

GM123   St Augustine's church (Old Change or Watling Street), now St Paul's Cathedral Choir School, New Change, EC4, 1965   72

GM124   New Change, EC4, 1957   73

GM125   Fresh Wharf, 1–6 Lower Thames Street, EC4, 1937   73

GM126   New Fresh Wharf, 1–6 Lower Thames Street, EC4, 1950   73

GM127   Cripplegate, Bastion 12, EC2, 1953   73

GM128   6–9 Newgate Street, EC4, 1965   73

GM129   Westminster Bank, 21 Lombard Street (site of St Nicholas Acon church, Nicholas Lane), EC4, 1963–4   74

GM130   Shelley House, 3 Noble Street (formerly no. 1), EC2, 1959   74

GM131   Central Criminal Court, Old Bailey / Warwick Square, EC4, 1966–9   75

GM132   Hillgate House, 27–34 Old Bailey, 50–62 Ludgate Hill, EC4, 1959   75

GM133   33–34 Old Jewry (Price Waterhouse), Frederick's Place, EC2, 1952   76

GM134   27–32 Old Jewry (Bank of Sydney), EC2, 1953   76

GM135   160 Queen Victoria Street (Printing House Square, site of former Times offices), EC4, 1960   76

GM136   Paternoster Square development (including 10–14 Newgate Street and 61–70 St Paul's Churchyard), EC4, 1961–2   77

GM137   Upper Thames Street / St Peter's Hill (site of St Peter Paul's Wharf church), EC4, 1961   78

GM138   Pilgrim Street (sewerworks west end), EC4, 1925–6   78

GM139   32–33 Lombard Street, Plough Court (Bank of New York), EC4, 1955 6   79

GM140   33–35 Poultry, EC2, 1936   79

GM141   6–8 Princes Street, EC2, 1970   79

GM142   Aldermary House, 10–15 Queen Street, 61–62 Watling Street, EC4, 1960   79

GM143   Queen Victoria Street / Poultry (Bank Underground Station), EC4, 1959–60   80

GM144   40–66 Queen Victoria Street, 82 Queen Street (formerly Bank of London and South America), EC4, 1953–4   80

GM145   Guildhall, EC2, 1968   81

GM146   Bastion 19, General Post Office Yard, Giltspur Street, EC1, 1908–9   82

GM147   Sugar Loaf Court, Garlick Hill, EC4, 1959   82

GM148   39 Threadneedle Street (site of St Martin Outwich church), EC2, 1927   82

GM149   1–4 Threadneedle Street, EC2, 1965   83

GM150   8 Old Bailey, EC4, 1900   83

GM151   Upper Thames Street (sewer on north side between Queen Street and Dowgate Hill), EC4, 1958–9   83

GM152   Baynard House, Queen Victoria Street (Upper Thames Street, site of second Baynard's Castle), EC4, 1972–3 (=BC72)   84

GM153   25 Upper Thames Street (Fur Trade House), EC4, 1969   85

GM154   Central Criminal Court, Newgate Street, EC4, 1903   85

GM155   61 Queen Street / Upper Thames Street (site of St Martin Vintry church), EC4, 1956–7   85

GM156   Walbrook Wharf, Upper Thames Street (Public Cleansing Depot), EC4, 1959–60   86

GM157   Bucklersbury House, 11–12 Walbrook, EC4, 1954–5   87

GM158   St Swithin's House, 30–37 Walbrook, EC4, 1949–50   87

GM159   10 Warwick Square, EC4, 1925   88

GM160   Gateway House, 1 Watling Street (including the site of St John Evangelist church), EC4, 1954   89

GM161   67–69 Watling Street, EC4, 1961   90

GM162   4–9 Wood Street (Mitre Court), EC2, 1953   90

GM163   St Dunstan's Hill, 84 Lower Thames Street, EC3, 1967   90

GM164   160 Queen Victoria Street (south-east corner; site of Times offices), EC4, 1935   90

GM165   Shoe Lane, open space at rear of 2 Charterhouse Street / 10 Holborn Viaduct, EC1, 1954   90

GM166   6–12, 15, 16–45 Cheapside (Bank of England) / New Change, EC4, 1957   91

GM167   Barber-Surgeons' Hall Gardens (formerly Windsor Court, Monkwell Street), Wood Street, EC2, ?19th century   91

GM168   Old Change House, 4–6 Cannon Street, EC4, 1955   91

GM169   22–25 Farringdon Street (Amalgamated Press site), EC4, 1955   91

GM170   City Institute of Marine Engineers war memorial, 56–59 Fenchurch Street, EC3, 1956   92

GM171   8–18 Cannon Street (rear of Bracken House; Financial Times site), EC4, 1955   92

GM172   50 Mark Lane, EC3, 1957   92

GM173   London Wall (Route 11) between Coleman Street and Basinghall Street, EC2, 1957 (=GM109)   93

GM174   11–13 Crosswall / Vine Street, EC3, 1957   93

GM175   Cannon Street Station (south-west corner by Upper Thames Street), EC4, 1959   93

GM176   20 Cannon Street (Wates site), EC4, 1959   93

GM177   Girdlers' Hall, Basinghall Street, EC2, 1960   94

GM178   Mansion House Underground Station, Queen Victoria Street, EC4, 1960   94

GM179   Barber-Surgeons' Hall and Lee House (Cripplegate corner), Monkwell Square, EC2, 1960   94

GM180   Swan Lane car park, 95–103 Upper Thames Street (Dyers' Hall Wharf), EC4, 1961   94

GM181   Blackfriars underpass (Blackfriars Wreck 2), EC4, 1962 (=GM302)   95

GM182   Blackfriars underpass, Puddle Dock (Cofferdam 1: Roman ship), EC4, 1962   95

GM183   Blackfriars Bridge (road) (Cofferdam 4: Blackfriars Wreck 4), EC4, 1970   95

GM184   9–12 Pancras Lane (site of St Pancras church), EC4, 1963 (=GM36)   95

GM185   97–101 Cannon Street (Gallagher Ltd), EC4, 1964   95

GM186   Playground, Portsoken Street (south side), E1, 1965   96

GM187   Suffolk House, 154–156 Upper Thames Street (Suffolk Lane), EC4, 1969 (?=GM52)   96

GM188   2–3 New London Street, 34–35 Crutched Friars, EC3, 1973   96

GM189   Mermaid Theatre, Upper Thames Street (Puddle Dock), EC4, 1957   96

GM190   9 Great Swan Alley (Copthall Close) / Copthall Avenue, EC2, 1961 (=GM45)   97

GM191   20–30 Aldgate, EC3, 1972 (=CASS72)   97

GM192   14–20 St Mary Axe (Baltic Exchange Co), EC3, 1952–3   97

GM193   Winchester House, 74–77 London Wall, EC2, 1963 (=GM74)   97

GM194   Milton Court, 1–13 Moor Lane (Public Services Building), EC2, 1963   98

GM195   City of London unstratified finds from various sites   98

GM196   24–30 St Swithin's Lane (London Assurance), EC4, 1953   98

GM197   ?66–75 Aldermanbury (fort ditch section on west side of Aldermanbury RMLEC site 14), EC2, 1963   98

GM198   Barclay's Bank site, [?Old] Broad Street, EC2, c 1953   98

GM199   St Mary le Bow church, Cheapside, EC4, 1955   99

GM200   St Lawrence Jewry church, Gresham Street, EC2, 1952, 1954 and 1955   99

GM201   Falcon Street (north turret of fort), EC2, 1955   99

GM202   36–38 Botolph Lane, EC3, 1959   99

GM203   20–21 Lawrence Lane, EC2, 1965   100

GM204   Gutter Lane (south of Saddlers' Hall), EC2, 1959   100

GM205   St John Zachary Gardens, Gresham Street, EC2, 1960   100

GM206   Thames foreshore at Billingsgate, EC3, 1960   100

GM207   Thames foreshore, 1963   101

GM208   Lambeth Hill east road scheme (now west), EC4, 1960 (=GM91)   101

GM209   1–3 St Alphage Highwalk, EC2, 1960 (=GM11)   101

GM210   9–11 Bush Lane, EC4, 1960–1   101

GM211   Dowgate Hill House, Upper Thames Street / Little College Lane, EC4, 1959   102

GM212   St Alban's church, Wood Street, EC2, 1962   102

GM213   Watling House, 12–16 Watling Street, 31–37 Cannon Street, EC4, 1954   102

GM214   10–12 Cooper's Row (site of Barber's Warehouse), EC3, 1935   103

GM215   Cripplegate Buildings (now Roman House), Wood Street, EC2, 1947   103

GM216   Guildhall, EC2, 1954–5   103

GM217   7–8 (formerly 3–8) King Street, EC2, ?1926–7   103

GM218   67 Lombard Street, Birchin Lane, EC3, 1929   104

GM219   11 Ironmonger Lane, EC2, 1949   104

GM220   Ironmonger Lane or St Olave's Court (sewer trench), EC2, 1932   104

GM221   10–12 Little Trinity Lane, EC4, 1929 (=GM321)   105

GM222   Wallside Monkwell Square (formerly 63–64 Wood Street), EC2, 1932   105

GM223   St Mary le Bow church, Cheapside, EC4, 1934 and 1959   105

GM224   39 St Andrew's Hill, EC4, 1935   105

GM225   53 Cornhill, EC3, 1937   106

GM226   2 Moorgate (Founders' Court), EC2, 1927 and 1930   106

GM227	London Electricity Board Ludgate main substation (?Seacoal House), Seacoal Lane, EC4, 1952	106
GM228	?Haberdashers' Hall, Gresham Street, EC2, 1953	107
GM229	Brook's Wharf (south end of Stew Lane), Upper Thames Street, EC4, 1953	107
GM230	Mincing Lane, EC3, ?1955	107
GM231	Windsor Court (RMLEC site WFG3; now gardens south of Barber-Surgeons' Hall, Monkwell Square), EC2, 1955	107
GM232	?7–17 Jewry Street (almost directly opposite Roman Wall House), EC3, 1955	107
GM233	General Steam Navigation Company, Lower Thames Street, EC3, 1957	108
GM234	Addle Street / Aldermanbury (?1 Aldermanbury Square), EC2, 1957	108
GM235	Red Bull Yard, All Hallows Lane, Upper Thames Street (?Mondial House), EC4, 1957	108
GM236	Philip Lane (?Royex House, Aldermanbury Square), EC2, 1960	108
GM237	Bush Lane (sewer at south end), EC4, 1964	109
GM238	Fleet Lane (corner with Seacoal Lane), EC4, 1955	109
GM239	Huggin Hill (east side, bath-house site II), EC4, 1969	109
GM240	Huggin Hill (Roman bath-house), EC4, 1964 and 1969	109
GM241	Leadenhall Street / St Mary Axe (Commercial Union and P&O site), EC3, 1964	110
GM242	Site of Bastion 7, Duke's Place, EC3, 1949	110
GM243	Bartholomew Lane, EC2, 1932	111
GM244	Bartholomew Close, Little Britain, EC1, 1934	111
GM245	St Mary Aldermanbury church, Aldermanbury, EC2, 1967–8	111
GM246	28–30 Cornhill, EC3, 1934	111
GM247	Roman Wall House, Crutched Friars, EC3, ?1905	111
GM248	King William Street / Fish Street Hill (Regis House), EC3, 1930	112
GM249	King William Street (junction with Cannon Street opposite nos 116–126), EC4, 1935	112
GM250	40 Mitre Street, EC3, 1898 and 1967	112
GM251	37 Ludgate Hill, EC4, 1969	112
GM252	3–6 Lothbury, EC2, 1930	113
GM253	London Wall (opposite nos 108–115), EC2, 1930	113
GM254	Blossoms Inn Yard, EC2, 1930	113
GM255	69–73 Cannon Street, EC4, 1933	114
GM256	Temple of Mithras, Walbrook, EC4, 1952–4	114
GM257	Bank of England, Princes Street, EC2, 1933–4	114
GM258	'Temple House', Queen Victoria Street, EC4, 1959 (probably=GM31)	115
GM259	Noble Street (west side), EC2, 1972	115
GM260	GPO site (Mondial House), Upper Thames Street, EC4, 1969	115
GM261	129–130 Upper Thames Street, EC4, 1931	116
GM262	St Mary le Bow church, Cheapside, EC2, 1932	116
GM263	St Stephen Walbrook church, Walbrook, EC4, 1960s or 1970s	116
GM264	Bastion 14, Barber-Surgeons' Hall Gardens (150 London Wall), EC2, 1947	116
GM266	*Daily News* site, 22 Bouverie Street, EC4, 1924	117
GM268	4–6 Lime Street (Lloyd's), EC3, 1925	117
GM276	42 Lombard Street, EC4, 1925	117
GM280	50 Fleet Street (rear) (Serjeants' Inn), EC4, c 1950	117
GM287	205 Upper Thames Street / Lambeth Hill, EC4, 1924	118
GM288	58–60 Houndsditch / Camomile Street, EC3, 1926	118
GM292	77 Leadenhall Street, EC3, 1924–5	118
GM293	Gracechurch Street (east of St Peter Cornhill church), EC3, 1922	118
GM294	Gracechurch Street (shaft), EC3, 1978	119
GM295	54–58 Lombard Street (Barclay's Bank), EC3, 1960–1 (=GM100)	119
GM296	Lombard Street (south of All Hallows Lombard Street church), EC3, 1933 (=GM102)	119
GM297	22 Lime Street, 168–170 Fenchurch Street (Barclay's Bank) (site of St Dionis Backchurch church), EC3, 1968–9	119
GM298	5–8 Birchin Lane, EC3, 1935	119
GM299	25–29 Camomile Street, EC3, 1958 (=GM28)	119
GM301	Blackfriars Riverside Wall, Wreck 3, EC4, 1970 (=GM19)	120
GM302	Blackfriars Riverside Wall, Wreck 2, EC4, 1970 (=GM181)	120
GM303	Fetter Lane (adjoining Neville's Court), now 15–17 New Fetter Lane, EC1, 1921	120
GM305	Aldersgate Street / London Wall (Museum of London rotunda), EC2, 1972	120
GM306	Carter Lane, EC4, pre-1939	121
GM307	St Paul's Cathedral, north of north portico, EC4, 1970	121
GM308	Cripplegate and city wall nearby, EC2, 1947–66	121
GM309	Cross Lane (south of Cannon Street), EC4, 1945	121
GM310	Falcon Street, EC2, 1957	121
GM311	20–23 Fenchurch Street, EC3, 1964	122
GM312	Fenchurch Street, EC3, pre-1927	122
GM313	Fetter Lane, EC4, 1896	122
GM314	Cannon Street (*Financial Times* site), EC4, 1955	122
GM315	12–16 Finsbury Circus, EC2, 1920	122
GM316	Fore Street, EC2, 1954	123
GM317	'Fort' and 'Fort West Gate' excavations, Cripplegate, EC2, c 1955	123
GM318	'GPO' (presumably east side of St Martin's le Grand), EC2, 1913–14 and 1925	123
GM319	Leadenhall Street, EC3	123
GM320	Lime Street, EC3, 1945–7	124
GM321	10–12 Little Trinity Lane, EC4, 1929–30 (=GM221)	124
GM322	6 Lloyd's Row, St John's Street, EC1	124
GM323	Mercers' Hall, Cheapside, EC2, probably post-War	124
GM324	Miles Lane, EC4, 1926–7	124
GM325	Nicholas Lane, EC4, c 1926	125
GM326	7 Leadenhall Market, EC3, 1924	125
GM327	2–5 Fenchurch Buildings, and west side of Fenchurch Buildings, Fenchurch Street, EC3, 1924–5	125
GM328	26–27 Paternoster Square, EC4, 1925	125
GM329	28–30 Gracechurch Street, EC4, 1928	126

DEPARTMENT OF URBAN ARCHAEOLOGY SITE CODES, 1973–1991

For these site codes, the last two digits indicate the year of excavation, or the first year of a project which lasted several years. These codes include two sites started in 1972 by the Guildhall Museum (BC72, CASS72), one undertaken by the City of London Archaeological Society (MIL72) and one by Ove Arup & Partners (FNS72); all these took place before the creation of the DUA in 1973.

Code	Description	Page
BC72	Baynard's Castle, Baynard House, EC4 (=GM152)	126
CASS72	Sir John Cass School, 20–30 Aldgate, EC3 (=GM191)	126
FNS72	110–114 Fenchurch Street, EC3	128
MIL72	7–10 Milk Street, EC2	128
AFR73	Africa House, 39–42 Leadenhall Street, EC3	129
BLH73	Bush Lane House, 80 Cannon Street, EC4	129
CUS73	Custom House, Sugar Quay, Lower Thames Street, EC3	129
GF73	Christchurch Greyfriars, Newgate Street, EC1	130
LPL73	Laurence Pountney Lane, EC4	130
MC73	Site of St Mildred Bread Street church, now 84–94 Queen Victoria Street, EC4	131
ML73	24–27 Martin Lane, 4–8 Arthur Street, EC4	131
NOB73	29 Noble Street, EC2	131
ACW74	1–8 Angel Court, 30–35 Throgmorton Street, EC2	131
AL74	Wingate Centre, 62–64 Aldgate High Street, E1	132
BC74	Baynard House, Queen Victoria Street / White Lion Hill, EC4	133
FSH74	Fish Street Hill (west side), EC3	133
HL74	14–21 St Dunstan's Hill, Cross Lane (Harp Lane), EC3	133
LH74	42–46 Ludgate Hill, 1–6 Old Bailey, EC4	134
MM74	Baynard House, Queen Victoria Street (site of Upper Thames Street), EC4	134
MN74	Bain Dawes House, 15 Minories, EC3	134
MON74	Monument Street, 16 Fish Street Hill, EC3	134
NFW74	New Fresh Wharf, 2–6 Lower Thames Street, EC3	135
SH74	Seal House, 106–108 Upper Thames Street, EC4 (including SH76)	137
SPS74	St Paul's Cathedral Choir School, New Change, EC4	137
TL74	2–3 Trig Lane, Upper Thames Street, EC4	138
TR74	Billingsgate Buildings, 101–110 Lower Thames Street, EC3	140
UPP74	Upper Thames Street (south side, near Fishmongers' Hall), EC4	140
UT74	Upper Thames Street (now Baynard House, Queen Victoria Street), EC4	140
BC75	Upper Thames Street (Baynard's Castle), now Baynard House, Queen Victoria Street, EC4	140
BIL75	Billingsgate bath-house, 100 Lower Thames Street, EC3	141
CAS75	3–4 Jewry Street, EC3	142
CS75	48–50 Cannon Street, EC4	142
GPO75	76–80 Newgate Street (former GPO; now British Telecom Headquarters, 81 Newgate Street), EC1	142
KW75	8–12 King William Street, EC4	144
PIL75	5 Pilgrim Street, EC4	144
SL75	10 St Swithin's Lane, EC4	145
SM75	[St Magnus] New Fresh Wharf, 2–6 Lower Thames Street, EC3	145
BG76	190 Bishopsgate, EC2	145
BON76	16–28 Tabernacle Street, Bonhill Street, EC2	145
CAM76	Camomile Street (south pavement at west end), EC3	145
CHR76	Christchurch Greyfriars, Newgate Street, EC1	146
FET76	113–137 Fetter Lane (rear of St Dunstan's House), EC4	146
FSE76	160–162 Fenchurch Street, 22–23 Lime Street, EC3	146
GSA76	Great Swan Alley, 68–71 Coleman Street, EC2	147
LC76	2–3 Lombard Court, 39–40 Lombard Street, EC3	147
MAR76	St Margaret Lothbury church, Lothbury, EC2	147
MFS76	Modern foreshore, River Thames, EC3 & EC4	148
MLK76	1–6 Milk Street, 5–6 Russia Row, EC2	148
NH76	4–8 Northumberland Alley, EC3	150
PEN76	Peninsular House, 112–116 Lower Thames Street, EC3	150
BXA77	St Botolph Bishopsgate churchyard, Bastion 10A, EC2	150
CGT77	Cripplegate Gardens, London Wall and Wallside, EC2	150
DUK77	St James Passage subway, 2–7 Dukes Place, EC3	151
GST77	Gracechurch Street, GPO tunnel, EC3	151
KSC77	Kingscote Street, tunnel, EC4	151
BRI78	9–12 Bridewell Place, 13–16 New Bridge Street, EC4	152
CUT78	Cutler Street PLA Warehouses, Harrow Place, E1	152
FRE78	New Fresh Wharf (watching brief), 1–6 Lower Thames Street, EC3	153
HOU78	Chatsworth House, 48–56 Houndsditch, 66–70 St Mary Axe, EC3	153
LLO78	Lloyd's, 12–19 Leadenhall Street, EC3	153
MAS78	1–9 Masons Avenue (Butler's Head), 10–14 Masons Avenue, 23 Moorgate, EC2	154
TST78	Upper Thames Street, tunnel, EC4	154
TUD78	1–3 Tudor Street, EC4	154
WAT78	Watling Court, 10–14a Bow Lane, 39–53 Cannon Street, 19–28 Watling Street, EC4	155
AGT79	174–176 Aldersgate Street, EC1	156
BAR79	Medical School, St Bartholomew's Hospital, EC1	156
BLL79	Bull Wharf, 14–15 Queenhithe, EC4	157
CRE79	33 Creechurch Lane, 16a Bevis Marks, EC3	157
FCH79	78–79 Fenchurch Street, EC3	157
FRR79	22–25 Farringdon Street, EC1	157
HEN79	6–10 Heneage Lane, EC3	158
HTP79	Mitre Square, 10–14 Mitre Street, EC3	158
ILA79	Miles Lane, 132–137 Upper Thames Street, 15–17 Arthur Street, EC4	158
PEN79	Peninsular House, 112–116 Lower Thames Street, EC3	159
POM79	Newgate Street, GPO site, middle area, EC1	160
THE79	Mermaid Theatre, Puddle Dock, EC4	160
WEL79	5–10, 12a–13 Well Court, 44–48 Bow Lane, EC4	161
WOW79	128–133 Cheapside (Woolworths), 1 Gutter Lane, 130 Wood Street, EC2	161
XWL79	8–10 Crosswall, EC3	162
BEV80	1–9, 10–16 Bevis Marks, 15–18 Bury Street, EC3	163
CAN80	62–64 Cannon Street, EC4	163
CCN80	Christchurch Greyfriars, Newgate Street, EC1	163
FEC80	47–49 Fenchurch Street, EC3	164
FSP80	60 Fenchurch Street, Post Office, EC3	164
HAG80	46 (Hoop and Grapes) and 47 Aldgate High Street, EC3	164
IRO80	24–25 Ironmonger Lane, 9–12 King Street, EC2	165
MOO80	GPO tunnel, Moorgate, EC2	165
NIC80	12 Nicholas Lane, EC4	165
PUB80	The George public house, 86 Fenchurch Street, EC3	166
SPC80	St Paul's churchyard, EC4	166
ADM81	Alderman's House, 34–37 Liverpool Street, EC2	166
APO81	Apothecaries' Hall and 22–26 Blackfriars Lane, EC4	166
ARC81	9 The Arches, Crutched Friars, EC3	167
BYD81	South-east corner tower of Baynard's Castle, City of London Boys' School, Upper Thames Street, EC4	167
CLE81	29–32 Clements Lane, 33–36 Lombard Street, EC4	168
CNL81	68–73 Cornhill, EC3	169
COL81	19–20 College Hill, EC4	170
FIN81	Finsbury House, 23 Blomfield Street, EC2	170
LOV81	9–9½ and 21–24 Lovat Lane, 8–19 St Mary at Hill, 29–40 Botolph Lane, EC3	171
OPT81	2–3 Cross Keys Court, Copthall Avenue, EC2	171
PDN81	11–11A Pudding Lane (now Namura House), 22–26 Monument Street, 121–127 Lower Thames Street, EC3	173
PET81	St Peter's Hill and 223–225 Upper Thames Street, EC4	174
PHI81	5–7 Philpot Lane, EC3	175
SWA81	Swan Lane car park, 95–103 Upper Thames Street, EC4	176

Code	Description	Page
ALD82	Museum of London rotunda, junction of Aldersgate and London Wall, EC2	177
APY82	Apothecary Street (north side), near junction with New Bridge Street, EC4	177
BIG82	Billingsgate Market lorry park, Lower Thames Street, EC3	177
BIS82	76–80 Bishopsgate, EC2	180
BOP82	28–34 Bishopsgate, 2–3 Crosby Square, 2–3 Great St Helens, EC2	181
BSA82	Billingsgate bath-house, 4–9 St Dunstan's Hill, 100 Lower Thames Street, EC3	182
CRC82	Opposite 22 Creechurch Lane, EC3	182
FLE82	180–183 Fleet Street, 140–143 Fetter Lane, EC4	182
LAT82	1–6 Ludgate Circus Buildings, EC4	182
LIB82	119–121 Cannon Street, 1–3 Abchurch Yard, 14 Sherbourne Lane, EC4	183
LOG82	84–85 Long Lane, EC1	183
LON82	London Wall, junction with Blomfield Street, EC2	184
LUD82	1–6 Old Bailey, 42–46 Ludgate Hill, EC4	184
MAN82	21–29 Mansell Street, E1	185
OST82	7–10 Foster Lane, 5–6 Rose and Crown Court, EC2	185
POT82	9–10 Philpot Lane, EC3	186
RAG82	1–12 Rangoon Street, 61–65 Crutched Friars, 2–4 Carlisle Avenue, 11–13 Northumberland Alley (now Friary Court), EC3	187
SLO82	14 Garlick Hill (Sugar Loaf Court), EC4	187
TAV82	Horn Tavern, 29–33 Knightrider Street, EC4	188
ACE83	77–79 Gracechurch Street, EC3	188
ARK83	42–46 Houndsditch, 24–25 Bevis Marks, EC3	189
BID83	St Bride's House, 10–12 Salisbury Court, 1–4 Dorset Buildings, EC4	189
BIR83	18 Birchin Lane, 62 Lombard Street, EC3	190
BOA83	Bank of Argentina, 11 Ironmonger Lane, EC2	190
BWB83	Billingsgate Market lorry park (watching brief), Lower Thames Street, EC3	190
CLO83	24–37 Cloth Fair, 62–67 Long Lane, EC1	192
CUL83	154–156 Fenchurch Street, 15–16 Cullum Street, EC3	192
EST83	23–29 Eastcheap, 14–15 Philpot Lane, EC3	192
FEN83	5–12 Fenchurch Street, 1 Philpot Lane, EC3	193
HOP83	3–5 Bishopsgate, EC2	194
IME83	27–30 Lime Street, EC3	195
KEY83	15–35 Copthall Avenue, 45–50 London Wall, 2–3 Cross Keys Court, EC2	195
LIM83	25–26 Lime Street, EC3	196
OMB83	37 Lombard Street, EC3	197
SKI83	2–4 Skinner's Lane, 36–39 Queen Street, 19–20 Garlick Hill, EC4	197
TEL83	8 Telegraph Street, EC2	197
WAY83	7–9 Pilgrim Street, 10–13 Ludgate Broadway, EC4	198
WIT83	18–23 St Swithin's Lane, 113–117 Cannon Street, 13 Sherbourne Lane, EC4	198
ALG84	7–12 Aldersgate Street, EC1	199
CHL84	4–6 Copthall Avenue, EC2	199
DEL84	6–7 New Bridge Street, 16–17 and 21 Bride Lane, EC4	200
ECP84	23–39 Eastcheap, 14–15 Philpot Lane, EC3	200
ETH84	St Ethelburga Bishopsgate church, Bishopsgate, EC2	200
FSS84	Fenchurch Street Station, EC3	201
GCH84	1–2 Gracechurch Street, EC3	201
GRA84	77–79 Gracechurch Street, EC3	201
HIL84	7–8 Philpot Lane, EC3	202
LCT84	99–100 Gracechurch Street, 1–6 Leadenhall Street, 2–12 Whittington Avenue (now Leadenhall Court), EC3	203
LDW84	44 London Wall, EC2	204
LEA84	71–77 Leadenhall Street, 32–40 Mitre Street, EC3	204
LWA84	43 London Wall, EC2	206
MAH84	St Mary at Hill church, St Mary at Hill, EC3	206
MIR84	12–14 Mitre Street, EC3	207
NBS84	35–38 New Bridge Street, EC4	208
SSL84	18, 19, 21–23 St Swithin's Lane, 13 Sherbourne Lane, EC4	208
TIG84	Trig Lane, Upper Thames Street (watching brief), EC4	209
ADT85	131 Aldersgate Street, 14 Carthusian Street, EC2	209
AGS85	Carthusian Street, junction with Aldersgate Street, EC2	209
ATR85	10 Arthur Street, EC4	209
BBT85	4 Brabant Court, EC3	210
BMK85	Billingsgate Market, Lower Thames Street, EC3	210
CME85	West side of Coleman Street, near Woolgate House, EC2	210
CRH85	2–20 Creechurch Lane, 24–31 Mitre Street, EC3	210

Code	Description	Page
CST85	6–7 Crescent, 41–42 Trinity Square, EC3	211
FMO85	37–40 Fish Street Hill, 16–20 Monument Street, EC3	211
FST85	94–97 Fenchurch Street, EC3	212
GDH85	Guildhall House, 81–87 Gresham Street, EC2	213
KHN85	6–9 Kinghorn Street, EC1	214
KNG85	36–37 King Street, EC2	214
LAU85	6 Laurence Pountney Hill, EC4	215
LBY85	7 Ludgate Broadway, EC4	215
LSM85	Little Somerset Street, E1	216
LSS85	Liverpool Street Station, Broad Street Station, EC2	216
NWG85	Newgate Street (south side), outside Central Criminal Court, EC1	216
OLC85	St Margaret's Rectory, St Olave's Court, Ironmonger Lane, EC2	217
PCH85	1–3 St Paul's Churchyard, 1–9 Ludgate Hill, 15 Creed Lane, 40 Carter Lane, EC4	217
PLM85	7–8 Plumtree Court, 26–30 Holborn Viaduct, 54–55 Farringdon Street, EC1	218
QUN85	61 Queen Street, EC4	218
QVS85	167–179 Queen Victoria Street, EC4	219
SMN85	St Martin's le Grand, junction with Newgate Street, EC2	219
SON85	Mansion House, Poultry, EC4	219
STW85	St Stephen Walbrook church, Walbrook, EC4	220
ABS86	St Alban's House, 124 Wood Street, EC2	220
APG86	The city wall at St Alphage Garden, 4 Fore Street, 4–10 Alphage High Walk, EC2	220
AXE86	St Mary Axe House, 56–60 St Mary Axe, 1–3 Goring Street, EC3	221
BFT86	Beaufort House, 29–55 Middlesex Street, 15 St Botolph Street, E1	221
BHO86	Bible House, 146 Queen Victoria Street, EC4	222
BLA86	36–38 Botolph Lane, EC3	222
BOT86	St Botolph Aldgate church, Aldgate High Street, EC3	222
BOY86	Former City of London Boys' School, 60 Victoria Embankment, 5–17 Tudor Street, EC4	222
BUS86	8–14 Brushfield Street, EC1	223
CAP86	Capel House, 54–62 New Broad Street, EC2	224
CAT86	52–54 Carter Lane, EC4	224
CFA86	43–44 Cloth Fair, 8 Cloth Court, EC1	224
CIL86	62–64 Cornhill, EC3	225
COA86	16 Coleman Street, EC2	225
CON86	76 Cannon Street, EC4	225
CRU86	9–13 Crutched Friars, 1–7 Crosswall, EC3	226
CTN86	10–13 Carthusian Street, EC1	226
CUE86	9–19 Cutler Street, E1	226
DGH86	Dowgate Hill House, 14–16 Dowgate Hill, EC4	227
DOW86	3–7 Dowgate Hill, EC4	228
FRD86	17–21 Farringdon Street, EC4	228
GTO86	Great St Thomas Apostle (north side), junction with Queen Street, EC4	228
HEL86	St Helen Bishopsgate church, Bishopsgate, EC3	228
JBL86	Jubilee Gardens, Houndsditch, EC3	229
LBT86	Little Britain, 14–14a Bartholomew Close, EC1	229
LLN86	Long Lane (east end, south side), EC1	230
LMB86	1–6 Lombard Street, EC3	230
MIO86	118 Minories, EC3	230
MIT86	32–34 Mitre Street, EC3	230
MLL86	14–16 Mansell Street, E1	231
MOG86	49–53 Moorgate, 72–74 Coleman Street, EC2	231
MRS86	2–5 Minories, EC3	232
NEH86	Automated Public Convenience, south side of St Paul's Cathedral Choir School, New Change, EC4	232
NHA86	9 Northumberland Alley, EC3	232
ORG86	St Martin Orgar churchyard, 24–32 King William Street, EC4	232
PAL86	56–66 Carter Lane, 1–3 Ludgate Square, EC4	233
PUT86	1–19 Poultry, 2–22 Queen Victoria Street, EC2	233
QNV86	74–82 Queen Victoria Street, EC4	233
SNL86	Sunlight Wharf (north end only), Upper Thames Street, EC4 (see SUN86)	233
STO86	Stothard Place, 284–294 Bishopsgate, EC2	234
SUN86	Sunlight Wharf, Upper Thames Street, EC4 (and SNL86)	234
SWH86	1–3 Snow Hill, EC1	236
TRM86	9–19 Throgmorton Avenue, 21 Austin Friars, EC2	236

VLT86	Liverpool Street Station booking hall, Liverpool Street, EC2	236
WOD86	22 Wormwood Street, EC2	237
WTS86	34 Watling Street, EC4	237
ABC87	Abacus House, 33–39 Gutter Lane, EC2	237
AHA87	The Warehouse, Apothecaries' Hall, Blackfriars Lane, EC4	238
AMB87	Aldermanbury House, 58–63 Aldermanbury, EC2	238
ASQ87	12 America Square, 15–17 Crosswall, 15 Cooper's Row, EC3	239
AST87	22–25 Austin Friars, EC2	240
AUS87	2–6 Austin Friars, EC2	240
BAA87	Barnard's Inn, Holborn, 78–81 Fetter Lane, 7–13 Norwich Street, EC1	240
BBH87	Billingsgate bath-house, 100 Lower Thames Street, 1–8 St Dunstan's Lane, EC3	241
BHS87	192–200 Bishopsgate, E1	242
BLM87	Blomfield House, 85–86 London Wall, 53 New Broad Street, EC2	242
BOS87	274–306 Bishopsgate, EC2	243
BRL87	19–25 Birchin Lane, EC3	244
BUC87	Docklands Light Railway shaft, Bucklersbury, near 3 Queen Victoria Street, EC4	244
CMA87	80 Coleman Street, EC2	245
COV87	10–12 Copthall Avenue, EC2	246
CWN87	City wall, Noble Street, EC2	246
DOC87	Docklands Light Railway shaft, Lombard Street, EC3	246
EAG87	Eagle House, 86–96 Cannon Street, 31–33 Bush Lane, EC4	247
FCS87	107 Fenchurch Street, EC3	247
FUR87	40–41 Furnival Street, EC4	248
GAG87	Guildhall Art Gallery, Guildhall Yard, EC2	248
HND87	Houndsditch Warehouse, 123–137 Houndsditch, 3–31 Stoney Lane, EC3	249
HOS87	Catering Block, St Bartholomew's Hospital, EC1	249
IFF87	Wood Street (west carriageway), London Wall (north side) (Lee House, Monkwell Square), EC2	250
LFE87	65–68 Leadenhall Street, 98 Fenchurch Street, EC3	250
LGA87	41–43 Ludgate Hill, 8 Pilgrim Street, EC4	250
LWL87	British Telecom shaft, opposite 48 London Wall, EC2	251
MCO87	109–117 Middlesex Street, 1–4 Cock Hill, E1	251
MDX87	110–116 Middlesex Street, E1	252
MFI87	Monument Street and 17 Fish Street Hill, EC4	252
MGT87	55–61 Moorgate, 75–79 Coleman Street, EC2	252
MKB87	Market Buildings, 26–28 Mincing Lane, EC3	253
MTH87	Merchant Taylors' Hall, 2 White Lion Court, 30 Threadneedle Street, EC3	253
NAV87	Navigation House, 1–18 Aldgate, EC3	254
NEB87	35–45 New Broad Street, EC2	254
NOW87	1–19 Whitefriars Street, 63–67 Fleet Street, 23–24 Bouverie Street, 4 Britton's Court, EC4	254
PIC87	56–66 Carter Lane, 1–3 Pilgrim Street, 29–33 Ludgate Hill, EC4	255
PLY87	Thames Water Authority main, 18 Poultry, EC2	256
PPO87	2–3 Philpot Lane, EC3	256
RIV87	Riverplate House, 7–11 Finsbury Circus, EC2	257
SAB87	St Botolph Aldgate church, Aldgate, EC3	257
SBG87	St Bartholomew the Great churchyard, Cloth Fair, EC1	258
SKN87	Skinners' Hall kitchen, 8–9 Cloak Lane, EC4 (=CKL88)	258
UTA87	Cannon Street Station south, Upper Thames Street (Cousin Lane), EC4	259
WOC87	Ye Olde Cheshire Cheese, Wine Office Court, 145 Fleet Street, EC4	260
YHA87	Youth Hostel, 36–38 Carter Lane, EC4	260
AGE88	158–170 Aldersgate, EC1	260
ANT88	9–10 Angel Court, EC2	261
AUF88	13–14a Austin Friars, EC2	261
BAS88	55 Basinghall Street, EC2	261
BIP88	41–63 Bishopsgate, EC2	262
BOU88	6–8 Bouverie Street, EC4	262
BPA88	Bishopsgate, junction with Brushfield Street, EC2	262
BRD88	Opposite 80 Lombard Street, EC3	263
BRT88	St Bartholomew's crypt, Cloth Fair, EC1 (see SBG87)	263
BSL88	28 and 30 Bush Lane, 2 Suffolk Lane, EC4	263
BUN88	Bunge House, 53–71 St Mary Axe, EC3	264
CEM88	80 Coleman Street, EC2	264
CKL88	8–9 Cloak Lane, EC4 (=SKN87)	264
CNN88	108 Cannon Street, EC4	264
COT88	Cotts House, 27–29 Camomile Street, EC3	265
DMT88	Dominant House, 85 Queen Victoria Street, EC4	265
DUH88	23–26 St Dunstan's Hill, EC3	266

EAS88	14–18 Eastcheap, EC3	266
ECH88	30–40 Eastcheap, 37–39 St Mary at Hill, EC3	267
ELD88	Liverpool House, 15–17 Eldon Street, EC2	267
FIB88	12–15 Finsbury Circus, EC2	267
FNC88	88–93 Fenchurch Street, 5–7 Carlisle Avenue, EC3	268
FRI88	10 Friar Street, 69 Carter Lane, EC4	268
GAM88	52 Gresham Street, 14 Ironmonger Lane, EC2	269
GRL88	21–26 Garlick Hill, EC4	269
GUY88	Guildhall Yard, EC2	270
HAR88	British Telecom shaft, Harp Lane (south end), EC3	270
HON88	123–125 Houndsditch, 22–26 Cutler Street, 7–8 Exchange Buildings, EC3 & E1	270
ISH88	168–170 Bishopsgate, 14–15 New Street, EC2	271
LAH88	80–84 Leadenhall Street, EC3	271
LDL88	Albion House, 34–35 Leadenhall Street, 4 Billiter Street, EC3	271
LHY88	Docklands Light Railway works in Lothbury, near Moorgate, EC2	272
LLA88	60–61 Long Lane, EC1	272
LOM88	Docklands Light Railway shaft, Lombard Street (near Pope's Head Alley), EC3	273
LOW88	52–63 London Wall, 20–56 Copthall Avenue, EC2	273
LSO88	Leith House, 47–57 Gresham Street, EC2	274
LYD88	Cannon Street Station north, Upper Thames Street (Dowgate Hill), EC4	274
MCT88	Dunster Court, 21–38 Mincing Lane, 85 Great Tower Street, 12–18 Mark Lane, EC3	275
MDE88	6–9 Middle Street, 24–26 Newbury Street, EC1	275
MOH88	Moorgate Hall, 143–171 Moorgate, EC2	276
MSE88	109–115 Middlesex Street, E1	276
MYA88	46 St Mary Axe, EC3	276
OBA88	18–25 Old Bailey, 10–18 Bishop's Court, 29–37 Fleet Lane, EC4	277
OPS88	158–164 Bishopsgate, EC2	277
ORM88	Ormond House, 62–63 Queen Victoria Street, EC4	278
PTD88	72–73 Basinghall Street, EC2	278
PWB88	Pilgrim Street, EC4	279
QUE88	32–35 Queen Street, 6A Great St Thomas Apostle, EC4	279
SAY88	25–51 St Mary Axe, 9 St Helen's Place, EC3	280
SEA88	2 Seething Lane, EC3	280
SHO88	Salisbury House, 8 Salisbury Square, EC4	281
SMY88	St Mary at Hill church, St Mary at Hill, EC3	281
SXE88	Cayzer House, 2–4 St Mary Axe, EC3	281
TEX88	Thames Exchange, 78 Upper Thames Street and Bull Wharf Lane, EC4	282
TRY88	Trinity House, Savage Gardens, EC3	283
VAL88	Fleet Valley between Blackfriars and Holborn Viaduct stations, EC4	283
WAP88	5a–10 Wardrobe Place, 146a Wardrobe Chambers, EC4	287
WHO88	Wren House, 13–23 Carter Lane, EC4	287
WIV88	1–7 Whittington Avenue, EC3	287
ALN89	26–30 Artillery Lane, E1	288
ARY89	4–10 Artillery Lane, E1	289
ATL89	Atlantic House, 45–50 Holborn Viaduct, EC1	289
BOG89	298–306 Bishopsgate, EC2	289
BTB89	British Telecom shaft, Bishopsgate and Wormwood Street, EC2	289
CED89	64–66 Cheapside, EC4	290
CIS89	Christchurch Greyfriars, Newgate Street, EC1	290
CLY89	76 Carter Lane, 9 Ludgate Broadway, EC4	290
COE89	Coleman Street (outside Armourers' Hall), EC2	291
CRT89	8–11 Crescent, EC3	291
ETA89	7–11 Bishopsgate, EC2	291
FRS89	2 Fore Street, EC2	291
FUL89	32 Furnival Street, EC4	292
GDS89	Goldsmiths' Hall, Foster Lane, EC2	292
GTA89	13–14 Great St Thomas Apostle, EC4	292
GWS89	Pinners' Hall, Great Winchester Street, 8 Austin Friars Square, 105–108 Old Broad Street, EC2	293
HSD89	58–60 Houndsditch, EC3	293
IHA89	Innholders' Hall, 29–30 College Street, EC4	293
LEN89	145–146 Leadenhall Street, EC3	294
LHN89	78–79 Leadenhall Street, EC3	294
LWB89	London Wall, junction with Blomfield Street, EC2	294
MHS89	Mansion House Underground Station, 38 Cannon Street, EC4	295
PEP89	Colchester House, Savage Gardens, Pepys Street; Woodruffe House, Cooper's Row, EC3	295

27

QSK89	40 Queen Street, 1 Skinner's Lane, EC4	295
REC89	Rectory House, 7a Laurence Pountney Hill, 9 Laurence Pountney Lane, EC4	296
TCP89	King's Bench Walk, Inner Temple, EC4	296
THM89	1–7 Great St Thomas Apostle, 29–30 Queen Street, EC4	296
TWR89	1–4 Great Tower Street, EC3	297
VHA89	Vintry House (Vintners' Place) (watching brief), 68–69 Upper Thames Street, EC4	297
VRY89	Vintry House (Vintners' Place), 68–69 Upper Thames Street, EC4	298
WES89	24–30 West Smithfield, 18–20 Cock Lane, 1–4 Giltspur Street, EC1	298
BEX90	Baynard's Castle, [new] City of London Boys' School, EC4	299
BGA90	Broadgate, phases 12–13: Norton Folgate and Primrose Street, EC2	299
BHD90	Brooks Wharf, 48 Upper Thames Street, EC4	299
BRO90	Boston House, 90–94 Old Broad Street, 63–64 New Broad Street, EC2	300
BSS90	Blossoms Inn, 3–6 Trump Street, 20–27 Lawrence Lane, 2–4 Russia Row, EC2	300
BUF90	Bull Wharf, 16–19 Queenhithe, 66–67 Upper Thames Street, EC4	300
CAE90	1 Carter Court, 77–79 Carter Lane, EC4	301
CBY90	8 Crosby Square, 4 Great St Helens, EC3	301
CCT90	20–26 Cutler Street, 123–125 Houndsditch, 5–8 Clothier Street, E1	302
CID90	72–80 Cheapside, 83–93 Queen Street, 12 Pancras Lane, EC2 & EC4	302
COH90	75–77 Cornhill, EC3	303
CPG90	Cripplegate House, Golden Lane, EC1	303
CTL90	Cutlers' Hall, 4 Warwick Lane, EC4	304
FAO90	75–82 Farringdon Street, EC4	304
FRN90	32 Furnival Street, EC4	304
FUS90	34–35 Furnival Street, EC4	304
GOG90	2–4 Gough Square, EC4	305
GRM90	50 Gresham Street, EC2	305
GTR90	Opposite 1 Gutter Lane, sewer trench, EC2	305
HAS90	Hand and Shears public house, 1 Middle Street, EC1	305
LIE90	20–21 Lime Street, 8–11 Ship Tavern Passage, EC3	305
LOA90	54 Lombard Street, 15–17 Gracechurch Street, EC3	306
ORN90	Opposite 1 Cornhill, EC3	306
PAT90	Paternoster Square, EC4	306
PEM90	1–3 Pemberton Row, EC4	306
PSO90	274–280 Bishopsgate, EC2	307
PTE90	St Peter Cornhill church, Cornhill, EC3	307
RAC90	55–58 Gracechurch Street and Brabant House, St Benet's Place, EC3	307
RON90	Corn Exchange, 51–60 Mark Lane, and Cereal House, 58 Mark Lane, EC3	308
SAK90	Sackville House, 143–149 Fenchurch Street, 17–20 Cullum Street, EC3	308
SHL90	34–35 Great St Helens, EC3	309
SOB90	British Telecom tunnel, Old Broad Street, EC2	309
TAH90	Tallow Chandlers' Hall, 4 Dowgate Hill, EC4	309
TED90	Opposite 1 Threadneedle Street, EC2	310
TIM90	High Timber Street and Stew Lane, EC4	310
UPT90	Bull Wharf Lane, 66–67 Upper Thames Street, EC4	310
BSP91	6 Broad Street Place, EC2	311
BSY91	Bishopsgate, pedestrian subway near Liverpool Street Station, EC2	311
COC91	35–37 Cock Lane, EC1	312
CTW91	City wall at Barbican Waterside and next to Bastion House, London Wall, EC2	312
DEN91	104–106 Leadenhall Street, EC3	312
ETL91	Equitable House, 47–51 King William Street, EC4	312
JAS91	St James Garlickhithe church, Garlick Hill, EC4	313
MEN91	1 and 5–6 Amen Court, EC4	313
NIB91	Niblett Hall, King's Bench Walk, Inner Temple, EC4	313
OBS91	119–122 Old Broad Street, EC2	313
PUM91	5–6 Pump Court, EC4	314
SEN91	25–26 Savage Gardens, EC3	314
SMT91	57a–59 West Smithfield, EC1	314
TEE91	41–53 Threadneedle Street, 1–17 Old Broad Street, EC2	314
WOL91	Devlin Tower, Tower of London, EC3	314

GAZETTEER OF SITES INVESTIGATED BY THE

GUILDHALL MUSEUM

BEFORE 1973

GM1

A Oswald, 1939
NGR: TQ 32815 81040
SMR: 041529–30

Post Office Court, 1–3 Abchurch Lane, EC4

Three Roman pits were observed. The S end of a medieval cellar or possibly a large cesspit was found at the S end of the site, aligned parallel with Abchurch Lane. It was 10ft wide and more than 11ft N–S. The tops of the walls lay at 10ft below street level, and their bases at 20ft below street level; the walls were 4ft thick and of chalk with some tiles. Silt lay in the bottom of the cellar, and was overlaid first by a deposit of burnt wood 1ft thick, and then by another silt layer. Green-glazed pottery, perhaps of 14th–15th-c date, and encaustic tiles were found in this deposit, along with a bronze cauldron, Venetian glass and the base of a stone mortar. Subsequent layers of burning and silt contained pottery of the 16th and 17th c, indicating that the cellar or cesspit had been filled in either before or immediately after the Great Fire of 1666.

For observations on this site in 1958–9, see GM98 below.

EN I, 37–9; site file
PRG, 1047

GM2

P Marsden, 1961
NGR: TQ 32480 81562
SMR: 041256–8

Aldermanbury (junction with London Wall), EC2

A section across Aldermanbury was revealed when the new London Wall road was built across its line. Two small silt-filled gullies with a post-hole between them were found cut into natural gravel, containing pottery of the Late Saxon or early medieval period. Above were three layers of gravel, extending across the whole width of the modern street, probably road surfaces. Between the bottom and the middle layers of gravel was a thin layer of silt. Above the gravel layers were dumps of rubbish 8ft thick extending to within 3ft of the modern street. These contained sherds of the second half of the 13th c, and many pieces of slag and bronze suggesting metalworking. At the bottom of the dumps were the remains of a decayed wooden pipe which, with the dumping, suggests a deliberate attempt to raise the ground level, probably in response to local marshy conditions. This part of Aldermanbury was known as Gayspur Lane in 1332–3 (Ekwall 1954, 137).

ER numbers 684, 783, 849, 898, 899, 900, 1263, 1264, 1265, 1266, 1267
EDN VII, 46; VIII, 65; IX, 12, 36; XI, 4–5
PRG, 616
Ekwall, E, 1954 *The street-names of London*
Marsden, P, 1967 'Archaeological finds in the City of London, 1963–4', *Trans London Middlesex Archaeol Soc,* 21.3, 215–16

GM3

P Marsden, 1965–6
NGR: TQ 32487 81453
SMR: 041323–8

Three Nun Court (formerly Church Alley), Aldermanbury, EC2

Excavation in 1965–6 found Roman pits and gullies immediately E of the E ditch of the Cripplegate Roman fort. They were dug in the 1st c and were in use until the mid-4th c.

Excavation here, W of the site of St Michael Bassishaw church (see GM13 below), also revealed many medieval rubbish pits; a well, chalk lined at the bottom and brick lined at the top, about 2ft 9in. wide; and several brick-lined post-medieval cesspits. A large circular 'tank' 9ft in diameter and with a surviving depth of 4ft 6in., into which drains flowed, was lined with chalk and mortar, and included a blind arch exposing the natural brickearth behind. The lower part of the tank was filled with silt containing 15th-c pottery, and sherds of c 1500 above. The main upper fill was of brick rubble containing 17th-c objects, and was perhaps debris of the Great Fire. Foundations of a medieval building were found nearby, following the alignment of modern Aldermanbury. They were 4ft thick and built of chalk and gravel, but could not be dated. The earliest pits E of (behind) the building were of 13th-c date.

This site is also called Area B of the Guildhall Precinct (or Extension) excavations (a site plan (photo 2943–50) shows Areas A–C; see also GM4 and GM13 below).

ER numbers 992, 993, 994, 995, 996, 997, 998, 999, 1000, 1001, 1002, 1003, 1004, 1005, 1006, 1007, 1008, 1009, 1010, 1011, 1012, 1013, 1014, 1015, 1016, 1017, 1220, 1220A, 1220B, 1220C, 1221, 1221A, 1221B, 1222, 1223, 1224, 1225, 1226, 1227, 1228, 1229, 1230, 1231, 1232, 1233
EDN X, 26–30, 69–70; site file
PRG, 754
Medieval Archaeol, 11, 1967, 294
Marsden, P, 1968 'Archaeological finds in the City of London, 1965–66', *Trans London Middlesex Archaeol Soc,* 22.1, 4–5

Guildhall Library (formerly Guildhall car park), Aldermanbury, EC2

GM4

P Marsden, 1965
NGR: TQ 32425 81430
SMR: 041327–8

Excavation revealed the E defences of the Cripplegate Roman fort. A short length of the foundation of the wall of the fort and about 50ft of the ditch were recorded. The fill of the ditch contained sherds of AD120–30.

At least 29ft 6in. of the foundation of the E wall of the fort had been robbed of ragstone, and the trench filled with 12th-c material. The robbing ceased where the wall began to pass beneath Aldermanbury, as if the street was in use. Several 12th- and 13th-c rubbish pits were excavated; in one was a decayed wooden box 3ft 5in. square by 3ft deep, containing a mass of mostly broken jugs of the 12th–13th c.

This site is also called Area A of the Guildhall Precinct (or Extension) excavations (see also GM3 and GM13).

ER numbers 988, 1069, 1069A, 1069B, 1069C, 1070, 1071, 1072, 1073, 1074, 1075, 1076, 1076A, 1076B, 1076C, 1077, 1078, 1079, 1080, 1081, 1082, 1083, 1084, 1085, 1086, 1087, 1088, 1089, 1090, 1091, 1092, 1093, 1094, 1095, 1096, 1097, 1098, 1099, 1100, 1101, 1102, 1103, 1104, 1105, 1106, 1107, 1108, 1109, 1238, 1239, 1240, 1241, 1242, 1243
EDN X, 25, 42–52, 72–3; site file (2 files)
PRG, 755
Crowfoot, E, Pritchard, F, & Staniland, K, 1992 *Textiles and clothing,* Medieval finds from excavations in London 4, 209 [a 12th-c piece of linen textile in ER 1069]
Marsden, P, 1968 'Archaeological finds in the City of London, 1965–66', *Trans London Middlesex Archaeol Soc,* 22.1, 12–13

Aldersgate, EC1

GM5

A Oswald, 1939
NGR: TQ 32142 81463
SMR: 040465, 081543

A mass of ragstone masonry was found in the centre of the street, projecting to the N of the Roman city wall. No original facing remained. The bottom rested on black silt which had apparently accumulated after the building of the city wall. In places the structure seemed to have been keyed roughly into the wall, but it overlay the wall footings and was clearly of later date. To the E were two massive piers of characteristically Roman ragstone masonry, with yellow mortar like that of the projection. These lay on the line of the wall, but set at an angle to it, and the foundations of the N pier had been cut through the flint and clay footings of the wall. There seems little doubt that the piers formed the central spine of a double gateway, and the projection part of its W tower. The gate was apparently inserted after the building of the city wall.

The foundation of the 17th-c gate projected more than 5ft beyond the external N face of the city wall, and more than 2ft 6in. beyond the inner face. It was built of brick in extremely hard grey mortar, and included fragments of medieval tracery. The foundations lay from 6ft to 33ft W of the frontage of Alder House (1 Aldersgate). They may be the same fragments observed by A Clapham in 1923.

Merrifield, R, 1965 *The Roman city of London,* gazetteer G8

GM6

Q Waddington, 1924
NGR: TQ 31244 81475
SMR: 040466, 041310, 082100

Aldersgate Street, EC1

The medieval city ditch was found during excavations for a new sewer 23ft beneath Aldersgate Street, 'a few feet to the N' of the city wall. The sewer tunnel revealed that the ditch extended 70ft N of the wall, where gravel was recorded. The filling was 'black mud, still oozing in some places, and very foul smelling', so that 'fresh air had to be pumped in to the men working. The mud was full of the bones of domestic animals, including the skull of a horse.' The tunnel did not apparently reach the bottom of the ditch, and gave no clue to the means of access to the gate in the medieval period. A side tunnel to the SE corner of St Botolph's church revealed a chalk foundation, presumably of the church.

EN 1, 2; with a plan
PRG, 757

GM7

P Marsden, 1967
NGR: TQ 33556 81160
SMR: 041954–5

Aldgate, junction with Duke's Place (east corner, site of Post Office), EC3

Excavation revealed parts of four successive N towers of Aldgate (Roman, Saxon or early medieval, later medieval, and the gate of 1607); and of three successive defensive ditches, the earliest of which was possibly Roman.

The square Roman gate tower had a foundation of clay and flints, and projected about 3m from the city wall. About 3m beyond it was the surviving edge of a defensive ditch, most of which had been cut away by the early medieval ditch. The post-Roman gate tower apparently standing during the 12th c was built of ragstone, roughly square in shape, and projected about 1.5m beyond the city wall. The steeply sloping side of a ditch more than 2.5m deep, and perhaps V-shaped in section, lay just beyond the gate. The grey earth filling of the ditch contained pottery dating to the late 12th or early 13th c.

The N edge of another gate tower was located, the robbed face of which suggested that it might have been D-shaped. It is possible that this was the gate built in 1215. The tower projected at least 7.3m from the wall, and overlay the filled-in early medieval ditch. Associated with the gate was the butt end of a later medieval ditch, filled with waterlaid sands containing pottery of the second half of the 13th c. Unlike the earlier ditches, which probably passed in front of the gate, the later medieval ditch terminated immediately N of the gate, so that the roadway out of the gate was built on solid ground.

The latest gate was represented by part of the N tower of the gate built in 1607–9. Its foundation of ragstone and reused stones projected 8.5m from the city wall, and its interior comprised a basement room with a clay floor.

ER numbers 1268, 1269, 1270, 1271, 1272, 1273, 1274, 1275, 1276, 1277, 1278A, 1278B, 1278C, 1278D, 1278E, 1278F
EDN XI, 5–8 (including annotated photographs); site file
PRG, 1607
Medieval Archaeol, 12, 1968, 184
Marsden, P, 1969 'Archaeological finds in the City of London, 1966–8', *Trans London Middlesex Archaeol Soc,* 22.2, 20–6

GM8

Q Waddington, 1925
NGR: TQ 33615 81190
SMR: 041454

Opposite 78 Aldgate High Street, E1

In excavating opposite the Rose and Crown public house in July 1925, the Corporation's contractors discovered an old, abandoned pump, chamber and well. The well was dry and partly filled in; it was 14ft deep from a point 5ft below road level. The City Engineer had the well filled in and concreted over. It is shown on the Ordnance Survey map of 1873–5, but not on later editions.

EN 1, 20 (letter of City Engineer to Librarian, 14 July 1925)

52 Aldgate High Street, E1

GM9

F Cottrill, 1938
NGR: TQ 33712 81233
SMR: 041096

Excavations in connection with the extension of Aldgate East Underground Station exposed sections of the ancient thoroughfare outside the city gate. The lowest layers of road-metalling, resting on virgin clay at a depth of 10ft below the present street level, were said to be undoubtedly Roman. During excavations for a District Railway tunnel, the SW angle of a Roman structure was found about 7ft S of the building-line on the S side of Aldgate High Street. The wall is said to have been entirely of Roman brick, about 3ft high and 1ft 6in. thick. It was described by F Cottrill who did not however see it himself. Within the angle was Roman debris which contained a micaceous hemispherical bowl with a flange (cf T May, *The pottery found at Silchester,* 1916, pl. xlviii, 61). It is likely that this roadside structure was a Roman tomb.

GM, *Annual Report* 1938; site file
Merrifield, R, 1965 *The Roman city of London,* gazetteer 362–3

St Botolph's churchyard / Botolph Street, EC3

GM10

P Marsden, 1965
NGR: TQ 33580 81215
SMR: 041453

A large undated pit was found beneath the churchyard on the NE side of the church, in which were layers of burnt clay moulded to shape and evidently used for casting bells. There were also some wood, ash and brownish-yellow clay. The only finds from the pit were a few thin roof tiles. The base of a samian mortarium was also found.

ER numbers 990, 991
EDN X, 25
PRG, 1608

Fore Street / 2 St Alphage Garden / St Alphage House (St Alphage churchyard), EC2

GM11
(=GM209)

P Marsden, 1960
NGR: TQ 32450 81640
SMR: 041898, 040486–7

Excavations immediately N of St Alphage church and E of the churchyard revealed a section through the foundations of a ragstone wall 3ft 6in. thick. This was in line with the wall of the Roman fort 37ft to the W and was presumably its continuation. Everything above the bottom 2ft of the foundation had been removed, and there was no trace here of the foundation of the inner thickening wall which was added to the fort wall when the later city wall was built; it may have been later removed, since its foundation was normally at a higher level. A V-shaped cutting which may have been the bottom of the fort ditch was seen immediately to the N, though its relationship to the ragstone foundation was puzzling as it appeared in the section. Its filling contained shells of land mollusca so it was probably dry. Further N, about 17ft N of the wall, was the bottom of a V-shaped depression which appeared to be the Roman city ditch. Excavation also exposed the broad medieval–16th-c ditch.

This is the same site as GM209; the details are given here, but the finds are reported under GM209 in case the division into two observations has meaning.

EDN VII, 30, 34; site file
There are no ER groups from this site as GM11. The EDN contains bound-in correspondence comprising a short report on mollusca from the silt at the base of the Roman ditch (C P Castell, BMNH) and a letter discussing the findings by W F Grimes. See GM209, which is the same site, also in 1960, which has finds.
Schofield, J, 1994 'Saxon and medieval parish churches in the City of London: a review', *Trans London Middlesex Archaeol Soc,* 45, 92 [summary of observations on the site of St Alphage church]

GM12

I Noël Hume, 1954–5
NGR: TQ 32785 80782
SMR: 041001–2, 041430

Minster House, 12 Arthur Street / Laurence Pountney Lane, EC4

In the NE corner of the site were traces of two successive Roman buildings, the first of which had a floor of rough but evenly set white tesserae laid on a bed of concrete 2ft thick. The later building had been raised 1ft above this by a layer of concrete through which ran moulded channels capped by red building tiles. These were evidently flues through which passed furnace-heated air to warm a floor above. A small number of pottery sherds from one of the channels suggested that this part of the hypocaust had ceased to operate by the mid-3rd c.

A medieval chalk wall in the NE of the site overlay a Roman wall 3ft 9in. wide which had been used as its foundation. The medieval wall was in turn used as the base for an 18th-c wall. A large cesspit near the S side of the site contained a large number of objects up to the period 1660–80, including a hoard of jetton-like coins called billon placks of James IV/V of Scotland (c 1515).

ER numbers 262A, 262B, 264, 266, 269, 269B, 270, 270A
EDN II, 86–93, 97; III, 26, 28–31
PRG, 934
Merrifield, R, 1965 *The Roman city of London*, gazetteer 302

GM13

P Marsden, 1965
NGR: TQ 32513 81448
SMR: 041501–3

Guildhall offices formerly Bassishaw House (site of St Michael Bassishaw church), Basinghall Street, EC2

Excavations revealed the foundations of the E end of the 12th-c church of St Michael Bassishaw. They were of chalk and gravel, about 3ft 3in. wide. The church had a nave 13ft wide and at least 32ft long, with an apsidal chancel 6ft 6in. deep internally. The foundations overlay earlier rubbish pits containing 11th–12th-c pottery. Traces of later medieval foundations of chalk and yellow mortar were also found, though they did not form a coherent plan.

The earliest documentary reference to the church is in the latter half of the 12th c. It was rebuilt in the 15th c, burnt in 1666, rebuilt in 1671–9, and demolished in 1897. The church was also investigated during and after demolition, in 1899.

This site was Area C of the Guildhall Precincts (or Extension) excavations (see also GM3 and GM4 above).

ER numbers 1036, 1037, 1038, 1039, 1040, 1041, 1042, 1043, 1044, 1045, 1046, 1047, 1048, 1049, 1050, 1051, 1052, 1053, 1054, 1055, 1056, 1057, 1058, 1059, 1060, 1061, 1062, 1063, 1064, 1065, 1066, 1067, 1068, 1068A
EDN X, 37–41; site file
PRG, 1040 (PRG, 1027 for discoveries of 1899)
Cohen, N, 1995 'The birth of church archaeology in London', *London Archaeol*, 7, 315–20
Marsden, P, 1968 'Archaeological finds in the City of London, 1965–66', *Trans London Middlesex Archaeol Soc*, 22.1, 14–16; cf *Trans London Middlesex Archaeol Soc*, II, 1910, 158–78
Schofield, J, 1994 'Saxon and medieval parish churches in the City of London: a review', *Trans London Middlesex Archaeol Soc*, 45, 121

GM14

P Marsden, 1962
NGR: TQ 32480 81517
SMR: 041444–6

40 Basinghall Avenue (Route 11), EC2

Silt deposits reflecting marshy conditions during the 11th–12th c were recorded.

ER numbers 784, 799, 803
EDN VIII, 66, 86; IX, 5

19 Bevis Marks, EC3

GM15

F Cottrill, 1935
NGR: TQ 33416 81295
SMR: 041943

A length of more than 19ft of the city wall, running right across the site, was exposed and subsequently destroyed. The outer face was about 25ft 6in. from the Bevis Marks frontage, and the thickness of the wall above the plinth was 7ft 11in. The Roman masonry in parts came up to the underside of the ground floor of the modern building, 2ft 6in. below pavement level. The top of the plinth was 4ft 4in. lower than this. A double bonding-course ran through the wall, with its top 4ft below pavement level, and on the inner face of the wall there was an offset of 3in. at this level, with an additional single course of bricks immediately above it, only one brick deep.

J Roman Stud, 26, 1936, 254
Merrifield, R, 1965 *The Roman city of London*, gazetteer W22

St Mary Axe House, 56–60 St Mary Axe, 1–3 Goring Street, EC3

GM16

P Marsden, 1961
NGR: TQ 33350 81370
SMR: 041937

Traces of the black earth fill of the city ditch, containing pottery of the 16th–17th c, were noted. The observed SW edge of the ditch lay parallel to and 52ft NE of the frontage of Bevis Marks.

EDN VIII, 43
PRG, 1328
Marsden, P, 1963 'Archaeological finds in the City of London, 1961', *Trans London Middlesex Archaeol Soc*, 21.1, 77

Billiter Street (sewer tunnel), EC3

GM17

I Noël Hume, 1953
NGR: TQ 33300 81115
SMR: 041814

A square chalk-lined pit containing a group of 16th–17th-c pottery found by a workman while digging a new sewer tunnel in Billiter Street, at a point approximately 45–50ft S of its junction with Leadenhall Street, beneath the centre of the road.

EDN II, 72; finds not traceable
PRG, 1329

19–21 Birchin Lane, EC3

GM18

F Cottrill, 1935
NGR: TQ 32900 81050
SMR: 040806–9

Road-metalling consisting of hard compact gravel with some brick fragments was seen in two places on the site. It contained some blocks of worked stone near the bottom, which was at an irregular depth varying from 15ft to 21ft below pavement level. It seemed to form part of a N–S road, which must have been more than 30ft wide. From occupation levels and refuse deposits below it came eight potters' stamps of the following dates: Tiberius–Nero (1), Tiberius–Vespasian (2), Claudius–Nero (1), Claudius–Vespasian (2), Claudius–Domitian (1), Nero–Vespasian (1). The construction of the road cannot therefore be earlier than the reign of Nero, and is more probably of Flavian date. E of the road was a robber trench 4ft wide, containing powdered cement and lumps of ragstone, apparently following the line of a N–S wall just E of the road.

The site is included in the recent study of the Roman fora by Marsden (1987, 79–82); the above summary is from Merrifield.

Marsden, P, 1987 *The Roman forum site in London: discoveries before 1985*, 79–82
Merrifield, R, 1965 *The Roman city of London*, gazetteer 225

GM19
(=GM301)

P Marsden, 1970
NGR: TQ 32068 80797
SMR: 041389 Wreck 3

Blackfriars Wreck 3, EC4

Wrecks of two boats were found. In this *Guide* GM19 is reserved for Blackfriars Wreck 3, and GM183 for Blackfriars Wreck 4.

A clinker-built sailing vessel (Blackfriars Wreck 3) was found wrecked in the bed of the Thames W of Trig Lane, and was excavated within a modern cofferdam. The vessel was originally about 16m long and 3m wide, and had a flat bottom (Fig 4). It was a river barge since it had a very low freeboard. Both bow and stern were pointed, and since there was no trace of a rudder it seems that the boat was steered by steering oar. The overlapping oak planks were held by iron rivets, and were made watertight with a luting of hair. In the centre was a broad but thin keel-plank. Ribs were held to the planks by wooden pegs. A longitudinal mast-step lay almost amidships, and wear marks on the timber show that the mast was frequently lowered. Pottery, shoes and two pewter pilgrim badges were found in the wreck and may have been deposited after it was sunk in the late 15th c. Many repairs to the oak planking suggest that the vessel had a long and hard usage. Nearly 2000 cylindrical lead weights from inside the vessel suggest that a fishing net of the late 15th c had been caught in the wreck.

The wreck of a second clinker-built ship (Blackfriars Wreck 4), carrying a cargo of Kentish ragstone, was found in the bed of the river close to the first wreck. It had probably sunk during the 15th c. It was not possible to record its full dimensions. See GM183 below.

Int J Naut Archaeol, 1, 1972, 130–2; *Medieval Archaeol,* 15, 1971, 176
Marsden, P, 1996 *Ships of the port of London: twelfth to seventeenth centuries AD,* 55–104
Peberdy, R B, 1996 'Navigation on the River Thames between London and Oxford in the late Middle Ages: a reconsideration',
   Oxoniensia, 61, 311–40 [the boat as an example of a river vessel used in trading up the Thames]
Tyers, I, 1992 'City: early to late medieval boats (BIG82, CUS73, TL74, Blackfriars Wreck 3)', Dendrochronology Report

Fig 4 GM19: the lower part of Blackfriars Wreck 3, shortly after discovery.

GM20

I Noël Hume, 1956
NGR: TQ 32432 81235
SMR: 041356–7

Blossoms Inn, 3–4 Trump Street, EC2

After excavation by W F Grimes for RMLEC on this site in 1955, I Noël Hume recorded further features in 1956. His examination followed the cutting of a retaining wall trench from E to W. At the W end of the trench, post-medieval features rested on a deposit of black gravel and organic clay containing exclusively Roman material. Noël Hume interpreted this as a pond or stream open in the Roman period.

A rectangular timber-lined well was excavated by workmen in the middle of the site. Finds included three buff-white jugs and other sherds of the mid-2nd c (ER 359).

Also in the section, a chalk-lined well 2ft 10in. in diameter and up to 9ft 5in. deep below the modern cellar floor was recorded. Its lining was 2ft 2in. thick. The lower fill of silt contained many objects of c 1500, including 78 buckle strap ends and many incomplete buckles, suggesting manufacture nearby. A roughly square chalk-lined cesspit, also at the S end of the site, measured 6ft 8in. x 5ft 9in., with walls 1ft 5in. thick, and its base at 6ft 6in. below the modern cellar floor. No dating evidence was recovered. Another chalk-lined well, of unknown dimensions, was found in the centre of the site, containing objects of the 16th and early 17th c.

ER numbers 318, 319, 323, 324, 327, 359, 361, 377
EDN III, 74–7; IV, 19, 23–4, 43–5
PRG, 775
See also GM254, the observations by G Dunning on this site in 1930.
Goodall, I, 1981 'The medieval blacksmith and his products', in Crossley, D (ed), *Medieval industry*, CBA Res Rep 40, 51–62
Shepherd, J, 1987 'The pre-urban and Roman topography in the King Street and Cheapside areas of the City of London', *Trans London Middlesex Archaeol Soc*, 38, 11–58

Bow Bells House, 11 Bread Street, 46–55 Cheapside, EC4

GM21

E Rutter, 1958
NGR: TQ 32318 81109
SMR: 041329

A chalk-lined well was found in the SW part of this site, close to Bread Street. It was 3ft 6in. in diameter internally, and the chalk lining, faced with neatly dressed blocks, was 1ft 4in. thick. No dating evidence was recovered.

ER number 415 (unstratified finds)
EDN IV, 62; V, 3a–4
PRG, 759

Rear of 72 Upper Thames Street, EC4

GM22

G Davies, 1961
NGR: TQ 32437 80709
SMR: 041375–7

A 10ft length of waterfront wall of ragstone was found about 40ft N of the existing modern riverside wall. The ragstone wall was 4ft thick, faced only on its S (river) side, and it lay on a raft of horizontal timbers overlying rows of upright timber piles. A sloping foreshore of soft grey mud lay in front of the wall, and this was overlaid by dumps of brick and cement. A sherd of 15th-c pottery was found in the grey foreshore mud, apparently predating the waterfront.

EDN VII, 51–2
PRG, 818

Colchester House, Pepys Street, EC3

GM23

Unknown, 1951
NGR: TQ 33530 80840
SMR: 040209

During post-War widening of Savage Gardens in 1951, several whole Roman pots were found. Some were retained by Trinity House and are on display at their offices in Colchester House, which is on the E side of the Gardens.

GM24

Q Waddington, 1926
NGR: TQ 31595 81061
SMR: 041227

4 Bridewell Place, EC4

A large well of unknown date was found under the roadway opposite the entrance of 4 Bridewell Place. It was 6ft in diameter internally and brick lined as far as could be observed. Soundings showed that it was about 126ft deep, with a water depth of 47ft. The well was approached by a vaulted passage 3ft high and 2ft 6in. wide from the W (according to a plan; 'E' according to the text). The floor of the passage and the top of the well were at a depth of 5ft below the roadway. The passage was 28ft long, and had been bricked off in front of the house on the W side of the street. The passage and well were filled in 1926.

Though the well is undated (apart from the use of bricks suggesting a date after c 1500), its size, position and construction details suggest it may have been part of Bridewell Palace (1515–23). Bridewell Place crosses the main courtyard of the palace (Gadd & Dyson 1981).

EN I, 31; Librarian's Annual Report, 1926
PRG, 436
Gadd, D, & Dyson, T, 1981 'Bridewell Palace: excavations at 9–11 Bridewell Place and 1–3 Tudor Street, City of London, 1978',
    Post-Medieval Archaeol, 15, 1–79

GM25

P Marsden, 1964–5
NGR: TQ 32643 80788
SMR: 041414

Site of Bush Lane, 152 Upper Thames Street, EC4

Excavations here revealed parts of large Roman masonry structures interpreted as the palace of the Roman governor. This site is published, for its Roman period, as Areas 4 and 5 in the Roman governor's palace report. The main structure was a N–S wing of rooms immediately E of the ornamental pool.

For the post-Roman period, excavation revealed three medieval chalk foundations, of buildings of unknown size and alignment since the builders had reused parts of the Roman structures beneath, and it was not possible to ascertain the medieval plan. They seem to have fronted onto Suffolk Lane. The E face of another wall of chalk and brown mortar was found aligned N–S just E of Cannon Street Station and N of Upper Thames Street. A stone-lined cesspit contained objects of the first half of the 17th c.

ER numbers 951, 952, 953, 954, 955, 956, 957, 958, 959, 960, 961, 962, 963, 964, 965, 966, 967, 968, 969, 970, 971, 972, 973, 974,
    975, 976, 977, 978, 979, 980, 981, 982, 983, 984, 1018, 1019, 1020, 1021, 1022, 1023, 1024, 1026, 1027, 1028, 1029, 1030, 1031,
    1032, 1033, 1034, 1035
EDN IX, 24; X, 1–22, 31–2, 33–6; site file
PRG, 926
Marsden, P, 1975 'The excavation of a Roman palace site in London, 1961–1972', *Trans London Middlesex Archaeol Soc*, 26, 1–102
Milne, G, 1996 'A palace disproved: reassessing the provincial governor's presence in 1st-century London', in Bird, J, Hassall, M, &
    Sheldon, H (eds), *Interpreting Roman London: papers in memory of Hugh Chapman*, 49–56

GM26

P Marsden, 1968
NGR: TQ 33335 80670
SMR: 044354–7

26–27 Byward Street (junction with Water Lane), EC3

A deep excavation into the natural gravel at the N end of Water Lane exposed several undated rubbish pits in section and part of a Roman building. It comprised walls forming the corner of a sunken room. Its floor of buff mortar lay about 4ft below the top of natural gravel. The N wall was 1ft 9in. wide, and the E wall was 2ft wide; both were built of ragstone with courses of bonding-tile.

Two lengths of chalk and ragstone wall were noted on the N side of the modern Bakers' Hall and to the E of the hall. They were of unknown thickness since they were encased in recent brick walls. They may be part of the 15th-c house of John Chichele, Chamberlain of London 1435–46, whose property passed to the Bakers to become their hall.

EDN XI, 15; site file
Marsden, P, 1969 'Archaeological finds in the City of London, 1966–8', *Trans London Middlesex Archaeol Soc*, 22.2, 20

4 Castle Court, EC3

GM27

P Marsden, 1976
NGR: TQ 32925 81075
SMR: 044358

A trench dug in November 1976 in the cellar of this building exposed the gravel metalling of a Roman street on the W side of the second Roman forum. The surviving top of the gravel lay 3.63m below the pavement level of the Court, and it extended downwards for more than 1.14m. The trench had been cut along the axis of the street so no camber could be observed.

Though the date of this observation is 1976, ie during the time of the DUA, it was subsequently added to P Marsden's area of work and therefore was given a GM number.

Marsden, P, 1987 *The Roman forum site in London: discoveries before 1985*, 82

25–29 (now 23–29) Camomile Street, EC3

**GM28
(=GM299)**

E Rutter, 1958
NGR: TQ 33301 81416
SMR: 041934, 041824

Traces of the broad medieval ditch were found extending from about 57ft N of Camomile Street as far as Houndsditch. The S part of the ditch contained grey-black earth which included tile, pottery and bone fragments. Further N the ditch was flat-bottomed at a depth of 9ft 3in. below the modern basement floor, and contained thick grey-blue clay which was completely sterile. The two types of fill suggest two phases in the history of the ditch. A few pottery sherds of the 16th or early 17th c were recovered from a ditch filling. A brick-lined cesspit containing 17th-c pottery was noted S of the ditch.

See also COT88 below, excavations on this site in 1988.

ER numbers 404, 405, 406, 407
EDN IV, 77–86
PRG, 1337

78–80 Cannon Street (site of Dyers' Arms), EC4

GM29

P Marsden, 1966
NGR: TQ 32670 80885
SMR: 041415

This site revealed walls interpreted as part of the Roman governor's palace, and the site is Areas 2 and 3 in the published report of the palace excavations (Marsden 1975).

Several Late Saxon/early medieval pits containing Badorf ware were recorded, suggesting the Late Saxon robbing of the Roman palace structures in the S half of the site. A chalk-lined well, 3ft in diameter, contained 14th-c pottery. Two cesspits were recorded: one contained objects of the mid-17th c, and the other, chalk lined, objects of the 16th and 17th c, including much fine glassware and a gold noble of Henry IV.

ER numbers 913, 1114, 1115, 1116, 1117, 1118, 1118A, 1118B, 1119, 1120, 1121, 1122, 1123, 1124, 1125, 1126, 1127, 1128, 1129,
    1130, 1131, 1158, 1159, 1160, 1161, 1162, 1200, 1201, 1202, 1203, 1204, 1205, 1206
EDN IX, 38, 40; X, 57–8, 62, 67; site file
PRG, 927
Medieval Archaeol, 20, 1967, 294–5
Marsden, P, 1975 'The excavation of a Roman palace site in London, 1961–1972', *Trans London Middlesex Archaeol Soc*, 26, 1–102

GM30

P Marsden, 1961
NGR: TQ 32680 80915
SMR: 040909, 040912–16

111 Cannon Street (site of St Swithun's church), EC4

A medieval grave-slab of Purbeck marble, 2ft 7in. square, was found reused in the foundation of the SE corner of Wren's church. It had an incised drawing of a lady holding a heart in her hands, and an inscription in Lombardic lettering (transcribed, EDN VIII, 22) referring to the burial of the heart of Joanna, wife of Fulke de St Edmond, sheriff of the City in 1289–90. A chalk and mortar wall (dimensions not recorded) aligned E–W and partly reused by Wren was noted beneath the W part of the Wren crypt.

EDN VII, 57–8; VIII, 1, 4–6, 8, 22, 41; site file
PRG, 942
Marsden, P, 1963 'Archaeological finds in the City of London, 1961', *Trans London Middlesex Archaeol Soc,* 21.1, 77; see also excavation by Grimes on this site at the same time: Grimes, W F, 1968 *The excavation of Roman and medieval London,* 199–203 (site WFG48)
Schofield, J, 1994 'Saxon and medieval parish churches in the City of London: a review', *Trans London Middlesex Archaeol Soc,* 45, 131

GM31
(probably=
GM258)

E Rutter, 1958
NGR: TQ 32500 81000
SMR: 040885–91, 040899

Temple Court, 77 Cannon Street, Queen Victoria Street and 4 Budge Row, EC4

This site is also sometimes called Temple House in the EDN. The present building on the site (1997) is called Temple Court.

A line of squared wooden piles was observed running just N of Budge Row, roughly in line with Watling Street, but as these probably formed part of a complex of posts their alignment may not signify much. Patches of clean ballast were seen where the grab had been working along the line of Budge Row, overlying a thin layer of black pebbly mud, from which an amphora handle was recovered. This layer was immediately above the clay subsoil. The patches of ballast may possibly indicate the continuation of the metalled Roman road seen on the E of the Walbrook.

In the trench for the retaining wall along the Cannon Street frontage, about 12–15ft N of the pavement, wooden piles were seen, not in even lines, running roughly E–W. The pile tops were about 7ft below the basement floor. A hoard of 1st-c coins was recovered from the site.

At the same general time as these observations (December 1958), on a site called 'Cantling/Bucklersbury House', what were probably the E and S walls of the pre-Fire St Antholin's church were revealed by a mechanical grab; they were constructed of chalk, ragstone and bricks, but details were impossible to obtain. The church site lay N of Watling Street. At the N end of the site a well with an internal diameter of 4ft 3in. was recorded; its wall was 1ft 7in. thick and constructed of chalk and flint with a facing of Kentish ragstone.

ER numbers 436, 440, 442, 444, 473, 474, 485, 439, 488, 410, 431, 441, 445, 470, 484
EDN IV, 90; V, 14, 18, 22–30, 35–6, 56–7, 62, 64
Merrifield, R, 1960 'A first-century coin hoard from Budge Row (London)', *Numismatic Chronicle* 6th series, 20, 279–82
Merrifield, R, 1965 *The Roman city of London,* gazetteer 255–6
Wilmott, T, 1991 *Excavations in the middle Walbrook Valley, City of London, 1927–1960,* London Middlesex Archaeol Soc Spec Pap 13, 18–33

GM32

F Cottrill, 1935
NGR: TQ 32740 80870
SMR: 041439

106 Cannon Street, EC4

A 3ft length of an undated wall was found in the NE part of the site. It was built of flint rubble and buff cement, faced only on its N side; 2ft 3in. thick and exposed 1ft 6in. in depth, its top was at about basement level.

Site file
PRG, 941

143–147 Cannon Street (Nicholas Lane site), EC4

GM33

P Marsden, 1961
NGR: TQ 32785 80885
SMR: 040949–52

On the E half of 143 Cannon Street, a gravel deposit 1ft thick was observed extending to about 6ft
N of the old building frontage. It overlay the natural brickearth and seemed to be an artificial deposit.
It had the appearance of Roman road-metalling, and probably represented either the N edge of the
Roman road or a spill of road material immediately adjacent to it. Elsewhere on the site was a fire-level
containing burnt daub and pottery of the Flavian period. In view of the presence of Hadrianic fire
deposits on sites immediately to the N and E, however, there seems little doubt (according to
Merrifield 1965) that this should also be attributed to the same fire. Cutting into it were ragstone
foundations of a later date. An earlier thin burnt level, possibly representing the Boudican fire, lay a
few inches above the natural soil.

ER numbers 734, 765, 766
EDN VIII, 29–30, 48
Marsden, P, 1963 'Archaeological finds in the City of London, 1961', *Trans London Middlesex Archaeol Soc,* 21.1, 70
Merrifield, R, 1965 *The Roman city of London,* gazetteer 283

67–69 Cheapside, 1–5 Queen Street, EC4

GM34

F Cottrill, 1937–8
NGR: TQ 32461 81129
SMR: 040527–9

The gravel metalling of a Roman road was observed in three places on this site, with its top at a depth
of about 13ft below the pavement level of Queen Street, and its bottom at a depth of about 17ft 3in.
resting on a layer of yellow clay 3–6in. thick, beneath which was greyish-brown natural clay. The gravel
was hard and coarse, with horizontal layering. From a low level in it came the base of a samian cup
(form Dr 27) with an encircling groove (a pre-Flavian feature). The road was at least 26ft 6in. wide.
To the S of it was a square timber-lined well.

A medieval foundation at least 5ft thick was seen at the N end of the site. It was built of ragstone,
chalk rubble and soft sandy mortar, and the recorded face was aligned roughly N–S. It was found in a
small trench, and not seen in other nearby trenches. It lay immediately beneath the modern cellar floor
and was at least 4ft 9in. in depth.

The site was excavated again in 1991 (see CED89 below).

Site file
PRG, 760
Merrifield, R, 1965 *The Roman city of London,* gazetteer 64

72–73 Cheapside, EC4

GM35

Unknown, presumably
Q Waddington, 1930
NGR: TQ 32480 81140
SMR: 040531–2

Oak piles and camp-sheathing, apparently associated with early Roman pottery, on this site suggest that
a tributary of the Walbrook may have lain here in Roman times. A very early occupation of this area
was indicated by the samian ware found, which included stamps of Claudian potters. The site was
excavated again in 1991 (CID90, see below).

Site file (drawings only)
GL Annual Report, 30 April 1931, 14
Merrifield, R, 1965 *The Roman city of London,* gazetteer 65
Shepherd, J, 1987 'The pre-urban and Roman topography in the King Street and Cheapside areas of the City of London', *Trans
London Middlesex Archaeol Soc,* 38, 11–58

GM36 (including GM184)

P Marsden, 1963
NGR: TQ 32525 81127
SMR: 040733, 040735–43; the church, 041516, SAM GL147

1–2 Bucklersbury, 76–80 Cheapside, 9–12 Pancras Lane (including site of St Pancras church), EC4

Note: the development site of 76–80 Cheapside included nos 9–12 Pancras Lane to the S, and therefore the site of St Pancras church. In some lists of GM sites the site of 9–12 Pancras Lane is given the site number GM184. In this document the two sites are summarised together under GM36 for convenience. This site in 1963 also included 1–2 Bucklersbury.

The gravel metalling of a Roman road was observed during builders' excavations in several places in the central part of the site. It overlay grey silt. The natural ground level descended sharply into the valley of a small stream which apparently flowed in a SE direction across the SW corner of the site. Unfortunately the whole area was much disturbed, and it was impossible to see how the road crossed the stream. There appeared to be a road surface just N of 9 Pancras Lane, with more metalling lying above it. The total surviving thickness was 4ft in the E part of the site, and 4ft 9in. further W. No edge of the road was seen, but from the distribution of the remaining patches of gravel, the road cannot have been less than 29ft wide, and could hardly have been more than 35ft. Piles indicated the presence of timber structures immediately to the N and S of it, and a curious feature was the presence of a few posts, 4in. or 5in. in diameter, in the silt and extending up into the gravel near the centre of the road itself. These must have formed part of a fairly slight structure which was earlier than the road, or contemporary with an early phase when the road was narrower.

The plan of the medieval church of St Pancras was also revealed. It had a simple plan and most of what was uncovered was of one period. It had a nave 19ft 4in. wide, with an apsidal chancel at the E end. The walls were about 3ft thick and mainly of ragstone and yellow cement. The N face of the N wall was built of roughly squared stone blocks above a well-tooled plinth. N of the chancel was the corner of a room rendered internally with white painted plaster. This rendering was also found on the interior of the nave. Since there were no traces of doorways in the N and S walls of the nave, it is probable that the entrance to the church lay in the unexcavated portion of the nave to the W. The church floor was mostly destroyed by burials, but some patterned floor tiles were recovered. At one point on the S side of the nave a patch of undisturbed tile flooring was found at some distance above the bottom of the plastered wall. The church is first mentioned in 1038, and was destroyed in 1666 and not rebuilt. Other chalk foundations were noted to the E of the church, with a well 3ft in diameter composed of a reused barrel, in which was 13th-c pottery. A second barrel-well at the W end of the site was undated, but since it lay in the line of the Roman road, it is probably also of post-Roman date. The site of 12 Pancras Lane was excavated again in 1991 as part of CID90 (see below).

Observation at 1–2 Bucklersbury, now part of 76–80 Cheapside, 1963: the grey silt in the S and central part of the Cheapside site did not extend over the NE area immediately S of Bucklersbury. Here the natural soil was brickearth. A few inches higher was a burnt deposit, and at a still higher level another burnt layer with its bottom about 4ft above the natural soil. About 16ft to the W was a square timber-lined well, the filling of which contained pottery of *c* AD200. The stratigraphical relationship with the two burnt layers could not be determined, and the latter could not be dated. A Roman quern was found in a burnt deposit a few feet to the SE of the well.

Nos 72–75 Cheapside, 83–93 Queen Street and 12 Pancras Lane were excavated by the DUA in 1991: see CID90 below. Nos 76–80 Cheapside were excavated again during redevelopment in 1994: MoLAS archive, site BOL94.

ER numbers 807–9, 851–3, 862 (St Pancras church)
EDN IX, 1, 6, 9, 13–15; site file
PRG, 1041
Medieval Archaeol, 9, 1965, 185
Marsden, P, 1967 'Archaeological finds in the City of London, 1963–4', *Trans London Middlesex Archaeol Soc,* 21.3, 216–18
Merrifield, R, 1965 *The Roman city of London,* gazetteer 191–2
Schofield, J, 1994 'Saxon and medieval parish churches in the City of London: a review', *Trans London Middlesex Archaeol Soc,* 45, 125–6
Shepherd, J, 1987 'The pre-urban and Roman topography in the King Street and Cheapside areas of the City of London', *Trans London Middlesex Archaeol Soc,* 38, 11–58

110–116 Cheapside (Sun Life Assurance), EC2

GM37

I Noël Hume, 1955–6
NGR: TQ 32412 81205
SMR: 040500–9, 040512–13

The main discovery on this site was a Roman bath house building, which is now published (Marsden 1976); post-Roman features remain unpublished, and will be dealt with here in greater detail.

In 1954–5 Professor Grimes excavated three trenches in the S part of the site, but missed the Roman building by a few metres (Grimes, site WFG40). The site was later watched during development by I Noël Hume for the Guildhall Museum (Fig 5).

In Phase I (Flavian), the bath-house had six rooms, two on hypocausts. In Phase 2 (2nd c), modifications resulted in an establishment of eleven rooms, four of which were heated. Other Roman features included a timber-lined tank NE of the building, the SE corner of a second Roman masonry building to the N of the bath-house, fragments of a N–S Roman road in the W of the site, pits and a well, a fragment of mosaic and traces of two further Roman buildings.

Fig 5 GM37: conditions on the Sun Life Assurance site, Cheapside. This view from the W shows the NW corner of the N room of the first bath-building overlaid by the stoke-hole platform of the second bath-building.

A hollow filled with black silt, evidently the bed of a stream or a pond, was seen in the builders' cutting on the N edge of the site. If the former, its general direction was apparently to the SE. The water-tank of the Roman bath-house was eventually submerged by black silt in which was a quantity of Roman pottery, none of it later than the 2nd c. All of this area seems to abound in springs, and a deposit of wet black gravel in the SE corner of the site suggested that there may have been an early stream which flowed into the channel seen on the opposite side of the Roman road under St Mary le Bow. If so, it was covered by dumped material and built over in the early Roman period, for a deposit of clay containing pottery of the early 2nd c overlay the gravel, and on this was burnt daub. The stream, whether dammed or driven underground, now presumably supplied the bath-house tank until the latter was swamped and submerged by the rising waterlevels of the later 2nd c.

The depression or pond on the N side of the site was probably open in the post-Roman period, though no dating evidence was found in its fill. A possible continuation of the depression was found over the Roman timber-lined tank serving the bath-house. A medieval timber-lined well, 2ft 1in. square, was found at the SE corner of the site. Another well, lined with chalk above a base of brick with timber lining and 2ft 7in. in diameter internally, contained 17th-c objects. Several cesspits lined with brick and stone, dating from the 15th to the 18th c, were found. Most had been backfilled before 1666. One cesspit had walls of brick and ragstone and measured 7ft x 8ft, and another had walls of chalk and brick and was 4ft 6in. wide internally. Another of ragstone and chalk measured 5ft 9in. x 6ft 8in., with walls 1ft 5in. thick. A chalk wall 2ft 2in. thick was found in the NE part of the site, close to Trump Street. It lay close to a chalk-lined well 2ft 10in. in diameter, that extended to a depth of 9ft 2in. below modern basement level.

Traces of burnt debris were found in the E half of the site, and were believed to be from the Great Fire of 1666, but the deposits were not described. From the sketches in the EDN book, there appear to be some good 17th–19th-c groups.

ER numbers 274, 275, 278, 280, 280A, 281, 286, 290, 290A, 290B, 292, 300, 303, 306, 306A, 306B, 306C, 306D, 307, 309, 310, 311, 312, 313, 314, 315, 316, 317, 317A, 317B, 317C, 320, 321, 322, 325, 326, 328, 329, 330, 331, 332, 332A, 332B, 332C, 332D, 332E, 332F, 332G, 333, 334, 335, 336, 337, 338, 339, 340, 341, 342, 343A, 343B, 344, 345, 346, 347, 348, 349, 350, 351, 352, 353, 354, 355, 356A, 356B, 367A, 367B, 368, 370
EDN III, 35, 41, 49, 53, 58–60, 63–5, 68, 72, 75–8, 83–6; IV, 4; 2 site files, containing some Roman pot drawings not published
PRG, 761
Marsden, P, 1976 'Two Roman public baths in London', Trans London Middlesex Archaeol Soc, 27, 1–70 [Roman levels only]
Merrifield, R, 1965 The Roman city of London, gazetteer 51–5

GM38

P Marsden, 1957
NGR: TQ 32214 81234
SMR: 040053

137–144 Cheapside, EC2

A patch of packed gravel was seen on the S edge of the site in the edges of the builders' trenches. It was dirty and packed in layers, and had the appearance of road-metalling. This was opposite the E end of St Vedast Foster Lane church. Another sighting recorded a similar patch of rammed gravel in a foundation trench about 10ft to the E. This metalling probably formed part of the main Roman road which has been detected at several points on the S side of Cheapside.

EDN IV, 59–60
Merrifield, R, 1965 *The Roman city of London,* gazetteer 37

GM39

P Marsden, 1964
NGR: TQ 32337 81195
SMR: 041358

Cheapside (opposite Milk Street), EC2

A lead waterpipe was found under the N carriageway of Cheapside at a depth of about 10ft 6in. It was aligned E–W, surrounded by puddled clay and was oval in section, about 2in. in diameter. It was possibly part of the medieval conduit system in Cheapside.

ER number 942; accession number 23842
EDN IX, 67
PRG, 776
Marsden, P, 1967 'Archaeological finds in the City of London, 1963–4', *Trans London Middlesex Archaeol Soc,* 21.3, 215

GM40

P Marsden, 1963–4
NGR: TQ 32155 81245
SMR: 041335

Cheapside (junction with New Change), EC4

Two stone walls, about 5ft apart and aligned E–W, were exposed for a length of 8ft 9in. beneath the centre of the present roadway at the W end of Cheapside, nearly opposite Old Change. They lay at a depth of 4ft 7½ in. below the modern street surface, extending below the bottom of the excavation at 7ft 3in. The N wall had a fine tooled S face of rectangular stone blocks, and the S wall, the faces of which had not survived, was built of ragstone and brown mortar. These were possibly remains of St Michael le Querne church, first mentioned in the 12th c and not rebuilt after its destruction in the Great Fire of 1666; or of the Little Conduit which adjoined the church at its E end (see S elevation of the church and conduit by Ralph Treswell, 1585, published in Schofield 1987).

EDN IX, 16; site file (plan only)
PRG, 762
Marsden, P, 1967 'Archaeological finds in the City of London, 1963–4', *Trans London Middlesex Archaeol Soc,* 21.3, 215
Schofield, J, 1987 *The London surveys of Ralph Treswell,* London Topographical Soc Publication 135

GM41

E Rutter, 1958
NGR: TQ 33208 81382
SMR: 041815–17

5 Clark's Place, Bishopsgate, EC3

A short length of chalk wall was noted on the E side of this site, aligned E–W, but no further details are recorded. Part of a chalk-lined pit, at least 9ft deep below the modern basement, was found with parallel walls 1ft 9in. thick and 8ft 3in. apart. The pit cut into an earlier circular timber-lined well 3ft 3in. in diameter. The chalk-lined pit produced pottery in two groups, of c 1300 and c 1500.

ER numbers 425, 426, 427, 429
EDN V, 13a–17
PRG, 1330

36–40 Coleman Street (site of St Stephen Coleman Street church), EC2

GM42

E Rutter, 1955–6
NGR: TQ 32609 81341
SMR: 041520, 04152001

Traces of the medieval church of St Stephen Coleman Street were noted during the clearance of burials of the post-Fire church (Fig 6). Walls predating those of Wren suggest several different building phases. One foundation under the S wall was constructed of chalk and gravel, while another under the S wall had arches of chalk and mortar. In general the medieval foundations were between 3ft 6in. and 4ft wide. Medieval foundations seemed to coincide with the N, S and E walls of the post-Fire church. The W end of the pre-Fire church seemed to align with the E side of Wren's tower, which itself evidently lay outside the pre-Fire alignment and structure. Inside the pre-Fire church part of a medieval pier, with traces of red colouring, were recorded; and a substantial L–W foundation 1ft wide following the centre line of the post-Fire church, indicating that a smaller church may have lain to one side or the other in a previous phase.

Stow says the church was previously a Jewish synagogue, but Kingsford thinks this is a confusion with the site of the Chapel of the Friars of the Sack, which became part of the site of Grocers' Hall (Stow i, 284; ii, 336).

Fig 6 GM42: Eve Rutter (later Eve Harris) at work on the site.

ER numbers 559, 561, 575, 576, 592, 600, 615, 625, 646, 650, 651, 660; ER 575 is a portion of a medieval pier with traces of red colouring on it.
EN II, 84; EDN VI, 32–3, 40–1, 43, 46, 55, 57–9; VII, 5, 10, 23, 26, 32; site file
PRG, 1042
Medieval Archaeol, 2, 1960, 143; *Trans London Middlesex Archaeol Soc*, 20, 1961, 223
Anon, 1981 'Finds identification'
Schofield, J, 1994 'Saxon and medieval parish churches in the City of London: a review', *Trans London Middlesex Archaeol Soc*, 45, 130
Stow, J, *Survey of London* (ed C L Kingsford), 1908 (3rd edn, 1971)

65–66 Coleman Street, EC2

GM43

E Rutter, 1953–4
NGR: TQ 32652 81431
SMR: 041521

A barrel-lined well 2ft 6in. wide was found containing 15th-c pottery. Another well was 3ft 9in. in diameter and of chalk, sandstone and ragstone. At its base, 8ft 7in. below the modern cellar, a decayed wooden structure was sunk into the natural gravel; possibly a cut-down barrel or tub 2ft 2in. in diameter. Pottery and clay pipes dated its filling to the mid-17th c.

ER numbers 68, 69, 71, 124
EDN I, 10–11, 13–15, 18, 81; Librarian's monthly reports, July–September 1953
PRG, 1043

GM44

P Marsden, 1962
NGR: TQ 33597 80858
SMR: 041916, 041976–8

8–10 Cooper's Row (and space at rear), EC3

Building excavations revealed a portion of an internal turret to the Roman city wall known to form the E side of this site. The walls of the turret were 3ft 7in. thick at foundation level, where they were of clay and flints, and 2ft 10in. above, of ragstone with courses of bonding-tiles. A small portion of the cement floor within remained. To the N, the bank behind the wall was seen as gravel with a layer of soil sandwiched in the middle. Fragments of Castor ware of Antonine date came from a layer of soil beneath the bank.

The city wall here, first observed in 1864, survives 110ft long and up to 35ft high. The Roman work survives well up to the third tile course about 10ft high. Medieval work above is of chalk and flint faced with ragstone, rising to the level of the parapet walk. Towards the S end are a window and four round-headed embrasures (?c 1200) and traces of a stair to the parapet. In 1962 a barrel-lined well containing 13th-c pottery was found at the S end of the site.

When the wall was restored by DoE in 1962, much of the stone refacing was removed and remortared. Phases of construction in the core were recorded by Marsden.

ER numbers 790, 793, 794, 795, 796, 797, 989
EDN IV, 76 (refers to a site inspection in 1957; 'No excavation is to be done'); VIII, 68, 72–83; X, 25; site file
PRG, 1501
Marsden, P, 1965 'Archaeological finds in the City of London, 1962', *Trans London Middlesex Archaeol Soc*, 21.2, 135, 139
Merrifield, R, 1965 *The Roman city of London,* gazetteer W9, W10

GM45 (=GM190)

P Marsden, 1962
NGR: TQ 32760 81420
SMR: 040646

5–7 Copthall Avenue, EC2

Builders' excavations on this site between Great Swan Alley and Copthall Close revealed black silt-like mud of a considerable thickness, containing pottery of the 3rd and 4th c. This seemed to indicate the close proximity of a large tributary of the Walbrook, although the actual stream-bed was not seen. It is most unlikely (according to Merrifield 1965) that such a thick deposit could be the result of flooding from the main stream about 120ft to the E.

This is the same site as GM190, and the GM190 number should not be used.

ER numbers 779, 780, 781, 782, 785
EDN VIII, 64–5, 67
Maloney, C, 1990 *The upper Walbrook Valley in the Roman period,* The archaeology of Roman London 1, CBA Res Rep 69
Merrifield, R, 1965 *The Roman city of London,* gazetteer 138; reference only to 'GM' as source, no further source material. For discussion of this site in the wider setting of recent discoveries in the area, see now Maloney 1990.

Corbet Court, 3–6 Gracechurch Street (1964): see GM67

GM46

G Dunning, 1930
NGR: TQ 32980 81109
SMR: 040788

52 Cornhill, EC3

Two ragstone walls 5ft and 6ft in thickness were found, 20ft apart, running E–W. Between them was an *opus signinum* floor 6in. thick, 11ft below the level of Cornhill. These were part of the second Roman basilica. Occupation continued into the 4th c. Roman objects from the site are GM acc nos 12486–9.

Site file
J Roman Stud, 21, 1930, 236–8
Marsden, P, 1987 *The Roman forum site in London: discoveries before 1985,* 82–5
Merrifield, R, 1965 *The Roman city of London,* gazetteer 214

69–73 Cornhill, EC3

Walls observed on the site in 1959 and observations of 1897 combine to indicate two rectangular rooms, of ragstone with squared blocks. These are from the second Roman forum. Part of the foundation and wall of the second basilica is preserved in a small chamber beneath the basement of 71 Cornhill. The site of 68–72 Cornhill was excavated again in 1981 as CNL81 (see below).

EDN V, 37
Marsden, P, 1987 *The Roman forum site in London: discoveries before 1985*, 85–7
Merrifield, R, 1965 *The Roman city of London*, gazetteer 211

GM47

E Harris and P Marsden, 1959
NGR: TQ 32963 81136
SMR: 040784

Cousin Lane (north end), EC4

A wall of chalk with a little flint was found at a depth of about 9ft in a sewer tunnel dug in the roadway at the junction of Upper Thames Street and Cousin Lane. It seemed to align roughly N–S, and was of considerable thickness, though no dimensions are given.

EDN V, 56

GM48

P Marsden, 1959
NGR: TQ 32554 80786
SMR: 041418

6 Crescent, EC3

A stretch of the Roman city wall, 40ft long and 11ft high, was uncovered and the inner slope of the Roman ditch was traced 12ft in front of it. The site was visited by Queen Elizabeth (the Queen Mother) (Fig 7). Merrifield reported in 1965 that 'a considerable portion of the external face of the wall can still be seen in the basement of the Toc H Club. It consists of plinth, four courses of squared ragstone, a triple bonding-course of brick and then six more courses of ragstone.' The building on the E, outside of the wall, was later demolished and the site excavated as CST85 (see below).

Site file; contains some photos
J Roman Stud, 29, 1939, 216
Merrifield, R, 1965 *The Roman city of London*, gazetteer W8

GM49

F Cottrill, 1938 (or 1935?)
NGR: TQ 33620 80815
SMR: 044260

Fig 7 GM49: Queen Elizabeth (the Queen Mother) visits the site of the Roman wall in the cellar at 6 Crescent (?1938, though a note with the original negative gives the date '12.5.35').

28–32 King William Street (formerly Crooked Lane), EC4

In several places gravel deposits about 1ft thick, containing indeterminable sherds of Roman pottery, were observed overlying the natural gravel when the modern roadway had been removed. These were possibly remains of the metalling of a Roman road, since Crooked Lane lay on the line of a S

GM50

P Marsden, 1961
NGR: TQ 32840 80801
SMR: 040993

continuation of the N–S road bounding the W side of the basilica and forum. Basements on both sides of Crooked Lane were deep, so that the gravel layers survived only beneath the narrow roadway, and gave no indication of the width of the original deposit.

ER number 767
EDN VIII, 54
Marsden, P, 1963 'Archaeological finds in the City of London, 1961', *Trans London Middlesex Archaeol Soc,* 21.1, 72
Merrifield, R, 1965 *The Roman city of London,* gazetteer 399

GM51

F Cottrill, 1932
NGR: TQ 32408 80864
SMR: 040218

2 Skinner's Lane, EC4

A fragment of a Roman cement floor was recorded 10ft 4in. below pavement level, on the N side of Skinner's Lane near its junction with Doby Court.

Site file

GM52 (?=GM187)

P Marsden, 1966
NGR: TQ 32707 80788
SMR: 041432

Suffolk House, Upper Thames Street (formerly 1–2 Ducksfoot Lane), EC4

A medieval wall of ragstone with a little chalk was discovered at the N boundary of this site, aligned E–W, and standing 10ft high; its facing possibly having been removed. As it supported a recent wall 70ft high, the City Engineer did not disturb the medieval work, even to discover its thickness.

This seems to be the same site as GM187 (observed 1969), which has two ER groups.

EDN X, 54 for site GM52

GM53

I Noël Hume, 1953
NGR: TQ 33479 81218
SMR: 041818

Duke's Place (opposite nos 32–38), EC3

A chalk-lined sewer was found crossing beneath Duke's Place, opposite the Great Synagogue. It lay at a depth of 14ft 6in. below modern street level, and was built of chalk blocks. The walls were 1ft 8in. thick, the internal height 4ft 6in., and the internal width 2ft 8in. It was filled with 'dirt' containing pottery of the 16th and 17th c, which was not retained.

This is probably part of the drainage system of Holy Trinity Priory, which occupied a large area inside the city wall at this point; the site is considered in a report on the priory (Schofield & Lea in prep.). The site of the drain lies N of the frater and kitchen of the priory. The direction of flow of the observed part is not known, but it seems likely that it drained northwards, through the city wall and into the ditch.

EN II, 66
PRG, 1331
Schofield, J, & Lea, R, in prep. *Holy Trinity Priory Aldgate*

15–16 St Dunstan's Hill, EC3

GM54

F Cottrill, 1937–8
NGR: TQ 33153 80678
SMR: 041086–8

Walling of ragstone rubble was seen at a depth of 10ft 6in. below the pavement adjacent to the curved frontage, which it is said to have followed, with its face about 1ft from the edge of the site. The mortar contained fragments of brick and tile and was presumably Roman.

On the E edge of the site, two Roman walls making a corner were seen. They were of ragstone rubble with light brown mortar containing brick fragments, and the faces were of coursed undressed blocks. The surviving top of each was at a depth of 3ft below basement level. Adjoining the N side of the E–W wall was a floor of plain red tesserae at a depth of 4ft below basement level, with a cement moulding at the junction of wall and floor. Another similar but narrower E–W wall ran across the site 8ft 6in. S of the first, extending from 5ft 9in. to 8ft 6in. below basement level.

Site file
Merrifield, R, 1965 *The Roman city of London,* gazetteer 355

Site of Bastion 6, Duke's Place, EC3

GM55

P Marsden, 1971
NGR: TQ 33515 81204
SMR: 041953, 044261–4

Bastion 6 was found standing more than 1m high, and in its structure were a number of large sculptured stone blocks perhaps originally parts of tombs. The only recognisable piece was a baluster-shaped piece which may have come from the top of the wall. The foundation of the bastion had been cut through a deposit of 4th-c date; a thicker layer of rubbish overlay the foundation, containing 4th-c pottery and bronze coins of 364–75. Another excavation close to the bastion found the early Roman ditch, filled in to allow the assumed wider late Roman ditch to be dug. In the fill was a coin of Constans of 341–4, indicating a *terminus post quem* for the later ditch (and bastion).

A broad medieval ditch was uncovered beside the city wall, and in the berm a medieval cesspit. Post-medieval pottery and kiln waste (including one kiln trivet) from delftware manufacture were also found; they may relate to the workshop of Jacob Johnson/Jansen, immigrant potter, known on documentary grounds to be nearby.

The post-medieval pottery and kiln material are in ER 1352–5, and are discussed by Noël Hume 1977, 111–14. See also Schofield & Lea in prep., and Edwards in prep. on other discoveries of delftware material in the area and Jansen.

ER numbers 1331, 1332, 1333, 1334, 1335, 1336, 1337, 1338, 1339, 1340, 1341, 1342, 1343, 1344, 1345, 1346, 1347, 1348, 1349, 1350, 1351, 1352, 1353, 1354, 1355
EDN XI, 40–6; site file
Edwards, J, in prep. *Tin-glazed wares,* Post-medieval pottery from London 3
Marsden, P, 1980 *Roman London,* 172 [source of the Roman summary]
Noël Hume, I, 1977 *Early English Delftware from London and Virginia,* Colonial Williamsburg Occasional Papers in Archaeology II
Schofield, J, & Lea, R, in prep. *Holy Trinity Priory Aldgate*

Noble Street (east side) / Falcon Square (south-east), EC2

GM56

Unknown, 1956
NGR: TW 32253 81530
SMR: 041265

This observation was N of what is now 3 Noble Street; in 1956, S side of Falcon Square.

A well containing 17th-c objects was noted; the precise location is uncertain. The well had an internal diameter of 3ft 6in. and sides 1ft 6in. thick, and was traced for a depth of 19ft from its surviving top (the depth below basement unknown). The sides of the well were carefully built of bands of limestone and brick on a timber base.

ER number 364
EDN IV, 29; site file

GM57

Unknown, 1955
NGR: TQ 33205 80960
SMR: 041872

125–135 Fenchurch Street, EC3

A chalk-lined cesspit was found at the corner of Fen Court and Fenchurch Street. The sole of an early 16th-c shoe and a small Bellarmine jug of c 1640 were recovered from inside it (not brought in to GM).

EN II, 85
PRG, 1429

GM58

P Marsden, 1964
NGR: TQ 33115 80918
SMR: 041065, 041824

22 Fenchurch Street, EC3

A piece of gravel metalling 7ft 6in. wide and 5ft thick was observed in a builder's excavation on the N edge of the site, 3ft S of the old building-line. This was the only sign of gravel metalling on the site, and it lies exactly on the S edge of the presumed course of the Roman road observed to the E and W. Sandwiched among the layers of gravel was a single layer of yellow clay.

EDN IX, 18–19
Marsden, P, 1967 'Archaeological finds in the City of London, 1963–4', *Trans London Middlesex Archaeol Soc*, 21.3, 213–14
Merrifield, R, 1965 *The Roman city of London*, gazetteer 344A

GM59

F Cottrill, 1935
NGR: TQ 33210 80895
SMR: 041060–4, 041066, 041875

31–34 Fenchurch Street, 23 Rood Lane and 4–8 Mincing Lane, EC3

Reddish gravel layers were seen in the E part of the site of 31–34 Fenchurch Street, extending for 2ft below basement level, ie from 13ft to 15ft below street level. This seems to be a continuation of the road-metalling seen on the site of 4–8 Mincing Lane (see below). Neighbouring Roman walls seem to be approximately at right angles to the line of roadway produced by joining these patches of metalling; if it continued to the W, this skirts the S front of the forum and would reach the Walbrook near the supposed crossing noted on the site of the National Safe Deposit Company, Queen Victoria Street, in 1872–3 (Merrifield 1965, gazetteer 195–6).

Portions of a Roman wall were seen in section in holes to the S of the road-metalling. It ran approximately N–S at right angles to the supposed alignment of the road. The foundation was of rubble, consisting of flints, yellow cement and Roman brick. S of the wall were traces of a rectangular timber structure on approximately the same alignment.

The site plans and photographs in the site file show that along the S side of the site, the arched chalk foundations of the N side of the adjacent church of St Margaret Pattens, Rood Lane, were revealed beneath the party wall. The site plan also indicates that the N side of the medieval tower, evidently at the NW corner of the church, lay at the W end of this foundation and protruded slightly to the N (ie into the site), but the photographs do not include this end.

This GM site number includes a separate observation at 4–8 Mincing Lane in 1936. Here, near the N end of the site, under no. 4, layers of gravel were seen, 4ft in thickness, extending from 11ft to 15ft below pavement level. Beneath them was grey sand with occasional flecks of charcoal. The gravel was hard, brown and laid in horizontal layers, evidently the metalling of a major E–W road.

Site file
31–34 Fenchurch Street: *J Roman Stud*, 26, 1936, 256; Merrifield, R, 1965 *The Roman city of London*, gazetteer 344, 345
4–8 Mincing Lane: *J Roman Stud*, 27, 1937, 241; Merrifield, R, 1965 *The Roman city of London*, gazetteer 343

112–114 Fenchurch Street, 17–18 Billiter Street, EC3

GM60

Q Waddington, 1925–6
NGR: TQ 33330 81020
SMR: 041819, 040149–50,
044436

The part of the site facing Fenchurch Street was excavated in the first half of 1925, and 18 Billiter Street at the beginning of 1926. On this site, when it was previously excavated in 1872 (according to the notes in EN I), was found an Early Iron Age sword with a bronze handle (in GM).

The excavation of 1925–6 produced the bases of two pedestal urns, one of 'pre-Roman type' (acc no. 1925.50, 51; RCHM 1928, 21, fig 2 nos 4 and 5) and much 1st-c Roman pottery, including samian form 29 and Ritterling 12. Below these in the gravel were a number of burials. Cinerary urns had been enclosed in cists of thick oaken planks, sometimes clamped with iron. One of them had as cover a thin slab of Purbeck marble, and on the wooden cover of another was a cross cut from a thin sheet of copper (acc no. 1925.45). All the cinerary and other urns had been broken at a remote date, the cemetery having been disturbed by the building of a series of underground chambers. These were excavated in the gravel, and the sides faced with well-built walls of squared blocks of chalk individually about 10in. x 6in. They were floored in the same manner, and seemed to have been 8ft or 9ft in height, their floor level being about 25ft or 26ft below the present street. During demolition of one a ring brooch of the early 14th c (acc no. 1926.9) was found.

Below the level of the Roman graves was the bottom of a well sunk into the gravel and lined to a height of about 4ft with blocks of roughly squared granite (*sic*; sometimes confused with Kentish ragstone). In it were several sherds of several large jugs of the 13th and 14th c. Scattered about the site were numerous other fragments of this period, as well as of the 4th and 5th c, and much undatable coarse ware.

For further work on the site of 110–114 Fenchurch Street in 1972, see FNS72 below.

EN I, 9
RCHM, 1928 *London III: Roman London*, 21–2

155 Fenchurch Street, EC3

GM61

F Cottrill, 1934
NGR: TQ 33110 80945
SMR: 044265

An undated ragstone wall was recorded (P Marsden note in 1981 listing). No other documentation has so far been located.

154–161 Fleet Street, EC4

GM62

Q Waddington, 1924–5
NGR: TQ 31370 81180
SMR: 041181

Four wells were found. One was possibly of late medieval date, lined with chalk blocks, with a diameter of 2ft 9in. A second well was built of brick. The third contained a dagger with a 'flame-shaped' blade and a hilt of some very hard wood, probably of oriental origin.

EN I, 10

St Vedast House, 150 Cheapside / Foster Lane, EC2

GM63

P Marsden, 1962
NGR: TQ 31269 81256
SMR: 040052

Traces of gravel metalling, presumably part of the main E–W Roman road beneath Cheapside, were observed during builders' excavations. It overlay the natural brickearth, and survived to a thickness of 18in. The upper levels had evidently been removed in post-Roman times.

EDN IX, 2; site file
Merrifield, R, 1965 *The Roman city of London*, gazetteer 36

GM64

Q Waddington, 1925
NGR: TQ 32259 81157
SMR: 041338

16–45 Cheapside (formerly 5 Friday Street), EC4

A wall of chalk and buff mortar was exposed in a shaft dug on the W side of Friday Street, at the NE corner of the passage leading to the former churchyard of St Matthew Friday Street. The wall was 5ft thick and seemed to extend N of the shaft. It was probably the SE corner of the church of St Matthew (demolished 1886). It was at least 7ft high and rested on clay at a depth of 14ft 6in. below street level; the distance from the exposed highest course to the street, 7ft 6in., was obscured.

EN I, 11
PRG, 764

GM65

P Marsden, 1961
NGR: TQ 32696 81034
SMR: 040749–50

8–10 Mansion House Place (formerly 13–14 George Street), EC4

In the N part of 14 George Street, deposits of gravel were found overlying natural brickearth and gravel. These were clearly artificial, for a thin spread of material from one of the gravel deposits extended to the S and overlay a pit containing 1st-c pottery, about 20ft S of the N edge of the site. It seems likely that these deposits were either part of the metalling of the expected E–W Roman road which should pass along the N side of the site, or related spreads.

ER numbers 744, 759
EDN VIII, 36, 47
[GM staff] 1963 'Archaeological finds in the City of London, 1961', *Trans London Middlesex Archaeol Soc*, 21.1, 70
Merrifield, R, 1965 *The Roman city of London*, gazetteer 197
Note: in the I Noël Hume collection of photographs is one of a small section of tessellated pavement, with tesserae of red brick and chalk, which 'was briefly exposed during site clearance. My recollection is that it was located in the vicinity marked 197 (George Street) on Merrifield's base map' (pers. comm. 1996). This must refer to a separate observation sometime in 1949–55 near the later site of GM65. Further investigation may find the address.

GM66

P Marsden, 1961
NGR: TQ 32294 81257
SMR: 040057–61, 041340

St Alban's House, 124 Wood Street (formerly Goldsmith House, Goldsmith Street), EC2

Fragmentary remains of several structures were seen. One consisted of portions of two parallel ragstone and chalk foundations 2ft 6in. thick and about 22ft apart. The S foundation terminated on the W with a return to the N, probably to form a compartment with the N wall. There was no dating evidence, but the alignment is approximately that of the Roman fort to the N and of the presumed line of the Roman road to the S. This building overlay a structure with a floor of *opus signinum* sunk into the natural brickearth; late 1st-c pottery was found on this floor. About 40ft to the SW was another fragment of ragstone wall. To the N of this, in the centre of the site, were the burnt remains of a daub and timber building, overlying a pit of the period Nero–Vespasian, and in the debris above was late 1st-c–early 2nd-c pottery. Under the building was a layer of brickearth and under that a pit containing pottery of the period of Nero.

Parts of a medieval stone building were found in the N part of the site. Ragstone and yellow mortar walls about 4ft thick enclosed a room measuring 16ft x 17ft with a white mortar floor. The inner wall faces had been painted white, and against one face was a fragment of 13th-c pottery. The room was probably an undercroft of a building fronting on to Wood Street or Gutter Lane, since Goldsmith Street was not established until the 17th c.

The site was excavated again in 1986 on demolition of the 1961 building: site code ABS86 (see below).

ER numbers 738, 739, 740, 741, 742, 750, 752, 753, 754, 755, 756, 761, 762, 763, 764
EDN VIII, 32–6, 43–5, 48; site file
PRG, 765
Marsden, P, 1963 'Archaeological finds in the City of London, 1961', *Trans London Middlesex Archaeol Soc*, 21.1, 71, 77
Merrifield, R, 1965 *The Roman city of London*, gazetteer 43

General note for GM67, GM68 and GM70: these sites, being chiefly investigations of parts of the second Roman basilica and forum, have extensive entries in Merrifield's 1965 gazetteer and have been discussed in the two forum publications: Marsden, P, 1987 *The Roman forum site in London: discoveries before 1985* and in general terms in Milne, G, 1992 *From Roman basilica to medieval market: archaeology in action in the City of London.* Their Roman results are therefore summarised briefly here.

Corbet Court, 3–6 Gracechurch Street (St Peter's Alley site), 53 Cornhill, EC3

GM67

P Marsden, 1964
NGR: TQ 33001 81070
SMR: 040819–23, 040868

Walls of the second basilica had been noted here in 1883–4 by Henry Hodge. In 1964 foundations of an E–W wall of the basilica, a buttress, other walls and a cement floor of the first basilica were recorded (Fig 8).

ER numbers 869, 869A, 903, 904, 905, 906, 864, 897
EDN IX, 17, 26, 29–31, 36, 38–9, 41–2, 44; X, 64
Marsden, P, 1987 *The Roman forum site in London: discoveries before 1985,* 101–6
Merrifield, R, 1965 *The Roman city of London,* gazetteer 221, 229A

Fig 8 GM67: Peter Marsden standing below a section of strata which includes the W wall of the first Roman basilica with its bonding courses of tiles (towards the top).

17–19 Gracechurch Street, EC3

GM68

F Cottrill, 1934
NGR: TQ 32970 81030
SMR: 040834–42, 041538–40

The walls and foundations of a small temple were recorded in the W half of the site. It was 10.66m wide and 20.7m long, aligned approximately N–S. It comprised a cella with an angular apse in its N wall, and a doorway in its S wall; to the S was a rectangular area mostly enclosed by walls with shallow foundations. The portico on the S side of the cella was flanked by two projecting walls which may have supported a staircase to a podium level within the cella. Traces of a possible walled enclosure or *temenos* were found to the W and N of the temple. A gravelled area was found on the building site immediately S of the temple in 1960–1, suggesting that the temple precinct extended beyond the S side of the site of 17 Gracechurch Street and onto the site formerly occupied by the church of All Hallows Lombard Street (Marsden 1987).

Marsden, P, 1987 *The Roman forum site in London: discoveries before 1985,* 106–16
Merrifield, R, 1965 *The Roman city of London,* gazetteer 234–6, 238

GM69

P Marsden and E Rutter, 1959
NGR: TQ 32978 80905
SMR: 040976–81, 041419–20

Midland Bank, 55–60 Gracechurch Street (site of St Benet Gracechurch), EC3

A burnt level containing mid-1st-c pottery, including a jug of coarse ware with stamp C.ALBUC, presumably of the period of the Boudican revolt, was found in the SW part of the site. In it were burnt remains of timber and daub houses. Towards the centre of the site, a fragment of Roman ragstone wall was seen, running N–S, approximately parallel with Gracechurch Street.

Several fragments of chalk walls and foundations were noted; some, including a vault, evidently from the medieval church of St Benet Gracechurch. The vault fragment, of chalk, formed the W end of the structure about 7ft S of the S wall of the Wren church. A circular chalk-lined well was recorded on the E side of the site; another was lined with chalk and brick. An unusual square chalk-lined pit 9ft x 9ft with walls 2ft thick was found just N of St Benet's Place. It extended into the natural gravel, and survived at least 14ft deep; at the bottom the insides had two internal offsets so that its internal diameter reduced from 5ft to 3ft. Its fill included 13th-c pottery. Although called a cesspit in the site notes, this seems to be a well.

The site of 55–58 Gracechurch Street was excavated again in 1990; see RAC90 below.

ER numbers 408, 408A, 408B, 408C, 409, 494, 495, 496, 492, 493, 498, 499, 500, 504, 505, 506, 509, 512, 513, 522, 523, 524, 525, 527, 528, 541, 542, 549, 560, 572, 573, 577
EDN IV, 86–90; VI, 3a, 8, 10, 13a, 14a, 15–17, 20a, 21, 25, 32, 42, 46; site file (comprises note on amphora by F Grew). Two photos of the arched vault of St Benet are in EDN VI, 21.
PRG, 929
Merrifield, R, 1965 *The Roman city of London*, gazetteer 293

GM70

F Cottrill, 1934
NGR: TQ 33040 81046
SMR: 040816–18, 040824–7, 041825

83–87 Gracechurch Street, EC3

The E end of the main building of the first forum was recorded, with extensive details of its construction. Finds were deposited in the GM, but though some were accessioned, most have since been lost.

The site of 85 Gracechurch Street was observed again in 1995–6 by MoLAS (site code GRC95).

Marsden, P, 1987 *The Roman forum site in London: discoveries before 1985*, 119–29
Merrifield, R, 1965 *The Roman city of London*, gazetteer 229–31

GM71

F Cottrill, 1934
NGR: TQ 32730 81380
SMR: 044359

11–16 Telegraph Street, EC2

At the NW corner of the basement on this site, 10ft below street level, layers of dark mud, sand and gravel, about 6ft deep, were seen in a builder's shaft.

Site file

GM72

F Cottrill, 1934
NGR: TQ 32785 81540
SMR: 044360

London Wall Street (opposite Copthall Avenue), EC2

In June 1934 a hole was observed in the roadway of London Wall, E of Moorgate, at about W24 on the plan in RCHM *Roman London* (1928). At a depth of 12ft 3in. the back of the city wall was exposed, and a 'tunnel' cut through it. The wall was just over 7ft thick. A double brick bonding-course could be seen on the back of the wall, 12ft 6in. down; the front was not excavated to this depth. Two feet above the course was a triple bonding-course with 1½ in. offset between top and middle bricks.

The core of the wall, at a depth of 10–12ft, was of rag, poorly mortared. The top of this work was not level, and above was rag with some brown sandstone, as in the plinth, in hard white mortar; a double bonding-course appeared in it, but was not visible on the outer face. Between this well-mortared work and that below was a layer, a few inches thick, and some feet long, in the middle of the wall, of loose red tiles about ³/₄ in. thick, one with a flange.

Site file

All Hallows Barking church, Great Tower Street, EC3

GM73

G Dunning and F Cottrill, 1928–32, 1936 and discoveries of 1951
NGR: TQ 33365 80690
SMR: 041091–2, 041853

In 1928 a pavement of tesserae was found beneath the tower of the church, and is preserved *in situ*. Part of a moulding in pink plaster with a light red surface remains next to a gully which crosses the floor, probably for a timber partition. Near the centre of the church, stone walls were found forming three sides of a room or corridor, 9ft wide and at least 20ft long. They were 2–3ft 6in. thick, and rested on footings of large squared blocks of chalk in hard yellow mortar. There was a single bonding-course of flanged tiles 4ft above the foundations, and above this the walls were built of ragstone and flints. The foundations cut into a layer of the Antonine period. Dunning thought the building was of 3rd-c date. The walls were on the same alignment as the ?partition gully in the tessellated floor beneath the tower. These alignments are different from those of the Saxon and medieval church.

In 1931–2 Dunning also observed what appears to be the foundation of the E wall of the chancel of the Norman church, about 3ft 6in. wide, 10ft 6in. W of the present 14th-c E wall. Two other walls ran W from each end of the discovered wall to form an area 14ft 6in. wide. The S arm was about 3ft wide while the original width of the N arm was uncertain as it had been strengthened at a later date. In the footings of the S and E walls were flints and pieces of Roman brick, with the upper wall fabric of chalk and ragstone rubble in a hard yellow mortar. The cores of the N and S walls also contained many architectural fragments with patches of hard white mortar attached, probably from the underlying Roman building. A length of rubble masonry set in hard yellow mortar and running N–S was observed about 30ft to the W of the 'Norman chancel wall'. The function and date of this wall are not clear, but it may be the E wall of the Saxon church. A wall was recorded in much the same place, under the pulpit, in 1708 during repairs. An alternative interpretation could be that this is the sleeper wall making the junction of the Norman nave and chancel, but as the S wall of the 'Norman' chancel extended a further 10ft 9in. to the W, this seems unlikely.

The church was burnt out to its shell by bombs in 1940. The bombing revealed several pieces of Saxon sculpture from two freestanding crosses of the first half of the 11th c; and that a wall at the SW corner of the church, running E–W, was a blocked-up arch of Roman tiles; this arch (Fig 9), perhaps of 11th-c date (proposed by Schofield 1994, 81–3), is now exposed in the rebuilt church (Kendrick & Radford 1943; Taylor &

Fig 9 GM73: the arch of reused Roman tiles at the SW corner of All Hallows Barking church, looking S.

Taylor 1965, 399–400, both suggesting an earlier date). In the adjacent church offices, at first-floor level, the NW corner of the church at a similar Late Saxon or 11th-c date is also preserved.

In December 1951 an inscribed stone was found beneath the nave. It is in two pieces, from the upper part of a wheeled cross-head, uniquely inscribed on one face, and with traces of black paint on the other face. The inscription is probably to be translated: 'Thelvar had [this] stone set up over Here[ ].'

For a watching brief at the SE corner of the church in 1996, see MoLAS site code ALH96.

PRG, 1413–16

Trans London Middlesex Archaeol Soc, 20, 1961, 222; Medieval Archaeol, 11, 1967, 249–51 [both notes concerning the
    Saxon cross-head; the second note by E Okasha]

Kendrick, T D, & Radford, C A R, 1943 'Recent discoveries at All Hallows Barking', Antiq J, 23, 14–18

Merrifield, R, 1965 The Roman city of London, gazetteer 358–9

Schofield, J, 1994 'Saxon and medieval parish churches in the City of London: a review', Trans London Middlesex Archaeol Soc, 45, 81–3

Taylor, H, & Taylor, J, 1965 Anglo-Saxon architecture, i, 399–400

GM74 (=GM193)

P Marsden, 1962–3
NGR: TQ 32950 81460
SMR: 040654

Winchester House, Great Winchester Street, EC2

The E tributary of the Walbrook was observed in the W part of the site. The stream-bed itself was not revetted and was ill-defined, but its position could be located fairly satisfactorily by noting the position of the lowest point in the mud-filled valley. The black silt of the flood deposits extended E to about the middle of the site.

When the building of 1962 was demolished in 1995, the site was recorded again: MoLAS archive, site WCH95.

Marsden, P, 1967 'Archaeological finds in the City of London, 1963–4', Trans London Middlesex Archaeol Soc, 21, 208–9

Merrifield, R, 1965 The Roman city of London, gazetteer 145

GM75

E Rutter and P Marsden,
1956–7
NGR: TQ 32291 81353
SMR: 041341, 044381–3,
044442

2–12 Gresham Street (site of Waxchandlers' Hall), EC2

The gravel metalling of a Roman road was seen in builders' excavations, but there is no record of its exact position or alignment. It is said to have run across the site in a NW direction towards Aldersgate.

A chalk-lined well 2ft 9in. in diameter produced sherds, clay pipes, all of the first half of the 17th c, and a coin of Charles I. The chalk lining was only 8in. thick, suggesting a post-medieval date. The well lay near the middle of the N side of the site, and its surviving top lay 12ft below street level. It was excavated for a further 12ft, at which depth excavation was abandoned.

A pit excavated by workmen during digging for the SW corner of the retaining wall produced fragments of large tubular-necked vessels, a crucible fragment and sherds of the mid-16th c (ER 360).

A brick-lined cesspit lay with a complex of 18th-c foundations at right angles to Wood Street (sic); finds inside contained pottery of 1730–40. A second pit or cellar abutting the first contained a quantity of late 19th-c leather trimmings from boots, belts, braces and other items.

ER numbers 258, 360, 373, 374, 374A, 374B, 374C, 379, 381, 383, 386, 399

EDN IV, 19, 40–2, 48–50, 52–3, 93; VI, 41–2, 93; site file, containing a list of material which was deemed property of the Goldsmiths'
    Company, but with GM acc nos 21076 and 21244–96.

PRG, 766

Merrifield, R, 1965 The Roman city of London, gazetteer 39

30 Gresham Street (formerly nos 20–38, and before that 26–27 King Street), EC2

GM76

P Marsden and E Harris, 1960
NGR: TQ 32466 81213
SMR: 040063, 041343–4

Traces of Roman ragstone walls 3ft thick, with courses of bonding-tiles, were recorded during builders' excavations. The position of the fragments observed, mostly in section, indicated the lines of two parallel walls about 10ft apart, apparently forming the corner of a room or courtyard around which ran a corridor. The alignment was unusual, being approximately NE–SW, suggesting that the remains were part of the same building as a wall observed on the same alignment on the opposite side of King Street (the site of nos 13–14) in 1956, and another fragment further S, on the site of no. 33, recorded in 1938. Groups of Roman and later pottery, unstratified, were also recovered.

ER numbers 457, 458, 460, 461, 462, 463, 464, 465, 471, 471A, 471B, 471C, 479, 449, 452, 641
EDN V, 41–3, 45, 47–51, 69; VII, 2, 22; site file
PRG, 767 (cf also 709)
Medieval Archaeol, 4, 1960, 149; *Trans London Middlesex Archaeol Soc,* 20, 1961, 220
Merrifield, R, 1965 *The Roman city of London,* gazetteer 45
Shepherd, J, 1987 'The pre-urban and Roman topography in the King Street and Cheapside areas of the City of London', *Trans London Middlesex Archaeol Soc,* 38, 11–58

Guildhall, EC2

GM77

I Noël Hume, 1951
NGR: TQ 32484 81386
SMR: 040629, 040632–3

This entry covers two separate observations, one on the S side, the other on the N side of Guildhall, in 1951.

On the S side:

A trial hole revealed a Roman foundation on the E side of buttress no. 3 on the S side of Guildhall. The medieval buttress terminated at a depth of about 10ft 6in. beneath the basement floor of the Comptroller's office, and under it were the remains of a substantial Roman wall, consisting of a course of squared ragstone blocks resting on two courses of bonding-tiles, one of which appeared to be a reused roof tile. Below these was a base of ragstone rubble bound with mortar. On the S side of the hole at the same depth was seen a level of broken Roman tiles on a similar base, springing from the N–S wall, and apparently forming part of an E–W wall at right angles to it.

On the N side:

Between the third and fourth buttresses of Guildhall from the W a stratum of silt was observed during builders' excavations. Rushes lying N–S suggested that the silt was in the bed of a stream flowing to the S. This was presumably drained or diverted when the first medieval Guildhall was built (?12th c), and the silt contained a few fragments of 12th-c pottery. Immediately to the W of the stream, Roman pottery of the 3rd c and a coin of Postumus were found in the filling of a medieval pit, which had been cut through Roman levels where another coin of the late 3rd c was found.

Several medieval stone walls were noted in the area immediately N of Guildhall. One, running E–W, was 46ft long, 9ft 6in. high and 3ft wide, on three foundation arches. Another N–S wall ran for 55ft 6in. Other features included a stone cesspit against the N wall of Guildhall and a number of medieval pits.

I Noël Hume also notes: 'I recall a good 2nd-c group containing at least one face pot. The principal finds from this area were the 1940-scorched records of the Corporation dating from the second half of the 18th c. Those that I was able to save were later returned to the Guildhall Library – where I hope they remain' (pers. comm. 1996; for the discovery, and research based on the saved documents, see Noël Hume 1974, 212–18).

For observations by P Marsden inside and on the S side of Guildhall in 1968, see GM145 below. For work in 1954 to the N of the medieval Guildhall, on the site of the Corporation Offices, see GM216 below. For summary of recording and restorations at Guildhall, see PRG 710 (restorations of 1909–10); PRG 711 (summary of post-War recording, including Barron 1974 and Wilson 1976).

Librarian's monthly reports June 1950, March 1951, November 1955
EN II, 23–7; EDN II, 46–7, 60–1
Barron, C, 1974 *The medieval Guildhall of London*
Merrifield, R, 1965 *The Roman city of London,* gazetteer 127 [the N site] and 129 [the S site]
Noël Hume, I, 1974 *All the best rubbish,* 212–18
Schofield, J, 1995 *Medieval London houses,* 14–19
Wilson, C, 1976 'The original design of the City of London Guildhall', *J Brit Archaeol Assoc,* 129, 1–14

GM78

I Noël Hume, 1950–1
NGR: TQ 33370 80860
SMR: 041873–4, 0200714

8 Hart Street, EC2

Several chalk foundations 3ft 3in. wide were found N of the tower and crypt of St Olave Hart Street church; they were undated. They had been reused by the foundations of the 18th-c rectory. Burials were found, believed to date from the 12th and 13th c. A circular chalk-lined well, 3ft in diameter and 16ft deep from the modern concrete floor, was found close to the church tower. It contained debris of the mid-16th and early 17th c. A circular chalk-lined cesspit or well 4ft in diameter contained pottery of the 16th and 17th c. Some of the finds are preserved on display at the church.

Site file, containing summary report
EN II, 32–44

GM79

F Cottrill, 1935
NGR: TQ 33444 81270
SMR: 041947

28–30 Houndsditch, EC3

The core of the city wall was exposed at the SE corner of the site, and was seen in section at several points. It consisted of ragstone rubble, roughly coursed in alternate layers of ragstone blocks and hard cream-coloured cement mixed with small flints. The footings were of flints and puddled clay, level at the bottom which was about 15ft below pavement level. The masonry above oversailed the footings on the N side by about 1ft. There was a triple levelling-course of bricks with the top bricks about 7ft 9in. below pavement level, and the bottom 4ft above the top of the footings.

Site file
J Roman Stud, 26, 1936, 254 [a note by Cottrill, referring to the site as 'Bevis Marks and Gracechurch Lane']
Merrifield, R, 1965 *The Roman city of London,* gazetteer W20

GM80

P Marsden, 1964
NGR: TQ 32261 80878
SMR: 040623, 041378–9

Huggin Hill (south-west corner), EC4

A medieval cellar or undercroft about 19ft wide was found immediately W of Huggin Hill. Its W wall parallel to the Hill was 1ft 9in. thick and constructed of ragstone and broken Roman tiles, presumably from the underlying Roman bath building, and both the W and E walls were roughly faced. The undercroft was aligned at right angles to Huggin Hill, and much of it survives in the public garden on the site. A note by P Marsden (1981 summary) adds that 'its wall face had a chequered design, and originally it had a vaulted roof the springer stones of which had survived. North of this was a late medieval or 16th-c stone wall with evidence of the post-1666 Fire rebuilding in brick.'

To the E of the cellar was a medieval well lined with squared chalk blocks and rubble. It was 2ft 10in. in diameter, and had been cut through the N wall of the Roman baths. Between the cellars and the well were two walls of ragstone and thin medieval tiles, about 1ft 6in. wide, and presumably forming the corner of a room.

ER numbers 907, 908, 909, 910, 911, 912, 914, 915, 916, 917, 918, 919, 920, 921, 922, 923, 924, 925, 926, 927, 928, 929, 930, 931, 932, 933, 934, 935, 936, 937, 938, 939, 940, 941, 943, 944, 947, 949, 950, 1427, 1428
EDN IX, 45; site file
PRG, 819

Sir John Cass College, 32–35 Jewry Street, EC3

GM81

F Cottrill, 1933
NGR: TQ 33567 81096
SMR: 041911–12

The Roman city wall was exposed for a length of 75ft. It was 8ft thick, surviving to a height of 4ft above the plinth. The foundations were cut through the filling of a stream-bed which contained pottery of the late 1st c. A culvert of bricks had been constructed below the plinth, evidently to carry the water of the stream through the wall. The Roman city ditch was observed in section at several points, but its relationship to the stream is not clear. A fragment of the wall has been preserved in the basement of the college. The medieval ditch was also recorded cutting into the natural gravel. The sloping inner side of the ditch was between 35ft and 44ft from the outer face of the city wall, and between 10ft and 15ft 6in. below the Roman plinth.

Site file
PRG, 1609
J Roman Stud, 24, 1934, 11
Merrifield, R, 1965 *The Roman city of London,* gazetteer W16

9–12 King Street and Prudent Passage (Atlas Assurance site), EC2

GM82

P Marsden, 1963–4
NGR: TQ 32485 81238
SMR: 040072–3, 041345–6

A layered deposit of gravel nearly 3ft thick was found in the S part of the site, overlying the natural soil. It was very similar to the deposits seen between King Street and Lawrence Lane (Merrifield 1965, gazetteer 46–7) and may form part of a Roman E–W road. A much thinner layer of metalling in the N of the site had the appearance of a minor N–S road, with a shallow drainage ditch along its W edge, and a width of about 20ft. It was not constructed until the early 2nd c and did not continue in use for very long. In neither case could the exact alignment of the supposed road be traced. No Roman buildings were found, but a scatter of burnt daub and fragments of red and white wall plaster showed that there were wattle and daub houses in the neighbourhood in the late 1st and early 2nd c.

A medieval cellar 11ft long by more than 5ft wide, with walls 2ft thick of mortared chalk, was also recorded in the W of the site, apparently aligned at right angles to Ironmonger Lane some distance to the E (ie at the back of a medieval property). It had an earth floor upon which 13th-c material was found. A late 15th-c pit cut into the cellar.

ER numbers 813, 814, 815, 816, 817, 818, 819, 820, 821, 822, 823, 824, 825, 826, 827, 828, 829, 830, 831, 832, 833, 834, 835, 836, 837, 838, 839, 840, 841, 842, 843, 844, 845, 846, 847, 848A
EDN IX, 10–11 (lists ER groups and gives positions in trenches); X, 10; site file
PRG, 768
Marsden, P, 1967 'Archaeological finds in the City of London, 1963–4', *Trans London Middlesex Archaeol Soc,* 21.3, 202–6, 216–17
Merrifield, R, 1965 *The Roman city of London,* gazetteer 49
Shepherd, J, 1987 'The pre-urban and Roman topography in the King Street and Cheapside areas of the City of London', *Trans London Middlesex Archaeol Soc,* 38, 11–58 [not including the finds]

13–14 King Street, EC2

GM83

P Marsden, 1956
NGR: TQ 32490 81246
SMR: 040069–70, 041342

The SE corner of a ragstone building was exposed, one wall running NE and the other NW. At a lower level on the same site was uncovered an earlier path of rammed gravel, apparently running approximately N–S.

The corner of a chalk-lined cesspit containing early 17th-c pottery and glass was found 10ft from the modern frontage. The walls were about 1ft 6in. thick.

EDN IV, 37, 42
ER numbers 369, 375
Merrifield, R, 1965 *The Roman city of London,* gazetteer 48
Shepherd, J, 1987 'The pre-urban and Roman topography in the King Street and Cheapside areas of the City of London', *Trans London Middlesex Archaeol Soc,* 38, 11–58

GM84

P Marsden, 1960
NGR: TQ 32463 81291
SMR: 044361

26 King Street, EC2

P Marsden's 1981 summary of sites includes a note, 'a chalk wall was recorded'. No further documentation has been located.

GM85

F Cottrill, 1938
NGR: TQ 32454 81235
SMR: 040064–5

33 King Street, 8–9 Lawrence Lane, EC2

A fragment of a wall, probably Roman, of ragstone rubble with light sandy mortar, was observed in a builder's excavation. It is said to have run approximately NW–SE. The bottom was in natural sand at a depth of 14ft 3in. below the level of the modern pavement of Lawrence Lane. A section to the S of the wall showed the top of the natural soil 1ft above this, and above were dark sandy and gravelly layers presumed to be Roman occupation levels or debris. In the extreme SW corner of the site, under the Lawrence Lane frontage, an underpinning hole, 4ft x 5ft, was dug through dumped gravel, resembling road material, 6ft thick with traces of horizontal layering. Its top was at a depth of 10ft 6in. below the pavement level of Lawrence Lane.

Site file
Merrifield, R, 1965 *The Roman city of London*, gazetteer 46
Shepherd, J, 1987 'The pre-urban and Roman topography in the King Street and Cheapside areas of the City of London', *Trans London Middlesex Archaeol Soc*, 38, 11–58

GM86

I Noël Hume, 1955
NGR: TQ 32449 81233
SMR: 040065–8

34–35 King Street, 6–7 Lawrence Lane, EC2

In the N central part of the site was a layered accumulation of gravel 4ft thick, which seemed to form part of a road or courtyard which had been remetalled nine times. A timber-lined well containing 3rd–4th-c pottery in its lower fill cut through the metalling near the N edge of the site. There seems to have been a trace of similar gravel metalling in the SW corner also. During trenching for the retaining wall on the W edge of the site, the workmen cut through a 14in. layer of burnt daub resting on wood-ash at a depth of 4ft below the level of the basement. It contained pottery of the first half of the 2nd c.

ER numbers 282, 283, 284, 285, 293, 294, 295
EDN III, 43–4; site file
Merrifield, R, 1965 *The Roman city of London*, gazetteer 47
Shepherd, J, 1987 'The pre-urban and Roman topography in the King Street and Cheapside areas of the City of London', *Trans London Middlesex Archaeol Soc*, 38, 11–58 [not including the finds]

GM87

F Cottrill, 1935
NGR: TQ 32465 81230
SMR: 040514

39 King Street, EC2

In the SE corner of the site were found two patches of coarse Roman cement flooring at a depth of 16ft below pavement level. Occupation and clay layers continued to a depth of 19ft.

Site file
J Roman Stud, 26, 1936, 256
Merrifield, R, 1965 *The Roman city of London*, gazetteer 58

1 King's Arms Yard (Bank of England Club), EC2

GM88

E Harris, 1959
NGR: TQ 32509 81312
SMR: 040693

Black mud containing 1st- and early 2nd-c pottery, leather and metal objects was found in builders' trenches in various parts of the site, resting on the ballast and brickearth. The ballast was higher on both W and E sides of the site, and dipped towards the centre, where the black silt was much thicker; evidently the stream-bed of the Walbrook. Wooden piles were observed on the W side of the stream, and two planks on their edges were seen in section 9ft 9in. apart, apparently extended in a S direction beside the stream. There were also remains of tree-trunks and branches, which may have been growing when they were submerged by the silt.

The note in EDN V, 33–4 includes two sketchplans of the site and two transcribed borehole logs. P Marsden's 1981 summary of sites adds a note: 'Medieval objects were recovered from the bed of the Walbrook stream.'

ER numbers 447, 448, 450, 453, 454, 455, 468, 476, 478, 487, 510, 511, 526, 530, 533, 451, 489, 537
EDN V, 33–4; no site file
Merrifield, R, 1965 *The Roman city of London,* gazetteer 158
Wilmott, T, 1991 *Excavations in the middle Walbrook Valley, City of London, 1927–1960,* London Middlesex Archaeol Soc Spec
   Pap 13, 55–8

King William Street / Nicholas Lane, EC2

GM89

Q Waddington, 1924
NGR: TQ 32815 80928
SMR: 041434

A chalk foundation was exposed in a sewer trench in the roadway where Nicholas Lane crosses King William Street. Neither the top nor the bottom of the foundation was exposed, even though the base of the trench lay at a depth of 19ft, and the foundation was first seen at a depth of 6ft. It seemed to be the foundation of a wall running at right angles to King William Street.

EN 1, 6

Old Change Court and Old Change House, Distaff Lane (rear of 128 Queen Victoria Street and formerly Knightrider Street), EC4

GM90

1 Noël Hume, 1956;
P Marsden, 1961
NGR: TQ 32070 80990
SMR: 040587–96, 040601,
040603

Merrifield's 1965 gazetteer records this site in six separate entries (gazetteer 93, 95–8, 100), further abbreviated here. All have now been reconsidered for the Roman period by Williams (1993, 72–87). A seventh part of the site, Old Change Court and Old Change House, Distaff Lane (Merrifield 1965, gazetteer 102), is here separated into GM168.

Peter's Hill, near Knightrider Street (Merrifield gazetteer 93): the E end of a large Roman wall, seen running along the N side of Knightrider Street in 1863, was recorded in 1961. The foundations cut through a 1st-c pit, and the foundation trench had originally been lined with timber. The wall survived 5ft 6in. high, but the upper portion had been rebuilt; against it lay late 3rd–4th-c debris.

Knightrider Street, W of Old Change, 1961 (gazetteer 95): a 24ft 6in. length of Roman wall was exposed running E–W, with squared ragstone blocks above a foundation.

Knightrider Street, at junction with Old Change, 1961 (gazetteer 96): another portion of this wall was uncovered in a sewer diversion. It extended W from the E edge of Old Change for 29ft. As elsewhere on this wall there were no traces of connecting walls to the N.

Knightrider Street, N side, opposite St Nicholas Cole Abbey church (site of Old Change House), 1955 (gazetteer 97): a Roman culvert was observed running through a ragstone wall. The wall ran from Distaff Lane to Old Change, over 125ft. It survived 6ft high, and had been used as foundations for walls in the 18th and 19th c. Photographs show a culvert through a substantial Roman wall, to the W of the *Financial Times* site. There are also two photographs of sunken-featured buildings on the *Financial Times* site, then being excavated by Grimes (site WFG35). An early 18th-c brick pit or well was also seen (EDN III, 38).

Knightrider Street, N side, opposite E end of St Nicholas Cole Abbey church (site of *Financial Times* building), 1956 (gazetteer 98): a continuation of the Roman wall was recorded for a further 6ft. Level with the uppermost remaining course was a small bronze knee brooch (Collingwood Group V) of the middle of the 2nd c. The wall here survived to a height of 9ft, and a length of 14ft 3in. extended W of Distaff Lane.

Peter's Hill, upper end, 1845 and 1961 (gazetteer 100): a Roman wall was seen in builders' excavations in 1961; foundations were 4ft 4in. wide and composed of ragstone and hard white cement, set into the undisturbed gravel. This wall was seen in 1845 and is marked on the City Sewers Plan.

ER numbers 746, 747, 748, 749, 786
EDN III, 38–40, 46; IV, 31–3; VIII, 22–4, 38–40, 62, 67; site file
Merrifield, R, 1965 *The Roman city of London,* gazetteer 93, 95–8, 100, 102
Williams, T, 1993 *Public buildings in the south-west quarter of Roman London,* The archaeology of Roman London 3, CBA Res Rep 88, 72–87

GM91 (=GM208)

P Marsden, 1961
NGR: TQ 32100 80900
SMR: 040660–1, 040663–5, 041380–3

101 Queen Victoria Street, Lambeth Hill (Salvation Army Headquarters), EC4

On the W side of Lambeth Hill two chalk platforms supported by piles formed an upper and lower terrace. The former, seen only in the NW of the site, had an E–W retaining wall of cement about 3ft thick on its S side. It contained a large squared block of stone, evidently reused. A sandstone block 3ft x 3ft x 1ft, with a bevel on its N side, lay on the platform 30ft N of the retaining wall. The lower terrace extended to the N frontage of Thames Street, and incorporated two reused stone blocks. The terraces appear to be Roman.

During excavations for the S end of the new line of Lambeth Hill, four parallel rows of oak piles about 1ft apart were uncovered, running E–W. Their tops were about 14ft 6in. below the level of Upper Thames Street. They presumably acted as piles for a foundation about 5ft thick. Building debris containing *opus signinum,* Roman bricks, a fragment of white tessellated pavement and wall plaster painted red, white and black, lay to the S of the piles, mixed with brown river silt. Similar rows of piles were subsequently found to the W.

On the S side of the E–W part of Lambeth Hill, near Queen Victoria Street, builders' excavations exposed two portions of Roman walls, 3ft thick, of ragstone with a double or triple course of bonding-tiles. Both ran approximately E–W, but were not quite in alignment. Refuse layers containing Pingsdorf pottery of the 11th–12th c lay piled against part of one wall; it also seems probable that the medieval boundary between the parishes of St Mary Mounthaw and St Mary Somerset followed these walls.

In the middle of the roadway at the bottom of the former Lambeth Hill (30ft E of its new alignment) a ragstone wall was seen running approximately N–S. It had three double courses of red bonding-tiles and stood about 7ft high. Nearly 10ft to the E and apparently parallel to it was the foundation of another, massive wall.

The opening part of this investigation is recorded in one list separately as Lambeth Hill Road Scheme, GM208; but the two sites should be merged. The GM208 documentation is catalogued here under GM91. The site file for GM208 contains one small sheet of notes, a plan of Roman walls and floors found W of St Mary Somerset.

ER numbers (GM91) 768, 778, 861; (GM208) 610, 611, 617, 619, 685
(GM91) EDN VIII, 41, 54–60, 68; IX, 16; site file
(GM208) EDN VIII, 1–3, 5, 7, 43, 47–8; site file (under GM208)
Merrifield, R, 1965 *The Roman city of London,* gazetteer 110–13, 116
Williams, T, 1993 *Public buildings in the south-west quarter of Roman London,* The archaeology of Roman London 3, CBA Res Rep 88, 63–71

Albion House, 34–35 Leadenhall Street, EC3

A trial hole revealed a Roman pavement of coarse red and yellow tesserae at a depth of about 16ft below the present street level. A Roman coin, unidentifiable, but of minim size and therefore of the late 3rd c or later, was found in a black filling 6in. above the pavement. At a level 3ft above it were traces of a daub structure destroyed by fire; this was presumably medieval, as a 12th-c sherd lay on it. At the N end of the site were traces of possible bronzeworking, associated with pottery possibly of the 14th–15th c. The industrial debris included slag, copper and daub-like mould fragments, similar to those used for bell-founding.

For excavation on this site again in 1988, see LDL88 below.

ER number 89
EDN I, 12–13, 37
Merrifield, R, 1965 *The Roman city of London,* gazetteer 332

GM92

I Noël Hume, 1953
NGR: TQ 33275 81128
SMR: 041045–6, 041820–1

77 Leadenhall Street, EC3

A deposit of lumps of chalk, which probably formed the foundation of some part of the monastic buildings of Holy Trinity Priory Aldgate, was found in 1924 in a small excavation in the basement at about 14ft below street level (see GM292 below, the same site); and again in 1968. The work in 1968 has not been described.

Site file pocket and note describing contents as 'one page of rough sketches' but this is missing.
Schofield, J, & Lea, R, in prep. *Holy Trinity Priory Aldgate*

GM93

P Marsden, 1968
NGR: TQ 33462 81131
SMR: 04169201009

139–144 Leadenhall Street, EC3

In a section beneath the old building-line of 139–144 Leadenhall Street was seen a thickness of 2–3ft of layers of gravel resembling Roman road-metalling which overlay natural brickearth over most of this site. A Bronze Age beaker possibly from this site was purchased by the GM in 1960 *(sic).*

EDN IX, 54

GM94

P Marsden, 1964
NGR: TQ 33128 81155
SMR: 041155

22–23 Lime Street, 160–170 Fenchurch Street (Barclay's Bank) (site of St Dionis Backchurch church), EC3

This site is at the corner of Fenchurch Street and Lime Street, the address of which (OS Map, 1988) is: 161 and 168–170 Fenchurch Street, 22, 23 and 23a Lime Street. The site has been examined a number of times as its component parts were developed. Only in the 1970s did the site take on its present overall (and largest) form.

At 22 Lime Street (then Barclay's Bank) in 1969, works were recorded both by B Philp (Kent Archaeological Rescue Group) and P Marsden (Marsden 1987, 90–2). In 1976 at the corner site to the S, then addressed as 160–162 Fenchurch Street, A Boddington excavated for the DUA (site code FSE76; see below for summary, and summarised in context and discussed in Marsden 1987, 92–100). The two sites together gave information on buildings prior to the Boudican fire of AD60–1, and the SE parts of both Flavian and second fora.

GM95

P Marsden, 1969
NGR: TQ 33055 80960
SMR: 040163

The corner site is also the site of St Dionis Backchurch, the medieval and Wren church. Foundations probably of the medieval tower were recorded in the FSE76 excavation. A study of the church is in Schofield 1994.

The site code GM95 should be used for the observations by P Marsden in 1969 only. The observations by B Philp, which generated both records and finds, should be allocated the site code GM297.

Marsden, P, 1987 *The Roman forum site in London: discoveries before 1985*, 90–100
Schofield, J, 1994 'Saxon and medieval parish churches in the City of London: a review', *Trans London Middlesex Archaeol Soc*, 45, 100–1

GM96

I Noël Hume, 1951–2
NGR: TQ 33195 81065
SMR: 041041–4

41–51 Lime Street / Billiter Street (Lloyd's site), EC3

Traces of a substantial ragstone building, with a room heated by a hypocaust at the N end, were recorded. Near the SW corner of the site, at the corner of Lime Street and Fenchurch Avenue, were pavements of coarse red tesserae. The building seems to have been destroyed by fire after AD350. There was some evidence of a late 1st–early 2nd-c origin, with a major reconstruction and extension of the N part of the building in the late 3rd c. A small hoard of barbarous radiate coins was buried apparently at the time of the reconstruction.

A medieval floor of crushed chalk on puddled clay was found covering an area more than 5ft x 6ft. It lay adjacent to Lime Street, and at a depth of 12ft. No walls were found; associated pottery dated to the 15th c. A circular chalk-lined pit or well was found near the middle of the site. It had been repaired with wood and brick, but only the lowest 7ft 6in. of it survived. It was 3ft wide at the top, tapering to 2ft wide at the bottom. Its fill contained Roman material and a few objects of the period 1600–20. There were also 12th-c and 13th-c pits.

ER numbers 1, 2, 3, 4, 5, 6, 7, 8, 9, 10, 11, 12, 13, 14, 15, 16, 17, 18, 19, 20, 21, 22, 23, 24, 25, 26, 27, 28, 29, 30, 31, 32, 33, 34, 35, 36, 37, 38, 39, 40, 42, 43, 44, 45, 46, 47, 48, 49, 50, 51, 52, 55, 56, 57, 58, 60, 61, 62, 62A, 87, 865
EDN I, 35; see also EDN IX, 20, where ER 865 is 'early medieval pottery, unstratified from the site probably' accessioned in 1963.
Site file contains a typed list of the contents of ER groups 1–62A; Roman, '5th c' (ER 29), 12th/13th-c, 15th-c and 17th-c groups.
PRG, 1336
Merrifield, R, 1965 *The Roman city of London*, gazetteer 331

GM97

F Cottrill, 1932
NGR: TQ 33090 81010
SMR: 040828–33

15–18 Lime Street, EC3

The gravel metalling of a Roman N–S road was observed in the NW corner of the site. It was at least 25ft wide and made up to 8ft thick. It overlay an early occupation layer resting on the brickearth, containing pottery of AD50–80, including potters' stamps. W of the road, in the extreme NW corner of the site, were the footings of a wall running parallel with the road. This probably represented the E boundary of the forum.

Part of a rectangular compartment, possibly part of a bath-building, measuring 11ft x 8ft internally, was found about 50ft E of the Roman road. It had a thick concrete floor and solid tile walls 3ft thick, standing to a height of 2ft above the floor. The alignment seems to have been that of buildings within the forum rather than that of the forum and basilica.

Marsden's 1981 summary of sites also notes: 'A well, possibly medieval, was found on this site.'

J Roman Stud, 23, 1933, 205
Marsden, P, 1987 *The Roman forum site in London: discoveries before 1985*, 129–33
Merrifield, R, 1965 *The Roman city of London*, gazetteer 232–3

15 Lombard Street (Coutt's Bank), EC3

GM98

P Marsden, 1958–9
NGR: TQ 32805 81027
SMR: 040758–63, 041435,
041451

A wall of ragstone, chalk and flint was found running parallel with Abchurch Lane, and part of a wall, apparently of the same building, was found at right angles to this in the N part of the site. The bottom of the foundations was at a depth of 18ft and the top was 14ft 6in. below Abchurch Lane. Overlying these walls was fire debris containing pottery of the late 1st–early 2nd c. At the NW corner of the site was found a deep room, with walls of ragstone with a small quantity of chalk, their base being at a depth of about 20ft below street level. This was on the same alignment, and may have formed part of the same building.

A short length of wall or foundation 2ft wide was found at the S end of the site; built of ragstone and flint, it was faced with pieces of knapped flint, and is likely to be of post-Roman date. It was founded on some Roman metalling.

For observations on this site in 1939, see GM1 above.

ER numbers 437, 443, 446, 482
EDN V, 21, 23, 33, 36, 41; site file
PRG, 1054
Marsden, P, 1968 'Archaeological finds in the City of London', 1965–66, *Trans London Middlesex Archaeol Soc,* 22.1, 38
Merrifield, R, 1965 *The Roman city of London,* gazetteer 201–2

30–32 Lombard Street, EC3

GM99

P Marsden, 1962
NGR: TQ 32947 80962
SMR: 040970–3

Gravel metalling more than 6ft thick was observed during builders' excavations, overlying the trampled surface of natural brickearth. The metalling was in layers which were slightly cambered to the S. Among these were two distinct road surfaces, part of the main E–W Roman street. A short distance to the S, the trampled surface of the natural brickearth was overlaid by a manmade layer of brickearth and charcoal, and over this was a layer of burnt daub containing red and white painted wall plaster.

A chalk-lined well 4ft in diameter, and presumably medieval, was recorded near the centre of the S end of the site. ER 805 is ?12th-c pottery from the filling of a pit in the middle of the E end of the site.

ER numbers 805, 806
EDN VIII, 87; IX, 3–5; site file
J Roman Stud, 54, 1963, 140
Marsden, P, 1965 'Archaeological finds in the City of London, 1962', *Trans London Middlesex Archaeol Soc,* 21.2, 138
Merrifield, R, 1965 *The Roman city of London,* gazetteer 290

54–58 Lombard Street (Barclay's Bank), EC3

**GM100
(=GM295)**

P Marsden, 1960–1
NGR: TQ 32920 80980
SMR: 041431

Parts of several successive Roman buildings were recorded. The first was perhaps pre-Boudican; the second, part of the first forum building; and several parts of the second forum of the early 2nd c. The outer portico of the second forum was located with a stone structure lying in it. Parts of the forum walls were robbed in the 12th c.

ER numbers 613, 620, 621, 622, 623, 629, 630, 631, 632, 633, 635, 636, 637, 639, 648, 649, 653, 661, 665, 666, 667, 668, 669, 670, 675, 676, 677, 678, 682, 683, 726, 728, 757, 770, 771, 772, 774, 775
EDN VII, 4–5, 7–9 12–14, 16–19, 26, 29, 32, 35, 40–2, 46, 53; VIII, 20, 22, 46, 53, 58–9, 61
Trans London Middlesex Archaeol Soc, 20, 1961, 221
Marsden, P, 1987 *The Roman forum site in London: discoveries before 1985,* 140–7
Merrifield, R, 1965 *The Roman city of London,* gazetteer 243–5

GM101

A Oswald, 1939; E Rutter, 1957
NGR: TQ 32970 80990
SMR: 040844–53

54 Lombard Street (site of All Hallows Lombard Street church), EC3

Roman levels: walls and piers of both basilicas of the successive Roman fora were discovered; these have recently been reinterpreted and analysed (Marsden 1987).

Saxon and medieval levels: an early stone church with overall dimensions of 66ft x 22ft was recorded (Fig 10). A stagger in the N wall may indicate the division between nave and chancel; there was no crosswall between them. The walls were of ragstone with reused Roman tiles and bricks between layers of clean gravel, between 3ft 6in. and 5ft wide. At the W end were two fragmentary walls of pitched ragstone in soft mortar, 2–2ft 6in. wide. These might have been a W porch or part of an earlier structure.

In the 13th c a narrow N aisle (about 10ft wide) was added, of chalk walls on ragstone piers, with pointed foundation arches of chalk at the W end. This aisle was widened in the late 14th or early 15th c and further rebuilt c 1500 with ragstone walls on chalk and sandstone arches. The E wall of the chancel was also built on chalk foundation arches. The tower at the W end of the nave was probably constructed at the time of the later rebuilding of the N aisle (c 1500 on documentary evidence). In his rebuilding Wren positioned a new tower in the SW corner (Bloe 1948; Schofield 1994). A number of Spanish floor and ceiling tiles, recovered in 1939–40, have recently (1998) been identified as from Seville, dating to 1500–50.

Fig 10 GM101: medieval foundations of one of the aisle arcades of All Hallows Lombard Street church. The view is perhaps of the N arcade, looking NE.

In 1940 workmen digging just outside the SE corner of the church broke through an old chalk wall at a depth of 18ft below Gracechurch Street. To the E of this wall, between it and Gracechurch Street, were deposits backfilling a cellar including pottery, tobacco pipes and over 1,000 fragments of glass vessels. The assemblage is mainly of the first half of the 17th c, with some 16th-c pieces, and was covered with what is probably debris of the Great Fire of 1666 (Oswald & Phillips 1949).

What was probably the foundation of the tower was observed by E Rutter in February 1957: EDN IV, 56. This observation does not have a separate GM site number, and is here combined with GM101.

For later excavation of the site, see LOA90 below.

PRG, 908
Antiq J, 20, 1940, 510–11 [a note by A Oswald]
Bloe, J, 1948 'Report on a visit made to the site of All Hallows Lombard Street', *Trans London Middlesex Archaeol Soc*, ns 9, 181–6
Marsden, P, 1987 *The Roman forum site in London: discoveries before 1985*, 135–40 [reproducing a draft text on the Roman levels by A Oswald (1946)]
Merrifield, R, 1965 *The Roman city of London*, gazetteer 239–40
Oswald, A, & Phillips, H, 1949 'A Restoration glass hoard from Gracechurch Street, London', *Connoisseur*, Sept, 30–6
Schofield, J, 1994 'Saxon and medieval parish churches in the City of London: a review', *Trans London Middlesex Archaeol Soc*, 45, 85–6

GM102 (=GM296)

F Cottrill, 1933
NGR: TQ 32940 80975
SMR: 040854, 040856, 040860, 040863

54 Lombard Street, EC3

Outside All Hallows church, Roman walls were observed about 7ft S of the building-line.

Marsden, P, 1987 *The Roman forum site in London: discoveries before 1985*, 133
Merrifield, R, 1965 *The Roman city of London*, gazetteer 242

79 Lombard Street, EC3

A ragstone wall running N–S was seen in section at a depth of 4–6ft 3in. below basement level. It was assumed to be Roman.

Site file
J Roman Stud, 26, 1936, 256
Merrifield, R, 1965 *The Roman city of London,* gazetteer 189

GM103

F Cottrill, 1933
NGR: TQ 32758 81079
SMR: 044362

Lombard Street (opposite St Clements Lane), EC3

During sewer excavations a portion of Roman walling 3ft thick, running in the direction of the line of Lombard Street, was seen. It was suggested that it may have met, at a right angle, a wall observed in 1785 crossing the street opposite the church of St Edmund the King (Merrifield 1965, gazetteer 205), if both were contemporary.

GL Report, 1937, 17
Merrifield, R, 1965 *The Roman city of London,* gazetteer 206

GM104

G Dunning, 1937
NGR: TQ 32890 80995
SMR: 040767, 040769–70

Lombard Street / Nicholas Lane, EC3

During excavations for a new sewer, a piece of Roman walling running at right angles with the street was found a few feet W of Nicholas Lane. It stood 7ft 6in. high, and had five courses of bonding-tiles. Another account of the wall says it ran N–S at a depth of 14–15ft below the modern street level, and gave its position as about 11ft W of the corner of Birchin Lane.

GL Report, 1937, 17
J Roman Stud, 29, 1939, 217
Merrifield, R, 1965 *The Roman city of London,* gazetteer 204

GM105

?G Dunning, 1937
NGR: TQ 32856 81018
SMR: 040768–9

Site of London Bridge, River Thames

Dredging to the E of the Rennie bridge disclosed the remains of two starlings of the medieval bridge, the 12th and 13th starlings from the N end, but only their pile foundations were recovered (Fig 11). Many piles of oak and elm were seen; they were mostly about 15ft long, though one was 22ft 9in. long. The earlier piles seemed to be of pointed tree-trunks, while the later were squared and found at the E ends of the starlings where they had evidently been extended. The dredger also raised much chalk and ragstone rubble, presumably from the masonry parts of the starlings (though disturbed).

A wide range of finds was recovered: spurs, weights, pins, locks, coins, grappling hooks, nails and two iron fragments of pistols.

ER numbers 1279, 1279A, 1279B
EDN XI, 9–11
PRG, 930
Marsden, P, 1970 'Archaeological finds in the City of London, 1966–9', *Trans London Middlesex Archaeol Soc,* 22.3, 12–14

GM106

P Marsden, 1967
NGR: TQ 32850 80500
SMR: 090688, 0213463, 0222695, 0222475, 041409

Fig 11 GM106: timber piles and carved stones dredged from the Thames near London Bridge. In the background, the Rennie bridge, now in Arizona.

GM107

P Marsden, 1971–2
NGR: TQ 32200 81600
SMR: 040474, 04047401,
044443

150 London Wall (Museum of London), EC2 (formerly EC1)

Two adjacent sites have been combined in the present listing.

A section, parallel to the N side of London Wall street, and just south of B14, revealed a sequence of the outer part of the city ditches, and possibly includes parts of the main Roman, medieval and post-medieval ditches. The section began 11.35m W of the face of the city wall, and disclosed the outer part of a flat-bottomed ditch between 6.5m and 12m W of the start-point. The ditch appears to have been recut and deepened by 1.5m with a dish-shaped profile. It had silted up and was recut with its new outer limit about 14m W of the city wall. A timber revetment built into the ditch from the W side suggests a bridge or landing-stage. Post-medieval pottery was found in the black silt filling of the latest ditch, and above it a row of street cobbles indicated that the ditch had been backfilled. The ditches recorded seem to be the medieval and late medieval ditches (eg the recutting of 1477).

In 1972 the Museum site was developed. A number of wells were noted in outline but not recorded in detail. ER 1371 is early 19th-c material retrieved by workmen from a circular brick-built well.

ER number 1371
EDN XI, 49 for MoL site
PRG, 618

GM108

P Marsden, 1961
NGR: TQ 32650 81560
SMR: 044363

London Wall (opposite Coleman Street), EC2

A length of about 45ft of the core of the Roman city wall was uncovered immediately below the street frontage of the buildings on the N side of London Wall (street) at the corner with Moorgate (now London Wall Buildings). The wall had been underpinned presumably when the building was constructed in 1882, as modern work was found both beneath and above the wall for its whole observed length. At a depth of about 6ft from the modern pavement an irregular double course of Roman bonding-tiles in yellow cement was seen (EDN VIII, 51). This is the same piece as was observed in 1882: it was then 9ft 2in. thick, but this included 2ft of medieval thickening on the inner face. It then stood to a height of 4ft above the modern ground level and extended to a depth of at least 8ft below it (Merrifield 1965, gazetteer W35; the 1961 sighting is not mentioned in Merrifield).

EDN VIII, 51
Merrifield, R, 1965 *The Roman city of London*, gazetteer W35

GM109
(=GM173)

E Rutter, 1956–7
NGR: TQ 32470 81570
SMR: 040490–2, 044371

London Wall (north-west of Aldermanbury), EC2

During clearance for the new Route 11 road (the present London Wall carriageway), about 210ft of the Roman and medieval city wall was exposed, extending from about 60ft W of Coleman Street. Much of the external N face had survived, standing 2–6ft above the footings with its chamfered sandstone plinth and levelling tile course. The thickness of the wall was 8ft 3in.–8ft 6in. A portion has been preserved in the underground car park beneath the present London Wall. The Roman city ditch was seen to be about 12ft wide and 4ft deep here. There may also have been a Roman intramural street at this point.

Professor Grimes recorded in this area at the same time (1957; WFG22).

This site has also been numbered GM173, but the latter number should not be used.

ER numbers 357, 358, 400, 400A, 400B, 400C, 400D, 400E
EDN IV, 56–9, 69–73; site file
PRG, 605
J Roman Stud, 48, 1958, 144
Merrifield, R, 1965 *The Roman city of London*, gazetteer W37

Lothbury (opposite no. 5), EC2

GM110

P Marsden, 1963
NGR: TQ 32668 81271
SMR: 040697

A tunnel in the roadway between no. 5 and the public lavatories revealed a Roman wall of ragstone with a double course of bonding-tiles. It was about 2ft thick, with an offset of 2in. immediately above the bonding-course on the S side. The base of the tunnel was at a depth of 12ft 9in., and the wall continued below this level, and to a height of 2ft above it.

EDN IX, 12; site file
Merrifield, R, 1965 *The Roman city of London*, gazetteer 161

Coal Exchange, 100 Lower Thames Street (Billingsgate Roman bath-house site), EC3

GM111

I Noël Hume, 1951;
P Marsden, 1968–71
NGR: TQ 33110 80680
SMR: 041079–85

The only meaningful plan of a Roman dwelling of the 3rd c so far found is that excavated at Billingsgate bath-house. The entire brick-built bath suite, discovered in 1848 and 1859, was uncovered in 1968–71; a water-tank nearby was recorded in 1975 (BIL75), further walls in 1982 (BSA82), and a conservation exercise was undertaken in 1987–90 (BBH87). The bath-house was attached to a house of at least two and possibly three wings which surrounded it; the house was probably built in the late 2nd c, and had been deeply set into the terrace of the hillside. Each wing was bordered by a corridor, with a plain red mosaic floor, off which were a number of living-rooms; those in the E wing all heated, and originally probably floored with mosaic pavements. The bath was a separate building entered through a covered porch from the N wing of the house. The late Roman pottery from the site has been partly published (Symonds & Tomber 1991).

I Noël Hume also recovered 'two if not three intact Roman pots' from the hypocaust, 1951 (pers. comm.; EN II, 21–2).

The DUA work of 1987–90 has resulted in a two-volume assessment of the site and finds, but not including the GM site or finds material (Rowsome 1993).

ER numbers 252, 1280, 1281, 1282, 1283, 1284, 1285, 1286, 1287, 1288, 1289, 1290, 1291, 1292, 1293, 1294, 1295, 1296, 1297, 1298, 1299, 1300, 1301, 1302, 1303, 1304, 1305, 1306, 1307, 1308, 1309, 1310, 1311, 1312, 1313, 1314, 1315, 1316, 1317, 1320, 1321, 1322, 1323, 1324, 1325, 1326, 1327, 1328, 1329; there are also approximately 60 boxes of uncatalogued finds
EN II, 21–2 (the observations of 1951)
EDN XI, 17–32, 34–9; site file (2)
Marsden, P, 1980 *Roman London,* 151–5
Merrifield, R, 1965 *The Roman city of London,* gazetteer 335
Pringle, S, 1990 'GM111', Building Materials Appraisal
Rowsome, P, 1993 'Billingsgate bath-house', Post-excavation Assessment [of the DUA work only]
Symonds, R P, & Tomber, R S, 1991 'Late Roman London: an assessment of the ceramic evidence from the City of London', *Trans London Middlesex Archaeol Soc,* 42, 59–99

Lower Thames Street (west side of Billingsgate Market), EC3

GM112

P Marsden, 1960
NGR: TQ 33022 80662
SMR: 041876

A wall of ragstone and chalk 4ft 6in. wide was found aligned E–W under Thames Street, and was presumably of medieval date. Its S edge lay 6ft N of the former building-line, and 33ft 6in. W of the NW corner of Billingsgate Market. The bottom line of the wall lay at a depth of about 14ft and overlay a foundation of oak piles 10in. in diameter.

This was presumably part of the S frontage of medieval Thames Street; it will be plotted in the study, in preparation, of the Billingsgate lorry park excavations (BIG82), medieval periods (Schofield & Dyson, in prep.).

EDN VII, 33
PRG, 1432
Schofield, J, & Dyson, T, in prep. *Medieval waterfront tenements*

GM113

P Marsden and E Harris, 1960
NGR: TQ 31870 81150
SMR: 041229–32

18–28 Ludgate Hill, EC4

A medieval undercroft measuring 11ft 3in. wide and more than 17ft 6in. long E–W was found towards the N end of this site, its axis parallel with Ludgate Hill to the S. Its walls were of chalk and lime mortar, 2ft 6in. thick. In the SE corner was part of a stone spiral stair. The undercroft was found immediately beneath the modern basement floor, and extended downwards for about 5ft, at which level there was a floor of puddled chalk 3–4in. thick covered by a layer of 'powdery damp' ragstone. This was sealed by a floor of bricks and reused stone. A hole in this later floor contained pottery and clay pipes of the early 17th c.

In the SE part of the site were fragments of chalk masonry, one wall being 2ft 6in. thick, and a chalk-lined well 2ft 9in. in diameter.

ER numbers 627, 628, 634, 638, 640
EDN VII, 10–12, 15, 18, 21; site file
PRG, 438
Trans London Middlesex Archaeol Soc, 20, 1961, 222

GM114

F Cottrill, 1935
NGR: TQ 33291 80835
SMR: 041070–2, 41869–71

26–28 Mark Lane, 28–29 Mincing Lane, EC3

On the N edge of the site, a Roman bath or tank was found. It was 5ft wide with a cement floor, and adjoining it to the N was a mass of masonry 6ft thick.

Site file
J Roman Stud, 26, 1936, 255–6
Merrifield, R, 1965 *The Roman city of London*, gazetteer 348

GM115

I Noël Hume, 1950–1
NGR: TQ 33280 81333
SMR: 041826–8

43–51 St Mary Axe (site of St Mary Axe church), EC3

The site of the church of St Mary Axe at 37, 43 and 45 St Mary Axe street (street numbers as in 1918) was observed during redevelopment in 1950–1. Disturbed medieval burials were observed on the sites of nos 43 and 45, the S part of the site. Also in this part was a chalk foundation pier 5ft 9in. long N–S, 5ft wide at the N end and 4ft wide at the S end. About 12ft to the E was a further fragment of chalk walling. These are presumably parts of the church. The church is shown on the copperplate map of 1559 as having an axial tower and a chancel.

Notes on City Excavations, 1949–1955, 9–10; site file
Schofield, J, 1994 'Saxon and medieval parish churches in the City of London: a review', *Trans London Middlesex Archaeol Soc*, 45, 118

GM116

?E Rutter, 1955
NGR: TQ 32604 81371
SMR: 041552001001

1 Masons Avenue (Butler's Head), EC2

Human bones were found in a pit on the Butler's Head public house site but close to the site of the N wall of St Stephen Coleman Street church. The bones had probably been redeposited from the churchyard which originally lay on the N side of the church. A 17th-c sherd was found with the bones, though their reburial could have occurred in more recent times.

EDN II, 84
PRG, 1052

St Michael's House, 1–2 St Michael's Alley, EC3

GM117

G Dunning, 1932
NGR: TQ 32941 81061
SMR: 040812–47, 041532–3

Two ragstone walls 5ft thick and another 3ft thick to the E of them were found crossing the site N–S. They seemed to belong to a series of Roman rooms and a colonnade overlooking the forum from the W. The foundations cut through an occupation layer and rubbish pit of middle or late 1st-c date.

Several walls of chalk rubble with occasional pieces of ragstone, flint and brick, in poor light brown mortar, were recorded on the W half of the site. Their thicknesses were not recorded, though one was over 2ft 3in. wide. They aligned with or were at right angles to St Michael's Alley, and at the W end of the site was a 16th-c cellar floor and associated walls, at a depth of 19ft below the Alley. This was dated by associated pottery and shoe fragments.

Librarian's Monthly Report, May 1932
PRG, 1049

Opposite 140–150 London Wall (west gate of Roman fort), EC2

GM118

Unknown, 1956
NGR: TQ 32246 81557
SMR: not necessary

A site file contains only seven black and white photographs of the excavation of the W gate of the Roman fort by W F Grimes (site WFG5); medieval and later walls (Neville's Inn) are shown. There was no GM excavation on this site.

20–28 Moorgate, 1–4 Copthall Close, 10–11 Great Swan Alley, EC2

GM119

F Cottrill, 1936
NGR: TQ 32704 81415
SMR: 040645

Towards the E end of the site large quantities of Roman coarse pottery wasters were found, indicating the proximity of a kiln. They included shouldered jars of grey ware, open pans with reeded horizontal rims, and platters with upright walls. There were also wasters of fine micaceous ware, and of black glossy ware imitating samian bowls, and decorated with incised designs of concentric circles and parts of circles. The damaged pots all seemed to belong to the late 1st or early 2nd c. The ground sloped rapidly E towards the bed of the Walbrook.

Site file
GL Report, 1936, 14–15
Merrifield, R, 1965 *The Roman city of London,* gazetteer 137

30 Moorgate, EC2

GM120

I Noël Hume, 1951
NGR: TQ 32702 81455
SMR: 040644, 041522–3

A bed of black, peat-like silt was seen in a small excavation, overlying the natural ballast. From its lower levels, down to 14ft below street level, came a few sherds of Roman coarse pottery with animal bones and shells of whelks and oysters. A Roman bronze coin of the 4th c was said by workmen to have been found on the site, but its patina was unlike that of coins from similar deposits. It seems likely that a tributary of the Walbrook flowed across the site, but on an unknown alignment.

The upper silt levels contained medieval floor tiles and wood. Two medieval chalk walls were recorded cutting into the silt layers in the middle of the S of the site. The walls formed a corner of a subterranean room, one side of which was parallel to Great Swan Alley. It had a floor of crushed chalk 6in. thick, above which lay a mixed filling containing pottery of the 13th–14th c. Fragments of Pingsdorf ware were found in a gravel layer at the bottom of the foundation trench of one of the walls.

Notes on City Excavations, 1949–1955, 18–20
Merrifield, R, 1965 *The Roman city of London,* gazetteer 136

GM121

G Dunning, 1929
NGR: TQ 32672 81500
SMR: 040641

55–61 Moorgate, EC2

The embankments of what were apparently brooks running E into the Walbrook were observed. The bottom was of river gravel with a layer of black mud above it. Above this was a Roman deposit 5ft thick, in the lower part of which was a rectangular system of camp-sheathing held together by piles driven into the gravel. From this site came a small votive silver plaque with repoussé figures of the Mother Goddesses. The pottery was almost all of the 2nd c, and earlier forms were rare.

For later work on this site, in 1987, see MGT87 below.

Site file
GL Annual Report, 1929–30
J Roman Stud, 19, 1929, 199
Merrifield, R, 1965 *The Roman city of London,* gazetteer 134

GM122

Q Waddington, 1925
NGR: TQ 32982 81548
SMR: 040659, 041921

46–47 New Broad Street, EC2

A line of stout oak posts, irregularly placed but roughly parallel with Blomfield Street, was seen in the N part of the site. This might be the remains of the embankment of the Walbrook, and the bed of the stream was believed to be between the posts and Blomfield Street. Merrifield thought the stream was more likely to be W of the site, and that the supposed stream-bed here was the E edge of the flood silt. In the silt W of the posts were found fragments of Roman pottery, including a ring-necked jug of the 1st c, and samian ware of the 1st and 2nd c, together with an iron knife and the linch-pin of a cart.

Marsden's 1981 listing notes: 'a medieval city ditch was recorded, and also a stream-bed containing medieval objects, which had presumably once flowed into the medieval city ditch'; but there is no PRG gazetteer entry for the site.

Merrifield's entry for this site refers to 'MS notes by Q Waddington in Guildhall Museum', but there is no site file.

Maloney, C, 1990 *The upper Walbrook Valley in the Roman period,* The archaeology of Roman London 1, CBA Res Rep 69 ('site 8')
Merrifield, R, 1965 *The Roman city of London,* gazetteer 149

GM123

P Marsden, 1965
NGR: TQ 32150 81110
SMR: 041336–7

St Augustine's church (Old Change or Watling Street), now St Paul's Cathedral Choir School, New Change, EC4

Roman gravel metalling was observed. The N half of St Augustine's church (destroyed in the Second World War) was recorded; the S half remains *in situ.* The foundations of the medieval church, of chalk and yellow mortar, suggest a building 61ft long. The church was extended to the N, on foundations of chalk and white mortar; the extension measuring 59ft long and 16ft wide. This is presumably a N aisle, added on documentary grounds in the 1250s. The Wren tower has been restored and survives on the site, with three bays of the S wall, as part of the Cathedral Choir School. For a trench dug on the site in 1974, see SPS74 below. The site was refurbished in 1997 and walls of the church exposed.

ER number 1025; site file
EDN X, 32, 36
PRG, 763
Marsden, P, 1968 'Archaeological finds in the City of London, 1965–66', *Trans London Middlesex Archaeol Soc,* 22.1, 2–3, 11
Schofield, J, 1994 'Saxon and medieval parish churches in the City of London: a review', *Trans London Middlesex Archaeol Soc,* 45, 94

New Change, EC4

Marsden's 1981 summary notes 'a chalk-lined well was found', but there is no entry in PRG and no site file.

GM124

Unknown, 1957
SMR: 044420

Fresh Wharf, 1–6 Lower Thames Street, EC4

The W part of a cutwater of the medieval London Bridge was recorded. The surviving top was 7ft 6in. below the street, and it was founded on elm piles which started at 19ft below the street.

For later excavations on this site see GM126 and NFW74 below.

Site file
Schofield, J, & Dyson, T, in prep. *Medieval waterfront tenements*

GM125

F Cottrill, 1937
NGR: TQ 32880 80615
SMR: 04140901

New Fresh Wharf, 1–6 Lower Thames Street, EC4

Deep silt deposits covered the whole site, and within this was a timber revetment 60ft N of the present river frontage, 18ft below street level. It comprised large square oak piles standing vertically, their sharpened bases packed with rubble in which were a few sherds of 15th-c pottery. Many sherds of similar date were found in the surrounding silt at this depth, and it seems likely that the structure was a quay. A chalk sewer had been cut through the revetment, and it extended to within at least 10ft of the present waterfront. It measured 2ft x 3ft 6in. internally, and in it were many objects dating from the early 17th to the early 18th c.

For observation of the northern cutwaters of the medieval London Bridge on this site in 1937, see GM125 above; for excavation of the whole site in 1974–8, see NFW74 below.

EN II, 7
PRG, 933
Schofield, J, & Dyson, T, in prep. *Medieval waterfront tenements*

GM126

I Noël Hume, 1950
NGR: TQ 32927 80612
SMR: 041427–9

Cripplegate, Bastion 12, EC2

Site file, containing only two photographs of the bastion in 1953 (a note on the back of one reads: 'the lady in the photograph became Mrs Merrifield').

GM127

?R Merrifield, 1953
NGR: TQ 32301 81671
SMR: 040480

6–9 Newgate Street, EC4

Piling operations on the site disclosed black silt along the E side on the Warwick Lane frontage, and the foreman reported that black silt was found in the SW corner. The former deposit must have been part of the W arm of the stream discovered on the site of the Paternoster Square development to the E in 1961.

EDN X, 33
Marsden, P, 1968 'Archaeological finds in the City of London, 1965–66', *Trans London Middlesex Archaeol Soc*, 22.1, 1–2

GM128

P Marsden, 1965
NGR: TQ 31867 81362
SMR: 044364

GM129

P Marsden, 1963–4
NGR: TQ 32825 80985
SMR: 041422–3

Westminster Bank, 21 Lombard Street (site of St Nicholas Acon church, Nicholas Lane), EC4

In the centre of the site were fragmentary traces of the E–W Roman road which originally went past the S frontage of the forum. It overlay natural brickearth. A deposit of burnt daub and clay about a foot thick was cut into by square post-holes and overlaid by dark earth. The site was partly occupied in the Late Saxon and medieval period by the church of St Nicholas Acon.

Excavations revealed Late Saxon pits, post-holes and a ragstone wall 2ft 3in. thick retaining the W side of a hollow, probably of the 11th c, containing debris and white-painted plaster. One pit containing a coin of the second quarter of the 11th c was overlaid by a foundation of the church, which originally comprised a nave and square chancel on foundations of chalk and gravel about 4ft thick. Later a S aisle and a square chamber (suggested by Marsden to be a tower, but more likely to be a vestry (Schofield 1994)) at the NE corner were added, on foundations of mortared chalk. The addition of the S aisle, when the existing S wall was replaced by two piers on foundations of mortared chalk, may have been at the same time as a lengthening of the nave from 46ft to about 59ft long.

Finds include many floor tiles. Some of the church walls survive beneath the modern courtyard.

A typescript history (c 1957) in the site file of one of the banks on the site mentions that in 1909 a fragment of fresco, said to have been found during one of several reconstructions of bank buildings on the site of St Nicholas in the 19th or early 20th c, was given by the London and County Bank to the parish of St Edmund (which had incorporated that of St Nicholas after the Fire). This fragment is now in the parish room of St Edmund, and shows a life-sized head of a saint, probably St Dominic, in a black habit placing his finger on his lips. Dr Sharon Cather of the Courtauld Institute of Art examined the piece in 1995 and concluded it was probably a 19th-c production (details in Schofield 1994).

ER numbers 866, 870, 873, 874, 875, 876, 877, 878, 879, 880, 881, 882, 883, 884, 885, 886, 887, 888, 889, 890, 891, 892, 893, 894, 945, 946
EDN IX, 20, 26–7, 32–5, 54, 70; site file
PRG, 931
Marsden, P, 1967 'Archaeological finds in the City of London, 1963–4', *Trans London Middlesex Archaeol Soc*, 21.3, 208, 219–20
Schofield, J, 1994 'Saxon and medieval parish churches in the City of London: a review', *Trans London Middlesex Archaeol Soc*, 45, 123

GM130

P Marsden, 1959
SMR: 040033, 040036,
041266, 049999
NGR: TQ 32269 81499

Shelley House, 3 Noble Street (formerly no. 1), EC2

A small portion of a ragstone wall, over 9in. thick, was found running approximately N–S. On the E side was a yellow clay containing many pieces of Roman wall plaster surrounding and overlaying the wall. About 23ft E of this wall was an area of gravel metalling, up to 6in. thick. Two sherds of the 2nd c were found above it at the S end; cutting into the gravel was a 12th-c pit. The metalling, believed to be of Roman date, may have formed part of the surface of the Cripplegate Roman fort, probably a courtyard rather than a road.

A medieval chalk cesspit 4ft wide and more than 4ft long was found at the N end of the site. The surviving top lay 3ft 10in. below the basement and below this it was 5ft deep. It contained a 2in. solid layer of mussel shells and below this many oyster shells and a few clams (pottery is part of ER 480, which also includes general workmen's finds).

This site was also excavated by W F Grimes (site WFG20) in 1957; and again by MoLAS in 1996 (site NST94).

ER numbers 480, 481, 587A, 587B, 594
EDN V, 59–60; site file
Trans London Middlesex Archaeol Soc, 20, 1961, 221
Merrifield, R, 1965 *The Roman city of London*, gazetteer 30

Central Criminal Court, Old Bailey / Warwick Square, EC4

GM131

P Marsden, 1966–9
NGR: TQ 31814 81304
SMR: 040437–42, 040465,
041223–5, 041890–4

Excavation in 1966 exposed two Roman burials and the corner of a Roman stone building (Fig 12). Part of the adjacent Roman and medieval city wall, the bank and a Roman internal turret were also recorded; the medieval bank overlay a small intramural roadway of ragstone chippings. Finds from the turret included pottery and forged coins which gave a *terminus ante quem* of 220–5 for the building of the Roman defences.

Two medieval defensive ditches were found beyond the wall, the earlier V-shaped in section, and probably of the 12th or 13th c; the later extended at least 62ft from the wall, and its base was 19ft 6in. below the Roman wall plinth. Its final filling dated to the 16th

Fig 12 GM131: view of the excavation at Central Criminal Court / Warwick Square, one of the earliest area excavations in the City, looking W. The foundations between modern stanchions are those of the medieval buildings.

c, and this was overlaid by brick walls and wood pile foundations. A large 13th-c internal earth bank, so far unique in London, was found against the wall.

Between the city wall and Warwick Lane three phases of large stone buildings and many pits of the 12th and 13th c were recorded. The plan of the first 13th-c building was fragmentary, but it included a room 12ft wide and 33ft long; foundations were of chalk and gravel, and one surviving wall of ragstone. This was rebuilt into a range with two rooms, one a cellar 15ft x 29ft with white painted walls and an entrance at the S end; occupation debris and the demolition fill of the cellar contained pottery of the second half of the 13th c. A third building with foundations of ragstone and chalk overlay the second-period structure. It was evidently part of the medieval house also recorded in 1880; a large hall 19ft 7in. wide and 57ft long, with a small external chamber, possibly a garderobe, at the W end. This latest phase may have been the town house of the earls of Warwick.

This excavation was assisted by a grant of £3000 by the Corporation (Central Criminal Court Committee), arranged by Mr Jeff Moulden.

ER numbers 1132, 1133, 1134, 1135, 1136, 1137, 1138, 1139, 1140, 1141, 1142, 1143, 1144, 1145, 1146, 1147, 1148, 1149, 1150, 1151, 1152, 1153, 1154, 1155, 1156, 1157, 1163, 1164, 1165, 1166, 1167, 1168, 1169, 1170, 1171, 1172, 1173, 1174, 1175, 1176, 1177, 1178, 1179, 1180, 1181, 1182, 1183, 1184, 1185, 1186, 1187, 1188, 1189, 1190, 1191, 1192, 1193, 1194, 1195, 1196, 1197, 1198, 1199, 1207, 1208, 1209, 1210, 1211, 1212, 1213, 1214, 1215, 1216, 1217, 1218, 1219, 1234, 1235, 1236, 1237A, 1237B, 1244, 1245, 1246, 1247, 1248, 1249, 1250
EDN X, 55, 59–61, 68, 71–3; site file (2 folders)
PRG, 439, 443
Medieval Archaeol, 11, 1967, 295–6
Armitage, P, 1979 'The mammalian remains from the Roman and medieval levels', Animal Bone Report (AML Report 2805)
Marsden, P, 1969 'Archaeological finds in the City of London, 1966–8', *Trans London Middlesex Archaeol Soc*, 22.2, 2–10
Merrifield, R, 1983 *London city of the Romans*, 162–3

Hillgate House, 27–34 Old Bailey, 50–62 Ludgate Hill, EC4

GM132

P Marsden, 1959
NGR: TQ 31735 81233
SMR: 041228

A chalk and ragstone wall 3ft 6in. thick was found at the S end of this site, and in spite of its thickness appeared to be part of a cesspit. The external courses of another chalk-lined structure were found on the E side of the site adjacent to Seacoal Lane and may have been part of another cesspit. No dating evidence was found in either case. A section at the SW corner of the site revealed evidence of a stream, presumably an unknown tributary of the Fleet river to the W.

ER numbers 529, 554
EDN VI, 17, 30
Site file includes a drawn section across the tributary of the Fleet
PRG, 437

GM133

I Noël Hume, 1952
NGR: TQ 32552 81212
SMR: 040675, 040679–81,
041506, 041524–8

33–34 Old Jewry (Price Waterhouse), Frederick's Place, EC2

In a small excavation, approximately 12ft W of the building line of Old Jewry, the gravel metalling of a Roman road or courtyard was recorded at a depth of 6ft 2in. below modern basement level. The camber suggested that it might be part of an E–W road.

Cut into the street was a Late Saxon or early medieval structure; two timbers formed a corner foundation of a sunken building. The depth of the beams was about 7ft 8in. below the modern basement floor, and about 1ft 6in. cut into the Roman street. Rubbish pits of the 12th and 13th c had also been cut into the street. Medieval chalk foundations perhaps over 3ft thick were found at the S end of the site adjacent to Frederick's Place. Near the centre of the site was a medieval cellar over 20ft long N–S and 8ft 6in. wide internally; it had ragstone walls of unknown thickness. The latest structures included a brick-lined well 3ft 3in. in diameter containing objects of the late 18th c and a chalk-walled cesspit or well probably 5ft x 4ft containing early 18th-c objects. The site overlay the former St Olave's graveyard, and at the NE corner was found a 'medieval grave lined with Roman tiles' containing a human skeleton.

ER numbers 217, 219, 248
EDN 1, 12, 19; site file
PRG, 1045
Merrifield, R, 1965 *The Roman city of London*, gazetteer 154

GM134

I Noël Hume, 1953
NGR: TQ 32560 81240
SMR: 040676–8

27–32 Old Jewry (Bank of Sydney), EC2

Trial holes revealed a wall foundation of ragstone and tiles running roughly N–S approximately at right angles to St Olave's church, in the SW corner of the site. The foundation trench had been cut into a refuse deposit of the early 2nd c at the S edge of the site, and into a refuse pit of Flavian date. Roman pits were also observed in other cuttings on the site, for instance against Old Jewry. Traces of human burials were noted, no doubt associated with the church of St Olave to the S.

ER numbers 70, 72, 73, 192, 193, 194, 195, 196, 247
EDN 1, 12, 16–20; II, 27–30
PRG, 1046
Merrifield, R, 1965 *The Roman city of London*, gazetteer 153

GM135

P Marsden, 1960
NGR: TQ 31745 80990
SMR: 040029, 040039, 041196

160 Queen Victoria Street (Printing House Square, site of former *Times* offices), EC4

In the N of the site, a natural stream-bed was found cutting into waterlaid gravels. The bottom of the bed was filled with a black mud which had a maximum thickness of 1ft.

Two walls of ragstone and fragments of Roman brick were found on the N edge of Printing House Lane. There was no evidence of date, but the E–W wall lay beneath two later stone walls, presumably medieval. This wall was battered on its S face, which was covered with yellow cement ³/₄in. thick. Lying against it were two horizontal timbers, one above the other. The wall was 5ft 4in. thick at one point, but at least 7ft thick at the E end; this thickness may have been the start of another N–S wall. To the SW were wooden piles in black gravelly mud.

A number of medieval walls were recorded during the watching brief. One was built over the earlier stream-bed, and two, as noted, were on top of the presumed Roman masonry structure. An E–W wall and a well of post-medieval date were found to contain many moulded stones. The well, though built of brick, contained fragments of tracery from a notable medieval window. The medieval walls and moulded stones probably come from the Blackfriars friary which stood on the site.

An evaluation of the site in 1994 by W McCann of MoLAS suggests: (i) that the 'Roman' wall, lying outside the city wall, may have been built to stand river erosion; (ii) it has similarities to monumental foundations further E; (iii) the medieval walls coincide with the position of St Anne's Chapel within the Blackfriars (as mapped by Clapham).

See also GM164 below, observations of 1935 on the site of the *Times* offices.

ER numbers 652, 659, 662, 664, 671
EDN VII, 25–36; site file
PRG, 310
Trans London Middlesex Archaeol Soc, 20, 1961, 222–3
Clapham, A W, & Godfrey, W H, [1913] *Some famous buildings and their story*, 254

Paternoster Square development (including 10–14 Newgate Street and 61–70 St Paul's Churchyard), EC4

GM136

P Marsden, 1961–2
NGR: TQ 32053 81298
SMR: 040004–7, 040010–17,
040024, 040034

This large site was watched during development by both GM (P Marsden) and Professor Grimes (WFG26–9). Following Merrifield's 1965 gazetteer, the summary here is in a number of sections (gazetteer 3–6, 9–17, 20, further conflated here).

Newgate Street, S side, E of Warwick Lane, 1961: the S edge of the main Roman E–W road, about 8ft 6in. S of the building frontage, and a possible ditch. To the S of the probable road-edge, gravel layers extended for at least 17ft. A culvert of Roman bricks lay on the W side of an ancient watercourse, towards which it ran (Merrifield 1965, gazetteer 3–4; not W of the Lane as in titles to both gazetteer entries).

Newgate Street, 10–13, 1962: a layer of Roman gravel seen in section below the old building frontage, immediately above natural brickearth; also probably a trace of the main Roman road (gazetteer 5).

Newgate Street, S side, 1961: a portion of a Roman building, with a ragstone wall running N–S towards an E–W wall. To the W was a floor of brick tiles through which an open drain ran to the W. Above this were two more floors. To the S was another N–S wall, a pavement of small tiles set in *opus signinum*, another brick drain, and traces of a pottery kiln with sherds of the late 1st c (gazetteer 6; for the kiln and pottery, Marsden 1969).

Paternoster Square, approximately 190ft E of Warwick Lane, and behind 14–29 Newgate Street, 1961: a mass of gravel metalling indicated a Roman N–S road; a drainage gully adjoined it on the E side. It was not possible to ascertain the road's width (gazetteer 9–10).

Newgate Street, W of Ivy Lane, opposite Greyfriars' Passage, 1961: a possible fragment of the N–S road was observed, but not enough to help significantly with the road's alignment (gazetteer 11).

Newgate Street, S side, N of Paternoster Row, 1961: the course of an ancient stream was recorded running N–S. Its bed was defined by a band of black mud. Its E limit coincided with the boundary between the wards of Farringdon Within and Castle Baynard in the central and S parts of the site. In the N part towards Newgate it curved from the NE, and another branch apparently joined it from the NW, probably following approximately the boundary at the N end of Castle Baynard ward (gazetteer 12).

Ave Maria Lane, E side, 1962: a continuation of the stream just mentioned was observed here; the W edge was 63ft E of the old building-line, 105ft N of the junction of Ave Maria Lane and Ludgate Hill (gazetteer 13).

Newgate Street, S side, opposite Roman Bath Street [now lost, beneath British Telecom Headquarters on N side of street], 1961: wooden piles may represent the edge of the main Roman road beneath Newgate Street, which was otherwise not seen (gazetteer 14).

Newgate Street, 48, W of St Paul's Underground Station, 1961: a thick deposit of gravel was observed in section, 18–20ft S of the building-line. It may have been part of the E–W Roman road beneath Newgate or of the N–S road seen to the S (see gazetteer 17 below) (gazetteer 15).

Newgate Street/Paternoster Row, W of Panyer Alley, 1961: gravels resembling road-metalling seemed to form a N–S Roman road running in the direction of Aldersgate. Metalling was found further E, but this would make a N–S road 40ft wide. The latter may have been a courtyard (gazetteer 16–17).

Paternoster Row, E of Canon Alley, 1961: a Roman pavement of coarse red tesserae under the N frontage of Paternoster Row was recorded. There were no signs of associated walls (gazetteer 20).

Post-Roman: pending further work, the PRG entry is given here. It summarises all the sites without dividing them. Many chalk walls, presumably of medieval date, were seen but could not be recorded because of the rapid method of excavation. Two undercrofts were noted: one near the E end of Paternoster Row was recorded by Professor Grimes (not mentioned in Grimes 1968), and the other, near the middle of the E half of the site, by P Marsden. The latter measured 16ft wide and more than 24ft long. It was built of ragstone with a facing of greenish sandstone with traces of mouldings and an arch. Seventeenth-c pottery and clay pipes from its brick rubble fill may be debris of the Great Fire. At the E end of the site, close to St Paul's Underground Station, was a ragstone foundation with hard yellowish-white mortar. This overlay a rubbish pit containing Saxon and early medieval pottery. At the NW corner of the site a medieval or later barrel-well was noted.

Though no archaeological evidence for post-Roman use of the N–S stream was noted, its correspondence with the ward boundaries suggests that it was open in early medieval times.

For later observations on the site, see PAT90 below.

ER numbers 696, 697, 698, 699, 700, 701, 702, 703, 704, 705, 706, 707, 708, 709, 710, 711, 712, 713, 714, 715, 716, 717, 718, 719, 720, 721, 730, 731, 732, 735, 743, 745, 751, 751F, 760, 787, 776, 777, 773, 789, 788, 791, 985, 986
EDN VIII, 7, 9–18, 26–8, 30, 36–7, 45, 47–8, 52, 59, 61, 71–2; IX, 1; X, 24
PRG, 440
Grimes, W F, 1968 *The excavation of Roman and medieval London*, 148–9
Marsden, P, 1963 'Archaeological finds in the City of London, 1961', *Trans London Middlesex Archaeol Soc*, 21.1, 75–6
Marsden, P, 1969 'The Roman pottery industry of London', *Trans London Middlesex Archaeol Soc*, 22.2, 39–44
Merrifield, R, 1965 *The Roman city of London*, gazetteer 3–6, 9–17, 20

GM137

Unknown, 1961
NGR: TQ 32356 81530
SMR: 041384

Upper Thames Street / St Peter's Hill (site of St Peter Paul's Wharf church), EC4

Workmen clearing the churchyard to a depth of 10ft below street level uncovered chalk walls up to 2ft deep. A sketchplan indicates that the walls formed the NE corner of the church, with two other fragments forming a chamber attached to the N wall at the corner.

Further details of the church have been excavated here or nearby since 1961. Excavation of the site of 223–225 Upper Thames Street in 1981 recorded the foundations of the W end of the church (PET81 below). A separate watching brief associated with the building of the City of London Boys' School to the S in 1984 recorded details of the S and W walls, early graves, and traces of the post-1666 graveyard (TIG84 below).

ER number 694
EDN VIII, 2, 5
PRG, 821
Schofield, J, 1994 'Saxon and medieval parish churches in the City of London: a review', *Trans London Middlesex Archaeol Soc*, 45, 127–8

GM138

Q Waddington, 1925–6
NGR: TQ 31670 81125
SMR: 040420

Pilgrim Street (sewerworks west end), EC4

Excavation in Pilgrim Street, just E of Waithman Street, exposed the inner or S face of the medieval city wall, and penetrated it. The wall extended beneath the pavement on the N side of Pilgrim Street, about 2ft below the pavement, and a pit dug to a depth of 10ft failed to reach its base. The wall was faced with squared stones, the core being of Kentish rag or similar stone. Another fragment was noted 60ft to the W, beneath the railway arch which crosses Pilgrim Street. This wall seemed to form an angle turning S. The core here was less homogeneous, containing a mixture of flint, chalk and ragstone, as well as two small yellow bricks each measuring 6in. x 3in. x 1½in.

For work in the street in 1988, see PWB88 below.

EN I, 19.1
PRG, 441

32–33 Lombard Street, Plough Court (Bank of New York), EC4

GM139

P Marsden, 1955–6
NGR: TQ 32944 80935
SMR: 040963–9, 041436–8

Post-holes of Claudian date were found in many parts of the site. There were also traces of foundations of a later 1st-c ragstone building, its alignment approximately that of Plough Court, except in the SE corner of the site where a wall of a similar character ran NW–SE. The walls were about 2ft thick, and there may have been an entrance from the W. This building was succeeded by a much smaller building on a different alignment, approximately that of the forum, apparently before the end of the 1st c. There were also traces of brick walls and an *opus signinum* floor of a building apparently destroyed in the Hadrianic fire.

A bone comb probably of Saxon date was found in a small pit at the W side of the site. Two lengths of medieval chalk foundations, 2ft thick and aligned parallel with Plough Court, were recorded. A human skeleton was found in the NW corner of the site, apparently of post-Roman date.

The comb, now in P Marsden's private collection, is a rare example of a handled Saxon comb from the City; it is of a type common in the Middle Saxon period, but also known in the Late Saxon (Riddler 1990, 13–14).

PRG, 940
Marsden, P, 1968 'Some discoveries in the City of London, 1954–59', *Trans London Middlesex Archaeol Soc*, 22.1, 36
Merrifield, R, 1965 *The Roman city of London,* gazetteer 289
Riddler, I, 1990 'Saxon handled combs from London', *Trans London Middlesex Archaeol Soc*, 41, 9–20

33–35 Poultry, EC2

GM140

F Cottrill, 1936
NGR: TQ 32604 81147
SMR: 040718, 041542

A number of oak piles were found in the SW corner of the site. They stood in black mud which probably indicated the position of a tributary of the Walbrook. Nearby was a square timber-lined well, from the bottom of which came a sestertius of Commodus. The Roman features from this site have been published and discussed (Wilmott 1991).

Part of a chalk-lined well, presumably of medieval date, was found near the NW corner of the site. Its position and dimensions are not recorded, but its lining rested on a circle of wood.

Site file
J Roman Stud, 27, 1937, 241
Merrifield, R, 1965 *The Roman city of London,* gazetteer 177
Wilmott, T, 1991 *Excavations in the middle Walbrook Valley, City of London, 1927–1960,* London Middlesex Archaeol Soc Spec Pap 13, 49–50

6–8 Princes Street, EC2

GM141

P Marsden, 1970
NGR: TQ 32641 81196
SMR: 041531

Several walls of chalk, ragstone and mortar were noted on the W side of the site. One was 1.2m thick, another was more than 1.5m thick, and a third had a face of knapped flint.

Site file; includes a log of four boreholes
PRG, 1048

Aldermary House, 10-15 Queen Street, 61-62 Watling Street, EC4

GM142

E Rutter, 1960
NGR: TQ 32490 81060
SMR: 040582, 041350

Seven Roman wells were recorded on this site. They were of two types: square wells with sides formed of boxes of planks, and round barrel-wells. On the N edge of the site adjacent to Well Court was a hollow filled with black peat-like mud, resembling a pond or stream-bed. It may have determined the boundaries between Cheap and Cordwainer wards as it flowed E to the Walbrook.

Two medieval and two post-medieval wells were also recorded. The medieval wells were formed from barrels, 0.76m and 0.61m in diameter, and lay on the E side of the site. Both contained 13th-c pottery, but one also contained 14th-c pottery. One of the two post-medieval wells was 1.4m in diameter and had brick, chalk and wood in its lining. The other was chalk-lined, and although it contained 18th-c pottery, the chalk lining suggests it was constructed in the medieval period. It was 0.99m in diameter.

ER numbers 585, 586, 589A, 589B, 590, 595, 596, 597, 598, 599, 602A, 602B, 603, 604, 605, 606, 606A, 607, 608, 612, 616, 618, 624, 626, 642, 643, 644, 645, 647
EDN VI, 50, 54, 56–62; VII, 4–6, 9, 10, 22–4; site file
PRG, 772
Marsden, P, 1961 'Archaeological finds in the City of London, 1960', *Trans London Middlesex Archaeol Soc*, 20.4, 220
Merrifield, R, 1965 *The Roman city of London*, gazetteer 89
Wilmott, T, 1982 'Excavations at Queen Street, City of London, 1953 and 1960, and timber-lined wells in London', *Trans London Middlesex Archaeol Soc*, 33, 21–2

GM143

Unknown, 1959–60
NGR: TQ 32700 81111
SMR: 040732

Queen Victoria Street / Poultry (Bank Underground Station), EC4

During tunnelling excavations for the Travelator at the Bank Underground Station, black Walbrook mud containing metal antiquities and pottery of the early Roman period was encountered, as well as substantial wooden piles and horizontal timbers. The piles were closely set in rows running not quite at right angles with the kerb-line of Queen Victoria Street. These presumably were to support the foundations of Roman buildings immediately to the W of the Walbrook, and were situated to the N of the mosaic pavement found when Queen Victoria Street was constructed in 1869. Both sites have now been published and discussed in their Roman setting in the Walbrook Valley (Wilmott 1991).

Trans London Middlesex Archaeol Soc, 20, 1961, 221
Merrifield, R, 1965 *The Roman city of London*, gazetteer 190 [quoting 'Information from Engineer's plan, British Railways']
Wilmott, T, 1991 *Excavations in the middle Walbrook Valley, City of London, 1927–1960*, London Middlesex Archaeol Soc Spec Pap 13, 44–7

GM144

I Noël Hume, 1953–4
NGR: TQ 32480 81050
SMR: 040585, 041349

40–66 Queen Victoria Street, 82 Queen Street (formerly Bank of London and South America), EC4

Fourteen Roman timber-lined wells were found during builders' excavations. They were both square and round, the former having the upper portion supported by a box-like frame of oak planks, and the latter by a barrel-like structure. In a square well near the N edge of the site, filled before the end of the 1st c, were found a wooden ladder, a pair of leather trunks, a wooden spoon and a wooden dipper. The Roman levels from this site have now been published (Wilmott 1982).

Three medieval barrel-lined wells were also recorded; they were 0.61m, 0.76m and 1.02m in diameter. Pottery dated them respectively to the 13th, late 13th or 14th and 15th c. There was also a chalk-lined well 2.67m in diameter in which was found pottery of the late 14th c. Three post-medieval wells were also found. One had a brick lower lining overlaid by a barrel and chalk blocks, and was 1.14m in diameter. Another was chalk-lined, 0.99m in diameter, and although it contained pottery of the 18th c it was probably of earlier date. The third was lined with brick and wood, and was 1.02m in diameter. This contained objects of the early 17th c, and burnt debris believed to be of the Great Fire.

ER numbers 78, 79, 80, 81A, 81B, 81C, 81D, 82, 83, 84, 85, 88, 90, 91, 92, 92B, 92C, 93, 93B, 93C, 93D, 94, 95, 96, 97, 98, 99, 100, 102, 103, 104, 105, 106, 107, 108, 109, 110, 111, 112, 113, 114, 115, 116, 117, 118, 119, 120, 120A, 121, 122, 125, 232, 254, 254A, 254B, 255

EDN I, 25–32, 38–54, 78, 80, 84, II, 66

PRG, 771

J Roman Stud, 45, 1955, 138–9

Armitage, P, & West, B, nd, 'The mammalian remains from the two Roman wells, Queen Street, 1954', Animal Bone Report

Merrifield, R, 1965 *The Roman city of London,* gazetteer 91

Wilmott, T, 1982 'Excavations at Queen Street, City of London, 1953 and 1960, and timber-lined wells in London', *Trans London Middlesex Archaeol Soc,* 33, 1–78

Guildhall, EC2

GM145

P Marsden, 1968
NGR: TQ 32484 81386
SMR: 041301, 04130101

In 1232–46 *Gildhalla* can be placed in the parish of St Lawrence Jewry, and deeds of the later 13th c fix it on or about the present site. The earliest comprehensive remains date to the late 13th c, but at two places works preceding this phase have been noted. In the N wall of the W crypt a pilaster of the crypt blocked a recess with a carefully prepared white plaster surface, suggesting that the crypt was a modification of an earlier stone building, at least along its N side. The lower of two different wall fragments below the 15th-c porch to the SE, of ragstone on a mortared ragstone foundation, is also probably of a building two phases before the 15th c. This wall had a dressed rag face on the W, 1.2m below the floor level of the 15th-c porch. Together these two fragments suggest a stone building preceded the late 13th-c rebuilding, but there is no further indication of date. Excavations of 1987–8 and 1992–7 beneath and E of Guildhall Yard uncovered a Roman amphitheatre and 11th-c timber buildings above it (see GAG87 below).

The surviving W undercroft, now much restored, is of three aisles five bays long, the easternmost bays truncated by the W wall of the later E undercroft. The windows of the W undercroft in their present form probably date from alterations in the late 15th c, and the vaulting alone can be dated, though only roughly, to 1200–1340. Documentary evidence would suggest dates of either the 1280s, since work on the adjacent chapel began in the 1290s, or 1333–5, when repairs are recorded; the closest architectural analogy, an undercroft of *c* 1290 at Penshurst Place, Kent, suggests the former date (Barron 1974).

Archaeological observation in 1968 recorded a length of walling, of ragstone and bands of knapped flint, beneath the W wall of the 15th-c porch which may be part of this wing; the use of knapped flint in this way would suggest a date in the 14th c (Marsden 1981).

Guildhall was rebuilt in 1411–30 by John Croxton, mason, whose previous work is not known. Work on the roof was in progress in 1418, and in 1423 Richard Whittington left money to pave the hall with Purbeck marble; construction may have been finished by 1430. Croxton inserted buttresses in the W undercroft (necessary support for the new unaisled hall if the previous hall had been aisled), cut off the easternmost bay of the undercroft and built a new E undercroft of three aisles, four bays long (summary from Schofield 1995).

The GM records include photographs (eg Fig 13), but no finds or EDN references.

Barron, C, 1974 *The medieval Guildhall of London*

Marsden, P, 1981 'The pre-1411 Guildhall of London', *London Archaeol,* 4, 115–20

Merrifield, R, 1965 *The Roman city of London,* gazetteer 125

Schofield, J, 1995 *Medieval London houses,* 14–19

Fig 13 GM145: one of the medieval windows in the S wall of the W crypt of Guildhall, from the outside.

GM146

P Norman and F Reader,
1908–9
NGR: TQ 31850 81440
SMR: 040412, 041896,
040449, 041900; SAM
GM26U

Bastion 19, General Post Office Yard, Giltspur Street, EC1

During rebuilding work in 1908–9, P Norman and F Reader recorded parts of the city wall and three bastions, now numbered B17 to B19. Some photographs (eg Fig 14) are in the GM collection.

Bastion 19 was preserved in a chamber beneath the Yard. It was resurveyed and some trial work conducted into the surviving deposits by MoLAS in 1992 (KEB92).

PRG, 419–21
Norman, P, & Reader, F, 1912 'Further
discoveries relating to Roman London,
1906–12', *Archaeologia*, 63, 277–344

Fig 14 GM146: the uncovering of Bastion 19, later preserved as a monument beneath the ground surface and still accessible.

GM147

E Rutter, 1959
NGR: TQ 32340 80870
SMR: 041386

Sugar Loaf Court, Garlick Hill, EC4

The SW part of a medieval undercroft was recorded in 1959; it extended under Sugar Loaf Court (it was on the S side). It measured more than 13ft by more than 10ft, and was parallel to the Court. On the S wall was the springer for a vault. The chalk walls were faced with blocks on the inside and were rough outside, showing that the undercroft was originally below ground level. The W wall was 2ft thick and the S wall 3ft thick.

Two samples were submitted for geological analysis to the Geological Survey. The first, from a wall, was similar to chert from the Lower Greensand, Hythe Beds at Godstone, Surrey; the second, from a vault springer, was similar to calcareous sandstone from Reigate, Surrey.

This undercroft is almost certainly the one recorded in 1982 (SLO82, see below).

EDN V, 30a, 31–31a
PRG, 823

GM148

Unknown, 1927
NGR: TQ 33045 81235
SMR: 04181101

39 Threadneedle Street (site of St Martin Outwich church), EC2

An entry in the diary of the Librarian for 21 September 1927 reads: 'Inspected excavation in Threadneedle Street on site of St Martin Outwich, opened up by the P.H.D. [Public Health Department] for sewerage work. Large quantity of skulls and bones built in behind the foundation of a medieval wall, with a superstructure in red brick of much later date.' These must have been from vaults as the churchyard was separate.

PRG, 1335
Notes on Excavations in the City, 1924–1939, 15.1

1–4 Threadneedle Street, EC2

GM149

P Marsden, 1965
NGR: TQ 32900 81185
SMR: 041535; see also 41534

Fragments of a Roman building were exposed at the SE corner of the site. A portion of the foundation of a wall 2ft thick and aligned approximately E–W was constructed of flints and buff mortar, with three courses of tiles at the top. On the S side was a floor of white mortar and small fragments of brick. Another fragment of wall was later exposed in a section further E. On the N side of this part was a hypocaust.

Marsden, P, 1968 'Archaeological finds in the City of London, 1965–66', *Trans London Middlesex Archaeol Soc*, 22.1, 10–11

8 Old Bailey, EC4

GM150

Unknown (?P Norman), 1900
NGR: TQ 31780 81230
SMR: 040436

A fragment of the Roman city wall was found at the rear of 8 Old Bailey in 1900, standing 8ft high, with the top 18in. below pavement level.

Merrifield, R, 1965 *The Roman city of London*, gazetteer W59
Norman, P, & Reader, F, 1912 'Further discoveries relating to Roman London, 1906–12', *Archaeologia*, 63, 295

Upper Thames Street (sewer on north side between Queen Street and Dowgate Hill), EC4

GM151

E Rutter, 1958–9
NGR: TQ 32527 80821
SMR: 040900–1

The bed of the Walbrook stream was seen in section in a sewer trench N of Upper Thames Street, about 130ft W of Dowgate Hill. The stream was 20–21ft wide, with the W bank marked by vertical wooden piles about 2ft apart, and the E bank by two large horizontal timbers placed one above the other. The stream-bed lay at a depth of 22–25ft below modern street level, but the bottom was not reached. Pottery was 1st–3rd c in date.

Traces of an E–W foundation of chalk, with a mixture of mortar and earth, were also recorded beneath what is now (1994) the N carriageway of Upper Thames Street between Little College Hill and Dowgate Hill. The foundation was at least 7ft wide, and was traced for a length of more than 40ft. It was presumably of medieval date.

A barrel-well (also recorded as of wickerwork) was seen in the NE corner of the junction between Dowgate and Thames Street. The wattle was set into grey clay containing bones, shells and tile fragments.

ER numbers 389, 412, 413A, 413B, 414, 416, 417, 418, 419, 420, 421, 422, 428, 582, 583, 584, 588, 601
EDN IV, 63; V, 1–3, 5, 8–11, 56
PRG, 937
J Roman Stud, 49, 1959, 125
Merrifield, R, 1965 *The Roman city of London*, gazetteer 260–1

GM152 (=BC72)

P Marsden, 1972–3
NGR: TQ 31930 80840
SMR: 041200–4

Baynard House, Queen Victoria Street (Upper Thames Street, site of second Baynard's Castle), EC4

Excavations here in 1972 found the foundations of the 15th-c and Tudor Baynard's Castle, overlying earlier tenements and the East Watergate, a dock-like public watergate. This is the second Baynard's Castle; the earlier, Norman castle lay on a separate site 100m to the N, within what was later the precinct of the Blackfriars. It seems likely that the name of this castle lingered on after it was destroyed c 1275, and transferred to the nearby waterfront area; and a prominent waterfront town house, rebuilt 1428, then took the name up again.

Saxon and early medieval river deposits were recorded W of the castle, S of the Roman riverside city wall (the wall lay below and along the S edge of medieval Thames Street, and was reused as a foundation by the N wall of the late medieval house and castle). Reclamation began in the 13th c when the riverbed was deepened in front of a revetment containing reused parts of timber buildings. A timber-lined dock may have existed at this stage, to be replaced during the 14th c by a stone-lined dock basin; an area to the W was reclaimed to form an open dockside service area. Part of a medieval stone building, originally with an arcaded open front, opened onto the service area.

The N wall of the dock was formed by using an earlier timber structure, and the E wall was a pre-existing stone wall. The W wall was formed by reclaiming an area of foreshore within a stone wall. The dump behind this wall can be dated by jettons to the 1330s or later. Other finds include a pewter ampulla of late 13th-c date and two lead tokens of Rigold type D2–4. The dock was backfilled in the last quarter of the 14th c. There were many finds in these two major dumps, both pottery and objects such as textiles, knives, shears and scabbards. These have been mostly catalogued in the various *Medieval finds from London* volumes (see bibliography below). There was also evidence of the working of amber, probably into beads (Mead 1977; Fig 15).

The castle, built entirely on reclaimed land, had foundations of chalk, ragstone and mortar. The original shape was trapezoidal, with four wings built around a courtyard. It was extensively modified by Henry VII, who refaced the river frontage with a series of five projecting towers between the two pre-existing multi-angular S corner towers. The N side of the castle lay on Thames Street, and excavations of 1972 and 1975 (BC75) found the entrance and a chamber on the E side of it. The SE tower was subsequently re-excavated in 1981: BYD81 below. In c 1550 the castle was enlarged to the W with three new wings of brick, faced with stone along the waterfront.

Fig 15 GM152: pieces of unfinished amber, and beads rejected during manufacture, from the Baynard's Castle site.

Though excavated by P Marsden for GM before the creation of the DUA in December 1973, this site was subsequently given the site code BC72. This code is used in several publications, particularly on medieval finds, which have analysed and published groups from the site.

The site archive also includes notes on sections of medieval alleys S of Thames Street, E of Baynard's Castle, recorded by J Haslam in 1972–3.

ER group 1356; most of the finds are stored under the site code BC72. Many of the individual finds have been accessioned by MoL. Site notes and drawings in MoL archive.
PRG, 311–12
London Archaeol, 1, 1972, 315–16
Bramwell, D, 1974 'The bird bones', Archive Report
Clark, J (ed), 1995 *The medieval horse and its equipment c 1150–c 1450,* Medieval finds from excavations in London 5 [medieval horseshoes and horse equipment]
Cowgill, J, de Neergaard, M, & Griffiths, N, 1987 *Knives and scabbards,* Medieval finds from excavations in London 1

Crosby, D D B, & Mitchell, J G, 1987 'Potassium-argon determinations of some London medieval honestones', *Trans London Middlesex Archaeol Soc,* 38, 159–64

Crowfoot, E, Pritchard, F, & Staniland, K, 1992 *Textiles and clothing c 1150–c 1450,* Medieval finds from excavations in London 4

Egan, G, 1998 *The medieval household,* Medieval finds from excavations in London 6

Egan, G, & Moir, D, in prep. 'Post-medieval finds c 1450–c 1700: a selection from the City of London sites 1972–82'

Egan, G, & Pritchard, F, 1991 *Dress accessories c 1150–c 1450,* Medieval finds from excavations in London 3

Grew, F, & de Neergaard, M, 1988 *Shoes and pattens,* Medieval finds from excavations in London 2

Marsden, P, 1972 'Baynard's Castle', *London Archaeol,* 1, 315–16

Mead, V K, 1977 'Evidence for the manufacture of amber beads in London in the 14th–15th century', *Trans London Middlesex Archaeol Soc,* 28, 211–14

Pringle, S, 1990 'Baynard's Castle', Building Materials Appraisal

Pritchard, F, 1990 'Missing threads from medieval textiles in north-west Europe', in *Archaeological Textiles,* Occ Pap 10, 15–17, United Kingdom Institute of Conservation

Spencer, B, in prep. *Pilgrim souvenirs and secular badges,* Medieval finds from excavations in London 7

Thornton, J H, 1976 'The leather', AML Report

Vince, A, nd, 'The dating of the three main finds groups', Dating Report

25 Upper Thames Street (Fur Trade House), EC4

GM153

P Marsden, 1969
NGR: TQ 32300 80875
SMR: 041387

A large group of 17th-c objects was recovered from a brick-lined cesspit on the N side of the E caldarium of the Huggin Hill Roman baths. The cesspit had been damaged by recent activities on the site, and its dimensions are uncertain.

EDN XI, 37 (no ER group)
PRG, 824

Central Criminal Court, Newgate Street, EC4

GM154

Unknown (?P Norman), 1903
NGR: TQ 31797 81296
SMR: 040444

Photographs of excavations which uncovered the Roman and medieval Newgate, and parts of the adjacent medieval and post-medieval prison, in 1903. They are filed under two headings: Newgate and Newgate Prison. The latter group is said to be from the LAMAS slide collection.

Norman, P, 1904 'Roman and later remains found during the excavations on the site of Newgate Prison, 1903–1904', *Archaeologia,* 59, 125–42

61 Queen Street / Upper Thames Street (site of St Martin Vintry church), EC4

GM155

I Noël Hume and E Rutter, 1956–7
NGR: TQ 32452 80843
SMR: 041385

Roman levels: a Roman pier was found resting on a sleeper wall running E–W which consisted of three courses of ragstone capped by a double course of tiles. Over the top was a layer of pink *opus signinum.* The pier was constructed of Roman tiles, some whole and others broken, set in yellowish mortar. The sides were covered with a layer of *opus signinum* covered with plaster. A concave moulding at the top was painted red. A few sherds of the late 1st or early 2nd c came from the loose filling around the pier. Several other walls were seen in builders' trenches in the N part of the site.

Post-Roman levels: foundations of the church of St Martin Vintry were recorded. Walls were generally of mortared ragstone and chalk. The church had a nave about 21ft wide, with N and S aisles. The N wall was not recorded, but the aisle was probably about 12ft wide; the S aisle was about 15ft wide. The foundations of the tower were located at the W end of the S aisle, suggesting a tower about 24ft square. Immediately N of the tower, within the W end of the nave, may have been a separate room. The E end was not recorded. Debris of the Great Fire was found overlying the church foundations at a depth of 6ft below street level. The remains of a path were found running along the N boundary of the graveyard and opening into Queen Street (so says report in EDN IV, 43: but Queen Street was built after the church was destroyed in the Great Fire, so presumably 'running up to and under Queen Street' is more likely). The site was excavated again in 1985 when the 1957 building was demolished: see QUN85 below.

Finds in 1956–7 included a complete London delftware plate of c 1680 inverted over the abdomen of a male skeleton in a coffin (the plate now on display in MoL; photograph in Noël Hume 1974, 170).

ER numbers 378, 380, 382

EDN IV, 43, 46–8, 51–2

Cohen, N, 1995 'The birth of church archaeology in London', *London Archaeol*, 7, 315–20

Noël Hume, I, 1974 *All the best rubbish*, 169–70

Schofield, J, 1994 'Saxon and medieval parish churches in the City of London: a review', *Trans London Middlesex Archaeol Soc*, 45, 116

GM156

E Rutter and P Marsden, 1959–60

NGR: TQ 32615 80975

SMR: 041097–1100, 041424–6

Walbrook Wharf, Upper Thames Street (Public Cleansing Depot), EC4

Roman river gravels formed two distinct layers. The lower consisted of lenses of large pebbles and pottery of the 1st and 2nd c, evidently dumped from boats. It included a considerable amount of samian, including over 200 potters' stamps. The upper gravel consisted of smaller pebbles and was more muddy, suggesting sluggish water. This contained pottery of the 3rd and 4th c in smaller quantities.

A Late Saxon waterfront was found between 20ft 6in. and 54ft S of the N frontage of the site. It comprised a raft of logs in a clay bank 4ft thick, aligned with the river. A sherd of Late Saxon pottery was found under the bank, while above was a great amount of pottery of the 10th–13th c. Much of this was imported red-painted ware, Pingsdorf and other German types. The clay bank thinned out to the S of the logs. At 150ft S of Thames Street a clay layer contained a concentration of pottery of the 10th–13th c, and may have marked the shoreline. This pottery was also largely imports, including red-painted, Paffrath and yellow-glazed wares, perhaps a cargo broken in transit.

The embankment is presumably part of the port of Dowgate recorded as belonging to the men of Rouen in the reign of Edward the Confessor. The large quantity of German pottery probably reflects the proximity of the Steelyard site immediately to the E, where the Germans were established by the 12th c.

A timber revetment of upright posts and horizontal planks supported by raking struts was found 250ft S of Thames Street, and is earlier than 15th-c pottery associated with it. The medieval bed of the Walbrook was also found, with possible traces of a revetment about 19ft 6in. W of Dowgate Dock. Various ragstone and chalk foundations were also recorded, some built on piles.

ER numbers 430, 432, 433, 438, 456, 466, 472, 477, 486, 490, 491, 491A, 491B, 497, 501, 502, 503, 507, 508, 514, 515, 516, 517, 518, 519, 520, 521, 534, 535, 536, 538, 540, 543, 544, 545, 546, 547, 548, 550, 551, 552, 553, 555, 556, 557, 558, 563, 564, 565, 566, 567, 568, 569, 571, 574, 579, 580

EDN V, 17, 18–21, 24, 48, 51, 54–6, 58, 63, 65; VI, 1, 4, 6, 8, 11–14, 16, 19–20, 23–7, 29–31, 34–40, 42–3, 45, 47, 51

PRG, 932

Cowgill, J, de Neergaard, M, & Griffiths, N, 1987 *Knives and scabbards*, Medieval finds from excavations in London 1

Crowfoot, E, Pritchard, F, & Staniland, K, 1992 *Textiles and clothing*, Medieval finds from excavations in London 4

Grew, F, & de Neergaard, M, 1988 *Shoes and pattens*, Medieval finds from excavations in London 2

Merrifield, R, *The Roman city of London*, gazetteer 260–2

Vince, A, 1985 'Saxon and medieval pottery in London: a review', *Medieval Archaeol*, 29, 25–93 [Saxon pottery]

Bucklersbury House, 11–20 Walbrook, EC4

GM157

I Noël Hume, 1954–5
NGR: TQ 32534 81046
SMR: 040870–83

Excavations on this large site (also known as Temple House) were undertaken both by I Noël Hume for GM and by Professor Grimes for the RMLEC in 1954–5. This is the site of the Walbrook Mithraeum, which first became evident in 1952 (site WFG44/45). The GM site has now been published (Wilmott 1991) and publication of the Mithraeum excavations is advanced (Shepherd 1998a). Only a brief outline of the Roman deposits will therefore be given here. Very few post-Roman features were recorded.

The entire width of the Walbrook stream in the Roman period was traced from N to S through the Bucklersbury House site (Fig 16). From the earliest phase of Roman occupation the stream was enclosed or canalised between timber-revetted banks. On the E side of the stream lay the Mithraeum, walls and floors of several scattered Roman buildings, and wells; at the S end of the site the Roman road along Cannon Street to the E was seen in section, with a timber platform on its S side. The expected bridge across the Walbrook for this road was not seen, but in the general position of the stream crossing were revetments. The temple was built c 240–50. One well and a pit (both unplanned) produced 3rd-/4th-c pottery. Wilmott (1991) suggests that

Fig 16 GM157: an alignment of Roman piles, probably associated with a Roman road, appearing during large-scale earth moving.

the large amount of Roman metalwork found in the silts of the Walbrook stream at this point (and elsewhere) was the result of normal rubbish-dumping from all over the city; Merrifield (1995) contests that it may instead have been a ritual practice.

The account by Wilmott (1991) shows some features not plotted by Merrifield (1965).

A few post-Roman features were noted: a 13th-c pit (ER 238), clay pipes (ER 234) and a 13th- or 14th-c mortar (ER 263).

ER numbers 212, 213, 214, 215, 216, 218, 220, 222, 233, 234, 235, 235B, 235C, 236, 237, 238, 239, 240, 241, 242, 243, 244, 245, 246, 249A, 249B, 250, 251, 253, 287, 259A, 259B, 259C, 259D, 261, 263, 267, 268, 268A, 268B, 268C, 268D, 268E, 268F, 268G, 268H, 268K, 268L, 291, 296, 297, 298, 299, 301, 302, 304, 305

Greep, S, 1981 'A model sword from Bucklersbury House, London', *Trans London Middlesex Archaeol Soc*, 32, 103–6

Merrifield, R, 1965 *The Roman city of London*, gazetteer 246–7, 249–53

Merrifield, R, 1995 'Roman metalwork from the Walbrook — rubbish, ritual or redundancy?', *Trans London Middlesex Archaeol Soc*, 46, 27–44

Shepherd, J, 1998a *The temple of Mithras in London: excavations by W F Grimes and A Williams at the Walbrook*

Wilmott, T, 1991 *Excavations in the middle Walbrook Valley, City of London, 1927–1960*, London Middlesex Archaeol Soc Spec Pap 13, 18–33

St Swithin's House, 30–37 Walbrook, EC4

GM158

I Noël Hume, 1949–50 (Fig 17)
NGR: TQ 32632 81005
SMR: 040902–4, 040906–8,
040910–11, 041400–2

The mortar-covered skirting moulding and wall plaster of two walls forming the angle of a room were found in approximate alignment with the modern street of Walbrook. The *opus signinum* rested on a wooden 'builder's raft'. The remains of a timber partition wall were also found; associated pottery suggested a date late in the 1st c.

Walls of ragstone blocks interspersed with courses of bonding-tiles were observed, standing in one corner to a height of 3ft; evidently a Roman building on the approximate alignment of modern Walbrook street. The *opus signinum* floor overlay a sherd of samian of Antonine date. From the building a square wooden gutter ran towards the Walbrook. A little to the N was a square timber-lined well, 10ft in depth. The bottom was lined with chalk rubble, in which was a sestertius of Postumus (AD259–68), probably deposited during construction of the well.

Approximately midway between Walbrook and St Swithin's Lane were the remains of a wattle and daub hut with a clay floor, on which lay pottery of the early 2nd c. It had apparently been destroyed by fire, probably the Hadrianic fire.

Fig 17 GM158:1 Noël Hume at work, watched by members of the public.

The ragstone foundations of a fairly large house with remains of coarse red tesserae laid on *opus signinum* were revealed in small portions at the E end of the St Swithin's House site, on approximately the same alignment as the lower part of St Swithin's Lane. The house seemed to have been destroyed by fire, and quantities of burnt wattle and ash lay on the floor. It may have been burnt in the Hadrianic fire, as pottery of the late 1st and early 2nd c seemed to be associated with it.

Many Roman pits were recorded summarily, but only two in detail. Of these, Feature 55 was a pit filled with debris of Boudican date (Noël Hume & Noël Hume 1954; Wilmott 1991).

Parts of several medieval buildings were also noted. Along the Walbrook frontage was a large structure with chalk walls about 4ft 6in. thick; its overall dimensions were 75ft N–S x 65ft E–W. Along the frontage to St Swithin's Lane were chalk foundations about 4ft wide associated with a crushed chalk floor. At the E end of St Stephen Walbrook were chalk foundations only 3ft wide, which adjoined the E wall of the church.

The Roman levels have now been published and discussed (Wilmott 1991).

PRG, 907

Merrifield, R, 1965 *The Roman city of London,* gazetteer 263–6

Noël Hume, I, & Noël Hume, A, 1954 *Discoveries in Walbrook, 1949–50* [GM booklet]

Wilmott, T, 1991 *Excavations in the middle Walbrook Valley, City of London, 1927–1960,* London Middlesex Archaeol Soc Spec Pap 13, 34–43

GM159

Q Waddington, 1925
NGR: TQ 31857 81274
SMR: 040439

10 Warwick Square, EC4

A massive stone wall of medieval character was found on the W boundary of this site. There are no further details.

EN 1, 26
PRG, 442

Gateway House, I Watling Street (including the site of St John Evangelist church), EC4

GM160

I Noël Hume, 1954
NGR: TQ 32263 81054
SMR: 040536–52, 041351–5

The Roman levels from this site have now been published (Shepherd 1986), and only a summary will be given here; but see below about Roman artefacts.

Three main periods of development were recorded. Period I (Neronian/Flavian) was represented only by pits, which included evidence of glassworking. In Period II (Flavian to Hadrianic) substantial buildings with mortar and *opus signinum* floors were recorded, similar to those excavated immediately to the E in 1978 (see below, WAT78). They were destroyed in the Hadrianic fire. There followed, at an unknown date, the construction of larger buildings (Period III) which might represent a single structure. Rooms were decorated with plain red and decorated mosaics and one room at least had a hypocaust. A 4th-c pit cut through the floor of one room and dark earth accumulated on parts of the site. In the N of both this site and of Watling Court to the E, the constant adherence to an E–W alignment suggests a road or thoroughfare outside the areas examined. This would be along the medieval Watling Street at this point.

The site of the church of St John Evangelist, in the NW corner of the site, was also investigated. The church was destroyed in the Great Fire and not rebuilt. The earliest church appeared to have a small nave 27ft x 17ft internally, and a chancel about 10ft 3in. wide and probably of the same length. A further wall of the first period was traced running S at right angles to the nave and half way along it, for about 6ft. The foundations included ragstone and reused Roman building material laid in gravel, and were 3ft 6in.–4ft wide. The ragstone and mortar walls above, recorded on the N side at junction of nave and chancel, were rendered, and 2ft 9in. wide. The excavator dated this first phase to possibly the 11th c. In the 13th or 14th c, apparently in two distinctly different phases, all three walls of the nave were rebuilt on the original alignment; and the chancel was widened by having new foundations laid alongside and outside the old on the N and S sides. This included a protruberance which may be the base of a buttress on the S side. Within the church were recorded several burials, in coffins and chalk-lined graves; and to the S, the E end of a brick and chalk vault containing 18th-c coffins, a relic of the post-Fire period when the church site was used as a graveyard. Glazed and decorated floor tiles were found in and around the church.

A number of other medieval foundations were recorded, including a small cellar measuring 12ft x 6ft. This had walls of chalk 2ft thick, and contained stratified rubbish from the early 16th to the 17th c, overlaid by a burnt deposit 2in. thick of the mid-17th c (?the Great Fire). Eleven cesspits were found, containing pottery of the 13th, 15th, 16th and 17th c. Two wells were also noted, one containing pottery of the 16th or 17th c. Extensive traces of burnt debris, believed to be from the Fire of 1666, were found in various cesspits.

The finds from the site were numerous, and apart from a group of Roman glassworking waste (Shepherd 1986, 141–3), and articles on the 16th- and 17th-c glass, they have not been studied or published.

An evaluation of the site was carried out in 1996 when Gateway House was demolished: MoLAS, site code CAO96. Roman pits and parts of the medieval Friday Street were recorded, along with traces of medieval and post-medieval buildings on Friday Street and Watling Street.

ER numbers 182, 184, 191, 191A, 191B, 207, 207A, 207B, 207C, 207D, 144, 145, 146, 147, 148, 149, 150, 151, 152, 153, 154, 1 55, 156, 159, 160, 161, 161A, 161B, 162, 163, 164, 166, 166A, 166B, 166C, 166D, 167, 168, 169, 171, 172, 173, 174, 175, 176, 188, 189, 126, 127, 128, 129, 130, 131, 132, 133A, 133B, 134, 135, 136, 137, 205, 205A; the medieval tiles are MoL acc nos 21516–24

EDN I, 85–92, 100; II, 5–15, 20, 22–7, 34, 44–6; site file. For a concordance between ER numbers and the context numbers used by Shepherd (1986), see MoL archive under this site.

PRG, 773–4

Cohen, N, 1995 'The birth of church archaeology in London', *London Archaeol*, 7, 315–20

Merrifield, R, 1965 *The Roman city of London*, gazetteer 68–80

Schofield, J, 1994 'Saxon and medieval parish churches in the City of London: a review', *Trans London Middlesex Archaeol Soc*, 45, 106–8

Shepherd, J, 1986 'The Roman features at Gateway House and Watling House, Watling Street, City of London (1954)', *Trans London Middlesex Archaeol Soc*, 37, 127–44

GM161

P Marsden, 1961
NGR: TQ 32408 81063
SMR: 040581

67–69 Watling Street, EC4

A small excavation at the rear of this building revealed the remains of a tessellated pavement, much disturbed and broken. It lay 65–75ft behind the frontage of Watling Street.

EDN VII, 40; site file
Merrifield, R, 1965 *The Roman city of London,* gazetteer 88

GM162

I Noël Hume, 1953
NGR: TQ 32218 81270
SMR: 041347–8

4–9 Wood Street (Mitre Court), EC2

A trial hole revealed N–S and E–W walls of ragstone, believed to be of medieval date.

Immediately beneath the modern basement was a cesspit (construction materials not recorded) 5ft x 5ft 6in., containing objects of the first half of the 18th c. It was set in the middle of a long E–W wine cellar, which terminated in a bricked-up doorway originally connecting with existing wine cellars in Mitre Court. The pit was apparently in the passage between wine bins on either side.

ER numbers 67, 74, 77, 86
EDN I, 8–9, 20–4
PRG, 770

GM163

P Marsden, 1967
NGR: TQ 33150 80675
SMR: 044365, 044434

St Dunstan's Hill, 84 Lower Thames Street, EC3

A small temple-like building was recorded, alongside a N–S Roman street. It formed a single room with an entrance on the E side; on its walls were traces of red lines on a pink background speckled with red splashes. It seemed to be contemporary with the Billingsgate bath-house, immediately to the E.

ER numbers 1251, 1252, 1253, 1254, 1255, 1256, 1257, 1258, 1259, 1260, 1261, 1262; site file
Marsden, P, 1980 *Roman London,* 155

GM164

F Cottrill, 1935

160 Queen Victoria Street (south-east corner; site of *Times* offices), EC4

See GM135 above, observations on the same site during redevelopment in 1960. There is no immediately available documentation on work in 1935.

GM165

Unknown, 1954
NGR: TQ 31503 81610
SMR: 040242

Shoe Lane, open space at rear of 2 Charterhouse Street / 10 Holborn Viaduct, EC1

A Roman cremation was found. Bones were contained in the lower half of a decorated grey ware olla set in natural clay. A chalk cesspit produced a group of artefacts of the first quarter of the 18th c: glass and clay tobacco pipes (ER 140).

ER numbers 123, 139, 140, 141, 142, 143, 157A, 157B, 158; MoL 21450, 21471; GM acc nos 21454–63

6–12, 15, 16–45 Cheapside (Bank of England) / New Change, EC4

GM166

E Rutter, 1957
NGR: TQ 32183 61163
SMR: 041359

(Nos 6–10 were to the W of Old Change, the other numbers to the E. Nos 6–10 are now beneath the E carriageway of New Change as it meets Cheapside.)

A rectangular chalk-lined cesspit was found to the S of the main entrance of the Bank of England building, in the E half of the new E carriageway of New Change. An apparently brick-lined pit was also seen, and the finds recovered by workmen.

For excavations to the rear of 16–45 Cheapside, formerly Friday Street, in 1925, see GM64 above.

ER numbers 384, 390; one almost complete late 13th-c green-glazed jug is GM acc no. 20737
EDN IV, 53, 63–4, 69 ('New Change')
PRG, 777

Barber-Surgeons' Hall Gardens (formerly Windsor Court, Monkwell Street), Wood Street, EC2

GM167

Unknown, ?19th c
NGR: TQ 32300 81600
SMR: 044366

The site file contains one plan, a groundplan of the estate belonging to the Barbers' Company; it is on paper, dated 1818. There is also a finds group, ER 257.

ER number 257

Old Change House, 4–6 Cannon Street, EC1

GM168

I Noël Hume, 1955
NGR: TQ 32160 80990
SMR: 044367

This is part of a larger site, summarised in Merrifield 1965 as follows:

Queen Victoria Street, W of St Nicholas Cole Abbey church, 1961 (gazetteer 102): a continuation of a wall seen in 1845 (gazetteer 101) was seen in section 80ft W of the W wall of St Nicholas church. It was 4ft thick; the surviving N edge, cut away by later work, was 32ft 4in. S of the S edge of the Knightrider Street wall noted in gazetteer 96. The two walls were very similar in construction.

ER numbers 276, 277, 279
EDN III, 38–40, 46; site file
Merrifield, R, 1965 *The Roman city of London,* gazetteer 101–2

22–25 Farringdon Street (Amalgamated Press site), EC4

GM169

I Noël Hume, 1955
NGR: TQ 31629 81345
SMR: 044368–9

A brick-walled late 17th-c cellar had been turned into a domestic refuse pit c 1720–30 and then filled with rubble to street level. It lay in the SE area of the site directly against the walls of the railway viaduct. ER 288 combines all material from the initial cellar filling: Delft, stoneware, pipes and coarse pottery. In the NE corner of the cellar was a brick-lined cesspit 5ft 6in. x 3ft 6in. x 2ft 6in. at a depth of 8ft below street level. The pit retained its refuse chute at the NW corner, in which a complete pitcher (ER 289A) had become wedged. It contained a quantity of pottery and bottles of 1680–1780 (ER 289B).

ER numbers 288, 289A, 289B
EDN III, 47–8

GM170

P Marsden, 1956
NGR: TQ 33340 80940
SMR: 044370

City Institute of Marine Engineers war memorial, 56–59 Fenchurch Street, EC3

ER 372 is a group of 1st-c pottery found in a rubbish pit dug into natural at the S side of the site.

ER number 372
EDN IV, 40
Marsden, P, 1974 'Two pit groups in the City of London', *Trans London Middlesex Archaeol Soc,* 25, 282–4

GM171

GM staff on site excavated by
W F Grimes, 1955
NGR: TQ 32190 80980
SMR: 040597–9

8–18 Cannon Street (rear of Bracken House; *Financial Times* site), EC4

Some watching evidently took place by GM staff on the site which was excavated by Professor Grimes (site WFG35); the visits by GM staff were in August 1955.

The builders' excavations were in strips around the four sides of the *Financial Times* site. Two walls are noted: one of stone running E–W for some distance, lying N of St Nicholas Cole Abbey church; and a continuation of this wall, in brick, running for a short distance E into the site. The stone wall was composed of limestone, well bonded. Only the core remained, the facing stones being absent. The brick wall was joined onto the E end of the stone wall. The stone wall was equated with that found in Friday Street (RCHM, 1928, 120).

A small knee brooch of early 2nd-c type was found by 'W.F. Rector and myself' (?I Noël Hume, but in 1996 he had no recollection of this) in close association with the Roman wall (ER 365). On a separate visit, pottery found in excavation of the same wall at the SE corner of the site produced pottery of unspecified date (ER 376).

ER numbers 365, 376
EDN IV, 31–3, 42; site file
RCHM, 1928 *London III: Roman London,* 120

GM172

E Rutter, 1957
NGR: TQ 33327 80758
SMR: 041839

50 Mark Lane, EC3

A stone undercroft was recorded about 60ft to the E of Mark Lane, measuring 24ft N–S and 15ft 6in. E–W internally. The walls survived up to 6ft high. They were 2ft wide on the N and E sides and 2ft 6in. wide on the W. The interior facing was of dressed chalk and the core of chalk and flint. In the middle of the E and W walls, dividing the structure into two bays, were semicircular attached shafts of limestone with moulded bases with hollow chamfers, and in the four corners were round engaged limestone shafts. All these rested on foundations of tightly packed flint and sandstone. Several fragments of chamfered sandstone ribs and a moulded abacus were found in later walls, and may have been parts of the vault reused. A layer of chalk chippings indicated the construction level, and above this was a floor surface of gravel with finds of Roman, 13th- and 15th-c date. Traces of decayed wood at a higher level possibly indicate a subsequent planked floor. From the architectural evidence the undercroft was built in the mid-13th c, and was in use, on archaeological grounds, until the Great Fire.

A chalk-lined well was found towards the NW corner of the site, and on the N side a thick layer of burnt debris, containing pottery of the early 17th c.

ER numbers 391, 392, 393, 394, 396, 397, 398
GM acc nos 21155–60 (pieces of the ribs and imposts)
EDN IV, 64–8; site file
PRG, 1401
Medieval Archaeol, 2, 1958, 178–82

London Wall (Route 11) between Coleman Street and Basinghall Street, EC2

GM173 (=GM109)

E Rutter, 1957

This is a duplicate number for GM109, and should be discontinued.

11–13 Crosswall / Vine Street, EC3

GM174

E Rutter, 1957
NGR: TQ 33615 80960
SMR: 044372

On 3 October 1957 a tombstone, with a Greek inscription beneath figures in relief, having been found on this site by workmen, was collected by GM staff. It was allegedly found approximately 18in. below the old cellar floor. Some 17th-c material was seen during subsequent building works. The site file contains a letter from Jocelyn Toynbee, of January 1958, suggesting that the stone is a Greek stele and similar to one of the late 4th or early 3rd c BC in Italy. It had been reinscribed by one Ti.Claudius, probably before it was taken from an east Mediterranean place to Britain.

ER numbers 401 (the tombstone), 402
EDN IV, 73–5; site file

Cannon Street Station (south-west corner by Upper Thames Street), EC4

GM175

E Rutter, 1959
NGR: TQ 32555 80780
SMR: 044373

A trench 'in a cellar just off Dowgate Hill' in August 1959 revealed horizontal Roman timber beams, four or five high. One of three site plans in the site file shows the trench or inspection pit near the junction of Dowgate Hill and Upper Thames Street. The beams ran N–S in the E side of the pit. This site was excavated again in 1988 (LYD88 below).

Site file contains: borehole logs for the site; four photographs of the trench (a shuttered rectangular hole); and photographs and negatives of a Roman hairpin, ER 531.

Note: Roman timbers probably from the surface of a wharf were seen in the same year in a hole dug in the pavement on the S side of Upper Thames Street, under the arch of the bridge. One timber was recorded *in situ,* 24ft below the street; plan and section in EDN VI, 28.

ER numbers 531, 532
EDN VI, 18

20 Cannon Street (Wates site), EC4

GM176

Unknown, 1959
NGR: TQ 32555 81587
SMR: 044432

A builder's trench cut through a 13th-c rubbish pit. A few pieces of pottery were recovered, but the upper portion of a jug had to be left in the section to avoid undercutting. On a second visit to the site a month later, a limited number of sherds was recovered from a rubbish pit cut into the gravel ballast at the S (Queen Victoria Street) end of the site. Animal bones and a human skull were also found. The pit appeared to be about 5ft in diameter and surviving 6ft deep.

ER numbers 539, 570
EDN VI, 24, 41

GM177

P Marsden, 1960
NGR: TQ 32564 81413
SMR: 044374

Girdlers' Hall, Basinghall Street, EC2

Three unstratified finds (a stoneware jug base, a 17th-c clay pipe and an iron knife) were collected by 'Messrs Marsden and Chaplin'.

ER number 581
EDN VI, 48

GM178

Unknown, 1960
NGR: TQ 32560 80965
SMR: 044375

Mansion House Underground Station, Queen Victoria Street, EC4

A rim sherd of a sagging-base cooking pot was recovered by workmen from black fill in a trial hole. It could have come from a rubbish pit but the hole was too small to give any indication of a pit's area.

For observations on the site in 1990, see MHS89 below.

ER number 614
EDN VII, 4

GM179

Unknown, 1960
NGR: TQ 32285 81640
SMR: 044444

Barber-Surgeons' Hall and Lee House (Cripplegate corner), Monkwell Square, EC2

No summary is available for this site; it is adjacent to Bastions 13 and 14. The ER groups attributed to the site contain Roman pottery dating from the Flavian period to the 4th c.

ER numbers 654, 655, 656, 657, 658A, 658B
EDN VII, 29, 32

GM180

Unknown, 1961
NGR: TQ 32720 80680
SMR: 044376

Swan Lane car park, 95–103 Upper Thames Street (Dyers' Hall Wharf), EC4

In clearance of the rubble-filled site and two N–S lanes which ran across it, a section of the W of the two (Dyers' Hall Wharf) was exposed next to Upper Thames Street. Twelve layers are briefly described in the EDN, but no drawing appears to survive. Two photographs are pasted into the Notebook, but the negative numbers are not known. One of them shows Dyers' Hall Wharf, the other George Alley.

This is the site of the DUA excavation SWA81 in 1981 (before and during demolition of the multi-storey car park constructed in 1961); see below under that code.

ER numbers 687, 688, 769
EDN VII, 54–6; VIII, 55

Blackfriars underpass (Blackfriars Wreck 2), EC4

GM181 (=GM302)

P Marsden, 1962
NGR: TQ 32050 80803
SMR: 041388

The wreck of a 17th-c boat (known as 'Blackfriars Wreck 2') was found in the bed of the river off Paul's Stairs. It was flat-bottomed and clinker built, the overlapping planks held by iron rivets. The planks were of oak, and the keel of elm. The vessel was roughly 14m long and perhaps 3m broad, and was carrying a cargo of bricks. Pottery, clay pipes and wineglass stems suggest that the sinking was around the time of, and possibly after, the Great Fire of 1666.

ER numbers 800, 801, 854, 855, 856, 857, 858, 859, 860, 868, 871, 901, 902, 850, 798
EDN IX, 4, 8, 13, 15, 25, 27–8, 35; site file
PRG, 825
Marsden, P, 1971 'A seventeenth-century boat found in London', *Post-Medieval Archaeol*, 5, 88–98
Marsden, P, 1996 *Ships of the port of London: twelfth to seventeenth centuries* AD, EH Archaeol Rep 5, 145–79

Blackfriars underpass, Puddle Dock (Cofferdam 1: Roman ship), EC4

GM182

P Marsden, 1962
NGR: TQ 31690 80820
SMR: 040030

A large part of a Roman ship was discovered in 1962. It sank in about AD150 while carrying a cargo of building stone quarried near Maidstone (Kent), though *Teredo* infestation showed that mostly it sailed at sea. It was constructed in a Romano-Celtic shipbuilding tradition, and its flat bottom made it ideally suited to being beached on tidal shores. It could carry up to 50 tonnes of cargo.

Marsden, P, 1967 *A Roman ship from Blackfriars*, GM
Marsden, P, 1994 *Ships of the port of London: first to the eleventh centuries* AD, EH Archaeol Rep 3, 33–96

Blackfriars Bridge (road) (Cofferdam 4: Blackfriars Wreck 4), EC4

GM183

P Marsden, 1970
NGR: TQ 32074 80795
SMR: 041390

A second wreck ('Blackfriars 4') was found a few metres E of Blackfriars ship 3. It was a clinker-built vessel, probably of the 15th c, with a cargo of Kentish ragstone. Only a few details were recorded, as the wreck was exposed by a mechanical grab.

ER numbers 802, 812
PRG, 826, 827
Marsden, P, 1996 *Ships of the port of London: twelfth to seventeenth centuries* AD, EH Archaeol Rep 5, 105–6

9-12 Pancras Lane (site of St Pancras church, EC4, 1963

GM184

This is a duplicate entry for GM36, and the summaries are there.

97–101 Cannon Street (Gallagher Ltd), EC4

GM185

Unknown, 1964
NGR: TQ 32635 80940
SMR: 044377

ER 987 is a group of unstratified finds from excavation for a lift-shaft on this site. There is no documentation as to their date.

ER number 987
EDN X, 24

GM186

P Marsden, 1965
NGR: TQ 33545 80930
SMR: 044423

Playground, Portsoken Street (south side), E1

Site file has correspondence between GM and the GLC about the possibility of GM digging trenches across this site to locate the expected Roman cemetery. There are four ER groups, but the results are otherwise not known.

ER numbers 1110, 1111, 1112, 1113
Site file

GM187
(?=GM52)

P Marsden, 1969
NGR: TQ 32700 80780
SMR: 044424, 044445

Suffolk House, 154–156 Upper Thames Street (Suffolk Lane), EC4

Two finds groups were recovered from this site, with the location 'between Suffolk Lane and Ducksfoot Lane and north of Upper Thames Street'.

The first group (ER 1318) is the contents of a brick-lined cesspit near the NW corner of the site: a considerable quantity of pottery and glass, toys, glass bottles, probably from the site of the Merchant Taylors' School, and dated to the early 18th c.

The second group (ER 1319) is a fragment of Roman mosaic found *in situ* on the site. Mostly destroyed by the mechanical excavator, it had tesserae in red, white, yellow and black, and had a guilloche border.

This site was excavated again by MoLAS during redevelopment in 1994–6: site code SUF94. See also GM52 above.

ER numbers 1318, 1319
EDN VI, 33

GM188

H Chapman, 1973
NGR: TQ 33385 80890
SMR: 044378

2–3 New London Street, 34–35 Crutched Friars, EC3

A cesspit group was recovered from this site. It was excavated from the side of a narrow trench dug to insert a diaphragm wall. It consisted of pipes, Delft, Tudor-Green bowls and Surrey ware, and glass; mid-17th c.

A second cesspit group was recovered apparently six months later (ER 1359); this was dated 1840–50.

ER numbers 1357, 1359
EDN XI, 47–8

GM189

E Rutter, 1957
NGR: TQ 31825 80940
SMR: 04350201

Mermaid Theatre, Upper Thames Street (Puddle Dock), EC4

A N–S trench was cut in the NW corner of the site, 66ft x 6ft, but it was abandoned 'owing to the presence of very thick concrete rafts which were continuing at a depth of 2–3ft' (note in site file). This site was excavated again as the Mermaid Theatre site in 1979 (THE79, see below).

Site file

8 Great Swan Alley (Copthall Close) / Copthall Avenue, EC2

See GM45 above for details of this excavation and its reports.

**GM190
(=GM45)**

P Marsden, 1961
NGR: TQ 32760 81403
SMR: 040644, 040646

20–30 Aldgate, EC3

Evidence of 1st-c military occupation (a V-shaped ditch and two, possibly three timber buildings) was overlaid by Flavian/early 2nd-c buildings on different alignments. Evidence for the later Roman period was sparse. There were also medieval and post-medieval pits, some brick lined.

ER number 1358; the site records and all other finds are stored under CASS72

Armitage, P, 1979 'The mammalian remains from the Roman, medieval and post-medieval refuse pits', Animal Bone Report (AML Report 2804)

Chapman, H, & Johnson, T, 1973 'Excavations at Aldgate and Bush Lane House in the City of London, 1972', *Trans London Middlesex Archaeol Soc*, 24, 1–73

**GM191
(=CASS72)**

H Chapman, 1972
NGR: TQ 33500 81170
SMR: 042100

14–20 St Mary Axe (Baltic Exchange Co), EC3

The recording was only at no. 18. Three trial pits along the front, middle and back of the N wall were recorded, and a short length of wall along the middle of the S side. The trial hole midway along the N side exposed the E face of a substantial chalk wall and a deposit of decayed wood, containing a 13th-c sherd and a length of plaited human hair. The hole at the back of the N wall produced burnt bronze-smelting waste and sherds of the late 15th c. The third hole at the front of the site on the N side produced 18th-c material, but was backfilled before it could be examined. A large charnel pit of uncertain date was also observed.

The site was excavated by MoLAS in 1995–6 (site code BAX95), and extensive remains of several periods recorded.

ER numbers 63, 63B, 63C, 64, 65, 66, 165

GM192

I Noël Hume, 1952–3
NGR: TQ 33297 81259
SMR: 044379–80

Winchester House, 74–77 London Wall, EC2

A length of a Walbrook tributary was seen, cut into natural gravel; it flowed from NE to SW, with a slight bend in its course on the site. The first few feet of deposit were grey silt (pre-Roman), above which was a dark grey sandy silt deposit which contained pottery ER 810.

This is the same site as GM74, but the finds are noted under GM193.

ER number 810

EDN IX, 7; site file

Marsden, P, 1967 'Archaeological finds in the City of London, 1963–4', *Trans London Middlesex Archaeol Soc*, 21, 208–9

Merrifield, R, 1965 *The Roman city of London*, gazetteer 145

**GM193
(=GM74)**

P Marsden, 1963
NGR: TQ 32960 81450
SMR: 040653

GM194

1963
NGR: TQ 32516 81870
SMR: 044384

Milton Court, 1–13 Moor Lane (Public Services Building), EC2

ER 811 is a group of pottery given in 1963 by Mr Holder the Clerk of Works on this site, from the NE corner of the new Public Services Building, under (sic) Moor Lane, at the boundary of the City and Finsbury.

ER number 811
EDN IX, 7

GM195

City of London unstratified finds from various sites

This number relates to unstratified finds from several sites in the City, brought together in 1963.

ER number 863
EDN IX, 17

GM196

I Noël Hume, 1953
NGR: TQ 32740 80970
SMR: 044385–6

24–30 St Swithin's Lane (London Assurance), EC4

A pit was observed in a trial hole, 15ft below cellar level, about 20ft E of St Swithin's Lane, in a corner of the site. Roman pottery probably came from the pit; medieval material was also recovered, but from workmen, not by archaeologists.

ER numbers 75, 76, 170
EDN 1, 24

GM197

W F Grimes, 1953
NGR: TQ 32400 81400

?66–75 Aldermanbury (fort ditch section on west side of Aldermanbury RMLEC site 14), EC2

This group is evidently a mixture of elements from observation of a Grimes site (WFG14), and correspondence about GM4 and GM13.

ER number 101

GM198

Unknown, c 1953
NGR: TQ 3300 8133
SMR: 044387–8

Barclay's Bank site, [?Old] Broad Street, EC2

A group of Roman pottery, perhaps of 2nd-c date, was recovered by workmen from a pit or well, boarded at the base. Finds included sherds of amphorae, 'metallic-surfaced poppyhead beaker', a large vessel of similar ware and other fragments.

It is not known what address in (presumably Old) Broad Street is meant here, though it could possibly be traced through Barclay's records. The NGR is therefore approximate, being placed in the middle of the street.

ER number 230
EDN 2, 65

St Mary le Bow church, Cheapside, EC4

GM199

R Merrifield, 1955
NGR: TQ 32382 81154
SMR: 041303

The site file contains two photographs of an early 13th-c column base taken by Ralph Merrifield in 1955. The lower part is now kept in the vestibule of the church. A note by D Keene in the file, June 1983, records that Mr Pickett, one of the architects associated with Lawrence King in the post-War restoration of the church, recollects that the stones were found in the crypt near the opening between the central compartment and the S aisle. This cannot have been their original position, but it is possible that they originally supported a pier in the arcade separating the nave from the S aisle in the church above. They would thus be evidence for an otherwise unrecorded period of major building in the church. For further discoveries in 1959, see GM223 below.

ER 271 is a group of 17th-c finds from 'a cellar W of the tower': evidently the medieval undercroft excavated by Grimes on the same site, WFG39.

ER number 271
EDN III, 32–3
Schofield, J, 1994 'Saxon and medieval parish churches in the City of London: a review', *Trans London Middlesex Archaeol Soc,* 45, 118–19

St Lawrence Jewry church, Gresham Street, EC2

GM200

I Noël Hume, 1952, 1954;
?E Rutter, 1955
NGR: TQ 32471 81311
SMR.: 200707, 20070701

This entry covers several post-War pieces of recording at the church:

(i) GM photographs: of steps found on the S side of the church, 1952, which may be of the pre-Fire church or for a vault in the Wren church, later sealed up; (ii) in 1954, a list of coffin plates from the 'great vault' beneath the church was made; they were of 18th- and 19th-c date (EDN II, 67–8); (iii) in 1955 a carved stone from a tomb or lintel was found reused in the core of the wall of the Wren church, at the SE corner, at the junction of wall with roof. The top of the E wall also appeared to have a number of late medieval and 16th-c flooring tiles reused as a bonding-course; three examples were recovered and retained (ER number 273; EDN III, 34).

Schofield, J, 1994 'Saxon and medieval parish churches in the City of London: a review', *Trans London Middlesex Archaeol Soc,* 45, 118–19

Falcon Street (north turret of fort), EC2

GM201

Unknown, 1955
NGR: TQ 32260 81570
SMR: 044389

EDN has note: 'From Falcon Street. Found by a Mr Banks digging near the West gate, north turret of the Fort. Two 18th-c chamber pots — one complete and sherds of two other 18th-c vessels. All glazed.

ER number 366
EDN IV, 34

36–38 Botolph Lane, EC3

GM202

E Harris, 1959
NGR: TQ 33030 80755
SMR: 044390

A selection of 16th-c tumbler ware (glass), 17th-c drug pots and bottles, coarseware, Delft and 18th-c pipes were found on the site of Turban House, and sent in by the site owners, Field & Co, for identification; note in EDN says 'to be returned to them' but there is an ER group.

ER number 459
EDN V, 48

GM203

P Marsden, 1965
NGR: TQ 32434 81273
SMR: 044391

20–21 Lawrence Lane, EC2

On this site the natural subsoil was pebbly brickearth about 4ft thick which overlay the natural gravel. A Roman jug neck of the 1st c was recovered.

ER number 948
EDN IX, 70

GM204

Unknown, 1959
NGR: TQ 32250 81245
SMR: 044392

Gutter Lane (south of Saddlers' Hall), EC2

A 17th-c jug and a pipkin were found by workmen constructing a sewer pipe in Gutter Lane, just S of Saddlers' Hall.

ER number 578
EDN VI, 46

GM205

Unknown, 1960
NGR: TQ 32221 61408
SMR: 044425

St John Zachary Gardens, Gresham Street, EC2

One small brass coffin plate was recovered from a coffin lid lying in the easternmost of the three vaults partially cleared by the road-widening scheme (?of Gresham Street). The inscription (transcribed in EDN VI, 55) is of a Henry Drax, and the date is apparently 1682.

The site file contains a list of coffin plates found during clearance of the vaults. Twenty plates are described, dating from 1759 to 1833.

ER number 591 (the first brass plate)
EDN VI, 55; site file

GM206

Unknown, 1960
NGR: 33030 80600
SMR: 044433, 04443301

Thames foreshore at Billingsgate, EC3

This number covers two ER groups:

(i) A mixed group of pottery, metalwork and coins recovered from mudlarking on material dredged up during the alterations to the quay and wharf alongside Billingsgate Fish Market. The note does not say which side of the market; it is possibly the extension of the wharf on the W side (the area which became Billingsgate lorry park, the site of the DUA excavation BIG82 in 1982): ER 593.

(ii) The handle and upper part of the blade of a sword of c 1600, found in 1961 about 20ft S of the middle of the market in the bed of the Thames at a depth of about 3–4ft (ER 672: GM 23885).

ER numbers 593, 672
EDN VI, 56

Thames foreshore

GM207

Unknown, 1963

A note in the EDN says: 'ER 872: part of Noël Hume collection of objects from bed of the Thames. For find spots see list within box.'

ER number 872
EDN IX, 27

Lambeth Hill east road scheme (now west), EC4

**GM208
(=GM91)**

P Marsden, 1960

This site is the same as GM91, and should be combined with it.

1–3 St Alphage Highwalk, EC2

**GM209
(=GM11)**

P Marsden, 1960
NGR: TQ 32471 81616
SMR: 040486

Site file contains only five photographs of the city wall at both St Alphage Highwalk (four) and at Trinity Place (one), c 1960. This is the same as GM11, and should be added to it.

ER number 663

9–11 Bush Lane, EC4

GM210

P Marsden, 1960–1
NGR: TQ 32650 80840
SMR: 040930–7

This site, recorded under difficult conditions (Fig 18), is part of the site of large Roman buildings interpreted by the excavator as the Roman governor's palace, and now published (Marsden 1975); but later commentators have questioned this interpretation.

During the Flavian period the hillside was terraced in three levels for the construction of a large complex of buildings arranged around an ornamental garden court and an elongated central pool. The N wing fronted onto the Roman predecessor of Cannon Street, and possibly included a monumental entrance which might have incorporated the stone known as London Stone. The W wing survives in part beneath Cannon Street Railway Station, and timber waterfront structures lie underneath Thames Street at the foot of the terrace.

Fig 18 GM210: pneumatic drills uncovering the S wall of Room D in the complex interpreted by Marsden as the Roman provincial governor's palace.

ER numbers 673, 674, 679, 680, 681, 686, 689, 690, 691, 692, 693, 695, 722, 723, 724, 725, 727, 729, 733, 758, 792
EDN VI, 34
Site file includes one sheet of sketch sections from St Swithun's site (Grimes), being excavated at the same time (WFG48).
Trans London Middlesex Archaeol Soc, 20, 1961, 220–1
Marsden, P, 1975 'The excavation of a Roman palace site in London, 1961–1972', Trans London Middlesex Archaeol Soc, 26, 1–102
Merrifield, R, 1965 The Roman city of London, gazetteer 273

GM211

E Rutter, 1959
NGR: TQ 32317 81052
SMR: 044393

Dowgate Hill House, Upper Thames Street / Little College Lane, EC4

At the corner of Thames Street and Little College Lane, workmen dug a small trial hole. Fragments of Pingsdorf ware were thrown out of a layer of black mud, at a depth of about 15ft.

ER number 562
EDN VI, 33

GM212

W F Grimes and P Marsden, 1962
NGR: TQ 32346 81462
SMR: 04004503

St Alban's church, Wood Street, EC2

In April 1962 the cemetery against and outside of the N wall of the church, then being excavated by Grimes (WFG22), produced five lead coffin plates of the first half of the 19th c, which were transcribed: the transcriptions are in both EDN and the site file. In May 1962 a further three were found, and they are transcribed in EDN.

EDN VIII, 69–70, 82; site file

GM213

I Noël Hume, 1954
NGR: TQ 32304 81074
(slightly E of ref for GM160)
SMR: 040554–70

Watling House, 12–16 Watling Street, 31–37 Cannon Street, EC4

This site has been paired in publication of the Roman levels with the adjacent Gateway House site (GM160).

The earliest identifiable remains on both sites were a small number of Neronian-period pits, followed by Flavian buildings. In a further period two buildings were constructed on the Watling House site; both had floors either of mosaics or *opus signinum,* and at least five rooms could be identified. These buildings were damaged and probably destroyed in the Hadrianic fire. Post-Hadrianic structures, one on a slightly different alignment, were also summarily recorded, as was the presence of dark earth on the Watling House site (Shepherd 1986). This sequence mirrors that on the Watling Court site (WAT78), dug by the DUA in 1978 immediately to the E of Watling House.

The Roman finds from this site have not been published, except for a group of glassworking waste from Watling House (ER 181): Shepherd 1986, 141–2.

Post-Roman features and finds recorded included incomplete vessels of Siegburg and Cologne stonewares, clay pipes, two brick-walled cesspits, a fragment of E–W ragstone wall, a chalk-lined cesspit, and a rectangular ragstone cesspit or cellar divided in the 15th c by a chalk partition. This cesspit was recorded in the slit trench for the E retaining wall of the new building; and was probably within the grounds of *La Rouge Sale,* a prominent tenement, whose grounds to the E were explored on the Watling Court (WAT78) site (Schofield, Allen, & Taylor 1990). The Watling House cesspit seems to have lain at the S end of the medieval court of the house, and therefore probably under the main range.

ER numbers 183, 185, 185A, 185B, 185C, 185D, 185E, 186, 190, 190A, 190B, 190C, 197, 198, 200, 201, 203, 203A, 203B, 204, 221, 225, 226, 227, 228, 231, 177, 178, 179, 180, 181, 187, 208A, 208B, 209, 210, 272
EDN II, 16–27, 34, 44
PRG, 785
Schofield, J, Allen, P, & Taylor, C, 1990 'Medieval buildings and property development in the area of Cheapside', *Trans London Middlesex Archaeol Soc,* 41, 39–238
Shepherd, J, 1986 'The Roman features at Gateway House and Watling House, Watling Street, City of London (1954)', *Trans London Middlesex Archaeol Soc,* 37, 127–44

10–12 Cooper's Row (site of Barber's Warehouse), EC3

GM214

F Cottrill, 1935
NGR: TQ 33580 80840
SMR: 041916, 041976–8

In 1935 F Cottrill made observations of the inner side of the city wall within the bonded warehouse on its W side. These are descriptive only, and do not record any intervention in the fabric.

Site file
See GM44 above for later observations

Cripplegate Buildings (now Roman House), Wood Street, EC2

GM215

A Oswald, 1947
NGR: TQ 32410 81650
SMR: 044394–7

Site file contains a photocopy of both sides of a N–S section across the city ditch at Cripplegate Buildings (ie immediately N of medieval Cripplegate, on the E side). The main strata recorded are of the ditch c 1600; there is also a well of c 1720–60 in section, and the N side of the ditch includes a timber revetment and 'Saxo-Norman floor levels'. These sketches are by A Oswald, and are of a trench dug by Grimes, site code WFG18.

Site file

Guildhall, EC2

GM216

I Noël Hume, 1954–5
NGR: TQ 33180 80680
SMR: 040216

Site file contains photographs of the bomb-damaged cellars on the N side of Guildhall, one interpretation plan and a photographic reproduction of a pencil view by H Hodge, 1882–3, of the site during a previous demolition to make the New Council Chamber of Guildhall. Some medieval features are evident in the photographs, including doors, fragments of windows, and foundation arches.

Some observations were made on site by I Noël Hume: a large brick cesspit containing a quantity of china, porcelain and clay pipes; a pit containing late 1st-/early 2nd-c pottery and a fragment of human cranium; another pit of similar date formed at its base by boards; an 'osier basket' pit (like the wicker-lined early medieval pits) N of the W end of Guildhall; a chalk-lined well containing late 15th- and 16th-c pottery; and a pit-group of bottles of 1660–70.

For other work around Guildhall, see GM77 and GM145 above; for excavation in 1987–9 to the E of Guildhall Yard and beneath the Yard itself, see GAG87 and GUY88 below.

ER numbers 199, 202, 206, 211, 223, 224, 229
EDN II, 34, 39, 46–7, 60–1, 64
Site file
PRG, 711
See also GM77

7–8 (formerly 3–8) King Street, EC2

GM217

G Dunning and G Home,
?1926–7
NGR: TQ 32485 81238
SMR: 040074

Seven or eight Roman occupation levels, none apparently later than the reign of Trajan, were found between 14ft and 18ft below the surface. On the original gravel surface were fragments of pre-Flavian samian, including a stamp of Murranus, coarse pottery and the stumps of bushes. There was evidence of two fires, one above the earliest occupation level and one over the fourth. A small stream apparently flowed ESE in the S part of the site.

Site file
Summary from Merrifield, R, 1965 The Roman city of London, gazetteer 50, where source is given as RCHM, 1928 Roman London, 123 and an article by G Home in Morning Post, 27 January 1927; the site is there numbered only '7 King Street'. Presumably this was the site to which Dunning's notes refer.

GM218

G Dunning, 1929
NGR: TQ 32850 81040
SMR: 040194

67 Lombard Street, Birchin Lane, EC3

Roman levels were found intact below the basement over the greater part of the site, but structures were disappointingly meagre. One wall was found on the E side of the site, parallel to Birchin Lane, the E face 11ft from the modern frontage. It was exposed for a length of about 10ft but only to a height of 2ft 6in.; it was 3ft 9in. wide and built of Kentish rag set in hard yellow mortar. Pottery nearby indicated a 1st-c date for the wall.

Site file
Not in Merrifield, R, 1965 *The Roman city of London*

GM219

I Noël Hume and A Oswald, 1949
NGR: TQ 32532 81244;
32546 81243
SMR: 040670–1 (Roman features), 041473–8 (medieval features)

11 Ironmonger Lane, EC2

Recording was undertaken on this site by both I Noël Hume and A Oswald.

During builders' excavation, a tessellated pavement with a geometrical pattern and traces of three ragstone walls were found. Pottery of the mid-2nd c was found in rammed gravel beneath the pavement. Further W on the site, however, were traces of another tessellated pavement on the same level, and this overlay a pink floor dated by an underlying pit of the first half of the 3rd c. The building is therefore probably of the later 3rd c. Near the SW corner of the site, black silt containing late Roman pottery was found in an underpinning hole, apparently indicating the presence of a stream. A portion of the first pavement was preserved *in situ* in the basement of the new buildings.

Post-Roman: Aligned N–S on the ?boundary was a 'massive' chalk wall at least 2ft wide which had been used as a foundation for later brick walls. At the S, running E–W, was a 20ft length of wall about 4ft wide with pointed foundation arches of chalk. It appeared to turn S at the W end, and beneath it were human burials. In the centre of the site were two parallel chalk walls aligned NE–SW, probably parts of the same building. To the E was a 40ft length of wall about 3ft 3in. wide with a short length of a smaller wall, 1ft 6in. wide, to the W; the date of these was early 14th c. Medieval pits were also recorded. The wall on arched foundations may have been attached to the church of St Martin Pomary.

Strata on this site have been recorded a further two times: during refurbishment of the *in situ* mosaic (BOA83) and during redevelopment in 1995 (MoLAS, site code IRL95); see below for the BOA83 recording.

EDN III, 1; site file
PRG, 1010
Dawe, D, & Oswald, A, 1952 *11 Ironmonger Lane*
Merrifield, R, 1965 *The Roman city of London*, gazetteer 151
Shepherd, J, 1987 'The pre-urban and Roman topography in the King Street and Cheapside areas of the City of London', *Trans London Middlesex Archaeol Soc*, 38, 11–58

GM220

F Cottrill, 1932
NGR: TQ 32530 81225;
32526 81230
SMR: 040217 ('pottery assemblage'); 041491

Ironmonger Lane or St Olave's Court (sewer trench), EC2

In June 1932 a sewer tunnel along St Olave's Court was observed on several visits. The floor of the tunnel was about 16ft below street level. In the N face, some courses of undressed chalk blocks and modern brick above were seen. At the W end, for 2–3ft above the floor, a black deposit, and in it a horizontal layer of white material, 1–2in. thick; from the deposit, probably below the white layer, came part of an amphora neck. In subsequent days three worked stones, perhaps from the church of St Martin Pomary, were found; one may have gone to Guildhall. Roman pottery including samian was also found. In a hole connected with the sewer, dug in the E pavement of Ironmonger Lane, a N–S chalk wall with brick above was observed. This also may have been part of the church or its curtilage.

Site file
PRG, 1024; Librarian's Monthly Report, October 1932

10–12 Little Trinity Lane, EC4

A ragstone wall with courses of tiles, 5ft thick, with its base in London Clay at a depth of 15ft 6in. below the modern surface, was observed running E–W from Huggin Hill across the site for over 36ft. Ten feet to the S of this was a 2ft wall parallel with it, and there were traces of other walls at right angles. The two E–W walls rose almost to the surface where they passed under Huggin Hill, and the larger was pierced with an arched culvert of voussoir tiles. About 40ft to the N was another Roman ragstone wall parallel with these, underlying the S wall of Painter-Stainers' Hall, and over 20ft long. Its W end abutted against a wall built entirely of large tiles set in mortar containing crushed tile. These foundations were at a considerably higher level than the two walls found further S and must have belonged to another building. Merrifield suggested that the S building formed part of the Huggin Hill bath-house, found to the W of the Hill in 1964 (GM240).

Merrifield, R, 1965 *The Roman city of London*, gazetteer 121

**GM221
(=GM321)**

G Dunning, 1929
NGR: TQ 32260 80900
SMR: 040623

Wallside Monkwell Square (formerly 63–64 Wood Street), EC2

A square chalk-walled structure, probably a cesspit, was recorded at the SW corner of this site. It was roughly built, bonded with buff mortar, cut through natural brickearth into gravel, with walls about 1ft 3¹/₂in. wide surviving to a height of 3ft. The structure measured 6ft 6in. E–W and 6ft 10in. N–S. Finds illustrated in the records appear to be of late 13th–early 14th-c date.

PRG, 614

GM222

F Cottrill, 1932
NGR: TQ 32372 81533
SMR: 041255

St Mary le Bow church, Cheapside, EC4

A spiral stair in the NW corner of the 11th-c crypt had been noted in 1934. After War damage, during restoration in 1959, this stair was uncovered. The top of the remaining portion of the stair lay 3ft 6in. below the floor level and Wren's church wall lay centrally across it (ie had disregarded it). The newel posts have two carvings of interlace designs; these are still extant. The site file contains only photographs of the uncovering of the stair and close-ups of the carvings.

See also GM199 above.

EDN V, 39; site file
PRG, 727; *City Press*, 5 October 1934, 13
Schofield, J, 1994 'Saxon and medieval parish churches in the City of London: a review', *Trans London Middlesex Archaeol Soc*, 45, 118–19

GM223

Unknown, 1934; E Rutter and R Merrifield, 1959
NGR: TQ 32390 81140
SMR: 041303

39 St Andrew's Hill, EC4

During rebuilding works parts of a medieval wall aligned N–S, about 4ft wide and of chalk, ragstone and flint with stone facing and pieces of moulded stone were noted. The wall is presumed to be part of Blackfriars, but this site is to the E of the friary precinct, on the site of the King's or Great Wardrobe.

Site file
PRG, 402
Librarian's Monthly Report, October 1935

GM224

F Cottrill, 1935
NGR: TQ 31813 80971
SMR: 041198

GM225

Unknown (probably
F Cottrill), 1937
NGR: TQ 32989 81114
SMR: 044398

53 Cornhill, EC3

This site lay at the W end of Corbet Court. Two pieces of walling were observed. The first was near the E side of the site, near the SE corner. It was of rag rubble with yellow sandy mortar, including chalk and Roman brick, and ran NE–SW. Against the E face and under it was black soil. A height of 1ft 9in. was observed; it was disturbed above this. The top was 13ft 6in. below pavement level. Similar walling appeared in section at right angles to and against the S wall of the site, about 13ft from the SW corner. This may be a W part of the same structure. A few days later a second wall was observed more to the N. These fragments were thought to be of post-Roman date.

Site file

GM226

G Dunning, 1927 and 1930
NGR: TQ 32680 81300
SMR: 040685–92

2 Moorgate (Founders' Court), EC2

W of Founders' Court was found the base of a wall of chalk and flint rubble, about 4ft 3in. thick, running approximately N–S, with a pink cement floor on either side, 13ft 6in. below the modern pavement. A second pink pavement capped the wall 7in. above the first. There were indications of the brick pillars of a hypocaust on the W side of the wall. About the middle of the site the wall appeared to turn to the W, and the line of this return wall was continued to the E by a double row of piles. The foundations of the building had been laid in the black sludge, and other groups of piles were found to the N and W.

At the NE corner of the Court a tessellated pavement was found at a depth of 19ft 8in. It consisted of a border 3ft 6in. wide of red tesserae, with a fragment of the edge of a pattern in smaller black tesserae at the SE corner of the excavation. At the W edge the red border came to a well-defined end, indicating the former presence of a wall running approximately N–S, but inclined slightly more towards the NE than the modern building-line. A deposit described as alluvial, sealed by the floor, contained pottery of the 1st and early 2nd c with burnt animal bones and oyster shells. The pre-Antonine date of the pottery from this layer was confirmed by further finds in 1930. Fragments of the mosaic were preserved in the London Museum (A.30.157).

Merrifield, R, 1965 *The Roman city of London*, gazetteer 156–7
RCHM, 1928 *London III: Roman London*, 130–2

GM227

Unknown, 1952
NGR: TQ 31711 81246
SMR: 044427

London Electricity Board Ludgate main substation (?Seacoal House), Seacoal Lane, EC4

A computer file allocates ER 53 and ER 54 to this site, but there is no other documentation. The notes on the contents of ER groups (on cards in MoL) describe ER 53 as material from a pit, including a buckle, tiles and 15th-c sherds; and ER 54 as material from a second pit containing cockle shell, iron bars and 15th-c sherds.

ER numbers 53, 54

?Haberdashers' Hall, Gresham Street, EC2

GM228

Unknown, 1953

Several finds were recovered 'from a pit of the first 30 years of the 17th century, in a cellar at Haberdashers' Hall, Gresham Street' (GM Accession Register, nos 21340–8); pottery and clay tobacco pipes.

The site of 31–45 Gresham Street (Garrard House), adjacent to the site of the medieval and present Haberdashers' Hall, was excavated by MoLAS in 1996: site code GAH95. It is possible that some features were in the hall grounds.

ER number 59

Brook's Wharf (south end of Stew Lane), Upper Thames Street, EC4

GM229

Unknown, 1953

A computer file allocates ER 59A to this site, but there is no other documentation.

?ER number 59A

Mincing Lane, EC3

GM230

Unknown, ?1955

In EDN II, 86 is a note: 'ER 256. K.40. Mincing Lane' (the words 'Windsor Court' have been crossed out, and they are the title of the following group 257). The previous entry is dated 16 February 1955. There is no other documentation.

ER number 256
EDN II, 86

Windsor Court (RMLEC site WFG3; now gardens south of Barber-Surgeons' Hall, Monkwell Square), EC2

GM231

Unknown, 1955
NGR: TQ 32270 81600

A computer file assigns ER 41 to this site. This is presumably an error, and the number GM231 is not known to have any significance. Professor Grimes was digging on this site in 1955 (site WFG3).

?ER number 41

?7–17 Jewry Street (almost directly opposite Roman Wall House), EC3

GM232

I Noël Hume, 1955
NGR: TQ 33545 81045
SMR: 044329

Workmen dug up animal skulls (not collected), 17th-c sherds and glass.

ER number 362
EDN IV, 27

GM233

E Rutter, 1957
NGR: TQ 33380 80610
(approximately)
SMR: 044428–9

General Steam Navigation Company, Lower Thames Street, EC3

In April 1957 pile-driving on the site of the General Steam Navigation Company in Lower Thames Street 'next to the Tower' produced workmen's finds of a Delft drug jar containing pipes and various sherds from a brick sewer visible in a pile hole in the centre E of the site. Medieval sherds and miscellaneous finds were perhaps from the same hole. The drug jar and one pipe were accessioned as GM 20574 and 20573. A second visit in June 1957 produced a group of knives, a spear and other finds (ER 395).

ER numbers 385, 395
EDN IV, 58, 62, 67

GM234

E Rutter, 1957
NGR: TQ 32420 81480
SMR: 044400

Addle Street / Aldermanbury (?1 Aldermanbury Square), EC2

A group of pottery including a paint pot, of possible 18th-c date, was brought in by Mr J A Buttery of the Corporation Surveyor's Department, from a site noted as 'Addle St/Aldermanbury', which is taken to be 1 Aldermanbury Square. The site was visited and there was then nothing to see, but the foreman handed over a considerable quantity of 17th- and 18th-c pottery found earlier.

ER numbers 387, 388
EDN IV, 61, 63

GM235

N Cook, 1957
NGR: TQ 32660 80710
SMR: 044401–2

Red Bull Yard, All Hallows Lane, Upper Thames Street (?Mondial House), EC4

A trial hole by builders produced a group of pottery, bone and leather fragments which was brought to GM. The hole in 'All Hallows Lane' was beneath the roadway, and exposed a 'vaulted ?cellar', but water filled and obscured the hole.

ER number 403
EDN IV, 76–7

GM236

Unknown, 1960
NGR: TQ 32400 81502
SMR: 044430

Philip Lane (?Royex House, Aldermanbury Square), EC2

A small group of 13th- and 14th-c pottery was recovered from a builder's trench immediately W of Philip Lane (W of Brewers' Hall) and S of Route 11 (now London Wall).

ER number 609

Bush Lane (sewer at south end), EC4

GM237

P Marsden, 1964
NGR: TQ 32624 80786
SMR: 040940

Several Roman walls of ragstone with double and triple courses of bonding-tiles were encountered during tunnelling for a sewer. They mostly stood more than 6ft 6in. high, and the only foundation reached consisted of rows of timber piles. From N to S, the remains comprised: (i) three sides of a room in which was a brick construction like a drain; (ii) two walls with a facing of *opus signinum*, apparently curving and possibly part of an apse; (iii) several more walls, one of which had a construction of bricks and cement resembling a hypocaust against it. No dating material was found.

ER numbers 867, 895, 896
Marsden, P, 1975 'The excavation of a Roman palace site in London, 1961–1972', *Trans London Middlesex Archaeol Soc*, 26, 47–9
Merrifield, R, 1965 *The Roman city of London*, gazetteer 277

Fleet Lane (corner with Seacoal Lane), EC4

GM238

I Noël Hume, 1955
NGR: TQ 31715 81300
SMR: 044403

A lead cylinder, completely sealed, was found in a brick pier at the corner of Fleet Lane and Seacoal Lane about 4ft below present ground level by workmen. It contained a glass tube with a heavy stopper, sealed by wax and intact. The contents of this tube or bottle were a sixpence of 1874; a charter recording the laying of the foundation stone for Messrs Cattell, Petter & Galpin on 1 January 1874; a Literary Year Book Catalogue and Illustrated Catalogue of the above firm for 1874; copies of the *Echo* newspaper for 1 January and 2 January 1874; and of *The Daily News* for 1 January 1874.

ER number 363
EDN IV, 28 (sketch of cylinder and description of contents)

Huggin Hill (east side, bath-house site II), EC4

GM239

P Marsden, 1969
NGR: TQ 32276 80875
SMR: 041387

The SMR entry 041387, which cites GM239, is for a brick cesspit of uncertain dimensions with 17th-c pottery in its lower fills and a Victorian coin in the upper fill. This cesspit was cut into the E caldarium of the Roman baths, and the site address is given as 'Fur Trade House, Huggin Hill East Corn[er]'. This code (GM239) should therefore be used for this cesspit only, not for any feature from the bath-house below (see GM240). Features of the bath-house were found on both sites (both sides of Huggin Hill), but it is suggested here that records of the bath-house be kept together under GM240.

ER number 1330
EDN XI, 37
PRG, 824

Huggin Hill (Roman bath-house), EC4

GM240

P Marsden, 1964 and 1969
NGR: TQ 32260 80900
SMR: 040623

In 1964 it was confirmed that a large Roman bath-house complex lay on both sides of Huggin Hill at its S end; in that year the apsidal wall of a caldarium and other features were uncovered W of the lane (Fig 19). Further observations followed during construction work in 1969.

The baths were initially constructed not earlier than the Flavian period, and were extended to the E after the end of the 1st c. At a date possibly in the latter half of the 2nd c the baths were systematically demolished. Thereafter at least two Roman buildings were constructed on the site; no satisfactory dating evidence for them was recovered (Marsden 1976).

In 1987–9 the building erected on the site W of Huggin Hill in 1969 was itself the site of further excavations by the DUA (site code DMT88, below). Extensive evidence of the bath-house was recovered. The intended publication of the later and wider DMT88 excavations will include a review of the earlier discoveries.

Post-Roman: the site is probably that known as *Hwaetmundes Stan* in the late 9th c; a Roman stone building (so far unidentified archaeologically) may have been still standing (Dyson 1978).

A medieval cellar or undercroft about 19ft wide was found immediately W of and alongside Huggin Hill in 1964. Its W wall was 1ft 9in. wide, and constructed of ragstone and broken Roman tiles presumably from the baths beneath. W of it was a medieval well

Fig 19 GM240: view of the Roman bath-house site with S to the top. The heated Room 30 is in the middle.

lined with squared chalk blocks and rubble, 2ft 10in. in diameter internally, cut through the N wall of the Roman baths. Between the cellar and the well were two other walls of ragstone and thin medieval tiles, about 1ft 6in. wide.

ER numbers 1372, 1373, 1374, 1375, 1376, 1377, 1378, 1379, 1380, 1381, 1382, 1383, 1384, 1385, 1386, 1387, 1388, 1389, 1390, 1391, 1392, 1393, 1394, 1395, 1396, 1397, 1398, 1399, 1400, 1401, 1402, 1403, 1404, 1405, 1406, 1407, 1408, 1409, 1410, 1411, 1412, 1413, 1414, 1415, 1416, 1417, 1418, 1419, 1420, 1421, 1422, 1423, 1424, 1425, 1426
EDN IX, 45–53, 55–6, 68–80; XI, 50–2 (brief context notes for ER groups 1372 to 1433); site file
PRG, 819
Dyson, T, 1978 'Two Saxon land grants for Queenhithe', in Bird, J, Chapman, H, & Clark, J (eds), *Collectanea Londiniensia,* London Middlesex Archaeol Soc Spec Pap 2, 200–15
Marsden, P, 1976 'Two Roman public baths in London', *Trans London Middlesex Archaeol Soc,* 27, 1–30

GM241

Unknown, 1964
NGR: TQ 33207 81185

Leadenhall Street / St Mary Axe (Commercial Union and P&O site), EC3

No records traceable.

GM242

Unknown, 1949
NGR: TQ 33460 81270
SMR: 041948

Site of Bastion 7, Duke's Place, EC3

Engravings of mid-18th-c date show a polygonal, or possibly rectangular, tower, probably of stone, built on top of a semicircular bastion with four regularly spaced triple bonding-courses of tile. This may be a partly schematic representation of the Roman and medieval fabric of the bastion; tile courses were recorded by Woodward in 1711 when the total height of the bastion was 26ft.

A small portion of the N side of the bastion was seen during building excavations on the site of 23–27 Houndsditch (S end, near Duke's Place) in 1949. It contained a reused piece of worked limestone, probably a portion of a coping stone. The rest of the bastion had evidently been removed by this date.

PRG, 1316
Merrifield, R, 1965 *The Roman city of London,* gazetteer B7
RCHM, 1928 *London III: Roman London,* 100, pl 28

Bartholomew Lane, EC2

GM243

G Dunning, 1932
NGR: TQ 3280 8123
SMR: 044404–5

The site file contains a single sheet of notes about the finding of a cannon in a hole at the SE corner of the site, with a sketch drawing of the cannon; and a separate drawing of what appears to be a Roman altar, 2ft 6in. high, but otherwise not described. The location of this site in Bartholomew Lane is uncertain.

Site file

Bartholomew Close, Little Britain, EC1

GM244

F Cottrill, 1934

No records traceable.

St Mary Aldermanbury church, Aldermanbury, EC2

GM245

Unknown, 1967–8
NGR: TQ 32412 81443
SMR: 04131401–3

The RMLEC excavations on this site in April 1968 (site WFG22A) were visited and photographs taken; in addition some recording of Wren-period and later features took place.

A sketchplan of brick vaults in the Wren church is in EDN. Nineteenth-c coffin plates were recorded from vaults at the NE corner of the church, one a short distance to the W in the N aisle, in the S aisle near the SE corner of the church, and from the Hog family vault at the W end of the nave abutting the tower. The sketchplan includes outlines of a burial pit under the nave containing '?Wren's excess bones from the rebuilding', a charnel house at the SE corner of the church, and an unopened vault running N–S from the SW corner of the church (ie outside the S wall).

Three photographs of the RMLEC excavations on the site include one of the 'pre-1666 Fire floor tiles of church *in situ* in chancel'.

EDN XI, 13–14
Schofield, J, 1994 'Saxon and medieval parish churches in the City of London: a review', *Trans London Middlesex Archaeol Soc*, 45, 117

28–30 Cornhill, EC3

GM246

F Cottrill, 1934

No records traceable.

Roman Wall House, Crutched Friars, EC3

GM247

Unknown, ?1905
NGR: TQ 33570 81005
SMR: 041964

The GM photograph archive includes seven photographs of the preserved section of Roman city wall, presumably from its exposure on the site in 1905.

RCHM, 1928 *London III: Roman London*, 85

GM248

G Dunning, 1930
NGR: TQ 32885 80725
SMR: 041012–14

King William Street / Fish Street Hill (Regis House), EC3

Timber structures, believed to be part of a wharf, and similar to those found on both sides of Miles Lane a short distance to the W, were exposed in pits dug down to the gravel. There were massive oak baulks 18in. square, some 20ft long, running E–W. In some cases other timbers joined with these at right angles. To the S were camp-sheathing and piles. There was a mass of oyster shells filling the spaces between the timbers, and this contained samian of a date later than AD100. Spread over the S part of the site was a layer about 8ft thick of burnt debris containing pottery. It appeared to be a dump, overlying the timbers, from a wide area occupied by wattle and daub huts, destroyed in the great fire of AD120–30.

Two walls, 2ft thick and 20ft apart, built of solid Roman brick with chalk foundations were found on the landward side of the timber embankment. They may have been part of a warehouse or shed adjoining the embankment. Between the walls was found a moulded column base, not *in situ*.

In 1994 the building erected in 1929, Regis House, was demolished. For further excavations on the site, see MoLAS archive, site KWS94.

J Roman Stud, 19, 1929, 200; 21, 1931, 239
Merrifield, R, 1965 *The Roman city of London,* gazetteer 308–9

GM249

F Cottrill, 1935

King William Street (junction with Cannon Street opposite nos 116–126), EC4

No records traceable.

GM250

1898; P Marsden, 1967
NGR: TQ 33465 81146
SMR: 04169201004

40 Mitre Street, EC3

During demolition work in 1898, a medieval pointed arch was discovered on the S side of Mitre Street, which bisects the length of the site of the church within Holy Trinity Priory Aldgate. The arch was re-exposed in 1967 and noted by Marsden. The arch formed part of the S wall of a house fronting onto Mitre Street. The site was excavated in 1984 (LEA84, see below) and the arch was restored during redevelopment; it is now in the foyer of the building on the site.

PRG, 1312; *Daily Graphic,* 13 January 1898, 13
Marsden, P, 1969 'Archaeological finds in the City of London, 1966–8', *Trans London Middlesex Archaeol Soc,* 22.2, 20
Schofield, J, & Lea, R, in prep. *Holy Trinity Priory Aldgate*

GM251

P Marsden, 1969
NGR: TQ 31790 81155
SMR: 040430

37 Ludgate Hill, EC4

Cutting into brickearth were several Roman pits and a foundation. This was of flints, freshly mined from chalk, set in sticky puddled clay. It was either the foundation of the Roman city wall or part of the S tower of the Roman gate of Ludgate (fragments of edges observed suggested it was the SE part). No continuation of the foundation was seen, reinforcing the suggestion that it was part of the gate and not the wall.

The E boundary of the site included a ragstone wall in yellow mortar which extended below the basement floor and up to 4m above the ground floor, a height of 7m. About halfway along the boundary wall was seen, at basement level, the edge of a relieving arch.

This is suggested to be the E wall of the S tower of the rebuilt Ludgate of 1586 (Marsden 1970); or the E wall of the prison attached to Ludgate in 1435 (C Harding in PRG, 427). The prison and gate were surveyed by Leybourn in 1676 (CLRO, Leybourn's Survey); presumably the prison block was rebuilt after the Fire, but the E wall could be pre-Fire. The wall had also been described by Henry Hodge in 1889, during building works (drawings in GL, 373/LUD).

PRG, 427
Marsden, P, 1970 'Archaeological finds in the City of London, 1966–9', *Trans London Middlesex Archaeol Soc,* 22.3, 8–9

3–6 Lothbury, EC2

In the Royal Bank of Canada on the site of no. 6 in 1965, were preserved two fragments of tessellated pavement which had been found on the site in 1931–2 *(sic)*. The bank also possesses some iron tools and a bronze ligula, which, from their condition, came from the flood silt which lay beneath a similar pavement on the adjacent site in Founders' Court.

Merrifield, R, 1965 *The Roman city of London,* gazetteer 160

GM252

G Dunning, 1930
NGR: TQ 32692 81283
SMR: 040696

London Wall (opposite nos 108–115), EC2

A tunnel for telephone cables was cut through the Roman wall which was exposed for a length of more than 105ft immediately E of the junction of London Wall and Moorgate. It was of Kentish ragstone in yellowish-white mortar, faced with squared stones, and with three courses of red bonding-tiles passing right through the core. There was a single course of tiles at 4ft below street level, a double course at 6ft 6in. and a triple course at 10ft. The plinth and foundations were not uncovered.

Site file
Merrifield, R, 1965 *The Roman city of London,* gazetteer W34

GM253

G Dunning, 1930
NGR: TQ 32750 81540
SMR: 044406

Blossoms Inn Yard, EC2

In 1930 much Roman pottery was found on the site, ranging in date from the Claudian period to the 4th c, but no structures were detected. The site file also contains a one-page typewritten list of objects returned to the site owners, from Roman to 16th c in date. Excavations on the same site by Professor Grimes in 1955 revealed traces of Roman buildings and internal floors (site WFG41).

The site file contains two packets of small black and white photographs, which are of a Roman mosaic fragment, a wooden ?box or base of a timber-lined well and a half-sectioned chalk-lined well, both features probably recorded on this site in 1956 (GM20). One fragment of mosaic has a guilloche pattern and may be that uncovered on the Sun Alliance site S of Blossoms Inn in 1954. The packets are marked 'Blossoms Inn extension'.

An evaluation by MoLAS in 1995 produced some further observations: site code BLO95.

Grimes, W F, 1968 *The excavation of Roman and medieval London,* 135–7
Merrifield, R, 1965 *The Roman city of London,* gazetteer 44

GM254

G Dunning, 1930
NGR: TQ 32425 81236
SMR: 044407

GM255

G Dunning, 1933
NGR: TQ 32470 80950
SMR: 040134

69–73 Cannon Street, EC4

In the centre of the site a section comprising seven superimposed layers of Roman date was recorded. Natural gravel was overlaid by occupation levels and a red layer with burnt samian pottery in it.

Wilmott, T, 1991 *Excavations in the Middle Walbrook Valley, City of London, 1927–1960*, London Middlesex Archaeol Soc Spec Pap 13, 31

GM256

W F Grimes, 1952–4
NGR: TQ 32567 80995
SMR: 040871

Temple of Mithras, Walbrook, EC4

During excavations by Professor W F Grimes (site WFG44/45), a basilican temple was found. It had a rounded apse at the W end, a central nave and two side aisles separated from the nave by sleeper walls, bearing settings for seven columns on either side. At the W end within the apse was a raised sanctuary, and at the E end was a narthex with a double door; the narthex could not be excavated as it lay near and under Walbrook street. A succession of floors of beaten earth and gravel had been laid because of flooding from the adjacent Walbrook. The last but one of these, dated by coin evidence to the reign of Constantine, overlay carefully buried marble sculptures of Mithras and other deities. The temple was built, probably as part of an adjacent private house, c AD240–50. It was modified several times before being converted for use by the followers of another pagan cult, perhaps Bacchus, during the first decades of the 4th c; and fell into disuse towards the end of the 4th c.

Site file contains photographs of the sculptures (including one apparently on site), press cuttings, correspondence and a typed draft of a report on the smallfinds from the Grimes excavation called Cutting C (J Bird, not dated).

Grimes, W F, 1968 *The excavation of Roman and medieval London*, 92–117
Merrifield, R, 1965 *The Roman city of London*, gazetteer 248
Shepherd, J, 1998a *The temple of Mithras in London: excavations by W F Grimes and A Williams at the Walbrook*

GM257

F Cottrill, 1933–4
NGR: TQ 32720 81240
SMR: 040705–11

Bank of England, Princes Street, EC2

When development of the Bank of England began in 1926, the Society of Antiquaries began a rota system for site watching. Several archaeologists were involved: J P Bushe-Fox, A G K Hayter, P Norman, O F Parker, F Reader, Q Waddington, R E M and Mrs T V Wheeler. Their notes, and articles written at the time by G Dunning who conducted recording in 1929, have been brought together by Wilmott (1991).

This entry also covers several excavations on the site in 1933–4, mostly if not all conducted by Frank Cottrill. The parts are distinguished here by their numbers in Merrifield's gazetteer. For some of the discoveries and finds from 1926, see also RCHM 1928, 21–3 (Iron Age pedestal urns), 106–7 (structures).

Excavations revealed the stream-bed of the Walbrook running through the site NE–SW. Traces of piling were recorded lying in wet mud, with Roman pots; and two boards standing 4–5ft apart with their tops 15ft below floor level (168).

An oak waterpipe was found in the NE part of the site, south of the E entrance on Lothbury, lying approximately NE–SW (170).

A square tessellated pavement with a circular round panel, borders in meander and guilloche, and leaf ornaments in the spandrels, was found in 1933 at a depth of 20ft or more below modern street level. Pottery beneath it was of the early 2nd c, and the pavement is therefore of this date or later. About 60ft to the S, and 8ft higher, was another paved area with plain tesserae only. In 1934 a second patterned mosaic was found to the SE of the first, also at a depth of 20ft or so. The decorated portion is 4ft 6in. square, with floral ornaments in squares and a guilloche border, surrounded by plain red tesserae. It also overlay pottery of the early 2nd c. Both mosaics have been restored, and the first, larger pavement is now preserved in the basement of the bank, while the second is set in the floor of the bank's Cupola Museum (171). Wilmott (1991, 51–6) dates the second mosaic to the Antonine period (ibid, 146). To the S and E of the tessellated pavements were a number of Roman wells (172).

Merrifield, R, 1965 *The Roman city of London,* gazetteer 168, 170–2

Wilmott, T, 1991 *Excavations in the middle Walbrook Valley, City of London, 1927–1960,* London Middlesex Archaeol Soc Spec Pap 13, 51–6, 146

'Temple House', Queen Victoria Street, EC4

GM258 (probably= GM31)

E Harris, 1959

This site is probably the same as that usually known as Temple Court; see GM31 above.

Noble Street (west side), EC2

GM259

J Clark, 1972
NGR: TQ 32237 81536
SMR: 044408

A stretch of brick wall on the line of the city wall between Plaisterers' Hall and Noble Street was demolished to a level four courses above the visible Roman stonework on the E side, to open the view from the E window of the new hall (which is at basement level). Professor Grimes and J Clark (GM) supervised the work. The city wall was double. The E wall contained a great deal of reused stone in its lowest 1.5m; one tall narrow fragment of the original medieval wall (1.6m x 0.6m and 1.3m thick) survived *in situ* where the remains of an E–W brick wall met the N–S wall, but underpinned by brickwork. This could not be preserved and was demolished. It had a face of roughly squared and coursed Kentish ragstone, the core of random rubble, with a number of chalk blocks in the interior.

EDN XI, 47

GPO site (Mondial House), Upper Thames Street, EC4

GM260

P Marsden, 1969
NGR: TQ 32660 80710

Site file contains an engineer's site plan, and a plan with twelve borehole logs of the site. There are no records of any archaeological work here in 1969. For work possibly on this site earlier, in 1957, see GM235 above.

GM261

G Dunning, 1931
NGR: TQ 32800 80749
SMR: 044409

129–130 Upper Thames Street, EC4

Site file contains sketches and rough notes, not brought together; apparently observations of piles, which fits with the Roman topography known in the area of the site.

See Merrifield, R, 1965 *The Roman city of London,* gazetteer 306, which is the site to the N in Miles Lane, observed 1921 by F Lambert (but not in the GM site series as there are no records) and excavated again in 1979 as ILA79 (see below).

GM262

E Underwood, 1932
NGR: TQ 32388 81124
SMR: 041273

St Mary le Bow church, Cheapside, EC2

Surveying by E Underwood for GM in 1932 in the crypt of St Mary le Bow revealed, in the SE corner, a 'substantial' wall running along the S wall of the Wren church and S of the line of the Norman church (which stops short of the S wall as rebuilt by Wren; compare the plans of crypt and present church). The wall was 3ft 6in. wide and turned to the S 4ft 6in. W of the SE corner of the church. The wall was about 14ft high with its top about 2ft below pavement level. Its recorded length was 16ft. Underwood's coloured elevation, plan and sections are on a sheet in the site file. The structure appears to be the corner of a medieval or at least pre-Fire building adjacent to the church at its SE corner, with one wall running S along Bow Lane.

Librarian's Monthly Report, March 1932
PRG, 703
Schofield, J, 1994 'Saxon and medieval parish churches in the City of London: a review', *Trans London Middlesex Archaeol Soc,* 45, 118–19

GM263

Unknown, 1960s or 1970s
NGR: TQ 32650 81025
SMR: 041403

St Stephen Walbrook church, Walbrook, EC4

Site file contains two drawings on drawing film of what appear to be the sides of trial holes in the church: 'inside profile of church wall directly south of pillar' and 'foundations beneath 3rd columns (S wall), looking north'; and a plan of the church showing positions of three boreholes. This is undated but refers to the church architect of the 1960s and 1970s, Stephen Potter.

GM264

Unknown, 1947
NGR: TQ 32262 81582
SMR: 040476

Bastion 14, Barber-Surgeons' Hall Gardens (150 London Wall), EC2

The site of Bastion 14, next to the Museum, was excavated by Grimes in 1947 (sites WFG3–4) and is now preserved. Site file contains two photographs of Bastion 14, and a dyeline plan of the intended setting, post-War.

Grimes, W F, 1968 *The excavation of Roman and medieval London,* 64–5, 68–71

General note: there are intermittent gaps in the numbering of GM sites from 265 to 304 inclusive. These gaps arose during the compilation of the site records in 1980–4, and have no significance. The process of allocation of a site number to previously uncatalogued site records was continued by the present editor, starting at GM305.

Daily News site, 22 Bouverie Street, EC4

GM266

Q Waddington, 1924
NGR: TQ 31400 81000
SMR: 044410

The site, bounded by Bouverie Street, Tudor Street, Magpie Alley (to the N) and Glasshouse Alley (to the E), lay on the site of the gardens of the Carmelite Whitefriars. Sixteenth-c stoneware, a candlestick, and 17th- and 18th-c glass and pottery were recovered. During post-War redevelopment the two alleys have disappeared, and the site now forms part of 16–22 Bouverie Street.

EN 1, 5 (contains press cuttings including two photographs from the *Daily News*, 13 November 1924)

1–6 Lime Street (Lloyd's), EC3

GM268

Q Waddington, 1925
NGR: TQ 33130 81070
SMR: 040805

Clearance of this large site for the new Lloyd's building left a flat surface 18ft below street level. Excavations below this depth revealed, it seemed, that the previous buildings on the site had removed much of the archaeological evidence. A Roman chamber was then discovered in the NW part of the site with its floor at a depth of 19ft 6in. below the level of Leadenhall Street. A line of rubble, Roman pottery and tiles was noted at a depth of 17ft in the face of the W side of the excavation. This could be traced for many yards, and seemed to be the remains of a Roman pathway. On the E side of the site, against Lime Street, a wide trench had been dug down to a depth of 40ft, and 'a large bone of some antediluvian monster has been found in the blue clay' (EN 1, 8).

This site was excavated again in 1978, within the standing building, prior to the construction of the present Lloyd's building: see LLO78 below.

EN 1, 8
Merrifield, R, 1965 *The Roman city of London,* gazetteer 224
RCHM, 1928 *London III: Roman London,* 128

42 Lombard Street, EC4

GM276

Q Waddington and
W Martin, 1925
NGR: TQ 32970 80981
SMR: 041397

Building works monitored here revealed a medieval stone well on the E side of the site, the Gracechurch Street frontage, with an internal diameter of about 3ft 6in

EN 1, 22
PRG, 905
Trans London Middlesex Archaeol Soc, v, 1925, opp p322

50 Fleet Street (rear) (Serjeants' Inn), EC4

GM280

Unknown, c 1950
NGR: TQ 31328 81125
SMR: 041182

Building works revealed an E–W wall foundation about five courses high, constructed of ragstone and reused Roman building material. The foundation trench cut natural gravels and had been lined with clay, fragments of broken tile and *opus signinum.*

PRG, 107

GM287

Q Waddington, 1924
NGR: TQ 32220 80870
SMR: 040613

205 Upper Thames Street / Lambeth Hill, EC4

Sewer works revealed two parallel E–W rag walls. The S wall has been equated with the 'river wall' running along Knightrider Street in 1841. The walls were 15ft apart and about 14ft below the surface. The N wall was 8ft thick and the other 5ft thick, battered on both sides and possibly rendered with clay.

EN I, 3.1–3.3; *Times,* 18 June 1925
Merrifield, R, 1965 *The Roman city of London,* gazetteer 115

GM288

Unknown, 1926
NGR: TQ 33313 81387
SMR: 041935

58–60 Houndsditch / Camomile Street, EC3

Part of the city wall forming the rear (S) of 58–60 Houndsditch and dividing it from the graveyard of St Martin Outwich was recorded by P Norman and F W Reader in 1905, again in 1926, and in 1989 by the DUA (site code HSO89). In 1926 the bottom of the plinth was seen 8ft 4in. below street level. The fragment of wall stood in 1905 to a height of 14ft 6in. above the base of the plinth. The site records for 1926 have not been located.

Merrifield, R, 1965 *The Roman city of London,* gazetteer W25
Norman, P, & Reader, F, 1906 'Recent discoveries in connexion with Roman London', *Archaeologia,* 60, 187

GM292

Q Waddington, 1924–5
NGR: TQ 33443 81200
SMR: 04169201009

77 Leadenhall Street, EC3

A deposit of lumps of chalk, which probably formed the foundation of some part of the monastic buildings of Holy Trinity Priory Aldgate, was found in a small excavation in the basement at about 14ft below street level. For observations on this site in 1968, see GM93 above.

EN I, 8
PRG, 1352
RCHM, 1928 *London III: Roman London,* 128
Schofield, J, & Lea, R, in prep. *Holy Trinity Priory Aldgate*

GM293

Unknown, 1922
NGR: TQ 33030 81100
SMR: 040793

Gracechurch Street (east of St Peter Cornhill church), EC3

During excavations for telephone wires Roman walls were found under the roadway opposite the N portion of St Peter Cornhill church.

Merrifield, R, 1965 *The Roman city of London,* gazetteer 217

Gracechurch Street (shaft), EC3

GM294

P Marsden, 1978
NGR: TQ 32990 80995
SMR: 044431

A shaft on the E side of Gracechurch Street and 8m S of Ship Tavern Passage was monitored. There are no further details available. See also 'Gracechurch Street tunnel' (GST77 below), supervised by P Marsden at this time.

EDN XI, 71

54–58 Lombard Street (Barclay's Bank), EC3

**GM295
(=GM100)**

P Marsden, 1960–1

This is the same site as GM100, and the number GM295 should be discontinued.

Lombard Street (south of All Hallows Lombard Street church), EC3

**GM296
(=GM102)**

F Cottrill, 1933

This seems to be the same as GM102, and the number GM296 should be discontinued.

22 Lime Street, 168–170 Fenchurch Street (Barclay's Bank) (site of St Dionis Backchurch church), EC3

GM297

B Philp, 1960–9

During 1968–9 both P Marsden and B Philp recorded deposits on this site, at the SE corner of successive Roman fora. The site code GM297 should be used for the records of B Philp's observations. The chief features were traces of a gravel metalling, perhaps an E–W street, overlaid by burnt debris, probably from the Boudican fire of AD60–1. Subsequently the E wing of the second forum was built across the site and there was evidence for at least three or four superimposed floors in its outer portico (from the summary in Marsden 1987).

The site records and finds are in MoL.

Marsden, P, 1987 *The Roman forum site in London: discoveries before 1985,* 90–2
Philp, B, 1977 'The forum of Roman London: excavations of 1968–9', *Britannia,* 8, 1–64

5–8 Birchin Lane, EC3

GM298

F Cottrill, 1935
NGR: TQ 32880 81070

No records traceable.

25–29 Camomile Street, EC3

**GM299
(=GM28)**

E Rutter, 1958

This is a duplicate entry for GM28, and should be discontinued.

**GM301
(=GM19)**

P Marsden, 1970

Blackfriars Riverside Wall, Wreck 3, EC4

This is a duplicate entry for GM19, and should be discontinued.

**GM302
(=GM181)**

P Marsden, 1970

Blackfriars Riverside Wall, Wreck 2, EC4

This is a duplicate entry for GM181, and should be discontinued.

GM303

H S Gordon, 1921
NGR: TQ 31320 81340
SMR: 044703–6

Fetter Lane (adjoining Neville's Court), now 15–17 New Fetter Lane, EC1

A set of annotated black and white photographs indicate that the site, bordered on its S side by the 'Moravian Church', contained between 11ft and 12ft 6in. of humic deposits, the skeleton of a horse about 5ft down and a brick cellar. Finds included Roman coins, pottery and glass; oyster shells were also seen.

Neville's Court, before the last War, was in the area of 15–17 New Fetter Lane, on the E side of the Lane opposite the Public Record Office. The first OS map of 1875 shows the site of the Moravian church.

GM305

J Haslam, 1972
NGR: TQ 32147 81536
SMR 041242–5

Aldersgate Street / London Wall (Museum of London rotunda), EC2

In the excavation for what is now the rotunda forming the roundabout at the junction of Aldersgate Street and London Wall (and part of the site of the MoL), J Haslam noted a section across Roman and post-Roman Aldersgate, immediately N of the Roman and medieval gate; and medieval buildings on both sides of the road (Fig 20).

ER numbers 1360, 1361, 1362, 1363, 1364, 1365, 1366, 1367, 1368, 1369, 1370; 1371 is a group of clay pipes and early 19th-c jugs from a circular well on the site, given in by workmen (EDN XI, 49).

PRG, 601

Haslam, J, 1973 'The excavation of a section across Aldersgate Street, City of London, 1972', *Trans London Middlesex Archaeol Soc*, 24, 74–84

Fig 20 GM305: section across the Roman and medieval roads N of Aldersgate, with medieval buildings also in section on the right; looking N.

Carter Lane, EC4

GM306

Unknown, pre-1939

In the GM photographic archive are three photographs of the base of a medieval double-column pillar.

GM photos: 603–30, 686–30 to 687–30

St Paul's Cathedral, north of north portico, EC4

GM307

P Marsden, 1970
NGR: TQ 32020 81180
SMR: 044411

A medieval well was recorded N of the N portico of the Cathedral. This was capped and left untouched by the architect at the request of P Marsden, and is still to be seen inside the W gate to the churchyard on the N of the Cathedral.

ER number 1685
EDN XI, note in unnumbered pages towards rear

Cripplegate and city wall nearby, EC2

GM308

Unknown, 1947–66

In the GM photographic archive are 32 photographs of trenches near Cripplegate and of the wall and bastions nearby, at various times in the period 1947–66. They possibly include pictures of the RMLEC excavations.

Cross Lane (south of Cannon Street), EC4

GM309

Unknown, 1945

In the GM photographic archive is one photograph 'showing post-medieval cellars' on a cleared basement site.

Falcon Street, EC2

GM310

Unknown, 1957

In the GM photographic archive are photographs of the RMLEC excavation (WFG5) at Falcon Street in 1957.

GM311

P Marsden, 1964
NGR: TQ 33080 80905
SMR: 041065, 044432

20–23 Fenchurch Street, EC3

Excavations on this site revealed two sections. Section 'B' was exposed beneath the old cellar floor 3ft 3in. S of the old N frontage. It showed 5ft of hard dirty gravel metalling through the middle of which was a horizontal layer of yellow clay containing a few scattered lumps of burnt clay, between 2in. and 3in. thick. This gravel is on the line of the Roman road running E–W beneath Fenchurch Street. The road probably lay over natural, 17ft 4in. below street level. A fragment of Roman wall which seemed to be the E face of a N–S wall was found near the E boundary of the site, 51ft 10in. S of the corner, 10ft 1in. inside the Rood Lane boundary.

EDN IX, 18–19; no finds

GM312

Unknown, pre-1927

Fenchurch Street, EC3

In the GM photographic archive are two photographs of 'an aurochs bone split to obtain marrow'. The bone has a 1927 accession number, hard to read.

GM photos: 109–30, 110–30

GM313

Unknown, 1896

Fetter Lane, EC4

In the GM photographic archive are two photographs of two complete Roman pots, 'found 1896, photographed 1930'.

GM photos: 111–30, 112–30

GM314

Unknown, 1955

Cannon Street (*Financial Times* site), EC4

In the GM photographic archive are 17 photographs of the site under excavation by Professor Grimes (site WFG35).

GM photos: 2610–50 to 2626–50

GM315

Unknown, 1920
NGR: TQ 32900 81680
SMR: 044412

12–16 Finsbury Circus, EC2

In the GM photographic archive is a photograph of two Roman pots. The annotated negative envelope reads 'finds in the gravel'. In the GM Accession Register are many Roman and medieval objects recovered from works at this address in 1920, as well as a Neolithic stone axe (GM acc nos 10560–7, 10926–59).

The building now numbered 12–15 Riverplate House was the site of an excavation within the standing building in 1987: see RIV87 below.

GM photo: 132–30

Fore Street, EC2

GM316

Unknown, 1954

In the GM photographic archive are two photographs of a section through the 17th-c city ditch. This may be the excavation by Grimes, WFG17.

GM photos: 443–50, 444–50

'Fort' and 'Fort West Gate' excavations, Cripplegate, EC2

GM317

Unknown, c 1955

In the GM photographic archive are several photographs showing details of the excavation by Professor Grimes of the W gate of the Cripplegate fort, and other excavations in the Cripplegate fort area (the individual sites not located).

'GPO' (presumably east side of St Martin's le Grand), EC2

GM318

F Lambert, 1913–14; and observations of 1925
NGR: TQ 32160 81310
SMR: 044413

In 1913–14 contractors dug out, to basement level, an immense area between St Martin's le Grand, Foster Lane, Gresham Street and Cheapside. P Norman was successful in obtaining funds for archaeological recording from the Goldsmiths' Company and from the Court of Common Council of the Corporation, and F Lambert recorded the contents of many Roman pits dug into the gravel (Fig 21), a well and traces of a footpath. Traces of a 'wattle-and-daub house' were also found in the SW of the site.

In the GM photographic archive are three photographs of the site.

In 1925, in the centre of the E of the site, a group of Roman rubbish pits was observed; one produced a base of an Iron Age pedestal urn (RCHM 1928, 21, fig 2 no. 1); another two base fragments came from the SE corner of the same site (ibid, fig 2 no. 2).

Fig 21 GM318: view of the 'GPO' site from the NW. To the left is Goldsmiths' Hall in Foster Lane.

GM photos: 567–30, 623–30, 631–30
Merrifield, R, 1965 The Roman city of London, 8, gazetteer 35
RCHM, 1928 London III: Roman London, 21

Leadenhall Street, EC3

GM319

Unknown

In the GM photographic archive are photographs of a complete Roman beaker and a ?lamp with the head of Selena or Iris.

GM photos: 119–30, 120–30

GM320

Unknown, 1945–7

Lime Street, EC3

In the GM photographic archive are three photographs, one of a site, two of Roman lamps.

GM photos: 512–30, 1–40, 54–40

GM321 (=GM221)

Unknown (?G Dunning), 1929–30
NGR: TQ 32300 80900
SMR: 04062301

10–12 Little Trinity Lane, EC4

In the GM photographic archive are four photographs showing Roman strata and walls. These are presumably part of the observations on the site by Gerald Dunning (see GM221 above). This duplication of numbers was noticed only in a late stage of compiling this volume, and the separate SMR numbers have been retained. The GM321 number should not be used.

GM photos: 555–30, 575–30, 586–30, 606–30

GM322

Unknown
NGR: TQ 31500 82750
SMR: 044414

6 Lloyd's Row, St John's Street, EC1

In the GM photographic archive is one photograph showing a cylindrical structure of flints resembling a well, possibly medieval, apparently within a small space delimited by brick walls.

GM photo: 401–30

GM323

Unknown, probably post-War
NGR: TQ 32505 81180
SMR: 044415

Mercers' Hall, Cheapside, EC2

In the GM photographic archive are photographs of a Flemish 16th-c statue of the dead Christ, thought to have been originally in the pre-Fire Mercers' chapel. There are also said to be some finds from this site, but no records have been located for this *Guide*.

GM photos: 1017–50 to 1022–50, 2417–50 to 2421–50

GM324

Unknown, 1926–7

Miles Lane, EC4

In the GM photographic archive are three photographs of a piece of daub with wattle impressions, and a stoneware pot (?18th c) found at the same time, presented or shown to GM in 1930.

GM photos: 107–30, 493–30, 43–40

Nicholas Lane, EC4

In the GM photographic archive is a photograph of a fragment of a decorated samian bowl 'from the Ed. Yates collection', said to come from Nicholas Lane c 1926.

GM photo: 689–30

7 Leadenhall Market, EC3

An attempt to drill a hole from a floor of the basement of this small building on the N side of the W avenue of Leadenhall Market having failed, a hole 5ft x 3ft 6in. was excavated with pneumatic road-breakers.

For a depth of 11ft 6in. this shaft had to be made through Roman masonry 'of the hardest description', a concrete of Kentish ragstone. This was evidently the wall seen by Hodge in 1881–2. The masonry was homogeneous throughout, with no traces of tiles. The basement lay at 15ft 4in. below street level, and the Roman wall reached 27ft below street level. The upper part of the Roman structure had been made use of as the back wall of the present building. The soil beneath the Roman wall was gravel.

EN 1, 7

This observation appears not to have been reported for itself, but for the setting see RCHM, 1928 *London III: Roman London,* 127 and
   Merrifield, R, 1965 *The Roman city of London,* gazetteer 220

2–5 Fenchurch Buildings, and west side of Fenchurch Buildings, Fenchurch Street, EC3

The site of nos 2–5 was excavated down to the natural soil, here a 'red' gravel, and later in 1924 a little further excavation took place under the roadway. Among objects found were fragments of delftware drug jars, a small glass bottle of the 18th c, a portion of Roman quern, a clay 'net-sinker' and a bronze coin of Carausius.

The 'West side' of Fenchurch Buildings was excavated by builders in January 1925. Considerable remains of Roman pottery covering the whole Roman period were unearthed, along with stoneware and a number of delftware jars.

EN 1, 9

26–27 Paternoster Square, EC4

This site was excavated by builders to a depth of 20ft below street level. Made earth extended down to a depth of 15ft, and below that was brickearth. The gravel below this began to appear in one spot at the 20ft level.

No foundations of any early buildings were found, but the W portion of the site contained a Roman rubbish pit extending down to the full depth of the excavation. It appeared to be of late 1st-c date as it contained fragments of samian stamps of this period and vessels type 29 and Ritterling type 12, with fragments of an amphora of 'Graeco-Italian pointed form'. A fragment of medieval pitcher was also recovered.

EN 1, 14
RCHM, 1928 *London III: Roman London,* 135

GM329

Unknown, 1928
NGR: TQ 32940 80945
SMR: 041410

28–30 Gracechurch Street, EC4

In MoL Library is a set of drawings on a single sheet entitled 'A mediaeval vaulted chamber' with this address, dated 1928. There are some notes on the sheet, which includes a plan, section and elevation of the E end. A rectangular undercroft measuring 12ft 11in. E–W x 7ft N–S lay about 19ft below Gracechurch Street. The vault was at least 6ft 9in. high, but the original floor could not be determined. The walls and vault were constructed of 'hard white chalk' and the vault was of a four-centred form without ribs. At the E end, nearest to Gracechurch Street, a rectangular cavity with a low-arched head formed a light well up to the modern surface. The position of this undercroft within the modern property is not known, though the plan shows it was entered by a modern stair from the W.

GM files, box P8
Schofield, J, 1995 *Medieval London houses,* 187 and fig 222

GAZETTEER OF SITES INVESTIGATED BY THE

DEPARTMENT OF URBAN ARCHAEOLOGY

1973–1991

The following sites of 1972 have site codes in the manner used by the Department of Urban Archaeology (2–4 characters + 2 digits representing the year of starting the excavation), but have also at some time been given GM site numbers. Site summaries will be found above under their GM numbers:

GM152   BC72   Baynard's Castle (P Marsden)

GM191   CASS72   20–30 Aldgate (H Chapman)

But in each case the majority of the finds are stored under the '72' site code. The site at 110–114 Fenchurch Street, recorded in 1972, has the site code FNS72 but no GM number; and the site at 7–10 Milk Street, excavated by the City of London Archaeological Society in 1972, was given the site code MIL72 but no subsequent GM number. These two sites are given below before the main DUA series.

This part of the *Guide* includes eight sites set up in 1973 which were conducted, at least in excavation, by the curatorial staff of the GM before the DUA was created at the end of 1973. The excavations were finished by the end of 1973, and post-excavation and publication work was taken up for some of them by the DUA. For convenience this part also includes one excavation undertaken by an individual (FNS72) and another (FET76) undertaken by the Inner London Archaeological Unit, a predecessor of the DGLA.

FNS72

R Hughes
NGR: 33340 81300
SMR: 042103–9

110–114 Fenchurch Street, EC3

A watching brief was carried out by Ove Arup & Partners. Earliest activity consisted of a sequence of occupation surfaces which were sealed by fire debris dating to the second half of the 1st c. In the northern half of the site a cellar, disused in the early–mid-2nd c, was marked by an *opus signinum* floor. In the southern half of the site rough gravel surfaces were laid out in the mid–late 2nd c; these were sealed by an undated deposit which may have been dark earth. A chalk-lined cellar was then constructed and was possibly associated with a chalk-lined well and cesspits dated between the mid-12th to mid-14th/15th c.

For work on the site in 1925–6, see GM60 above.

Garratt, B, 1985 'Watching brief at 110–114 Fenchurch Street', Archive Report

MIL72

N Farrant (later N Fuentes)
NGR: TQ 32390 81280
SMR: 042110–15

7–10 Milk Street, EC2

This site was excavated by the City of London Archaeological Society for GM in 1972. The earliest activity above natural brickearth comprised late 1st-/early 2nd-c timber buildings and a timber drain. The line of the Roman street recorded later at 1–6 Milk Street immediately to the S in 1977 (see MLK76 below) crosses the site, but was not located here since it lay outside the area of excavation. In the Hadrianic period a new street was however laid S–N across the site, and a street junction constructed in the Antonine period, with new streets to N and W reflecting the development of the Cripplegate fort to the NW and the later buildings found on the MLK76 site to the S. The street was overlain by dark earth in the 4th c. Pits of the 9th–11th c, two stone buildings probably of the 12th or 13th c and stone-lined cesspits were also recorded.

London Archaeol, 2, 1973, 40
Betts, I, 1986 '10 Milk Street (MIL72), medieval and post-medieval building material', Archive Report
Egan, G, & Moir, D, in prep. 'Post-medieval finds c 1450–c 1700: a selection from the City of London sites 1972–82'
Farrant, N, 1975 'A Roman cross-roads in the City', *London Archaeol*, 2, 300–3
Perring, D, & Roskams, S, with Allen, P, 1991 *The early development of Roman London west of the Walbrook*, The archaeology of Roman London 2, CBA Res Rep 70 [Roman strata]
Schofield, J, Allen, P, & Taylor, C, 1990 'Medieval buildings and property development in the area of Cheapside', *Trans London Middlesex Archaeol Soc*, 41, 124–54 [Saxon and medieval strata]
Taylor, G W, 1986 'Dye tests on Saxon pot sherds', Archive Report

Africa House, 39–42 Leadenhall Street, EC3

AFR73

D Woods
NGR: TQ 33330 81100
SMR: 042116–22

Two sections were recorded here during construction work. One contained evidence of two periods of Roman buildings, medieval pits and an early medieval foundation; the other only medieval pits. The early medieval foundation has been proposed as a fragment of the lost chapel of St Michael Aldgate, which lay in this general area.

Schofield, J, 1995 *Medieval London houses*, 195–6
Woods, D, Rhodes, M, & Dyson, T, 1975 'Africa House sections London 1973', *Trans London Middlesex Archaeol Soc*, 26, 252–66

Bush Lane House, 80 Cannon Street, EC4

BLH73

T Johnson
NGR: TQ 32670 80870
SMR: 042125–7

First-c occupation in two phases was recorded: the first pre-Flavian, and probably pre-Boudican, timber buildings; the second masonry structures of Roman character.

London Archaeol, 2, 1973, 40
Chapman, H, & Johnson, T, 1973 'Excavations at Aldgate and Bush Lane House in the City of London, 1972', *Trans London Middlesex Archaeol Soc*, 24, 1–73

Custom House, Sugar Quay, Lower Thames Street, EC3

CUS73

T Tatton-Brown
NGR: TQ 33295 80590
SMR: 041829–36

The pre-Roman River Thames bank was represented by steeply rising London Clay in the N half of the site; to the S London Clay was overlaid by river gravels. Timber quays were built on the river bank in the Roman period, the first of which was recorded in the NE part of the site. This was constructed in the late 1st or early 2nd c of a series of horizontal E–W beams with a series of posts and planks in front and clay packing behind. Towards the end of the 2nd c the waterfront was advanced approximately 6m to the S in the E part of the site. Here much of the waterfront had been robbed out but it seems to have been constructed of a series of massive E–W beams at the front, tied in at the top with lesser N–S beams. In the W the waterfront consisted of a series of timber boxes composed of four or five tiers of massive oak beams. These boxes were not filled in. In front (and perhaps added later) was a series of posts and planks, possibly additional support for the revetment, or possibly foundations of buildings. By the 4th c this quay went out of use and was partly robbed. Erosion of the upper Roman levels and deposition of river gravels occurred from this time onwards (Tatton-Brown 1974a; revised in light of work on other sites by Brigham 1990).

Waterfront activity was resumed in the medieval period. A front-braced revetment was roughly constructed of reused timbers, including boat timbers, some 8m S of the Roman revetment in the late 13th or early 14th c. In the W of the site a large timber jetty, with internal scissor brace construction, was probably the main jetty for the medieval Wool Quay. The first revetment collapsed and was replaced in the mid-14th c with a well-built revetment which was front-braced, horizontally planked and supported on ground-plates and piles. In the E of the site, the area of Stone Wharf, the line of this waterfront was continued with a new revetment about 4.5m in front of the earlier one. Only a small part of this could be examined but it consisted of a series of posts and planks, some reused from a boat, on a massive ground-plate. The earlier jetty continued in use. S of the waterfront the foreshore was filled in, presumably after the waterfront had been moved forward. A chalk and ragstone foundation was identified as the SE corner of the Custom House of 1382. A large timber drain lay outside its E wall, partially demolished when an arched chalk foundation was constructed over it: this may have been the remains of an extension to the Custom House, dated to 1383.

Virtually all late and post-medieval deposits had been destroyed by modern basementing but foundations and cellars were recorded. Part of the projecting E wing of the Wren/Ripley Custom House was recorded as a series of brick arches and, in front of it, the surviving part of the contemporary riverwall. In the NE corner of the site, reverse-arched foundations for a building with a vaulted cellar may be the remains of either the early 18th-c (Ripley) extension to the Custom House or, more likely, the remains of an early 19th-c warehouse built after the Custom House site had been sold off in 1814. A series of later 17th- and early 18th-c walls and cellars was also located in this part of the site: these were almost certainly part of buildings constructed after the Great Fire on the property adjoining the Wren Custom House on the E, Hartshorn Quay (Tatton-Brown 1975).

Britannia, 5, 1974, 416; *Medieval Archaeol,* 18, 1974, 180, 202–4; *Post-Medieval Archaeol,* 8, 1974, 124–5

Brigham, T, 1990 'The late Roman waterfront in London', *Britannia,* 21, 99–183

Cowgill, J, de Neergaard, M, & Griffiths, N, 1987 *Knives and scabbards,* Medieval finds from excavations in London 1

Crowfoot, E, Pritchard, F, & Staniland, K, 1992 *Textiles and clothing,* Medieval finds from excavations in London 4

Fleck-Abbey, A, and King, A, nd, 'Animal bones', Animal Bone Report

Fletcher, J, 1982 'The waterfront of Londinium — the date of the quays at the Custom House site reassessed', *Trans London Middlesex Archaeol Soc,* 33, 79–84

Grew, F, & de Neergaard, M, 1988 *Shoes and pattens,* Medieval finds from excavations in London 2

Hillam, J, 1979 'Tree-ring analysis of further samples from the medieval Custom House', Archive Report

Locker, A, 1992 'The fish bones (1/92)', Archive Report

Pearce, J, Vince, A G, & Jenner, M A, 1985 *A dated type-series of medieval pottery part 2: London-type ware,* London Middlesex Archaeol Soc Spec Pap 6

Tatton-Brown, T, 1974a 'Excavations at the Custom House site City of London 1973', *Trans London Middlesex Archaeol Soc,* 25, 117–219

Tatton-Brown, T, 1974b 'Rescue excavations on the Old Custom House Site part I — medieval and later', *London Archaeol,* 2, 136–41

Tatton-Brown, T, 1974c 'Rescue excavations on the Old Custom House Site part II — Roman', *London Archaeol,* 2, 155–9

Tatton-Brown, T, 1975 'Excavations at Custom House — Part II', *Trans London Middlesex Archaeol Soc,* 26, 103–70

Tyers, I, 1992 'City: early to late medieval boats (BIG82, CUS73, TL74, Blackfriars Wreck 3)', Dendrochronology Report

Wilthew, P, 1984a 'Inlays and fittings on medieval iron knives and shears', Archive Report (AML)

Wilthew, P, 1984b 'Metallographic examination of medieval knives and shears', Archive Report (AML)

GF73

T Johnson
NGR: TQ 32020 81370
SMR: 042128–30

Christchurch Greyfriars, Newgate Street, EC1

An area within the E end of Wren's church was excavated in June 1973 prior to removal of the E end during road widening. The excavation was confined to a depth of 2m, the intended depth of destruction. Structural features of the 13th c were overlaid by deposits of the Greyfriars church; a portion of the medieval E wall and three pillar bases forming the S arcade. Both N and S aisles contained post-medieval brick vaults. A number of lead coffins were exposed and reburied on site.

For later work on the Christchurch Greyfriars site, see CHR76, CCN80 and CIS89 below.

London Archaeol, 2, 1974, 133; *Post-Medieval Archaeol,* 8, 1974, 120

Johnson, T, 1974 'Excavations at Christ Church Newgate Street 1973', *Trans London Middlesex Archaeol Soc,* 25, 220–34

LPL73

T Johnson
NGR: TQ 32780 80850
SMR: 044707–8

Laurence Pountney Lane, EC4

The precise site of this observation is not known. Building material of the Roman to post-medieval periods was recovered, including a fragment of Roman walling with plastered face and wattle impressions on the back.

Site of St Mildred Bread Street church, now 84–94 Queen Victoria Street, EC4

Two periods of 1st-c Roman buildings were observed, the earlier of timber, the second in masonry; the second was destroyed at the end of the 1st c. Part of a Late Saxon sunken-floored building, foundations of the medieval church and of the Wren church of St Mildred were also recorded.

London Archaeol, 2, 1974, 133; *Britannia*, 5, 1974, 445; *Post-Medieval Archaeol*, 8, 1974, 120

Marsden, P, Dyson, T, & Rhodes, M, 1975 'Excavations on the site of St Mildred's church, Bread Street, London, 1973–4', *Trans London Middlesex Archaeol Soc*, 26, 171–208

Pringle, S, 1989 'St Mildred Bread Street', Building Materials Appraisal

Schofield, J, 1994 'Saxon and medieval parish churches in the City of London: a review', *Trans London Middlesex Archaeol Soc*, 45, 123

MC73

M Guterres
NGR: TQ 32290 80990
SMR: 042131–8

24–27 Martin Lane, 4–8 Arthur Street, EC4

There are no site records for this site in the archive, but some Roman pottery was recovered (Davies 1993, table 18).

Davies, B, 1993 'Inter-site studies', in Milne, G, & Wardle, A, 'Early Roman development at Leadenhall Court, London and related research', *Trans London Middlesex Archaeol Soc*, 44, 135–50

ML73

T Johnson
NGR: TQ 32815 80820
SMR: 044446

29 Noble Street, EC2

Observations in 1973 and 1985 during landscaping works next to the standing fragment of city wall found that the brickearth bank associated with the original wall of the Roman Cripplegate fort was constructed, together with an intramural street and its drainage gully. Additions to the bank were then made; these encroached upon the street. The street was repaired and resurfaced and on two occasions a deliberate attempt was made to re-establish the original street edge by cutting into the tail of the bank. During this phase, it is presumed that the ragstone wall of the reinforcement of the fort wall (the city wall of c AD200) cut the original bank.

Allen, P, 1985 'A watching brief at 29 Noble Street', Archive Report

NOB73

P Ellis, G Milne, 1973; P Allen, 1985
NGR: TQ 32220 81490
SMR: 040471

1–8 Angel Court, 30–35 Throgmorton Street, EC2

A controlled excavation took place at the NE side of the site and sections were recorded in a number of mechanically excavated trenches further to the S. In the controlled excavation a small tributary stream of the Walbrook was found cutting the natural brickearth. It was canalised in the late 1st–early 2nd c by means of timber revetting and artificial banks, and a gravel path was provided on its S side. Silting, followed by a similar pattern of banking and relaying the path, continued at increasingly higher levels until the late 4th c when waterborne deposits covered the sequence. Possible supports for a timber footbridge were also located. Drainage activity did not recommence until the medieval period — in the late 12th–early 13th c — but the stream was no longer in evidence. Thereafter, organic deposits and dumping, dated to the 14th c, were overlaid by the modern basement. In the S area of the site Roman timber drains and substantial buildings were recorded in section.

ACW74

M Guterres
NGR: TQ 32810 81320
SMR: 042139–42

Part of the site, corresponding to 31–32 Throgmorton Street and 9–13 Copthall Court, became part of the estate of the Clothworkers' Company by 1592, and was surveyed by Ralph Treswell in 1612.

London Archaeol, 2, 1975, 256; *Britannia,* 6, 1975, 268

Blurton, R, 1977 'Excavations at Angel Court', Archive Report

Clutton-Brock, J, & Armitage, P, 1976a 'A system for classification and description of the horn cores of cattle from archaeological sites', *J Archaeol Science,* 4, 329–48

Clutton-Brock, J, & Armitage, P, 1976b 'Mammal remains from Roman and medieval levels (ACW74)', Archive Report

Dannell, G, nd, 'Report on the Samian pottery', Archive Report

Dannell, G, & Rhodes, M, 1977 'Catalogue of samian', Archive Report

Liversidge, J, 1976 'Burnt Roman–British painted wall plaster', Archive Report

Rhodes, M, & Blurton, R, 1977 'Excavations at Angel Court', *Trans London Middlesex Archaeol Soc,* 28, 14–100

Schofield, J (ed), 1987 *The London surveys of Ralph Treswell,* London Topographical Soc Publication 135, 123–5

Schofield, J, 1995 *Medieval London houses,* 225

Thornton, J H, 1976 'Angel Court leather', Archive Report

Wickham, D E, 1995 'A chronological account of Angel Court, a property of The Clothworkers' Company, and the Angel Court development of 1985', *London Topographical Record,* 27, 195–230

Young, C J, nd, 'Oxfordshire pottery from Angel Court', Archive Report

AL74

G A Thompson
NGR: TQ 3367 8120
SMR: 042143–52

Wingate Centre, 62–64 Aldgate High Street, E1

This site, to the S of Aldgate High Street and to the E of Minories, was used for sand- or brickearth-quarrying in the 12th c, but for most of the medieval period was open land. The first major development took place in the late 16th and early 17th c, and was represented by substantial, though fragmentary, lengths of wall. The ground was used for rubbish-tipping, including refuse from a nearby slaughter-yard, and waste and crucibles from a glass factory. A row of terraced properties was built on the site in the 1670s and demolished in the mid-18th c. To the S of these lay a further building whose cellar was the only room surviving. All these structures are visible on contemporary maps; the archaeological evidence shows that they included both domestic units (houses of two-room plan with axial chimneys) and workshops. In one workshop a fragmentary clay pipe kiln was found. The associated household finds and faunal remains enable a distinction of status to be made between the main block of houses and the richer building to the S.

Post-Medieval Archaeol, 10, 1976, 164

Armitage, P, 1983 'The mammalian bones from the post-medieval contexts', Archive Report

Betts, I, nd, 'AL74 Bricks', Archive Report

Egan, G, nd, 'AL74 Leaden cloth seal', Archive Report

Grew, F, nd, 'AL74 Cutlery', Archive Report

Grew, F, nd, 'AL74 Objects of iron', Archive Report

Grew, F, nd, 'AL74 Pipeclay hair-curlers', Archive Report

Jones, A, nd, 'AL74 Coins', Archive Report

Locker, A, 1982 'Fish bone from Aldgate 1974', Archive Report

Moore, D, 1982 'AL74 Hone stone', Archive Report

Orton, C, nd, 'The post-medieval pottery', Archive Report

Shepherd, J, nd, 'AL74 The glass', Archive Report

Smith, B, & Gilmour, B, 1986 'Lead content in glass', Archive Report

Thompson, A, 1975 'An excavation at Aldgate', *London Archaeol,* 2, 317–19

Thompson, A, 1978 'A clay pipe-kiln at Aldgate', *Industrial Archaeol,* 13, 319–24

Thompson, A, 1979 'Excavations at Aldgate', Archive Report

Thompson, A, 1981 'The Aldgate clay-pipe kiln', in Davey, P, *Archaeology of the clay tobacco-pipe,* British Archaeol Reps 97, 3–13

Thompson, A, Grew, F, & Schofield, J, 1984 'Excavations at Aldgate, 1974', *Post-Medieval Archaeol,* 18, 1–148

Vince, A, 1982 'AL74 Ceramic building materials', Archive Report

Vince, A, & Egan, G, 1981 'The contents of a late eighteenth-century pit at Crosswall, City of London', *Trans London Middlesex Archaeol Soc,* 32, 159–81 [comparison of AL74, CUT78 and XWL79 sites in pottery assemblages]

Weinstein, R, nd, 'AL74 Copper alloy', Archive Report

Weinstein, R, nd, 'AL74 Pipe clay figurines', Archive Report

West, B, 1978 'The bird bones from Aldgate', Archive Report

Young, B R, nd, 'Provenance of pipe clays', Archive Report

Baynard House, Queen Victoria Street / White Lion Hill, EC4

BC74

P Marsden
NGR: TQ 3194 8092
SMR: 04120005–6,
044613–14

Excavations revealed part of the N wing of the medieval Baynard's Castle, including the N gate and gate tower (Fig 22); the frontages of medieval houses between the medieval castle and the East Watergate dock; part of the N wing of the 16th-c addition to the castle; the cobbled entrance to the castle from Thames Street; and evidence for Thames Street before the Great Fire of 1666, such as its construction and narrow width.

See also BC72/GM152, BC75 and BYD81.

Fig 22 BC74: looking W along the N side of Baynard's Castle. The 19th-c cellar walls are based on the medieval walls, including the N gate where the closer human figure stands. The Roman riverside wall (Fig 26) lay on the same alignment beneath, forming the S side of Thames Street (marked here by the trench dug by machine).

Fish Street Hill (west side), EC3

FSH74

No supervisor
NGR: TQ 3281 8070

A site code was issued but no useful structural or topographical information gained. Some finds were recovered.

14–21 St Dunstan's Hill, Cross Lane (Harp Lane), EC3

HL74

R Jones and A Boddington
NGR: TQ 33190 80680
SMR: 042153–4

Excavation revealed two Roman buildings on terraces, apparently of later Roman date. From 17th-c contexts came a number of medieval moulded stones from an ecclesiastical context; the site lies immediately S of the parish church of St Dunstan in the East. A watching brief was also carried out on the site in 1977.

London Archaeol, 2, 1975, 256; Britannia, 6, 1975, 268

Boddington, A, & Jones, R, 1982 'Excavations at Harp Lane 1974–1977', Archive Report

Lea, R, 1981 'Moulded stones from Harp Lane (HL74)', notes and drawings

Pringle, S, 1990 'Harp Lane', Building Materials Appraisal

Richardson, B, 1988 'The Roman pottery from Harp Lane (HL74)', Archive Report

Williams, T, in prep. The development of Roman London east of the Walbrook, The archaeology of Roman London 4, CBA Res Rep [Roman strata]

LH74

C Hill
NGR: TQ 3178 8118
SMR: 040433, 043457

42–46 Ludgate Hill, 1–6 Old Bailey, EC4

A flat-bottomed ditch was located near the alleged position of a bastion and to the S the butt ends of two successive ditches were traced. The presence of the butt ends of the ditch suggests that the approach to Ludgate was a causeway rather than a bridge.

See LUD82 below for later excavation of the same site.

London Archaeol, 2, 1975, 256; *Britannia*, 6, 1975, 265
Ancient Monuments Laboratory, nd, 'Wood identification and dates report'
Pringle, S, 1989 '44–46 Ludgate Hill (LH74)', Building Materials Appraisal

MM74

M Millett
NGR: TQ 3194 8090
SMR: 042155–8

Baynard House, Queen Victoria Street (site of Upper Thames Street), EC4

A trench across Upper Thames Street 20m E of the Mermaid Theatre (before its moving to a new site nearby in 1979) found a fragment of Roman masonry, evidence of river erosion and surface of Thames Street from the 12th c. The masonry is identified as part of the Roman riverside wall, dated on the adjacent Baynard's Castle site (BC75) to 255–70.

London Archaeol, 2, 1975, 256
Betts, I, 1987 'Baynard House/Queen Victoria Street (BC75 and MM74) ceramic building materials', Archive Report
Egan, G, & Moir, D, in prep. 'Post-medieval finds c 1450–c 1700: a selection from the City of London sites 1972–82'
Marsh, G, 1979 'Three "theatre" masks from London', *Britannia*, 10, 263–5
Millett, M, 1974 'A trench across Upper Thames Street — Roman riverside wall discovered', *London Archaeol*, 2, 232–3
Millett, M, 1975 'The excavation of a section across Upper Thames Street', Archive Report

MN74

A Thompson
NGR: TQ 33655 81090
SMR: 044447–9, 04444901

Bain Dawes House, 15 Minories, EC3

A N–S wall, composed of chalk blocks, may have been medieval in date. Garden soil of medieval or later date was followed by arch-founded brick walls, considered to be the S side and SE corner of the Ordnance Factory of 1706. A cellar with a stepped window light seems to have been part of this building. After its demolition the area was apparently left open; debris and domestic rubbish were dumped and some external surfaces were laid. A system of drains was then constructed above which was the remains of a brick floor, set in rectangular patterns, and a brick foundation. This is considered to be the remains of the horse stables of the goods railway yard of the London and Blackwall Railway Company which bought the site in 1851. Warehouses were then built on the site, represented by concrete floors laid in the 20th c.

Egan, G, & Moir, D, in prep. 'Post-medieval finds c 1450–c 1700: a selection from the City of London sites 1972–82'
Moir, D, 1989 'Bain Dawes House', Finds Appraisal

MON74

NGR: TQ 32910 80787

Monument Street, 16 Fish Street Hill, EC3

A site code was issued but no useful structural or topographical information gained. Photographs under this code in the archive show a hole dug by machine.

New Fresh Wharf, 2–6 Lower Thames Street, EC3 (NFW74)
St Magnus trench, New Fresh Wharf, 2–6 Lower Thames Street, EC3 (SM75)
Fresh Wharf, New Fresh Wharf, 2–6 Lower Thames Street, EC3 (FRE78)

NFW74; also SM75, FRE78

G Clewley/L Miller (NFW74)
J Schofield (SM75)
L Miller (FRE78)
NGR: TQ 32950 80660
SMR: 042159–66

The excavation of New Fresh Wharf (2–6 Lower Thames Street) was carried out in three stages in 1974–8. Two areas, named Areas I and II during excavation, were supervised by G Clewley (NFW74). In 1975 a third trench was excavated to relocate the Roman quay discovered in Area II; this third trench was called the St Magnus excavation, though it was several metres E of the church (SM75, supervised by J Schofield). In 1975–8 NFW74 and SM75 were written to archive level by J Schofield and L Miller, under the overall title New Fresh Wharf; the St Magnus trench was termed Area III.

In 1978 the postponed redevelopment of the site resulted in a watching brief around and incorporating all three areas (resulting in the creation of Areas IV and V) by L Miller (FRE78). The archive report for FRE78 Roman period (ie the quayside) is a separate volume, but post-Roman periods for FRE78 are added to the relevant parts of the New Fresh Wharf archive report (shelved under NFW74). The fitting together of the three sites is also developed in the various publications.

The redeveloped site was named St Magnus House, and this name appears in some of the archive reports and in the main excavation report for the Roman period.

The main discoveries were as follows:

Period 1: traces of a timber revetment, probably an early 2nd-c quay, were followed by silting and then a land revetment probably contemporary with a timber quay (Fig 23) dated by dendrochronology to 209–24 or 209–44 and ceramically to c 235–45; a considered date of 225–45 is proposed. The structure was infilled, probably during construction; the dumping containing a large group of unused samian and Lezoux wares. Further silting preceded the robbing of the quay in the late 3rd c or later. In the late 3rd c a section of the Roman riverside wall was built across the N of the site from W to E, underneath the present S pavement of Lower Thames Street.

Fig 23 SM75: the 3rd-c Roman quay, looking E. The large timbers forming the sill-beam had over 200 rings.

Period 2: after silting a mid-10th-c rubble bank extended 4m S of the decayed Roman quay and extended 18m E–W; W of it a grid of oak stakes (Fig 24) may have been the posts of a jetty leading to the riverside wall. After mid-10th–11th-c silting further embankments of clay and timber were built, dated by dendrochronology to 991–1000. This embankment was divided into plots by rough fences.

Period 3: after further 11th-c silting a further revetment, the first with a vertical face, was built in the late 11th c. After silting of the 11th c, a front-braced revetment dated by dendrochronology to 1188±9 was erected. Masonry foundations for late 12th-c buildings were recorded on five of the plots (Buildings A–E). After internal modifications to the buildings (12th/13th c) the plots were extended to new revetments in the early–mid-13th c.

Fig 24 SM75: part of the grid of stakes driven into the Late Saxon foreshore, around the submerged and partly robbed beams of the 3rd-c Roman quay. The large timber with the ridge at the back is the sill-beam of the Roman quay.

Period 4: from this point assumed associated revetments must have lain S of the recorded areas. Dumps probably behind new revetments in the 13th/14th c were followed by a phase of rebuilding on all plots (Buildings F–H, K–L). After two phases of piecemeal alterations one property was rebuilt (Building J) in the 16th c, and after two phases of development in the 16th and 17th c the site was destroyed in the Great Fire.

Period 5: several phases of building from immediately post-Fire to 1952 were recorded.

For earlier observations on this site in 1937 and 1950, see GM125 and GM126 above.

Britannia, 6, 1975, 265; 7, 1976, 347; *Medieval Archaeol,* 19, 1975, 224; 20, 1976, 165–6; *Post-Medieval Archaeol,* 10, 1976, 163

Armitage, P, 1979 'The mammalian remains from the Roman, medieval and early modern levels — St Magnus', Archive Report

Betts, I, 1983 'Ceramic Building Material — New Fresh Wharf/St Magnus', Archive Report

Bird, J, 1985 'Roman quay at St Magnus House — catalogue of samian wares', Archive Report

Boyd, P, 1981 'Report on the qualitative analysis of diatoms from sediments associated with the Roman waterfront', Archive Report

Calnan, C, 1985 'Roman quay at St Magnus House — analysis of leather for presence of dyes', Archive Report

Carey, G, & Armitage, P, 1979 'The bird bones from the Roman, medieval and early modern levels St Magnus 1975', Archive Report

Chapman, H, 1985a 'Roman quay at St Magnus House — additional metal objects (NFW74)', Archive Report

Chapman, H, 1985b 'Roman quay at St Magnus House — amber bead (NFW74)', Archive Report

Clark, J, 1983 'New Fresh Wharf small finds metal/bone medieval', Archive Report

Dearne, M J, & Branigan, K, 1995 'The use of coal in Roman Britain', *Antiq J,* 75, 71–106

Evans, J, 1985a 'Roman quay at St Magnus House — slags and firedistorted leaden waste (NFW74)', Archive Report

Evans, J, 1985b 'Roman quay at St Magnus House — mortar sample analysis (NFW74)', Archive Report

Evans, J, 1985c 'Roman quay at St Magnus House — resin (NFW74)', Archive Report

Ganiaris, H, & Starling, K, 1985 'Roman quay at St Magnus House — painted wall plaster (scientific analysis)', Archive Report

Greep, S, 1985 'Roman quay at St Magnus House — bone objects (NFW74)', Archive Report

Hall, J, 1985 'Roman quay at St Magnus House — coins (catalogue)', Archive Report

Hassall, M, nd, 'Roman quay at St Magnus House — inscriptions and graffiti', Archive Report

Henig, M, 1974 'Two inscribed finger rings from the City of London', Archive Report

Henig, M, 1984 'Two inscribed finger rings from the City of London', *Trans London Middlesex Archaeol Soc,* 35, 17–18

Hillam, J, 1981 'An English tree-ring chronology, AD404–1216', *Medieval Archaeol,* 25, 31–44

Hillam, J, & Morgan, R, 1981 'Tree-ring analysis of timbers from New Fresh Wharf', Archive Report

Jobbins, E, 1985 'Roman quay at St Magnus House — jet and shale objects (material identification)', Archive Report

Locker, A, 1979 'New Fresh Wharf — fish bones', Archive Report

Locker, A, 1982 'St Magnus (SM75) City of London — the fish bones', Archive Report

MacConnoran, P, 1985 'Roman quay at St Magnus House — catalogue of the shoes', Archive Report

Marsden, P, 1994 *Ships of the port of London: first to eleventh centuries AD,* EH Archaeol Rep 3, 141–52 [Saxon boat fragments]

Marsh, G, & Rhodes, M, 1985 'Roman quay at St Magnus House — miscellaneous ceramic objects', Archive Report

Miller, L, 1977 'New Fresh Wharf — 2', *London Archaeol,* 3, 47–53

Miller, L, 1985 'Excavations at New Fresh Wharf 1978 (FRE78)', Archive Report

Miller, L, Schofield, J, & Rhodes, M, 1986 *The Roman quay at St Magnus House, London,* London Middlesex Archaeol Soc Spec Pap 8

Morris, C, 1981 'Saxon and medieval wooden objects from New Fresh Wharf', Archive Report

Rhodes, M, 1983 'Painted wall plaster (NFW74)', Archive Report

Rhodes, M, 1985a 'Roman quay at St Magnus House — jet and shale objects (description)', Archive Report

Rhodes, M, 1985b 'Roman quay at St Magnus House — additional items of leather', Archive Report

Rhodes, M, 1985c 'Roman quay at St Magnus House — additional stone objects', Archive Report

Rhodes, M, 1985d 'Roman quay at St Magnus House — nails', Archive Report

Rhodes, M, 1985e 'Roman quay at St Magnus House — other building materials', Archive Report

Rhodes, M, 1985f 'Roman quay at St Magnus House — painted wall plaster', Archive Report

Schofield, J, 1977 'New Fresh Wharf — 3, the medieval buildings', *London Archaeol,* 3, 66–73

Schofield, J, 1981 'Medieval waterfront buildings in the City of London', in Milne, G, & Hobley, B (eds), *Waterfront archaeology in Britain and northern Europe,* CBA Res Rep 41, 24–31

Schofield, J, 1995 *Medieval London houses,* 221

Schofield, J, & Dyson, T, in prep. *Medieval waterfront tenements*

Schofield, J, & Miller, L, 1976 'New Fresh Wharf — 1', *London Archaeol,* 2, 390–5

Schofield, J, & Miller, L, 1982 'Excavations at New Fresh Wharf', Archive Report

Seeley, N, 1985 'Roman quay at St Magnus House — coins (analysis of forged denarius of Elagabalus)', Archive Report

Shepherd, J, 1985 'Roman quay at St Magnus House — additional glass items', Archive Report

Smith, A, 1985 'Roman quay at St Magnus House — coal', Archive Report

Steedman, K, Dyson, T, & Schofield, J, 1992 *Aspects of Saxo-Norman London III: the bridgehead and Billingsgate to 1200,* London Middlesex Archaeol Soc Spec Pap 14 [Saxon and medieval embankments]

Tyers, I, 1988 'Dendrochronological spot date report: interim report (SPT/07/88)', Dendrochronology Report

Vince, A (ed), 1991 *Aspects of Saxo-Norman London II: finds and environmental evidence,* London Middlesex Archaeol Soc Spec Pap 12 [Saxon smallfinds]

Weeks, J, 1985 'Roman quay at St Magnus House — additional wooden items', Archive Report

West, B, 1985 'Roman quay at St Magnus House — human bone', Archive Report

Seal House, 106–108 Upper Thames Street, EC4

SH74 (and SH76)

J Schofield
NGR: TQ 3278 8070
SMR: 043440–2

This excavation was undertaken by arrangement with the Fishmongers' Company. It comprised a N–S trench 26m x 3m with a 14m x 1m extension to the N; the N end lay 1m S of the S side of Upper Thames Street. Subsequently in 1976 a watching brief was undertaken on the whole site. A 1m wide section of a Roman waterfront was recorded in the trench, but not excavated below the upper timbers, which included horizontal beams from a quay floor or possibly a building on the quayside. The waterfront was dated by dendrochronology to AD171+, and early 3rd-c material lay around it. Subsequent analysis and comparison of the structure with those recorded at Swan Lane to the E (SWA81) suggest that three separate Roman structures were recorded at Seal House (Brigham 1990, 107).

Excavations also located three successive medieval revetments (dated by dendrochronology to c 1140, c 1170 and c 1210) (Waterfronts I–III) and several periods of medieval buildings (Buildings A–G). In one of them was a damaged *in situ* floor of decorated medieval floor tiles, of late 13th-c or early 14th-c date. After the Great Fire a row of late 17th-c houses (Buildings H and J) occupied the site; these are also known from a plan in the Fishmongers' Company archives. The watching brief on the site in 1976 (coded SH76) recorded more of the Roman quay and further medieval revetments to the S of the 1974 trench (Waterfronts IV–VIII).

London Archaeol, 2, 1975, 256; 3, 1977, 36; *Medieval Archaeol*, 20, 1976, 190

Barnes, M, 1976 'Report of the feasibility of studying pollen from Seal House and other sites in the City of London', Archive Report

Brigham, T, 1990 'The late Roman waterfront in London', *Britannia*, 21, 99–183

Clark, J (ed), 1995 *The medieval horse and its equipment c 1150–c 1450*, Medieval finds from excavations in London 5 [medieval horseshoes and horse equipment]

Cowgill, J, de Neergaard, M, & Griffiths, N, 1987 *Knives and scabbards*, Medieval finds from excavations in London 1

Crowfoot, E, Pritchard, F, & Staniland, K, 1992 *Textiles and clothing*, Medieval finds from excavations in London 4

Egan, G, 1998 *The medieval household*, Medieval finds from excavations in London 6

Egan, G, & Moir, D, in prep. 'Post-medieval finds c 1450–c 1700: a selection from the City of London sites 1972–02'

Grew, F, 1985 'Seal House (SH74) Part I — Roman', Finds Appraisal

Grew, F, & de Neergaard, M, 1988 *Shoes and pattens*, Medieval finds from excavations in London 2

Jones, A, nd, 'Seal House (SH74) fish bones', Archive Report

Leddy, A., & Betts, I, 1986 'Seal House — Roman and medieval building material', Archive Report

Locker, A, nd, 'The fish bones', Archive Report

Milne, G, 1992 *Timber building techniques in London, c 900–1400*, London Middlesex Archaeol Soc Spec Pap 15 [joints and carpentry]

Morgan, R, nd, 'Tree-ring dating of the medieval waterfront at the Seal House site', Archive Report

Pearce, J, Vince, A G, & Jenner, M A, 1985 *A dated type-series of medieval pottery part 2: London-type ware*, London Middlesex Archaeol Soc Spec Pap 6

Richardson, B, 1989 'The Roman pottery from Seal House (SH74)', Archive Report

Ruddle, J, 1991 'An investigation of the potential of tooth cement annuli for ageing zooarchaeological material, with special consideration to cattle mandibular first molars (DIS/02/91)', MSc Dissertation, Dept of Human Environment, Institute of Archaeology, University College London

Schofield, J, 1975 'Seal House', *Current Archaeol*, 49, 53–7

Schofield, J, 1977 'Excavations at Seal House', Archive Report

Schofield, J, 1981 'Medieval waterfront buildings in the City of London', in Milne, G, & Hobley, B (eds), *Waterfront archaeology in Britain and northern Europe*, CBA Res Rep 41, 24–31

Schofield, J, 1995 *Medieval London houses*, 219

Schofield, J, & Dyson, T, in prep. *Medieval waterfront tenements*

Schofield, J, & Morgan, R, 1978 'Tree rings and the archaeology of the Thames waterfront in the City of London', in Fletcher, J (ed), *Dendrochronology in Europe*, British Archaeol Reps International Series 51, 223–38

Steedman, K, Dyson, T, & Schofield, J, 1992 *Aspects of Saxo-Norman London III: the bridgehead and Billingsgate to 1200*, London Middlesex Archaeol Soc Spec Pap 14 [Saxon and medieval embankments]

Vince, A, 1985 'Saxon and medieval pottery in London: a review', *Medieval Archaeol*, 29, 25–93

St Paul's Cathedral Choir School, New Change, EC4

SPS74

P J Muir
NGR: TQ 32140 81150
SMR: 044709

One trench, located on the W side of the school, revealed a Roman pit cut into the natural brickearth. It was severely disturbed by modern construction.

For earlier work on the Choir School site, see GM123 above.

TL74

M Harrison; later G Milne
and C Milne
NGR: TQ 32030 80830
SMR: 042167–72

2–3 Trig Lane, Upper Thames Street, EC4

Excavations in 1974–6 revealed a series of timber and stone riverfront revetments and associated features erected on the Thames foreshore from the mid-13th–mid-15th c (Fig 25). It was possible to plot the differing development and rates of riverfront extension during this period on three adjacent properties.

Fig 25 TL74: a view looking NW across the Trig Lane excavations. Several successive phases of timber revetments are shown; that on the right, of late 13th-c date, was later used to coincide with the stone foundations of a building which functioned with the next revetment, shown here by the few vertical timbers supported by metal scaffolding.

The earliest feature was a freestanding structure or platform which was built on the foreshore possibly c 1250. During the mid-13th and 14th c a series of closely datable revetments successively advanced the waterfront to the S into the Thames. These revetments were horizontally planked and both front- and back-braced; one survived to a height of 2.5m. Behind the waterfronts and above the contemporary infilling, surfaces of gravel and stone chips, and buildings were laid out.

In about 1346 the E section of the earlier revetment was advanced about 3m to the S with the erection of a back-braced revetment, several of the timbers of which were reused boat strakes. Its W limit may have marked a property boundary. A substantial building was erected behind this waterfront, the chalk rubble of its S wall encasing the earlier revetment. At about the same time 2m to the W of the timber revetment a riverwall of irregular courses of dressed ragstone was constructed, the inlet between the two waterfronts being aligned on the S end of Bosse Alley. In about 1370 a back-braced 'stave wall' advanced the timber waterfront in the W; in the E it replaced the earlier revetment. About 6.5m of the foreshore was reclaimed c 1383 when the E end of the waterfront was advanced with the construction of a back-braced revetment. The 'stave wall' was then heightened or a second storey replaced. A new building was erected above the demolished earlier one, one wall of its earliest phase being constructed of uncoursed greensand and chalk rubble; there seems to have been a yard to its S (ie at the water's edge). A number of jetties, landing-stages and other features were recorded on the foreshore.

The subdivided waterfront then underwent a major rebuild c 1483. A massive ragstone-faced riverwall was constructed to the S of the timber revetments to produce a common frontage and stair which functioned with the earlier riverwall. Associated with this riverfront was a narrow building fronting E onto Trig Lane which may have been used for industrial purposes. This riverfront lasted until the 17th c.

Reclamation was resumed in the 17th c, in the areas to the W and S of the riverwall. Buildings were constructed above the earlier waterfronts, represented by brick and rubble walls, brick or mortar floors, and hearths. Other post-medieval features included drains and a well.

The watching brief on the site during construction works in 1984 is recorded under TIG84. For the revised finds dating of the major waterfront groups, see Vince 1985, 85–6.

The TL74 excavations of 1974–6 were next to the Thames and S of the new alignment of the widened Upper Thames Street (from 1974, in this area, the street was rebuilt as a ground-level tunnel under the site of the intended new City of London Boys' School). Some observation of the N ends of Trig Lane and adjacent alleys S of the former Upper Thames Street took place in 1972–3 before the construction of the tunnel, by J Haslam. The records of these observations are kept in the archive under the site code BC72 (Baynard's Castle, which was the main excavation in the area at the time of the first construction).

Medieval Archaeol, 19, 1975, 245–6; 20, 1976, 190; 22, 1978, 176; *Post-Medieval Archaeol,* 10, 1976, 163

Armitage, P, 1980a 'Report on the animal hairs found attached to metal "leaves" from the medieval levels', Archive Report

Armitage, P, 1980b 'Report on the study carried out on the spectacles from Trig Lane', Archive Report

Brett, D, 1978 'Medieval and recent elms in London', in Fletcher, J (ed), *Dendrochronology in Europe,* British Archaeol Reps International Series 51, 195–9

Cherry, J, 1976 'A bronze seal matrix from Trig Lane', *Antiq J,* 56, 253

Clark, J (ed), 1995 *The medieval horse and its equipment c 1150–c 1450,* Medieval finds from excavations in London 5 [medieval horseshoes and horse equipment]

Cowgill, J, de Neergaard, M, & Griffiths, N, 1987 *Knives and scabbards,* Medieval finds from excavations in London 1

Crosby, D D B, & Mitchell, J G, 1987 'Potassium-argon determinations of some London medieval honestones', *Trans London Middlesex Archaeol Soc,* 38, 159–64

Crowfoot, E, Pritchard, F, & Staniland, K, 1992 *Textiles and clothing,* Medieval finds from excavations in London 4

Egan, G, & Moir, D, in prep. 'Post-medieval finds c 1450–c 1700: a selection from the City of London sites 1972–82'

Gale, R, 1987 'The identification of wood from artefacts excavated by the DUA at London sites — Trig Lane', AML Report 59/87

Grew, F, & de Neergaard, M, 1988 *Shoes and pattens,* Medieval finds from excavations in London 2

Harrison, M, 1975 'Trig Lane', *Current Archaeol,* 49, 57–9

Heyworth, M, 1988 'Amber samples analysis', AML Report 125/88

Jones, A, nd, 'Trig Lane — Fish Bones (TL74)', Archive Report

Milne, C, & Milne, G, 1977 'Excavations at Trig Lane 1974–6', Archive Report

Milne, G, 1979 'Medieval riverfront revetment construction in London', in McGrail, S (ed), *Medieval ships and harbours in northern Europe,* British Archaeol Reps International Series 66, 145–53

Milne, G, 1981 'Medieval waterfront reclamation in London', in Milne, G, & Hobley, B (eds), *Waterfront archaeology in Britain and northern Europe,* CBA Res Rep 41, 32–6

Milne, G, 1982 'Recording timberwork on the London waterfront', in McGrail, S (ed), *Woodworking techniques before AD 1500,* British Archaeol Reps International Series 129, 7–23

Milne, G, 1991 'Waterfront archaeology and vernacular architecture: a London study', in Good, G L, Jones, R H, & Ponsford, M W (eds), *Waterfront archaeology: proceedings of the third international conference, Bristol, 1988,* CBA Res Rep 74, 116–20

Milne, G, 1992 *Timber building techniques in London, c 900–1400,* London Middlesex Archaeol Soc Spec Pap 15 [joints and carpentry]

Milne, G, & Milne, C, 1978 'Excavations on the Thames waterfront at Trig Lane 1974–76', *Medieval Archaeol,* 22, 84–104

Milne, G, & Milne, C, 1979 'The making of the London waterfront', *Current Archaeol,* 66, 198–204

Milne, G, & Milne, C, 1981 'Medieval buildings at Trig Lane', *London Archaeol,* 4, 31–7

Milne, G, & Milne, C, 1982 *Medieval waterfront development at Trig Lane,* London Middlesex Archaeol Soc Spec Pap 5

Pearce, J, Vince, A G, & Jenner, M A, 1985 *A dated type-series of medieval pottery part 2: London-type ware,* London Middlesex Archaeol Soc Spec Pap 6

Rhodes, M, 1980a 'A pair of late medieval spectacle frames from the Trig Lane site', *London Archaeol,* 4, 23–5

Rhodes, M, 1980b 'The earliest European spectacles — a remarkable discovery from the City of London', *The Optician,* 180, 32–4

Rhodes, M, 1981 'Spectacular find', *Sunday Times Magazine,* 37

Rhodes, M, 1982 'A pair of fifteenth-century spectacle frames from the City of London', *Antiq J,* 62, 57–73

Rhodes, M, 1985 'The Trig Lane spectacles', *Bull Opthalmic Antiques Collectors Club,* 10, 3–4

Schofield, J, 1981 'Medieval waterfront buildings in the City of London', in Milne, G, & Hobley, B (eds), *Waterfront archaeology in Britain and northern Europe,* CBA Res Rep 41, 24–31

Schofield, J, 1995 *Medieval London houses,* 213–14

Spencer, B, 1982 'Pilgrim souvenirs from the medieval waterfront excavations at Trig Lane', *Trans London Middlesex Archaeol Soc,* 33, 304–23

Spencer, B, in prep. *Pilgrim souvenirs and secular badges,* Medieval finds from excavations in London 7

Tyers, I, 1992 'City: early to late medieval boats (BIG82, CUS73, TL74, Blackfriars Wreck 3)', Dendrochronology Report

Vince, A, 1985 'Saxon and medieval pottery in London: a review', *Medieval Archaeol,* 29, 25–93

Willcox, G, nd, 'Trig Lane (TL74) [environmental archaeology]', Archive Report

Wilthew, P, 1984 'Metallographic examination of medieval knives and shears', Archive Report (AML)

TR74

D Jones
NGR: TQ 33013 80685
SMR: 042173–9

Billingsgate Buildings, 101–110 Lower Thames Street, EC3

Excavations found a series of artificial terracings of the riverbank of the late 1st and early 2nd c, comprising three sets of post and plank revetments, backfilled with a variety of rubbish and artefacts; environmental remains were particularly well represented in waterlogged conditions. A masonry foundation crossed the site from W to E in the late Roman period. Post-Roman features included a Saxo-Norman wicker-lined pit and a timber-lined well. The site was informally known as 'The Triangle'; hence the site code of TR74 and the use of the name in some reports.

London Archaeol, 2, 1975, 256; Britannia, 6, 1975, 268; Medieval Archaeol, 19, 1975, 224
Ancient Monuments Laboratory, nd, 'Wood identification', Wood Identification Report
Armitage, P, nd, 'The mammalian remains', Archive Report
Armitage, P, 1982 'Report on the animal bone with the ballista bolt', Archive Report
Jones, A, nd, 'Triangle fish remains (TR74)', Archive Report
Jones, D, 1975 'Excavations at Billingsgate Buildings (Triangle)', Archive Report
Jones, D, & Rhodes, M, 1980 Excavations at Billingsgate Buildings (Triangle) Lower Thames Street 1974, London Middlesex Archaeol Soc Spec Pap 4
Liversidge, J, nd, 'Wall-painting', Archive Report
Morgan, R, nd, 'Tree-ring analysis of timber piles from the Triangle', Archive Report
Orton, C, nd, 'Saxo-Norman and early medieval pottery', Archive Report
Wilcox, G, nd, 'The environmental evidence', Archive Report

UPP74

No supervisor
NGR: TQ 32810 80700

Upper Thames Street (south side, near Fishmongers' Hall), EC4

Some finds were recovered.

UT74

D Jones
NGR: TQ 31900 80910
SMR: 043859

Upper Thames Street (now Baynard House, Queen Victoria Street), EC4

A trench 30m E of the Mermaid trench (see MM74) disclosed two parallel E–W 'limestone' walls which may be part of Baynard's Castle II (built from 1428 onwards). The more S of the two was surmounted by brick facing with a rubble core to which a rectangular pier was attached. The excavator suggests that the N wall was 'the pre-1428 curtain wall of Baynard's Castle' and the S wall was a post-1428 replacement. A late 17th-c cellar with several phases of walls and floors was also recorded. For other excavations of Baynard's Castle, see BC72/GM152, BC75, BYD81 and BEX90.

London Archaeol, 2, 1975, 256; Britannia, 6, 1975, 266
Clark, J (ed), 1995 The medieval horse and its equipment c 1150–c 1450, Medieval finds from excavations in London 5 [medieval horseshoes and horse equipment]
Jones, D, 1974 'Excavations in Upper Thames Street', Archive Report
Pringle, S, 1989 'Baynard House', Building Materials Appraisal

BC75

C Hill
NGR: TQ 31940 80910
SMR: 044451

Upper Thames Street (Baynard's Castle), now Baynard House, Queen Victoria Street, EC4

Observation and limited excavation on this site recorded 115m of the Roman riverside city wall (Fig 26). Carbon 14 and dendrochronological dating suggested a building date in the 4th c, probably after 330 (this has been modified to 255–70 by Sheldon & Tyers 1983). In the western part of the wall were 52 sculptured blocks reused as building material (Fig 27). They are derived from at least two major monuments, a freestanding monumental arch and a Screen of Gods (Fig 28), both of early 3rd-c style.

Also recovered were two mid-3rd-c altars from temples. Fragments of the wall had been undermined by the rising Thames in the post-Roman period; one section had fallen northwards, suggesting demolition. The earliest levels of Thames Street over these fragments dated to the 12th c. Parts of medieval timber waterfronts were recorded to the W of the East Watergate of the Tudor Baynard's Castle (see BC72/GM152 and BC74 above).

The late Roman riverside wall on this site is compared to that found on other sites in 1973–85 by Brigham (1990).

Britannia, 7, 1976, 347; *Post-Medieval Archaeol,* 10, 1976, 163

Armitage, P, 1978 'A system for recording and processing of data relating to animal remains from archaeological sites', in Brothwell, D, *et al* (eds), *Research problems in zooarchaeology,* Institute of Archaeol Occ Pub, 3, 39–45

Armitage, P, 1980 'Report on the study of the diptych showing the Crucifixion of Christ', Archive Report

Betts, I, 1987 'Baynard House/Queen Victoria Street (BC75 and MM74) ceramic building materials', Archive Report

Bramwell, D, 1975 'Bird remains from medieval London', *The London Naturalist,* 54, 15–20

Brigham, T, 1990 'The late Roman waterfront in London', *Britannia,* 21, 99–183

Crowfoot, E, 1976 'Baynard's Castle textile', Archive Report

Crowfoot, E, Pritchard, F, & Staniland, K, 1992 *Textiles and clothing c 1150–c 1450,* Medieval finds from excavations in London 4 [medieval textiles]

Hill, C, 1975 'The Roman riverside wall in the City', *London Archaeol,* 2, 260–2

Hill, C, & Blagg, T, 1977 'The London riverside wall and the London arch', *Current Archaeol,* 57, 308–15

Hill, C, Millett, M, & Blagg, T, 1980 *The Roman riverside wall and monumental arch in London,* London Middlesex Archaeol Soc Spec Pap 3

Hillam, J, & Morgan, R, 1979 'The dating of the Roman riverside wall at three sites in London', *London Archaeol,* 3, 283–8

Mead, V, 1977 'Evidence for the manufacture of amber beads in London in 14th–15th century', *Trans London Middlesex Archaeol Soc,* 28, 211–14

Pain, C, 1975 'Baynard's Castle molluscan survey', Archive Report

Pringle, S, 1989 'Building material', Appraisal Report

Sheldon, H, & Tyers, I, 1983 'Recent dendrochronological work in Southwark and its implications', *London Archaeol,* 4, 355–61

Wilmott, T, 1982 'A medieval armorial brooch or pendant from Baynard's Castle', *Trans London Middlesex Archaeol Soc,* 33, 299–302

Fig 26 BC75: a section through the Roman riverside wall of the late 3rd c. It was based on piles in a layer of rammed chalk. Towards the top of the surviving wall, the stones have fallen or have been pushed forward over organic dumps on the riverbank (to the right).

Fig 27 BC75: the head of Mars, one of the sculptured blocks from a 3rd-c monument; see Fig 28 for reconstruction.

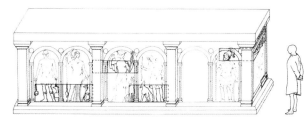

Fig 28 BC75: reconstruction of the Screen of Gods. It originally comprised niches with three male and (probably) three female deities on one side; on the other side were other mythological figures. From left to right, the main panels showed Vulcan, Minerva, Mercury, Diana, probably Venus, and Mars (the stone in Fig 27).

Billingsgate bath-house, 100 Lower Thames Street, EC3

BIL75

J Maloney
NGR: TQ 33125 80705
SMR: 041079–85, 043452–6

Two ragstone walls of the 1st c were set into natural clay. To the W was an early phase of timber piles and planks and an area of natural hillside revetted to prevent landslip. Post-dating this was a 1st-c dump in which a timber-lined water-tank with a hollow log pipe had been placed.

For earlier work at the site, see GM111 above; for later work, BSA82 and BBH87 below.

London Archaeol, 2, 1975, 256; *Britannia,* 7, 1976, 350

Jones, A, nd, 'Billingsgate (BIL75) — fish remains', Archive Report

Pringle, S, 1989 'Billingsgate bath-house, Lower Thames Street', Building Materials Appraisal

Prior, R, 1990 'Finds appraisal for 100 Lower Thames Street', Finds Appraisal

CAS75

D Woods, 1975; watching
brief in 1980 by P Rowsome
NGR: TQ 33545 81085
SMR: 043574–82

3–4 Jewry Street, EC3

Though a small excavation took place on this site in 1975, the records have not been traced, apart from photographs.

An extensive watching brief in 1980 was able to record several sections across the site, over a larger area than the excavation trench. First- and 2nd-c stratigraphy up to 1.8m deep was recorded. An early road or alley surface was found in the SW of the site; and dark earth recorded in various sections. Later intrusive activity included large pits of ?Saxon and medieval date and two wells.

London Archaeol, 4, 1981, 45; *Britannia*, 7, 1976, 350; 12, 1981, 351
Moir, D, 1989 'Finds Appraisal for 3–4 Jewry Street', Archive Report
Rowsome, P, nd, 'Excavations at 3–4 Jewry Street EC3', Archive Report
Williams, T, in prep. *The development of Roman London east of the Walbrook*, The archaeology of Roman London 4, CBA Res Rep [Roman strata]

CS75

A Boddington
NGR: TQ 32425 80960
SMR: 042180–5

48–50 Cannon Street, EC4

Excavations on this small site to the S of Cannon Street located three Roman water channels revetted with timber, probably for drainage rather than for water supply. Numerous post-holes were found, mostly associated with the channels, though one group may represent a Late Saxon building. Pits of Roman, Saxon and medieval date were recorded.

Britannia, 7, 1976, 347
Bird, C, & Armitage, P, nd, 'Mammalian remains from the Roman and medieval contexts', Archive Report
Boddington, A, nd, 'The effect of slumping on the 1st- and 2nd-century levels', Archive Report
Boddington, A, 1976 'Roman drains and a possible Saxon building in Cannon Street', *London Archaeol*, 2, 426–7
Boddington, A, 1978 'Excavations at 48–50 Cannon Street', Archive Report
Boddington, A, 1979 'Excavations at 48–50 Cannon Street City of London 1975', *Trans London Middlesex Archaeol Soc*, 30, 1–38
Hayes, K, & Rhodes, M, 1980 'Roman nails (CS75)', Archive Report
Johns, C, 1976a 'A note on the Cannon Street necklace (CS75)', Archive Report
Johns, C, 1976b 'A Roman gold and enamelled necklace from Cannon Street', *Antiq J*, 56, 247–8
Morgan, M, nd, 'Human bones (CS75)', Archive Report

GPO75

A Thompson and S Roskams
NGR: TQ 32050 81350
SMR: 043338–48

76–80 Newgate Street (former GPO; now British Telecom Headquarters, 81 Newgate Street), EC1

This large site was excavated in several stages in 1975–9; the site code GPO75 alludes to the site being formerly part of the General Post Office (GPO) building complex on both sides of King Edward Street. The first stage, under Thompson, had three main components:

(i) a N–S trench which ran through most of the available site; (ii) an investigation of the church of St Nicholas Shambles and its graveyard, expanding from the S part of the exploratory trench (Fig 29); (iii) a northern area by Angel Street (the N boundary of the site).

The second stage, under Roskams, continued excavation of the southern area (ii) into Roman levels beneath the church. A third stage of excavation, between the southern and northern areas, was excavated in 1979 under the separate site code POM79 (see below).

Bronze Age pottery, not associated with any structural feature, was found in the northern area.

In the Roman period, part of a circular hut and boundary ditch (Period I, c 50–5) seems to predate the establishment of the Roman street beneath Newgate Street, which formed the frontage of the seven succeeding periods. After establishment of drains running perpendicular to the street (Period II, 50–5) two rectangular buildings were constructed at the S end by the street with other circular huts to the N (Period III, 50–60). They were destroyed by fire, probably Boudican. After a short interval properties were re-established but not built upon (Period IV, 60–70). An integrated rebuilding on these two strip properties followed, with brickearth quarrying behind the street frontage (Period V, 65–85). The buildings were totally rebuilt in Period VII (c 90–125), with commercial premises to the front and smaller chambers behind. These were destroyed by fire, probably Hadrianic (Fig 30). In Period VIII (120–60) the properties were rebuilt on the same alignments, and dismantled before the end of the 2nd c (Roskams 1982).

The church of St Nicholas Shambles comprised five main phases. A nave and chancel of the ?11th c was extended in the second half of the 12th c or later; in a third phase chapels were added to the extended chancel, in the period 1340–1400; in a fourth phase, a N aisle was added to the nave and extended chancel in the first half of the 15th c; and fifthly the E end was rebuilt and a sacristy added on the N side, also in the first half of the 15th c. The church was dissolved in 1547 and the site converted into a court of small post-medieval houses (Bull Head Court), which survived as scattered foundations and a well (Thompson 1979a, 1979b; Tyler 1991; Schofield in prep.).

Fig 29 GPO75: overall view (Newgate Street) looking S in 1976. Excavation of the northern cemetery of St Nicholas Shambles (closed 1551) is in progress. The foundations of the parish church were to be excavated later in the area beyond.

Fig 30 GPO75: collapsed wall of clay blocks from an early 2nd-c Roman building (Newgate Street).

London Archaeol, 2, 1976, 369–70; Britannia, 7, 1976, 345; 8, 1977, 408; 10, 1979, 311; 11, 1980, 379–80; Medieval Archaeol, 20, 1976, 165, 183; 22, 1978, 165; Post-Medieval Archaeol, 10, 1976, 163; 12, 1978, 113

Davies, B, 1993 'Inter-site studies', in Milne, G, & Wardle, A, 'Early Roman development at Leadenhall Court, London and related research', Trans London Middlesex Archaeol Soc, 44, 135–50

Davies, B, Richardson, B, & Tomber, R, 1994 A dated corpus of early Roman pottery from the City of London, The archaeology of Roman London 5, CBA Res Rep 98 [contribution to early Roman pottery corpus]

Dyson, T, 1984 'St Nicholas Shambles and cemetery — documentary survey', Archive Report

Egan, G, & Moir, D, in prep. 'Post-medieval finds c 1450–c 1700: a selection from the City of London sites 1972–82'

Halpin, C, 1980 'GPO75 pottery', Archive Report

Henig, M, nd, 'A tripod mount from the GPO site', Archive Report

Henig, M, nd, 'Intaglio (GPO75)', Archive Report

Henig, M, 1976 'A Roman tripod mount from the GPO site', *Antiq J*, 56, 248–9

Henig, M, 1978 *Corpus of Roman engraved gemstones from the British Isles,* British Archaeol Rep 8, 314 [intaglio from site]

Macdonald, J, 1975 'Note on collared urn', Archive Report

Macphail, R, 1980 'Soil report on the dark earth at GPO75', Archive Report

Macphail, R, 1981 'Soil and botanical studies of the dark earth', in Jones, M, & Dimbleby, G (eds), *The environment of man — the Iron Age to Anglo-Saxon period,* British Archaeol Rep 87, 309–32

Morgan, M, 1978 'Excavation and recording techniques used at the cemetery of St Nicholas Shambles London 1975–8', *London Archaeol,* 3, 213–16

Perring, D, & Roskams, S, with Allen, P, 1991 *The early development of Roman London west of the Walbrook,* The archaeology of Roman London 2, CBA Res Rep 70 [Roman strata]

Reece R, 1975 'Coin identification <82>', Archive Report

Roskams, S, 1980 'GPO Newgate Street', *London Archaeol,* 3, 403–7

Roskams, S, 1982 'Excavations at the GPO site', Archive Report

Schofield, J, in prep. 'Excavations on the site of St Nicholas Shambles, City of London, 1975–9', *Trans London Middlesex Archaeol Soc*

Stephens, D, nd, 'Pits', Archive Report

Taylor, C, 1983 'Documentary survey', Archive Report

Thompson, A, 1979a 'St Nicholas in the Shambles and the cemetery', Archive Report [see also Tyler 1991]

Thompson, A, 1979b 'St Nicholas in the Shambles', *Current Archaeol,* 65, 176–9

Tyers, P, 1984 'Roman pottery from GPO', Archive Report

Tyler, K, 1991 'Excavations at the GPO75 site, post-Roman levels', Archive Report

Wells, C, nd, 'Note on a burial from GPO site', Archive Report

West, B, 1983 'Human, animal and bird bones from early Roman buildings', Archive Report

White, W, 1984 'The cemetery of St Nicholas in the Shambles', Archive Report

White, W, 1988 *Skeletal remains from the cemetery of St Nicholas Shambles, City of London,* London Middlesex Archaeol Soc Spec Pap 9

KW75

NGR: TQ 32790 80930

8–12 King William Street, EC4

A site code was issued but no useful structural or topographical information gained.

PIL75

J Schofield, 1975; B Watson, 1990

NGR: TQ 31780 81110

SMR: 042186, 042192–3

5 Pilgrim Street, EC4

A salvage brief on this small site recorded a brick cesspit with a garderobe chute and recovered a group of pottery, including Delft and Westerwald stoneware, clay pipes and glass dated to c 1640. The E side of the site followed the alignment of the Roman city wall S of Ludgate, but no traces of Roman work were observed below 19th-c foundations.

A watching brief in 1990 during reduction and underpinning found, on the W, cesspits and rubbish pits cut into natural gravel and cut in turn by a N–S feature, perhaps the robbing of a medieval or post-medieval wall.

Post-Medieval Archaeol, 10, 1976, 163

Egan, G, & Moir, D, in prep. 'Post-medieval finds c 1450–c 1700: a selection from the City of London sites 1972–82'

Schofield, J, 1982 'Watching brief at 5 Pilgrim Street', Archive Report

10 St Swithin's Lane, EC4

SL75

L Miller
NGR·TQ 32704 80980
SMR: 043332–7

Boudican and Hadrianic fire levels were succeeded by a ragstone building, later Roman pits, medieval and post-medieval tenements.

London Archaeol, 2, 1976, 370; Britannia, 7, 1976, 347; Post-Medieval Archaeol, 10, 1976, 163–4
Egan, G, & Moir, D, in prep. 'Post-medieval finds c 1450–c 1700: a selection from the City of London sites 1972–82'
Marschner, J, 1983 'Ten fragments of bone fan sticks', Archive Report
Miller, L, 1976 '10 St Swithin's Lane', Archive Report
Southall, B, nd, 'Finds appraisal report'
Williams, T, in prep. The development of Roman London east of the Walbrook, The archaeology of Roman London 4, CBA Res Rep
   [Roman strata]

[St Magnus] New Fresh Wharf, 2–6 Lower Thames Street, EC3

SM75: see
NFW74

NGR: TQ 32930 80605
SMR: 042159–66

Britannia, 10, 1979, 313; Medieval Archaeol, 20, 1976, 165–6; Post-Medieval Archaeol, 10, 1976, 163
For summary and all reports, see NFW74.

190 Bishopsgate, EC2

BG76

R Blurton
NGR: TQ 33330 81630
SMR: 044453–4

No site records of this watching brief can be located. Correspondence (in site file) refers to 14th- and 16th-c pits. The finds include an Antonine group, late Roman amphora, residual 12th-c roof tile, early 13th-c residual pottery, some late 14th–15th-c material and a late medieval Syrian alkaline-glazed jar sherd.

16–28 Tabernacle Street, Bonhill Street, EC2

BON76

A Boddington
NGR: TQ 32870 81280
SMR: 080488

A deposit of black peaty material was recorded over most of the site to a depth of about 1m below the Victorian slab. It contained organic debris, leather shoes and cloth fabric besides oyster shells and large amounts of bone.

Camomile Street (south pavement at west end), EC3

CAM76

L Miller
NGR: TQ 33240 81430
SMR: 044455

A ?Roman timber and clay walled building on a timber raft, associated flooring and destruction levels were observed beneath the pavement on the S side of the street.

Miller, L, 1987 'Excavations at Camomile Street (west end, south pavement) EC3', Archive Report
Williams, T, in prep. The development of Roman London east of the Walbrook, The archaeology of Roman London 4, CBA Res Rep [Roman strata]

CHR76

P Herbert
NGR: TQ 32010 81350
SMR: 044456–7

Christchurch Greyfriars, Newgate Street, EC1

Excavations were carried out in advance of the digging of a shaft 5m square for works connected with the nearby St Paul's Underground Station. Earliest activity consisted of quarry and other pits, followed by the construction of a building founded on brickearth sills and aligned on the Roman Newgate road. It was destroyed by fire, possibly the Hadrianic, in the early 2nd c. Levelling above the fire debris was covered by dark earth which was later cut by medieval pits dated to the late 12th–mid-13th c. Above these the traces of five buildings may represent occupation of the site by the Franciscan (Grey) Friars in the early 13th c; they were probably demolished for the construction of the church (1306–53). The arched foundations of the S wall and a pier base of the S aisle of the friary church were recorded. Five graves are considered to have been contemporary. Constructed onto the truncated foundations of the friary church was an external wall of Wren's post-Fire parish church; three brick piers were also recorded. Relocated lead coffins, dating to 1764–1803, were found in a 19th-c cut feature.

For earlier work on the Christchurch Greyfriars site, see GF73 above; for later work, CCN80 and CIS89 below. For work in the Greyfriars' garden W of the church, see POM79 below.

London Archaeol, 3, 1977, 36
Egan, G, & Moir, D, in prep. 'Post-medieval finds *c* 1450–*c* 1700: a selection from the City of London sites 1972–82'
Herbert, P, 1979 'Excavations at Christchurch Greyfriars', *London Archaeol,* 3, 327–32
Herbert, P, 1981 'Excavations at Christchurch Greyfriars', Archive Report

FET76

J Siegel
NGR: TQ 31212 81233
SMR: 200593

113–137 Fetter Lane (rear of St Dunstan's House), EC4

Observation by the Inner London Archaeological Unit after demolition of St Dunstan's House revealed that extensive basements of this building had destroyed all archaeological strata. An initial trial trench immediately W of St Dunstan's House recorded foundations and other structural features of several of the pre-Fire chambers of Clifford's Inn, an Inn of Chancery which was affiliated with the Inner Temple from the late medieval period. Prior to the construction of these chambers, the site appears on 16th- and mid-17th-c maps as open ground, probably a garden. A layer of garden soil containing mainly 16th- and 17th-c pottery sealed 16th-c pits and ditches, some of which were excavated. During subsequent development of the site a possible Roman ditch or pit was recorded.

Siegel, J, 1978 'Excavations at Fetter Lane, 1976', *Trans London Middlesex Archaeol Soc,* 29, 73–90

FSE76

A Boddington
NGR: TQ 33055 80965
SMR: 043420

160–162 Fenchurch Street, 22–23 Lime Street, EC3

This site lay over the SE corner of successive Roman fora. Six major Roman phases were identified: Phase 1 comprised the initial occupation of the site, represented by gravel and brickearth surfaces, occupation layers and a small gully. In Phase 2 these features were levelled and an extensive building or buildings with mudbrick walls was constructed. During Phase 3 these were destroyed in the Boudican fire of AD60–1. This was followed in Phase 4 by the construction of gravel and brickearth surfaces with little evidence of associated structures; and subsequently in Phase 5 a series of levelling deposits was laid down which apparently preceded the construction of the walls and floor surfaces of the second forum during Phase 6. In Phase 7 the forum walls were robbed, and this was followed by the construction of the church of St Dionis Backchurch (first mentioned between 1089 and 1108). The foundations of the S aisle and of the SW tower were recorded. See GM95 above.

Betts, I, 1988 '22–23 Lime Street/161 Fenchurch Street (FSE76)', Archive Report [building materials]

Boddington, A, 1979 'Excavations at 160–162 Fenchurch Street 1976', Archive Report

Boyd, P, 1980 'Carbonised cereals and associated weed seeds from Roman London AD60', Archive Report

Davies, B, 1993 'Inter-site studies', in Milne, G, & Wardle, A, 'Early Roman development at Leadenhall Court, London and related research', *Trans London Middlesex Archaeol Soc,* 44, 135–50

Marsden, P, 1987 *The Roman forum site in London: discoveries before 1985,* 92–100

Schofield, J, 1994 'Saxon and medieval parish churches in the City of London: a review', *Trans London Middlesex Archaeol Soc,* 45, 100–1

Straker, V, 1983 'First and second century carbonised cereal grain from Roman London', in Van Zeist, W, & Casparie, W A (eds), *Proceedings of the sixth symposium of the International Work Group for Paleoethnobotany, Plants and Ancient Man — Studies in Palaeoethnobotany,* 323–9

Williams, T, in prep. *The development of Roman London east of the Walbrook,* The archaeology of Roman London 4, CBA Res Rep [Roman strata]

Great Swan Alley, 68–71 Coleman Street, EC2

GSA76

R Blurton
NGR: TQ 32650 81450

A site code was issued but no useful structural or topographical information gained.

2–3 Lombard Court, 39–40 Lombard Street, EC3

LC76

J Maloney
NGR: TQ 32940 80940
SMR: 043436–9

Refurbishment of the property in February 1976 involved the excavation of one trench and a watching brief over the rest of the site to the N. The Roman period was represented by a substantial layer of burnt debris which contained a collapsed brick wall, faced with painted plaster, and the remains of a tessellated floor. These are dated to the late 1st/early 2nd c and could be the result of the Hadrianic fire. For the medieval period, two large pits — possibly quarry pits — were recorded. They are dated to the 13th c and one of the pits yielded a large mortarium sherd which had been refired and covered with a green glaze; it had probably been used as kiln furniture. Borehole records indicate the presence of similar pits over the rest of the site.

London Archaeol, 3, 1977, 36

Maloney, J, 1977 'A green glazed mortarium from the City of London', *Trans London Middlesex Archaeol Soc,* 28, 276–7

Williams, T, in prep. *The development of Roman London east of the Walbrook,* The archaeology of Roman London 4, CBA Res Rep [Roman strata]

St Margaret Lothbury church, Lothbury, EC2

MAR76

A Thompson
NGR: TQ 32710 81270
SMR: 043426–7

During repairs at the NE corner of the Wren church, foundations of a medieval extension to the E were recorded; it comprised an arch over a channelled tributary of the Walbrook stream.

London Archaeol, 3, 1977, 36

Schofield, J, 1994 'Saxon and medieval parish churches in the City of London: a review', *Trans London Middlesex Archaeol Soc,* 45, 109–10

Thompson, A, nd, 'Excavations at St Margaret Lothbury EC2', Archive Report

MFS76

Modern Foreshore, River Thames, EC3 & EC4

This code was created in 1976 to deal with artefacts found on the N bank of the River Thames within the City of London, recovered both by the Museum and by members of the public (often the Society of Mudlarks). It continues in use.

MLK76

1–6 Milk Street, 5–6 Russia Row, EC2

S Roskams, P Allen and J Schofield
NGR: TQ 32380 81270
SMR: 043372–81

Seven periods of Roman occupation were recorded. In Periods I and II (both pre-Neronian), two distinct structures were evidenced by slots and post-holes. One of these did not align with the N–S gravelled Roman street found in the E of the site, and both structures are thought to predate its setting-out. In Period III (Flavian) at least two buildings, one of which included concrete floors and a tessellated pavement, fronted onto the street, and were bounded by an open area to the S and W. In Period IV (Trajanic), these were replaced by a structure interpreted as a lean-to against a larger structure off site to the W, and the area adjacent to the street on the E now became external. The suggested lean-to was replaced in Period V (c 120–5) by another light structure which was destroyed in the Hadrianic fire. In Period VI (c 125–30), slots of a massive building cut into the fire debris may represent temporary reuse of the area, before extensive rebuilding in Period VII (mid-2nd c). The back of a timber building including a tessellated floor

Fig 31 MLK76: cleaning a 2nd-c Roman mosaic; the mosaic is now on show in the Museum's Roman gallery. In the top right of the picture is the Saxon dark earth which overlay Roman buildings on this site (as on many others); in the top left, a Victorian foundation which lay over an 11th-c property boundary at right angles to Milk Street, just off the top of the picture. There is no evidence that the medieval boundaries in this area were influenced by the underlying Roman buildings, which had been long forgotten.

(Fig 31; now on display in MoL) lay in the W of the site, and was bounded on the E by a gravelled yard. A well was sunk to the N of the building. The building was dismantled by the end of the Antonine period, and the site was covered with dark earth (Period X). The street probably remained in use beyond the 2nd c, although its later surfaces were less well laid.

In Period VIII (10th c) a sunken-floored structure was cut through the W side of the Roman street, with an entrance porch actually on the street itself, suggesting that the latter survived in some form, if only as a rough track. The structure became filled with rubbish, but was later cleared out and reoccupied before its final disuse. In Period IX (?10th c) a second sunken-floored structure cut a corner of the first and lay on top of the Roman street. Both sunken-floored structures were truncated, but they presumably lay in or above the dark earth horizon. Above the dark earth were traces of a light timber structure (Period XI, 10th c), along the Milk Street frontage, and a large number of medieval pits (Period XII, late 9th–12th c), some with plank or wattle linings. In Period XIII (12th–15th c) stone buildings were constructed along the Milk Street frontage. A substantial early medieval stone building (Fig 32), medieval cesspits and wells, and the foot of a stair of a medieval undercroft in the N of the site were recorded. A late 17th-c house on Russia Court was recorded by the GLC Historic Buildings Division before demolition.

Fig 32 MLK76: Building 6 of c 1100, looking S. This was one of the City's earliest recorded medieval stone buildings; foundation layers were traced between 19th-c concrete stanchions, forming a rectangular building at right angles to Milk Street (upper right).

London Archaeol, 3, 1977, 140; Post-Medieval Archaeol, 9, 1975, 246 [the post-Fire building, recording by A F Kelsall & R W Weston]

Armitage, P, 1983 'Report on the animal hair fibres from medieval textiles', Archive Report

Bayley, J, 1985 'Some crucibles from Milk Street', Archive Report

Betts, I, 1985a 'MLK76 (Milk Street residual Roman) Important Roman tile', Archive Report

Betts, I, 1985b 'Medieval building material — MLK76', Archive Report

Clark, J, nd, 'MLK76 — An early carpenter's axe', Archive Report

Clark, J, 1978 'MLK76 — Bone comb identification <41>', Archive Report

Crowfoot, E, Pritchard, F, & Staniland, K, 1992 Textiles and clothing c 1150–c 1450, Medieval finds from excavations in London 4

Davis, A, 1992 'Plant remains from a medieval garderobe at Milk Street', Archive Report

Davis, A, & Straker, V, 1982 'Milk Street — plant remains from early medieval pits', Archive Report

Davis, A, Jones, G, & Straker, V, 1984a 'Early medieval plant use and ecology in the City of London', Archive Report

Davis, A, Jones, G, & Straker, V, 1984b 'Saxon plant use and botanical evidence for plant function', Archive Report

Davies, B, 1993 'Inter-site studies', in Milne, G, & Wardle, A, 'Early Roman development at Leadenhall Court, London and related research', Trans London Middlesex Archaeol Soc, 44, 135–50

Egan, G, 1998 The medieval household, Medieval finds from excavations in London 6

Egan, G, & Pritchard, F, 1991 Dress accessories c 1150–c 1450, Medieval finds from excavations in London 3 [medieval dress accessories]

Grew, F, & de Neergaard, M, 1988 Shoes and pattens, Medieval finds from excavations in London 2

Groves, C, & Hillam, J, 1985 'Tree ring analysis of oak timbers from Milk Street London', Archive Report

Groves, J, nd, 'The Milk Street pits (MLK76)', Archive Report

Hillam, J, 1980 'Milk Street — interim dendrochronology report', Archive Report

Horsman, V, Milne, C, & Milne, G, 1988 Aspects of Saxo-Norman London I: building and street development, London Middlesex Archaeol Soc Spec Pap 11 [Saxon buildings and streets]

Locker, A, 1985 'The fish bones', Archive Report (AML Report 4460)

Orton, C, 1983 'Statistical analysis of seed samples from the Milk Street pit project', Archive Report

Perring, D, & Roskams, S, with Allen, P, 1991 The early development of Roman London west of the Walbrook, The archaeology of Roman London 2, CBA Res Rep 70 [Roman strata]

Roskams, S, 1978 'The Milk Street excavation — 1 [Roman]', London Archaeol, 3, 199–205

Roskams, S, Schofield, J, & Allen, P, 1986 'Excavations at Milk Street EC2 (MLK76)', Archive Report

Schofield, J, 1995 Medieval London houses, 203–5

Schofield, J, & Roskams, S, 1978 'Milk Street excavations — 2 [post-Roman]', London Archaeol, 3, 227–34

Schofield, J, Allen, P, & Taylor, C, 1990 'Medieval buildings and property development in the area of Cheapside', Trans London Middlesex Archaeol Soc, 41, 39–237 [Saxon and medieval strata, documentary report]

Smith, D, nd, 'A mosaic from Milk Street', Archive Report

Spencer, B, nd, 'Leaden bulla of Pope Urban VI 1378–89 [context 1003 <111>]', Archive Report

Straker, V, & Davis, A, 1982 'Interim report on the analysis of environmental samples (ASS/02/82)', Archive Report

Taylor, C, 1985 'Milk Street documentary survey', Archive Report

Vince, A (ed), 1991 Aspects of Saxo-Norman London II: finds and environmental evidence, London Middlesex Archaeol Soc Spec Pap 12 [Saxon smallfinds]

Vince, A, & Hurman, B, 1982 'The Saxon pottery', Archive Report

West, B, nd, 'Milk Street — animal bone', Archive Report

NH76

A Boddington
NGR: TQ 33470 81020
SMR: 044710–12

4–8 Northumberland Alley, EC3

Natural brickearth was cut by a series of rubbish pits, one of which may originally have been for brickearth extraction. This latter pit was sealed by one of three areas of internal brickearth and trampled surfaces, although there were no recorded structural elements. A possible well cut through one of the areas of floor surfaces. These features are not dated in the summaries produced so far, but Roman material was found.

Rivière, S, 1987 '4–6 Northumberland Alley', Post-excavation Assessment
Williams, T, in prep. *The development of Roman London east of the Walbrook*, The archaeology of Roman London 4, CBA Res Rep [Roman strata]

PEN76

L Miller
NGR: TQ 32950 80695
SMR: 043491, 043496

Peninsular House, 112–116 Lower Thames Street, EC3

A single section was drawn after contractors had dug a hole by machine on this site; traces of a Roman building with a drain and a medieval foundation were observed. The site was excavated three years later as PEN79.

**SH76: see
SH74**

Seal House, 106–108 Upper Thames Street, EC4

BXA77

J Schofield
NGR: TQ 33160 8148
SMR: 041928

St Botolph Bishopsgate churchyard, Bastion 10A, EC2

Cartographic and documentary sources between 1529 and c 1558 indicate a hitherto unrecognised bastion on the city wall, for which the number 10A is proposed, between All Hallows on the Wall church and Bishopsgate. A resistivity survey carried out over the proposed site of the bastion in the churchyard of St Botolph Bishopsgate could not firmly identify the feature, though a slight anomaly was registered. There are no finds from this site.

Schofield, J, 1978 'Bastion 10A — a newly identified bastion in the City of London', *Trans London Middlesex Archaeol Soc*, 29, 91–8

CGT77

D Gadd
NGR: TQ 32250 81610
SMR: 040477

Cripplegate Gardens, London Wall and Wallside, EC2

A short report on the remaining archaeology of the ditches outside the city wall between Bastions 12 and 14 was prepared; and the landscaping of terraced earth over a surviving fragment of the post-medieval churchyard of St Giles Cripplegate, immediately S of Bastion 12, was monitored.

St James Passage subway, 2–7 Dukes Place, EC3

DUK77

J Maloney
NGR: TQ 33520 81190
SMR: 041910, 041949–51

The recording of a 30m section across the defences revealed a sequence of activity from before AD120 to the 17th c. The earliest dated feature was a shallow flat-bottomed ditch (probably a pre-wall boundary), the fill of which contained pottery of c AD120 and the remains of two human skeletons. The foundation trench for the city wall was cut through a deposit which yielded pottery of c 180, as did the internal bank and deposits dumped against the external face of the wall. The wall survived to its full width of 2.7m and to a height of 1.7m above the plinth. A longitudinal section through the wall facilitated the recording of details of its construction: a singular feature was an offset on its external face. A V-shaped ditch, 3.5m from the wall, was possibly contemporary with its construction. A localised change in the construction of the wall proved to be the blocking of a doorway and passage, and it is likely that this medieval postern was a private thoroughfare for the incumbents of Holy Trinity Priory. Other features of the priory recorded include a doorway and undercroft in the dorter. An arched brick wall constructed parallel to and up against the internal face of the city wall is probably part of a medieval renovation. Two large medieval ditches and a ?Civil War ditch were cut into by a series of post-medieval pits which contained substantial groups of pottery including six pots (four containing paint), a stoneware sherd dated 1591, delftware wasters, kiln furniture and a vitrified brick. A stoneware Bellarmine jug containing the remains of pins is thought to have been a witch bottle.

London Archaeol, 3, 1978, 159
Bimson, M, 1979 'Analysis of early 17th-c paints from Duke's Place', Archive Report
Crowfoot, E, Pritchard, F, & Staniland, K, 1992 Textiles and clothing c 1150–c 1450, Medieval finds from excavations in London 4
Egan, G, & Moir, D, in prep. 'Post-medieval finds c 1450–c 1700: a selection from the City of London sites 1972–82'
Gale, R, 1986 'The identification of wood from sites excavated by the DUA', AML Report 60/87
Harding, C, & Maloney, J, 1979 'Duke's Place and Houndsditch — the medieval defences', London Archaeol, 3, 347–54
Lea, R, nd, 'Moulded stone', Archive Report
Maloney, C, 1980 'A witch bottle from Duke's Place', Trans London Middlesex Archaeol Soc, 31, 157–8
Maloney, J, 1979 'Excavations at Duke's Place — the Roman defences', London Archaeol, 3, 292–7
Rhodes, M, 1983 'Spectacle lens (DUK77)', Archive Report
Schofield, J, & Lea, R, in prep. Holy Trinity Priory Aldgate
Vince, A, 1985 '2–7 Duke's Place (DUK77) — medieval pottery from cesspit', Archive Report

Gracechurch Street, GPO tunnel, EC3

GST77

P Marsden and J Maloney
NGR: TQ 33010 81040
SMR: 043406–11

A traverse of the Roman basilica and forum was made in a GPO tunnel dug 4.5m below and along Gracechurch Street. It crossed first the S wing of the forum and then found the forum entrance; then the courtyard, with a structure, perhaps a decorative pool, near the middle; thirdly, the basilica floor in the hall and side aisles. S of the forum the tunnel passed through three Roman roads, the frontages of several Roman buildings, a 15th-c conduit and the W end of St Benet Gracechurch. The Roman levels recorded in the tunnel are reported in Marsden 1987; this includes a plan of the location and extent of the tunnel (his fig 48).

London Archaeol, 3, 1978, 159
Marsden, P, 1987 The Roman forum site in London: discoveries before 1985, 57–60

Kingscote Street, tunnel, EC4

KSC77

C Milne and G Milne
NGR: TQ 31600 80990
SMR: 044460

A tunnel to construct a sewer along Kingscote Street was monitored and a section in the tunnel drawn as it crossed Tudor Street. The section showed two horizontal timber base-plates on piles, driven into waterlain gravels, aligned N–S; above was ragstone rubble.

Hillam, J, 1980 'Kingscote Street (KSC77) — final tree-ring report', Archive Report
Milne, C, & Milne, G, 1977 'Watching brief on Kingscote Street', Archive Report

BRI78

D Gadd
NGR: TQ 31610 81030
SMR: 044461–3

9–12 Bridewell Place, 13–16 New Bridge Street, EC4

Excavation recorded large-scale reclamation on the W bank of the Fleet in the medieval period; a revetment included part of a boat. The main findings were parallel brick foundations (including brick arches on pile-supported chalk piers, Fig 33). Documentary and cartographic evidence identifies these as the S half of the E range of the principal courtyard of Bridewell Palace (1515–23). The beginning of the S range, the base of a corner stair and traces of the brick courtyard surface were also recorded; in the E of the site, later brick foundations were perhaps associated with the chapel of the Bridewell Hospital.

Fig 33 BRI78: arched brick foundations of Henry VIII's Bridewell Palace, 1523.

This site is published with evidence from the watching brief at 1–3 Tudor Street (TUD78), which uncovered foundations of the gallery of the palace.

Egan, G, & Moir, D, in prep. 'Post-medieval finds c 1450–c 1700: a selection from the City of London sites 1972–82'

Gadd, D, nd, 'Excavations at 9–12 Bridewell Place EC4', Archive Report

Gadd, D, & Dyson, T, 1981 'Bridewell Palace: excavations at 9–11 Bridewell Place and 1–3 Tudor Street, City of London, 1978', Post-Medieval Archaeol, 15, 1–79

Hillam, J, 1980 'Bridewell — dendrochronology (BRI78)', Archive Report

Rhodes, M, 1983 'Objects of slate (BRI78)', Archive Report

Thompson, A, & Gadd, D, 1979 'Bridewell Palace', London Archaeol, 3, 255–60

Vince, A, 1980 'Pottery from Periods 3C and 3D at Bridewell Place (BRI78)', Archive Report

CUT78

S O'Connor Thompson
NGR: TQ 33470 81490
SMR: 043511–22

Cutler Street PLA Warehouses, Harrow Place, E1

At the former PLA warehouses situated between Bishopsgate, Houndsditch and Middlesex Street, about 200sq m were excavated in plan within standing buildings and a watching brief maintained on the remaining 4 acres. On the W of two excavation sites a number of human bones were recorded and dated to the Roman period. Though no grave was discovered, it seems probable that these represent part of the Roman cemetery outside Bishopsgate from the 1st c. The Saxon and medieval periods were represented by a deposit of dark earth recorded throughout the site. A pond had silted up by 1500 to become a dumping ground for a variety of rubbish including a number of 15th-c shoes. During the 16th c and first half of the 17th c the site saw an increased amount of activity, though the land remained agricultural. By 1700 a large number of buildings had been erected, of which substantial remains of 13 were recorded, with cesspits and wells. The debris from several small-scale industries including clay pipemaking, bell-founding, glassmaking and hornworking, was widespread. One industry involved the use of pits lined with cattle horn cores; a dozen of these pits were found.

During the subsequent watching brief three E–W aligned inhumation burials of the 3rd c were recorded in the NW part of the site. These overlay shallow brickearth quarries of 2nd- or 3rd-c date, and were in turn cut by early medieval pits filled with dark earth.

London Archaeol, 3, 1981, 385; Britannia, 11, 1980, 379; 12, 1981, 351; Medieval Archaeol, 24, 1980, 254

Armitage, P, 1979 'Preliminary report on the cattle horn cores from the trial hole No. 2, Cutler Street warehouses', Archive Report (AML Report 2803)

Armitage, P, 1980 'A system for ageing and sexing the horn cores of 17th- and early 18th-century unimproved British longhorn cattle', Archive Report (AML Report 3132)

Davis, A, & Straker, V, 1981 'Cutlers Gardens environmental report', Archive Report

Drummond-Murray, J, & Greig, I, 1991 'Cutler Street', Archive Report, draft

Egan, G, & Moir, D, in prep. 'Post-medieval finds c 1450–c 1700: a selection from the City of London sites 1972–82'

Gale, R, 1987 'The identification of wood from artefacts excavated by the DUA at London sites — Cutler Street', Archive Report

Giorgi, J, Rackham, J, & Smith, D, 1996 'The environmental samples from post-medieval deposits at Cutler Street (ENV/REP/13/96)', Archive Report

Girling M, nd, 'Eighteenth-century records of human lice and fleas', Archive Report

Girling, M, 1982 'The arthropod assemblage from Cutlers Gardens', Archive Report (AML 3670)

Richardson, B, 1988 'The Roman pottery from Cutler Street (CUT78)', Archive Report

Vince, A, & Egan, G, 1981 'The contents of a late eighteenth-century pit at Crosswall, City of London', Trans London Middlesex Archaeol Soc, 32, 159–81 [comparison of AL74, CUT78 and XWL79 sites in pottery assemblages]

New Fresh Wharf (watching brief), 1–6 Lower Thames Street, EC3

FRE78

NGR: TQ 32940 80640
SMR: 042159–66

See NFW74 above for details of this excavation and its reports.

Chatsworth House, 48–56 Houndsditch, 66–70 St Mary Axe, EC3

HOU78

C Harding
NGR: TQ 33370 81370
SMR: 041937

Five periods of activity were observed in two sections cut by machine at right angles. An undated NW–SE gully was overlaid by an E–W ditch, perhaps of 13th-c date, which was in turn sealed by surfaces of sand and pebbles. This was cut by a further ditch, sometime after the 14th c, which was ``not filled (or backfilled) until after the end of the 16th c. This was cut by an early modern brick sewer.

Cassely, V, 1989 'Chatsworth House, 47–56 Houndsditch', Finds Appraisal

Giorgi, J, Rackham, J, & Smith, D, 1996 'The environmental samples from post-medieval deposits at Chatsworth House, Houndsditch (ENV/REP/06/96)', Archive Report

Harding, C, 1978 'A recent excavation in the City', Taywood News, 17, 26–8

Harding, C, 1979 'Excavations at Chatsworth House', Archive Report

Harding, C, & Maloney, J, 1979 'Duke's Place and Houndsditch — the medieval defences', London Archaeol, 3, 347–54

Lloyd's, 12–19 Leadenhall Street, EC3

LLO78

K Flude
NGR: TQ 33150 81090
SMR: 044466–71

Excavation took place within the basement of the standing building. Roman features investigated included early Roman pits predating post-holes. The post-holes consisted of two types. The first were aligned E–W and were large square features with no sign of a post-pipe, the second were aligned slightly N of E–W, and contained a square post-pipe. Early medieval pits investigated included a rectangular soak-away, or well, a clay-lined pit, and a presumed rubbish pit containing a bone skate. The latter postdated a mortar-lined feature with a charcoal and ash primary fill, also containing slag, suggesting an industrial use.

This site was also observed during the construction of the building in 1925: see GM268 above.

London Archaeol, 3, 1979, 262

Cassely, V, 1989 'Lloyd's, Leadenhall Place', Finds Appraisal

Davies, B, 1993 'Inter-site studies', in Milne, G, & Wardle, A, 'Early Roman development at Leadenhall Court, London and related research', Trans London Middlesex Archaeol Soc, 44, 135–50

Flude, K, nd, 'Excavations at Lloyd's', Archive Report, draft

Macphail, R, 1980 'Report on a soil in a Romano-British context at Lloyd's Insurance Building excavations', Archive Report

Vaughan, D, nd, 'Plant remains', Archive Report

Williams, T, in prep. The development of Roman London east of the Walbrook, The archaeology of Roman London 4, CBA Res Rep [Roman strata]

MAS78

P Herbert
NGR: TQ 32570 81370 and
32610 81370
SMR: 044472–3

1–9 Masons Avenue (Butler's Head), 10–14 Masons Avenue, 23 Moorgate, EC2

This site code covers salvage observations on three sites in close proximity. At Site A (12–14 Masons Avenue) in 1978, a N–S trench exposed two box drains, running approximately E–W, dating to the 2nd c or later. Beneath them was a natural stream-bed, silted up before the Roman period. At Site B (Butler's Head public house) in 1980 a timber-lined drain was observed and sampled. At Site C (23 Moorgate) in 1978 an ancient stream-bed was observed.

London Archaeol, 3, 1979, 262
Herbert, P, 1980 'Excavations at Masons Avenue and 23 Moorgate', Archive Report
Hillam, J, 1980 'Masons Avenue — interim dendrochronology report (MAS78)', Archive Report

TST78

K Flude
NGR: TQ 32380 80840
SMR: 044474–6

Upper Thames Street, tunnel, EC4

Sections were recorded through an E–W GPO tunnel along the N carriageway of Upper Thames Street, from Dowgate Hill House W to Garlick Hill (the main shaft at the E end about 6m W of the W end of St James Garlickhithe church). Deposits recorded ranged from early Roman river gravels to medieval foundations. Among several timber constructions found were two box-type quay structures of Roman date. One at Garlick Hill had its main baulk aligned N–S, the other at St James Garlickhithe was aligned E–W. At the time of excavation they were the first such structures found W of the Walbrook, and were N of the presumed line of the late Roman riverside wall.

London Archaeol, 3, 1979, 261
Flude, K, nd, 'Excavations in the Thames Street tunnel', Archive Report, draft
Hillam, J, 1980 'Thames Street tunnel — interim dendrochronology report', Archive Report

TUD78

A Thompson
NGR: TQ 31590 80970
SMR: 04119104001

1–3 Tudor Street, EC4

A watching brief on this large site recovered evidence of the Fleet Valley in Pleistocene and prehistoric times; reclamation and revetting of the W side of the valley in the medieval period; and fragmentary brick arched foundations of the gallery of Bridewell Palace (1515–23).

Armitage, P, & West, B, 1980 'The faunal remains from the medieval and Tudor levels', Archive Report
Boyd, P, 1981 'The micropalaeontology and palaeoecology of medieval estuarine sediments from the Fleet and Thames in London', in Neale, J, & Brasier, M (eds), *Microfossils from recent and fossil shelf seas,* British Micropalaeontological Association, 274–92
Clark, J (ed), 1995 *The medieval horse and its equipment c 1150–c 1450,* Medieval finds from excavations in London 5 [medieval horseshoes and horse equipment]
Gadd, D, & Dyson, T, 1981 'Bridewell Palace: excavations at 9–11 Bridewell Place and 1–3 Tudor Street, City of London, 1978, *Post-Medieval Archaeol,* 15, 1–79
Hillam, J, 1980 'Tudor Street — interim dendrochronology', Archive Report
Hillam, J, 1981 'An English tree-ring chronology, AD404–1216', *Medieval Archaeol,* 25, 31–44 [contribution of a timber from TUD78]
Locker, A, 1980 'Tudor Street — the fish bones', Archive Report
Thompson, A, 1979 'Excavations at 1–3 Tudor Street', Archive Report
Thompson, A, & Gadd, D, 1979 'Bridewell Palace', *London Archaeol,* 3, 255–60

Watling Court, 10–14a Bow Lane, 39–53 Cannon Street, 19–28 Watling Street, EC4

WAT78

D Perring
NGR: TQ 32355 81045
SMR: 043616–25

Fig 34 WAT78: excavation at Watling Court begins as demolition contractors finish their work and withdraw. The top 3m of strata have been lost to 19th-c basements. Between the 19th-c footings which cross the site, Roman strata and the lower parts of Saxon and medieval buildings, cesspits and wells can be seen. On sites away from the waterfront, this is the usual character of deposits from each period.

An area 32m x 30m (Fig 34) was examined in detail, and a watching brief held on a wider area about 40m square. After a period of shallow brickearth-quarrying (Period I, before 70), two Flavian buildings were constructed in the SE corner of the site (Period II, before c 85). These were destroyed by fire and the site used for further quarrying (Period III, 70–95). In Period IV (70–120) buildings divided by alleys were constructed over the whole site; the S building fronted off the site to the S. They were also destroyed by fire (probably Hadrianic). These buildings included *opus signinum* and tessellated floors. A further period of less substantial building (Period V, 125–60) reproduced Period IV boundaries on a smaller scale; this period was also ended by a fire. A further building is possibly represented (Period VI, c 160), and a small number of stake-holes below the dark earth (Period VII) may be of Roman date (Perring & Roskams 1991).

The report on the Saxon to post-medieval levels uses post-Roman Ceramic Phases (CP) instead of periodisation. In CP1 (850–1020), lines of rubbish pits ran about 10m W of Bow Lane, and to a less extent a similar distance N of medieval Basing Lane (now beneath Cannon Street on the S of the site), indicating ground-level buildings in the strips between them and the streets. In CP2 (1000–30) or CP3 (1020–50), a timber building with a sunken floor was part of probably continuous ground-level buildings along Bow Lane. In CP4 (1050–1100), three more and larger sunken-floored timber buildings were constructed away from the frontages. In CP5–6 (1100–80), stone buildings appeared on the site (one square foundation on the site of the largest previous timber cellar), and in CP7–11 (1180–1400) several cesspits. A number of rebuildings and further cesspits followed in CP12–21 (1400–1740), but the remains of these periods were fragmentary (Schofield, Allen & Taylor 1990).

The published report on the Late Saxon and medieval periods (ibid) includes a documentary report by C Taylor. The W part of the site was in the medieval period part of the large tenement called *La Rouge Sale;* some of the 12th-c and later foundations and an open area which was probably a garden lay within the reconstructed boundaries of the tenement.

London Archaeol, 3, 1979, 261; *Britannia,* 10, 1979, 313–17; 12, 1981, 351; *Medieval Archaeol,* 23, 1979, 267–8; 25, 1981, 210
Betts, I, 1986 'Watling Court / 41–53 Cannon Street WAT78 — medieval and post-medieval building material', Archive Report
Burnett, A, 1982 'The Watling Court hoard', Archive Report
Crowley, N, 1990 'Watling Court', [Roman] Building Materials Appraisal
Davies, B, 1993 'Inter-site studies', in Milne, G, & Wardle, A, 'Early Roman development at Leadenhall Court, London and related research', *Trans London Middlesex Archaeol Soc,* 44, 135–50
Davies, B, Richardson, B, & Tomber, R, 1994 *A dated corpus of early Roman pottery from the City of London,* The archaeology of Roman London 5, CBA Res Rep 98 [contribution to early Roman pottery corpus]
Egan, G, & Moir, D, in prep. 'Post-medieval finds c 1450–c 1700: a selection from the City of London sites 1972–82'

Ganiaris, H, 1985 'Treatment and display of diplomas', in Roxan, M H (ed), *Roman military diplomas,* Institute of Archaeol Occ Pap 9, 213–16

Giorgi, J, Rackham, J, & Smith, D, 1996 'The environmental samples from post-medieval deposits at Watling Court (ENV/REP/10/96)', Archive Report

Hillam, J, 1980 'Watling Court — interim dendrochronology report', Archive Report

Horsman, V, Milne, C, & Milne, G, 1988 *Aspects of Saxo-Norman London I: building and street development,* London Middlesex Archaeol Soc Spec Pap 11 [Saxon buildings and streets]

Perring, D, 1981 'Excavations at Watling Court — Part 1', *London Archaeol,* 4, 103–8

Perring, D, 1982a 'Excavations at Watling Court — Part 2', *London Archaeol,* 4, 208–12

Perring, D, 1982b 'Housing in Roman London', *Popular Archaeol,* 3, No. 12, 36–9

Perring, D, 1983 'Excavations at Watling Court 1978', Archive Report

Perring, D, & Roskams, S, with Allen, P, 1991 *The early development of Roman London west of the Walbrook,* The archaeology of Roman London 2, CBA Res Rep 70 [Roman strata]

Rhodes, M, 1979 'Note on wooden barrel <1158>', Archive Report

de Rouffignac, C, 1987 'The effects of sample storage conditions on the preservation of human parasite remains in soil samples from Roman, medieval and post-medieval deposits at Watling Court and Monument Fish Street (DIS/01/87)', Archive Report

Roxan, M, nd, 'A Roman military diploma from London', Archive Report

Schofield, J, 1995 *Medieval London houses,* 164–6

Schofield, J, Allen, P, & Taylor, C, 1990 'Medieval buildings and property development in the area of Cheapside', *Trans London Middlesex Archaeol Soc,* 41, 39–238 [Saxon and medieval strata]

Taylor, C, 1985 'Watling Court documentary survey', Archive Report

Vince, A, 1983 'Saxon and early medieval pottery from WAT78', Archive Report

AGT79

M Barker
NGR: TQ 32120 81620
SMR: 043602–7

174–176 Aldersgate Street, EC1

A N–S section to the rear of this extramural property revealed a possibly Roman horizon of redeposited natural, overlaid by a series of make-ups/dumps which in turn were cut by an E–W ditch. The ditch is provisionally dated to the 12th/13th c. Gravel and silty clay dumps were laid across the site over the ditchfills. These were sealed by a medieval tile-based hearth which predated chalk block wall foundations. Post-medieval brick foundations were also noted.

London Archaeol, 3, 1981, 45; *Britannia,* 12, 1981, 350; *Medieval Archaeol,* 25, 1981, 210

Barker, M, 1985 'Excavations at 174–176 Aldersgate Street', Archive Report

BAR79

D Bentley
NGR: TQ 31870 81510
SMR: 040293

Medical School, St Bartholomew's Hospital, EC1

During excavations at St Bartholomew's Hospital in April 1979 evidence was found of several 2nd–4th-c burials in an area known to have been a Roman cemetery. The site, 50m N of the city wall, also produced evidence of a 1st-/2nd-c building, representing at least three phases of activity. Several brickearth occupation surfaces were bounded by major and minor E–W aligned brickearth sills. The laying of an *opus signinum* floor followed a rearrangement of internal divisions. Evidence indicates the continued use of this mortar floor after the building was destroyed and the debris removed. Sixteen inhumations of men, women and children found in dark earth deposits overlying the building suggest that the immediate area was not intensively used as a cemetery. Coin evidence suggests burials from the early 3rd to mid-4th c. Of note was one grave, a female, containing a small bronze bell and a series of simply decorated bronze amulets apparently placed on her chest.

London Archaeol, 3, 1980, 364; *Britannia,* 11, 1980, 381

Armitage, P, 1980a 'Historical note', *Bart's J,* 27–8

Armitage, P, 1980b 'Identification of mammalian bone from Roman levels', Archive Report

Bentley, D, nd, 'Excavations at St Bartholomew's Hospital Medical School EC1', Archive Report

Bentley, D, 1979 'Archaeology at Barts', *Bart's J,* 25

Bentley, D, 1980 'Archaeology at Barts', *Bart's J,* 19

Bentley, D, & Pritchard, F, 1982 'The Roman cemetery at St Bartholomew's Hospital', *Trans London Middlesex Archaeol Soc,* 33, 134–72

Downs, D, nd, 'Human skeleton remains', Archive Report

Downs, D, 1980 'Archaeology at Barts — human skeletal remains', *Bart's J,* 20–3

Macphail, R, 1980 'Soil report on dark earth at St Bartholomew's Hospital', Archive Report

Rhodes, M, 1982 'Painted wall plaster (BAR79)', Archive Report

West B, nd, 'Sawn human bone', Archive Report

West, B, 1980 'The sawn human bone of St Barts', *Bart's J,* 24–6

Bull Wharf, 14–15 Queenhithe, EC4

BLL79

C Milne
NGR: TQ 32320 80760
SMR: 043504

A watching brief conducted during the contractors' redevelopment of the site produced evidence of medieval and post-medieval riverfront reclamation incorporating both front-braced timber revetments and stone riverwalls.

The site was excavated again as part of BUF90 (see below).

London Archaeol, 3, 1985, 385; Medieval Archaeol, 24, 1980, 254
Hillam, J, 1981 'Bull Wharf — interim dendrochronology report (BLL79)', Archive Report

33 Creechurch Lane, 16a Bevis Marks, EC3

CRE79

G Egan
NGR: TQ 33430 81260
SMR: 044478–80

Cutting into natural brickearth was a ditch 4m long, aligned NW–SE, which was infilled in the 4th c. Fragments of chalk and ragstone wall foundations seem to be from the NW part of the precinct of Holy Trinity Priory, while a series of six medieval pits aligned N–S down the centre of the site presumably indicate a property boundary, probably that of the W edge of the priory's precinct. Several ?late medieval or post-medieval wall foundations were recorded, and a brick-arched culvert which may date from the first half of the 19th c.

Britannia, 11, 1979, 301
Egan, G, 1979 'Excavations at Creechurch Lane', Archive Report
Schofield, J, & Lea, R, in prep. Holy Trinity Priory Aldgate
Williams, T, in prep. The development of Roman London east of the Walbrook, The archaeology of Roman London 4, CBA Res Rep
  [Roman strata]

78–79 Fenchurch Street, EC3

FCH79

L Watson
NGR: TQ 33460 81070
SMR: 044483–5

Two testpits were recorded in a basement before demolition. Roman stratigraphy consisted of alternate bands of discoloured light tan brickearth and silts. Medieval pits and a corner of a post-medieval brick-lined cesspit were also recorded.

Watson, L, nd, 'Excavations at 78–79 Fenchurch Street EC3', Archive Report
Williams, T, in prep. The development of Roman London east of the Walbrook, The archaeology of Roman London 4, CBA Res Rep
  [Roman strata]

22–25 Farringdon Street, EC1

FRR79

A Thompson and M Barker
NGR: TQ 31650 81340
SMR: 043663–4

Natural clay was cut by a channel or ditch, possibly Roman in date. Its waterlogged fill accumulated over a period of time. Modern make-up sealed the ditch.

London Archaeol, 3, 1980, 385

HEN79

L Watson
NGR: TQ 33380 81240
SMR: 044486–93

6–10 Heneage Lane, EC3

Quarry pits of 1st-/2nd-c date were followed by possible brickearth surfaces and dark earth. Occupation in the medieval period was represented by pits and chalk or chalk and ragstone foundations, together with garden soil. These were followed by brick-founded buildings in the post-medieval period, a brick-lined cesspit and a well.

Watson, L, 1980 'Watching brief at 6–10 Heneage Lane EC3', Archive Report
Williams, T, in prep. *The development of Roman London east of the Walbrook*, The archaeology of Roman London 4, CBA Res Rep [Roman strata]

HTP79

J Schofield
NGR: TQ 33440 81190
SMR: 043506–10

Mitre Square, 10–14 Mitre Street, EC3

Excavations on the W side of Mitre Square revealed foundations of the range on the W side of the cloister of Holy Trinity Priory (founded 1108). Three main phases were identified: an initial building on the W side of the cloister, with medieval burials to the S, some in chalk and mortar cists; a phase of adaptation at the time of a new building, probably the W end of the priory church, to the S and E; and a third phase of internal adaptation, probably at the time of a doubling in width of the range to the W which is deducible from the post-Dissolution plan of the priory by John Symonds (formerly dated on internal evidence to 1592, but proposed now (Schofield & Lea in prep.) as c 1586). Beneath the priory foundations lay disturbed levels of humic silt and evidence of small-scale digging for brickearth in the 1st and 2nd c. The watching brief on this site produced evidence of 17th-c pottery wasters, possibly from a kiln of the 'Aldgate potter', Jacob Jansen.

London Archaeol, 3, 1980, 385
Downs, D, 1979 'Human skeletal remains from Holy Trinity Priory 1979', Archive Report [later combined with a report on human remains at LEA84; the edited report by J Conheeney, MoLAS Environmental Archaeology Section, Human Bone Report HUM 02/93, 1993]
Lea, R, nd, 'Moulded stone', Archive Report
Schofield, J, 1985 'Excavations at Mitre Square EC3', Archive Report
Schofield, J, 1993 'Building in religious precincts in London at the Dissolution and after', in Gilchrist, R, & Mytum, H (eds), *Advances in monastic archaeology*, British Archaeol Reps 227, 29–42
Schofield, J, & Lea, R, in prep. *Holy Trinity Priory Aldgate*
Williams, T, in prep. *The development of Roman London east of the Walbrook*, The archaeology of Roman London 4, CBA Res Rep [Roman strata]

ILA79

L Miller
NGR: TQ 32800 80740
SMR: 043523–32

Miles Lane, 132–137 Upper Thames Street, 15–17 Arthur Street, EC4

A Roman building with timber terracing to the S was observed in construction trenches for a building in 1920. The remaining archaeology was sealed beneath the slab of the previous 19th-c building and this awaited an opportunity for excavation. The site was opened at the beginning of September 1979 and was available, from Land Securities Ltd, for four months. The medieval layers were truncated by the 19th-c slab but the bottoms of several Saxon pits survived. The building observed by Frank Lambert in 1920 (Lambert 1921) was found in two parts, with the northern end being completely of tile and the southern of dressed rag with tile courses. Floors of *opus signinum* were found associated with the northern part but very patchy mortar floors with the southern. An eaves drip gully ran down the outside wall bordering a gravel pavement on the further side. A drain ran down the other side of this pavement. A fragment of timber-lined drain 2m deep was found preserved below the water table. Of Hadrianic date, this cut through the timber terracing, which consisted of two beams side by side running at right angles to the front which was parallel with the front of the building. The timber boxes formed were then packed with dumps of mortars and clays.

Subsequent excavation on the E side of Miles Lane showed that the Roman building excavated in 1979–80 was Flavian in date. During the watching brief following the demolition of a large area to the W of the lane several further Roman buildings were traced, with more of the Flavian quayfront (Fig 35). Foundations and cesspits of medieval buildings fronting onto both Upper Thames Street and St Martin's Lane were also recorded.

London Archaeol, 3, 1980, 384; *Britannia,* 11, 1980, 380; 12, 1981, 351–3; *Medieval Archaeol,* 25, 1981, 210

Armitage, P, 1981 'Roman horse skeleton from Miles Lane 1979', Archive Report

Grew, F, 1983a 'Copper objects from Miles Lane (ILA79)', Archive Report

Grew, F, 1983b 'Glass from 1st- and 2nd-century contexts from Miles Lane (ILA79)', Archive Report

Grew, F, & Pritchard, F, 1983 'Miles Lane (ILA79)', Finds Appraisal

Henig, M, & Jones, C, 1992 'A cornelian intaglio from Miles Lane, City of London', *Trans London Middlesex Archaeol Soc,* 43, 1–2

Hillam, J, 1982 'Miles Lane — dendrochronology', Archive Report

Lambert, F, 1921 'Some recent excavations in London', *Archaeologia,* 71, 62–72

Miller, L, 1982 'Miles Lane — the early Roman waterfront', *London Archaeol,* 4, 143–7

Miller, L, 1985 'Excavations at Miles Lane and 132–137 Upper Thames Street', Archive Report

Milne, G, 1985 *The port of Roman London* [Roman waterfronts]

Orton, C, 1996 'Dem dry bones', in Bird, J, Hassall, M, & Sheldon, H (eds), *Interpreting Roman London: papers in memory of Hugh Chapman,* 199–208 [comparative statistical study of animal bones]

Pritchard, F, 1983a 'Bone objects from Miles Lane (ILA79)', Archive Report

Pritchard, F, 1983b 'Stone objects from Miles Lane (ILA79)', Archive Report

Richardson, B, & Tyers, P, 1984 'Roman pottery (ILA79)', Archive Report

Ruddle, J, 1991 'An investigation of the potential of tooth cement annuli for ageing zooarchaeological material, with special consideration to cattle mandibular first molars (DIS/02/91)', MSc Dissertation, Dept of Human Environment, Institute of Archaeology, University College London

Fig 35 ILA79: working conditions on the Miles Lane site while recording Roman quay timbers hauled out by machines.

Peninsular House, 112–116 Lower Thames Street, EC3

PEN79

G Milne
NGR: TQ 32970 80705
SMR: 043489–98

A four-month controlled excavation on Areas A–F was followed by a watching brief. The truncated remains of a Mesolithic marsh were sampled beneath a foundation raft associated with one of the five Roman masonry buildings (Area D). Part of a 1st-c timber quay was observed in the watching brief and the 1st–5th-c development of two bays of an associated warehouse building was examined in the excavation (Areas B, C), together with evidence for 2nd–3rd-c fish processing (Areas A, D). Overlying dark grey silt deposits (Area E) were a series of Saxon internal floors and hearths, representing buildings along Botolph Lane to the E, the early medieval surfaces of which were sectioned (Area F). A number of medieval pits were excavated, and a brick-lined cellar on Pudding Lane in which barrels of tar were being stored at the time of the Great Fire was recorded in detail (Area B). The main conclusions reached in the archive report are integrated with those of the Pudding Lane excavation (see PDN81 below).

Britannia, 11, 1980, 380

Bimson, M, 1980 'Report on the scientific examination of a red pigment RL13608T from PEN79', Archive Report

British Carbonization Research Association, 1980 'Tar and tar products', Archive Report

Egan, G, & Moir, D, in prep. 'Post-medieval finds *c* 1450–*c* 1700: a selection from the City of London sites 1972–82'

Giorgi, J, Rackham, J, & Smith, D, 1996 'An environmental sample from a post-medieval drainfill at Peninsular House (ENV/REP/09/96)', Archive Report

Hillam, J, 1982 'Peninsular House — dendrochronology', Archive Report

Horsman, V, Milne, C, & Milne, G, 1988 *Aspects of Saxo-Norman London I: building and street development,* London Middlesex Archaeol Soc Spec Pap 11 [Saxon buildings and streets]

Locker, A, 1982 'The fish bones from context 700', Archive Report (AML Report 3686)

Locker, A, 1986 'The fish remains: context 619 (FIS/01/86)', Archive Report

Locker, A, & Bateman, N, 1982 'The sauce of the Thames', *London Archaeol,* 4, 204–7

Milne, G, 1980a 'Excavations at Peninsular House/112–116 Lower Thames Street EC3', Archive Report

Milne, G, 1980b 'Saxon Botolph Lane', *London Archaeol*, 3, 423–30

Milne, G, 1981 'Peninsular House', *Popular Archaeol*, 2, No. 7, 35

Milne, G, 1983 'Archaeology and the Great Fire of London', *Popular Archaeol*, 5, No. 6, 32–6

Milne, G, 1985 *The port of Roman London* [Roman waterfronts]

Milne, G, & Milne, C, 1985 'A building in Pudding Lane destroyed in the Great Fire of 1666: excavations on the Peninsular House
site, 1979–80', *Trans London Middlesex Archaeol Soc*, 36, 169–82

Pritchard, F, 1983a 'Bone objects from Peninsular House (PEN79)', Archive Report

Pritchard, F, 1983b 'Ceramic objects from Peninsular House (PEN79)', Archive Report

Pritchard, F, 1983c 'Stone objects from Peninsular House (PEN79)', Archive Report

Richardson, B, 1984 'Peninsular House Roman pottery (PEN79)', Archive Report

Scaife, R, 1983 'Stratigraphy and preliminary palynological results of peats', Archive Report

Tyers, P, 1984a 'Roman pottery (PEN79)', Archive Report

Tyers, P, 1984b 'The Roman pottery from PEN79 Areas B and C', Archive Report

POM79

P Allen, I Blair,
J Burke-Easton, M Lee,
C Midgley and J Norton
NGR: TQ 32060 81380
SMR: 044494–501, 04449601

Newgate Street, GPO site, middle area, EC1

Early Roman activity in the form of intercutting pits for rubbish and brickearth extraction to the E, and a sequence on the W following the pattern established during earlier excavations to the rear of the properties fronting onto Newgate Street to the S (see GPO75 above) was sealed by a thick deposit of dark silts covering the whole area. A series of hearths, mostly of tile and brickearth construction, was concentrated in three separated areas of the site during the early medieval period, the western group probably being associated with a flimsy structure. This was followed on the E side by a series of large rubbish pits mostly of 13th-c date, and by fragmentary remains of a building with chalk and ragstone foundations and associated with a chalk-lined well and cesspits to the W, the contemporary differences in land use probably relating to property boundaries across the site. Immediately below the level of the Victorian basement, a substantial stone-founded building covering an area 12m x 10m is provisionally dated to the 14th c.

London Archaeol, 3, 1980, 384; *Medieval Archaeol*, 24, 1980, 253

Armitage, P, nd, 'Small wild mammals', Archive Report

Armitage, P, & West, B, 1985 'Faunal evidence from a late medieval garden well of the Greyfriars, London', *Trans London Middlesex
Archaeol Soc*, 36, 107–36

Brown, G, in prep. 'Excavations in the Greyfriars' garden (POM79)'

Clarke, B T, nd, 'Amphibian bones', Archive Report

Cowgill, J, de Neergaard, M, & Griffiths, N, 1987 *Knives and scabbards*, Medieval finds from excavations in London 1

Crosby, D D B, & Mitchell, J G, 1987 'Potassium-argon determinations of some London medieval honestones', *Trans London Middlesex
Archaeol Soc*, 38, 159–64

Davies, B, 1991 'POM79', Summary Roman Pottery Appraisal

Egan, G, & Moir, D, in prep. 'Post-medieval finds c 1450–c 1700: a selection from the City of London sites 1972–82'

Locker, A, 1982 'GPO Middle (POM79) fish bone (post-medieval)', Archive Report

Macphail, R, 1980 'Soil report on dark earth at GPO Middle (POM79) London', Archive Report

Midgley, C (ed), 1981 'Excavations at Post Office Middle (POM79)', Archive Report (MS)

West B, nd, 'Bird bones', Archive Report

West B, nd, 'Large mammal bones', Archive Report

THE79

P Herbert
NGR: TQ 31810 80910
SMR: 043502

Mermaid Theatre, Puddle Dock, EC4

A small excavation on the site of the N end of the theatre and the adjacent Puddle Dock failed to find the Roman riverside wall, which was found immediately to the E in 1974–6. The wall must turn to the NW, as probably did Upper Thames Street, at this point. Timber base-plates for a front- and back-braced timber revetment were found turning from the line of the Dock on the W side to form a frontage to the river, initially datable on carpentry joints to the late 13th or early 14th c but by dendrochronology to c 1240. With this revetment were noted traces of buildings forming units of reclamation S of Thames Street.

London Archaeol, 3, 1980, 384; *Medieval Archaeol*, 24, 1980, 254

Clark, J (ed), 1995 *The medieval horse and its equipment c 1150–c 1450,* Medieval finds from excavations in London 5 [medieval horseshoes and horse equipment]

Herbert, P, nd, 'Excavations at Mermaid Theatre Puddle Dock EC4', Archive Report

Hillam, J, 1979 'Tree-ring dating in London — the Mermaid Theatre site', Archive Report

Hillam, J, & Herbert, P, 1980 'Tree-ring dating — the Mermaid Theatre', *London Archaeol*, 3, 439–44

Jones, S, 1975 'Mermaid Theatre — fish bones (THE79)', Archive Report

Vince, A, 1980 'Ceramic finds from Mermaid Theatre 1979 (THE79)', Archive Report

5–10, 12a–13 Well Court, 44–48 Bow Lane, EC4

WEL79

D Perring and P Rowsome
NGR: TQ 32410 81095
SMR: 043474–88

A shallow ditch (Period I) marked out the line of a N–S Roman street (Period II), probably laid out in the Flavian period. The area to the W of the street may initially have been external (Period II) but subsequently a series of Flavian buildings, the latest of which was destroyed by fire, fronted onto the street (Periods III–IV). In Period V (late Flavian–Hadrianic) successive buildings on the W side of the street had a portico at the frontage and were probably shops, while a cellared building immediately to the N had a large storage tank built into its front wall. By contrast, development on the E side of the street during Periods I–V was limited to pits and gravelled external areas, and further E still, where the ground fell away into the Walbrook Valley, stone-founded Roman domestic buildings were set well back from the street. Buildings across the entire site were destroyed in the Hadrianic fire at the end of Period V, but in Period VI (Hadrianic–early 3rd c) the site was redeveloped much as before. Further shops, one of which had amphorae set inside its front wall, were constructed on the W side of the street, but the area to the E remained open except for a stone building at the extreme E of the site. Apart from flooding in Period IV, the street was frequently resurfaced to keep pace with the rising buildings. In Period VII (3rd c and later) however a series of crude timber buildings erected near the street did not align with it, suggesting its disuse sometime before dark earth was deposited over the site in Period VI.

Above dark earth a second N–S Late Saxon street was laid out immediately to the W of its predecessor, and represents the forerunner of Bow Lane. The first street surfaces with structures on their E edge (Periods IX–X) are undated, but later wattle and daub buildings (Periods XI–XII), one of which incorporated an oven, are dated to the 10th–12th c. A sunken-floored structure set well back from the street became disused in the late 10th c, but two other sunken structures may have predated the street. Various rubbish pits (Period XIII) were dug in the central part of the site in the early medieval period, but by the 14th c the site was covered by a series of medieval stone-cellared buildings (Period XIV), two of which were refurbished in the post-medieval period (Period XV).

London Archaeol, 3, 1980, 384; *Britannia*, 11, 1980, 381; 12, 1981, 351–3; *Medieval Archaeol*, 24, 1980, 254; 25, 1981, 210

Allen, P, 1985 'A plan for the City?', *Popular Archaeol*, 6, No. 12, 2–6

Betts, I, 1985 'Well Court/44–48 Bow Lane WEL79 — building material', Archive Report

Grew, F, 1983 'Quernstones from Well Court', Archive Report

Millner, J, & Allen, P, 1986 'Excavations at Well Court', Archive Report

Perring, D, & Roskams, S, with Allen, P, 1991 *The early development of Roman London west of the Walbrook,* The archaeology of Roman London 2, CBA Res Rep 70 [Roman strata]

Schofield, J, 1995 *Medieval London houses,* 166–7

Schofield, J, Allen, P, & Taylor, C, 1990 'Medieval buildings and property development in the area of Cheapside', *Trans London Middlesex Archaeol Soc,* 41, 39–238 [Saxon and medieval strata, documentary report]

Vince, A, 1983 'Saxon pottery from Well Court (WEL79)', Archive Report

128–133 Cheapside (Woolworths), 1 Gutter Lane, 130 Wood Street, EC2

WOW79

J Millner
NGR: TQ 32300 81240
SMR: 044502–9

A watching brief on the site of a former Woolworths' store produced evidence of activity from the 1st c onwards. The Roman sequence included three phrases of occupation, the first and third of them terminated by fire-destruction horizons which may represent the mid-1st-c Boudican and early 2nd-c Hadrianic fires respectively. The structures destroyed by these fires were probably aligned with the main Roman E–W road to the S beneath modern Cheapside and possibly, in one case, to a N–S road to the W: that leading to the S gate of the Roman fort (note that this road is different to that found at OST82).

Above these deposits was a band of dark soil indicating a prolonged interruption of the sequence between Roman and medieval periods. The latter was represented by pits and traces of timber buildings, followed by a series of 13th- and 14th-c stone foundations, possibly of the medieval Cross Keys Inn on Wood Street and the alley which divided it from the churchyard of St Peter Cheap. A post-medieval well and drains were almost certainly from the Inn, which occupied the site until it was replaced in the 1860s by the building demolished for the present redevelopment.

Millner, J, nd, 'Excavations at 130–131 Cheapside EC2', Archive Report

Perring, D, & Roskams, S, with Allen, P, 1991 *The early development of Roman London west of the Walbrook*, The archaeology of Roman London 2, CBA Res Rep 70 [Roman strata]

XWL79

J Maloney
NGR: TQ 33590 80980
SMR: 041965–8

8–10 Crosswall, EC3

Excavations were carried out in the N and at the S end of the site. The earliest indication of activity occurred in the N area where the natural gravels were cut by a drainage ditch of early 2nd-c date, and by the construction of the Roman defensive wall (which is dated elsewhere to the late 2nd–early 3rd c). On this site the wall had become incorporated into a property boundary, its outer face forming part of the western boundary of the site. A total length of about 22.5m was recorded, with a 10m stretch surviving 3m in height up to the third tile course and with numerous post-Roman repairs. Some 3m in advance of the wall the contemporary V-shaped ditch was recorded in both the N and S areas of the site: it was about 2m deep and about 4m wide. The remains of Bastion 4 were located in the S and a hitherto unknown bastion, to be called B4A, was discovered in the N area. The foundations of these bastions were rectangular in shape and projected 5.4m (B4A) and a minimum 4.7m (B4) from the wall, B4A's foundations — coursed chalk and ragstone — being 'stepped' into the bottom of the V-shaped ditch. The solid, D-shaped superstructure of B4A was partly at least composed of reused monumental masonry — including fragments of an inscribed Roman tombstone, probably of early 3rd-c date — and was not keyed into the wall. The 3m high stretch of wall and the foundation of B4A have been preserved within the present building.

In the medieval period, a defensive ditch was constructed and infilled in the late 12th–13th c when B4A was demolished and B4 apparently demolished, though since documentary evidence indicates that B4 survived into the 17th c, this may only have been partial. During a watching brief on the E side of the site, the W edge of a ditch was recorded at a low level and is likely to have been part of a later medieval defensive ditch: the city ditch. Post-medieval horncore lined pits dating to the late 16th–17th c were found, two of which were associated with the casting of gun-metal. Towards the end of the 17th-c domestic properties were established. In the S a basement containing a brick water channel and well were recorded: they possibly represented the remains of a wash-house. The backfill of the well contained a substantial quantity of material associated with glassmaking in the late 17th–early 18th c. In the N area, two brick-lined cesspits were constructed against the city wall where they probably demarcated two properties. Both were disused by the early–mid-18th c. One of the cesspits was infilled about 1770, probably as the result of a household clearance: it contained a large collection of pottery and glassware — many near-complete items — and an animal bone assemblage which included an angora rabbit and a linnet. In the later 19th c the Metropolitan Bonded Warehouse was constructed, storing tea and cork; features connected with this and the Irongate sewer, which ran N–S beneath the warehouse, were recorded.

London Archaeol, 3, 1980, 385; *Britannia*, 11, 1980, 379

Armitage, P, nd, 'Report on the faunal remains from the sieved soil samples from the Roman ditch', Archive Report

Armitage, P, nd, 'The faunal remains from context 220 (post-medieval cesspit)', Archive Report

Armitage, P, 1981 'Remains of an Angora rabbit from a late 18th-century pit at Crosswall', *London Archaeol*, 4, 87–95

Egan, G, & Moir, D, in prep. 'Post-medieval finds c 1450–c 1700: a selection from the City of London sites 1972–82'

Locker, A, 1981 'The fish bones', Archive Report (AML Report 3276)

Maloney, C, & Egan, G, 1981 'Excavations at Crosswall', Archive Report

Maloney, J, 1980 'The discovery of Bastion 4A and its implications', *Trans London Middlesex Archaeol Soc*, 31, 68–76

Maloney, J, 1981 'Crosswall — the Roman wall and bastion foundation', *Popular Archaeol*, 2, No. 7, 35

Maloney, J, 1983 'Recent work on London's defences', in Maloney, J, & Hobley, B (eds), *Roman urban defences in the west*, CBA Res Rep 51, 96–117

Vince, A, & Egan, G, 1981 'The contents of a late eighteenth-century pit at Crosswall, City of London', *Trans London Middlesex Archaeol Soc*, 32, 159–82

1–9, 10–16 Bevis Marks, 15–18 Bury Street, EC3

BEV80

C Midgley
NGR: TQ 33370 81300
SMR: 043550–7

Site 1 (10–16 Bevis Marks): all horizontal stratigraphy had been destroyed by Victorian basements. Surviving features included Roman rubbish and brickearth-quarrying pits of the late 2nd–4th c; 11th–early 13th-c rubbish pits and two linear cuts running E–W, possibly marking a property boundary; a late 16th-c brick and chalk lined well; and a late 17th-c brick basement having at least three phases of use.

Site 2 (1–9 Bevis Marks): machine-cut trenches along the front and down one side of the site revealed a cut feature of possible late 3rd-c date at least 40m long and 4m wide, running the length of the street frontage. To its S were a complex sequence of Roman and medieval pits and horizontal deposits. No structural remains survived except a medieval chalk-lined cesspit.

London Archaeol, 4, 1981, 44; *Britannia,* 12, 1981, 350; *Medieval Archaeol,* 25, 1981, 210
Egan, G, & Moir, D, in prep. 'Post-medieval finds *c* 1450–*c* 1700: a selection from the City of London sites 1972–82'
Giorgi, J, Rackham, J, & Smith, D, 1996 'Environmental samples from post-medieval deposits at 13–16 Bevis Marks (ENV/REP/05/96)',
    Archive Report
Midgley, C, 1982 'Excavations at 5–9 Bevis Marks', Archive Report
Williams, T, in prep. *The development of Roman London east of the Walbrook,* The archaeology of Roman London 4, CBA Res Rep
    [Roman strata]

62–64 Cannon Street, EC4

CAN80

D Perring
NGR: TQ 32510 80940
SMR: 040088–90

Two tile-capped walls running N–S were provisionally assigned to the 4th c. In a second trench fire debris, probably of 2nd-c date, was recorded but not excavated. A sequence of late medieval and post-medieval features was also recorded.

Britannia, 12, 1981, 351; *Medieval Archaeol,* 25, 1981, 210
Perring, D, Price, J, & Rowsome, P, nd, 'Excavations at 62–64 Cannon Street EC4', Archive Report

Christchurch Greyfriars, Newgate Street, EC1

CCN80

R Lea
NGR: TQ 31000 81370
SMR: 043774–9

Details of the Wren church were recorded when the turf inside the church (now an open space) was stripped: floors, pier bases, a brick vault containing lead coffins, other brick vaults and a pulpit base. Finds included medieval moulded stonework from the pre-Great Fire Greyfriars church and fragments of the font of the Wren church. Further work by the Corporation of London took place at the E end of the church in 1982 when brick features and architectural fragments, apparently from the Wren church, were observed.

For previous work inside the church see GF73 and CHR76 above; for later work, CIS89 below.

Lea, R, 1987 'Watching brief at Christchurch Greyfriars Newgate Street EC1', Archive Report

FEC80

M Barker
NGR: TQ 33265 80950
SMR: 040091–5

47–49 Fenchurch Street, EC3

Remains of 1st- and 2nd-c structures were excavated, together with fire debris (possibly Hadrianic) lying *in situ,* but the upper levels were truncated. To the S lay further 1st-c levels, cut by a pit and sealed by more deposits. An early medieval pit, a medieval chalk cesspit and a fragment of a 16th-c or 17th-c brick foundation were also recorded. This last may be a fragment beneath one of the walls surveyed on the site in 1612 by Ralph Treswell.

Britannia, 12, 1981, 351; *Medieval Archaeol,* 25, 1981, 210
Barker, M, nd, 'Excavations at 47–49 Fenchurch Street EC3', Archive Report
Keily, J, nd, '47–49 Fenchurch Street', Building Materials Appraisal
Price, P, 1990 'Finds appraisal for 47–49 Fenchurch Street, EC3', Finds Appraisal
Schofield, J (ed), 1987 *The London surveys of Ralph Treswell,* London Topographical Soc Publication 135, 72–3
Schofield, J, 1995 *Medieval London houses,* 181
Williams, T, in prep. *The development of Roman London east of the Walbrook,* The archaeology of Roman London 4, CBA Res Rep
    [Roman strata]

FSP80

C Guy
NGR: TQ 33360 80980
SMR: 040096–100

60 Fenchurch Street, Post Office, EC3

A 1st-c (probably Flavian) structure, probably of timber-framed construction, was observed; its S limit running E–W across the area. This building was replaced by a similar structure, possibly after its destruction by fire. In the late 1st or early 2nd c a stone-founded wall, represented by a mid-2nd-c robber trench, was constructed along the same line. This wall was robbed after an early 2nd-c fire, presumably Hadrianic. Later pits apparently respected the boundary indicated by these walls until the 3rd c, after which the pits were apparently randomly distributed.

London Archaeol, 4, 1981, 45
Guy, C, 1981 'Excavations at 60 Fenchurch Street', Archive Report
Williams, T, in prep. *The development of Roman London east of the Walbrook,* The archaeology of Roman London 4, CBA Res Rep
    [Roman strata]

HAG80

J Schofield and A Upson
NGR: TQ 33730 81220
SMR: 040102–3

46 (Hoop and Grapes) and 47 Aldgate High Street, EC3

These two timber-framed buildings date from the middle of the 17th c. During conversion so that no. 47 could expand into the storeys above the ground-floor public house at no. 46 (the Hoop and Grapes), details of the timber-framing were noted. The rear elevation of no. 47, from first floor upwards, was dismantled under the direction of Dr Richard Harris and stored at MoL.

Sections were also recorded in a lift pit in the cellar of no. 47. These revealed that the earliest exposed deposits consisted of a series of horizontal strata, possibly levelling, which was cut by a large rectangular pit containing cattle horn cores. Above this was the damp coursing and construction cuts for the standing building.

24–25 Ironmonger Lane, 9–12 King Street, EC2

IRO80

J Norton
NGR: TQ 32500 81220
SMR: 040104–13, 043558–71

A small site (8m x 8m) on the W side of Ironmonger Lane provided evidence of a Roman street of Flavian date and associated buildings. The first occupation on this site comprised large gravel quarry pits, backfilled with Neronian material (Period I). Structures of Period II were divided into seven phases. In phase I a ditch and E–W street were laid out, with a timber building on its N side, presumably of immediately post-Boudican (Neronian) date. In phase 2 (69–79) this was replaced, and a further replacement in phase 3 had four successive hearths, possible sunken containers/tanks, and a porch; a remetalling of the street was the occasion for a verandah on the S side. This was replaced in the fourth phase (late 1st/early 2nd c), and the yard on the W of the building given a tiled pathway and a gate to the street. This was dismantled and rebuilt in phase 5 and again in phase 6 (Trajanic). By this time the street was cambered and 5–6m wide. The building was again rebuilt (phase 7), internally adapted almost continually, and the porch removed. The building was destroyed by fire, probably Hadrianic. In Period III dark earth overlay the building, but a stone wall divided the site of the building from the street, which apparently continued in use.

The remains of two interconnecting Saxon sunken structures, dug into the Roman road gravels, were filled with 9th-c debris; robber trenches of about the same date removed much of the Roman masonry. Medieval pits were encountered over the site; one contained an almost complete horse skeleton. The excavation was funded by Guardian Royal Exchange Assurance.

London Archaeol, 4, 1981, 44; Britannia, 12, 1981, 351; Medieval Archaeol, 25, 1981, 173

Armitage, P, 1981 'Late Anglo-Saxon horse skeleton from Ironmonger Lane 1980', Archive Report

Betts, I, 1985 'Building material (IRO80)', Archive Report

Davies, B, 1993 'Inter-site studies', in Milne, G, & Wardle, A, 'Early Roman development at Leadenhall Court, London and related research', Trans London Middlesex Archaeol Soc, 44, 135–50

Davies, B, Richardson, B, & Tomber, R, 1994 A dated corpus of early Roman pottery from the City of London, The archaeology of Roman London 5, CBA Res Rep 98 [contribution to early Roman pottery corpus]

Norton, J, 1982 'Ironmonger Lane', London Archaeol, 4, 171–6

Norton, J, 1985 'Excavations at 24–25 Ironmonger Lane', Archive Report

Perring, D, & Roskams, S, with Allen, P, 1991 The early development of Roman London west of the Walbrook, The archaeology of Roman London 2, CBA Res Rep 70 [Roman strata]

Rackham, D J, 1995 'Physical remains of medieval horses', in Clark, J (ed), The medieval horse and its equipment c 1150–c 1450, Medieval finds from excavations in London 5, 19–22

Schofield, J, Allen, P, & Taylor, C, 1990 'Medieval buildings and property development in the area of Cheapside', Trans London Middlesex Archaeol Soc, 41, 39–238 [Saxon and medieval strata]

Vince, A (ed), 1991 Aspects of Saxo-Norman London II: finds and environmental evidence, London Middlesex Archaeol Soc Spec Pap 12 [Saxon smallfinds]

GPO tunnel, Moorgate, EC2

MOO80

D Perring
NGR: TQ 32710 81540
SMR: 040498

A GPO tunnel beneath the S carriageway of London Wall near its junction with Moorgate probably went through the brick foundations of the 15th-c Moorgate. A substantial brick wall was recorded: possibly the W wall of the 17th-c rebuild of Moorgate, as it projected N from the city wall, or a building fronting onto the road N of the gate.

12 Nicholas Lane, EC4

NIC80

D Bowler
NGR: TQ 32802 80907
SMR: 040101

Substantial Roman wall footings and at least two layers of fire debris were observed.

Britannia, 12, 1981, 351

Williams, T, in prep. The development of Roman London east of the Walbrook, The archaeology of Roman London 4, CBA Res Rep [Roman strata]

PUB80

A Upson
NGR: TQ 33490 81093
SMR: 040114–23

The George public house, 86 Fenchurch Street, EC3

Excavation revealed a series of 1st- and early 2nd-c timber buildings, the earliest of which was possibly sub-circular in plan, being replaced by a series of rectangular structures lying roughly parallel to the forerunner of Fenchurch Street. The earliest rectangular structure was destroyed by fire. Subsequent deposits clearly related to an E–W division, with a sequence of internal brickearth floors and occupation accumulations to the S, and a series of well-surfaced exterior gravel courtyard or lane-metallings to the N. The Roman sequence was cut along the E side of the site by a N–S line of early medieval pits.

London Archaeol, 4, 1981, 45; *Britannia,* 12, 1981, 351; *Medieval Archaeol,* 25, 1981, 210

Crowley, N, 1988 'George Public House 86 Fenchurch Street (PUB80) Roman building material', Archive Report

Davies, B, 1987 'Excavations at the George Public House 86 Fenchurch Street EC3 1980: Roman pottery', Archive Report

Davies, B, 1993 'Inter-site studies', in Milne, G, & Wardle, A, 'Early Roman development at Leadenhall Court, London and related research', *Trans London Middlesex Archaeol Soc,* 44, 135–50

Upson, A, 1981 'Excavations at The George Public House (PUB80)', Archive Report

Vince, A, 1985 'George Public House', Archive Report

Waller, R, 1989 'Finds Appraisal for the George Public House 86 Fenchurch Street (PUB80)', Finds Appraisal

Williams, T, in prep. *The development of Roman London east of the Walbrook,* The archaeology of Roman London 4, CBA Res Rep [Roman strata]

SPC80

R Lea
NGR: TQ 32020 81106
SMR: 043651–3

St Paul's churchyard, EC4

A trench 2m square and 1.3m deep was cut for tree planting in St Paul's churchyard 10m S of the S facade of the W transept and 20m E of the line of the W front. In the W half of the trench a brick structure at least 0.8m wide, possibly a burial vault, was observed running on a NNW–SSW axis about 0.45m below the present ground surface. A blocked round arch of four orders was found in its E face. Limestone blocks were used in the blocking and in the main structure itself, which was overlaid by demolition debris including limestone, mortar, brick, tile and ash containing no finds.

London Archaeol, 4, 1982, 162

Lea, R, 1986 'Watching brief at St Paul's churchyard EC4', Archive Report

ADM81

H White
NGR: TQ 33200 81530
SMR: 044510–14

Alderman's House, 34–37 Liverpool Street, EC2

A possible quarry pit was succeeded by an E–W aligned burial of 3rd-c date. Two medieval and one post-medieval cess- or rubbish pits were recorded and, at the W end of the site, a 17th-c brick walled cellar had been set into the natural brickearth.

APO81

D Bluer
NGR: TQ 31760 81050
SMR: 040426, 041194,
042500, 043784, 043800–1

Apothecaries' Hall and 22–26 Blackfriars Lane, EC4

A short watching brief was conducted in 1981 as a result of the discovery of human bones while digging trial holes in a basement floor. Two holes, each about 1m square, were examined. The first yielded 11 stratified but disarticulated bones, but the grave fill had been much disturbed by the workmen and no grave cut was identified. The bones were of an adult, possibly male. The second contained two grave cuts, only one of which contained stratified material, viz. 17 very disturbed and disarticulated bones and one skull, an adolescent of 14–18 years, and a child of about ten.

The grave fill was truncated by a pit, which contained building material and a sherd, of hitherto unrecorded form, of Guy's Hospital ware, provisionally dated to the 16th or 17th c. The area in which these two trenches were situated is known, from excavations of 1926–7, to have been beneath the floor of the 13th-c church of the Blackfriars.

In 1983 a watching brief was funded by St Anselm Properties and the Apothecaries' Company. A steep cut in the W part of the site was probably the W edge of an early phase of the medieval city ditch, which is known from documentary sources to have been filled in the late 13th c for the building of the Blackfriars. It was backfilled with sandy gravels with some domestic rubbish. Cutting into these gravels were several substantial ragstone walls and masonry features, but no occupation surfaces or floors. Correspondence with a reconstructed groundplan of the friary enables identification of the recorded fragments as part of the S wall of the church, four foundation piers forming the S aisle arcade, the E wall of the guest house/outer wall of the W cloistral range. Several brick cesspits and a well from the post-Dissolution period were also observed.

London Archaeol, 4, 1982, 162–3; *Medieval Archaeol,* 26, 1982, 191; 28, 1984, 227–8
Allen, P, & Bluer, R, 1985 'Excavations at Apothecaries' Hall', Archive Report
Fabrizi, M, 1990 'Apothecaries' Hall', Finds Appraisal
Vince, A, 1984 'The medieval and post-medieval pottery from Apothecaries' Hall (APO81)', Archive Report
West, B, 1985 'APO81, Human bone report (HUM 01/85)'

9 The Arches, Crutched Friars, EC3

ARC81

R Lea
NGR: TQ 33500 80900
SMR: 043650

During refurbishment a human skeleton was discovered, aligned E–W 1m E of a chalk foundation about 1.1m wide which ran N–S immediately below the modern cellar floor. The site falls within the NE corner of the precinct of the Crutched Friars.

Summaries *London Archaeol,* 4, 1982, 162; *Medieval Archaeol,* 26, 1982, 191
Lea, R, nd, 'Watching brief at 9 The Arches Crutched Friars EC3', Archive Report

South-east corner tower of Baynard's Castle, City of London Boys' School, Upper Thames Street, EC4

BYD81

J Burke-Easton
NGR: TQ 31980 80870
SMR: 043780–4

Four periods of medieval and post-medieval E–W river frontages were recorded. Period I was timber; horizontal planks edge-on-edge were nailed to the back of large vertical posts which were supported on their front by angled struts jointed into them. Period II was represented by the construction of a stone rubble, ashlar-faced wall whose front line was little over 5m S of the previous structure. It was at least 2.3m wide at its base and partly founded on timber base-plates which were supported by piles set into the foreshore. Although the structure was extensively robbed, evidence of a N–S drain was recorded on the E of the area. It exited through an intact arch in the wall, and timber abutting it suggests some sort of sluice gate. Also recorded to the W during 1972/3 (see GM152 above), but outside this excavation, was a line of chalk rubble running N, similar to the remains of the E–W wall, perhaps suggesting a N–S return marking the W limit. Period III was the rebuilding of Baynard's Castle, historically dated to 1428, of which only the SE corner tower was within the area (Fig 36). It was roughly an octagonal shape, had a diameter of about 8m, and survived to a maximum height of 2.5m. Built as integral features on the E end of the tower were firstly a garderobe, the sump of which was *in situ,* with evidence of a system of chutes which allowed disposal from three floors, and exited into the river through, secondly, an E–W riverwall which ran for at least 10m. An arch was also incorporated in and through the E end of the wall which allowed the flow of the Period II drain to continue, having been extended 6m. The tower, wall and drain were founded on large timber plank base-plates which were supported by piles.

Although this part of the castle was pulled down in 1666, the river frontage stayed in use, and was subject to a rebuild on the front of the tower, while the garderobe was blocked off and converted into a cesspit. Period IV was the construction of a 19th-c brick wall. Its back face was only 0.5m S of the tower, but to its E cut through the Period III riverwall.

The site of Baynard's Castle had been excavated previously in 1972: see GM152 above. For a further watching brief which exposed more of the castle adjacent to the BYD81 site, see TIG84 below; and for further excavation on the BYD81 site, see BEX90 below.

Fig 36 BYD81: the SE corner tower of Baynard's Castle, 1428; excavated in 1972 (BC72/GM152) and 1981 (BYD81). The view is looking W; the River Thames would have come up to the tower and its frontage from the left.

London Archaeol, 4, 1982, 160; Medieval Archaeol, 26, 1982, 192

Burke-Easton, J, 1982 'Excavations at the south-east corner tower of Baynard's Castle 1981', Archive Report

Crowfoot, E, Pritchard, F, & Staniland, K, 1992 Textiles and clothing c 1150–c 1450, Medieval finds from excavations in London 4

Davis, A, 1982 'Baynard's Castle: environmental analysis (ASS/01/82)', Archive Report

Egan, G, & Moir, D, in prep. 'Post-medieval finds c 1450–c 1700: a selection from the City of London sites 1972–82'

Giorgi, J, Rackham, J, & Smith, D, 1996 'An environmental sample from a post-medieval sewage system at Baynard's Castle (BYD81): (ENV/REP/08/96)', Archive Report

Grew, F, & de Neergaard, M, 1988 Shoes and pattens, Medieval finds from excavations in London 2

Pritchard, F, 1983 'Baynard's Castle 1981 textiles', Archive Report

Vince, A, 1983 'The medieval pottery from Baynards Castle 1981', Archive Report

Vince, A, 1985 'Saxon and medieval pottery in London: a review', Medieval Archaeol, 29, 25–93

CLE81 | 29–32 Clements Lane, 33–36 Lombard Street, EC4

C Evans
NGR: TQ 32890 80945
SMR: 043349–55, 043665–75

Excavations funded by Guinness Peat Properties Ltd were conducted in an E–W trench (15m x 3m) inside the standing building of 32 Clements Lane. The initial occupation of the site, of Neronian date, consisted of slot trenches with associated stake-holes cut into a brickearth slab. There followed a sequence of 1st- and early 2nd-c interior and exterior surfaces. A sunken Flavian tile and ragstone stairway had been cut through these surfaces in the W of the site, and apparently led to a cellar which must have been situated immediately N of the site. One side of this stairway was incorporated into, and its alignment followed, the construction of a major N–S wall of mid-2nd-c date. Associated with this later redevelopment was a parallel and corresponding wall and a tile drain. Throughout the site, in situ burning and collapse of an early–mid-2nd-c fire were found. In the eastern portion there was a N–S alleyway or minor road which predated this burnt horizon. The W side of this thoroughfare was bordered by two successive ditches, the earlier being of Flavian date and the second of late 1st- or early 2nd-c date; in the later ditch was evidence of a plank-revetted drain. Only a narrow strip of dark earth survived on the site and produced 3rd–4th-c pottery. While no Saxon features were found, a massive, early medieval, robbing shaft produced substantial quantities of Late Saxon pottery. All post-Roman horizontal stratigraphy except two medieval cesspits had been removed by the modern development of the site.

A watching brief was conducted on the enlarged site (including an area to the E of Plough Court) in April–December 1982. Evidence was found of Neronian timber buildings and an early fire, apparently Boudican. These buildings were succeeded by brickearth sill, wattle and mudbrick structures; in one instance 11 courses of a scorched mudbrick wall survived. A sequence of drains, indicating a property division, was found to the E of Clements Lane. A large early 2nd-c building was recorded beneath Plough Court. Here ragstone walls survived to a height of 0.8m and the interior of this rectangular structure had been made up to at least 0.9m above the exterior level. The base of a stairway leading up to the internal level was noted at one side. Mortar and red plaster surfaces covering its exterior faces would suggest that this structure may have formed part of an extensive courtyard-plan building, perhaps of public use. It was burnt in a second, Hadrianic fire, and contemporary burnt collapse was found across the site. Mid-2nd-c ragstone and flint walls and foundations were found on both E and W sides of the site. Associated surfaces and floor make-ups were recorded, and numerous fragments of a destroyed tessellated pavement were found in robbing trenches.

A Late Saxon/early medieval rammed chalk and gravel foundation seemed to relate to Clements Lane. This was cut by medieval pits, many others being in the middle of the site, as was a chalk-lined well. Late medieval chalk and brick foundations, one of which was arched, were recorded on the Clements Lane/Lombard Court corner. This building was burnt in the Fire of 1666 and subsequently rebuilt.

London Archaeol, 4, 1982, 160; Britannia, 14, 1983, 311; Medieval Archaeol, 26, 1982, 192; 27, 1983, 192; Post-Medieval Archaeol, 17, 1983, 189

Davies, B, 1993 'Inter-site studies', in Milne, G, & Wardle, A, 'Early Roman development at Leadenhall Court, London and related research', Trans London Middlesex Archaeol Soc, 44, 135–50

Egan, G, & Moir, D, in prep. 'Post-medieval finds c 1450–c 1700: a selection from the City of London sites 1972–82'

Evans, C, 1989 'Excavations at 29–32 Clements Lane EC4', Archive Report

Evans, C, & James, P, 1983 'The Roman Cornhill', Popular Archaeol, 5, No, 6, 19–26

Williams, T, in prep. The development of Roman London east of the Walbrook, The archaeology of Roman London 4, CBA Res Rep [Roman strata]

68–73 Cornhill, EC3

CNL81

P James
NGR: TQ 32990 81140
SMR: 040784

An area 6m x 7m on the site of no. 68 was excavated in plan, adjacent to the N side of the second Roman basilica, and four contractors' trenches were also monitored. In Period I a linear flat-bottomed ditch, 3m wide by 0.6m deep, ran for at least 9.5m E–W across the site. To the N of it lay an area of accumulated tread with two small (?domestic) hearths. The ditch was infilled and the whole area levelled up with redeposited brickearth c AD85. In Period II groups of stake-holes within rectangular cuts (about 0.6m x 0.5m) are thought to have been pile foundations for a timber building. The lack of survival of the Period II building remains is attributed to a large-scale horizontal truncation which marked the beginning of Period III. Immediately following this truncation the second Roman basilica was built. A previously unrecorded 3.5m length of its N wall, part of an internal partition wall and an external buttress, were uncovered and destroyed by the contractors, and showed the foundations to have been 2.4m deep. At the same time a metalled Roman street, about 5m wide, was laid down along the N side of the basilica. This street had flanking drains on either side N–S, and fronting onto its N side were timber buildings. A sequence of five superimposed street surfaces, several drain recuts, and ?four phases of timber buildings to the N survived, dating from AD85 to c 120. The later Roman and post-Roman material had largely been truncated by Victorian basements (Period V) but a late 3rd-/early 4th-c drain in the same position as earlier ones on the N side of the Roman street provided evidence for continuity of that street. Further N however the timber building remains had been cut through by two late Roman wells. The medieval period (Period IV) was represented only by a large refuse pit and part of a stone and brick built cellar.

London Archaeol, 4, 1983, 277; Britannia, 14, 1983, 311; Medieval Archaeol, 27, 1983, 182

Betts, I, 1988 '66–73 Cornhill (CNL81) Roman building material', Archive Report

Davies, B, 1993 'Inter-site studies', in Milne, G, & Wardle, A, 'Early Roman development at Leadenhall Court, London and related research', Trans London Middlesex Archaeol Soc, 44, 135–50

Davies, B, Richardson, B, & Tomber, R, 1994 *A dated corpus of early Roman pottery from the City of London,* The archaeology of Roman London 5, CBA Res Rep 98 [contribution to early Roman pottery corpus]

Evans, C, & James, P, 1983 'The Roman Cornhill', *Popular Archaeol,* 5, No. 6, 19–26

Ford, B, 1982 'Cornhill finds report (CNL81)', Archive Report

James, P, 1983 'Excavations at 68 Cornhill', Archive Report

Marsden, P, 1987 *The Roman forum site in London: discoveries before 1985,* 85–8

Richardson, B, 1987 'Cornhill Roman pottery report (CNL81)', Archive Report

Tyers, P, 1982 'Report on the Roman pottery from seven contexts in Phase IIIA', Archive Report

Williams, T, in prep. *The development of Roman London east of the Walbrook,* The archaeology of Roman London 4, CBA Res Rep [Roman strata]

COL81

M Barker
NGR: TQ 32495 80885
SMR: 043820–8

19–20 College Hill, EC4

From mid-January 1981 until the end of March a watching brief and excavation funded by Dundas Properties Ltd was carried out on the site of the almshouse built *c* 1426 under the terms of Richard Whittington's will. The contractors excavated an L-shaped trench in the yard area to the W (rear) of 19–20 College Hill and carried out investigations of the foundations of the standing building of the former Mercers' School adjacent to the NW corner of St Michael Paternoster Royal.

The earliest layers exposed were a series of gravels, recorded in a N–S section adjacent to the church, which may have represented a gravel alleyway or yard. These were overlaid by a series of early medieval occupation surfaces with horizontal, spaced medieval tiles. At one horizon a wedge of burnt daub may have represented a hearth area. The uppermost of the occupation surfaces had a well-built brickearth and green-glazed tile hearth. These layers had been cut into by burials contemporary with the Whittington almshouses.

The L-shaped trench exposed two phases of medieval wall construction. An earlier E–W wall was `probably contemporary with the occupation surfaces and was truncated by the late medieval burials. The later phase consisted of wall foundations probably of the almshouses *c* 1426. There were ragstone, sandstone and chalk walls forming part of a cellar, its inner walls faced with ashlar blocks and a scrim of whitewash. A carefully shaped Reigate stone block showed evidence of being used for the pivoting of the door leading down into the cellar, which had a fragmentary brick floor remaining.

During excavations adjacent to the S wall of 21 College Hill further truncated medieval walling was exposed together with a flagstone walkway with one flagstone carved to form a slot into which a beam could be laid flat. The walkway appeared to be of a phase of alteration postdating the almshouses.

Most of the S area had been truncated by burials, probably of inmates of the almshouses, which probably continued until 1666.

London Archaeol, 4, 1982, 160–1; *Medieval Archaeol,* 26, 1982, 192

Barker, M, 1986 'Excavations at 19–20 College Hill (COL81)', Archive Report

Stapley, E, 1989 'Finds appraisal for 19–20 College Hill', Archive Report

FIN81

C Maloney
NGR: TQ 32950 81570
SMR: 043413

Finsbury House, 23 Blomfield Street, EC2

A section was recorded through some fine river gravels, probably part of the bed of a tributary of the Walbrook. Immediately to the E was a N–S line of timber posts driven into the natural clay which may represent the remains of revetting, of unknown but possibly Roman date.

London Archaeol, 4, 1983, 275

Hillam, J, 1986 'Tree-ring dating in the City of London — Finsbury House', Archive Report

Maloney, C, 1983 'Excavations at Finsbury House 23 Blomfield Street EC2', Archive Report

Maloney, C, 1990 *The upper Walbrook Valley in the Roman period,* The archaeology of Roman London 1, CBA Res Rep 69 [Roman strata]

9–9¹/₂ and 21–24 Lovat Lane, 8–19 St Mary at Hill, 29–40 Botolph Lane, EC3

LOV81

D Gadd
NGR: TQ 33060 80740
SMR: 043421–5

Over the winter of 1981–2 the DUA carried out work on two sites in Lovat Lane: a small excavation at 22 Lovat Lane, and standing masonry was photogrammetrically recorded at 9 Lovat Lane. At the first site, no horizontal stratigraphy survived beneath the cellar slabs; only the truncated bottoms of half a dozen pits cut into the natural gravel. The pits dated from the 11th to the 18th c and the latest, a rectangular brick and tile lined cesspit, produced an interesting group of artefacts. Examination of the standing walls around the site demonstrated that the chalk, rag and brick walls claimed by Marjorie Honeybourne to be those of the late 12th-c Inn of the abbot of Waltham were in fact later, either post-medieval or post-Fire rebuilds.

At 9 Lovat Lane the stripping of the rendering and tiling from the basement walls of no. 9¹/₂ showed that it concealed a well-preserved chalk undercroft lining measuring 10m x 4.5m. The squared chalk blocks were accurately laid with very narrow mortar gaps. The lining survived to street level at the E end fronting onto Lovat Lane, and was pierced by two blocked openings, interpreted as a central entrance and a window. The rear, W end wall survived even higher with the remains of a spiral staircase in the NW corner squared-off by later modifications. It was built using a combination of materials: chalk for the spiralling barrel vault and containing wall, the latter with a brick facing. The door jamb of the entrance into the staircase was in Reigate stone and the treads of the surviving steps in hard Kentish rag. Alongside the entrance a recess had been cut into the W wall of the undercroft to house the door flush when it was swung right back.

The vault was replaced with a joist floor and the floor raised (by almost 1m) in 1620, and the basement was finally tiled over and used as a tank for live eels when the premises above were converted for the production of jellied eel. No dating evidence was recovered in association with the undercroft, and the only indications of its date of construction are stylistic. The door recess is a feature known from other buildings of the 13th c while the brickwork of the staircase was of an early type, possibly 14th c or earlier.

London Archaeol, 4, 1983, 276–7; *Medieval Archaeol,* 27, 1982, 193–4; *Post-Medieval Archaeol,* 17, 1983, 191
Ford, B, 1982 'Lovat Lane (LOV81)', Finds Appraisal
Gadd, D, 1982a 'Excavations at 9–9¹/₂ and 22–25 Lovat Lane', Archive Report
Gadd, D, 1982b 'Number Nine Lovat Lane', *Popular Archaeol,* 4, No. 1, 16–18
Gadd, D, 1983 'The London Inn of the abbots of Waltham — a revised reconstruction of a medieval town house in Lovat Lane', *Trans London Middlesex Archaeol Soc,* 34, 171–8
Pringle, S, 1989 'Lovat Lane (LOV81)', Building Materials Appraisal
Schofield, J, 1995 *Medieval London houses,* 200

2–3 Cross Keys Court, Copthall Avenue, EC2

OPT81

C Maloney
NGR: TQ 32750 81490
SMR: 043384–96

Excavation here (Fig 37) was funded by Commercial Union Properties Ltd. London Clay was overlaid by fine gravels and silts of a major tributary of the Walbrook stream; some of the silts were eventually colonised by small trees and vegetation. Environmental evidence indicates that the stream was fairly slow-flowing but clean. In the late 1st or early 2nd c the vegetation was cleared away, the stream infilled and a NE–SW road was constructed, with a drainage system laid out on its E side. Alterations to the drainage were undertaken on many occasions as flooding repeatedly occurred and by AD120–40 the road was completely rebuilt on a foundation of stacked turves above a brushwood raft. The drainage channels and dumps which continually raised the ground level during this period contained quantities of finds, particularly leather shoes, and some indicated industrial processes, including leather-, bone- and glassworking. Environmental evidence suggests that the landscape was still wet, but disturbed and grassy. Drainage seems to have been sufficiently under control by the early–mid-2nd c for the latest channel to be infilled with organic material and a building constructed above.

The clay and timber building, 12m long and possibly 4m wide, shared the same alignment as the road and was bordered on its S side by a path. Its external walls were supported on base-plates laid on piles, its internal walls on groundbeams, while evidence survived to suggest that the fabric of the walls had been wattle and daub. Inside the building the arrangement of rooms was frequently modified and clay or brickearth floors regularly relaid: it may have had an industrial function. The building continued, with alterations, into the 3rd c when it was demolished. Environmental evidence reflects the increasing urbanisation of the area that was, nevertheless, still wet. A thick dump then raised the ground level beside the road and a surface was laid, into which a number of large regular pits were cut throughout the 4th c. These pits may have been part of an industrial process: two of them contained a great quantity of furnace lining.

Fig 37 OPT81: excavation at Cross Keys Court comprised a trench within a former ward school hall (the internal height of which allowed sheet piling to be inserted in the floor to enable the excavation to be over 6m deep).

The road continued to be resurfaced throughout this period but it was bordered by a substantial revetted ditch and this, together with successive ground-raising dumps and ditches, indicates the resumption of drainage problems. Occupation then ceased in the late 4th c and a peaty deposit gradually formed over the site until the 11th–12th c when the site was reoccupied for a short while and wattle-lined pits and a drainage ditch were cut. The pits had been infilled in the early 12th c with organic material, including numerous leather off-cuts. After their abandonment the marshy formation resumed its deposition; environmental evidence confirms that wetter and more natural conditions prevailed. In approximately the early 12th c the marsh was reclaimed with thick dumps of clay which were cut by a complex of shallow pits or tanks, probably for an industrial usage. This sequence — of dumping followed by pit cutting — pertained throughout the medieval period; one series of pits, dated to the 15th c, was possibly associated with bronze casting. By the 17th and 18th c the site was in the backyards of properties fronting onto London Wall: the dumped deposits appeared to be garden soil and the pits for rubbish disposal. By the 19th c the alignment of drains indicates their association with properties along Cross Keys Court, probably the Coleman Street Ward School, and at the end of the 19th c the gymnasium of this school, within which the excavations took place, was built on the site.

London Archaeol, 4, 1982, 161; Britannia, 14, 1983, 311; 15, 1984, 309; Medieval Archaeol, 26, 1982, 192

Allison, E, & Kenward, H, 1987 'Insect remains from Copthall Avenue (INS/01/87)', Archive Report (AML Report 194/87)

Davies, B, 1987 'Cross Keys Court Roman pottery', Archive Report

Davis, A, & de Moulins, D, 1990 'Environmental analysis of the upper Walbrook in the Roman period: botanical evidence (PUB/03/90)', Archive Report

Egan, G, & Moir, D, in prep. 'Post-medieval finds c 1450–c 1700: a selection from the City of London sites 1972–82'

Egan, G, & Pritchard, F, 1991 Dress accessories c 1150–c 1450, Medieval finds from excavations in London 3 [medieval dress accessories]

Gale, R, 1985 'Wood identification for Cross Keys Court', Archive Report

Groves, J, nd, 'OPT81', Finds Appraisal

Hillam, J, 1986 'Copthall Avenue — tree-ring dating of Roman timbers from the upper Walbrook Valley', Archive Report

Maloney, C, 1981 'Digging back in time', Concord [house magazine of Commercial Union Properties], 12

Maloney, C, 1982 'Copthall Avenue — deep in the Roman backwaters', Popular Archaeol, 3, No. 12, 32–5

Maloney, C, 1987 'Excavations at 2–3 Cross Keys Court', Archive Report

Maloney, C, 1990 The upper Walbrook Valley in the Roman period, The archaeology of Roman London 1, CBA Res Rep 69 [Roman strata]

Merrifield, R, 1995 'Roman metalwork from the Walbrook — rubbish, ritual or redundancy?', Trans London Middlesex Archaeol Soc, 46, 27–44

Orton, C, 1996 'Dem dry bones', in Bird, J, Hassall, M, & Sheldon, H (eds), Interpreting Roman London: papers in memory of Hugh Chapman, 199–208 [comparative statistical study of animal bones]

Reece, R, nd, 'The mollusca', Archive Report

Ruddle, J, 1991 'An investigation of the potential of tooth cement annuli for ageing zooarchaeological material, with special consideration to cattle mandibular first molars (DIS/02/91)', MSc Dissertation, Dept of Human Environment, Institute of Archaeology, University College London

Scaife, R, nd, 'The pollen', Archive Report

Vince, A, Pearce, J, & Armitage, K, 1981 'A late medieval "bronze" mould from Copthall Avenue', Antiq J, 61, 362–4

Whittaker, J, 1982 'Copthall Avenue — analysis of ostracods from a medieval ditch fill', Archive Report

11–11A Pudding Lane (now Namura House), 22–26 Monument Street, 121–127 Lower Thames Street, EC3

PDN81

G Milne
NGR: TQ 32925 80715
SMR: 043397–405

An 11-month excavation of Areas A, B and C on the W side of Pudding Lane, a five-month excavation of Area F on the E side of Fish Street Hill and a subsequent watching brief produced evidence of natural topography and the line of the N bank of the pre-Roman River Thames. A Roman-piled embankment, timber landing-stage, and late 1st-c timber quay surviving to its full height (Fig 38), associated with two warehouse buildings (Areas C and F), were also found. Part of a possible timber bridge pier base (Fig 39) was recorded on the foreshore to the SW of the quay (Area F). On Area B, to the N, lay a mid- to late Roman masonry building which incorporated a tessellated bath, mosaic floor and hypocaust during its development. Roman activity was traced over the site from the 1st to the 5th c and was also represented by mudbrick buildings (some of which had been burnt in a major fire) and timber-lined drains. The Roman-period structures have formed the subject of a model in the Roman gallery of MoL (Fig 40).

The dark grey silts or waterlaid deposits sealing the latest Roman deposits were cut by many Saxon pits and two wells, and also by two sunken-floored buildings (Areas A and B).

Fig 38 PDN81: the 1st-c Roman quay at Pudding Lane, surviving to its full original height, preserved in waterlogged and anaerobic conditions.

Fig 39 PDN81: in front of the 1st-c quay (left) was one side of a timber structure, possibly a pier for a bridge; it could not be investigated further as it lies under Lower Thames Street.

A series of Saxon surface-laid buildings was also found (Area A); and details of floors, foundations, base-plates and a door were recorded. Stone foundations of later medieval buildings cut through this sequence. The final section of the archive report includes a discussion of relevant material from the neighbouring Peninsular House site (PEN79), to the E of Pudding Lane.

London Archaeol, 4, 1982, 161–2; 4, 1983, 275; Britannia, 13, 1982, 374; 14, 1982, 312; Medieval Archaeol, 26, 1982, 193

Bateman, N, Horsman, V, & Milne, G, nd, 'Excavations at Pudding Lane 118–127 Lower Thames Street EC3', Archive Report

Battarbee, R, nd, 'Diatom analysis of River Thames foreshore deposits exposed during the excavation of a Roman waterfront site at Pudding Lane', Working papers in palaeoecology 2

Betts, I M, 1995 'Procuratorial tile stamps from London', Britannia, 26, 220

Davies, B, 1993 'Inter-site studies', in Milne, G, & Wardle, A, 'Early Roman development at Leadenhall Court, London and related research', *Trans London Middlesex Archaeol Soc*, 44, 135–50

Egan, G, & Moir, D, in prep. 'Post-medieval finds *c* 1450–*c* 1700: a selection from the City of London sites 1972–82'

Grew, F, 1983a 'Copper objects from Pudding Lane', Archive Report

Grew, F, 1983b 'Glass from 1st and 2nd century contexts from Pudding Lane', Archive Report

Grew, F, & Pritchard, F, 1983a 'Bone objects from Pudding Lane', Archive Report

Grew, F, & Pritchard, F, 1983b 'Pudding Lane Part I', Finds Appraisal

Horsman, V, 1983 'Saxon buildings near Billingsgate', *Popular Archaeol*, 5, No. 4, 28–32

Horsman, V, 1985 'Rebuilding Saxon London', *Popular Archaeol*, 6, No. 12, 18–23

Horsman, V, Milne, C, & Milne, G, 1988 *Aspects of Saxo-Norman London I: building and street development*, London Middlesex Archaeol Soc Spec Pap 11 [Saxon buildings and streets]

Jenkins, F, 1983 'PDN81 — the ceramic figurines', Archive Report

Kerney, M, & Askew, P, 1983 'A molluscan fauna with Pomatias Elegans from an archaeological site in the City of London', *The Conchologist's Newsletter*, 84, 65–6

Locker, A, 1986 'The fish bones', Archive Report

Marsden, P, 1994 *Ships of the port of London: first to eleventh centuries AD*, EH Archaeol Rep 3, 15–32 [Roman ships, waterfronts and warehousing]

Marsh, G, & Bateman, N, 1983 'A model excavation', *Popular Archaeol*, 5, No. 4, 18–22

Milne, G, 1982a 'Further evidence for Roman London Bridge?', *Britannia*, 13, 271–6

Milne, G, 1982b 'On the waterfront at Pudding Lane', *Popular Archaeol*, 3, No. 12, 27–31

Milne, G, 1982c 'Recent work on London's Roman harbour', *Int J Naut Archaeol*, 2, 163–4

Milne, G, 1982d 'The hunt for London's bridge', *Popular Archaeol*, 3, No. 12, 22–5

Milne, G, 1985a 'Roman waterfront archaeology in London', in Herteig, A E (ed), *Conference on waterfront archaeology in north European towns no. 2, Bergen 1983, Historisk Museum Bergen*, 31–45 [includes contributions on horrea by N Bateman and on pottery by P Tyers]

Milne, G, 1985b *The port of Roman London* [Roman waterfronts and warehouses]

Milne, G, & Bateman, N, 1983 'A Roman harbour in London', *Britannia*, 14, 207–26

Pritchard, F, 1982 'PDN81 — Pudding Lane building material', Archive Report

Pritchard, F, 1983a 'Ceramic objects from Pudding Lane (PDN81)', Archive Report

Pritchard, F, 1983b 'Stone objects from Pudding Lane (PDN81)', Archive Report

Richardson, B, 1982 'A stone mortar from Pudding Lane (PDN81)', Archive Report

Richardson, B, 1984 'Pudding Lane Roman pottery report (PDN81)', Archive Report

Riddler, I, 1988 'Late Saxon or late Roman? A comb from Pudding Lane', *London Archaeol*, 5, 372–3

Taylor, G W, 1986 'Saxon pot sherds', Archive Report

Tyers, P, nd, 'Roman pottery', Appraisal Report

Vaughan, D, nd, 'Charred plant remains', Archive Report

Yule, B, Milne, G, Battarbee, R, & Straker, V, 1983 'The River Thames in London in the mid-1st century AD', *Trans London Middlesex Archaeol Soc*, 34, 19–30

Fig 40 PDN81: the model of the Roman quay in the Museum, based upon the excavations at Pudding Lane (compare Figs 38 and 39).

PET81

T Williams
NGR: TQ 32040 80920
SMR: 081384, 043829–41

St Peter's Hill and 223–225 Upper Thames Street, EC4

Excavations conducted over an eight-month period revealed a Roman to post-medieval sequence. There was little evidence of activity prior to a cutting of terraces into the hillside provisionally dated to the late 2nd or early 3rd c. The excavated area encompassed the lowest terrace and the retaining wall of a higher terrace, agreeing with the sequence found to the E by P Marsden underneath the present Salvation Army building in Queen Victoria Street (see GM91 above). On the lower terrace massive N–S and E–W foundations were constructed of oak piles, rammed chalk and limestone blocks. The N–S foundation was about 3.75m wide and the E–W foundation 8.5m wide. These formed the W and S segments of a massive structure for which the upper terrace wall formed the N element.

The internal surface consisted of a good quality *opus signinum* floor while to the W gravels were dumped to make up an external surface. These gravels sealed a lattice of timber possibly associated with the construction phase. The probably 4th-c riverside wall, which ran just to the S of the structure, was constructed after the monumental building was at least partially dismantled, though it may have used some of the latter's southernmost parts. Evidence of a later Roman timber building with beaten earth floors was uncovered on the N half of the site, again possibly utilising parts of the monumental structure.

Saxon activity survived only under St Peter's Hill and Upper Thames Street, both of which were sectioned as part of the excavation. Under the former a sequence of structural and occupational activity was identified, yielding a quantity of grass-tempered pottery, but the area was too small to allow firm conclusions. Both streets appear to have been laid out in the 12th c, Upper Thames Street using the Roman riverside wall as its S boundary. Medieval and post-medieval street surfaces survived on both streets from the 12th to 20th c. Various related medieval properties were excavated and although the pre-13th-c material is fragmented the spatial distribution of the early pits suggests various properties. The W wall of St Peter's church, possibly of the 12th c, was examined in relation to various phases of street surfaces of Peter's Hill. A sequence of Great Fire deposits consisted of burnt brick cellars, the destruction of the church and subsequent substantial dumping over the whole area, agreeing with documented raising of street levels by the Thames. A rebuilt wall on the site of the church incorporated a large quantity of moulded stonework which should allow considerable insight into the appearance of the pre-Fire church. A marked continuity of street frontages and property divisions can be traced from the 13th c to the post-Fire period and this continuity only ceased with the construction of a Victorian warehouse on the site.

London Archaeol, 4, 1982, 162; *Britannia,* 13, 1982, 374; *Medieval Archaeol,* 26, 1982, 193

Betts, I, 1987 'Peter's Hill PET81 Roman building material', Archive Report

Davies, B, 1986 'St Peter's Hill Roman pottery (PET81)', Archive Report

Egan, G, & Moir, D, in prep. 'Post-medieval finds c 1450–c 1700: a selection from the City of London sites 1972–82'

Grew, F, 1986 'St Peter's Hill (PET81)', Finds Appraisal

Locker, A, 1986 'The fish bones', Archive Report

Schofield, J, 1994 'Saxon and medieval parish churches in the City of London: a review', *Trans London Middlesex Archaeol Soc,* 45, 127–8

Williams, T, nd, 'Excavations at St Peter's Hill/Castle Baynard Street/Upper Thames Street EC4', Archive Report

Williams, T, 1991 'Allectus's building campaign in London: implications for the development of the Saxon shore', in Maxfield, V A, & Dobson, M J (eds), *Roman frontier studies 1989: proceedings of the XVth International Congress of Roman frontier studies,* 132–41

Williams, T, 1993 *Public buildings in the south-west quarter of Roman London,* The archaeology of Roman London 3, CBA Res Rep 88

[Roman strata]

5–7 Philpot Lane, EC3

PH181

F Hammer
NGR: TQ 33040 80895
SMR: 043676–84

A watching brief recovered information from 17 holes for concrete piling, spread over an area of about 220sq m to the W of Philpot Lane. The site lay about 60m S of the SE corner of the Hadrianic forum.

The sections showed seven periods of activity. In Period I were quarries of brickearth and sand, later levelling of the area and a few traces of a flimsy structure in the E and some construction in the W; a spread of destruction material appearing at the fringe seemed to come from a fire to the S or E outside the site.

Period II consisted of two buildings, of which the SW had substantial ragstone foundations and an inner flint foundation bonded with mortar. It seems to have survived into the late Roman period. The other, a timber and brickearth structure in the E running under modern Philpot Lane and having a gravelled area to the W, was extended in three phases until it reached a property boundary in the W marked by a stone foundation. After its destruction in Period III a new structure was built in the E with ragstone foundations and an *opus signinum* floor, also crossing the line of Philpot Lane. In Period IV dark earth and pitfills provided evidence of Saxon occupation, although much cut away. Two ragstone and chalk walls of Period V survived at the W and S boundaries of the site; they were perhaps contemporary with the surviving 15th-c vaulted undercroft S of the site. Evidence of post-medieval date (Period VI) consisted of two drains, a few portions of walls, a pit and a substantial levelling layer of destruction debris which was cut by Period VII Victorian stanchions.

London Archaeol, 4, 1982, 161; *Medieval Archaeol,* 26, 1982, 193; 28, 1984, 228

Hammer, F, 1983 'Excavations at 5–7 Philpot Lane', Archive Report

Williams, T, in prep. *The development of Roman London east of the Walbrook,* The archaeology of Roman London 4, CBA Res Rep [Roman strata]

SWA81

G Egan
NGR: TQ 32720 80685
SMR: 043802–17

Swan Lane car park, 95–103 Upper Thames Street, EC4

Excavation in the basement of the multi-storey car park at Swan Lane was made possible by a grant from the developers, Edger Investments, and through the co-operation of National Car Parks Ltd.

Some worn timber was found *in situ* at the edge of the River Thames in the Saxon period, immediately to the S of a consolidated surface of gravel and Roman building rubble. These features were overlaid by an eroded Late Saxon clay bank which foreshore material had accumulated.

To the S, 12th–13th-c dumping reclaimed at least 18m of land from the river, probably in more than 'one operation, but any revetting structures, with the exception of a single cruciform timber back brace, had been removed. The first activity on the newly made land was represented by a highly complicated series of at least 35 hearths, each constructed with a burning surface of mortar laid over vertically set roof tile fragments, surrounded by a keyhole-shaped kerb of ragstone and horizontal roof tile fragments. These hearths included a vertical series of six superimposed burning areas (from which samples were taken for archaeological dating by AML, but without clear result due to slumping), and up to five horizontal rows, though contemporaneity is difficult to demonstrate. The nature of this riverside industrial activity may be clarified by the analysis of samples recovered during excavation; these include some montmorillonite (fuller's earth) identified by the Mineralogy Department of the Natural History Museum. The hearths were truncated at the N by an early 13th-c undercroft, the stone-built entrance of which survived in detail, with the imprints from removed steps that would have led up towards medieval Thames Street to the N. After most of the usable building stone had been removed, the undercroft area had been backfilled with a series of dumps, including some substantial flints and a deposit of fine sandy material, perhaps from stoneworking. To the S the hearths were overlaid by several larger medieval stone, and post-medieval brick foundations. The implied N–S property boundaries seem to have shifted towards the end of the period represented in at least one area. Unusually for this part of London, no evidence of the Great Fire of 1666 was excavated. The latest feature uncovered was a brick-lined cistern, probably from the 18th- or 19th-c buildings on the site.

A seven-month watching brief on the 4000sq m site of the former Swan Lane car park took place during the early stages of redevelopment. It was made possible by grants from the City of London Archaeological Trust and the Museum of London Trust Funds, and with the co-operation of the contractor, Sir Robert McAlpine and Sons Ltd. The assistance and invaluable expertise of members of the Society of Thames Mudlarks and Antiquarians is gratefully acknowledged.

At the N end of the site a well-constructed ?late 2nd-c Roman quay, built of large beams, was found to have been partially dismantled. It was succeeded by structures with a different technique of construction: two post and plank revetments, and at least two other riverside structures which made secondary use of very large beams, but employed less sophisticated jointing than that in the earliest revetment. The alignments of these features apparently changed near the middle of the site, at a point where a N–S wooden drain was found. Deposits associated with these structures produced late Roman pottery.

Significant Roman finds from the site include leaden sealings, complete iron shears, fragments of about 100 leather shoes and sandals, and a large late 2nd-c–early 3rd-c samian group.

London Archaeol, 4, 1983, 276; *Britannia,* 14, 1983, 312; *Medieval Archaeol,* 26, 1982, 193; 27, 1983, 194–5; *Post-Medieval Archaeol,* 17, 1983, 191

Battarbee, R, 1981 'Diatom analysis — Swan Lane (SWA81)', Archive Report

Bayley, J, 1987 'Note on a medieval enamel from Swan Lane City of London', AML Report 242

Brigham, T, 1990 'The late Roman waterfront in London', *Britannia,* 21, 99–183

Clark, J (ed), 1995 *The medieval horse and its equipment c 1150–c 1450,* Medieval finds from excavations in London 5 [medieval horseshoes and horse equipment]

Cowgill, J, 1983 'Swan Lane 1981 — knives and scabbards', Archive Report

Cowgill, J, 1984 'Preliminary assessment of the straps and strap attachments from Swan Lane', Archive Report

Cowgill, J, 1986a 'Swan Lane (Excavation) (SWA81)', Finds Appraisal

Cowgill, J, 1986b 'Swan Lane (Watching brief) (SWA81)', Finds Appraisal

Cowgill, J, de Neergaard, M, & Griffiths, N, 1987 *Knives and scabbards,* Medieval finds from excavations in London 1

Crosby, D D B, & Mitchell, J G, 1987 'Potassium-argon determinations of some London medieval honestones', *Trans London Middlesex Archaeol Soc,* 38, 159–64

Crowfoot, E, Pritchard, F, & Staniland, K, 1992 *Textiles and clothing c 1150–c 1450,* Medieval finds from excavations in London 4

Egan, G, 1982 'Superb finds at the Swan Lane site', *McAlpine News,* 1

Egan, G, 1985/6 'Finds recovery on riverside sites in London', *Popular Archaeol,* 6, No. 14, 42–50

Egan, G, 1988 'Industry and economics on the medieval and later London waterfront', in Good, G L, Jones, R H, & Ponsford, M W (eds), *Waterfront archaeology: proceedings of the third international conference, Bristol, 1988,* CBA Res Rep 74, 9–18

Egan, G, 1998 *The medieval household,* Medieval finds from excavations in London 6

Egan, G, & Moir, D, in prep. 'Post-medieval finds c 1450–c 1700: a selection from the City of London sites 1972–82'

Egan, G, & Pritchard, F, 1991, *Dress accessories c 1150–c 1450,* Medieval finds from excavations in London 3

Gale, R, 1985 'Wood identification for Swan Lane (SWA81)', Archive Report

Giorgi, J, Rackham, J, & Smith, D, 1996 'An environmental sample from a post-medieval well at Swan Lane (ENV/REP/07/96)', Archive Report

Grew, F, & de Neergaard, M, 1988 *Shoes and pattens,* Medieval finds from excavations in London 2

Groves, C, & Hillam, J, 1987 'Tree-ring analysis of timbers from Swan Lane City of London 1981', AML Report 30/87

Harris, R, 1989 'Excavations at Swan Lane (SWA81), Groups 20–44', Archive Report (MS)

Locker, A, 1992 'The fish bones from Swan Lane (FIS/04/92)', Archive Report

Pearce, J, Vince, A G, & Jenner, M A, 1985 *A dated type-series of medieval pottery part 2: London-type ware,* London Middlesex Archaeol Soc Spec Pap 6

Pritchard, F, 1983 'Swan Lane medieval building material (SWA81)', Archive Report

Richardson, B, 1989 'The Roman pottery from Swan Lane (SWA81)', Archive Report

Shepherd, L, 1991 'Excavations at Swan Lane (SWA81), Groups 45–59', Archive Report (MS)

Spencer, B, in prep. *Pilgrim souvenirs and secular badges,* Medieval finds from excavations in London 7

Steedman, K, Dyson, T, & Schofield, J, 1992 *Aspects of Saxo-Norman London III: the bridgehead and Billingsgate to 1200,* London Middlesex Archaeol Soc Spec Pap 14 [Saxon and medieval embankments]

Vince, A, 1985 'Saxon and medieval pottery in London: a review', *Medieval Archaeol,* 29, 25–93

Wilthew, P, 1984 'Metallographic examination of medieval knives and shears', Archive Report (AML)

Museum of London rotunda, junction of Aldersgate and London Wall, EC2

ALD82

I Blair
NGR: TQ 32160 81570
SMR: 044515–16

In a British Telecom trench a sequence of road surfaces of Aldersgate street was recorded, the latest being a medieval or post-medieval cobbled surface. In another trench at the W end of London Wall a deposit of compacted brickearth was overlaid by thick deposits of scorched brickearth.

Apothecary Street (north side), near junction with New Bridge Street, EC4

APY82

J Norton
NGR: TQ 31670 81050
SMR: 044713–14

A gaspipe trench revealed a single course of masonry about 1m wide; it may have formed part of a N–S wall possibly composed of sandstone with some ragstone and chalk. Dark silt sealed the wall with silt and red brick fragments above, overlain by *in situ* burning, more silt and then the granite setts of the road surface.

Billingsgate Market lorry park, Lower Thames Street, EC3

BIG82

S Roskams
NGR: TQ 32980 80650
SMR: 043356–61

Excavation here (Fig 41) took place over a 12-month period, funded by DoE and the Corporation, with additional funding by the Manpower Services Commission, the City of London Archaeological Trust and help from several other sponsors.

The Roman quay was investigated in the closing weeks of the excavation, and enough was recorded to show that it was a continuation of the quay excavated in 1974–6 on the sites at New Fresh Wharf (NFW74, SM75) immediately to the E. The construction here however included what was probably the base for a crane. The principal quay timbers were dated by dendrochronology to AD201–28, which is in agreement with the structure being the same as that at New Fresh Wharf (AD209–44). After some robbing of the structure, part was rebuilt and this gave a later dendrochronological date of AD239–75 (Brigham 1990).

Fig 41 BIG82: the excavations at Billingsgate Market lorry park from the SW, after insertion of sheet piling to delimit the archaeological trench, 25m x 22m; initial clearance reveals medieval and post-medieval buildings which were shown to survive to an impressive extent in this waterfront area.

There was then a gap in occupation of the area until the 9th or 10th c; the areas behind and in front of the Roman waterfront silted up. The first signs of new constructional activity above this required the removal of elements of the quay in the E to give an inlet to the N formed by two very substantial stave-built revetments at least 2m high, and running off the site to the E and W behind which was packed clay with timber lacing. The revetment was strengthened by large tie-back braces in the body of the clay.

This arrangement was retained throughout the 10th and 11th c, although partial collapses, and perhaps rising river levels, required various additions to the front of the revetment. Eventually the inlet was filled in, but its position was preserved by a conspicuous property boundary which ultimately divided the areas of St Botolph's Wharf and Billingsgate.

From the 12th c, the waterfront made successive advances to the S, with a series of front-braced revetments (Fig 42). These showed extensive signs of prefabrication in the form of carpenters' marks and the reuse of timber from both contemporary buildings and boats. In the early 12th c, their configuration included a tongue of land projecting into the river, its position reflecting the now-filled inlet. The metallings of this projection constituted the earliest form of St Botolph's Wharf.

Fig 42 BIG82: the revetment at Billingsgate Market lorry park dated to the early 13th c by dendrochronology. This whole portion of revetment was later conserved for display.

In 1180 or later the waterfront was advanced about 3m southwards by the insertion of a new front-braced revetment. Timber buildings were constructed behind this in the NE part of the site. Subsequently the revetment was completely robbed out, and a front-braced revetment was inserted (1205 or later), with dumps behind it creating a new working surface. Later (1220+) a sequence of timber buildings with associated hearths was constructed immediately behind the revetment.

In 1250+ the waterfront advanced about 6m further S with the insertion of a new front-braced revetment. This was in turn sealed by further dumps (1250–70), presumably behind a new revetment which lay to the S of the limit of excavation. Over these dumps the gravel metallings of St Botolph's Lane were laid down. From the 13th c, the waterfronts lay off the site to the S, but the sequence of contemporary buildings behind them was examined; the buildings lay either side of the lane of St Botolph's Wharf, now evident. On the W side, it flanked the 12th-c masonry E end of the church of St Botolph, to the S of which probable secular buildings developed. In the early 15th c the latter included a well-preserved undercroft, and in the mid-15th c the church expanded S to incorporate this previously domestic structure, probably as a vestry (as suggested by documentary evidence), and the open area between it and the early church was made into a private chapel. This plan continued through until the 16th c (possibly as late as 1600) when the chapel was converted into the choir of the church.

To the E of the lane, by contrast, commercial buildings continued in use from the 13th c to the post-medieval period. The earliest of these were timber framed, with clay-infilled walls and containing hearths and in one case an associated timber drain. These buildings may have been structurally integrated with the waterfront revetments which bounded them in the S; this is significant for the study of the character of structural development in the medieval waterfront area, and fits with the way in which different forms of revetment construction match changes in property boundaries behind them.

For the watching brief on this site see BWB83 below.

London Archaeol, 4, 1983, 274; *Britannia,* 14, 1983, 311; 15, 1984, 308; *Medieval Archaeol,* 27, 1983, 191–2; 28, 1984, 226–7;
 Post-Medieval Archaeol, 17, 1983, 185
Betts, I, 1984 'Roman building material', Archive Report
Bird, J, 1986 'Billingsgate 1982 — Samian from phases II and III', Archive Report
Brigham, T, 1990 'The late Roman waterfront in London', *Britannia,* 21, 99–183
Brigham, T, 1991 'Excavations at Billingsgate lorry park, 1982–83: 1200 to the Great Fire', draft report
Clark, J (ed), 1995 *The medieval horse and its equipment* c 1150–c 1450, Medieval finds from excavations in London 5 [medieval
 horseshoes and horse equipment]
Cowgill, J, de Neergaard, M, & Griffiths, N, 1987 *Knives and scabbards,* Medieval finds from excavations in London 1
Crosby, D D B, & Mitchell, J G, 1987 'Potassium-argon determinations of some London medieval honestones', *Trans London
 Middlesex Archaeol Soc,* 38, 159–64
Crowfoot, E, Pritchard, F, & Staniland, K, 1992 *Textiles and clothing* c 1150–c 1450, Medieval finds from excavations in London 4
Dickinson, B, 1987 'Samian potters' stamps from Billingsgate', Archive Report
Egan, G, 1998 *The medieval household,* Medieval finds from excavations in London 6
Egan, G, & Moir, D, in prep. 'Post-medieval finds c 1450–c 1700: a selection from the City of London sites 1972–82'
Egan, G, & Pritchard, F, 1991 *Dress accessories* c 1150–c 1450, Medieval finds from excavations in London 3
Evans, J, & Gibson, J, 1985 'Some 18th-century pharmaceutical vessels from London', *Post-Medieval Archaeol,* 19, 151–5
Flude, K, 1982 'The use of computers in the Billingsgate excavation', *Bull Inst Archaeol Univ London,* 147–54
Gale, R, 1987 'The identification of wood from artefacts excavated by the DUA at London sites — Billingsgate', AML Report 55/87
Grew, F, 1984 'Billingsgate (BIG82) Part I — Roman', Finds Appraisal
Grew, F, & de Neergaard, M, 1988 *Shoes and pattens,* Medieval finds from excavations in London 2
Groves, C, & Hillam, J, 1985 'Tree-ring dating of waterfront structures from Billingsgate lorry park', Archive Report
Hillam, J, 1987 'Tree-ring analysis of timbers from Billingsgate lorry park City of London 1982', AML Report 47/87
Hillam, J, & Groves, C, 1985 'Tree-ring dating of waterfront structures from Billingsgate lorry park City of London',
 Archive Report
Lea, R, nd, 'Moulded stone', Archive Report
Marsden, P, 1994 *Ships of the port of London: first to eleventh centuries AD,* EH Archaeol Rep 3, 153–4 [fragments of two 11th-c boats]
Milne, G, 1991 'Waterfront archaeology and vernacular architecture: a London study', in Good, G L, Jones, R H, & Ponsford, M W
 (eds), *Waterfront archaeology: proceedings of the third international conference, Bristol, 1988,* CBA Res Rep 74, 116–20
Milne, G, 1992 *Timber building techniques in London,* c 900–1400, London Middlesex Archaeol Soc Spec Pap 15 [joints and carpentry]
de Neergaard, M, 1983 'Finds from Billingsgate', *Popular Archaeol,* 5, No. 6, 27–31
de Neergaard, M, 1984 'Billingsgate — the intricacies of urban excavation', *London Environmental Bulletin,* 2, 2–4
Pearce, J, Vince, A G, & Jenner, M A, 1985 *A dated type-series of medieval pottery part 2: London-type ware,* London Middlesex Archaeol
 Soc Spec Pap 6
Richardson, B, 1989 'The Roman pottery from Billingsgate lorry park (BIG82)', Archive Report
Roskams, S, 1989 'Excavations at Billingsgate lorry park (BIG82)', Archive Report
Ruddle, J, 1991 'An investigation of the potential of tooth cement annuli for ageing zooarchaeological material, with special
 consideration to cattle mandibular first molars (DIS/02/91)', MSc Dissertation, Dept of Human Environment, Institute of Archaeology,
 University College London
Schofield, J, 1982 'Billingsgate', *Popular Archaeol,* 4, No. 1, 31–4
Schofield, J, 1983 'Billingsgate', *Popular Archaeol,* 5, No. 4, 12–17
Schofield, J, 1986 'Billingsgate: diary of an excavation', in McIntosh, J, *The archaeologist's handbook,* 175–85
Schofield, J, & Dyson, T, 1980 'The need for archaeological investigation of the Billingsgate lorry park', internal DUA report
Schofield, J, & Dyson, T, in prep. *Medieval waterfront tenements*

Spencer, B, in prep. *Pilgrim souvenirs and secular badges,* Medieval finds from excavations in London 7

Steedman, K, Dyson, T, & Schofield, J, 1992 *Aspects of Saxo-Norman London III: the bridgehead and Billingsgate to 1200,* London Middlesex Archaeol Soc Spec Pap 14 [Saxon and medieval embankments]

Tyers, I, 1992 'City: early to late medieval boats (BIG82, CUS73, TL74, Blackfriars Wreck 3)', Dendrochronology Report

Vince, A, 1985 'The processing and analysis of the medieval pottery from Billingsgate lorry park 1982', in Herteig, A E (ed), *Conference on waterfront archaeology in north European towns no.2, Bergen 1983, Historisk Museum Bergen,* 157–68

Vince, A (ed), 1991a *Aspects of Saxo-Norman London II: finds and environmental evidence,* London Middlesex Archaeol Soc Spec Pap 12 [Saxon smallfinds]

Vince, A, 1991b 'Early medieval London: refining the chronology', *London Archaeol,* 6, 263–71

BIS82

H White
NGR: TQ 33190 81380
SMR: 044597–8, 044600–4

76–80 Bishopsgate, EC2

A four-month excavation funded by Pontsarn Investments Ltd was conducted on a 300sq m site on the E side of Bishopsgate street. The main purpose of the excavation was to trace the line of the Roman street suggested to run from the NE corner of the 2nd-c forum N to a gate on the site of Bishopsgate to the N of the site, and to investigate any relationship with the 1st-c N–S street found on a different alignment at 28–32 Bishopsgate in 1982. The natural brickearth had been truncated to a shallow depth by modern basements on the W part of the site, adjacent to Bishopsgate. Roman intrusive features suggested the presence of 1st- and 2nd-c buildings and pits relating to a frontage beneath the modern street. None of the features postdating this period showed any sign of having been inserted through a substantial metalled surface.

At the SE corner of the site stratigraphy survived to a greater height. Initial quarrying activities and ground preparation were followed by a rectangular timber-framed building of at least two rooms extending beyond the limits of the excavation, with a gravelled area to its N. One room had a floor of *opus signinum,* the other had carefully laid make-ups of crushed building material ending with a (robbed) brickearth slab. Overlying this were quantities of tesserae and painted wall plaster. The building's destruction was dated to the 3rd or 4th c.

A small rectangular sunken-floored structure respecting the alignment was recorded within the area of the building. Its construction was probably contemporary with the demolition of the by then derelict building. The dark earth overlying these structures produced 3rd- and 4th-c pottery and coins. All subsequent periods in this area were represented by intense pit digging and consequently few indications of surfaces or structures survived. Fragments of crucible, an early medieval hearth and quantities of demolished kiln material in medieval pits could suggest industrial activity in the vicinity. The remainder of the site, though heavily truncated, showed some pre-Roman features in the original ground surface with tree roots, overlaid by successive brickearth deposits and then medieval soils, suggesting this area remained open for long periods. Several medieval and post-medieval cesspits were recorded across the site.

During the excavation refurbishing of the N wall of St Ethelburga's church, on the S side of the site, afforded the opportunity of limited recording work. A 4m stretch of the N wall, revealed by removal of Victorian rendering, was recorded. A number of reused moulded stones incorporated in the 15th-c rebuild of the wall were noted. During underpinning of the party wall immediately N of the church a grave cut containing a skeleton was discovered, showing the N extent of the graveyard at the E end of the church.

Medieval Archaeol, 28, 1984, 227

Clark, J (ed), 1995 *The medieval horse and its equipment c 1150–c 1450,* Medieval finds from excavations in London 5 [medieval horse shoes and horse equipment]

Cowgill, J, de Neergaard, M, & Griffiths, N, 1987 *Knives and scabbards,* Medieval finds from excavations in London 1

Crowley, N, 1988 '76–88 Bishopsgate (BIS82) Roman building material Level III report', Archive Report

Davies, B, 1993 'Inter-site studies', in Milne, G, & Wardle, A, 'Early Roman development at Leadenhall Court, London and related research', *Trans London Middlesex Archaeol Soc,* 44, 135–50

Dunn, G, 1983 'Bishopsgate (BIS82)', Finds Appraisal

Egan, G, & Moir, D, in prep. 'Post-medieval finds c 1450–c 1700: a selection from the City of London sites 1972–82'

Steedman, K, nd, 'Excavations at 76–80 Bishopsgate EC2', Archive Report

Williams, T, in prep. *The development of Roman London east of the Walbrook,* The archaeology of Roman London 4, CBA Res Rep [Roman strata]

Wilthew, P, 1984a 'Inlays and fittings on medieval iron knives and shears', Archive Report (AML)

Wilthew, P, 1984b 'Metallographic examination of medieval knives and shears', Archive Report (AML)

28–34 Bishopsgate, 2–3 Crosby Square, 2–3 Great St Helens, EC2

BOP82

C Evans
NGR: TQ 33120 81260
SMR: 043362–83

Excavations funded by the Standard Charter Bank took place in a 280sq m L-shaped area. Possible evidence of later prehistoric activity was seen in a few minor features which survived extensive Roman truncation of the brickearth natural; worked flint flakes and a substantial amount of firecracked flint were recovered from the redeposited natural which covered the site.

The initial Roman development of this area (Neronian/Flavian) was certainly planned as was evident in the continuous brickearth slab which was cut by hacking-out ditches; quarry pits were found in the E area of the site. Contemporary with this initial development was a major N–S Roman road 7.5m wide. Its projected alignment would appear to be close to that of the first forum, running N from the approximate centre of the forum to the W of the Roman forerunner of Bishopsgate, though it need not necessarily have been straight. Successive drains were excavated on either side of the road. Truncated post-holes from E–W aligned timber structures which fronted upon this road were found, as was also an early pit which contained much scorched daub with wattle impressions. These early structures were succeeded by more substantial, later 1st-c, brickearth buildings, which followed the earlier property lines. The interior surfaces of these later buildings survived in only a limited area where a baked clay hearth was found. A sequence of associated exterior surfaces in the E end of the site would suggest rebuilding of these structures.

These buildings were destroyed or demolished probably in the early 2nd c; a horizon of large fragments of painted wall plaster and a large pit containing substantial quantities of building materials, some of which was scorched, were found. These were sealed by a thick brickearth dump perhaps arising from a redevelopment of the area. During the watching brief, a small portion of an *in situ* red tessellated floor was seen in the SE corner of Crosby Square, and apparently dated from this redevelopment phase as it was bedded on similar brickearth deposits. In the E of the site a remarkable mid-2nd-c pit was excavated which produced over 100 kilos of pottery and a large quantity of building materials and household goods. Though no later Roman horizontal stratigraphy survived on the site, fills from truncated roadside drains indicate that the road may have continued in use during the 3rd c. Only a few later Roman pits were present and their distribution would suggest that the early property boundaries had been maintained. One late Saxon pit and a number of 12th–14th-c cesspits were excavated. Two standing late medieval brick vaults, which had been part of the Crosby Place buildings (built *c* 1466) were examined and four main construction phases were recognised, dating from the 14th to the 17th c. A large brick-vaulted cesspit was found within one of the vaults which were contemporary with their late commercial use. A post-medieval well and cesspit were also excavated.

London Archaeol, 4, 1983, 274–5; *Britannia,* 14, 1983, 311; *Medieval Archaeol,* 27, 1983, 192; *Post-Medieval Archaeol,* 17, 1983, 189

Clark, J (ed), 1995 *The medieval horse and its equipment c 1150–c 1450,* Medieval finds from excavations in London 5 [medieval horse shoes and horse equipment]

Davies, B, 1993 'Inter-site studies', in Milne, G, & Wardle, A, 'Early Roman development at Leadenhall Court, London and related research', *Trans London Middlesex Archaeol Soc,* 44, 135–50

Davies, B, Richardson, B, & Tomber, R, 1994 *A dated corpus of early Roman pottery from the City of London,* The archaeology of Roman London 5, CBA Res Rep 98 [contribution to early Roman pottery corpus]

Dunn, C, 1983 'Bishopsgate (BOP82)', Finds Appraisal

Egan, G, & Moir, D, in prep. 'Post-medieval finds c 1450–c 1700: a selection from the City of London sites 1972–82'

Evans, C, nd, 'Excavations at 28–34 Bishopsgate EC2', Archive Report

Evans, C, 1990 'Power on silt: towards an archaeology of the East India Company', *Antiquity,* 64, 643–61

Gale, R, 1986 'The identification of wood from sites excavated by the DUA', AML Report 60/87

Giorgi, J, Rackham, J, & Smith, D, 1996 'Environmental samples from post-medieval deposits at 28–32 Bishopsgate (ENV/REP/11/96)', Archive Report

Grew, F, 1983 'The contents of a mid-2nd-century pit at Bishopsgate (BOP82)', Archive Report

Locker, A, 1992 'The fish bones from excavations at Billingsgate (FIS/06/92)', Archive Report

Orton, C, 1996 'Dem dry bones', in Bird, J, Hassall, M, & Sheldon, H (eds), *Interpreting Roman London: papers in memory of Hugh Chapman,* 199–208 [comparative statistical study of animal bones]

Schofield, J, 1995 *Medieval London houses,* 161–3 [Crosby Place]

Tyers, P, 1983 'BOP82 — the Roman pottery from contexts 140 and 1091 with a note on amphorae in 2nd-century London', Archive Report

Tyers, P, 1984 'An assemblage of Roman ceramics from London', *London Archaeol,* 4, 367–74

Vince, A, 1983 'The pottery from a brick-lined cesspit at 28–32 Bishopsgate', Archive Report

Williams, T, in prep. *The development of Roman London east of the Walbrook,* The archaeology of Roman London 4, CBA Res Rep [Roman strata]

BSA82

R Chapman
NGR: TQ 33330 80680
SMR: 044450

Billingsgate bath-house, 4–9 St Dunstan's Hill, 100 Lower Thames Street, EC3

Pile holes on the N and E of the Billingsgate bath-house site revealed two ragstone walls, one constructed on a piled foundation.

For earlier work on the bath-house site see GM111 and BIL75 above; for later work, see BBH87 below.

Chapman, R, nd, 'Watching brief at Billingsgate bath-house, EC3', Archive Report

CRC82

J Schofield
NGR: TQ 33400 81200
SMR: 044517

Opposite 22 Creechurch Lane, EC3

The site was a short tunnel dug at basement level into Creechurch Lane from the basement of no. 22. Medieval pottery was recovered from spoil from the tunnel, but no site records were made.

FLE82

C Guy
NGR: TQ 31260 81170
SMR: 043414–15

180–183 Fleet Street, 140–143 Fetter Lane, EC4

Excavation revealed the bottom of a late 14th-c chalk-lined feature and the bottom of an 18th-c brick-lined pit. The basement on this site had destroyed all other archaeological remains.

London Archaeol, 4, 1983, 276; *Medieval Archaeol,* 27, 1983, 193
Cowgill, J, 1984 'Fetter Lane (FLE82)', Finds Appraisal
Guy, C, 1983 'Excavations at 180–183 Fleet Street', Archive Report

LAT82

M Nally
NGR: TQ 31650 81210
SMR: 044518–19

1–6 Ludgate Circus Buildings, EC4

A N–S chalk, flint and Reigate stone-vaulted culvert was recorded in the watching brief at Ludgate Circus Buildings. The culvert extended 7m from the N limit of excavation to an E–W return wall or foundation. The N end of a N–S chalk, flint and ragstone wall or foundation was recorded 5m to the S, in section at the E edge of excavation. A fragment of N–S chalk wall or foundation was recorded 7m to the W. There was no dating evidence or associated occupation surfaces.

Dunn, G, 1984 'Ludgate Circus Buildings (LAT82)', Finds Appraisal
Giorgi, J, Rackham, J, & Smith, D, 1996 'An environmental sample from a post-medieval deposit at 1–6 Ludgate Circus (ENV/REP/03/96)', Archive Report
Nally, M, nd, 'Excavations at 1–6 Ludgate Circus Buildings EC4', Archive Report

119–121 Cannon Street, 1–3 Abchurch Yard, 14 Sherbourne Lane, EC4

LIB82

P Rowsome
NGR: TQ 32730 80925
SMR: 043443–51

Contractors' excavations on a large site just E of the Walbrook Valley and N of Cannon Street required archaeological coverage in January and February 1982. Preliminary trial holes had correctly shown the S and W areas of the site to be devoid of archaeological deposits, but in the E 1.2m of stratigraphy survived in a shallow basement area of 6m x 30m. Earliest recorded features were a Roman well and two square, vertical-sided cuts into natural. The well, to the extreme W of the site on the edge of the Walbrook Valley, survived to a 4m depth below natural and contained in a box at its base a human skull with the skeletons of two dogs and a large number of sherds of Neronian flagons and amphorae. The other square cuts were 2m square and 1.2m deep. Sealing these cuts were extensive dumps of Neronian and early Flavian date. To the E a sunken-floored masonry structure cutting down to natural was recorded. Its construction trench contained early to mid-Flavian pottery and the W wall was 6.5m long and 1m thick, the N and S walls running E off the site. The walls were of ragstone and tile-course construction in a matrix of hard cream mortar, faced on the inside. In a later phase of building a 3m long addition was made to the N. The structure continued in use until the early 4th c, subsequently filling with thick deposits of waterwashed clayey silts which sealed a quantity of fine marble tiles scattered over the mortar floor. The structure may be part of a bath complex or water reservoir for the nearby governor's palace.

To the W evidence of timber building and sealing fire debris was recorded. A V-shaped ditch of 1st-c date and cutting 2.5m into natural ran across the mouth of the site towards the SE and elsewhere five medieval wells, three with chalk linings, were observed in the natural. A sequence of late medieval–16th-c pits in the E of the site produced fine collections of pottery and glass.

London Archaeol, 4, 1983, 277; *Britannia,* 14, 1983, 311; *Medieval Archaeol,* 27, 1983, 192; *Post-Medieval Archaeol,* 17, 1983, 189
Armitage, P, 1983 'Report on a group of animal bones found with the human skull placed at the bottom of a Roman well', Archive Report
Crowley, N, 1988 '119 Cannon Street (LIB82) Roman building material Level III report', Archive Report
Davies, B, 1993 'Inter-site studies', in Milne, G, & Wardle, A, 'Early Roman development at Leadenhall Court, London and related research', *Trans London Middlesex Archaeol Soc,* 44, 135–50
Dunn, G, 1984 'Cannon Street (LIB82)', Finds Appraisal
Egan, G, & Moir, D, in prep. 'Post-medieval finds c 1450–c 1700: a selection from the City of London sites 1972–82'
Giorgi, J, Rackham, J, & Smith, D, 1996 'An environmental sample from a post-medieval pitfill at Cannon Street (LIB82): (ENV/REP/12/96)', Archive Report
Rowsome, P, nd, 'Excavations at 119–121 Cannon Street', Archive Report
Tyers, P, 1983 'The Roman pottery from LIB82', Archive Report
Vaughan, D, nd, 'Roman charred plant remains', Archive Report
Vince, A, 1982 'Post-Roman pottery summary report', Archive Report
Williams, T, in prep. *The development of Roman London east of the Walbrook,* The archaeology of Roman London 4, CBA Res Rep
[Roman strata]

84–85 Long Lane, EC1

LOG82

D Bentley
NGR: TQ 32030 81800
SMR: 044715–20

A small watching brief took place towards the NE corner of the precinct of St Bartholomew's Priory. Victorian basements had truncated the site but two rectilinear stone structures survived, cutting into the natural gravels. At least one was a cesspit, both of chalk and ragstone and aligned with Long Lane. Evidence from sections around the edge of the site revealed, on the N side, 2.5m of successive road-metallings and tread of medieval and post-medieval Long Lane, and on the S side horizontal deposits of garden soil disturbed only by N–S foundations of a 16th- or 17th-c brick wall under East Passage. Two N–S aligned adult skeletons were noted by contractors at a depth of 8ft.

In sections around the perimeter of the site the gravel street surfaces of Long Lane were recorded. The stone lining of a late medieval or post-medieval pit, probably a cesspit, was also recorded.

LON82

B Pye
NGR: TQ 32920 81500
SMR: 040499

London Wall, junction with Blomfield Street, EC2

Observations were carried out during work on a telephone manhole in London Wall street opposite no. 57. A 2m stretch of the Roman city wall was exposed, and full width of 2.5m at plinth level. The internal face of the wall survived up to the second tile course, 2.1m above the foundations. The defensive bank, consisting of dark grey earth, also survived to two ragstone courses above the red sandstone plinth. The wall foundations were unusually deep (about 1.6m), consisting of mortared ragstone footing, ragstone and puddled clay, with large unconsolidated ragstone at the bottom. In front of the wall to the N a ditch cut down to the natural gravels, and was filled with black peaty marsh deposits.

London Archaeol, 4, 1983, 277
Dunn, G, 1984 'London Wall (LON82)', Finds Appraisal
Pye, B, nd, 'Watching brief at London Wall, junction with Blomfield Street EC2', Archive Report

LUD82

P Rowsome
NGR: TQ 31770 81200
SMR: 040430–3, 041917

1–6 Old Bailey, 42–46 Ludgate Hill, EC4

Excavation and observation between April and December 1982 produced evidence of the city wall and defensive ditch sequence. Of the 51.5m stretch of the Roman city wall shown by trial holes to flank the E boundary of the site, a 17m section was revealed. This section was incorporated into the W wall of St Martin Ludgate in Wren's post-Fire rebuilding, and possibly into the pre-Fire church also. The city wall was observed surviving up to 3.1m above plinth level, the core having two double tile courses 0.7m apart, the lower of which was 0.7m above the top of the red sandstone plinth. The foundations of the wall were 0.95–1.0m deep and 2.45m thick. A 0.1m thick primary fill of silts in the base of the construction trench included tiles, chalk, ragstone, plaster, mortar and *opus signinum* suggesting that a previous building may have been demolished to make way for defensive work. The plinth and facing survived over a length of 11m and a height of 0.85m. Random single-tile courses, misplaced and broken plinth stones, two sandy limestone blocks and various mortars all suggest a medieval reconstruction of the face of the city wall N of Ludgate. The core material and foundation, definitely of Roman date, produced a samian bowl provisionally dated mid–late 2nd c. Underpinning work has allowed the recording of a massive ragstone and mortar foundation underneath the Ludgate Hill pavement and 8m W of the city wall which may well be the Roman gate.

Four separate areas of excavation on the site included three complete sections through the ditch sequence. The early Roman V-shaped ditch was not recorded, perhaps as a result of Victorian basement terracing into the Fleet Valley slope to a depth of 2.6m below the wall's plinth level, but Roman, Saxon and medieval ditches survived in truncated form. Furthest to the W a late Roman flat-bottomed and wide ditch was recorded. The Roman ditch was recut slightly to the E in the Late Saxon period and was in turn cut by a succession of three early medieval defensive ditches, each recut slightly to the E of its predecessor, the last being flat-bottomed, the first two roughly V-shaped. The latter, flat-bottomed, medieval ditch seemed well maintained and regularly cleaned but retained a V-shape in the area 35m N of Ludgate thereby leaving a 6m wide margin outside the city wall for a possible early medieval bastion (B21). A wealth of finds dating to *c* 1300–25 was preserved in the backfilling of the last ditch, including a large pottery group, horse skeletons and industrial waste suggestive of Fleet Valley industries, and a well-preserved wattle fence, perhaps representative of early suburban encroachment, crossing and blocking the ditch cut. The very early backfilling of the ditch N of Ludgate as excavated is supported by documentary evidence of encroachment.

London Archaeol, 4, 1983, 275; *Britannia,* 14, 1983, 312; *Medieval Archaeol,* 27, 1983, 194
Cowgill, J, de Neergaard, M, & Griffiths, N, 1987 *Knives and scabbards,* Medieval finds from excavations in London 1
Crosby, D D B, & Mitchell, J G, 1987 'Potassium-argon determinations of some London medieval honestones', *Trans London Middlesex Archaeol Soc,* 38, 159–64
Egan, G, & Pritchard, F, 1991 *Dress accessories c 1150–c 1450,* Medieval finds from excavations in London 3 [boneworking waste]
Ford, B, 1983a 'LUD82 — the ditch — industrial evidence', Archive Report
Ford, B, 1983b 'LUD82 — the mid-18th-century pit — pottery', Archive Report

Ford, B, 1983c 'LUD82 — the post-medieval pit group', Archive Report

Grew, F, & de Neergaard, M, 1988 *Shoes and pattens,* Medieval finds from excavations in London 2

Rowsome, P, 1985 'Excavations at 1–6 Old Bailey', Archive Report

Straker, V, 1982 'Report on the wooden hurdles from the medieval city ditch at Ludgate Hill', Archive Report

Vince, A, & Ford, B, 1983 'Ludgate Hill pottery (LUD82)', Archive Report

Wilkinson, T, 1983 'Report on the analysis of environmental samples taken from the medieval ditch at Ludgate Hill', Archive Report

Wilthew, P, 1983 'Examination of technological finds from Ludgate Hill (LUD82)', Archive Report

21–29 Mansell Street, E1

MAN82

A Upson
NGR: TQ 33810 81190
SMR: 043428–33

Excavation funded by A Peachey and Company in January–February 1982 found that all evidence of anticipated Roman burials on this extramural site had been removed by the digging of large quarry pits for the extraction of natural gravel. These pits had been backfilled over a long period between 1300 and 1700, and the whole area sealed by dumps of clayey silt in the 18th c. These dumps were dug into by several pits and a brick-lined well before a major property boundary was established with an E–W brick wall across the site, forming the N wall of a brick-lined cesspit. Another cesspit lay immediately adjacent to the S.

The area to the N of the boundary was used for the burial of over 100 bodies. These were mostly in wooden coffins which were stacked in rows to a maximum of nine per stack. Of the 74 whose ages could be estimated, 57 were adult, 7 children and 10 infants. Documentary sources suggest that this was a Non-Conformist burial ground in the 18th c.

London Archaeol, 4, 1983, 277; *Medieval Archaeol,* 27, 1983, 194; *Post-Medieval Archaeol,* 17, 1983, 191

Dunn, G, 1984 'Mansell Street (MAN82)', Finds Appraisal

Egan, G, & Moir, D, in prep. 'Post-medieval finds *c* 1450–*c* 1700: a selection from the City of London sites 1972–82'

Giorgi, J, Rackham, J, & Smith, D, 1996 'The environmental samples from post-medieval deposits at 21–29 Mansell Street (ENV/REP/04/96)', Archive Report

Upson, A, 1983 'Excavations at 21–29 Mansell Street', Archive Report

West, B, nd, 'Mansell Street — post-medieval human skeletons', Archive Report

7–10 Foster Lane, 5–6 Rose and Crown Court, EC2

OST82

I Blair
NGR: TQ 32200 81310
SMR: 043465 73

A two-month excavation and one-month watching brief funded by Wates Developments produced evidence of Roman and later periods from a small area of excavation and from a watching brief on building works. The earliest activity, recorded during the watching brief, consisted of quarry pits cut into the natural brickearth. Sealing the consolidation of at least one of these pits in the SE corner of the site was a succession of at least eight major road-metallings, the earliest of Flavian date, of a NE–SW road. It seems likely that this originally formed the W boundary of an insula which was bounded on the E by the Roman road found at Milk Street in 1977 (see MLK76 above).

Associated with the later road surfaces was a structure fronting directly onto the street to its W. This phase of activity was superseded by a series of linear roadside cuts which are interpreted as gullies. This means that subsequent buildings (which were not recorded) were pushed back behind the new lines of roadside ditches. In the main area of excavation the first series of buildings comprised four internal walls forming a room 3m x 2.5m, its axis parallel to the street, of brickearth sills probably for wattle and daub walls. This contained a domestic hearth similar to those on the GPO Newgate Street site (GPO75). The building was destroyed by fire in the mid–late 2nd c (the general date of the road widening) and was replaced by further structures which suffered the same fate in the early/mid-3rd c.

Cutting through the later fire dumps the NE corner of a Roman masonry structure was recorded on the W side of the site, running under Foster Lane. A second masonry structure in the N of the site comprised one N–S wall of rammed chalk, on the Roman alignment, which was not robbed until the early 11th c.

The dark earth was found slumped over 3rd-c surfaces, though its relationship to the masonry buildings and to the road was not established. External surfaces and stakes of the ?10th c suggest the establishment of Foster Lane. The medieval period was represented by two cesspits, which produced crucibles for metalworking, in one case (datable to the 14th c), with traces of goldworking upon it.

An important group of 14th-c Venetian glass beaker fragments (Fig 43) was recovered from one of the medieval cesspits.

Fig 43 OST82: one of the fragments of decorated glass beaker (14th c), of a rare type and indicative of a luxurious lifestyle in the goldsmiths' area around the W end of Cheapside.

London Archaeol, 4, 1983, 279; *Britannia,* 14, 1983, 312; *Medieval Archaeol,* 27, 1983, 193; *Post-Medieval Archaeol,* 17, 1983, 190

Armitage, P, 1982 'Faunal remains', Archive Report

Bayley, J, 1984 'Analyses of medieval enamelled glass found in London', Archive Report

Blair, I, 1983 'Foster Lane — the finding of the Foster Lane glass', *Popular Archaeol,* 5, No. 4, 23–7

Clark, J, 1983 'Medieval enamelled glasses from London', *Medieval Archaeol,* 27, 152–6

Egan, G, & Moir, D, in prep. 'Post-medieval finds c 1450–c 1700: a selection from the City of London sites 1972–82'

Tobert, N, 1982a 'Foster Lane (OST82)', Finds Appraisal

Tobert, N, 1982b 'Foster Lane — the crucibles', Archive Report

Tyers, P, 1982 'The Roman pottery from context 121', Archive Report

Vince, A, & Tobert, N, 1982 'The medieval pottery from context 190', Archive Report

POT82

S Rivière and A Westman
NGR: TQ 33030 80867
SMR: 044520–5

9–10 Philpot Lane, EC3

A watching brief during redevelopment by Wates Developments Ltd, who grant-aided recording work, was conducted from October 1982 to January 1983. Above natural gravel and brickearth, and redeposited natural brickearth, three successive sequences of internal surfaces were recorded, including floors of mortar and *opus signinum,* and tile. The sequences were interrupted by widespread mixed dumps, the whole dated by small quantities of pottery from the late 1st to the end of the 2nd c. Gravel metalling, which latterly extended over the eastern half of the site, was interpreted as external, but not a road.

No more definite evidence of structures was recovered than some traces of timber posts, fragmentary brickearth sills and one substantial cut feature. The last was either a Roman robber trench or the construction trench for a wall which in the event was not built. No fire horizons were recorded.

Intensive medieval pits were followed by or were partly contemporary with cellaring. The cellars were constructed mainly N of an implied property boundary which bisected the site. They showed considerable continuity with post-medieval and post-Great Fire cellars and with a standing post-Great Fire building to the immediate NW, in Brabant Court.

London Archaeol, 4, 1984, 401; *Britannia,* 15, 1984, 309; *Medieval Archaeol,* 28, 1984, 228

Dunn, G, 1984 'Philpot Lane (POT82)', Finds Appraisal

Westman, A, & Rivière, S, 1983 'Excavations at 9–10 Philpot Lane', Archive Report

Williams, T, in prep. *The development of Roman London east of the Walbrook,* The archaeology of Roman London 4, CBA Res Rep [Roman strata]

1–12 Rangoon Street, 61–65 Crutched Friars, 2–4 Carlisle Avenue, 11–13 Northumberland Alley (now Friary Court), EC3

RAG82

D Bowler
NGR: TQ 33500 81020
SMR: 043458–64

Commercial Union Properties generously funded a five-month excavation on this site from May to September of 1982.

The natural river gravels were uncovered over most of the site, together with a small area of the brickearth cap along the northern edge of the site. The earliest manmade features on the site were pits and gullies of the Roman period, from the 1st c onwards, and seen in the N part of the site. The unusually large area of excavation made it possible to trace the alignment and fall of the gullies over long distances. These features produced quite a large amount of animal bone, pottery and metalwork. The Rangoon Street site lay just within the walls of the Roman city, and well back from the main road (Fenchurch Street); it is likely that this area was taken up with gardens, or given over to industrial purposes, such as butchers' yards or even rubbish tips, as suggested by the plentiful animal bone and pottery.

In the N part of the site, the Roman features were sealed by about 0.3m of dark earth, deposited some time at the end of the Roman period, or later. It contained two human skeletons, buried together in the same grave, their heads to the N, the head of the upper (female) in the lap of the lower (male?). These unusual arrangements suggested some pagan burial practice.

Cut into the dark earth was a large medieval chalk-lined cesspit, containing fragments of painted window glass, decorated with a heraldic lion and foliage patterns; and a pattern of small rectangular pits, filled with rammed chalk and gravel, perhaps post-pads of a timber-framed structure.

South of Rangoon Street, the lower part of a timber-lined well survived, cut into the gravels and containing large amounts of 14th- and 15th-c pottery, including a watering-pot. The most conspicuous structure on the site was the East India Company's Tea and Drugs warehouse, built in 1796, whose massive brick and stone foundations covered most of the site. Surveyors' plans and elevations of this building survive in the India Office Archives. Associated with the warehouse, but not appearing on any surveyors' drawings, was an underground brick structure, identified as an ice-well. This consisted of a brick dome and cylinder, about 3m deep altogether, set in the natural gravel, down to the top of London Clay. It may originally have been built before the warehouse, but was retained when the warehouse was constructed. Rangoon Street was removed by the present redevelopment.

London Archaeol, 4, 1983, 279; Britannia, 14, 1983, 311–12; Medieval Archaeol, 27, 1983, 192–3; Post-Medieval Archaeol, 17, 1983, 189–90
Betts, I, 1988 'Rangoon Street/ 61–65 Crutched Friars (RAG82) Roman building material Level III report', Archive Report
Bowler, D, 1983 'Rangoon Street', Popular Archaeol, 5, No.6, 13–18
Bowler, D, 1984 'Excavations at Rangoon Street', Archive Report
Davies, B, 1993 'Inter-site studies', in Milne, G, & Wardle, A, 'Early Roman development at Leadenhall Court, London and related research', Trans London Middlesex Archaeol Soc, 44, 135–50
Davies, B, Richardson, B, & Tomber, R, 1994 A dated corpus of early Roman pottery from the City of London, The archaeology of Roman London 5, CBA Res Rep 98 [contribution to early Roman pottery corpus]
Dunn, G, 1984 'Rangoon Street (RAG82)', Finds Appraisal
Egan, G, & Moir, D, in prep. 'Post-medieval finds c 1450–c 1700: a selection from the City of London sites 1972–82'
Evans, C, 1990 'Power on silt: towards an archaeology of the East India Company', Antiquity, 64, 643–61
Giorgi, J, Rackham, J, & Smith, D, 1996 'An environmental sample from a post-medieval deposit at Rangoon Street (ENV/REP/02/96)', Archive Report
Locker, A, 1986 'The fish bones from context 1238', Archive Report (FIS/04/86)
Orton, C, 1996 'Dem dry bones', in Bird, J, Hassall, M, & Sheldon, H (eds), Interpreting Roman London: papers in memory of Hugh Chapman, 199–208 [comparative statistical study of animal bones]
Ruddle, J, 1991 'An investigation of the potential of tooth cement annuli for ageing zooarchaeological material, with special consideration to cattle mandibular first molars (DIS/02/91)', MSc Dissertation, Dept of Human Environment, Institute of Archaeology, University College London
Tyers, P, 1983 'The Roman pottery from Rangoon Street', Archive Report
Williams, T, in prep. The development of Roman London east of the Walbrook, The archaeology of Roman London 4, CBA Res Rep [Roman strata]

14 Garlick Hill (Sugar Loaf Court), EC4

SLO82

M Barker
NGR: TQ 32340 80867
SMR: 043317–20, 043416–19

Excavations on the S side of the Hudson's Bay Company's building Beaver House in 1982 recorded at least two phases of early Roman timber buildings; in the construction layers was Neronian pottery including wasters. The major part of the site was taken up by a large medieval undercroft with parts of the vault springers still *in situ*. During the 17th c a surface of London Clay was laid across the floor to form an impermeable barrier to rising water. Within the undercroft was a brick cesspit with an assemblage of 17th-c pottery including a Westerwald jug. During the post-Fire period the undercroft was backfilled with tile and timber debris, much of it burnt. To the W of the undercroft a chalk and gravel foundation of early medieval type was recorded.

The second part of the excavation took place between February and May 1983, with a further grant from the Hudson's Bay Company. Excavation continued of the trench opened in Sugar Loaf Court in October 1982, and in an extension to the S. In the Sugar Loaf Court trench, evidence of pre-Flavian and Flavian structures was recovered with direct correlations to others found to the S, which in turn produced evidence of a substantial timber structure on the same alignment as structures excavated to the E in 1982. Again pottery of Neronian date was in association.

The Sugar Loaf Court trench produced evidence of Saxon/early medieval pits and an oven-like structure with a small group of pottery provisionally dated 850–1000. A chalk foundation with associated occupation surfaces followed; the pottery from this phase dated to the 12th c. This building went out of use in the late medieval period and was followed by a phase of pits in the late 14th or 15th c. To the S of Sugar Loaf Court medieval surfaces were truncated by Victorian cellaring. The site is also called Beaver House in the records.

London Archaeol, 4, 1983, 276; *Britannia,* 14, 1983, 312; 15, 1984, 309; *Medieval Archaeol,* 27, 1983, 193; 28, 1984, 228; *Post-Medieval Archaeol,* 17, 1983, 191

Barker, M, 1989 'Excavations at Beaver House (Sugar Loaf Court) EC4', Archive Report

Betts, I, 1987 'Sugar Loaf Court/Beaver House (SLO82) Roman building material', Archive Report

Davies, B, 1993 'Inter-site studies', in Milne, G, & Wardle, A, 'Early Roman development at Leadenhall Court, London and related research', *Trans London Middlesex Archaeol Soc,* 44, 135–50

Davies, B, Richardson, B, & Tomber, R, 1994 *A dated corpus of early Roman pottery from the City of London,* The archaeology of Roman London 5, CBA Res Rep 98 [contribution to early Roman pottery corpus]

Dunn, G, 1984 'Sugar Loaf Court (SLO82)', Finds Appraisal

Richardson, B, 1987 'The Roman pottery from Beaver House (Sugar Loaf Court) (SLO82)', Archive Report

TAV82

J Burke-Easton
NGR: TQ 32030 81010
SMR: 0445256–7

Horn Tavern, 29–33 Knightrider Street, EC4

A small excavation on this site produced evidence of Roman and Saxon occupation, including a possible Late Saxon lime kiln. Early Saxon chaff-tempered pottery was also found, but in residual contexts.

Clark, J (ed), 1995 *The medieval horse and its equipment c 1150–c 1450,* Medieval finds from excavations in London 5 [medieval horseshoes and horse equipment]

Egan, G, & Moir, D, in prep. 'Post-medieval finds c 1450–c 1700: a selection from the City of London sites 1972–82'

Gale, R, 1986 'The identification of wood from sites excavated by the DUA', AML Report 60/87

Vince, A, & Jenner, A, 1991 'The Saxon and early medieval pottery of London', in Vince, A (ed), *Aspects of Saxo-Norman London II: finds and environmental evidence,* London Middlesex Archaeol Soc Spec Pap 12, 48

ACE83

A Upson
NGR: TQ 33020 81015
SMR: 043303–10

77–79 Gracechurch Street, EC3

A three-month excavation was carried out in the area of the E range of the first (Flavian) Roman forum, by arrangement with Land Securities Management Ltd. Excavation revealed some pre-Roman activity, although in the restricted area available no distinct structures could be identified. These deposits were bounded to the E by a steep-sided ditch which separated them from a sequence of well-surfaced gravel metallings, apparently representing a fragment of a N–S road.

The alignment established by these features was not respected by the subsequent building of the walls of the first (Flavian) forum. A N–S flint rubble wall foundation, capped by two tile courses, ran across the E of the site. Evidence from other sites suggests that it originally supported a continuous wall subsequently replaced by a series of square piers. These were used in conjunction with a new ragstone rubble foundation, capped by tiles, found in the present excavation approximately 2m to the W of the flint foundation. This would seem to be an extension of the E range into the courtyard area; the space between the two walls was well surfaced with hard mortar.

The superstructures of these features were thereafter carefully dismantled and the area covered with a thick deposit of clean sand and gravel to form a raised base for the courtyard surfaces of the second (early 2nd-c) forum.

Later features excavated included two pits of Saxon date, a coursed chalk foundation for an early medieval masonry building with its axis perpendicular to Gracechurch Street, and a large early 19th-c brick cesspit.

London Archaeol, 4, 1984, 385–6; Britannia, 15, 1984, 308; 16, 1985, 297; Medieval Archaeol, 28, 1984, 228
Marsden, P, 1987 The Roman forum site in London: discoveries before 1985, 117–19
Rivett-Carnac, A, 1983 'Gracechurch Street (ACE83)', Finds Appraisal

42–46 Houndsditch, 24–25 Bevis Marks, EC3

ARK83

A Westman
NGR: TQ 33410 81300
SMR: 041942

Redevelopment was monitored in October and November 1983 for traces of the NE sector of the city's defences: the wall there was demolished in 1923 (RCHM 1928, 85). Above natural gravel and possible natural brickearth was a brickearth bank, presumably originally behind the Roman wall. In front of the line of the wall, the bottom of a presumed ditch was recorded in section. Its primary fill contained pottery dated to the early 1st c, probably residual. More extensive features further away from the wall were identified as the bottom of the medieval ditch and silting within it.

Dunn, G, 1984 'Houndsditch/Bevis Marks (ARK83)', Finds Appraisal
RCHM, 1928 London III: Roman London, 85
Westman, A, nd, 'Excavations at 42–44 Houndsditch 23–25 Bevis Marks EC3', Archive Report

St Bride's House, 10–12 Salisbury Court, 1–4 Dorset Buildings, EC4

BID83

M Nally
NGR: TQ 31540 81090
SMR: 043288–9

A watching brief funded by Legal & General Insurance Ltd conducted at St Bride's House revealed clay and gravel which sloped S from St Bride's church and was truncated by the modern basement level. A series of brick and masonry foundations was observed in a piling trench along the S edge of the site. Several chalk and ragstone foundations of more than one phase of medieval construction were recorded; they were too fragmentary to give coherent plans. Brick and ragstone cellar lining walls were recorded 3m further W. No dating evidence was associated with these foundations. Construction details of the brick foundation in the SE corner were dated 1500–50. These brick foundations could be associated with Bridewell Palace, immediately to the SE; the remainder more probably with the Inn of the bishop of Salisbury to the W.

London Archaeol, 4, 1984, 385; Medieval Archaeol, 28, 1984, 229; Post-Medieval Archaeol, 18, 1984, 311
Dunn, G, 1984 'St Bride's Lane (BID83)', Finds Appraisal
Nally, M, 1984 'Excavations at St Bride's House (BID83)', Archive Report

BIR83

L Miller
NGR: TQ 32885 81037
SMR: 044528–31, 044477,
044606, 044608

18 Birchin Lane, 62 Lombard Street, EC3

A watching brief funded by Speyhawk and Scottish Equitable at this site immediately W of the forum showed that a number of early stake-holes were overlaid by dumped deposits of green sandy silts up to 1m thick dated to AD50–70. A succession of four brickearth slabs of building make-ups for internal floors but only one thin *opus signinum* floor was found and only one internal wall with a brickearth foundation. There was no dating evidence from this building, nor from the redeposited burnt debris which overlay the final Roman make-up. The stratigraphy was truncated at this level by modern disturbance but there were a number of Saxon, medieval and post-medieval pits.

London Archaeol, 4, 1984, 401; Britannia, 15, 1984, 308–9; Medieval Archaeol, 28, 1984, 227
Crowley, N, 1988 '18 Birchin Lane (BIR83) Roman building material', Archive Report
Davies, B, Richardson, B, & Tomber, R, 1994 *A dated corpus of early Roman pottery from the City of London,* The archaeology of Roman London 5, CBA Res Rep 98 [contribution to early Roman pottery corpus]
Dunn, G, 1984 'Birchin Lane (BIR83)', Finds Appraisal
Miller, L, 1984 'Excavations at Birchin Lane', Archive Report
Williams, T, in prep. *The development of Roman London east of the Walbrook,* The archaeology of Roman London 4, CBA Res Rep [Roman strata]

BOA83

P Allen
NGR: TQ 32530 81250
SMR: 044470–1

Bank of Argentina, 11 Ironmonger Lane, EC2

In December 1983 a small trench was excavated through stratigraphy sealed below the mosaic recorded by Adrian Oswald in 1949 (GM219 above), and subsequently preserved *in situ,* when it was lifted for relaying on a new base. Above the natural river gravels was a series of rough gravelled external surfaces dated by pottery to the later 1st and early 2nd c. Burnt material towards the bottom of the sequence, interpreted by Oswald as Boudican fire debris, was in fact dumped rubbish dated to at least the late 1st c. A thick layer of humic silt accumulated above the latest surface, possibly suggesting a period of disuse before the laying of the mosaic, identified by Oswald as belonging to a town house constructed in the 3rd c.

London Archaeol, 4, 1984, 402; Britannia, 15, 1984, 309
Allen, P, nd, 'Excavations at 11 Ironmonger Lane EC2', Archive Report
Allen, P, 1985 'Excavations at the Bank of Argentina', Archive Report
Dunn, G, 1984 'Ironmonger Lane (BOA83)', Finds Appraisal

BWB83

G Egan
NGR: TQ 32980 80640
SMR: 042995–8

Billingsgate Market lorry park (watching brief), Lower Thames Street, EC3

Agreement was reached with the developers at the end of January 1983 for access to the site for limited recording and observation, which was funded by EH, Museum of London Trust Fund and MoL Medieval Department. Dating is provisional, based on limited examination of the finds. No significant observation of Roman structures was possible. Riverine deposits of Roman date (bottomed only at the N) ran across the entire site, with no noticeable decrease in the frequency of finds from the N end (where an early 3rd-c wharf had been erected: see BIG82 above) to the S end, some 70m into the then river.

Limited recording was carried out on five probably successive post and plank timber revetments aligned E–W, located to the S of those recorded in 1982, and presumably marking successive phases of land reclamation from the river. Most, if not all five, of these structures were braced on the riverward side; the latest three at least appear to have been of 14th-c date. At the SE of the site, two opposed facing stone riverwalls aligned N–S probably represent a late medieval inlet some 6m wide. There appears to have been no land reclamation in the area since the early 15th c.

The W end of the 15th-c undercroft/vestry of the church of St Botolph Billingsgate (partly excavated in 1982) was recorded on the W boundary of the site. Survival here was to a higher level than at the E side of the structure, with possible evidence for a window in an upper storey; a lower window proved to be the same as that observed externally from the W on the adjacent New Fresh Wharf site in 1974 (NFW74; at that time thought to have been of the 17th c).

With the help of members of the Society of Thames Mudlarks and Antiquaries, Mepees Ltd and staff of GLC waste disposal services, apparently chronologically consistent assemblages of finds were recovered, both on and off the site. The Roman objects are the most varied series to have been recovered from the City for a generation, while the 14th-c group has no parallel from London archaeological excavations. From the Roman period are decorated dress fittings and pendants, leaden seals for merchants, several ear scoops/ligulae, and a flagon lid with a thumbpiece in the form of a duck. Medieval objects include series of pilgrims' and other badges (Fig 44), dress accessories, various lead tokens (some at different stages of manufacture, and others with pornographic overtones), late 14th-c cloth seals, a wooden buckler, various knives and tools, miniature vessels and other toys, mirror cases, a large group of shoes, and items of fishing equipment and weaponry. Of particular importance are a youth's sword of high quality with a decorated blade, and all four sections of a straight trumpet some 1.68m long when assembled.

Fig 44 BWB83: a pilgrim badge depicting the Madonna and Child, recovered from spoil removed en bloc from the Billingsgate Market lorry park site during construction.

London Archaeol, 5, 1985, 47–8; Britannia, 16, 1985, 296; Medieval Archaeol, 29, 1985, 173

Crowfoot, E, Pritchard, F, & Staniland, K, 1992 Textiles and clothing c 1150–c 1450, Medieval finds from excavations in London 4

Egan, G, 1985/6 'Finds recovery on riverside sites in London', Popular Archaeol, 6, No. 14, 42–50

Egan, G, 1986 'A late medieval trumpet from Billingsgate', London Archaeol, 5, 168

Egan, G, 1998 The medieval household, Medieval finds from excavations in London 6

Egan, G, & Pritchard, F, 1991 Dress accessories c 1150–c 1450, Medieval finds from excavations in London 3

Grew, F, & de Neergaard, M, 1988 Shoes and pattens, Medieval finds from excavations in London 2

Norton, C, 1993 'The export of decorated floor tiles from Normandy', in Stratford, J (ed), Medieval art, architecture and archaeology at Rouen, British Archaeol Assoc Conf Transactions for 1986, 81–97

Spencer, B, in prep. Pilgrim souvenirs and secular badges, Medieval finds from excavations in London 7

Wilthew, P, 1984a 'Inlays and fittings on medieval iron knives and shears', Archive Report (AML)

Wilthew, P, 1984b 'Metallographic examination of medieval knives and shears', Archive Report (AML)

CLO83

D Bentley
NGR: TQ 31950 81750
SMR: 043290–3

24–37 Cloth Fair, 62–67 Long Lane, EC1

During spring 1983 a watching brief was carried out with a grant from Harbour Group Developments Ltd on this site immediately N of St Bartholomew the Great church and within the precinct of the 12th-c priory. The earliest recorded features were a ditch system perhaps of the Roman period, which fell into disuse. This was overlaid by a large number of E–W aligned adult male burials of medieval date, confirming inference from documentary and archaeological sources that this was part of the site of the monastic cemetery. From the 14th c a succession of extensive but well-maintained gravelled yard surfaces covered the site, sealing the burials. A group of 15 very worn Penn floor tiles, dating to 1330–1400, were incorporated in the early part of the yard sequence. The surfaces correspond with the suggested site of the medieval Bartholomew Fair. The first structural evidence observed was a row of houses built in the late 16th c. The cellars of several of these houses were constructed of Reigate stone and brick with timbered floors; they cut through the latest gravelled surfaces, and fronted onto a metalled road (the origin of Cloth Fair) which was laid out across the S part of the site adjacent to the ex-priory church. This development was part of a larger scheme, known from documentary sources, involving all the land to the N and E of the church. It remained partially intact well into the 20th c.

London Archaeol, 4, 1984, 385; *Britannia,* 15, 1984, 309; *Medieval Archaeol,* 28, 1984, 228; *Post-Medieval Archaeol,* 18, 1984, 311
Dunn, G, 1983 'Cloth Fair (CLO83)', Finds Appraisal

CUL83

C Fenn, M Reid and T Williams
NGR: TQ 33115 80960
SMR: 043311–16

154–156 Fenchurch Street, 15–16 Cullum Street, EC3

A watching brief was conducted with funds from the Equitable Life Assurance Society. The earliest activity observed was a number of large gravel quarries (Period I) infilled prior to the first phase of structural activity; this consisted of a number of spatially isolated structures destroyed in a first fire (Boudican) (II). The site was subsequently levelled and a second, more extensive phase of structural construction took place: large masonry buildings with floors of *opus signinum* and plaster work (III). These were destroyed in a second widespread fire which was recorded in several areas immediately below modern basements. Due to this degree of disturbance only intrusive features survived postdating this fire. A number of medieval foundations were recorded, mostly in underpinning holes, conforming to the present property boundaries. Several wells, of a broad date-range, were recorded (IV).

London Archaeol, 4, 1984, 386; *Britannia,* 15, 1984, 308; *Medieval Archaeol,* 28, 1984, 228
Reid, M, 1983 'Excavations at 154–156 Fenchurch Street, 15–16 Cullum Street (CUL83)', Archive Report
Riddler, I, 1989 '154–156 Fenchurch Street, 15–16 Cullum Street', Finds Appraisal
Williams, T, in prep. *The development of Roman London east of the Walbrook,* The archaeology of Roman London 4, CBA Res Rep
   [Roman strata]

EST83

S Rivière
NGR: TQ 33055 80840
SMR: 043004–11

23–29 Eastcheap, 14–15 Philpot Lane, EC3

Excavation took place from November 1983 to January 1984 in the basement of a standing building by arrangement with Land Securities Ltd. The site covered an L-shaped area roughly 8m x 8m and to a depth of just under 2m.

Natural gravels were sealed by 0.2–0.3m of redeposited natural brickearth. There were four phases of Roman activity, none later than the mid-2nd c. The earliest consisted of several small rubbish pits (one of which contained four high-quality intaglios of approximately Neronian date) and trample surfaces, which were sealed by the first signs of a structure. This consisted of an E–W brickearth sill, and a N–S slot with several associated brickearth, gravel and plank floors. This was sealed by 0.2m of partially *in situ* fire debris, probably Boudican, which scorched and burnt the plank floors.

The fire debris was then levelled out to prepare for a 6m long N–S beam slot with four regularly spaced groups of four post-holes cutting into it. This piled foundation had one associated floor surface but no indication of the nature of the superstructure. The last structure was also a N–S slot with associated post-holes but no associated surfaces. Cutting into the Roman stratigraphy across the whole site was a sequence of medieval storage and rubbish pits, none earlier than the 12th c, and a large 4.5m x 2.5m 15th-c chalk-lined cesspit, from which came a complete 15th-c Italian Archaic Majolica jug. A 19th-c cesspit and a brick-arched sewer and modern drains completed the sequence.

London Archaeol, 8, 1985, 48; *Britannia*, 16, 1985, 296–7; *Medieval Archaeol*, 29, 1985, 173–4

Crowley, N, 1988 '27–29 Eastcheap (EST83) Roman building material Level III report', Archive Report

Davies, B, 1993 'Inter-site studies', in Milne, G, & Wardle, A, 'Early Roman development at Leadenhall Court, London and related research', *Trans London Middlesex Archaeol Soc*, 44, 135–50

Henig, M, 1984 'A cache of Roman intaglios from Eastcheap, City of London', *Trans London Middlesex Archaeol Soc*, 35, 11–15

Rivière, S, 1984 'Excavations at 27–29 Eastcheap', Archive Report

Simic, A, 1984 'Eastcheap (FST83)', Finds Appraisal

Tyers, P, 1984 'EST83 Roman pottery', Archive Report

Vaughan, D, nd, 'Charred plant remains (Roman)', Archive Report

Vince, A, 1984 'The Saxon medieval and post-medieval pottery from Eastcheap 1983', Archive Report

Williams, T, in prep. *The development of Roman London east of the Walbrook*, The archaeology of Roman London 4, CBA Res Rep [Roman strata]

5–12 Fenchurch Street, 1 Philpot Lane, EC3

FEN83

F Hammer
NGR: TQ 33030 80920
SMR: 043255–61

Excavation on the S side of Fenchurch Street, between Gracechurch Street and Philpot Lane (by arrangement with Land Securities (Management) Ltd) recorded 2m of Roman stratigraphy in an area of about 225sq m in plan; in addition a number of sections along and beneath the two roads forming the sides of the site showed the whole sequence of layers from natural to the modern road surface. The area is situated immediately S of the main E–W road through the Roman city, opposite the SE corner of the forum in the centre of the city.

Eleven periods of Roman occupation could be identified, comprising 30 buildings or structures. The first seven periods from c AD50 to the early/mid-2nd c were followed by slower development in four periods from the early/mid-2nd c to c 350.

The earliest timber and brickearth buildings (Periods I–III) comprised two or perhaps three properties, and had trading or manufacturing functions. The associated ceramics were of a remarkably high quality, including many cups and beakers in Lyon ware and at least two mould-made South-Gaulish colour-coated cups of a type which is otherwise almost entirely absent from the city. The coarser wares include products of the Neronian industry identified among the kiln waste recovered from Sugar Loaf Court in 1982.

Little Boudican fire debris was found, as the area was carefully cleared for a major building in Flavian times, including deep gravel, mortar and stone foundations and plastered mudbrick walls (Period IV). Nearly 20m long and at least 11m wide, it consisted of a big hall on pile foundations, with buttresses strengthening the N wall. Built on to it to the N lay a number of smaller rooms with many successive floors and partition walls of several phases (Periods IV–VII), with little evidence of inhabitation but with traces of slag and perhaps glassmaking in one case. They seem to have been used as shops or workshops.

On the E side a gravelled alleyway led from the main road to a side entrance with stairs. This was soon overbuilt towards the E: a room was found with a substantial *opus signinum* floor, divided by a plastered and polychrome-painted brickearth wall from a kitchen. This included a hearth and shelf, where the pots were still in position when the building burnt down, probably together with the adjoining building to the W, producing a thick layer of debris.

Cutting into it, the succeeding building (Period IX) only survived as N–S partition foundations of chipped ragstone and a very substantial ragstone-mortar foundation, which was seen in section along the eastern part of the S frontage of Fenchurch Street and returned under Philpot Lane. No traces of a road were seen behind the wall under Philpot Lane at the Roman level. Evidence of the late 3rd c came from two wells, constructed within one large pit in the NW; fire put them out of use when the charred timber construction collapsed into the shaft. One of these wells was thereafter used as a dump; of the small mammals which had fallen into it, bones of two black rats, *rattus rattus*, are the oldest found in Britain so far.

A pit cut into the backfill of this well contained three unbroken pots, upside down, all of which contained charcoal and one an eroded coin. No building was found in association with this foundation deposit or offering, as the upper layers were truncated.

Two further building periods (X–XI) followed at least in the NE of the site, above which was dark earth (Period XII), recorded in several parts of the site. In Period XIII above the dark earth seven successive road surfaces were recorded beneath modern Fenchurch Street and Philpot Lane. Pits dating from *c* 850 to 1700, several chalk foundations and a chalk-lined well, brick-lined wells and pits were also recorded.

London Archaeol, 4, 1984, 384; *Britannia,* 15, 1984, 308

Betts, I, 1984 'Summary of painted wall plaster designs and decoration', Archive Report

Davies, B, 1993 'Inter-site studies', in Milne, G, & Wardle, A, 'Early Roman development at Leadenhall Court, London and related research', *Trans London Middlesex Archaeol Soc,* 44, 135–50

Davies, B, Richardson, B, & Tomber, R, 1994 *A dated corpus of early Roman pottery from the City of London,* The archaeology of Roman London 5, CBA Res Rep 98 [contribution to early Roman pottery corpus]

Grew, F, & Groves, J, 1985 'Roman glass from pre-Flavian contexts (2802–3524) at 5–12 Fenchurch Street (FEN83)', Archive Report

Groves, J, 1984a 'Early Roman finds from 5–12 Fenchurch Street', Archive Report

Groves, J, 1984b 'Fenchurch Street (FEN83)', Finds Appraisal

Hammer, F, nd, 'Excavations at 5–12 Fenchurch Street EC3', Archive Report

Hammer, F, 1985 'Early Roman buildings in Fenchurch Street', *Popular Archaeol,* 6, No. 12, 7–13

Hammer, F, 1987 'A Roman basilican hall and associated buildings at Fenchurch Street', *Archaeol Today,* 8, 6–12

West, B, Steedman, K, & Armitage, P, 1984 'New evidence of Black Rat in Roman London', *London Archaeol,* 4, 375–83

Williams, T, in prep. *The development of Roman London east of the Walbrook,* The archaeology of Roman London 4, CBA Res Rep [Roman strata]

Wilthew, P, 1984 'Examination of technological material from Fenchurch Street', Archive Report

HOP83

G Milne, C Milne and N Bateman

NGR: TQ 33020 81170

SMR: 043262–70

3–5 Bishopsgate, EC2

Archaeological excavations were conducted in six basement rooms of a standing building during an eight-week period in advance of redevelopment. The work was generously funded by London & Edinburgh Securities.

The natural brickearth surface had been truncated and sealed by a redeposited brickearth slab. There was evidence to suggest that structural activity in the S of the site (Building 1) was burnt in the mid-/late 1st c, and that brickearth quarries were subsequently dug to the N of two superimposed timber buildings (Buildings 2 and 3). Structural divisions, a doorway, *opus signinum* floors and a hearth were associated with the final phase of this substantial structure. To the N was a timber Building 6. Both this and the masonry Building 5 were physically sealed by dark grey silts containing 3rd- and 4th-c pottery. These silts were cut by intrusive Late Saxon features including a hearth, a sunken-featured building, from which came three 11th- or 12th-c iron knives, and a backfilled well into which a sequence of 11 superimposed brickearth surfaces of a surface-laid building had slumped. Crucible fragments were associated with these floors. Provisional pottery analysis suggests that the site was certainly occupied by the early 11th c although the surface-laid building may not predate the Norman conquest.

London Archaeol, 4, 1984, 384; *Britannia,* 15, 1984, 309; *Medieval Archaeol,* 28, 1984, 227

Crowley, N, 1987 '3–5 Bishopsgate (HOP83) Roman building material Level III report', Archive Report

Davies, B, 1993 'Inter-site studies', in Milne, G, & Wardle, A, 'Early Roman development at Leadenhall Court, London and related research', *Trans London Middlesex Archaeol Soc,* 44, 135–50

Dunn, G, 1984 'Bishopsgate (HOP83)', Finds Appraisal

Milne, C, Milne, G, & Bateman, N, 1984a 'Bank deposits with interest', *London Archaeol,* 4, 395–400

Milne, C, Milne, G, & Bateman, N, 1984b 'Excavations at 3–5 Bishopsgate', Archive Report

Vince, A, 1983 'Saxon and medieval pottery (HOP83)', Archive Report

Williams, T, in prep. *The development of Roman London east of the Walbrook,* The archaeology of Roman London 4, CBA Res Rep
[Roman strata]

27–30 Lime Street, EC3

IME83

T Williams
NGR: TQ 33098 80977
SMR: 043130–6

A three-month excavation, funded by Trollope and Colls (City) Ltd, was conducted between June and August 1984. After initial levelling with a redeposited brickearth slab, a sequence of timber and brickearth buildings was recorded, dating from the mid-1st to mid-2nd c. There was evidence for two extensive fires within this sequence, probably the Boudican and Hadrianic. The structures were of strip-building form, aligned E–W and probably fronting onto a street to the W of the site. They exhibited a variety of decorative and internal forms, including rooms at the 'back' (E) of some quality.

The sequence was truncated at this level by the modern basement and only intrusive features survived. A late Roman pile foundation was recorded and is thought to form part of the complex excavated to the S on the 25–26 Lime Street site (LIM83). An E–W element of this was replaced with a deeper masonry foundation, possibly retaining elements of the pile foundation building. These walls were robbed in the early medieval period. Foundations of a c 14th-c undercroft were uncovered at the N end of the site, aligned according to the present curved street frontage rather than the straight N–S alignment of the Roman street. Two medieval wells and one post-medieval cesspit were also recorded.

London Archaeol, 5, 1985, 49; *Britannia,* 16, 1985, 297; *Medieval Archaeol,* 29, 1985, 174

Betts, I, & Crowley, N, 1988 '27–30 Lime Street (IME83) Roman building material Level III report', Archive Report

Davies, B, 1993 'Inter-site studies', in Milne, G, & Wardle, A, 'Early Roman development at Leadenhall Court, London and related research', *Trans London Middlesex Archaeol Soc,* 44, 135–50

Riddler, I, 1989 'Finds appraisal for 27–30 Lime Street (IME83)', Finds Appraisal

Williams, T, 1985/6 'Redevelopment in the City — What is new?', *Popular Archaeol,* 6, No. 14, 31–6

Williams, T, in prep. *The development of Roman London east of the Walbrook,* The archaeology of Roman London 4, CBA Res Rep
[Roman strata]

Williams, T, & Cocroft, W, 1986 'Excavations at 27–30 Lime Street (IME83)', Archive Report

15–35 Copthall Avenue, 45–50 London Wall, 2–3 Cross Keys Court, EC2

KEY83

C Maloney
NGR: TQ 32770 81500
SMR: 043271–6

A watching brief covered an area 60m x 60m, fronting onto London Wall and Copthall Avenue. The Roman road, recorded during the excavation within a standing building at Copthall Avenue in 1981–2 (OPT81), was traced for a distance of 50m, NNE–SSW; additional evidence of the associated timber-framed building indicated that it was at least 12m x 3.8m. Several series of posts, gravelled surfaces and various wooden structures, also Roman in date, were recorded.

In the NE corner of the site, natural gravels of a maximum depth of 3m gradually thinned towards the S, where, instead, waterlaid deposits of the Walbrook stream directly overlay the London Clay. During the Roman period the Walbrook was effectively regulated; thereafter the formation of peat indicated that the site reverted to a generally wet condition.

London Archaeol, 4, 1984, 385

Dunn, G, 1984 'Cross Key Court (KEY83)', Finds Appraisal

Maloney, C, 1987 'Excavations at 15–35 Copthall Avenue 45–49 London Wall the Coleman Street Ward School & Cross Key Court', Archive Report

Maloney, C, 1990 *The upper Walbrook Valley in the Roman period,* The archaeology of Roman London 1, CBA Res Rep 69 [Roman strata]

LIM83

T Williams
NGR: TQ 33095 80965
SMR: 044532–8, 044585

25–26 Lime Street, EC3

Excavation of an area 15m x 3m between January and April 1983 was followed by a watching brief on the whole site in May 1983, both exercises funded by the Worshipful Company of Clothworkers.

The first period of deposits comprised initial levelling with redeposited brickearth prior to the cutting of a N–S ?boundary ditch and a number of quarry pits (Period I). These were infilled as preparation for structural activity; the principal building being constructed of timber sills with a brickearth and daub superstructure, running E–W with a backyard area to the E. These structures were destroyed by fire, probably Boudican (II). Subsequently the area was levelled and left open (III); pottery from the Neronian levels is of interest as there was a higher proportion of amphorae than is usually found on sites away from the waterfront. A large fragment of a Sussex grog-tempered ware jar from a pit in this period may be the only well-dated stratified fragment found so far in London. Further extensive dumping took place for a second E–W building which bore no relation to the earlier property divisions. This building was also destroyed by fire, probably Hadrianic (IV). A substantial group of pottery was recovered from a gully to the E of this building, and a dump of this period produced the first example from a DUA site of stone inlay from Skyros in the Aegean.

Cutting through these deposits was a masonry cellar, well constructed and surviving to a height of 2.7m, with its floor at least 1.6m below contemporary ground level. A probable staircase entered the room from the S and the range continued in that direction. Twenty *tegulae* were found mortared in two rows on the interior face of the E wall, the first evidence in London of tiles being used as a wall facing. To the E of and respecting the structure was a N–S building which ended in a S-facing apse. It had substantial piled foundations which supported a course foundation of rammed chalk and ragstone, later extensively robbed (Period V). No associated horizontal levels survived due to the level of modern truncation.

The cellared area was reused during the 11th or 12th c, as attested by Late Saxon shelly ware, and was probably extended to the W in timber (to be replaced in the 14th or 15th c by masonry). This use continued, with numerous modifications, until it was destroyed and infilled in the Great Fire of 1666. Subsequently it provided the basis for property boundaries which persisted to the present (Period VI). A Spanish or N African lead-glazed water-jar in a good mid-17th-c assemblage is unique in the Museum's collection.

Various Late Saxon and medieval pits were recorded in the E of the site but due to modern truncation no horizontal activity survived from periods postdating the apsidal-ended building.

Britannia, 15, 1984, 309; *Medieval Archaeol,* 28, 1984, 228; *Post-Medieval Archaeol,* 18, 1984, 311

Betts, I, 1988 '25–26 Lime Street (LIM83) building material Level III report', Archive Report

Davies, B, 1993 'Inter-site studies', in Milne, G, & Wardle, A, 'Early Roman development at Leadenhall Court, London and related research', *Trans London Middlesex Archaeol Soc,* 44, 135–50

Nenk, B, 1983 'Lime Street (LIM83)', Finds Appraisal

Tyers, P, 1983 'The Roman pottery from Neronian levels at Lime Street', Archive Report

Vince, A, 1983 'LIM83 — Saxon and later pottery', Archive Report

Williams, T, nd, 'Excavations at 25–26 Lime Street EC3', Archive Report

Williams, T, 1984 'Excavations at 25–26 Lime Street', *London Archaeol,* 4, 426–30

Williams, T, in prep. *The development of Roman London east of the Walbrook,* The archaeology of Roman London 4, CBA Res Rep [Roman strata]

37 Lombard Street, EC3

OMB83

NGR: TQ 32915 80950
SMR: 044596

A site code was issued but no useful structural or topographical information gained.

2–4 Skinner's Lane, 36–39 Queen Street, 19–20 Garlick Hill, EC4

SKI83

P Rowsome
NGR: TQ 32400 80880
SMR: 043225–33

An excavation funded by Harbour Developments Ltd was conducted from December 1983 to March 1984 in two separate areas of excavation: one within the basement of 3 Skinner's Lane and the other in the courtyard to the N. Seven periods of activity were recorded overlying natural deposits of sand, gravel and brickearth which survived though truncated. At the N of the site natural was cut by pits filled with redeposited natural, and sealed by a sequence of dumped deposits. These were cut by a large ragstone foundation of late Roman date. The foundation was partially robbed and the robbing trench backfilled with a large quantity of roof tile, the backfill sealed by medieval pits and dumping. A post-Great Fire sequence sealed the medieval deposits and consisted of dumping and levelling in the N, and of a building sequence in the S. Here truncated natural was overlaid by a brick building with vaulted cellars which fronted onto Skinner's Lane. A contemporary brick-built drainage system was situated at the back of the structures. Several phases of 18th- and 19th-c rebuilding followed, all conforming to the same property boundaries; one incorporated a large group of 17th-/18th-c sugar-refining pottery vessels as backfill.

Observation of the large area of 36–39 Queen Street to the E during building works found that all manmade deposits had been very largely removed.

London Archaeol, 5, 1985, 50; *Britannia,* 16, 1985, 297; *Post-Medieval Archaeol,* 19, 1985, 167
Betts, I, 1987 'Skinner's Lane/Queen Street building materials', Archive Report
Dunn, G, 1984 'Skinner's Lane (SKI83)', Finds Appraisal
Rowsome, P, 1984 'Excavations at 3 Skinners Lane 36–39 Queen Street EC4', Archive Report

8 Telegraph Street, EC2

TEL83

P Chitwood
NGR: TQ 32700 81350
SMR: 043294–300

An excavation funded by Phoenix Assurance took place in July–August 1983 in a 2.3m x 2.5m area in the basement of a 19th-c listed building on the S side of what was formerly Great Bell Alley. Initial Roman development consisted of a series of dumps, contained to the N by a timber pile and plank revetment, presumably an attempt to raise the ground level. Further raising of ground surface followed, the first with a late 1st-/early 2nd-c stone-founded building, open to the E towards the Walbrook and then with a more substantial 2nd-c building with a sequence of interior floor surfaces. The raising dumps included fragments of leather garments and shoes. This building was probably demolished in the late 2nd or early 3rd c and its walls robbed (Period I). The robber trenches were cut by a ditch which may have been a drainage channel (Period II). A further series of dumps was followed by an 11th-/12th-c timber building, possibly wattle-walled, with several phases of gravel and clay occupation layers. Evidence was found for a second structure in approximately the same position as the first, with several associated hearths above dumps levelling the entire area (Period III). The uppermost activity was truncated by the modern basement (Period IV).

London Archaeol, 4, 1984, 385; *Medieval Archaeol,* 28, 1984, 229
Chitwood, P, 1983 'Excavations at 8 Telegraph Street', Archive Report
Davies, B, 1987 'The Roman pottery from Telegraph Street (TEL83)', Archive Report
Dunn, G, 1983 'Telegraph Street (TEL83)', Finds Appraisal
Gale, R, 1986 'The identification of wood from sites excavated by the DUA', AML Report 60/87
Maloney, C, 1990 *The upper Walbrook Valley in the Roman period,* The archaeology of Roman London 1, CBA Res Rep 69 [Roman strata]
Vince, A, 1983 'The medieval pottery from Telegraph Street 1983 (TEL83)', Archive Report

WAY83

P Rowsome
NGR: TQ 31765 81114
SMR: 040428

7–9 Pilgrim Street, 10–13 Ludgate Broadway, EC4

During January–February 1983 a small excavation was carried out to provide evidence of the city ditch S of Ludgate and to study the effect, if any, of the establishment of the Blackfriars. Six periods of activity were recorded, overlying natural and gravel. Natural was cut by a sequence of ditches, the earliest being badly truncated but surviving in the E to a depth of 3.6m. This, perhaps the late Roman defensive ditch, was cut by a wide, deep and steep-sided medieval ditch over 14m wide. Both major ditches ran N–S. The medieval ditch appeared to have been neglected from the mid-13th c and after initial silting was partially backfilled by large gravelly dumps, yielding a small quantity of 12th-/13th-c pottery, iron and copper objects, a small number of hone-stones, some beadmaking waste, an iron arrowhead and a bone comb.

There followed a horizon of Roman mortar and building debris, probably a by-product of the documented dismantling of the nearby city wall c 1278 to make way for the Blackfriars friary. Further dumps completed the backfilling of the medieval ditch by the late 13th c, a date corresponding to the establishment of the precinct.

The medieval ditch backfill was overlaid by a shallow ditch running N–S and E–W, which may have served as an inside perimeter or marking-out ditch for either the precinct or specifically its cemetery, to which a single burial recorded nearby c 1900 may have belonged. The sequence was completed by intercutting post-medieval pits and phases of brick building probably of post-Fire date; the latter were sealed by Victorian foundations.

London Archaeol, 5, 1984, 401; *Britannia*, 15, 1984, 309; *Medieval Archaeol*, 28, 1984, 229

Egan, G, & Pritchard, F, 1991 *Dress accessories c 1150–c 1450*, Medieval finds from excavations in London 3

Rowsome, P, 1984 (rev 1991) 'Excavations at 7–9 Ludgate Broadway (WAY83)', Archive Report

Vince, A, 1983 'Medieval pottery from Ludgate Broadway 1983 (WAY83)', Archive Report

Webber, M, 1983 'Ludgate Broadway (WAY83)', Finds Appraisal

WIT83

M Nally
NGR: TQ 32700 80910
SMR: 043277–87

18–23 St Swithin's Lane, 113–117 Cannon Street, 13 Sherbourne Lane, EC4

Excavations funded by Haslemere Estates Ltd were conducted in the basements of standing buildings at 18 and 20 St Swithin's Lane. A trench 1m x 2m in no. 20 revealed only modern backfill on top of natural brickearth. A standing medieval vaulted structure parallel to the street, immediately behind the pavement, was recorded.

In no. 18, two trenches, 3.6m x 6.8m and 5.7m x 7.9m, were excavated in plan. Two other smaller trenches were recorded in section. These disclosed a sequence of 1st- and 2nd-c Roman occupation, including a fence-line, wood-lined drain and masonry foundation in the W trench. Foundation trenches had been cut into the natural sand and gravel in the E trench, but there was no evidence of associated occupation surfaces. A large rectangular cut had also been made into natural, presumably for quarrying purposes. Later Roman activity included a sequence of make-up and floors associated with a collapsed wall. Medieval walls were recorded running parallel to the street frontage in no. 18, on the same alignment as the standing walls in no. 20. These walls were also observed continuing through no. 19 and presumably all represent a single structure over 20m long. The construction trench of the W wall produced pottery of 1150–1200, but the fabric of the vaulted structure contained occasional fragments of roof tile and is therefore likely to be of 13th-c or later date. A robbed medieval wall was recorded 7m to the E of this structure on the same alignment. A barrel-well and pits of the post-medieval period were also recorded.

London Archaeol, 4, 1984, 384–5; *Britannia*, 15, 1984, 309; 16, 1985, 297; *Medieval Archaeol*, 28, 1984, 229

Davies, B, 1984 'The Roman pottery from WIT83', Archive Report

Davies, B, 1993 'Inter-site studies', in Milne, G, & Wardle, A, 'Early Roman development at Leadenhall Court, London and related research', *Trans London Middlesex Archaeol Soc*, 44, 135–50

Dunn, G, 1984 'St Swithins Lane (WIT83)', Finds Appraisal

Harrison, J, 1988 '18–23 St Swithins Lane / 113–114 Cannon Street (WIT83) Roman building material', Archive Report

Vince, A, 1984 'Saxon and medieval pottery from St Swithins Lane 1983 (WIT83)', Archive Report

Williams, T, in prep. *The development of Roman London east of the Walbrook*, The archaeology of Roman London 4, CBA Res Rep [Roman strata]

7–12 Aldersgate Street, EC1

ALG84

G Egan
NGR: TQ 32180 81500
SMR: 040468

Four months' excavation on this extramural site was funded by Rush & Tompkins Developments plc. The earliest Roman features recorded were a series of large flat-bottomed ditches, apparently aligned N–S, parallel to the city boundary (as defined by the later wall) to the E. On the W side of the site, on a slightly differing alignment, was a heavily cambered metalled road or track just over 2m wide. The latest of three possible used surfaces bore grooves, interpreted as wheel ruts, about 1.2m apart. The orientation of this early Roman way was the same as that of the wider and later road (located immediately to the W of the site) leading to the N from Roman Aldersgate. Structural evidence from the Roman period was limited to a much truncated two-phase stone building at the NW of the site. On the E was part of a large ditch, presumably that alongside the city wall. Substantial silt and clay deposits were dumped, or accumulated, over most of the site, sealing the ditches and making up some 2m of ground from the 2nd c.

A series of mid-11th-c pits were the earliest traced medieval features. These, with later medieval pits and foundations, presumably represent occupation on the site (three properties are attested from the 14th c by documentary evidence). One of the earliest pits produced a leaden disc ineptly multiple-struck with a die apparently for the obverse of pennies of Edward the Confessor, issued in 1052–3. The medieval (?13th-c) city ditch was located at the E side of the site. Post-medieval brick cellars, foundations and drains and two chalk-lined wells bore little obvious correlation with a detailed plan from 1610 of the buildings on the site. The lower part of a substantial 18th-c oven, apparently operated at basement level, was uncovered. The fill of a late cellar produced a large assemblage of mid-19th-c glass and ceramic vessels, including pot lids with multicoloured transfer-printed rural and other scenes.

A watching brief on the remainder of the site provided further information about this extramural area. As in the previous year, all work was funded by Rush & Tompkins plc. The largest ditch along the E side of the site was found to be of Saxo-Norman date. The fill of this presumably defensive feature produced a pattern-welded knife and Saxo-Norman pottery. This is apparently the first time a substantial ditch of this date has been recorded immediately outside the city wall. Two 14th-c jugs, one of which was complete, were recovered from the fills of a medieval well. From the fills of a second chalk-lined well, which had been deepened with an addition to the shaft in brick in the post-medieval period, came an assemblage of finds datable to the mid-17th c. The group includes fragments of an Italian marbled-ware vessel and a plain pewter bowl of unusual form. This latter well is thought to be the one depicted on a detailed plan of 1610 by the surveyor Ralph Treswell, where it is shown in a courtyard, and was presumably shared by two households. If correctly interpreted, the plan places the well perhaps 0.50m away from its true position.

London Archaeol, 5, 1985, 47; *Britannia,* 16, 1985, 296; *Medieval Archaeol,* 29, 1985, 173; 30, 1986, 137; *Post-Medieval Archaeol,* 19, 1985, 165
Dunn, G, 1986 'Aldersgate ALG84', Finds Appraisal
Egan, G, 1985 'Excavations at 7–12 Aldersgate (ALG84)', Archive Report
Schofield, J (ed), 1987 *The London surveys of Ralph Treswell,* London Topographical Soc Publication 135, 34–5
Schofield, J, 1995 *Medieval London houses,* 153–4

4–6 Copthall Avenue, EC2

CHL84

C Maloney
NGR: TQ 32790 81400
SMR: 042999–3003

A watching brief, funded by London and Paris Properties, took place on this upper Walbrook site. The first major Roman development was represented by a dump of distinctive blue clay which has been noted elsewhere in the filling and levelling up of channels of the Walbrook stream. On the W side of the site a NNE–SSW road, bordered by a timber-lined drain, lay above further dumping. It seems to have fallen into disuse before the end of the Roman period. To the E of and level with the road, an E–W aligned drainage channel was banked and revetted with wattlework and raised the ground surface. Above, timber posts and piles were associated with internal and external surfaces. The ground surface was raised again and cut by a final drainage channel, truncated by the modern basement.

London Archaeol, 5, 1985, 48; *Britannia,* 16, 1985, 296
Davies, B, 1986 'The Roman pottery from 4–6 Copthall Avenue — watching brief CHL84', Archive Report
Dunn, G, 1985 'Copthall Avenue (CHL84)', Finds Appraisal
Maloney, C, 1984 'Excavations at 4–6 Copthall Avenue', Archive Report
Maloney, C, 1990 *The upper Walbrook Valley in the Roman period,* The archaeology of Roman London 1, CBA Res Rep 69 [Roman strata]

DEL84

B Pye
NGR: TQ 31600 81120
SMR: 043179–89

6–7 New Bridge Street, 16–17 and 21 Bride Lane, EC4

In February 1984 a watching brief funded by Taylor Woodrow Developments Ltd was conducted on this site on the W side of the River Fleet. Natural deposits were recorded sloping down the valley side from W to E at about 1 in 11. These deposits changed from gravels in the W through brickearth in the middle to London Clay in the E.

The W end of the site included a brick-built basement and cesspit truncating dumped deposits. These features were covered and filled by fire debris presumably, on the pottery evidence, from the Great Fire of 1666. Towards the E end of the site, natural brickearth was overlaid by medieval dumped material, possibly to raise the ground surface above the Fleet. These deposits had been truncated by a probably post-medieval brick and chalk block basement, with a decayed timber floor, and by two wells, one brick lined, the other lined with square chalk blocks. At the E end of the site were substantial chalk foundations with associated timber posts which overlay and were themselves overlaid by dumped materials. Timber platform structures on top of natural were overlaid by dumped material dated 1100–50. The purpose of these structures is uncertain, but they could be terracing of the Fleet Valley, probably of medieval date.

London Archaeol, 5, 1985, 49; *Medieval Archaeol,* 29, 1985, 174–5; *Post-Medieval Archaeol,* 19, 1985, 166
Dunn, G, 1984 'New Bridge Street/Bride Lane (DEL84)', Finds Appraisal
Pye, B, 1984 'Excavations at New Bridge Street/Bride Lane', Archive Report

ECP84

A Westman
NGR: TQ 33070 80845
SMR: 044615–21

23–39 Eastcheap, 14–15 Philpot Lane, EC3

Redevelopment was monitored in September–December 1984 by arrangement with Wates Construction Ltd and Taylor Woodrow Construction Ltd. In the S half of the site, natural gravel and brickearth were overlaid by at least two phases of gravel surfaces, floors and small post-holes. Dumping and levelling then preceded extensive buildings with wooden floors and brickearth sills, later burnt *in situ.* This phase of building probably corresponded to 1st-c structures excavated at 27–29 Eastcheap (EST83). The destruction was sealed by dumped burnt building debris, into which pits and other intrusive features were cut, later horizontally truncated. Other features elsewhere included one chalk-lined and one brick-lined well.

Cowgill, J, 1987 '23–39 Eastcheap/14–16 Philpot Lane ECP84', Finds Appraisal
Westman, A, 1986 'Watching brief at 23–39 Eastcheap 14–16 Philpot Lane', Archive Report
Williams, T, in prep. *The development of Roman London east of the Walbrook,* The archaeology of Roman London 4, CBA Res Rep [Roman strata]

ETH84

R Lea
NGR: TQ 33190 81350
SMR: 043301

St Ethelburga Bishopsgate church, Bishopsgate, EC2

Parts of the external base of the E wall and E window of the medieval church were revealed during repair work to the roof of the vestry. The face of the wall was of uncoursed rag and sandstone. The sandstone S jamb and sill of the E window were only partially revealed. The hollow chamfer on the jamb suggested a similar type of moulding to the one recorded in the N wall in 1982 (see BIS82 above). The window was blocked by post-Fire (probably 18th-c) brickwork. Quoinwork in the E face of the wall of the SE corner of the medieval church was also observed.

London Archaeol, 5, 1985, 50; *Medieval Archaeol,* 29, 1985, 175
Lea, R, 1985/6 'The archaeology of standing structures in the City of London', *Popular Archaeol,* 6, No. 14, 22–30
Lea, R, 1986 'Archaeological observations at St Ethelburga Bishopsgate (ETH84)', Archive Report

Fenchurch Street Station, EC3

FSS84

S P O'Connor Thompson
NGR: TQ 33430 80930
SMR: 043169

Between September 1984 and March 1985 a watching brief (funded by Norwich Union) was undertaken at this site. The redevelopment involved the sinking of 25 massive encaissoned concrete piles — up to 3m in diameter and over 30m deep — the shafts of which had to be hand dug. In the first six caissons it was possible to carry out some recording of the sections, but subsequently the introduction of different shoring techniques made that impossible. Excavations of the caissons were carried out 24 hours a day. Archaeologically it could be shown that the present alignment of streets and properties, as exemplified by French Ordinary Court which crosses the site, was in existence by at least the 15th c. Further, that activity in the area in all periods was fairly minimal up until the 18th c, and that perhaps by way of explanation for this it would seem that at least the southern fringes of the site were actually over the recently identified ancient valley in this part of the City. Certainly the quality of water encountered in four adjacent caissons indicates that there is still a stream flowing, albeit underground.

London Archaeol, 5, 1985, 158; Medieval Archaeol, 30, 1986, 137
Cowgill, J, 1986 'Fenchurch Street (FSS84)', Finds Appraisal
O'Connor-Thompson, S, 1984 'Excavations at Fenchurch Street Station (FSS84)', Archive Report
Williams, T, in prep. *The development of Roman London east of the Walbrook*, The archaeology of Roman London 4, CBA Res Rep
  [Roman strata]

1–2 Gracechurch Street, EC3

GCH84

T Brigham
NGR: TQ 33017 81093
SMR: 043093–5

Excavation by arrangement with Land Securities Ltd took place here in July 1984. A trench 17.5m x 1m wide was excavated by machine and hand, the chief evidence coming from sections.

The first phase of activity recorded above natural brickearth consisted of silty surfaces and brickearth slab layers, with gravel surfaces above, possibly part of an early Roman open area found on surrounding sites. In the E of the present site this was followed by the construction of two parallel N–S walls of ragstone and cobbles about 4.5m apart, probably part of the E wing of the Flavian forum. About 4m to the W lay a third N–S foundation of ragstone 1.8m wide; the W wall of the E wing was then demolished and 0.7m of sandy gravels laid on top of it. This suggests that the third foundation, used with the E of the two walls, constituted a doubling of the E forum range into the courtyard. The two walls of this second phase were subsequently demolished to foundation level, and covered with gravel, mortar and brickearth surfaces probably from the courtyard of the Hadrianic forum.

London Archaeol, 5, 1985, 48
Dunn, G, 1985 'Gracechurch Street (GCH84)', Finds Appraisal

77–79 Gracechurch Street, EC3

GRA84

B Pye
NGR: TQ 33015 81005
SMR: 043038–42

A watching brief, funded by the Trustees of the London Parochial Charities, was carried out in September–October 1984, on a small site adjacent to the church of St Peter Cornhill. Some 3.5m of Roman stratigraphy were recorded in section beneath 4m of 18th- and 19th-c make-ups. All the natural brickearth (normally 2m thick) had been removed during the 1st c AD, with no sign of natural gravels at the lowest point of excavation. This indicates either local quarrying or, more likely, trenching for a sub-basement of similar depth to one recorded by P Marsden at nos 3–6, within the first basilica (see GM67 above).

The lowest recorded deposits were gravelly green silts dated AD55–80 and sealed by a series of brickearth make-ups and slabs, with occasional thin mortar floors. These were divided centrally by a 0.3m gravel feature, possibly a path or corridor. This sequence was then overlaid by 1m thick brickearth slabs over the whole area, culminating in a thin fire horizon. This destroyed the existing building, which was broadly contemporary with the nearby first forum. After clearance of fire debris, a 0.7m concrete floor, part of the larger second forum-basilica, covered the site. This in turn was sealed by 0.5m of dark earth containing voussoir tiles from the collapsed basilica roof. All later deposits were destroyed by post-medieval activity.

London Archaeol, 5, 1985, 48; *Britannia,* 16, 1985, 297
Dunn, G, 1985 'Gracechurch Street (GRA84)', Finds Appraisal
Marsden, P, 1987 *The Roman forum site in London: discoveries before 1985,* 117
Pye, B, nd, 'Excavations at 77–78 Gracechurch Street (GRA84)', Archive Report

HIL84

R Lea and A Westman
NGR: TQ 33030 80880
SMR: 043219–24

7–8 Philpot Lane, EC3

A standing building at 7–8 Philpot Lane, EC3, was partly rebuilt and refurbished in January–June 1984, when a small excavation in the basement, recording of sections in underpinning trenches and a survey of the building were made possible by the developers, Wates Developments (City) Ltd.

Partial stripping of brickearth from the natural mixture of brickearth and gravel, and initial dumping of brickearth, was followed by at least three phases of construction, indicated by timber floors, post-holes and brickearth sills. These phases were divided by episodes of burning, probably *in situ*. The latest phase was sealed by an extensive dump of burnt building material. Dark earth then accumulated and pits, ditches and similar features were cut and eventually backfilled. Except for a possible internal floor, no contemporary surfaces were related to these intrusive features. Gravel surfaces to the E, possibly the precursor of Philpot Lane, preceded the construction of a stone-walled undercroft. The undercroft was aligned parallel to the street, from which it was lit by windows with moulded stone sills and jambs. It may have been entered by a spiral stair in the SE corner. Later, the walls and floor of the undercroft were partly, and the ceiling was wholly, rebuilt in brick. The shallow vaulted ceiling was divided into four bays by moulded green sandstone ribs, reusing springers of 14th-c type. A trace of a similar brick floor implied another cellar to the W.

Brick-lined cellars were added to the N and W, incorporating large, brick-lined cesspits. Larger, partly brick-lined pits within the undercroft were possibly for an industrial purpose or for underpinning. The undercroft and cellars survived the Great Fire of 1666, after which the former was used for storage of building and industrial materials. The building was rebuilt above ground respecting the undercroft in plan and incorporating an arched passage running between the street, Philpot Lane, and a courtyard to the W, Brabant Court.

In the second quarter of the 18th c this building was reconstructed but the undercroft and cellars, passage, and parts of the floors and S wall were retained. Above ground, the building was subdivided. Most of its original internal panelling, window frames and doors survived; the panelling was richest on the first floor. Eventual subsidence of the E side of this building probably prompted insertion of a subdividing wall across the undercroft, for reinforcement. Later modifications included construction of shop fronts, an extension to the NW which necessitated relocation of a staircase, and construction of a deep, brick-lined sewer under the passage and courtyard.

London Archaeol, 5, 1985, 49–50; *Britannia,* 16, 1985, 297; *Medieval Archaeol,* 29, 1985, 175; *Post-Medieval Archaeol,* 18, 1984, 311; 19, 1985, 166–7
Dunn, G, 1986 'Philpot Lane (HIL84)', Finds Appraisal
Lea, R, 1985/6 'The archaeology of standing structures in the City of London', *Popular Archaeol,* 6, No. 14, 22–30
Lea, R, & Westman, A, 1986 'Excavations, watching brief and archaeological survey of a standing building at 7–8 Philpot', Archive Report
Schofield, J, 1995 *Medieval London houses,* 208
Westman, A, & Lea, R, 1986 'Excavations at 7–8 Philpot Lane (HIL84)', Archive Report
Williams, T, in prep. *The development of Roman London east of the Walbrook,* The archaeology of Roman London 4, CBA Res Rep [Roman strata]

99–100 Gracechurch Street, 1–6 Leadenhall Street, 2–12 Whittington Avenue (now Leadenhall Court), EC3

LCT84

S P O'Connor-Thompson,
G Milne, T Brigham, G Brown
and P Wootton
NGR: TQ 33060 81090
SMR: 043060–93

Between September 1984 and February 1985 various investigations were undertaken on this site in advance of major archaeological excavations and subsequent redevelopment. This part of the project was generously funded by Legal and General Assurance Society Ltd. The investigations revealed over 4m of Roman stratigraphy in an area which overlies the NE corner of the early 2nd-c basilica. The earliest activity comprised brickearth quarrying succeeded by both industrial and domestic building deposits. These were superseded by the basilica of which at least three *opus signinum* floors were recorded. Following its demise the roof collapsed; this in turn was sealed by the fallen S wall of the nave and activity in the area appears to have ceased until the 10th c. Also recorded was the 14m high W wall of the mid-15th-c Leadenhall. The foundations comprised a series of relieving arches, which themselves are partially founded on the Roman foundations of the basilica.

From October 1985 to September 1986 extensive excavations were conducted, in addition to the preliminary work reported above. This part of the project, funded by the Legal and General Assurance Society and EH, was designed to examine a large area over and immediately N of the site of the suggested Roman basilica. The 11 trenches investigated below basements of the standing buildings on the S side of the site were supervised by P Wootton, and the three large external areas were supervised by T Brigham (S) G Brown (W) and G Milne (N) (Fig 45).

Evidence was found for the initial clearance of tree cover, quarry pits, ditches, a building with earth-fast posts and a thick fire-debris horizon. All these were sealed by six brickearth-walled buildings, pottery from which has been dated to c AD60–80; the associated pits, wells, alleys and middens were also excavated. All these features were swept away by a major redevelopment of the site which saw the introduction of a large masonry public building extending beyond the S, W and E limits of excavation. A well-made road lay to its N, with brickearth and timber buildings beyond that. Major structural modifications to the masonry building were recorded, as was the sequence of development in many of the rooms, together with the complex pattern of demolition and robbing. The Roman finds were typical of a Roman civilian settlement: nothing of a military character has yet been identified on the site. The Roman pottery constitutes a large assemblage, early Flavian–4th c in date, and including a great range of imports. There are very good examples of unusual types, for example hollow-foot amphora,

Fig 45 LCT84: foundations of the 2nd-c basilica of Roman London, looking W. The shelter and landscaping of the site around the excavations were provided by the developers; co-operation on the site was exemplary.

Rhineland mortaria, and glazed ware from central Gaul and SE England. Glass vessels included chariot and athletes' cups and a double-handed cup *(scyphos)*. Several iron waterpipe collars were recovered.

The road was resurfaced some nine times, but a thick layer of silt sealed the latest surface, into which a series of Saxon pits and other features were cut. Much structural evidence survived of the 15th-c Leadenhall market, as the trenches straddled the N part of the quadrangular market building, locating its truncated foundations. A fragment of the exterior wall of the W range survived to a height of 11.2m between modern buildings. It displayed evidence for an open ground floor for trade and, above, two floors for storage of wheat. Cellars built on the site of the N wing, after its demolition in 1795, incorporated over 100 dressed mouldings and blocks from the superstructure of the building (recording by M Samuel). Post-excavation work for the various published reports was funded by EH and the City of London Archaeological Trust.

London Archaeol, 5, 1986, 159; *Medieval Archaeol,* 30, 1986, 138; 31, 1987, 127–8

Betts, I, & Crowley, N, 1987 'Leadenhall Court/1–6 Leadenhall Street Roman building material — Level III report (LCT84)', Archive Report

Brigham, T, Brown, G, Milne, C, Milne, G, & Wootton, P, 1990 'Excavations at Leadenhall Court (LCT84)', Archive Report

Davis, A, 1991 'Plant remains from pre-basilica levels at Leadenhall Court (BOT/REP/01/91)', Archive Report

Groves, J, 1990 'Leadenhall Court', Finds Appraisal

Maloney, J, 1986 'Leadenhall — nineteen centuries of City life', *Lloyd's Log,* 44–7

Milne, G, 1992 *From Roman basilica to medieval market: archaeology in action in the City of London*

Milne, G, & Wardle, A 1993 'Early Roman development at Leadenhall Court, London, and related research', *Trans London Middlesex Archaeol Soc,* 44, 23–170

Milne, G, & West, B, 1993 'Owls in the basilica', *London Archaeol,* 7, 31–6

Milne, G, & Wootton, P, 1990 'Londinium, AD50–120: Leadenhall Court excavations 1984–6', *London Archaeol,* 6, 179–87

de Moulins, D, nd, 'Charred plant remains from a midden', Archive Report

Samuel, M, 1989 'The fifteenth-century garner at Leadenhall, London', *Antiq J,* 69, 119–53

Symonds, R P, & Tomber, R S, with Lakin, D, & Richardson, B, 1991 'Late Roman London: an assessment of the ceramic evidence from the City of London', *Trans London Middlesex Archaeol Soc,* 42, 59–100

LDW84

C Maloney
NGR: TQ 32790 81400
SMR: 043238–40

44 London Wall, EC2

Excavations were undertaken to locate and examine the W side of a Roman road first discovered in 1981 some 40m to the S. The NNE–SSW road was laid over the natural ground and was bordered by a timber-revetted drainage ditch. No construction date was obtained from this site but it had previously been dated to the late 1st/early 2nd c. The ditch had silted up and became waterlogged towards the second half of the 3rd c but the road remained in use until at least the end of the c. Surfaces were relaid above dumped deposits which continually raised the ground level possibly as a measure against a rising water table. The disuse of the road was marked by a sequence of undated brickearth floors and occupation deposits above the latest surface.

London Archaeol, 5, 1986, 160; *Britannia,* 17, 1986, 408

Davies, B, 1986 'The Roman pottery from 44 London Wall — watching brief (LDW84)', Archive Report

Maloney, C, 1987 'Excavations at 44 London Wall', Archive Report

Maloney, C, 1990 *The upper Walbrook Valley in the Roman period,* The archaeology of Roman London 1, CBA Res Rep 69 [Roman strata]

LEA84

S Rivière
NGR: TQ 33450 81150
SMR: 043107–16, 043234–7

71–77 Leadenhall Street, 32–40 Mitre Street, EC3

An excavation was carried out between July and November 1984, funded by Speyhawk Land and Estates Ltd. A cross-section of all periods from Roman to present day was examined including standing masonry of the priory of Holy Trinity Aldgate.

The Roman material suggested the presence of at least six successive 1st- and 2nd-c timber structures represented by lines of post-holes and slots which reused the same E–W line. Very few associated surfaces were uncovered and nearly all appeared to be external. One of these timber structures was a piled foundation within linear cuts identified in two areas to give a total length of at least 8m and consisting of deep timber piles, three to a row, supporting a masonry superstructure, which had been almost completely robbed out. In medieval contexts, large quantities of good-quality painted plaster, *opus signinum,* tessera cubes and other building material suggested the presence of a fine building nearby, and it is possible that the piled foundation could have supported such a building. One of the fragments of Roman building material found in a medieval context was the unusual survival, intact, of the join between the top of a wall and the first tiles of a roof: two *tegulae,* sealed by an *imbrex* and held in place by a wedge-shaped piece of mortar, on top of the top tile of the wall, giving the correct angle for the slope of the roof.

Heavily truncating the Roman stratigraphy across the whole length of the site (about 30m) there followed a deliberate preparation for a ?Late Saxon graveyard. No trace of an associated church was found. There were 42 articulated burials, of three basic types, buried within simple cuts, or within wooden coffins, or most commonly within stone and mortar lined cists. To the W, the burials cut one into another causing a build-up of a sequence of at least ten burials in one area. By contrast, the burials to the E were positioned carefully next to each other with very little disturbance. Unfortunately, the join between the areas was disturbed by later intrusions.

The site covered a portion of the S side of the church of the priory of Holy Trinity Aldgate, founded in 1108. The 12th-c foundations for the S wall of the church and the outline of almost the whole of the S transept foundations were excavated, together with foundations, and about 3.5m of superstructure, of a chapel with an apsidal E end on the outside of the NE corner of the transept. Part of the SW corner of a second chapel (to the E of the apsidal chapel) was recorded together with a later 14th- or 15th-c arch which formed the entrance from the church to the chapel. Only one small area of internal flooring survived: a series of mortar surfaces, possibly originally sealed by tiles. A small area of painted plaster inside the apsidal chapel remained on the wall. The apsidal chapel was squared externally and was founded on rough courses of chalk and mortar, with the superstructure of ragstone, flint, reused Roman tile and, more unusually, blocks of limestone, and possibly Caen stone. About 0.4m above floor level was a course, inside and outside, of chamfered stones and the corners were treated specially, with close-fitting ashlar blocks. Several architectural features on both the arch and the chapel have warranted the preservation of both within the new development. An external area between the two chapels contained material contemporary with and later than the priory. During the life of the priory it appeared to have no special status but received mixed dumps and some pits, and may possibly have been associated with medieval properties fronting on Leadenhall Street, perhaps as a backyard. In the 16th c the Dissolution was reflected in a change of use of the apsidal chapel to that of a cellar with a doorway and later a window knocked through the E wall. The external area to the E became covered with roof slates, probably from the church, and was then raised to a height level with the doorway in the chapel. A large timber structure was erected between the two still-standing chapels, respecting their S limits, and a series of external metallings formed an alleyway or courtyard to the S of the chapels and timber structure. The apsidal chapel continued to be reused, with several other additions into the 19th c, when a new series of basements and a cobbled courtyard finally truncated and sealed it. These buildings were dismantled after bombing in the Second World War.

Recording of the aboveground remains of Holy Trinity Priory Aldgate (the arch originally leading from the S aisle of the choir into a chapel) continued during 1985 following the excavation of the site in 1984. The medieval work was stabilised and where possible stripped of later brickwork. A pointed arch of two orders moulded in Reigate stone with

Fig 46 LEA84: the lifting of the 12th-c transept chapel of Holy Trinity Priory Aldgate prior to construction works. It was later lifted back into approximately the same position.

plain hollow chamfers which die into the jambs without capitals had been inserted into an earlier, probably 12th-c arch of which traces still survived in the core observed in the N face. Traces of a window in the wall E of the arch and a spiral staircase in the S face of the wall to the E of the arch were also observed.

During the first stage of the subsequent development, the S transept chapel remains were lifted temporarily across the site (Fig 46) to enable foundations to be dug, and then the chapel was lifted back into approximately its original place. The standing arch now forms a feature in the foyer of the new building.

London Archaeol, 5, 1985, 48–9; *Britannia,* 16, 1985, 297; *Medieval Archaeol,* 29, 1984, 174; 30, 1986, 138; 31, 1987, 128; *Post-Medieval Archaeol,* 19, 1985, 165–6; 21, 1987, 268

Dunn, G, 1985 'Leadenhall Street (LEA84)', Finds Appraisal

Hunting, P, nd [1990] *Archaeology and development* (Speyhawk and MoL), 32–8

Lea, R, nd, 'Preliminary report on reconstructing the arch', Archive Report

Lea, R, 1985/6 'The archaeology of standing structures in the City of London', *Popular Archaeol,* 6, No. 14, 22–30

Rivière, S, 1986a 'Excavations at 71–77 Leadenhall Street, 32–40 Mitre Street, EC3 (LEA84)', Archive Report

Rivière, S, 1986b 'The excavation at Mitre Street', *Popular Archaeol,* 6, No. 12, 37–41

Schofield, J, & Lea, R, in prep. *Holy Trinity Priory Aldgate*

West, B, 1986 'The late Saxon skeletons from Mitre Street (HUM/01/86)', Archive Report [later combined with a report on human remains at HTP79; the edited report by J Conheeney, MoLAS Environmental Archaeology Section, Human Bone Report HUM 02/93, 1993]

Williams, T, in prep. *The development of Roman London east of the Walbrook,* The archaeology of Roman London 4, CBA Res Rep [Roman strata]

LWA84

T Wilmott
NGR: TQ 32730 81530
SMR: 043170–3

43 London Wall, EC2

Excavations, funded by Gleesons Ltd, took place on the W edge of the Walbrook Valley just inside the line of the Roman city wall E of Moorgate and immediately W of a N–S aligned Roman road. In the mid-2nd c the natural ground surface was truncated and large open ditches dug, aligned NW–SE and N–S, the latter probably being part of the roadside ditch. The N–S ditch was replaced with a plank-lined drain, and on higher ground to the W of the road a post-built structure constructed. Occupation was brief and from the late 3rd c to the 11th c little activity was recorded. The drainage pattern was re-established in the 11th c by the cutting of an E–W aligned open ditch. No major development of the area is found until the post-medieval period. The complex drainage patterns of the site show the difficulty in maintaining a stable ground surface in this part of the Walbrook Valley. Until the post-medieval period this area, except for one short period of Roman development, can only be considered as marginal land within the city walls.

London Archaeol, 5, 1985, 49; *Britannia,* 15, 1985, 297

Davies, B, 1987 'The Roman pottery from 43 London Wall LWA84', Archive Report

Dunn, G, 1985 'London Wall (LWA84)', Finds Appraisal

Maloney, C, 1990 *The upper Walbrook Valley in the Roman period,* The archaeology of Roman London 1, CBA Res Rep 69 [Roman strata]

Orton, C, 1996 'Dem dry bones', in Bird, J, Hassall, M, & Sheldon, H (eds), *Interpreting Roman London: papers in memory of Hugh Chapman,* 199–208 [comparative statistical study of animal bones]

Spence, C, & Malt, D, 1985 'Excavations at 43 London Wall', Archive Report

MAH84

R Lea
NGR: TQ 33080 80760
SMR: 043302

St Mary at Hill church, St Mary at Hill, EC3

Part of the fabric of the medieval church of St Mary at Hill had surfaced during repairs to the roof timbers in the N aisle at the W end of the church. The work was funded by the GLC.

Parts of the pre-Fire N wall, faced in well-squared Kentish rag ashlar, and the heads of two pointed segmental arched windows were exposed when render and plaster were stripped from the external and internal elevations (Fig 47). A circular window above the N door was centred in the W of the two windows.

The E window was of the same type. The hood mouldings had been broken off but traces of the moulding and stops remained. The jamb and arch mouldings were only partially visible and had apparently been rendered prior to the insertion of the brickwork. Internally the face of the wall was rough-coursed rag and chalk. Above the W window there were no traces of a wall rib or shoulder for the support of a vault, implying a timber roof in the N aisle at least in this bay. The pre-Fire work would appear to be 15th or 16th c; the N aisle was built, according to documentary sources, in 1497–1501.

Fig 47 MAH84: at St Mary at Hill, it was found that the stone N wall of 1501 survived to eaves height, including several windows; one was later adapted, by Wren or later restorers, by inserting a circular window of brick.

At the time of recording, and in interim reports, the post-Fire alterations such as the circular window were thought to be of Wren's building. But further work in 1988 (SMY88 below) suggests that the alterations were by James Savage in 1848–9.

London Archaeol, 5, 1985, 50; *Medieval Archaeol,* 29, 1985, 175–6; *Post-Medieval Archaeol,* 19, 1985, 161

Jeffery, P, Lea, R, & Watson, B, 1992 'The architectural history of the church of St Mary at Hill in the City of London'. *Trans London Middlesex Archaeol Soc,* 43, 193–200

Lea, R, 1985 'Excavations at St Mary at Hill (MAH84)', Archive Report

Lea, R, 1985/6 'The archaeology of standing structures in the City of London', *Popular Archaeol,* 6, No. 14, 22–30

Schofield, J, 1994 'Saxon and medieval parish churches in the City of London: a review', *Trans London Middlesex Archaeol Soc,* 45, 119–20

12–14 Mitre Street, EC3

MIR84

B Pye
NGR: TQ 33420 81190
SMR: 043174–8

A watching brief was carried out in May and June 1984 on a site within the precinct of Holy Trinity Priory. Only cut features remained as the basement had truncated natural brickearth. The earliest features were a series of large quarry pits backfilled in the 2nd c. In the E half of the site these had been truncated by a medieval graveyard, presumably belonging to Holy Trinity Priory. Two small chalk, rag and greensand block foundations cut into the graveyard horizons. In the W half of the site the quarry pits were truncated by early medieval (1050–1150) and 18th-c rubbish pits; a brick cesspit produced a large group of early/mid-18th-c domestic material including a delftware (Lambeth) plate with the Hebrew word for 'milk' written across its central part before firing.

London Archaeol, 5, 1985, 49; *Medieval Archaeol,* 29, 1985, 174; *Post-Medieval Archaeol,* 19, 1985, 166

Dunn, G, 1984 'Mitre Street (MIR84)', Finds Appraisal

Pearce, J, in prep. 'A rare delftware Hebrew plate and associated assemblage from excavation in Mitre Street, City of London'

Pye, B, nd, 'Excavations at 12–14 Mitre Street (MIR84)', Archive Report, draft

Schofield, J, & Lea, R, in prep. *Holy Trinity Priory Aldgate*

Stone, J, 1990 'Finds appraisal for 12–14 Mitre Street', Finds Appraisal

Williams, T, in prep. *The development of Roman London east of the Walbrook,* The archaeology of Roman London 4, CBA Res Rep [Roman strata]

NBS84

P Chitwood
NGR: TQ 31670 81020
SMR: 040415–16

35–38 New Bridge Street, EC4

During May–June 1984 a small excavation within machine-cleared construction trenches produced evidence of early, probably Roman, development of the E bank of the Fleet, with two sequences of land reclamation extending the bank and stabilised with posts.

These dumps were truncated by the steep N–S construction cut for the Blackfriars city wall extension of between 1283 and 1320 which survives still in places. Generally 1.8m wide, with a randomly coursed chalk core, a sudden step out on the E face and a gradual increase in width towards the N could suggest buttressing for the bridge to the 16th-c Bridewell Palace (known to lie under Apothecary Street, immediately N of the site). The W face of the wall changes character frequently along its length, ranging from well-dressed monumental rectangular ashlar blocks to small irregular crudely worked ragstones with flints. Dressed blocks of chalk form the vertical E face, protected by constant backfilling during construction with steps-in corresponding very closely to changes in construction on the W side.

In the S the wall changes dramatically in both construction and alignment (NE–SW). There is no evidence for the continuation in a straight line of the N–S wall, so this portion, with its arched brick drain and the inclusion of brick in the core, probably represents a later rebuilding of the wall, possibly during the 17th-c construction of the Fleet Canal. This later use of bricks is also apparent in repairs to the W face of the N–S wall and in additions such as drains. The W face of the wall was eventually sealed by the mixed rubble dumps used to fill in the Fleet ditch in the 18th c.

London Archaeol, 5, 1985, 49; *Medieval Archaeol*, 29, 1985, 174–5; *Post-Medieval Archaeol*, 19, 1985, 166
Chitwood, P, 1984 (rev 1990) 'Excavations at New Bridge Street (NBS84)', Archive Report
Dunn, G, 1984 'New Bridge Street (NBS84)', Finds Appraisal

SSL84

K Steedman
NGR: TQ 32710 80940
SMR: 043321–31

18, 19, 21–23 St Swithin's Lane, 13 Sherbourne Lane, EC4

From mid-June to mid-August 1984 excavations, funded by Haslemere Estates, within the basement of a standing building, examined two contrasting sequences. In the larger trench (Area I), fence remains and quarrying cut into natural gravel were sealed by surfaces within a lean-to or verandah associated with an E–W post and trench foundation. This activity was truncated by a gravel quarry pit backfilled with redeposited material, including fire debris. Above this, evidence for external activity was sealed by two successive internal surfaces without associated structural divisions. The latest of these had an AD120 *terminus post quem,* while all earlier features contained 1st-c pottery. Dumps of redeposited material truncated by features dated to after 1050 including part of an internal surface and a rubbish pit. Several medieval pits and a post-Fire cellar completed the sequence.

In Area II, four successive N–S external divisions were sealed by internal features with minor structural divisions, similarly aligned to early features in Area I, and with a 1st-c *terminus post quem.* Evidence for further internal activity, but on a slightly different alignment and including some 2nd-c pottery, was truncated by the insertion of a medieval external surface overlaid by dumping and pits. The finds generally indicated a normal Roman domestic assemblage.

London Archaeol, 5, 1985, 50; *Medieval Archaeol*, 29, 1985, 175
Davies, B, 1985 'The Roman pottery from St Swithins Lane (SSL84)', Archive Report
Davies, B, 1993 'Inter-site studies', in Milne, G, & Wardle, A, 'Early Roman development at Leadenhall Court, London and related research', *Trans London Middlesex Archaeol Soc*, 44, 135–50
Keily, J, 1989 '19 St Swithins Lane (SSL84) Roman building material Level III report', Archive Report
Nenk, B, 1985 'St Swithins Lane (SSL84)', Finds Appraisal
Steedman, K, 1985 'Excavations at 19 St Swithins Lane', Archive Report
Williams, T, in prep. *The development of Roman London east of the Walbrook*, The archaeology of Roman London 4, CBA Res Rep [Roman strata]

Trig Lane, Upper Thames Street (watching brief), EC4

TIG84

B Pye
NGR: TQ 31980 80880
SMR: 041200, 044582–4,
044590–2, 044605, 044607,
044622–5

A watching brief took place in February–May 1984 on this large site (the future City of London Boys' School), which had already been excavated as the Trig Lane (TL74), Baynard's Castle (BC72/GM152 and BYD81) and St Peter's Hill (PET81) sites. On the W side of the site a 2m length of the S wall and foundation of Baynard's Castle was exposed, W of the SW corner tower (BYD81). The wall had been built on ash piles some 3m long. To the N of the Trig Lane excavation site a timber revetment of the 13th c or earlier was recorded, and to the W of the Trig Lane site a medieval ragstone-faced riverwall with a timber structure, possibly a stair, on its E side. Other recorded features in this area included large 18th-c arched brick cellars, wooden drains and a large oval wood-lined tank. Nearer Queen Victoria Street, the watching brief recorded the medieval S and W walls of St Peter Paul's Wharf church (also found in PET81), early graves cutting into a Roman chalk raft, and traces of the post-1666 graveyard. To the S of the church medieval Thames Street was seen as gravel surfaces topped with cobbles. The Roman riverside wall was briefly observed in one trial hole. On the W side of the site, near St Benet's church, was a series of Victorian brick vaults. Along the Queen Victoria Street frontage on the N a series of post-Great Fire dumps was recorded in the W and possibly dark earth overlying Roman mortar dumps in the E.

London Archaeol, 5, 1985, 63; *Medieval Archaeol,* 29, 1985, 176
Dunn, G, 1984 'Trig Lane (TIG84)', Finds Appraisal
Williams, T, 1993 *Public buildings in the south-west quarter of Roman London,* The archaeology of Roman London 3, CBA Res Rep 88
  [Roman strata]

131 Aldersgate Street, 14 Carthusian Street, EC2

ADT85

NGR: TQ 32065 81890

A site code was issued but no useful structural or topographical information gained.

Carthusian Street, junction with Aldersgate Street, EC2

AGS85

D Bentley
NGR: TQ 32090 81910
SMR: 044721

A trench revealed a sequence of horizontal gravel bands about 1m thick, which presumably represented earlier, probably medieval, street surfaces.

10 Arthur Street, EC4

ATR85

P Bethell
NGR: TQ 32790 80780
SMR: 043156–8

Excavations funded by London and Edinburgh plc were conducted here in April 1985. A Roman building with two successive floors of *opus signinum,* an external area and a ditch were recorded. A second building off the site to the N, from its demolition debris, had much painted wall plaster. The first building was demolished and further occupation attested by an alignment of stake-holes. Medieval pits and post-medieval features were also recorded.

London Archaeol, 5, 1986, 158; *Britannia,* 17, 1986, 407; *Medieval Archaeol,* 30, 1986, 137
Bethell, P, 1985 'Excavations at 10 Arthur Street', Archive Report
Dunn, G, 1985 'Arthur Street (ATR85)', Finds Appraisal

BBT85

NGR: TQ 33045 80880
SMR: 221064

4 Brabant Court, EC3

A site code was issued but no useful structural or topographical information gained. This house, with some original 18th-c features, was being refurbished. For the range in front of Brabant Court to Philpot Lane, see HIL84 above.

BMK85

T Brigham
NGR: TQ 33095 80630
SMR: 044595

Billingsgate Market, Lower Thames Street, EC3

A one-day investigation was conducted in a contractor's trench immediately E of the former Billingsgate Fish Market building during works associated with its refurbishment. This involved the digging by machine of a trench about 50m in length, alongside the E facade of the building. This was 3m deep with a further 6m sondage at the N end against Thames Street, 4m x 3m in plan. The main portion of the trench was filled with modern rubble to a depth of 3m. Within the deeper excavation at the N end, the remains of a substantial but badly eroded ragstone and mortar wall, thought to be part of the Roman riverside city wall, were recorded. The N face of this wall, which ran E–W, was intact, but the S side was eroded.

Brigham, T, 1985 'Billingsgate East watching brief (BMK85)', Archive Report
Brigham, T, 1990 'The late Roman waterfront in London', Britannia, 21, 99–183

CME85

C Maloney
NGR: TQ 32630 81440
SMR: 044722–4

West side of Coleman Street, near Woolgate House, EC2

Observations were made in an electricity trench. The earliest recorded deposit, over 0.5m thick, was a dark silty clay, apparently medieval or post-medieval in date. The N edge of the trench revealed a section through the road-metallings: these were recorded to a depth of 2.3m below ground level. E–W aligned brick arches were probably the remains of sewer tunnels. Modern services had caused much disturbance to the archaeological sequence.

CRH85

S Rivière
NGR: TQ 33400 81160
SMR: 043159–62

2–20 Creechurch Lane, 24–31 Mitre Street, EC3

A watching brief consisting of four testpits revealed 0.8m of Roman dumps, make-ups and brickearth surfaces which were cut into three groups of medieval rubbish pits and a disturbed burial all of which were sealed by extensive make-up for the standing building.

London Archaeol, 5, 1986, 158; Britannia, 17, 1986, 407; Medieval Archaeol, 30, 1986, 137
Rivière, S, 1986 'Excavations at 4–8 Creechurch Lane (CRH85)', Archive Report

6–7 Crescent, 41–42 Trinity Square, EC3

CST85

A Westman
NGR: TQ 33610 80820
SMR: 043163–8

Excavations took place in April–July 1985 immediately E of, and outside, the city wall N of the Tower of London, funded by the site developer, Arundell House Securities Ltd. The Roman wall, the face of which survived up to 2.45m in height, was associated with two successive ditches cut a short distance in front of it. The earlier, V-shaped in profile, was severely truncated by the later, flat-bottomed ditch. The backfill of the latter included debris which had tumbled from the wall. The berm in front of the wall was then reduced to the level to which most of the second ditch had been backfilled by the cutting of a third, more extensive flat-bottomed ditch which ran up to the face of the wall and initially exposed the upper courses of the foundations. The first deposits in this ditch were dated to the late 12th–13th c and suggested that the wall was being reconstructed. Later dumps of relatively clean gravel may have been upcast from cutting a fourth, much deeper ditch further E, the earliest fill of which was dated to the 13th–mid-14th c. The city wall, including its upper medieval construction, survived to an overall height of nearly 11m. Its disuse as a defence was implied by the cutting of two successive pits in the backfill of the latest ditch. They were lined with horn cores, perhaps for an industrial purpose, and were constructed and backfilled in the late 17th c. The wall then served as support for structures such as a furnace built in brick against its face. A cellar floor, other brick foundations and a brick-lined well were probably associated with the latest building on the site, known to have been built in 1767–70 as part of an elegant redevelopment designed by George Dance the younger.

London Archaeol, 5, 1986, 158; *Britannia,* 17, 1986, 407; *Medieval Archaeol,* 30, 1986, 137
Dunn, G, 1986 'Crescent (CST85)', Finds Appraisal
Westman, A, 1986 'Excavations at 6–7 Crescent', Archive Report

37–40 Fish Street Hill, 16–20 Monument Street, EC3

FMO85

N Bateman
NGR: TQ 32920 80730
SMR: 043190–200

Between July and September 1985 an excavation was carried out in advance of redevelopment of the site by Speyhawk, who sponsored the archaeological investigation. The site comprised the remaining quarter of a block which had produced evidence for London's early Roman waterfront in 1981 (PDN81). The area of excavation was about 20m x 15m and lay immediately adjacent to the expected alignment of the approach roads to both Roman and medieval London Bridge. In the early 1st c, the sloping hillside leading down to the Thames was sealed by a series of dumped deposits to create an artificial level terrace upon which a substantial building was constructed. The W wall and the SW corner of this building were masonry, but at least part of the S wall was probably timber framed. Internal brickearth surfaces in several large rooms and a corridor area along the W frontage were about 1m higher than the contemporary external ground level to the S.

After a fire in the mid-1st c, possibly associated with the Boudican revolt, the building was reconstructed to a similar plan but with timber walls replaced by masonry. Later modifications occurred when the SW corner was rebuilt, the S wall was strengthened and a deep E–W foundation, possibly reflecting the roof ridge alignment, was built across the site. In its latest form, the building was about 14.5m wide E–W with a 7.2m gap separating the S wall and the central bisecting E–W foundation. To the W of the building a series of compacted gravel surfaces and a series of intercutting drains and gullies which led off to the S were found. The highest of these was backfilled with redeposited fire debris of the early–mid-2nd c. The later development of the site after this date is not known in detail, since the horizontal sequence was truncated by a modern concrete slab. However, many cut features were recorded. Evidence of the two late Saxon/early medieval cellared buildings was found, cut through the underlying Roman deposits. One used earth-fast posts regularly spaced around the edge of a rectangular cut; the other had N and E walls of mortared rubble and an E wall represented by a probable robbed timber sill. Inside both buildings was a series of brickearth and beaten-earth floors.

A group of about 30 pits, ranging in date from mid-10th to early 13th c, was found along the E side of the site. The particular concentration is presumed to reflect the close packing of properties along the early medieval predecessor of Fish Street Hill. A complete 17th-c cellar, probably burnt in the Great Fire of 1666, was exposed, as well as a number of 17th-, 18th- and 19th-c wells, cesspits and wall foundations. These reveal the gradual evolution of the property boundaries which were extant until early 1985.

London Archaeol, 4, 1986, 276; Britannia, 17, 1986, 406–7; Medieval Archaeol, 30, 1986, 138

Bateman, N, 1986a 'Bridgehead revisited', London Archaeol, 5, 233–41

Bateman, N, 1986b 'Excavations at 37–40 Fish Street Hill — FMO85', Archive Report

Cowgill, J, nd, 'Fish Street Hill', Finds Appraisal

Davies, B, 1993 'Inter-site studies', in Milne, G, & Wardle, A, 'Early Roman development at Leadenhall Court, London and related research', Trans London Middlesex Archaeol Soc, 44, 135–50

Horsman, V, Milne, C, & Milne, G, 1988 Aspects of Saxo-Norman London I: building and street development, London Middlesex Archaeol Soc Spec Pap 11 [Saxon buildings and streets]

Tyers, P, 1986 'Fish Street Hill Roman pottery report (FMO85)', Archive Report

Vince, A (ed), 1991 Aspects of Saxo-Norman London II: finds and environmental evidence, London Middlesex Archaeol Soc Spec Pap 12 [Saxon smallfinds]

FST85

S Rivière
NGR: TQ 33450 81100
SMR: 043043–51

94–97 Fenchurch Street, EC3

Excavation took place here between October and December 1985. The earliest feature on the site was a 26m long Roman ditch, partly with the 'ankle-breaking' profile suggestive of a military function. It had a fairly short life and was backfilled and levelled over at one time, with the first indications of several flimsy timber structures sealing the levelling. These structures, and a large domestic oven, were themselves sealed by a further levelling up for the first of the more substantial buildings. These buildings, Buildings 1 and 2, were single storey, with wattle and daub walls supported by clay sills and roofed with thatch, and were confined to the E half of the site. To the W was an extensive external gravel area, possibly a courtyard, which covered an area at least 17m x 16m. The two buildings were completely destroyed by a major fire, probably Boudican. The new buildings and streets were deliberately laid out on a new alignment, at 45 degrees to the preceding buildings, employing slightly different building techniques but producing basically timber, with wattle and daub walls and thatched roofs. Each was subdivided into several rooms and was altered internally during its lifetime. They formed in plan the shape of a fairly typical strip building and appeared to front onto the street running to the S and E. To the W of these buildings lay a street composed of bands of gravel heavily compacted to form a smooth surface with a slight camber in the middle. The sides were revetted with timber, and a succession of roadside ditches ran along both sides. The street was resurfaced at least three times and was in use well into the 2nd c AD. This street must have met the street on which the buildings were fronting at an angle of less than 90 degrees, suggesting that the street found on the excavation may have been only a side street.

Any later Roman activity that may have existed across the site was destroyed by a large number of 12th-c and later rubbish pits, wells and three chalk-lined pits.

Britannia, 18, 1987, 333–4

Cowgill, J, 1987 'Fenchurch Street (FST85)', Finds Appraisal

Crowley, N, 1989 '94–97 Fenchurch Street Roman building material Level III report (FST85)', Archive Report

Davies, B, 1993 'Inter-site studies', in Milne, G, & Wardle, A, 'Early Roman development at Leadenhall Court, London and related research', Trans London Middlesex Archaeol Soc, 44, 135–50

Rivière, S, 1986 'Excavations at 94–97 Fenchurch Street (FST85)', Archive Report

Williams, T, in prep. The development of Roman London east of the Walbrook, The archaeology of Roman London 4, CBA Res Rep [Roman strata]

Guildhall House, 81–87 Gresham Street, EC2

GDH85

K Steedman
NGR: TQ 32510 81310
SMR: 043052–9

The excavation, funded by the Corporation of London, took place between December 1985 and March 1986. The underlying geology was a thick bed of Thames river gravels overlaid by a layer of natural brickearth. A number of 1st-c Roman buildings were identified, all of which had a NE–SW angle across the site. All of the structural remains of all the earliest buildings had been removed following destruction by fire, and it is unclear whether they had been timber or masonry. One of the buildings was partially terraced into natural and was at least 5m in width. Another rectangular building — at least about 6m x 7m — on the W of the site was also completely robbed and the trenches were backfilled with fire debris. There was evidence for either a third building immediately to the S, or possibly a corridor in front of the building to the N, with which it was parallel. The earliest building was apparently associated with pottery dated to c 50–60, and finds from associated destruction debris of all buildings have been provisionally dated to the immediately pre-Boudican period. Clearance of the area was succeeded by extensive levelling over with brickearth spreads which raised ground level by about 0.5m. This was sealed by the construction of a Flavian building, for which there was relatively little evidence, and metalled open areas in front of it.

In the early 2nd c extensive ground clearance and levelling occurred and a substantial wall was constructed across the previous external area, along the N of the site. This wall was about 1.4m wide and survived (in only very small patches) as two courses of Roman bonding brick on a shallow rubble foundation. Only two small stretches of extant wall were found, separated by more than 15m, with a larger extent of robbing trench around both areas but not conclusively linking the two together. Although too little survived to identify the building at the time (in 1985) it is now possible (after excavations to the N at GAG87, where more substantial remains of the Roman amphitheatre were recognised in 1989) to see both wall fragments as part of the outer wall of the amphitheatre. No associated surfaces survived though it has been suggested that the area S of the wall remained external for some time.

The area S of the amphitheatre may have remained external for a short period, but was quickly overlaid by a succession of probably timber buildings, one of which had at least three aisles. These are dated to the 2nd and 3rd c. A (robbed) wall about 1m wide and 17m long running up to the (?) amphitheatre wall was indicated. The amphitheatre and its surrounding buildings were all apparently disused by the 4th c judging by the date of the pottery from the robbing cuts.

All traces of the Roman buildings and any robbing deposits over them were covered by a thick deposit of grey silts which may be dark earth, cut by a number of Late Saxon pits, some of which contained carved bone trial pieces. Many (at least 18) of these pits produced pottery that has been provisionally dated to c 850–1000. The dark earth silts were also cut by two groups of 12th–13th-c chalk foundations, though contemporary surfaces and ground levels did not survive.

Those at the W side of the site enclosed an area to the NW, with what is assumed to have been a backyard area containing a unique chalk stone-built cellar, with steps leading down into it, measuring 1.65m x 1.15m internally. This was interpreted at the time as a possible strongroom but also suggested as a possible Jewish ritual bath or *mikveh* (Pepper 1992).

In the centre of the site substantial chalk foundations suggested another building running to the S and probably fronting on Catteaton (Gresham) Street. The size of the foundations (about 1.2m thick) imply more than one storey. The building must have been at least 6.6m E–W by at least 9.1m N–S externally (4.2m x 7.6m internally). If it indeed fronted on to Catteaton Street, it must have been about 15m long externally. It appeared to have a latrine cesspit added to its NW corner as a modification and the whole building was probably out of use by the 13th c. There were several wells and pits of post-medieval date but all other horizontal activity was truncated.

[summary by N Bateman]

London Archaeol, 5, 1987, 271; *Britannia*, 17, 1986, 335; *Medieval Archaeol*, 31, 1987, 128
Cowgill, J, 1986 'Guildhall House Gresham Street GDH85', Finds Appraisal
Pepper, G, 1992 'An archaeology of the Jewry in medieval London', *London Archaeol*, 7, 3–6
Sermon, R A, 1990 'Medieval mikveh or strong room?', *DUA Newsletter*, Sept, 12–14
Steedman, K, nd, 'Excavations at Guildhall House (GDH85)', Archive Report
Winder, J M, 1985 'Oyster shells', Archive Report

KHN85

D Bentley and D Lakin
NGR: TQ 31200 81740
SMR: 044725–9

6–9 Kinghorn Street, EC1

The site lay immediately E of the E end of St Bartholomew's Priory church. The earliest features recorded were a series of auxiliary buildings close to the church. Two substantial masonry E–W walls to the E of the Lady Chapel continued the line of the chapel: it was not clear whether these represented an earlier building or an unfinished part of the chapel. The E wall of the 15th-c Lady Chapel was exposed and recorded; it was found to have cut through the E end of some graves. Near the NE corner of the chapel was a chalk-lined well which contained a single block of reused Reigate stone on which survived the image of a painted face. It appeared to be a fragment of medieval fresco wall painting and, since it was found in association with the remains of brick buildings of late 16th or early 17th c, it may have derived from a nearby priory building, perhaps the Prior's Lodgings, during rebuilding after the Dissolution. Brick structures and walls represent the remains of 16th- and 17th-c domestic buildings; a cellar of 17th-c date was found to have been reused in the construction of a 19th-c building.

Cowgill, J, 1987 '6–9 Kinghorn Street KHN85', Finds Appraisal

KNG85

P Rowsome
NGR: TQ 32450 81206
SMR: 043201–11

36–37 King Street, EC2

Excavations funded by the Mercers' Company took place from January to June 1985 before demolition of buildings on the site. Two areas of excavation forming a total area of 20m x 10m were located immediately to the N of Roman Cheapside and to the E of the Cheapside baths. Two Roman roads crossed the excavated areas, one running NW–SE and the other NE–SW. The roads met to form a T-junction or crossroads at the NW corner of the site. Both were established around AD50–65 and were probably integral parts of the initial planning of this part of the Roman town which lay on the high ground to the N of the Roman street beneath Cheapside and to the W of the Walbrook stream. The alignment of the two roads, which differed from those of other Roman roads nearby, may have been influenced by the presence of a W tributary of the Walbrook. Evidence of a silt-filled stream-bed was found to the S of the road junction. The NW–SE aligned road may have converged with the Roman street beneath Cheapside to form an early bridgehead at the Walbrook. The earliest road-metallings were associated with shallow roadside drains bordered by simple domestic timber buildings. These were destroyed in a fire, perhaps Boudican. A short period of road disuse occurred at this point. Occupation was quickly re-established on the same alignments with timber- and brickearth-silled buildings and newly dug timber box drains lining remetalled road surfaces. The new buildings were more substantial, one Flavian building containing at least four rooms with plaster-faced sills and an *opus signinum* floor. All the roadside properties saw various modifications and rebuildings until the crowded timber structures were destroyed in the Hadrianic fire (c AD125). The tendency towards more substantial buildings was continued after the fire by a large structure with brickearth slabs and sills and one room containing a tessellated floor measuring 5m x 5m. This Antonine-period building was also destroyed by fire and was part of the last recorded phase of roadside occupation.

Throughout the 1st and 2nd c the road alignments and widths (3.5–4m) remained fairly constant with little roadside encroachment even though ground surfaces rose substantially and forced road levels to keep pace by regular resurfacing and drain replacement. The permanent abandonment of the two roads was shown by the site-wide deposit of dark earth. Sandwiched within the dark earth accumulations, directly over the NW–SE road, was a structural slot and brickearth slab of a building on a different alignment and dated to the late 3rd or early 4th c.

Two Late Saxon sunken buildings were recorded, one a small hut measuring 3m x 3m and the other a much larger structure at least 10m in length. Both were cut into dark earth deposits and were situated in part over the buried NW–SE Roman road. Fragments of chalk foundations also recorded may have been of medieval buildings fronting onto either Cheapside or Lawrence Lane.

London Archaeol, 5, 1986, 159; *Britannia,* 17, 1986, 408

Pringle, S, 1990 '36–37 King Street', Building Materials Appraisal

Riddler, I, 1989 '36–37 King Street (KNG85)', Finds Appraisal

Rowsome, P, 1987 '36–37 King Street', in Shepherd, J, 'The pre-urban and Roman topography in the King Street and Cheapside areas
   of the City of London', *Trans London Middlesex Archaeol Soc,* 38, 46–50

Rowsome, P, 1988 'Excavations at 36–37 King Street (KNG85)', Archive Report

6 Laurence Pountney Hill, EC4

LAU85

M O'D Shea
NGR: TQ 32750 00830
SMR: 043212–18

Excavations funded by Miller Buckley Ltd took place in a six-week period during November–December 1985 within a standing building and measuring 30m E–W x 6–10m N–S. The site lies immediately S of Cannon Street on a relatively steep gravel slope down to the Thames, and its main importance is its location on or near the sites of the church of St Laurence Pountney and the early 14th-c collegiate chapel of Corpus Christi, attached to the church in 1333/4. The site yielded evidence of Roman (N–S flint footings with a possible E–W return of a substantial building, a drain and sewer sequence and large pits, one possibly originally a well), medieval (chalk foundations, an area of burials and square pits) and post-medieval (foundations, walls and surfaces) periods.

London Archaeol, 5, 1986, 159; *Britannia,* 17, 1986, 408; *Medieval Archaeol,* 30, 1986, 138

Dunn, G, 1986 'Laurence Pountney Hill (LAU85)', Finds Appraisal

Shea, M, 1986 'Excavations at 6 Laurence Pountney Hill (LAU85)', Archive Report

7 Ludgate Broadway, EC4

LBY85

J Hill
NGR: TQ 31745 81080
SMR: 040427, 041194,
042502–5

The excavation, sponsored by Guardian Exchange, took place between 19 June and 25 August 1985. The site lies between 28m and 43m outside the Roman city wall. This wall-line was followed until the later 13th c when it was demolished to make way for the Dominican Blackfriars. Reconstructions of the friary made from observed walls and documentary evidence suggested that the NW corner of the nave should lie within the area of the site. The site had been terraced by the insertion of modern post-medieval cellars to a level at least 1.5m below that of pre-Roman natural. The W edge of a substantial cut feature running N–S was recorded in three sections. A paucity of material within the backfill hindered dating, but an absolute absence of medieval finds, the size of the cut and the distance of the W edge from the line of the city wall (about 37m) all suggested that it represented the late Roman city ditch, recorded at other sites. The backfilled ditch was overlaid by the substantial masonry foundations of the NW corner of the nave of the Dominican friary. No Lady Chapel, as suggested by Alfred Clapham in 1912, was evident. Measurements from foundations observed during a watching brief in 1983 (APO81) to those found at Ludgate Broadway indicate that dimensions quoted in a survey of 1551, hitherto regarded as external specifications, are in fact internal. The church is consequently larger than reconstructions to date have shown. A sequence of badly truncated late 17th-/early 18th-c brick and tile cellar floors and walls overlay the friary. Portions of foundations reusing moulded stone from the superstructure of the friary were incorporated within these brick features and are probably earlier, though reuse destroyed any dating evidence. Of particular interest were a large quantity of carved bone, ivory and tortoiseshell fan pieces of the late 17th/early 18th c found within material backfilling a cellar to the S of the site, and an extremely deep (3.2m), vaulted cesspit. Also from this feature was a large assemblage of mid-17th-/mid-18th-c pottery and glass, and a number of oyster shells used as paint palettes. Its earliest phase was of stone robbed from the friary.

London Archaeol, 5, 1986, 160; *Britannia,* 17, 1986, 407; *Medieval Archaeol,* 30, 1986, 139; *Post-Medieval Archaeol,* 20, 1986, 334–5

Clapham, A W, & Godfrey, W H, 1912 *Some famous buildings and their story,* 254–63

Dunn, G, 1986 'Ludgate Broadway (LBY85)', Finds Appraisal

Hill, J, 1986 'Excavations at 7 Ludgate Broadway (LBY85)', Archive Report

Holden, T, 1990 'Environmental appraisal report (ASS/01/90)', Archive Report

Smith, B, & Gilmour, B, 1986 'Lead content in glass', Archive Report

LSM85

P McCulloch
NGR: TQ 33740 81150
SMR: 044730–1

Little Somerset Street, E1

A trench for sewer- or waterworks revealed a grey silty or brickearth layer, sealed by an *opus signinum* floor. It was overlaid by a thick deposit of dark earth with modern make-up above.

LSS85

D Malt
NGR: TQ 33100 81700
SMR: 042900–5

Liverpool Street Station, Broad Street Station, EC2

A series of excavations, cutting and drawing of sections and inspections of testpits were in progress during 1985 on this large site, funded by Rosehaugh Stanhope plc. The earliest deposits comprised a stream-bed, one of the channels of the upper Walbrook, seen as a naturally eroded surface of sands and gravels occupying a shallow, broad channel running NE–SW across the site. Within this main channel were series of smaller stream channels interspersed with washouts of pea gravel and fine waterlaid silts. Brickearth and clay dumping during the Roman period on the E and W banks of the stream complement wooden revetments seen on other Walbrook sites to the S, implying control of the upper watercourse in the Roman period. Thereafter marsh and peat deposits up to 1.3m thick within the Walbrook Valley indicate part of the large marsh which accumulated in the area (later Moorfields) from the late Roman to the medieval period. A large 13th–14th-c N–S linear feature, probably a ditch, corresponds with a ditch shown on the copperplate map (c 1558) and one previously recorded nearer the city wall to the S. Wooden revetments running E–W were recorded near the assumed line of the precinct of St Mary Bethlem Hospital.

Excavations in the SW corner of the site were completed in April 1986. Excavation revealed considerable dumping over the marsh deposits and produced a section through the E bank of the Walbrook. The bank in this part of the site was constructed of compacted gravel, clay and building rubble. Tentative dating evidence from ceramic material places its construction to 180–230. Some 400 post-medieval burials were excavated from an area within the boundaries of the new churchyard, founded in 1569 by the City to relieve the congestion occurring in parish burial grounds. The burials were found in high density, some eight per cubic m. The cemetery was used up to at least 1720. Primary burials were mostly uncoffined but a large proportion of the later inhumations were coffined burials. A large brick vault contained six members of the Jenkes family, in lead coffins with highly decorated wooden inner coffins, dating from 1686 to 1714. Other finds included two Roman hipposandals and good groups of post-medieval pottery.

London Archaeol, 5, 1986, 160; *Britannia*, 17, 1986, 408; 18, 1987, 336; *Medieval Archaeol*, 30, 1986, 139; *Post-Medieval Archaeol*, 20, 1986, 333–4; 21, 1987, 267–8
Dyson, L, Malt, R, & Wellman, T, 1987 'Excavations at Broad Street Station (LSS85), Parts 1 and 2: the Walbrook and associated features', Archive Report
Gale, R, 1986 'The identification of wood from sites excavated by the DUA', AML Report 60/87
Malt, R, & White, W, 1987 'Excavations at Broad Street Station (LSS85), Part 3: the cemetery'
White, W, 1986 'The human skeletal remains from the Broadgate site LSS85 — some interim comments', Archive Report
White, W J, 1987 'The human skeletal remains from the Broadgate site (HUM 01/87)', Archive Report

NWG85

S Rivière
NGR: TQ 31820 81390
SMR: 040447

Newgate Street (south side), outside Central Criminal Court, EC1

A watching brief in a London Electricity Board trench uncovered the tops of three fragments of the S half of Newgate. A 2m length with a finished E face was constructed of chalk and ragstone and very heavily disturbed by later brick walls. The masonry can be fitted onto a plan of the known fragments of Roman and medieval Newgate, but the date of this fragment could not be established.

London Archaeol, 5, 1986, 160; *Medieval Archaeol*, 30, 1986, 139
Rivière, S, 1986 'Excavations at Newgate Street (NWG85)', Archive Report

St Margaret's Rectory, St Olave's Court, Ironmonger Lane, EC2

OLC85

E Shepherd
NGR: TQ 32540 81230
SMR: 043126–9

A watching brief and small excavation between October 1985 and June 1986 was funded by the Church Commissioners. In the SW corner of the site natural gravels were quarried in the mid-/later 1st c prior to a sequence of Roman clay and timber buildings. These apparently fronted onto a road running E–W to the S and had an external area to the N. A severe fire of 2nd-c date was indicated. A similar sequence was recorded over the rest of the site, although occupation was apparently less intensive towards the N.

Later deposits were truncated by the remains of the church of St Olave Jewry. At the S end of the site was a small church, its surviving fragments of nave measuring about 7.5m wide by 8m long, of 9th–11th-c date from constructional details such as use of Roman tiles for quoins. The church was enlarged and altered at various times in the medieval period, and was destroyed in the Great Fire of 1666. It was rebuilt in 1673–6 by Sir Christopher Wren; the tower survives.

London Archaeol, 5, 1987, 273; *Britannia*, 18, 1987, 335; *Medieval Archaeol*, 31, 1987, 129
Cowgill, J, 1987 'Saint Olave's Court (OLC85)', Finds Appraisal
Schofield, J, 1994 'Saxon and medieval parish churches in the City of London: a review', *Trans London Middlesex Archaeol Soc*, 45, 125
Shepherd, L, nd, 'Excavations at St Olave's Court (OLC85)', Archive Report, draft
Shepherd, L, 1987 'The Saxon church at St Margaret's Rectory', *Archaeol Today*, 8, 23–5

1–3 St Paul's Churchyard, 1–9 Ludgate Hill, 15 Creed Lane, 40 Carter Lane, EC4

PCH85

B Pye
NGR: TQ 31880 81105
SMR: 043246–52

During June–December 1985, a six-week excavation inside upstanding buildings, followed by a watching brief during demolition and groundworks, funded by UK Providence, was carried out on this large site. The excavation consisted of two areas. In the NW of the site, fronting onto Ludgate Hill (Area A), the truncated natural ground surface was directly beneath the concrete floor slab. However, above the slumped late 1st-c backfill of a quarry pit was a much altered Roman timber post and clay sill constructed building of the early 2nd c. This was destroyed in the Hadrianic period (although there was no evidence of it being burnt down) and replaced by a building of similar construction in the mid-2nd c which was covered by a dump of 3rd-c date. Other features recorded in this area include Late Saxon–post-medieval pits and a 17th-c brick-lined well. Fronting onto Creed Lane was the second area of excavation (B). Here the natural ground surface had been covered by a redeposited brickearth slab before a timber post and clay sill building was constructed in the late 1st c. This building was aligned N–S with a gravel yard to the S. It appeared to have been burnt down and replaced by a building of similar construction in the early 2nd c. When this building went out of use it was covered by a dump of 3rd-c material.

In the watching brief the major feature recorded was a large ditch about 5m deep and at least 15m wide (truncated to the E), running N–S from the St Paul's churchyard frontage. It cut into a late 1st-c quarry and was backfilled with Roman and medieval material. Other features recorded by section drawings include parts of Roman timber buildings with associated gravel yards and a small E–W running lane, and large pits of medieval–19th-c date. In the S part of the site, fronting onto Carter Lane, deep 19th-c basements had destroyed all archaeological deposits with the exception of pits.

Britannia, 17, 1986, 405; *Medieval Archaeol*, 30, 1986, 139
Grew, F, 1986 'St Paul's churchyard (PCH85)', Finds Appraisal
Pye, B, nd, 'Excavations at St Paul's churchyard (PCH85), Groups 12–40', Archive Report, draft

PLM85

P Durnford
NGR: TQ 31540 81490
SMR: 043103–6

7–8 Plumtree Court, 26–30 Holborn Viaduct, 54–55 Farringdon Street, EC1

Evidence ranging in date from the medieval to the post-medieval period was recorded on the site. The absence of finds and structures from the Roman period was marked. No Roman pottery was recovered and there was no sign of gravels or metalling which might be interpreted as the Roman road suspected in the NW corner. The medieval remains consisted of several wall fragments and one or two cut features associated with medieval pottery. Post-medieval structures in the form of walls, drains, floors and vaults were also recorded. In addition, the building-lines of pre-Viaduct structures were clearly seen on the W site of the site, along with associated drains running down to the N. Traces of a timber structure were recorded on the N edge of the site which also appeared to be post-medieval in date. A wide strip of greenish organic material was observed, running N–S down from the NE corner, and may be part of the original course of the River Fleet. Organic deposits were also seen in one section of a machine cut in the extreme SE corner, but no trace of timber revetments was recorded.

London Archaeol, 5, 1987, 273; Medieval Archaeol, 31, 1987, 128; notes by P Durnford in archive
Cowgill, J, 1987 '26–30 Holborn Viaduct/7–8 Plumtree Court PLM85', Finds Appraisal

QUN85

M Burch
NGR: TQ 32455 80845
SMR: 044539–45

61 Queen Street, EC4

Excavation here, funded by Greycoat Estates, was inside a building constructed in 1957 (for the excavation observed then, see GM155 above). A N–S trench 10m x 7m was excavated. The S edge of the trench was approximately 10m N of the 1st–2nd-c Roman waterfront structures recorded nearby in 1978 (see TST78 above).

Natural brickearth sloped down to the S with a marked (manmade?) step in the S third of the trench. Dumps raised the ground surface, and cut into these was a timber-lined pit 1m square and surviving 1.3m deep. It was subsequently filled with mixed silts and building material of late 2nd-c date. N of the pit was a building with a masonry foundation. The main Roman period of occupation then followed: a large terrace wall to the S, at least 5.6m E–W, with a protruding pier base of courses of tile at the E end. A similar pier had been recorded in 1957, 1.8m to the W. N of this was a second building, also on stone foundations. The small amount of dating evidence suggests a 3rd-c date. Later dump layers indicating decay included 15 examples of tiles stamped PP BR LON or variations; none was found in the surviving structure of the building.

In the N third of the trench was a sunken building cut into the Roman levels, and itself dated to 1000–1150. Part of the S wall and the SW corner were recorded. There was also one pit of 11th- or early 12th-c date. The church of St Martin Vintry, recorded in 1957, now lies largely under the N carriageway of Upper Thames Street, but the present site included the edge of the N graveyard. Eight badly disturbed graves were recorded, and one footing of probably early medieval date. Post-medieval brick foundations also crossed the site.

Perring (1991) has suggested that this building is a warehouse, but the presence of tesserae, painted wall plaster and hypocaust box-flue tile in a dump of debris over the building indicates a residential use.

Britannia, 18, 1987, 335; Medieval Archaeol, 31, 1987, 129
Betts, I M, 1995 'Procuratorial tile stamps from London', *Britannia, 26,* 219
Burch, M, 1987 'Roman and medieval occupation in Queen Street', *Archaeol Today, 8,* 9–12
Cowgill, J, 1986 'Queen Street (QUN85)', Finds Appraisal
Perring, D, 1991 *Roman London,* 98

167–179 Queen Victoria Street, EC4

QVS85

K Steedman
NGR: TQ 31670 80880
SMR: 042894–9

At the confluence of the Fleet and Thames in the late 13th or early 14th c, a substantial E–W wall was erected on the foreshore. Either during or shortly after the construction of this wall large amounts of mixed deposits were dumped behind it to reclaim the land. Stairs were probably constructed to the top of the wall from the new ground level. At the front of the wall, beaches of compacted gravel were deliberately laid, presumably to facilitate the beaching or mooring of boats, and several mooring timbers were found. This deposition began soon after or during the construction of the wall, and continued up until the first half of the 17th c when a set of wooden stairs was constructed from the top of the wall down to the foreshore. During this period, the area to the N of the wall yielded only traces of dumping and possible external activity from the 14th and 15th c. The stairs to the S of the wall appear to have had a relatively short life. They were dismantled and riverlain deposits sealed them. The foreshore area appears to have been used less intensively after this and the area was itself reclaimed in the second half of the 17th c, probably as part of the general redevelopment of this part of the City following the Great Fire of London in 1666. A sequence of brick cellars was constructed on this reclaimed land and use of the latest one dates from the mid- to late 18th c. To the N of the wall the earlier dumping was sealed by, and perhaps partly truncated by, activity associated with a setting for probable ladder access to the wall. This, and the layers which sealed it, were of 18th-c date. A brick cellar of uncertain date postdated them. Modern activity truncated the sequence on both sides of the wall.

London Archaeol, 5, 1986, 161; Medieval Archaeol, 30, 1986, 139
Dunn, G, 1985 'Queen Victoria Street (QVS85)', Finds Appraisal
Juggins, S, 1985 'Diatom analysis of foreshore deposits exposed during the Queen Victoria Street excavations: methods and preliminary results (DIA/01/85)', Archive Report
Steedman, K, 1985 'Excavations at 167–179 Queen Victoria Street', Archive Report
Vince, A, 1985 'The medieval and post-medieval pottery from Queen Victoria Street 1985', Archive Report

St Martin's le Grand, junction with Newgate Street, EC2

SMN85

C Harding
NGR: TQ 32120 81290
SMR: 044732

Human bones in the spoil from the NE end of a gas trench were noted; they were disarticulated, mainly long bones and were considered to be redeposited.

Mansion House, Poultry, EC4

SON85

D Bentley
NGR: TQ 32673 81080
SMR: 083241–5

A watching brief was carried out during August 1985 within trial trenches beneath the Mansion House. Natural gravels sloped down to the W, into the Walbrook Valley. On the E side seven metalled surfaces representing a yard or street were sealed by late Roman debris. This dump was overlaid by a chalk-mortar make-up which may have been associated with St Mary Woolchurch Haw which occupied part of the site in the medieval period. Further down the hill to the W a large accumulation of alluvial deposits overlay the natural gravels, containing undated industrial and domestic rubbish. These waterlogged levels were sealed by substantial clayey dumps. A Roman masonry structure in the immediate area is inferred from large fragments of semi-articulated building debris, which appeared to have collapsed or have been dumped over the sealing layers. This material may have derived from a Roman building recorded only 3m to the S during earlier underpinning work in 1917. There was no dating associated with this material.

London Archaeol, 5, 1986, 160; Britannia, 17, 1986, 408
Bentley, D, 1985 'Mansion House (SON85)', Archive Report
Groves, J, 1989 'Mansion House', Roman Pottery Appraisal
Robinson, J, 1989 'Mansion House', Post-Roman Pottery Appraisal

STW85

A Westman
NGR: TQ 32645 81026
SMR: 043253–4

St Stephen Walbrook church, Walbrook, EC4

Groundworks during partial underpinning and refurbishment of the church of St Stephen Walbrook were monitored in March–April 1985 by arrangement with the architects, Brandt Potter and Partners. Inside the church, beneath the floor, only brick burial vaults and brick rubble were observed. Outside, the chalk foundations of the medieval church were recorded up to 1.5m E of the E face of the foundations and superstructure built by Wren.

London Archaeol, 5, 1986, 161; *Medieval Archaeol*, 30, 1986, 139; *Post-Medieval Archaeol*, 20, 1986, 334

ABS86

P Chitwood and J Hill
NGR: TQ 32280 81500
SMR: 043117–24

St Alban's House, 124 Wood Street, EC2

Following the demolition of a post-War office building an archaeological investigation of the site between April and July 1986, sponsored by Eagle Star Insurance, recorded 3–5m of stratigraphy in two discrete areas, separated by a double basement.

In the E site an area of 300sq m (Area A) was excavated. Natural was immediately overlaid by 1st-c structures. Following destruction by fire, and extensive quarrying, these buildings were replaced by a sequence including an *opus signinum* floored cellar associating with clay and timber wall-lines. Much of the area would appear to have been external with only the backs of buildings lying to the S intruding into the area of excavation.

Some later 2nd-c surfaces survived, slumped over pitfills, but generally mid-2nd-c Roman deposits were sealed by dark organic dumps and a large concentration of pits. A substantial quarry pit containing 11th-/12th-c pottery and a bone trial piece was sealed by a ragstone foundation that still observed the Roman alignment. This was in turn cut by a 12th-c foundation which ran at right angles to Wood Street and disregarded Roman alignments. Some surfaces associated with this later foundation were recorded to its S. To the NE, medieval timber structures with patchy floorings were encountered.

To the W of the double basement an area of 75sq m was excavated (Area X), and a similar area recorded in section (Area B). Over natural, which was encountered at a level about 0.5m higher than on the E area, dumps and substantial pits analogous to the early activity in Area A were sealed by make-ups and surfaces, one of which was tessellated, associated with a ragstone dwarf wall. A substantial portion of the scorched and collapsed timber and clay superstructures of the wall was recorded *in situ*. Associated pottery suggested a 2nd-c date. Later Roman and medieval horizontal stratigraphy was destroyed by extensive pit digging.

London Archaeol, 5, 1987, 273; *Britannia*, 18, 1987, 335; *Medieval Archaeol*, 31, 1987, 129
Chitwood, P, 1987 'Excavations at St Alban's House, 125 Wood Street, EC2 (ABS86)', Archive Report
Chitwood, P, & Hill, J, 1987 'Excavations at St Alban's House Wood Street', *Archaeol Today*, 8, 13–16
Cowgill, J, 1987 'St Alban's House', Finds Appraisal
Crowley, N, 1989 'St Alban's House Wood Street', Building Materials Appraisal

APG86

A Westman
NGR: TQ 32440 81620
SMR: 040485

The city wall at St Alphage Garden, 4 Fore Street, 4–10 Alphage High Walk, EC2

An archaeological examination of part of the NW sector of the city wall at St Alphage Garden EC2, formerly London Wall, was undertaken in March and September 1986 for the Corporation of London. This work included photogrammetry by the Department of Civil Engineering of the City University. The earliest elements were identified as two phases of Roman defences: the inner face of the N wall of the 2nd-c fort, reinforced when this wall was incorporated in the defensive circuit built around the Roman city c AD200.

The dilapidated defences were then partly refaced to the N. This coarse refacing was slightly out of alignment with both the existing and subsequent defences and may have been associated with the foundation on the city wall of the church of St Alphage, probably in the 11th c. The N wall of the church was rebuilt decoratively in the late 14th c. The adjoining city wall was reconstructed at least twice, culminating in brick crenellations, dated to 1477 by documentary evidence. The church was dismantled in 1535–6, when the dedication was transferred to a larger building to the SE. Remaining masonry was partly incorporated in walls of adjacent premises and was exposed and consolidated in 1951–3.

London Archaeol, 5, 1987, 273; Britannia, 18, 1987, 336; Medieval Archaeol, 31, 1987, 129
Schofield, J, 1994 'Saxon and medieval parish churches in the City of London: a review', Trans London Middlesex Archaeol Soc, 45, 92
Westman, A, 1986 'Excavations at St Alphage Wall (APG86)', Archive Report
Westman, A, 1987a 'Archaeological examination of a standing monument at St Alphage Garden', Archive Report
Westman, A, 1987b 'The church of St Alphage', Archaeol Today, 8, 17–22

St Mary Axe House, 56–60 St Mary Axe, 1–3 Goring Street, EC3

AXE86

C Maloney
NGR: TQ 33360 81340
SMR: 041939

One section was recorded at the E end of the site after the walls of a basement had been removed. It revealed a thick band of mortar and ragstone fragments together with chalk, *opus signinum* and tile fragments. This is identified as the NW extremities of Bastion 9, or possibly material associated with the destruction of Bastion 9, since it was sealed by 16th-c deposits.

London Archaeol, 5, 1987, 273; Britannia, 18, 1987, 336
Cowgill, J, 1987 '56–60 St Mary Axe AXE86', Finds Appraisal

Beaufort House, 29–55 Middlesex Street, 15 St Botolph Street, E1

BFT86

I Blair
NGR: TQ 33630 81330
SMR: 044464–5,
044481–2, 044452

Natural gravels and gravelly brickearth were overlaid by clayey and silty marsh deposits, probably of Roman and early medieval date. Widespread and thick deposits resembling garden soil probably represented the Great Garden of Holy Trinity Priory which was located here from the 13th c. Above this lay soil and building debris of post-medieval date, probably indicating a change of land use after the Dissolution. This property passed into the possession of the De Vere family, earls of Oxford, and two substantial buildings are documented from the early 17th c onwards. The remains of a brick-lined well and cellars or wall foundations of brick and chalk were all that was observed for this period, succeeded by the foundations of the modern building.

BHO86

B Pye
NGR: TQ 31890 80970
SMR: 043953–6

Bible House, 146 Queen Victoria Street, EC4

A six-week excavation in November–December 1986 was followed by an intermittent watching brief during May–August 1987. Although all horizontal stratigraphy had been terraced away in the 1860s during construction of Queen Victoria Street, some cut features were recorded. The most important feature ran the entire length of the site N–S, 10.5m wide E–W and 2m deep. It was filled with a series of waterlaid silts; pottery from them has been provisionally dated to 1000–1100. This cut would appear to be a drainage ditch running S to the Thames.

Other features recorded on site included medieval, post-medieval and Victorian wells, Roman rubbish pits and the foundations of St Andrew by the Wardrobe church to the immediate W of the site.

Anon, nd, 'Bible House, Queen Victoria Street', Finds Appraisal
Hunting, P, nd [1990] *Archaeology and development* (Speyhawk and MoL), 59–60
Pye, B, 1988 'Excavations at Bible House, 146 Queen Victoria Street (BHO86)', Archive Report

BLA86

I Blair
NGR: TQ 33030 80755
SMR: 044733–4

36–38 Botolph Lane, EC3

Pits, probably medieval and post-medieval in date, were observed below the basement slab. They included chalk-walled and one brick-lined cesspits; other chalk walls were also noted.

BOT86

C Maloney
NGR: TQ 33590 81230
SMR: 043125

St Botolph Aldgate church, Aldgate High Street, EC3

During a watching brief in June and July 1986 — for which access was granted by the Parish Council of St Botolph, Aldgate — excavations alongside the eastern boundary wall of the churchyard revealed that this was built on an earlier stone wall. It was composed of coursed limestone and yellow sandstone blocks on a foundation of sandstone and chalk. Above a moulded string course, the face of the wall had been set back. At least 11m of its length and 1.1m of its height survive. Although all deposits relating to the wall had been destroyed, it can be dated to the 15th c and is identified as the W wall of the Crowne Inn, a property dating back to the 12th c; the wall is shown on the survey of 1610 by Ralph Treswell.

London Archaeol, 5, 1987, 273; *Medieval Archaeol*, 31, 1987, 129
Maloney, C, 1988 'Watching brief at St Botolph's churchyard E1', Archive Report
Schofield, J, 1995 *Medieval London houses*, 157–8 [Treswell's survey of the Crowne]

BOY86

C Spence
NGR: TQ 31540 80920
SMR: 043988–94

Former City of London Boys' School, 60 Victoria Embankment, 5–17 Tudor Street, EC4

Between October 1986 and February 1987 excavations were undertaken within the playground of the school, funded by the Morgan Bank. Natural deposits across the site consisted of alluvial deposits, one of which contained a number of eroded tile and pottery fragments of Roman date. The earliest well-dated material (12th c) was recorded at the N end of the site; this was composed of a series of dumps and naturally accumulated flood deposits. A gravel bank which ran from the NE to SW probably represents the confluence of the Fleet River and the Thames at this period.

In the main trench the earliest structural activity was dated to the mid-14th c. This was composed of a massive reclamation dump, associated with a Thames riverside wall constructed in chalk and built on the contemporary foreshore. The construction of the wall was aided by the digging of a shallow foundation trench which was shored with a large wattle fence. The dumping and the wall construction were contemporary in date. The reclamation activity extended the Thames waterfront towards the S by about 50m.

Sporadic features recorded on the top of the dumped deposits were sealed by a fire horizon of late 17th-c date, probably the Great Fire. The area to the S of the site appeared to have been reclaimed around this period with a timber revetment recorded at the S limit of excavation. This revetment and associated reclamation is thought to represent the construction of the new quays during the post-Fire rebuilding of this area of the waterfront. The area behind the revetment was reclaimed and consolidated by the driving of more than 700 timber piles. The timbers, when examined, were identified as being reused and were considered to have been originally derived from one or more 17th-/18th-c vessels. Many of the timbers were painted and several were moulded.

On the reclaimed land a series of post-medieval brick walls, foundations and cellar floors was recorded. One later cellar floor included a series of three brick-built (baking?) oven bases. During the early 19th c the City Gas Works was constructed on the site, and several structures associated with the gasworks were recorded. Completing the sequence was a forgotten Second World War public air-raid shelter.

Waterfront dumps produced several important groups of medieval organic material. The shoes and pattens from the site are an important addition to the collection of medieval footwear from London. One of the shoes was stuffed with seeds of *cannabis sativa*. A number of scabbards, a glove and some highly decorated fragments from unidentified leather objects were also recovered. Copper-alloy material appears to come from a later medieval workshop, including a copper-alloy coil and a rod, which may be the forms in which the metal was traded in the medieval period. An important find relating to this was a pilgrim's badge of St Eloi, the patron saint of smiths and other metalworkers. Pottery includes some late medieval imports, from Spain and the Southern Netherlands.

London Archaeol, 5, 1988, 387; *Medieval Archaeol*, 32, 1988, 249–50

Clark, J (ed), 1995 *The medieval horse and its equipment c 1150–c 1450*, Medieval finds from excavations in London 5 [medieval horse shoes and horse equipment]

Goodburn, D, 1991 'New light on early ship- and boatbuilding in the London area', in Good, G L, Jones, R H, & Ponsford, M W (eds), *Waterfront archaeology: proceedings of the third international conference, Bristol, 1988*, CBA Res Rep 74, 105–15 [ships' timbers]

Hunting, P, nd [1990] *Archaeology and development* (Speyhawk and MoL), 39–47

Keys, L, 1988 'Finds appraisal for City of London Boys' school controlled excavation (BOY86)', Finds Appraisal

Schofield, J, 1995 *Medieval London houses*, 183

Spence, C (ed), 1989 *Digging in the City: the annual review 1988* (DUA, MoL), 28–9

Spence, C, 1990 'Excavations at the former City of London Boys' School and former Guildhall School of Music and Drama, 60 Victoria Embankment, 5–17 Tudor Street (BOY86)', Archive Report

Spencer, B, in prep. *Pilgrim souvenirs and secular badges*, Medieval finds from excavations in London 7

Tyers, I, 1988 'Dendrochronological spot date report: interim report (SPT/16/88)', Archive Report

8–14 Brushfield Street, E1

BUS86

C Maloney and
C Sparey-Green
NGR: TQ 33410 81740
SMR: 044546–8

Natural brickearth was overlaid by a dump of clay dated to the late Roman period, followed by more dumping in the late 14th c and in the late 17th–early 18th c. This was capped by the York stone basement floor of the standing building.

Cowgill, J, 1987 '8–14 Brushfield Street BUS86', Finds Appraisal

CAP86

I Blair
NGR: TQ 33040 81500
SMR: 041907, 041923

Capel House, 54–62 New Broad Street, EC2

During a ten-week period between January and March 1986, a total of seven N–S trenches were excavated across the line of the city ditches. The work was generously funded by Haslemere Estates. The earliest features, which were cut into natural gravels, comprised a series of predominantly E–W stream and drainage channels running W towards the Walbrook. Following their natural silting and consolidation during the 2nd c, the ground level was raised across the N half of the site by upwards of 1.2m, with the large-scale dumping of mainly gravel-based make-ups. Running parallel to, and lying 6m from, the external face of the city wall (which formed the S boundary of the site) were the truncated remains of the associated early 3rd-c V-cut defensive ditch. Cut into its berm was a solitary grave of Roman date.

During the 12th c, the ground level was raised by a further 1.5m. The absence of any clear sign of a medieval ditch cut and the presence, instead, of a series of substantial dumped make-ups (which were waterlogged at the time of deposition) suggest that the marshy area around Moorfields precluded the cutting of a ditch during this period. It therefore seems likely that an artificial N bank was raised in order to delineate the line of the outer defensive circuit.

In the 16th c, a massive city ditch (which survived to a depth of 2m and extended E–W across the entire site) was cut into the reclamation dumps. The ditch was relatively short lived and was backfilled by the middle of the 17th c; the fill contained a fine 16th-c intaglio ring. Following its consolidation, a series of linear E–W horncore-filled land drains was cut into its uppermost fills. A large assemblage of 17th-c pottery included a range of delftware, Saintonge ware, bellarmines and other imported wares. The later encroachment of properties across the N edge of the ditch during the 18th c was indicated by a group of brick-lined wells and drains.

London Archaeol, 5, 1987, 272–3; *Medieval Archaeol*, 31, 1987, 128
Blair, I, 1987 'Excavations at 54–62 New Broad Street (CAP86)', Archive Report
Henig, M, 1986a 'An intaglio ring from the city ditch London', Archive Report
Henig, M, 1986b 'An intaglio ring from the city ditch', *London Archaeol*, 5, 192

CAT86

B Watson
NGR: TQ 31823 81087
SMR: 043013, 043019–20

52–54 Carter Lane, EC4

The excavation, sponsored by Waterglade International Holdings Ltd, took place in September and October. The N side of a large, truncated, ditch (2.6m deep) aligned NW to SE, on the same alignment as the oblique northern boundary of 52 and 54/56 Carter Lane, was recorded. It can be estimated from testpits on the adjoining properties (see PAL86 below) that the ditch is about 13m wide. The finds from the primary backfill of the ditch suggest it is of early medieval date and possibly, from its location, part of the defences of Montfichet's Tower. The S part of the site was occupied by the foundations of a later 17th-c building, fronting onto Carter Lane. An internal part of this building was a small, rectangular, brick-built ice-house, with a vaulted roof.

London Archaeol, 5, 1987, 270–1; *Medieval Archaeol*, 31, 1987, 126
Watson, B, 1992 'The excavation of a Norman fortress on Ludgate Hill', *London Archaeol*, 6, 371–7

CFA86

D Bentley
NGR: TQ 31910 81707
SMR: 043923

43–44 Cloth Fair, 8 Cloth Court, EC1

A watching brief was carried out during the refurbishment of this pair of late 18th-c houses in June 1986. The internal timber structure supported by an outer brick wall showed no evidence for reuse of materials and no trace of *in situ* decorative features. The plans and elevations were similar and in both instances chimneys and staircases were located against flanking walls. Basement fireplaces were marked by modern blocking although in one instance a series of finely chamfered limestone fragments was used which must have derived from a grander structure, as must an unusually decorated block of Caen stone retrieved from the basement floor make-up, attributed on stylistic grounds to the 17th c.

London Archaeol, 5, 1988, 383

62–64 Cornhill, EC3

CIL86

F M Meddens
NGR: TQ 31910 81790
SMR: 043685–90

Archaeological investigations were carried out between February and May 1986, funded by Greycoat Group plc. Of the five trenches opened up, three revealed up to 4m of stratigraphy.

The site was situated near the intersection of the N–S Roman road along present-day Bishopsgate with the Roman road passing E–W along the N side of the second basilica complex, roughly across the present Cornhill. No remains of either of these roads were uncovered. A large quarry had been dug in order to extract both brickearth and gravel. It appears likely to have been located in an open yard area.

The heavily truncated remains of several mudbrick structures were located. The robbed foundations of a number of stone buildings were present; in one area, three phases of stone construction appear to have been robbed in the Roman period. The last of these consisted of a building with an apsidal end, which would have fronted onto the main N–S road.

Elsewhere what may have been a broken crucible with quantities of liquid mercury rested on a hearth set on a floor which was sealed by a dump of Roman date. Where the Roman deposits were not truncated by later developments they were sealed by a mixed layer of what appeared to be garden soil and destruction rubble. This suggests that in the immediate post-Roman period the site was abandoned.

When the site was occupied again the evidence suggests an open area, possibly at the back of properties or in a courtyard space, primarily employed for rubbish disposal from early medieval times to the 16th c. It appears that from the 16th or 17th c to the late 19th/early 20th c buildings occupied the site, of which basement and cellar remains were uncovered. Fragments from two Roman Purbeck marble mortars, several medieval hone-stones and a quantity of post-medieval glass which included both bottles and phials were recovered.

Meddens, F, 1987 'Excavations at 62 Cornhill EC3', Archive Report

16 Coleman Street, EC2

COA86

C Spence
NGR: TQ 32590 81470
SMR: 043027–31

During February 1986 a watching brief was undertaken during groundworks. Natural gravel was truncated over the whole site; however, a number of pits were recorded. The earliest were rubbish pits of early 2nd-c date. In the NE corner of the site was a square wooden structure set within a pit, with an external clay packing. This was backfilled in the 3rd c and was later disturbed by a mid-4th-c NW–SE gully. Further pits of the 11th–17th c were recorded. A possible post-medieval cellar sequence was recorded at the E site limit.

London Archaeol, 5, 1986, 271; Britannia, 18, 1987, 335; Medieval Archaeol, 31, 1987, 127
Cowgill, J, 1987 'Coleman Street COA86', Finds Appraisal
Spence, C, 1986 'Excavations at 16 Coleman Street EC2', Archive Report

76 Cannon Street, EC4

CON86

A Stephenson
NGR: TQ 32570 80915
SMR: 042990–4

An excavation about 2.5m square, funded by Peachey Properties, took place during September–November 1986. The earliest deposits were of the stream-bed of the lower Walbrook. In the 1st c the E bank was consolidated with a N–S aligned revetment. Land to the W was subsequently reclaimed by further piling and dumping of organic material and brickearth to receive three successive Roman buildings, associated with glass- and ironworking. A 4th-c timber box-well cut the last of these and the 3m of Roman stratification were sealed by 0.5m of dark earth filled pits. A large group of mid–late 4th-c pottery was recovered.

London Archaeol, 5, 1987, 270; Britannia, 18, 1987, 336; Medieval Archaeol, 31, 1987, 127
Oakley, N, nd, 'Finds appraisal for 76 Cannon Street', Finds Appraisal
Stephenson, A, 1987 'Excavations at 76 Cannon Street', Archive Report

CRU86

A B Thomas
NGR: TQ 33550 80954
SMR: 041051, 043924–31

9–13 Crutched Friars, 1–7 Crosswall, EC3

Between December 1986 and March 1987 excavations funded by Hartstreet Properties Ltd were carried out at 9–13 Crutched Friars which is just inside the line of the Roman city wall.

Excavations suggested that the earliest activity on site was related to the construction of the defensive wall of c 200. The area appears to have been levelled by dumps and later sealed by a roughly N–S aligned compacted mixed mortar/gravel surface. To the E a small section of surviving Roman wall revealed in the main property boundary of the site gave clear indications that the gravel/mortar surface was constructed after the lower courses of the wall. Above this surface the internal bank survived to a height of approximately 1.4–1.5m, and a width of 8.5m. The bank was constructed using alternate dumps of brickearth/gravels, the tip-lines of which suggested that the dumping sequence was from S to N; the bank tended to slope down from E to W. Apart from the defensive wall and bank there was little late Roman activity noted on site.

By the medieval period the area of the bank was being encroached upon by a large N–S aligned foundation, possibly for a stone building to the W. To the E of this building a series of N–S aligned timber post-holes showed a possible lean-to structure or covered area between the building and the defensive wall. Once this timber structure went out of use, a N–S aligned yellow tile pathway was laid down between the building and the wall. During the post-medieval period the yellow tile path was incorporated into a larger cobblestone surface which covered most of the excavated area. By this period it is possible that the defensive wall had been demolished, for mixed in with the cobbled surface were stone fragments similar to those noted in the Roman wall construction.

Later a large N–S aligned brick wall crossed the site. This building had internal rooms to the W, but still incorporated the yellow tile path and its cobblestone surrounds to the E.

Thomas, T, nd, 'Excavations at 9–13 Crutched Friars/1–7 Crosswall EC3', Archive Report

CTN86

D Bentley
NGR: TQ 32040 81880
SMR: 043021–6

10–13 Carthusian Street, EC1

A watching brief was carried out here during July 1986. The site produced evidence of 13th-c occupation and lies 450m N of the city wall at Aldersgate demonstrating the extent to which London's suburbs had already grown by this period. The earliest identified activity was a deposit of heavily pitted early medieval agricultural or garden soil over which a large building provisionally of 13th-c date was erected with walls founded on arches of chalk and flint. This building was extended with the construction of shallow foundations extending 6m to the W whose associated chalk-lined pits and a well were found. The well was partially rebuilt using carved medieval stonework which may have come from the chalk-founded building.

During the 16th c a replacement brick building was erected but used the earlier foundations and followed the same property boundaries. It too underwent development and extension to the W over what had become a large metalled yard. The content of the associated rubbish pits produced large quantities of wine jars, bottles, cups and plates and reinforces the 17th-c documentary evidence that shows this to be the site of the Red Lion Inn which fronted onto Aldersgate Street 20m to the E.

London Archaeol, 5, 1987, 271; Medieval Archaeol, 31, 1987, 127
Cowgill, J, 1987 '10–13 Carthusian Street CTN86', Finds Appraisal

CUE86

S Cole
NGR: TQ 33410 81420
SMR: 043932–3

9–10 Cutler Street, E1

A watching brief of October 1986–January 1897 revealed one crushed chalk inhumation, not datable, cut into natural brickearth together with evidence of others disturbed by modern building works. Testpits and ground reduction showed extensive post-medieval pits sealed by a brick floor and foundations for the standing building.

Dowgate Hill House, 14–16 Dowgate Hill, EC4

DGH86

M Shea
NGR: TQ 32540 80815
SMR: 043938–46

A watching brief was conducted on site from the beginning of November 1986 until early February 1987 to oversee piling operations at Dowgate Hill House. A reasonably detailed survey of approximately 140 pile-borings was undertaken. This provided site-wide topographical information on the levels of the natural clay and subsequent siltings, as well as a three-dimensional record of the position of the site. This latter operation included the retrieval of about 50 samples for dendrochronological purposes.

From late January to late March 1987, excavations, sponsored by London and Edinburgh Trust, were conducted in the NE area of Dowgate Hill House in the proposed lift-shaft, approximately 8.5m x 5.5m x 5m. A natural streamlet or manmade channel cut through the N portion of the site, diagonally NE–SW. After this watercourse had filled with successive sand and gravel deposits, probably in the early Roman period, the ground was terraced into a slightly sloping surface to allow construction to commence. A large E–W clay-bank (possibly with timber lacing) was thrown up with a timber-piled channel running along its N flank; the latter construction was superseded by a NE–SW aligned drainage-channel, just S of it, when the earlier channel had fallen into disuse.

This apparent Thames embankment, with successive drainage-channels running along its N flank, later fell into disrepair and was bisected by a large erosion cutting, running diagonally (NE–SE) through the bank. Following this, the site was completely sealed by a thick horizon of waterlaid material; and the area witnessed the dumping of approximately 2m+ of material, probably within a relatively short period of time (late 3rd–early 4th c). This substantial dumping activity, very probably land reclamation, produced an exceptional collection of artefacts (even by Walbrook standards), including late Roman ceramic types. This apparent later Roman land reclamation could conceivably be associated with major public works in this area of the mouth of the Walbrook.

Subsequent activity was represented by several cut features which may originally have been masonry walls for building(s) running E–W across the site, and one circular-shaped group of cluster-piles which probably served as footing for an arched foundation. Environmental column samples were taken through the stratification to complement the archaeological data.

Following the excavations, a second watching brief was carried out on site between late April and the end of May 1987. This oversaw the reduction of the site to make way for pile-caps and the lift-shaft of new British Telecom offices. The work largely entailed the recording of numerous sections of chalk and ragstone walls, often resting on timber piles and/or chocks, very likely representing medieval tenement buildings, along the N side of the precursor of modern-day Upper Thames Street.

The excavations produced a large assemblage of finds dating to the late Roman period. The majority of the material was recovered from dumping horizons. A large proportion of the pottery from the dumps dates from the late 3rd to early 4th c. Oxfordshire, Colchester and Nene Valley wares are present, along with sherds of late Roman glazed ware thought to be of an eastern Mediterranean or Italian origin. Several crucible fragments of oxidised ware were also recovered. Of the 177 Roman coins found during excavations, 82% were recovered from the dumping levels. All the coins which have so far been identified date to the late 3rd c. The site also produced over 100 leather shoes and sandals, also of later 3rd-c date. This assemblage is particularly important as it provides evidence for the continued use of one-piece shoes into the 3rd c, a style which was previously thought to have gone out of fashion by the end of the 2nd c. As well as nailed shoes and evidence for shoemaking there is a unique example of the upper strapwork of a sandal. Other Roman finds include bone and jet pins and shale bracelets. Metalwork includes knives, locks, finger-rings, a stylus and fragments of a lead dish or platter.

Brigham, T, 1990 'The late Roman waterfront in London', *Britannia*, 21, 99–183

Davies, B, 1987 'Dowgate Hill (DGH86)', Roman Pottery Appraisal

Keily, J, 1987 'Dowgate Hill House', Finds Appraisal

Shea, M, 1987 'Excavations at 14–16 Dowgate Hill/Upper Thames Street/Dowgate Hill House EC4', Archive Report

Symonds, R P, & Tomber, R S, with Lakin, D, & Richardson, B, 1991 'Late Roman London: an assessment of the ceramic evidence from the City of London', *Trans London Middlesex Archaeol Soc*, 42, 59–100

Tyers, I, 1988 'Dendrochronological spot date report: interim report (SPT/02/88)', Archive Report

DOW86

C Maloney, L Shepherd and A Stephenson
NGR: TQ 32560 80885
SMR: 043032–4

3–7 Dowgate Hill, EC4

A watching brief (by C Maloney) in a number of exploratory pits prior to refurbishment by Taylor Woodrow took place in February–March 1986. They revealed internal rooms of a heated Roman building. In one pit a tessellated floor was recorded, associated with a wall rendered with *opus signinum* and faced with thin slabs of Purbeck marble. In a pit nearby, the internal corner of a room with a hypocaust system was located. Two walls survived up to 2.45m in height, composed of tile rendered with *opus signinum,* the bottom of the wall being lined with vertically set tiles. It was constructed on a concrete floor onto which *pilae* had been set and above which lay another concrete floor. In other pits a collapsed tile wall, ragstone walls and concrete floors were recorded.

Excavation of a trench (by L Shepherd and A Stephenson) subsequently revealed a very large N–S wall whose ragstone foundation was set deeply into the natural brickearth and gravels in a series of offsets stepped in to the W. It was roughly rendered on its E side. Above the foundation was a wall constructed of roof tiles and roof tile fragments. This may have been a retaining wall, probably for the room with the hypocaust system.

London Archaeol, 5, 1987, 271; *Britannia,* 18, 1987, 336

FRD86

P Durnford
NGR: TQ 31650 81320
SMR: 043035–7

17–21 Farringdon Street, EC4

Finds of the Roman, medieval and post-medieval periods testify to the continuing interest shown in this valley site from an early period. Although a number of possibly medieval timbers and wall fragments were observed and plotted, only tentative building-lines can be suggested. The earlier course of the River Fleet may have been further to the E, hence the presence of typical waterfront dumps and possible revetment features in the W of the site. Brick floor and wall fragments, together with several portions of post-medieval drain or pitfill from 17th-c contexts were also recorded. A drain or channel may formerly have existed in the centre of the site, feeding down the Fleet.

London Archaeol, 5, 1987, 271; *Medieval Archaeol,* 31, 1987, 127; notes by P Durnford in the archive

GTO86

C Maloney
NGR: TQ 32440 80940
SMR: 044735–6

Great St Thomas Apostle (north side), junction with Queen Street, EC4

In this trench dug in the modern pavement, human long bones were observed, apparently in backfill-type material: they are considered to be a disturbed part of the graveyard of St Thomas Apostle. At the same depth a possible E–W chalk foundation was observed.

HEL86

R Lea
NGR: TQ 33210 81270
SMR: 04188413

St Helen Bishopsgate church, Bishopsgate, EC3

Archaeological recording took place in December 1986 to February 1987, when the exteriors of the S wall of the nave and the W wall of the S transept were stripped of render and the mortar joints raked out prior to repointing. Areas of early 13th-c masonry were identified in both of the elevations. The masonry included wall facings, a lancet window and a relieving arch for a door in the S wall of the nave together with facings and two lancet windows in the W wall of the S transept. The lancet windows correspond with those in the S wall of the S transept.

Probably in the 14th or early 15th c the elevations were altered by the addition of knapped flint at parapet level, probably replacing eaves. The easternmost lancet window in the S wall of the nave was blocked, and a two-light window was inserted at a low level. A wall, probably the churchyard wall, was constructed to abut the SW corner of the S transept and a two-storey building was constructed against the S half of the W wall of the S transept, ie in the SE corner of the churchyard. This building incorporated a piscina at first-floor level and squints at ground and first-floor level into the S transept.

The body of the church underwent major alteration late in the 15th c, when the nave was heightened and the walls were refenestrated with plain three-light windows moulded without cusping. The present S door, inscribed with the date 1633, was inserted on the site of the earlier door in the S wall of the nave. Various brick buildings were constructed against the W wall of the S transept in the 17th and subsequent c. The S wall was rendered in the 19th c with Parker's Roman Cement.

Medieval Archaeol, 32, 1988, 245–6; *Post-Medieval Archaeol*, 22, 1988, 189
Lea, R, nd, 'Archaeological recording of standing elevations at St Helen Bishopsgate', Archive Report
Schofield, J, 1994 'Saxon and medieval parish churches in the City of London: a review', *Trans London Middlesex Archaeol Soc*, 45, 104–7

Jubilee Gardens, Houndsditch, EC3

JBL86

C Maloney
NGR: TQ 33330 81460
SMR: 044737–42

Natural brickearth was cut by shallow brickearth extraction pits, probably Roman in date. Their infill, which contained wall plaster, was sealed by a metalled surface. This surface may be the remains of an access road to the known Roman cemetery along Bishopsgate. At the N end of the site 4th-c deposits, which may have formed part of the cemetery, were recorded. Above the Roman deposits, thick soil horizons developed, probably representing the agricultural use of the site until the late medieval period. Two large fragments of crucible with slag adhering to them were recovered; they are dated to the mid-14th–late 16th c. Numerous cellar walls and floors were recorded, many of which seemed to be post-Great Fire in date; these were infilled with modern material, presumably in preparation for the Gardens.

Cowgill, J, 1987 'Jubilee Gardens JBL86', Finds Appraisal
Maloney, C, 1988 'Jubilee Gardens — archaeological investigations', Interim Archive Report

Little Britain, 14–14a Bartholomew Close, EC1

LBT86

M Nally
NGR: TQ 32100 81600
SMR: 042615–63, 044154–8

Between October 1986 and January 1987 excavations, funded by Wimpey Property Holdings, were undertaken following the first phase of demolition in the Little Britain development. Four areas were investigated, three along the Aldersgate frontage and one in the angle between Aldersgate and Little Britain. Extensive truncation by modern buildings meant that in some areas only intrusive features dug into natural brickearth survived; these included three medieval wells, one of which was barrel lined.

Effort was concentrated on the northernmost trench where horizontal stratigraphy survived to a depth of up to 1m. Here two well-built chalk foundations were found. One of these formed the side of a cellar, the backfill of which contained a medieval glass urinal. Another prominent feature of this trench were the wattle and plank lined pits which produced textile fragments and a quantity of leatherwork, including one nearly complete shoe with decorative silk stitching down the central vamp. All or some of this N area may have been within the precinct of St Bartholomew's Priory.

Despite the proximity of the site to the N–S Roman road along Aldersgate, the only potentially Roman features were two linear ditches running E–W and similar to the ditches found at Museum House to the N of the site in 1979 (see AGT79 above); but there thought possibly to be 12th c or 13th c.

Medieval Archaeol, 32, 1988, 247–8
Edwards, J, 1989 'Little Britain (LBT86)', Medieval Pottery Appraisal, draft
Greig, I, 1990 'Report on a trial trench at Little Britain', Archive Report
Greig, I, & Lakin, D, 1990 'Excavations at Little Britain EC1', Archive Report
Tyers, I, 1988 'Dendrochronological spot date report: interim report (SPT/14/88)', Archive Report

LLN86

D Bentley
NGR: TQ 32070 81825
SMR: 044743

Long Lane (east end, south side), EC1

Near the junction of Long Lane with Cloth Street, banded gravels were observed about 0.6m below ground level; they were probably the medieval or post-medieval metalled surfaces of Long Lane.

LMB86

C Maloney
NGR: TQ 32710 81060
SMR: 044790

1–6 Lombard Street, EC3

Engineers' holes for replacement foundations in the light well were examined during refurbishment. A depth of 2m of archaeological deposits was observed in section, half of which appeared to be the fill of a feature cutting the natural gravels. The deposits were not datable.

MIO86

P McCulloch
NGR: TQ 33640 80920
SMR: 043969–75

118 Minories, EC3

Archaeological investigation funded by Wimpey Property Holdings consisting of five testpits, one controlled excavation (approximately 10m x 10m) and a watching brief was carried out between October and December 1986 in advance of redevelopment.

Natural deposits were truncated by a large N–S medieval ditch which was backfilled and recut probably in the 17th c to accommodate a line of stakes. The fill of the second cut was itself truncated by a series of features which were succeeded by a humic ground surface. Later dumping and cut features were surmounted by another ground and dumping surface through which a large trench was cut. A timber structure housing a brick furnace was discovered in the trench. Backfilling over the destroyed furnace allowed another cut and fill phase.

Later shallow brick footings indicated the presence of at least one structure immediately preceding the Victorian basement of the latest building.

McCulloch, P, 1987 'Excavations at 118 Minories', Archive Report

MIT86

S Rivière
NGR: TQ 33430 81160
SMR: 043078–84

32–34 Mitre Street, EC3

A watching brief, funded by Speyhawk, was carried out in Mitre Street in March and April 1986, in an area which, prior to the watching brief, was part of the graveyard of St Katherine Cree church. The trench was 15m x 3.5m with a survival of 6m of stratigraphy. The natural brickearth was sealed by a series of patchy Roman surfaces and a possible quarry pit, sealed in turn by a series of homogeneous dumps. Cutting into the dumps were burials, in stone and mortar cists, probably a continuation of the Late Saxon graveyard excavated to the east at LEA84 which were themselves disturbed by the construction of massive chalk foundations for the wall of the nave of Holy Trinity Priory. The ground level to the S of the nave rose, and further burials continued to be made.

Three buttresses (one of which was itself later enlarged) were added to the S of the S wall. Burials continued to be made, to give a rise of 2.6m to the destruction horizon of the priory from the construction level. Parts of the superstructure of the priory must have remained standing in the late 16th c, as a new N–S wall was constructed to abut the S wall of the nave, probably forming the new E boundary for the graveyard for the parish church of St Katherine Cree which lay to the S. The area continued to be used as a graveyard to the present day, with burials being made in wooden and lead coffins and the ground level rising steadily. The area was sealed by a layer of topsoil.

London Archaeol, 5, 1987, 272
Cowgill, J, 1987 '32–34 Mitre Street/St Katherine Cree MIT86', Finds Appraisal
Rivière, S, 1986a 'The excavation at Mitre Street', *Popular Archaeol*, 6, No. 12, 37–41
Rivière, S, 1986b 'Watching brief at Mitre Street (MIT86)', Archive Report
Schofield, J, & Lea, R, in prep. *Holy Trinity Priory Aldgate*
Stone, J, 1990 '32–34 Mitre Street', Finds Appraisal

14–16 Mansell Street, E1

MLL86

I Blair
NGR: TQ 33720 81200
SMR. 044549

A deposit of mortar and building debris, dated to the post-medieval period, was recorded.

Cowgill, J, 1987 '14–16 Mansell Street MLL86', Finds Appraisal

49–53 Moorgate, 72–74 Coleman Street, EC2

MOG86

C Spence
NGR: TQ 32670 81470
SMR: 043085–92

Excavation took place between March and May 1986 funded by Wates City Ltd. Although most of the site was truncated by modern basements, a small area to the NE of the site retained horizontal stratigraphy. The natural gravels sloped down in this corner, but were truncated elsewhere on the site. The earliest activity on the site was the cutting of a gravel quarry pit, backfilled in the early 2nd c. This was immediately S of a metalled surface, possibly an alley or road, of contemporary date. In the NE corner of the site the downward slope of natural was levelled and a brickearth building constructed during the early 2nd c. The structure had at least three rooms and a narrow corridor; one room had a gravelled floor while the others used brickearth. The internal walls were of wattle and daub construction. The building, and an associated external area, with a wooden box-section drain and boundary fence, were occupied for a relatively short period as stages of disuse were dated to the mid-2nd c. By the late 2nd c a substantial NW–SE fence alignment ran across this area; to be followed in the early 3rd c by an E–W tile pathway. Late 3rd-c dumping completed the horizontal sequence. A large number of truncated pits were recorded, with a date-range of early 2nd c–c 1500. Of note were two very large square rubbish pits and a smaller wattle-lined pit, probably at the rear of a property fronting Coleman Street, all dated to the 12th c. A medieval chalk well, backfilled in the 18th c, and other post-medieval activity completed the sequence. Finds included a notable group of post-medieval metalwork.

London Archaeol, 5, 1987, 271; *Britannia*, 18, 1987, 335; *Medieval Archaeol*, 31, 1987, 128
Keily, J, 1990 '49–53 Moorgate, 72–73 Coleman Street', Building Materials Appraisal
Spence, C, 1988 'Excavations at 49–53 Moorgate (MOG86)', Archive Report, draft
Winder, J M, 1987 'Marine mollusc shells', Archive Report

MRS86

I Blair
NGR: TQ 33630 81160
SMR: 043075–7

2–5 Minories, EC3

In the basement of 3 Minories a single trench (measuring 6m x 2.5m) was excavated over a two-week period immediately prior to demolition. The earliest sequence, of Roman date, comprised a series of massive brickearth quarries, up to 2.5m deep, which bottomed out at 3.5m beneath the basement slab. Following their backfilling and consolidation, the area seems to have been given over to open fields during the medieval period and to have been extensively ploughed. This was evident by a well-sorted group of level-surfaced layers which extended across the entire trench. Intruding through the plough horizons was a large circular cut (about 1.7m in diameter) which seems to have functioned as a bell-casting pit and contained large quantities of smashed clay bell mould and some 14th-c pottery.

London Archaeol, 5, 1987, 272; Britannia, 18, 1987, 336; Medieval Archaeol, 31, 1987, 128
Cowgill, J, 1987 '2–5 Minories MRS86', Finds Appraisal

NEH86

C Maloney
NGR: TQ 32160 81110
SMR: 044550–2

Automated Public Convenience, south side of St Paul's Cathedral Choir School, New Change, EC4

The lowest recorded feature was a cut feature, sealed by a possible gravel surface, succeeded by a ragstone wall foundation. A chalk structure was also recorded.

NHA86

T Thomas
NGR: TQ 33470 81030
SMR: 043096–102

9 Northumberland Alley, EC3

In July and August 1986 excavations funded by R J Kiln Co Ltd were carried out in the basement of a standing building. Excavations revealed a sequence of gully and ditch activity dated to the early Roman period, including a major NNE–SSW linear V-shaped ditch with an associated post-pit alignment along its E side. Later in the Roman period a gravel strip and timber post structural activity running NNE–SSW spread across the site. These were sealed by major dumps and later Roman pits, including a large assemblage of late 3rd-/mid-4th-c pottery.

Due to the modern basement, medieval and later periods were reduced to truncated remains of a chalk-lined well and a square-cut pit. One pit produced a bone coin balance, possibly medieval.

London Archaeol, 5, 1987, 273; Britannia, 18, 1987, 336; Medieval Archaeol, 31, 1987, 128
Pitt, F, nd, '9 Northumberland Alley', Finds Appraisal
Rivière, S, & Thomas, A, 1987 'Excavations at 94–97 Fenchurch Street and 9 Northumberland Alley', *Archaeol Today*, 8, 13–17
Thomas, T, 1986 'Excavations at 9 Northumberland Alley EC3', Archive Report

ORG86

D Power
NGR: TQ 32820 80820
SMR: 043910–22

St Martin Orgar churchyard, 24–32 King William Street, EC4

In addition to pre- and post-excavation watching briefs, excavations were undertaken between February and May, funded by Lazard Property Unit Trusts. The use of the site as a churchyard since the Fire ensured the preservation of a rich variety of deposits.

In the NW area, cut into the natural brickearth, were two associated shallow features which were overlaid by a deposit containing several Late Bronze Age/Iron Age pottery sherds and a number of flint flakes.

The subsequent site-wide levelling preceded a mid-1st-c building to the SW. This was truncated by pits representing quarrying, and by a ditch running N–S through the W part of the site which contained the semi-articulated skeleton of a pony or mule. A rubbish dump associated with one phase in the sequence of later 1st-c clay and timber structures that followed produced a bronze figurine of the goddess Victory. In the E area layers representing a similarly intense period of Roman building activity were sealed by a deposit of 0.3m of dark earth. This was truncated by medieval pits which were in turn sealed by a series of horseshoe-shaped tile and clay hearths, dated to the 13th c, and cut by insubstantial chalk foundations.

Deposits later than the Roman period to the W were destroyed by the E end of a church. The flint and gravel foundations of the E apse of a church of Saxo-Norman date were replaced in the 13th c by a square-ended building founded on arches of chalk and ragstone. A number of alterations and extensions on the S and E were made in the medieval period. Overlying a vaulted crypt in the area of the S chapel a portion of the floor surface survived. It consisted of large glazed Flemish tiles arranged to form a chequerboard design around a series of moulded Reigate stone bases. The church was destroyed in the Great Fire of 1666 and not rebuilt.

Medieval Archaeol, 32, 1988, 247; *Post-Medieval Archaeol,* 22, 1988, 189
Power, D, 1990 'Excavations at St Martin Orgar churchyard', Archive Report, draft [Roman levels only]
Schofield, J, 1994 'Saxon and medieval parish churches in London: a review', *Trans London Middlesex Archaeol Soc,* 45, 110–11

56–66 Carter Lane, 1–3 Ludgate Square, EC4

PAL86

Bruce Watson
NGR: TQ 31820 81110
SMR: 042672–3

A watching brief was carried out during underpinning of a late 19th-c warehouse, where medieval masonry was uncovered and recorded in 1986–7 (see CAT86 above). Archaeological recording, funded by Eagle Star Properties Ltd, was suspended when the building burnt down in February 1990. An unlined well of Roman date and several cesspits and rubbish pits of uncertain date were cut into natural brickearth and, in turn, truncated by the foundations and basement of the latest building.

London Archaeol, 6, 1991, 276
Watson, B, 1989 'Testpit survey at 1–3 Ludgate Square, EC4 (PAL86)', Archive Report
Watson, B, 1992 'The excavation of a Norman fortress on Ludgate Hill', *London Archaeol,* 6, 371–7

1–19 Poultry, 2–22 Queen Victoria Street, EC2

PUT86

C Maloney and
C Sparey-Green
NGR: TQ 32600 81110
SMR: 044744–5

Roman timbers and waterlogged deposits, typical of those found in the Walbrook Valley, were recorded in two engineers' testpits. The findings are to be incorporated in the report on the major excavation later on the site by MoLAS, ONE94.

74–82 Queen Victoria Street, EC4

QNV86

H White
NGR: TQ 32390 81020
SMR: 043976–83

A small excavation and watching brief on this site, funded by Rowntree Mackintosh, took place in February–March 1986. In the western corner of the site the earliest activity recorded comprised a 1st-c building with brickearth sills and a floor of *opus signinum;* an associated cesspit on its E side contained an assemblage of rare vessels, almost all complete, from *c* AD55 to 70: a large two-handled flagon in Sugar Loaf Court ware, representing an early form of native grog-tempered ware made in or close to the city, and samian cups and plates which included a rare example from the Montans kiln.

Following this, a substantial masonry building was constructed. It comprised a N–S wall with a room to the E containing a concrete floor. In the external area to the W lay a robust platform of rammed gravels, mortar and ragstone overlaid by tiles set in brickearth. Running E–W through it lay a scorched channel or furnace suggesting that the platform could have supported a water-tank. The furnace was rebuilt twice in a reduced form and inside a shelter. The furnace was later dismantled and part of the tile platform adapted into a small room.

Following destruction by fire a gully was built to the W; its disuse, represented by spreads of mortar, may indicate robbing of the adjacent building. This was followed by pits and an accumulation of dark organic dumps. Medieval activity was represented by the base of a N–S chalk foundation.

Cowgill, J, 1987 'Queen Victoria Street QNV86', Finds Appraisal

SNL86: see SUN86

NGR: TQ 32100 80820

Sunlight Wharf, Upper Thames Street, EC4

STO86

C Sparey-Green
NGR: TQ 33410 81860
SMR: 043137–45

Stothard Place, 284–294 Bishopsgate, EC2

Excavations and a watching brief funded by County and District Properties Ltd were conducted between April and July 1986. The site lay 0.5km outside Bishopsgate, immediately S of the site of St Mary Spital, and in an area known to contain Roman cemeteries. The earliest activity was represented by a shallow brickearth quarry containing 2nd-c material, to the W of which lay three wood-lined tanks set in the natural brickearth and containing occupation debris of similar date. Thereafter a group of between seven and nine extended and oriented inhumation burials in wooden coffins was bounded on the N and E by at least four phases of ditches; both burials and enclosure dating to the late 3rd or 4th c. One burial contained 13 glass beads. In the early medieval period a timber structure 6.5m x 7m was surrounded by a complex of small pits and then succeeded by a group of large cesspits. In the late medieval period the W side of the site was occupied by a barrel-lined well and fragmentary gravel footings of timber buildings; the E side by cesspits. The E wall of an early post-medieval brick building had been incorporated in the rear of the existing E frontage of Bishopsgate, the coursed brick and chalk footings of which had previously been wrongly identified in the 19th c as of Roman date. This wall had later been incorporated into the terrace of the 18th-c houses forming the S side of Stothard Place.

Thirty-six fragments of moulded stone reused in the footings of this building included a richly moulded 14th-c traceried and glazed window fragment, possibly from the priory and hospital of St Mary; fragments of a plainer 14th-c window, 13 fragments from a 16th-c oriel window and a second, plainer, 16th-c window.

London Archaeol, 5, 1987, 273–4; *Medieval Archaeol*, 31, 1987, 129–30
Sparey-Green, C, 1987 'Excavations at Stothard Place (STO86)', Archive Report

SUN86 and SNL86

R Bluer and K Tyler
NGR: TQ 32120 80820
SMR: 043146–50, 043848–52

Sunlight Wharf, Upper Thames Street, EC4

During July and August 1986 LEP Ltd sponsored the excavation of five areas at the N limit of the Sunlight Wharf building site, S of the Salvation Army World Headquarters. In the two W areas the SW corner of a substantial piece of Roman masonry was discovered. The element aligned E–W measured approximately 17m E–W and 2m N–S. The element aligned N–S measured approximately

2.8m N–S and 6m E–W. The masonry feature was constructed upon a rammed chalk platform supported by a series of dumps and vertically piled timbers. The area E of this contained a masonry feature aligned N–S, butted by a masonry feature aligned E–W. These were constructed upon the same sort of platform, dumps and piles as the masonry feature to the W. The two areas to the N of this contained platform, dumps and piles only, with an isolated tile setting for a wooden pile. Dating evidence for the Roman features above will be obtained from dendrochronological samples of the piles. These Roman features may align with those recorded in 1981 at excavations at St Peter's Hill; masonry recorded in 1961–2 during the construction of the Salvation Army Headquarters; and masonry recorded in 1841 by Roach Smith between the foot of Lambeth Hill and Queenhithe.

Post-Roman features included a series of N–S and E–W aligned masonry features at the N limit of the excavation. To their S a series of deposits interpreted as road surfaces aligned E–W were recorded. Still further S a substantial masonry feature aligned E–W was recorded. This series of features has been interpreted as buildings to the N and S sides of a road.

Between April 1986 and March 1987 the DUA conducted a controlled watching brief, funded by the LEP Group, during reduction of the ground S of Upper Thames Street between the 19th-c LEP House and the new City of London Boys' School, an area encompassing four medieval tenements. Each property produced a sequence of timber revetments along with a number of late medieval arched foundations and post-medieval brick foundations. The earliest recorded revetment, provisionally dated by dendrochronology to the late 12th c, was of substantial staves inserted into a base-plate, and displayed excellent survival to a height of 3.6m. The property to the E subsequently reused some of the staves as uprights in a post and plank revetment.

For the remainder of the medieval period, a succession of repairs and reclamations was made on each property, resulting in the kind of piecemeal advancement of the waterfront identified in the Trig Lane excavations of 1974–6 (TL74, which lay within the area of these investigations). No two revetments seen at Sunlight Wharf were identical; they included techniques not previously seen in London, such as the use of diagonal members parallel to the face of the revetment, half-lapped to the uprights.

Evidence was recovered for lanes leading down to the river from Thames Street. Nineteen metres (two properties) to the E of Trig Lane was a lane which, in the second half of the 13th c, ended in a river inlet probably associated with the construction of a building immediately to the E. This was built on substantial arched foundations and was almost certainly the London residence of the dukes of Norfolk. It was razed to the ground by the Great Fire.

Finds included a large quantity of metalwork including decorative dress fittings and some pieces of popular medieval jewellery; fixtures and fittings such as hinges, keys and locks; knives (14th and 15th c), buckles, pilgrim badges and candlesticks; a large number of coins and tokens, cloth seals and mounts; a quantity of leather and a group of decorated medieval floor tiles.

The Roman-period remains (all at the N end of the site) have been reported as SNL86, and the remainder of the discoveries as SUN86.

In 1973 a section across an alley in this area called George Yard, leading from Upper Thames Street to the riverside, was recorded (see GM152 above). The section would have been on the N edge of the SNL86/SUN86 site.

London Archaeol, 5, 1987, 274; *Britannia,* 18, 1987, 335; *Medieval Archaeol,* 31, 1987, 130

Bluer, R, 1988 'Excavations at Sunlight Wharf Upper Thames Street EC4', Archive Report

Hunting, P, nd [1990] *Archaeology and development* (Speyhawk and MoL), 58

Milne, G, 1992 *Timber building techniques in London, c 900–1400,* London Middlesex Archaeol Soc Spec Pap 15 [joints and carpentry]

Schofield, J, 1995 *Medieval London houses,* 215

Spence, C (ed), 1989 *Digging in the City: the annual review 1988* (DUA, MoL), 24–5

Spencer, B, in prep. *Pilgrim souvenirs and secular badges,* Medieval finds from excavations in London 7

Tyers, I, 1988 'Dendrochronological spot date report: interim report (SPT/04/88)', Archive Report

Tyler, K, 1988 'Sunlight Wharf north area (SNL86)', Archive Report

Williams, T, 1993 *Public buildings in the south-west quarter of Roman London,* The archaeology of Roman London 3, CBA Res Rep 88 [Roman strata]

SWH86

C Maloney and I Blair
NGR: TQ 31740 81480
SMR: 044553–4

1–3 Snow Hill, EC1

A number of pits, possibly for quarrying, were cut into the natural gravel and are dated mainly to the 1st and 2nd c, with one to the mid-3rd/4th c. In one section pits were succeeded by two 'plaster' burials dating to the 4th c.

Cowgill, J, 1987 '1–3 Snow Hill SWH86', Finds Appraisal
Keily, F, 1988 'Analysis of two skeletons', Archive Report
Maloney, C, 1988 'Watching brief at 1–3 Snow Hill EC1', Archive Report

TRM86

P Durnford
NGR: TQ 32890 81410
SMR: 043151–4

9–19 Throgmorton Avenue, 21 Austin Friars, EC2

A limited excavation funded by MEPC was carried out in the S half of this large site from July to September 1986. A short watching brief was carried out immediately afterwards when the piling contractors were on site. McGee (Demolition) provided help throughout the excavation. The main objective was to try and establish, if possible, the line of the original channel of a Walbrook tributary which was known to have crossed the area. It was predicted that the Walbrook should traverse the SW quarter of the site, from NE to SW. The depth of the double basements in the N of the site determined the eventual size of excavation. In the S half of site, massive Victorian foundations also dictated the areas to be excavated. As modern footings crossed the site, E–W, three discrete areas of excavation were created.

During the excavation, up to 2m of stratigraphy were encountered over the S area of the site. Substantial remains of a timber revetment and part of a wooden trackway were uncovered. It proved possible to plot the probable alignment of the Walbrook tributary in the early Roman period. Finds included a large quantity of Roman vessel glass, a group of Roman leather shoes and sandals, and a Roman wooden writing tablet in very good condition with writing on it.

London Archaeol, 5, 1987, 274; *Britannia,* 18, 1987, 336; two typescript summaries by P Durnford in the archive
Davies, B, 1987 'TRM', Roman Pottery Appraisal
Durnford, P, nd, 'Excavations at 19 Throgmorton Avenue (TRM86)', Archive Report, draft
Ganiaris, H, 1990 'Examination and treatment of a wooden writing tablet from London', *The Conservator,* 14, 3–9
Hunting, P, 1987 *The Garden House*
Tomlin, R, 1987 'Roman wax writing tablet Throgmorton Street', Archive Report

VLT86

C Sparey-Green
NGR: TQ 33150 81570
SMR: 044555–9

Liverpool Street Station booking hall, Liverpool Street, EC2

Natural gravels were overlaid by disturbed or redeposited brickearth above which lay a metalled surface, possibly an E–W Roman road, with Roman occupation debris to its N at a similar level. The metalled surface was cut by a large feature, probably a pit, and the site then covered by a thick dark deposit which contained medieval material. This was succeeded by a N–S chalk wall foundation and, to its W, an E–W brick wall on a foundation of chalk and flint. Truncating the post-medieval brick wall was 19th-c brickwork which is assumed to be part of the underground railway tunnel.

22 Wormwood Street, EC2

WOD86

A Westman
NGR: TQ 33190 81450
SMR: 041927

The back wall of the cellar of the standing building was found to be the city wall with a 19th-c refacing, perhaps of the original core, which reused original stones, occasional Roman tile and bricks older than the 19th c. The inner face seemed to have been cut back and refaced in one operation in more than one property, and the cellar and superstructures built immediately afterwards.

34 Watling Street, EC4

WTS86

M Samuel
NGR: TQ 32430 81030
SMR: 043155

A two-week programme of recording determined the position of a large undercroft known to exist at 34 Watling Street. Prior to partial destruction when Queen Victoria Street was laid out in the 19th c, it had been recorded to a high standard, but it was unclear how these records related to the single vault springer still visible. Study revealed that plastered recesses in the W wall of the modern cellar corresponded to window splays in the old drawings, making possible their orientation. This reveals that the undercroft possibly survives extensively under both Watling Street to the N and Queen Victoria Street to the S, and that the floor of the Victorian cellar lies on top of a thick accumulation of undercroft floors. Stylistically, the details of the vault suggest a date-range of 1350–1500.

London Archaeol, 5, 1987, 274; Medieval Archaeol, 31, 1987, 130
Samuel, M, 1986 'Watching brief at 34 Watling Street EC4', Archive Report
Samuel, M, 1987 'The undercroft at 34 Watling Street', London Archaeol, 5, 286–90
Schofield, J, 1995 Medieval London houses, 227

Abacus House, 33–39 Gutter Lane, EC2

ABC87

I Blair
NGR: TQ 32220 81300
SMR: 041695–704

The heavily truncated remains of the E edge of a Roman road and its associated drainage ditches were uncovered in the extreme NW corner of the site, thus verifying the alignment of this road, first recorded at OST82, to the W. The road ran from SW to NE, presumably to the S gate of the Cripplegate fort. Fronting the road and extending to the E were 1st- and 2nd-c clay-walled buildings, some separated by narrow alleyways. All these buildings reflected the road alignment, including the earliest which were probably destroyed in the Boudican sack of London in AD60–1. Many had plastered internal walls. Floors were predominantly of clay, with one notable exception: a polychrome mosaic uncovered to the SE. This mosaic, in a room possibly with an apsidal end, consisted of a square central panel of small white tesserae, in the centre of which a square within a circle was picked out in black. Alternating bands of black and white tesserae formed a narrow edge around the central panel, outside which larger squared red tesserae extended 1m to the walls of the room. The structure was destroyed by fire during the 2nd c. Later Roman activity was represented by the NE corner of a substantial but heavily robbed masonry structure, possibly dating to the 3rd c and similar to those found at OST82.

Overlying the Roman sequence, dark earth survived only in small pockets. The site was extensively pitted during the medieval period and occupied from 1520, according to documentary sources, by Embroiderers' Hall (Schofield 1995). Near the Gutter Lane frontage, a single brick-lined cesspit, containing an assemblage of fine glass and pottery, appeared to be related to the hall.

The rich finds are predominantly Roman and post-medieval. The many Roman bone objects include a good selection of needles and pins, some complete, and, among less usual finds, a whole bone ligula, half a bone skate, a whole spindle-whorl and part of a double-sided ivory comb. Roman ceramics include many samian stamps, mortaria stamps, and several counters and lamps. Roman copper-alloy objects include a brooch, coins, and a lock and key. Roman glass includes flagons, jars and unguentaria. Among post-medieval pottery are many whole vessels. Post-medieval pins, studs and rings were recovered, and post-medieval glass comprised a range of forms, including many wine glasses, some with unusual decoration.

London Archaeol, 6, 1990, 164
Groves, J, 1990 'Abacus House, 33–39 Gutter Lane', Roman Pottery Appraisal
Pringle, S, 1990 '33–39 Gutter Lane (ABC87)', Building Materials Appraisal
Robinson, J, 1989 'Abacus House, 33–39 Gutter Lane', Post-Roman Pottery Appraisal
Schofield, J, 1995 *Medieval London houses,* 188

AHA87

B Pye
NGR: TQ 31730 81030
SMR: 043891–4

The Warehouse, Apothecaries' Hall, Blackfriars Lane, EC4

A three-month watching brief in the basement during refurbishment of this Grade I Listed Building during February–April 1987 was followed immediately by a three-month standing building survey.

The site is also a Scheduled Ancient Monument as Apothecaries' Hall was built on the site of the Dominican (Blackfriars) friary. However, no buildings of medieval date were found under the Warehouse. This area, external to the Roman city wall, was used for the digging of rubbish pits during the medieval period. The Society of Apothecaries purchased the site in the 1630s but their buildings were destroyed in the Great Fire of 1666. In the 1670s building work was carried out on the site with the evidence of a smaller three-roomed basement with brick floors and associated brick rubbish pits. This was recorded in the basement of the present building which was built in 1783. Incorporated within this later building was a 17th-c brick vaulted cellar under Playhouse Yard.

London Archaeol, 5, 1988, 383

AMB87

G Brown
NGR: TQ 32430 81490
SMR: 043865–8

Aldermanbury House, 58–63 Aldermanbury, EC2

Following the demolition of a post-War building on the S side of Aldermanbury Square an archaeological investigation funded by Heritable City Investments was conducted between June and mid-September 1987, and 300sq m of the site were excavated. The depth of the basement slabs of the post-War building was such as to have destroyed all archaeological features except for the intrusions: pits, wall foundations, post-holes and wells. The highest surviving fragment of natural brickearth had also been truncated by the modern slab.

Intrusive features of differing functions were recorded from Roman, medieval and post-medieval periods; though many of the medieval pits were cesspits. Foundations for two different structures were also recorded, their alignments reflecting the pre-War street pattern. These structures appear to have been established after 1350. From the fills of a post-medieval well several near complete pottery vessels were recovered dating between 1550 and 1750.

An extensive watching brief was conducted on underpinning holes around the N and E perimeters of the site. While features similar to those in the excavation trench were recorded, there was no evidence for the E defences including the E gate of the Cripplegate Roman fort thought to be located at this point on the perimeter.

London Archaeol, 5, 1988, 382; *Britannia,* 19, 1988, 461; *Medieval Archaeol,* 32, 1988, 245
Brown, G, nd, 'Aldermanbury House', Archive Report, draft
Harriss, N, 1988 'Aldermanbury House', Finds Appraisal

12–16 America Square, 15–17 Crosswall, 15 Cooper's Row, EC3

ASQ87

C Goode, A Stephenson and
T Nixon
NGR: TQ 33570 80910
SMR: 041914, 041973–4,
043869–73

Preliminary excavation work, funded by Central and City Properties Ltd, underneath the railway viaduct leading out of Fenchurch Street Station was undertaken in the summer of 1987 in two areas, each measuring about 25sq m to a depth of 2.5m below the warehouse basement slab.

In the S area the internal face of the Roman city wall was exposed immediately below the concrete slab, standing to a height of 1.7m above its clay, flint and *opus signinum* foundations, and showing the usual pattern of dressed ragstone blocks and tile courses. A series of deposits of sand, gravel and brickearth, tipped from E to W, were banked against the wall, containing pottery of mostly mid-2nd-c date. Below the 1.5m of rampart deposits was a layer of hard rammed gravel containing ragstone chippings and pottery up to 0.2m thick and with a distinct camber down towards the wall, presumably a road built either as part of the construction sequence of the defensive system or predating it. Below it lay a further 0.3m of dumping containing earlier Roman pottery.

In the N area, the Roman wall's external face was exposed to slightly less than 2m above foundation level. Above natural ballast lay a dump of material containing Roman tiles, chalk and ragstone fragments, through which cut the curving foundations of a later projecting bastion abutting the wall. The foundations were of gravel below undressed stone rubble, in rough courses, above which up to 1m of neat masonry superstructure survived. The core of the bastion, which was not dismantled, contained a coping stone and another partially moulded stone. Above this lay a series of dumps of 1650–1800, through which was cut a brick-lined cesspit abutting both wall and bastion and containing material provisionally dated to the same period. In a large testpit in the adjacent car park to the N, the wall survived intact to a height of 3m above foundations.

Following these preliminary excavations underneath the railway viaduct, a series of excavations took place between October 1987 and January 1988, also funded by Central and City Properties Ltd. Of 39 trenches sited where pile-caps were to be inserted to support a new building above the railway, 20 were excavated archaeologically and the rest by contractors.

The Roman city wall ran N–S across the site and, to the N, a 32m length was exposed (to be consolidated and displayed in the future building); it survived up to 2m high above original ground level on the E side. A change in build was evident on the inner face. N of this change a tile drain ran through the wall. A gravel metalled surface on the berm survived intact 0.6m below the sandstone plinth on the wall face, and the V-profile of the base of the original ditch was recorded.

In the W a hard gravel surface, dated to the late 2nd/early 3rd c, and probably a construction road for the wall, was sealed by dumps of sand, gravel and brickearth originally banked up against the inside of the wall, containing 2nd-c pottery.

Very thick deposits of dark earth or similar strata extended W, cut by pits, wells and lines of stake-holes, probably fencing. Datable finds suggest that occupation was continuous from the 11th c. A large pitched stone medieval culvert was inserted through the wall and remained in use until the 19th c. To the E, a medieval or later ditch cut sloped down further E than the recorded Roman ditch. It was backfilled and the area levelled up with dumps of homogeneous gravel containing 17th-c pottery, cut in turn by post-medieval horncore-lined pits. No evidence was found of substantial buildings before the 17th c, and parts of the site remained open until the construction of the railway viaduct in the 1840s, when much of the city wall was also demolished.

Roman finds included a bow brooch and quantities of glass from bottles, flasks and a pillar-moulded bowl; bone counters and fragments of two slate bracelets. Late medieval lead tokens and two cloth seals came from metal-detecting. There was also a range of post-medieval glassware, including wine glasses, phials and a near-complete beaker with chequered spiral decoration. Other post-medieval finds included an ivory comb and several knives.

London Archaeol, 5, 1988, 382; 6, 1990, 160; *Britannia,* 19, 1988, 461–2; 22, 1990, 265; *Medieval Archaeol,* 34, 1990, 176

Sankey, D, & Stephenson, A, 1991 'Recent work on London's defences', in Maxfield, V A, & Dobson, M J (eds), *Roman frontier studies 1989: proceedings of the XVth International Congress of Roman frontier studies,* 117–24

Spence, C, & Grew, F (eds), 1990 *The annual review 1989* (DUA, MoL), 24–5

AST87

D Dunlop and A Shotliff
NGR: TQ 32890 81370
SMR: 041567–76

22–25 Austin Friars, EC2

Excavations here were funded by MEPC Developments Ltd. Natural gravels and brickearth were cut in the W by a tributary of the Walbrook which was aligned NE–SW. During the Roman period, the area underwent large-scale drainage prior to revetting which, allied with dumping and levelling across the site, provided ground suitable for construction.

A complex sequence of waterlogged timber pipes, tanks and wells served buildings located to the S and E of the site. Two of these buildings had masonry walls and tessellated floors, indicating high status. The larger building contained at least nine rooms. Evidence for extensive rebuilding during its life included the replacement of earlier tessellated floors. Tile drains ran beneath the floors in both buildings, crossing one room diagonally.

Chalk and ragstone walls founded on timber piles formed part of an early medieval building, possibly related to the Augustinian friary nearby. Two brick-lined wells and a section of chalk cellar were probably of 17th-c date.

Finds from the site are almost entirely of Roman date. They include copper-alloy pins, jug lids, ligulae and styli, as well as 76 coins from the infill of a wooden drain feature. A pipeclay figurine of Venus also came from this feature. Other items include an enamelled zoomorphic mount, a wooden bowl and comb, a bow brooch and a bronze handle cast in the form of a lion.

London Archaeol, 6, 1990, 160
Moreno-Garcia, M, 1991 'Environmental appraisal report AST87 (ASS/10/91)', Archive Report
Nayling, N, 1990 'Dendrochronological spot date report: interim report (SPT/03/90)'
Shotliff, D, & Dunlop, D A, 1990 'Excavations at 22–25 Austin Friars (AST87)', Archive Report
Spence, C, & Grew, F (eds), 1990 *The annual review 1989* (DUA, MoL), 14–15

AUS87

O Beazley
NGR: TQ 32930 81330
SMR: 043876–81

2–6 Austin Friars, EC2

Excavations within the building in August and September, funded by Guardian Royal Exchange, recorded 0.5–0.7m of stratigraphy in three discrete areas.

Natural, consisting of river gravels to the W (Areas A and B) and brickearth to the E (Area C), was overlaid by redeposited natural deposits. Residual finds of a significant number of flint flakes from subsequent dumpings include flint blades and a fabricator and may suggest nearby prehistoric activity.

The paucity of structural or building evidence suggests that much of the site continued in use as an external area throughout the Roman period. Dumps and pits representing the earliest activity across the site were sealed by deposits indicative of internal activity but only in Area B. During the 2nd/3rd c an oven was constructed, replaced by possible surfaces, and thereafter overlaid by a second oven/hearth.

Later Roman and medieval horizontal stratigraphy was horizontally truncated by recent activity. The medieval period was represented by pits in all areas, finds from which provide an 11th–14th-c date-range and include a bone skate.

London Archaeol, 5, 1988, 382; *Britannia*, 19, 1988, 463; *Medieval Archaeol*, 32, 1988, 245
Beazley, O, 1987 'Excavations at 2–6 Austin Friars EC2', Archive Report
Stone, J, 1989 '2–6 Austin Friars', Finds Appraisal

BAA87

N J Elsden
NGR: TQ 31270 81510
SMR: 043731–40

Barnard's Inn, Holborn, 78–81 Fetter Lane, 7–13 Norwich Street, EC1

Five trenches, both inside standing buildings and outside, were excavated between March and June 1988, in advance of demolition work, and funded by the Mercers' Company.

An initial phase of gravel-pit digging in the S of the site was followed by a levelling of redeposited natural gravels, probably during the 1st and 2nd c. This was followed by three burials dating from the

2nd to possibly the 4th c; to the W a possible stake and wattle fence-line was separated from the burials by a N–S ditch. These features were covered by an accumulation representing disuse of the area until the gardens of the medieval and later periods. This deep layer of garden soil was cut by pits throughout its life, mostly for domestic rubbish, but including a large cesspit or soak-away.

In the centre of the site the earliest features were two large gravel pits, or possibly E–W ditches, and smaller pits. These were later levelled with a clay dump, which was in turn cut by more pits and by a ditch or pit with a chalk lining used as a cesspit or a sewer. These features were in turn levelled with the make-up for a chalk-walled building. A section of wall of similar construction was preserved to the N, within the basement of the hall of Barnard's Inn (early 15th c), where large and small post-holes indicated internal features, possibly medieval. The modern wall-line cut across a chalk-walled cesspit, probably lying originally half underneath and half outside the hall. A large circular pit may have been a robbed-out well, and later features included a post-pad over the backfill of one of the large post holes, and the burial of a cat, or its skin, in a wooden box.

To the S of the medieval hall, a large gravel pit was cut through the garden soil, and post-medieval dumps and disturbed garden soil covered most of the site. Brick cellars were constructed in the 17th and 18th c, along with, in the 18th c, a brick-lined well. Features were disturbed by the 19th-c reconstruction of the hall and construction of other standing buildings, including the Mercers' School in 1892–4.

Excavations here produced a number of burials of Roman date. A complete Verulamium white-slipped face pot contained a cremation burial and a further cremation was enclosed within a cist formed of six complete lydion bricks. An inhumation burial was accompanied by a necklace of 66 jet beads, a jet finger-ring and a bone pin.

London Archaeol, 6, 1989, 50; *Britannia,* 20, 1989, 308; *Medieval Archaeol,* 33, 1989, 182

Elsden, N, 1989 'Excavations at Barnard's Inn 78–81 Fetter Lane 7–13 Norwich Street EC1 (BAA87)', Archive Report

Keily, J, 1989 'Barnard's Hall', Building Materials Appraisal

Keys, L, 1989 'Barnard's Inn, Holborn', Finds Appraisal

Ruddle, J, 1987 'Environmental appraisal report (ASS/01/91)', Archive Report

Schofield, J, 1995 *Medieval London houses,* 190–1

Spence, C (ed), 1989 *Digging in the City: the annual review 1988* (DUA, MoL), 26–7

Billingsgate bath-house, 100 Lower Thames Street, 1–8 St Dunstan's Lane, EC3

BBH87

N Jaffa and J Oetgen
NGR: TQ 33100 80690
SMR: 041079–85

Recording and surveying of the Roman remains were carried out in 1987 and in 1989–90 for the Corporation of London. The site, originally excavated in 1968, now lies in the basement of a modern building. Despite previous consolidation the Roman structures need restorative treatment. Recording was to prepare for this, and for possible eventual public display. For earlier work on the bath-house site, see GM111, BIL75 and BSA82 above.

London Archaeol, 5, 1988, 385; 6, 1991, 275–6

Bates, M, 1990 'Billingsgate bath-house (BBH87): field report and sedimentological assessment (SED/03/90)', Archive Report

Davis, A, 1993 'Environmental remains (ENV/ASS/22/93)', Archive Report

Hibberd, H, 1992, 'Billingsgate bath-house (BIL75, BBH87)', Dendrochronology Report

Newton, L, & Sharman, B, 1993 'Environmental assessment (ENV/ASS/21/93)', Archive Report

O'Connor-Thompson, S, and Rowsome, P, 1994 'Case study 8.1: Billingsgate Roman bath-house', in Harrison, R, *Manual of heritage management,* 85–7

Oetgen, J, 1990 'Roman bath-building at 100 Lower Thames Street EC3: archaeological report October 1989 to May 1990', Report [superseded by Rowsome 1993]

Pearson E, nd, 'Environmental archive report', Archive Report

Pringle, S, 1990 'Billingsgate bath-house (BBH87)', Building Materials Appraisal

Rowsome, P, 1993 'Billingsgate Roman house and bath', Post-excavation Assessment

Rowsome, P, 1996 'The Billingsgate Roman house and bath — conservation and assessment', *London Archaeol,* 7, 415–23

BHS87

R Brown
NGR: TQ 33360 81630
SMR: 043542–9

192–200 Bishopsgate, E1

Chase Property Holdings funded excavation of seven trenches within the basement of the standing building, conducted between March and May 1988.

After an initial site-wide levelling of the area in the early Roman period three linear cuts and several brickearth or gravel quarries were dug. One ditch running N–S to the extreme W of the site, bordering the Bishopsgate frontage, may have had an association with the Roman road, Ermine Street, running N–S in the vicinity of the site to the W. In the centre of the site lay a badly truncated pebbled surface which was possibly a track or yard.

A second major phase of levelling followed, which prepared the area for use as a Roman cemetery. In total eight definite inhumations were found along with two cremation pits and another eight possible graves. Severe truncation by the modern basement and pipe trenches meant that only one inhumation was complete; several other disturbed fragments of human bone were distributed throughout the area. The graves were, with one exception, aligned E–W; four displayed evidence of coffins, and two were chalk or plaster burials. A linear cut associated with the cemetery may have been a boundary ditch.

After the cemetery fell into disuse the site seems to have been given over to agriculture punctuated by medieval rubbish pits and cesspits. This continued into the post-medieval period from which two wells and a brick-lined pit were recorded.

London Archaeol, 6, 1989, 46
Brown, R, 1988 'Excavations at 192–200 Bishopsgate (BHS87)', Archive Report

BLM87

D Sankey
NGR: TQ 32970 81510
SMR: 041918–20

Blomfield House, 85–86 London Wall, 53 New Broad Street, EC2

Between January and April 1988 an investigation sponsored by Trafalgar House Developments was undertaken which included the excavation of two, broadly linear, areas through the defences outside the city wall, a watching brief concurrently on site groundwork, and photogrammetric recording of the city wall.

Beneath and therefore preceding the city defences on the E side of the site were found two successive wooden buildings of the 1st and 2nd c. The first was aligned with the Walbrook tributary to the W (the line of Blomfield Street) and had one wall built in an interlocking upright plank technique previously assumed to be typically medieval. Adjacent to this building was a substantial box drain over 1m deep.

The development of a drainage system was traced from a small land drain running NE–SW on the E side of the site, through the box drain mentioned above, via a system of parallel ditches to a large defensive ditch 5m wide and 1.5m deep that accompanied the construction of the Roman city wall, immediately to the S. This drainage system was subject to extreme fluctuations in flow, presumably reflecting changes in land use upstream, leading to the deposition of up to 1.5m of sediments on the W side of the site.

During this period of natural aggradation, burials were inserted many of which were then subject to disturbance by erosion, leading to a mixed deposit of human bone, leather sandals, and funerary pots holding offerings of chickens and coins; also recovered was a scatter of over 500 forger's coin moulds, some of which were of later 3rd-c low-denomination bronze coins. After more silting in this area, a masonry structure was built against the outer face of the city wall. This badly truncated structure was apparently at first a bastion and was then altered, perhaps for a non-defensive purpose.

More fluvial deposition followed, deriving from the Walbrook tributary to the W, and continued in the medieval period, when drier parts of the site were used for agriculture and perhaps for grazing, evidenced by a fence-line. This was followed by the cutting of a large city ditch, 1m deep and 12.5m wide, in the early 17th c, reversing the flow of the drainage system, and taking water from the Walbrook around the outside of the City. It may also have removed any evidence for a medieval ditch.

Above the ditch sediments the area was covered by large landfill dumps of domestic waste and building debris, possibly from buildings postdating the Great Fire. A well in the NW corner was perhaps part of the 18th-c housing development known as Petty France.

The lengths of the upstanding city wall exposed along the S side of the site revealed details of both face and core. The face of the Roman wall includes the ferruginous sandstone plinth, four ragstone courses and the first tile string course, but the core of this wall survives to above the second tile string course. The core of the Roman wall was poured from above, leaving clear tip-lines at 45 degrees, the angle of repose. The medieval face of the wall used reworked Roman core blocks of ragstone and tiles, and the medieval core used new materials such as flint and chalk. A post-Great Fire redbrick church precinct wall on a sandstone plinth, visible from the pavement, was recorded directly above the sequence. The wall is preserved as a Scheduled Ancient Monument and a panel exposing the face of the medieval wall is to be left uncovered for public inspection.

Other finds from this site included part of a ceramic Langewehe horn, and most of a decorated Montelupo plate.

London Archaeol, 6, 1989, 51–2; *Britannia,* 20, 1989, 307; *Medieval Archaeol,* 33, 1989, 183

Crowley, N, 1990 '85–86 London Wall', Building Materials Appraisal

Moir, D, 1988 'Finds appraisal for 85–86 London Wall 52–53 New Broad Street (BLM87)', Finds Appraisal

Sankey, D, 1989 'Excavations at Blomfield House 85–86 London Wall and 53 New Broad Street EC2 (BLM87)', Archive Report

Sankey, D, & Stephenson, A, 1991 'Recent work on London's defences', in Maxfield, V A, & Dobson, M J (eds), *Roman frontier studies 1989: proceedings of the XVth International Congress of Roman frontier studies,* 117–24

Spence, C (ed), 1989 *Digging in the City: the annual review 1988* (DUA, MoL), 20–1

274–306 Bishopsgate, EC2

BOS87

Sarah Gibson
NGR: TQ 33410 81870
SMR: 08093412

Between November 1987 and February 1988 excavations took place, funded by County and District Properties Ltd. Two main trenches were opened up, one to the N of Stothard Place and the other to the S. It was anticipated that Roman burials would be discovered as the site is located beyond the boundary of the Roman city.

In the N area, post-medieval building activity had truncated the earlier deposits; all that remained was a possible early Roman ditch. In the S area, the larger of the two trenches, early Roman quarrying and levelling activity of the 1st and 2nd c was recorded. Five Roman burials, probably of the 4th c, were excavated to the E of the site, but subsequent medieval pits had disturbed any others. A medieval chalk cesspit, possibly within the precinct of St Mary Spital, was found to the N of this trench. Foundations of post-medieval buildings were also located, some with discernible rooms and floors. One of the floors was made from reused glazed and patterned medieval tiles.

This multi-period site produced a good deal of Roman material: many fragments of glass, including a basal fragment of a green phial and an assortment of beads; and a complete Roman ceramic vase. Also recovered were many whole, decorated medieval floor tiles, of varying designs, with one unique tile possibly depicting the tiler himself or a medieval 'green man'.

Sites immediately to the N and S were excavated in 1989–90, see PSO90 below (which incorporates BOG89).

London Archaeol, 6, 1989, 46; *Britannia,* 20, 1989, 308

Gibson, Sarah, 1989 '284–296 Bishopsgate E1', Archive Report

Keily, J, 1990 '282–296 Bishopsgate', Building Materials Appraisal

Norton, C, 1993 'The export of decorated floor tiles from Normandy', in Stratford, J (ed), *Medieval art, architecture and archaeology at Rouen,* British Archaeol Assoc Conf Transactions for 1986, 81–97

BRL87

E Shepherd and A Westman
NGR: TQ 32895 81060
SMR: 043882–90

19–25 Birchin Lane, EC3

An excavation, funded by City Merchant Developers Ltd, was conducted during February–March 1987. The depth of archaeological survival was found to be considerably greater than originally anticipated. As the length of the excavation could not be extended, the site was carried out under a two-shift system.

No excavation was undertaken in nos 19–21, as the insertion of basements in this area had removed all archaeological levels. The six trenches dug in nos 24–25 provided little information, again due to heavy truncation. Only a number of pits (of varying date) and ragstone foundation (of unknown date) survived.

In contrast, archaeological deposits survived to a depth of over 3m in nos 22–23. The earliest feature here (mid-1st c) was a band of gravel 6m wide (running E–W), retained within timber posts and planking. Its function is uncertain, although it may have formed an alleyway. It was flanked by external yards. A complex sequence of Roman clay and timber buildings, spanning the late 1st/2nd c followed. The discovery of two ovens and carbonised grain within the rooms of one of these buildings suggests that it was a bakery. It was destroyed by a major fire in the early/mid-2nd c. Late Roman buildings were truncated, although two pits and large masonry and piled foundations may have been of this date.

Roman pottery from the site included some rare types such as marbled samian, a glazed flagon and a face pot. There was also a large Antonine group as well as a large, high-quality group of mid-/late 4th-c wares. A shale platter from a late 2nd-c context was also recovered. Subsequent features, which were few, included cesspits, a chalk-lined well and a brick drain.

London Archaeol, 5, 1988, 382–3; *Britannia,* 19, 1988, 463; *Medieval Archaeol,* 32, 1988, 245

Davies, B, 1993 'Inter-site studies', in Milne, G, & Wardle, A, 'Early Roman development at Leadenhall Court, London and related research', *Trans London Middlesex Archaeol Soc,* 44, 135–50

Davies, B, Richardson, B, & Tomber, R, 1994 *A dated corpus of early Roman pottery from the City of London,* The archaeology of Roman London 5, CBA Res Rep 98 [contribution to early Roman pottery corpus]

Harrison, J, 1988 '22–25 Birchin Lane (BRL87) Roman building material interim report', Archive Report

Holden, T, 1990 'Environmental appraisal report (ASS/05/90)', Archive Report

Mason, S L R, 1988 'A preliminary experimental investigation of some aspects of the charring process in cereal grains (DIS/03/88)', MSc Dissertation, Dept of Human Environment, Institute of Archaeology, University College London

de Moulins, D, nd, 'Charred plant remains', Archive Report

Shepherd, L, & Westman, A, 1990 'Excavations at 19–25 Birchin Lane EC3 (BRL87)', Archive Report

BUC87

J Hill and P Rowsome
NGR: TQ 32590 81070
SMR: 041608–13

Docklands Light Railway shaft, Bucklersbury, near 3 Queen Victoria Street, EC4

Excavations (Fig 48) were funded by Olympia and York and DLR. This site was situated immediately to the W of the Walbrook stream; an archaeological sequence 8m in depth was recorded. Natural consisted of a clay-silt, possibly deposited within a prehistoric Walbrook channel. This horizon was sealed by deposits of sand-silt, which contained some Roman pottery and raised the ground surface. The earliest extant evidence of occupation was an earth and timber building of Neronian date, with wattle and brickearth walls. Parts of four room areas were recorded.

Fig 48 BUC87: excavation of Roman buildings in progress in the DLR shaft.

A revetted open area, which was prone to flooding from the Walbrook, lay immediately to the E. To the N of the building was an external area of planking, interpreted as a boardwalk along the S side of the main E–W Roman road which bridged the stream. In a second phase of use, the building was modified internally and the boardwalk covered by a gravel metalling. The building was destroyed by the Boudican fire in AD60–1, and the area was levelled using redeposited fire debris. The roadside was resurfaced and a poor-quality timber building constructed on the site, probably before c AD70. The area was then reterraced and a new earth and timber building of at least six room areas was constructed. The N rooms of the building were extended further N than the pre-Boudican roadside property, indicating that the Roman road had been shifted a short distance northwards, perhaps as a consequence of the bridge across the Walbrook being rebuilt on a slightly different position after the Boudican revolt.

A more substantial, multi-roomed building with timber base-plates set on oak piles, was dendrochronologically dated to c AD79. The first three phases of post-Boudican building were bordered to the E by the retained open area next to the stream, part of which was encroached upon by the next phase of building, a late 1st-c post and sill-beam structure with plank floors raised on joists. This building was demolished and the ground surface raised, perhaps at the start of the 2nd c. Massive oak-piled wall-lines were the only elements of a new building to survive subsequent truncation to ground level; it was replaced by a less substantial structure c AD120, which was sealed by redeposited Hadrianic fire debris containing samian pottery dated to AD120–5. A series of less well-preserved buildings was constructed on the site after the Hadrianic fire and up until the early 3rd c: the majority of these were of earth and timber construction, but one may have been built of masonry which was subsequently robbed. A mid-3rd-c, multi-room timber building with plank floors and an internal grain-storage bin was sealed by redeposited fire debris and was the latest extant evidence of Roman structures on the site. After that date the area remained external, with occasional pitting and dumping interspersed with rudimentary gravel surfaces during the 4th c.

Ephemeral structural evidence of two phases of Late Saxon buildings was followed by pitting in an external area. Much of the Saxo-Norman sequence was truncated by the ragstone foundations and undercroft of a medieval gatehouse on the W side of *Barge Yard,* both associated with the medieval residence *le Barge* (known on documentary grounds from the 12th c). The sequence was completed by the cellar of 3 Queen Victoria Street, constructed in 1870 and destroyed in the Blitz.

The Roman pottery includes a good assemblage of early Neronian groups, and amphora, mortaria and samian stamps. Among well-preserved metal objects are craftsmen's tools made of forged iron: styli, awls and split pins. A stud decorated with a bearded male figure in profile may have been associated with a copper-alloy leaf-shaped pendant, in a military garment. Copper-alloy jewellery, a wooden writing tablet and an amber-coloured glass flask with white marvered trails were also recovered. Medieval finds include a local grey-ware lamp of mid-11th–mid-12th-c date, almost complete.

London Archaeol, 6, 1990, 161; *Britannia,* 22, 1991, 266; *Medieval Archaeol,* 34, 1990, 176

Mason, S L R, 1988 'A preliminary experimental investigation of some aspects of the charring process in cereal grains (DIS/03/88)', MSc Dissertation, Dept of Human Environment, Institute of Archaeology, University College London

Moore, A, 1988 'Finds appraisal for the Docklands Light Railway shaft at Bucklersbury', Finds Appraisal

Rhodes, M, nd, 'The leather', Archive Report

Spence, C (ed), 1989 *Digging in the City: the annual review 1988* (DUA, MoL), 22–3

80 Coleman Street, EC2

CMA87

A T Mackinder
NGR: TQ 32670 81520
SMR: 044746–50

In June–July 1988 partial demolition allowed a seven-week excavation, funded by City Holdings Ltd. This revealed two parallel, E–W Roman ditches, which were backfilled with domestic rubbish and sealed by a dump containing evidence of burning. There were also traces of a brickearth building disturbed by extensive digging of pits to the S. In the medieval period another E–W ditch was dug and partly lined with timber; there was also a pit containing slag.

COV87

D Lees
NGR: TQ 32790 81420
SMR: 043654–62

10–12 Copthall Avenue, EC2

Between October and early December 1987, London and Edinburgh Trust plc funded excavations which revealed up to 2m of undisturbed Roman stratigraphy. The L-shaped trench on the N of the site covered roughly 35sq m; a section to the S was also investigated.

A Walbrook tributary is recorded in the area, and, although the excavations did not reveal the river channel, the sequence began with river-lain sands and gravels. Into this tributary area material had been dumped to level up the ground for 2nd-c Roman building works. In the W portion of the site ran a NE–SW gravel road. Fronting onto this road were well-preserved base-plates and floors of two timber-framed buildings. Between the two buildings ran a gravel alley and a timber-lined gully lying E–W. These ran off into another timber-lined drain running along the E edge of the road. The two buildings went out of use sometime before the mid-3rd c when the two drains were recut and the road resurfaced.

The area appears to have become increasingly wet and during the mid–late 3rd c flood deposits covered the site, the road and drains falling out of use. The site appears to have been open land with some possible agricultural activities taking place until the mid-4th c when large-scale dumping covered the entire site, probably to raise the ground surface above the water table. The basement of the modern building truncated the stratigraphy at this level.

Notable finds from this site were numerous fragments of various glass vessels which included jars, jugs, bottles and an indented glass bowl. The samian was of good quality with some ten stamps. Of the metal objects an almost complete copper-alloy ligula and an iron horse-bit were the most outstanding.

London Archaeol, 6, 1989, 48
Lees, D, nd, 'Excavations at 10–12 Copthall Avenue', Archive Report, draft
Tyers, I, 1988 'Dendrochronological spot date interim report (SPT/11/88)', Archive Report

CWN87

A Westman
NGR: TQ 32220 81490
SMR: 040471, 042912–15

City wall, Noble Street, EC2

Archaeological examination of a standing monument W of Noble Street, part of the NW sector of the city wall, was undertaken in May–June 1987 for the Corporation of London. The W wall and SW corner of the 2nd-c Cripplegate fort, with internal turrets, was reinforced when the city was enclosed by defences *c* AD200. The new city wall ran W from the corner of the fort over a tile-lined drain. The foundations of these features and portions of the medieval rebuild of the city wall, including a fragment of Bastion 15, excavated and identified by Grimes (site WFG8), were recorded by the DUA in conjunction with a photographic survey by the Department of Civil Engineering of the City University.

London Archaeol, 5, 1988, 386–7
Grimes, W F, 1968 *The excavation of Roman and medieval London*, 21–9
Westman, A, 1988 'Archaeological examination of the city wall at Noble Street EC2 (CWN87)', Archive Report

DOC87

P Rowsome
NGR: TQ 32780 81045
SMR: 043934–7

Docklands Light Railway shaft, Lombard Street, EC3

Excavations were funded by Olympia and York (Canary Wharf Development Company Ltd) and facilitated by Docklands Light Railway. The earliest recorded activity above the natural gravels was dumping and levelling in an external area, followed by a sequence of structures of 1st- and 2nd-c date which are interpreted as elements of clay and timber buildings. Towards the end of the 2nd c the area reverted to external use and dumping took place. A masonry building was erected above, of late Roman date, and this was sealed by dark earth. Overlying the dark earth, a series of street-metallings of 9th–11th-c date may have been associated with a Saxon forerunner of Lombard Street. The street was encroached upon by occupation or external activity on at least two occasions. It was truncated by a construction cut associated with the 18th-c rebuild of St Mary Woolnoth church and by modern cuts.

London Archaeol, 5, 1988, 385; 6, 1989, 51; *Britannia*, 20, 1989, 306
Tough, E, 1990 'Docklands Light Railway shaft at Lombard Street', Finds Appraisal

Eagle House, 86–96 Cannon Street, 31–33 Bush Lane, EC4

EAG87

J Oetgen
NGR: TQ 32710 80870
SMR: 043589–93

Excavations were carried out in the basement of Eagle House during July and August 1988. The work was funded by MEPC. The site lies within the scheduled area of the Roman governor's palace and, although the existing basements had truncated the stratigraphy to within 0.3m of the natural brickearth, evidence for Roman foundations and more deeply cut post-medieval features survived.

The natural brickearth was located. The earliest phase of activity consisted of a site-wide levelling of homogeneous sandy gravel, capped with fine, hard, silty redeposited brickearth, which produced no finds but is assumed to be Roman. These layers were cut by the foundations of timber-framed structures and mortared flint-rubble footings. The extensive ground preparation and certain similarities of alignment suggest that the structures were elements of a single building. No floors survived, although a number of tesserae were recovered from intrusive contexts.

The building, or buildings, were succeeded by a series of rectangular shafts which could not be fully excavated as they were more than 2m deep. These are interpreted as wells and were probably timber lined, although no trace of timbers survived. The fills produced finds of predominantly Roman date.

Due to the depth of truncation, there was no evidence for early medieval activity on the site. Later features consisted of a chalk-built cellar or cesspit, which contained finds of 15th–16th-c date, and a chalk-lined well, over 5m deep. The well was backfilled in the early 18th c and contained complete wine bottles and pharmaceutical jars in impressive quantities. A late medieval gold finger-ring was also recovered.

London Archaeol, 6, 1989, 46–7; *Britannia,* 20, 1989, 306
Hibberd, H, 1989 'Well matrix (environmental archaeology)', Archive Report
Oetgen, J M, 1989 'Excavations at 86–96 Cannon Street (EAG87)', Archive Report

107 Fenchurch Street, EC3

FCS87

H Bishop
NGR: TQ 33380 81040
SMR: 043705–15

An area 15m x 15m was excavated between April and July 1988, funding coming from the developers, the Corporation of London.

The earliest feature, an E–W road linking the Aldgate area to the forum, was laid directly onto the natural brickearth. This road was delimited on its N side by a ditch which was later scoured out and recut to take an enclosed wooden drain. The road gravels were then extended over the drain to link up with a courtyard area, to the N. Five road surfaces were discernible, all probably 1st c.

The partition wall of a clay and timber building was found at the edge of the site above an area of yard gravels. A small area of associated floor surface had been badly burnt. A NNW–SSE ditch, probably a property division of the 2nd c, cut through all the gravel surfaces of court and road, but unfortunately modern truncation had removed any relationship between the building and the ditch. On the W side a structure represented by posts set into the yard surface N of the road, was 2m wide and ran N for at least 4m before being truncated by a late 2nd- or 3rd-c ditch. This ran ENE–WSW across the whole site, cutting the earlier ditch at right angles; it was in use for some time, being continually cut back and repaired as its retaining posts collapsed or rotted. The last phase of Roman activity was a series of almost perfectly circular pits; there was no sign of dark earth.

The only surviving medieval features were a chalk well and intrusive pits, some single, some complex, recut five or six times, the earliest producing 11th- or perhaps 10th-c pottery. Brick cellar floors of post-medieval buildings survived immediately above the Roman road surfaces. In two instances very deep strongrooms survived: one was probably vaulted, extending under an alley to the W, Fenchurch Buildings; the other to the E was originally reached by ladder, and later was refloored and provided with a brick stair.

London Archaeol, 6, 1989, 49; *Britannia,* 20, 1989, 306; *Medieval Archaeol,* 33, 1989, 182
Edwards, J, 1989 '107 Fenchurch Street, medieval and post-medieval pottery appraisal report (FCS87)', Pottery Appraisal
Groves, J, 1988 'The Roman pottery from 107 Fenchurch Street (FCS87)', Archive Report

FUR87

K Tyler
NGR: TQ 31210 81540
SMR: 043905–9

40–41 Furnival Street, EC4

Between May and July 1987 excavations funded by Prudential Assurance plc were undertaken. The earliest activity, of medieval or earlier date, was the quarrying of natural gravels. The quarry pits had been backfilled with brickearth. A series of 13th–15th-c rubbish pits and chalk-lined cesspit postdated these quarries. The remains of the basement, ground floor and three upper storeys of a late 17th-c L-shaped building were identified on the S half of the site. In the basement three brick vaults survived with fragments of brick flooring. One fireplace was recorded on the first floor, and two on the second floor. The original height of this building is unknown. N of the building was a contemporary brick-lined well and the remains of a brick-lined cesspit.

London Archaeol, 5, 1988, 384; Medieval Archaeol, 32, 1988, 246; Post-Medieval Archaeol, 22, 1988, 210
Tyler, K, nd, '40–41 Furnival Street EC1', Archive Report

GAG87

N Bateman
NGR: TQ 32510 81360
SMR: 04128902, 041690–5

Guildhall Art Gallery, Guildhall Yard, EC2

Between June 1987 and May 1988 an excavation sponsored by the Corporation of London took place on the site of the Guildhall Art Gallery, which was being demolished as part of a major redevelopment along the E side of Guildhall Yard. An area about 30m x 30m was available in this first phase, but not all of this could be excavated because of the presence of large masonry foundations crossing the site and dividing it up into seven discrete areas of excavation.

Through most of the site, natural gravel and brickearth were truncated by the construction of a very large Roman masonry building (c AD 125) which has been identified as an amphitheatre (Fig 49). Substantial lengths of the inner perimeter wall, and the walls forming the ceremonial entrance at the E end of the arena with two flanking chambers, were recorded in the separate areas. Sequences up to 1m thick of internal

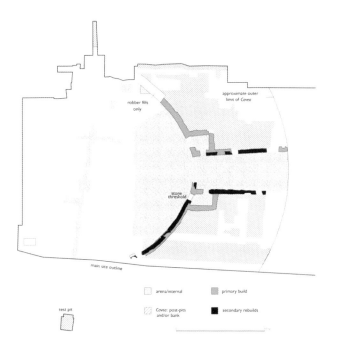

Fig 49 GAG87: plan of the E end of the rebuilt amphitheatre in the 2nd c.

and external surfaces were also recorded. A number of substantial timber features were associated with the amphitheatre, including several revetted drains with plank tops; two related settling tanks; at least two phases of very large sill-beams marking a porch-like structure in front of the ceremonial entrance; a number of threshold beams in the main entrance and subsidiary doorways; and a row of timber posts in front of the main perimeter wall. The row of posts and some of the lowest surfaces may belong to a phase of activity preceding the amphitheatre, possibly a timber amphitheatre, of the late 1st c.

The amphitheatre was evidently still in use (though not necessarily as an amphitheatre) in the mid-4th c, but was then robbed and the site was apparently abandoned. The whole site was sealed by up to 1.5m of dark earth, which was itself sealed by early medieval rubbish pits of very different sizes and orientations. A group of interconnecting medieval gullies and trenches in the S of the site may have been industrial. In the N of the site the substantial remains of the 15th-c Guildhall Chapel were recorded: these comprised foundations of the S aisle and of all four walls of the nave, up to 3m high.

A number of substantial but isolated chalk foundations which may have been part of other buildings connected with the 15th-c Guildhall were also recorded. All contemporary ground levels, internal and external, had been truncated by the insertion of the 19th-c basement of the former Art Gallery.

From this multi-period site medieval finds were the most noteworthy: 20 medieval buckles and a buckle plate, four copper scales, a pendant and a whole pair of tweezers; a bone weaving comb fashioned from a cattle metapodial; two counters and two dice. Ninety-six coins were retrieved, some of which were Roman. A most unusual object was a tortoiseshell weaving tablet; these are usually made from bone.

For excavations immediately to the W, beneath Guildhall Yard, see GUY88 below. Guildhall Yard East (GYE92) was undertaken by MoLAS in 1992–7, but is not reported in detail here. Excavations revealed more of the Roman amphitheatre and its surroundings, including metalled areas and timber buildings. Dark earth over the central arena was sealed by well-preserved 11th-c wattle and timber buildings. Substantial masonry foundations of several medieval buildings were also recorded.

London Archaeol, 5, 1988, 384–5; 6, 1989, 50; 6, 1990, 164; 7, 1994, 199–200; Britannia, 19, 1988, 461–2; 20, 1989, 305; 25, 1994, 281–2; Medieval Archaeol, 32, 1988, 246; 37, 1993, 259–60; Post-Medieval Archaeol, 27, 1993, 230

Bateman, N, 1989 'The Guildhall Art Gallery site (GAG87 and GUY88)', Archive Report

Bateman, N, 1990 'The discovery of Londinium's amphitheatre: excavations on the old Art Gallery site, 1987–8 and 1990', London Archaeol, 6, 232–41

Bateman, N, 1991 'The proposed development at Guildhall Yard', Assessment Report

Bateman, N, 1994a 'Guildhall: beyond the amphitheatre', London Archaeol, 7, 258–62

Bateman, N, 1994b 'The London amphitheatre', Current Archaeol, 137, 164–71

Bateman, N, 1997 'The London amphitheatre: excavations 1987–1996', Britannia, 28, 51–86

Betts, I M, 1995 'Procuratorial tile stamps from London', Britannia, 26, 207–29

Betts, I M, Bateman, N, & Porter, G, 1995 'Two late Anglo-Saxon tiles and the early history of St Lawrence Jewry, London', Medieval Archaeol, 38, 165–70

Ebbatson, L, 1990 'The London amphitheatre', London Archaeol, 6, 22

Egan, G, & Pritchard, F, 1991 Dress accessories c 1150–c 1450, Medieval finds from excavations in London 3 [medieval dress accessories]

Hassall, M W C, & Tomlin, R S O, 1995 'Roman Britain in 1994: inscriptions — the City', Britannia, 26, 382

Maloney, J, 1988 'Fun and games in Roman London', Illustrated London News, May, 46–9

Robinson, J, 1990 'Guidhall Yard', Post-Roman Pottery Appraisal

Spence, C (ed), 1989 Digging in the City: the annual review 1988 (DUA, MoL), 11–12

Tyers, I, 1988 'Dendrochronological spot dates: interim report (SPT/03/88)', Archive Report

Tyers, I, 1994 'Guildhall Yard — spot dates and sample lists (DEN/07/94)', Dendrochronology Report

Houndsditch Warehouse, 123–137 Houndsditch, 3–31 Stoney Lane, EC3

HND87

D Sankey and A Woodger
NGR: TQ 33470 81350
SMR: 044791

Natural gravels were truncated and no archaeological deposits survived.

Catering Block, St Bartholomew's Hospital, EC1

HOS87

D Bentley
NGR: TQ 31940 81616
SMR: 043952

A brief examination of this site on the W side of Little Britain in January 1987 revealed traces of cellared 15th–16th-c chalk-walled buildings within an area largely destroyed by modern foundations. These former buildings probably fronted onto medieval Duck Lane and the earlier W continuation of Little Britain prior to their destruction in the 18th and 19th c. No evidence of Roman activity was found.

London Archaeol, 5, 1988, 387

LEE87

G Brown
NGR: TQ 32370 81570
SMR: 043957–62

Wood Street (west carriageway), London Wall (north side) (Lee House, Monkwell Square), EC2

As part of the Lee House redevelopment in Monkwell Square a small trench was dug in the middle of Wood Street just to the N of the junction with London Wall. The contractors removed all material within the trench to the depth of the lowest modern service trench. An archaeological excavation for four weeks was funded by MEPC. The trench measured 7m x 3m, the E third having been totally truncated by a deep Victorian cellar.

Cutting through the natural brickearth was a very disturbed Roman sequence which included several elements of a timber structure. There was no evidence of a road leading to the N gate of the Cripplegate fort.

Overlying the Roman features was a deposit of dark earth. Directly over this was the first of at least seven building phases, represented within the trench by clay floors and occupation debris. Each floor surface had a hearth built on it in the N, more or less occupying the same position in each instance. The pottery from these surfaces had a date-range of c 1000–1150.

Constructed directly onto the final building remains was the first of a long sequence of road surfaces, the majority of which were recorded only in section because of the depth of the service trenches. The earliest road levels were recorded in plan along with N–S rut marks cut into the surface. These were the earliest surfaces of Wood Street and pottery evidence suggests it was established in the late 12th/early 13th c. Later medieval surfaces were also recorded in section.

London Archaeol, 5, 1988, 385; Britannia, 19, 1988, 461; Medieval Archaeol, 32, 1988, 248
Harriss, N, 1988 'Lee House', Finds Appraisal

LFE87

J Brown
NGR: TQ 33430 81100
SMR: 043741–6

65–68 Leadenhall Street, 98 Fenchurch Street, EC3

Excavations funded by Gable House Estates took place in December 1987 and January 1988 in the basement of the standing building. Natural brickearth sloped up from S to N which meant that horizontal stratigraphy survived only at the Fenchurch Street end. The initial activity on the site consisted of a V-shaped ditch of early 1st-c date, aligned E–W; this was devoid of finds, but by analogy with a length of the same ditch excavated on the neighbouring site (94–97 Fenchurch Street, FST85) is thought to have had some military function. After partial backfilling of the ditch, rubbish pits were dug and some flimsy timber structures erected. There followed a succession of strip buildings of clay and timber construction, dated to the 1st and early 2nd c. To the E of most of these buildings, which were all aligned NW–SE, was evidence for an external area, probably a courtyard. These buildings were replaced in the 2nd c by a building, probably of masonry construction, which underwent later robbing. The site was then used for rubbish and cesspits in both the Roman and medieval periods, and was built on again in the 17th c, as shown by cellar walls.

Among the few finds of note from this site were a shale bracelet and a stone spindle-whorl, both of Roman date.

London Archaeol, 6, 1989, 50; Britannia, 20, 1989, 305–6; Medieval Archaeol, 33, 1989, 182
Anon, 1988 '65–68 Leadenhall Street', Finds Appraisal
Brown, J, 1988 'Excavations at 65–68 Leadenhall Street 98 Fenchurch Street EC3 (LFE87)', Archive Report
Holden, T, 1990 'Environmental appraisal report (ASS/10/90)', Archive Report

LGA87

W McCann
NGR: TQ 31770 81140
SMR: 040423, 044006

41–43 Ludgate Hill, 8 Pilgrim Street, EC4

An archaeological investigation between September and November, sponsored by Crown Estate Commissioners, recorded 3m of stratigraphy in three discrete areas in the basement in this later 19th-c building.

Natural sands and gravels survived. In the E, the truncated remains of a N–S ditch were cut into this. Five metres wide and flat-bottomed, it seems to have been a recut of an earlier, possibly V-shaped, ditch. A small area of surviving primary fill contained 10th-/11th-c pottery.

In the S, a 7m length of the N face of the E–W late 13th-c extension of the city wall around the Blackfriars was uncovered. It was constructed of faced ragstone blocks with occasional blocks of Reigate stone and chalk and irregular tile courses, possibly reused Roman material. A 0.25m wide offset delimited the foundation from the wall, the latter surviving 0.9m above the level of the offset. The foundation had a maximum depth of 1.9m and contained five irregular and narrow offsets. A foundation arch was used to carry the wall over the E bank of the earlier ditch, whose W bank lay outside the limit of excavation in this area. Partial excavation of the arch showed the wall to be 3.12m wide.

No evidence of a ditch associated with this wall was found. However, a series of dumps, which contained late 13th-c pottery and a complete jet chess piece, were laid so as to produce a steep incline from the Ludgate road to the base of the wall.

Evidence of later occupation consisted of the N, E and S chalk foundations of a medieval building. Associated with these were a small chalk-lined well and a chalk-lined cesspit which used the ragstone wall as its S limit. This occupation made substantial use of gravel dumping to eliminate the incline from Ludgate Hill to the city wall. A series of timber and brick foundations represented occupation on the site immediately prior to the construction of the present building.

London Archaeol, 5, 1988, 385–6; Medieval Archaeol, 32, 1988, 248

British Telecom shaft, opposite 48 London Wall, EC2

LWL87

A T Mackinder and
A Woodger
NGR: TQ 32760 81540
SMR: 040499

In January 1988 contractors' work for British Telecom in the middle of the road revealed a stone-built culvert which conducted a tributary of the Walbrook through the Roman wall. This was 1.2m wide at its base and 0.9m from roof to floor. It extended S from the inner face of the wall and was probably of medieval date. It probably connected with an identical culvert recorded in 1983, further to the S at 15–35 Copthall Avenue, 45–50 London Wall (see KEY83 above).

London Archaeol, 6, 1989, 51; Medieval Archaeol, 33, 1989, 183

109–117 Middlesex Street, 1–4 Cock Hill, E1

MCO87

J Stevenson
NGR: TQ 33480 81580
SMR: 044458–9

Testpits on the Middlesex Street site indicated that redeposited brickearth sealed the natural gravels and was truncated by 17th-c activity or by modern foundations; on the Cock Hill site this redeposited brickearth slab contained Roman pottery. A series of 17th–18th-c pits also survived on the Cock Hill site.

Britannia, 19, 1988, 464
Cowgill, J, 1987 '117 Middlesex Street and 1–4 Cock Hill MCO87', Finds Appraisal
Stevenson, J, 1987 'Watching brief at 1–4 Cock Hill (MCO87)', Archive Report

MDX87

R Brown
NGR: TQ 33440 81650
SMR: 043963–8

110–116 Middlesex Street, E1

Following the demolition of the Salvation Army Hostel, an excavation and watching brief were conducted on the site in August and September 1987, funded by AMEC. Five testpits and three areas of controlled excavation were investigated.

There was apparently little activity in the area prior to the 3rd c when the site was levelled with dumps of brickearth. The expected Roman extramural cemetery was represented by one 3rd-c inhumation in poor condition, possibly indicating that the site was on the fringe of the main burial ground.

A series of parallel gullies running NW–SE across the W of the area and large pits and hollows to the E was succeeded by another site-wide levelling with a brickearth slab. Subsequently, a second series of gullies appeared in the E of indeterminate date and preceding post-medieval pit activity.

There was no structural evidence of any period before the 19th c, and all the surviving material had been truncated to a greater or lesser extent by modern basements.

London Archaeol, 5, 1988, 386
Brown, R, nd, '110–116 Middlesex Street E1', Archive Report
Keily, F, 1988 'Skeletal report (HUM/01/88b)', Archive Report
Riddler, I, 1989 '110–116 Middlesex Street', Finds Appraisal

MFI87

M Burch and P Rowsome
NGR: TQ 32900 80790
SMR: 043984–7

Monument Street and 17 Fish Street Hill, EC4

A five-week excavation sponsored by the Docklands Light Railway was carried out from the end of August 1987, before work on a new station at Monument. Truncated natural gravels were cut by a large quarry pit of 1st-c date and then sealed by a brickearth dump to form a terrace or platform for building construction. At least two major phases of Roman building could be identified from E–W and N–S post-holes and brickearth foundation lines; they probably fronted the known Roman road to the E (beneath Fish Street Hill) which ran N–S from the bridgehead to the forum and basilica to the N. No associated occupation levels survived. A square, timber-lined well of Flavian date was aligned with the buildings and survived to a depth of about 6m. Modifications to the buildings appeared to enclose the well within a yard for a time. Following its demise in the late 1st c, the well was used for rubbish disposal, its contents including fine ceramics, glass and large amounts of bird, fish, mammal bone and other environmental material in a manner which strongly suggests that all the material came from a nearby inn or restaurant. Post-Roman activity consisted of a succession of external areas which contained two possible wells, pits and chalk foundations of one or more medieval structures. The pits were located around the periphery of the site, possibly reflecting property boundaries and land use. Two post-Great Fire brick soak-aways or wells were also recorded. The site was truncated during the 1829–32 construction of King William Street and the new London Bridge. During this work burials from the graveyard of St Michael's Crooked Lane were reinterred within the area of the site: a total of 26 were recovered for reburial.

London Archaeol, 5, 1988, 386; *Britannia,* 19, 1988, 462–3
Davies, B, 1993 'Inter-site studies', in Milne, G, & Wardle, A, 'Early Roman development at Leadenhall Court, London and related research', *Trans London Middlesex Archaeol Soc,* 44, 135–50

MGT87

J Drummond-Murray
NGR: TQ 32680 81490
SMR: 043995–4005

55–61 Moorgate, 75–79 Coleman Street, EC2

The site, excavated between May and August 1987, was funded by Pearl Insurance. A total of 3m of archaeological deposits were preserved. Nine trenches were excavated, varying in size between 8m x 4m and 2m x 2m.

The earliest features recorded on site were designed to control drainage. A timber-lined drain led to a timber-lined structure, possibly a tank. Two phases of post and plank revetment running N–S, were found, the later provisionally dated to AD120–40. They appear to have revetted the banks of a Walbrook tributary. In the central area of excavation a brickearth and timber Roman building, provisionally mid- to late 1st c, contained at least three rooms, in one of which was a timber tank. This feature may have had an industrial function. After the abandonment of this building another, similar structure, in use until AD120–40, was built on the same site. An important collection of Roman glassworking debris, including part of a 'tank' furnace was found associated with this building.

In the N part of one trench a large dump of Roman leather shoemaking waste was found. The leather and glassworking material constitute a collection likely to provide considerable new insights into the industry of Roman Britain. The most spectacular individual find, associated with a metalled yard and timber tank, was a damaged stone statue of a god, possibly Mercury. The metalling has a provisional date of AD100–200. S of the yard lay the robbed foundations of a large masonry building, which fell into disuse by AD120.

The Roman occupation of this site finished with a phase of deep dumping in the late 2nd to early 3rd c. Evidence of medieval activity, truncated by the recent basements, consisted of a well and a series of wattle-lined pits. The pits appeared to lie along a property boundary parallel with the modern line of Nun Court. Several post-medieval features were also found.

For earlier work on this site, in 1929, see GM121 above.

London Archaeol, 5, 1988, 386; Britannia, 19, 1988, 463; Medieval Archaeol, 32, 1988, 248–9
Drummond-Murray, J, 1988 'Excavations at 55–61 Moorgate EC2 (MGT87)', Archive Report
Kaye, I, 1989 '55–61 Moorgate', Finds Appraisal
Spence, C (ed), 1989 Digging in the City: the annual review 1988 (DUA, MoL), 11

Market Buildings, 26–28 Mincing Lane, EC3

MKB87

M Nally
NGR: TQ 33270 80830
SMR: 044751

Natural gravels in one of three testpits were cut by a feature containing silt and oyster shells. This, and the gravels in the other pits, were truncated by modern make-up and the basement slab.

Merchant Taylors' Hall, 2 White Lion Court, 30 Threadneedle Street, EC3

MTH87

S Gibson and D Sankey
NGR: TQ 32980 81170
SMR: 043691

A watching brief funded by Greycoat plc was carried out in December 1988 during the excavation of a lift-shaft base, as part of the refurbishment of the standing 18th-c building. This revealed an L-shaped length of coursed chalk and rubble masonry standing over 2.9m high, interpreted as the SW corner of a 15th- or 16th-c undercroft, with a floor of crushed chalk rubble and mortar. This structure was cut into a homogeneous garden soil of uncertain date.

London Archaeol, 6, 1989, 49
Gibson, S, & Sankey, D, 1987 'Site investigations at Merchant Taylors' Hall (MTH87)', Archive Report
Schofield, J, 1995 Medieval London houses, 223–5

NAV87

D Dunlop
NGR: TQ 33530 81120
SMR: 043533–4

Navigation House, 1–18 Aldgate, EC3

Between May and July 1988 a post-demolition watching brief was carried out during development, funded by AMEC Properties Ltd. Natural deposits consisted of sand and gravel overlaid by brickearth. The earliest activity on site was extensive dumping of Roman date. While there was some structural evidence of Roman occupation, widespread late medieval and post-medieval truncation had occurred, although in one section a chalk wall running approximately E–W survived.

London Archaeol, 6, 1989, 46
Dunlop, D A, 1990 'Excavations at Navigation House, 1–18 Aldgate (NAV87)', Archive Report
Riddler, I, 1990 'Navigation House, 1–18 Aldgate', Finds Appraisal

NEB87

A Woodger
NGR: TQ 33030 81530
SMR: 043765–73

35–45 New Broad Street, EC2

A series of 20 testpits dug during 1987 prompted a controlled excavation of this large extramural site between March and June 1988. The investigation was generously funded by Norwich Union.

The site was in a low-lying part of the upper Walbrook Valley just to the E of one of the main stream channels which ran on the line of the present Blomfield Street. The site was cut through by a network of small tributaries running down a natural slope in the gravels which lay at 9.5m to the E of the site and 7.5m to the W. During the 2nd c the lower terrace was reclaimed from the stream and the upper terrace was extensively quarried. Roman inhumation burials were found in a small cemetery in the central S part of the site. The site was apparently abandoned from the time of the construction of the city wall c AD200 until it was drained in the 14th c.

A substantial E–W ditch at least 4m wide along the N of the site was replaced by a line of earth-fast posts 0.3m in width, probably by the early 17th c. These features most likely represent the S boundary of the St Mary Bethlem Hospital (later Bedlam) which stood from 1247 to 1676 approximately on the site of the present Liverpool Street Station. During most of the 17th c the area was used as a rubbish dump; a group of tenements called Petty France, mentioned by Stow (1598), was represented on site by brick cellars and wells, as well as brick and wood lined rubbish pits. These features were used into the 19th c and probably until the site was developed as offices in 1905. The facades of these offices were retained to the S and E in the present redevelopment.

Finds from this site include a large assemblage of post-medieval kitchen ware, a large Stuart cloth seal, a silver half groat of 1561–77 and a highly decorated bone handle of late 16th- or early 17th-c date with Renaissance motifs.

London Archaeol, 6, 1989, 52
Woodger, A, 1988 'Excavations at 35–45 New Broad Street EC2 (NEB87)', Archive Report

NOW87

J Stevenson
NGR: TQ 31410 81100
SMR: 043853–5

1–19 Whitefriars Street, 63–67 Fleet Street, 23–24 Bouverie Street, 4 Britton's Court, EC4

An excavation and watching brief funded by Kumagai Gumi UK Ltd were undertaken between January and March 1988. A central area of the site had been truncated down to the London Clay. At the S end of the site were a number of Roman clay quarry pits; to the N, along the Fleet Street frontage, was recorded a sequence of brick features, including a post-medieval brick cellar that truncated the natural gravel. A late medieval undercroft in Britton's Court was recorded by EH, and removed to be restored in the basement of the new development.

London Archaeol, 6, 1989, 53
Stevenson, J, 1988 'Excavations at 1–19 Whitefriars Street, 63–67 Fleet Street, 23–24 Bouverie Street and 4 Britton's Court (NOW87)', Archive Report

56–66 Carter Lane, 1–3 Pilgrim Street, 29–33 Ludgate Hill, EC4

PIC87

M Gavin and B Watson
NGR: TQ 31800 81110
SMR: 04119407007,
042666–71

Excavations funded by Eagle Star Assurance and London and Paris Properties were undertaken in two phases during November 1987 to March 1988 and June to July 1988.

The earliest features on site were the truncated pits and portions of the ditches of a Norman-period (1050–1200) fortress (perhaps Montfichet's Tower). Two phases of ditch aligned broadly E–W were located along the N side of Carter Lane. Both ditches terminated along the line of Cobb's Court alley at the W side of the site, approximately on the line of the N–S Roman and Norman city wall. The earliest S ditch did not extend right across the site; it was over 7m long, some 5m wide and 1.2m deep. The terminal at its E end may mark the position of an entrance into the fortress. The later S ditch (which presumably destroyed the rest of the earliest ditch), represents a realignment and widening of the defences. It was 16m wide and over 4m deep. This ditch has now been traced for 41m to the E along Carter Lane. The lowest excavated fills date to 1050–1200.

The N ditch was aligned E–W, parallel to the Ludgate Hill street frontage. The ditch was 6.8m wide, 2.8m deep and at least 11.5m long; the W extent of the ditch is unknown, but it did not reach the city wall-line as it was not found during salvage recording at 37 Ludgate Hill (see GM251 above). The dating evidence for these ditches was limited as only the later S ditch produced Norman material; the others produced only Roman finds. The great quantity of Roman material probably derived from the reduction of the earth bank behind the city wall. Within the area between the two sets of ditches (the bailey) were a number of cess- and rubbish pits cut into natural gravel and brickearth. Some of these pits contained Norman material, but many contained only Roman finds.

This fortress was probably a motte and bailey complex on Ludgate Hill inside the city walls. The fortress was defended by ditches on three sides approximately in line with modern streets (N, Ludgate Hill; E, probably Creed Lane; S, Carter Lane) and with the city wall on the fourth side. The existence of a motte, towards the E side of the fortress, can be postulated from the volume of material the excavation of the ditches would have produced.

It is documented that the fortress was in ruins by 1272, and in either 1274 or 1276 the Dominicans acquired it as a stone quarry to provide materials to help build their new friary nearby. The later S ditch was systematically infilled (dated by pottery to 1150–1350), then used as part of the friary cemetery. Sixty articulated inhumations were excavated on the present site, thirteen of which were in a mass grave, two in a double grave and the rest were single burials. Twenty-five had evidence of wooden coffins; there was also one lead coffin. There were five possible empty or unused graves. The overall plan of the graves showed a regular layout. Finds from the grave fills indicate a 13th- or 14th-c date; two graves may be as late as c 1500.

After the Dissolution, a rectangular chalk-walled cellar (internal dimensions 3.1m x 2.4m) was built during the late 16th c. The cellar was used as a lead-smelting or casting workshop. It was damaged by fire during the mid-17th c and a brick paved floor and stairs were added. The cellar was then used as a coal store and became a rubbish dump during the 18th c. Contemporary with the later use of the cellar were a number of brick-lined cesspits of 17th- and 18th-c date. Almost all traces of the associated buildings were destroyed by Victorian basements. The major exception to this destruction was an area of standing masonry (party wall between 54/56 Carter Lane and 1/3 and 6 Ludgate Square) which was surveyed. The earliest masonry was ragstone rubble containing a number of medieval moulded stones; above this was a large area of late 17th–18th-c brickwork, containing no architectural features except part of a chimney flue.

No Roman features were identified on this site and the Roman finds, which include a copper-alloy belt, a shale bowl and two brooches, were residual within later deposits. Several of the medieval burials were accompanied by gravegoods, in the form of belt-fittings, pins, a spindle-whorl and a prunted glass beaker. Quantities of later medieval moulded stones were retrieved from post-medieval contexts, which included also a glass vessel, wig-curlers and an axe.

London Archaeol, 6, 1989, 47; 6, 1991, 276; *Medieval Archaeol,* 33, 1989, 180–1

Gavin, M R, 1990 'The medieval cemetery at 54–66 Carter Lane (PIC87)', Archive Report

Keily, F, 1989 'Carter Lane (PIC87) skeleton report', Archive Report

Waller, R, 1989 'Finds appraisal for 25–33 Ludgate Hill 1–3 Pilgrim Street 56–66 Carter Lane (PIC87)', Finds Appraisal

Watson, B, 1987 'The excavation of the Dominican friary cemetery in Carter Lane, EC4: assessment', Assessment Report

Watson, B, 1990 'Excavations at 54–66 Carter Lane, 1–3 Pilgrim Street and 25–33 Ludgate Hill (PIC87)', Archive Report

Watson, B, 1992 'The Norman fortress on Ludgate Hill in the City of London, England, recent excavations 1986–90', *Chateau Gaillard,* 15, 335–45

PLY87

D Bentley
NGR: TQ 32620 81120
SMR: 043947–51

Thames Water Authority main, 18 Poultry, EC2

Observations were made during March–April 1987 in a service trench along Poultry and Cheapside by Thames Water. Archaeological deposits were recorded at two points: outside Mappin and Webb in Poultry and at the Queen Street junction with Cheapside.

At the former site chalk foundations, probably representing buildings on the S frontage of Poultry, were interrupted by a substantial and very worn ragstone-lined culvert. Documentary sources show this to be a branch of the medieval Walbrook which is recorded as running beneath St Mildred Poultry immediately to the N. The culvert was found to cut 12th–13th-c road surfaces while restoration of the fabric in the 17th and again in the 19th c show the important role that this stream played until fairly recently. Roman levels were not reached.

At the N end of Queen Street a succession of 17 road surfaces extended down to at least 4m beneath Cheapside. The earliest of these were cobbled, reusing Roman building material and were accompanied by E–W roadside drains. They appear to represent an uninterrupted sequence of medieval Cheapside although the earliest surfaces produced exclusively Roman dating.

To the S several phases of medieval chalk walling cut through 12th-c deposits, the earliest levels reached here. The walls represented a building which stood on the S side of Cheapside at the junction with Soper Lane prior to the construction of Queen Street in the 17th c.

London Archaeol, 5, 1988, 387; Medieval Archaeol, 32, 1988, 249

PPO87

A Thomas
NGR: TQ 33030 80900
SMR: 043792–9

2–3 Philpot Lane, EC3

Between November 1987 and January 1988 a series of 38 underpinning holes was excavated in preparation for conversion of a standing building by Philpot Management Ltd. Apart from three small areas, the holes were excavated by the contractors on site and recorded as sections by DUA staff.

The site was extensively truncated by the basement and sub-basement of the existing building, and the surviving archaeological strata varied in depth across the site from approximately 1.5m to 4m.

The Roman sequence started with a major brickearth dump across the site. Above this lay a timber building with possible associated floor surfaces to the W and discrete building areas to the N and E. After the timber building went out of use a subterranean tile and brickearth double flue was constructed on the W side of the site. The purpose of this structure was not established but it was possibly the fire box and vaulted entrance area for either a hypocaust or an aboveground kiln or oven. Once the flue structure went out of use the whole site was redeveloped: a series of major masonry buildings, with at least three successive floors of *opus signinum,* extended to both the E and W sides of the site.

Medieval activity comprised a series of large deeply cut pits, occasional chalk foundations aligned both N–S and E–W and gravel surfaces across the site.

During the post-medieval period the NE corner of the site was truncated by a large chalk-lined pit approximately 5m E–W and 5m deep, backfilled with cess and general rubbish on disuse. This was apparently associated, to the S and N, with a deep basement wall built of chalk, moulded ragstone and brick. A brick building was constructed over much of the site in the 18th c, and this survives with some later modifications.

There were few finds of note from this site although a bone skate and numerous fragments of the outer cope of a ceramic bell-mould were recovered.

London Archaeol, 6, 1989, 52–3; Britannia, 20, 1989, 306–7; Medieval Archaeol, 33, 1989, 183

Riverplate House, 7–11 Finsbury Circus, EC2

RIV87

P Askew and D Lees
NGR: TQ 32830 81700
SMR: 043895–903

During April 1987 an excavation funded by the Hammerson Group took place inside a standing building. The purpose of the excavation was to investigate evidence of prehistoric activity, Walbrook tributaries, a Roman road, possibly the continuation of one found at Copthall Avenue in 1981 (see OPT81 above), any evidence of a Roman cemetery, a marsh deposition and later medieval and post-medieval dumping activity.

A similar sequence was recorded in all the areas. Natural sands and gravels were located; a few fragments of Late Iron Age pottery were found in one of the areas. Immediately over this lay brickearth which showed evidence of naturally formed silted-up stream-beds cutting into it. A brown fibrous organic marsh deposit approximately 0.2m deep containing freshwater snails had formed over the brickearth. This phase on the site marks the last naturally formed deposition and probably represents the Roman and medieval marsh deposits which had built up outside the N perimeter of the Roman wall in the 2nd c. The final sequence of deposits consisted of medieval and post-medieval dumps; in one of the dumps a few fragments of a Valencian Lustre ware altar vase (1380–1650) were found, the form of which is quite rare in Britain.

During this phase of excavation a series of six underpinning holes, 8m to the S of the excavation and fronting onto Finsbury Circus, were investigated. Waterlogged black silts and organic material underlay the post-medieval dumping sequence, of which one bore certain evidence of a V-shaped channel 1.2m wide filled with these waterlogged deposits, cut into brickearth and gravel. This was the only evidence of a possibly manmade channel cut to divert or drain one of the Walbrook tributaries in the vicinity.

A further period of excavation took place to the N of the first excavation, fronting onto South Place. The same sequence of medieval and post-medieval dump deposits was located on top of the brown organic 'marsh' deposit as found earlier. In the area to the S a redeposited brickearth was found to overlie a cobbled and metalled surface consisting of gravel and coarse ragstone and chalk blocks with broken red tiles. A slight camber on the surface may indicate a road surface and could possibly be the continuation of the Roman road found at Copthall Avenue in 1981. Further investigation was not possible due to lack of time.

The area to the N contained three inhumations which had been truncated by the deep foundations, and a cremation within the underlying brickearth. Grave cuts were impossible to see possibly due to later marsh flooding which had resorted the deposited brickearth. Associated with one of the burials was a Verulamium Region White ware flask with bands of rouletted decoration around the rim, neck and shoulder and probably dates to the mid–late 2nd c. No other occurrences of this vessel type have been found in London to date.

The site was also observed when the building was erected in 1920; see GM315 above.

London Archaeol, 5, 1988, 384; *Britannia*, 19, 1988, 464; *Medieval Archaeol*, 32, 1988, 246
Askew, P, 1988 'Excavations at River Plate House', Archive Report
Keys, L, nd, '7–11 Finsbury Circus', Finds Appraisal

St Botolph Aldgate church, Aldgate, EC3

SAB87

J Ayre and S O'Connor
NGR: TQ 33580 81200
SMR: 04145202–3, 042694–7

Excavations took place between April and July 1990 inside a crypt at the S end of the church of St Botolph-without-Aldgate (by G Dance the elder, mid-18th c), before conversion of the crypt into offices. These excavations, sponsored by the London Diocesan Fund, augmented watching briefs conducted in 1986–7, before clearance of burials from the crypt.

Natural brickearth was overlaid by brickearth dumps and a clay and timber building of Roman date. This burnt down and the site was levelled, becoming a yard or open area. Later cess- and rubbish pits were in turn truncated by foundations of rammed gravel and chalk for an E–W wall and, to the S, by a series of at least 17 burials aligned E–W. The latter may date from the 10th–11th c and were probably associated with the wall, indicating that the church was in existence then. Another E–W wall built further to the S, including two courses of a wall face in Kentish rag and part of a door sill in Reigate stone, probably marked the later addition of a S aisle or porch, encroaching onto the cemetery.

The church became dilapidated and was rebuilt in the mid-18th c on a different alignment, nearly N–S, to a plan by George Dance the elder; this is the existing brick building. The brick-vaulted crypt added to the S included in its foundations and lower courses stone fragments of c 14th-c window tracery and 17th-c tomb monuments, presumably reused from the previous church. This crypt was filled with burials and sealed in the 19th c, except for the later interment of a head, reputedly that of Henry Grey, duke of Suffolk, executed in 1554. The excavators recovered this head and the parish reinterred it in the churchyard.

London Archaeol, 6, 1991, 276; *Britannia*, 22, 1991, 272; *Medieval Archaeol*, 31, 1987, 129; 35, 1991, 152; *Post-Medieval Archaeol*, 25, 1991, 116
O'Connor, S, 1990 'Excavations at St Botolph without Aldgate church, Aldgate High Street, EC3 (SAB87)', Archive Report
Schofield, J, 1994 'Saxon and medieval parish churches in the City of London: a review', *Trans London Middlesex Archaeol Soc*, 45, 95–7

SBG87

K Wooldridge
NGR: TQ 31968 81734
SMR: 043639–43

St Bartholomew the Great churchyard, Cloth Fair, EC1

For five weeks in April–May 1988 excavations were carried out within the churchyard of St Bartholomew the Great church, jointly funded by EH and the parish. The archaeological excavation preceded the development by the parish of part of the churchyard. The area of excavation, measuring approximately 75sq m, was located between the 14th-c Lady Chapel of the church on the S and Cloth Fair on the N.

The earliest features on the site were two linear ditches running in an approximate E–W direction. The ditches were sealed by a metalled surface containing some sherds of abraded Roman pottery. It was sealed by deposits through which a large number of inhumations had been made.

Sixty-six articulated and seventy-five disarticulated inhumations were recorded. In addition to the inhumations, two rectangular chalk and mortar features, adjacent to the N wall of the Lady Chapel, may have been tombs or burial vaults. All of the inhumations and the possible tombs are presumed to date from after the foundation of the priory in 1123.

The earliest wall foundation recorded was a semicircular chalk and rammed gravel structure predating the main foundations of the 14th-c Lady Chapel. The position of the semicircular structure suggests that it may have been an apsidal chapel to the chancel of the 12th-c church.

Two phases of construction were identified in the exposed foundations of the 14th-c Lady Chapel. The different phases of foundation suggested that at least part of the Lady Chapel had been constructed prior to the demolition of the E end of the 12th-c church.

Following the dissolution of the priory, the Lady Chapel was sold for private use. Some evidence for the post-Dissolution use of the Lady Chapel came from a pit adjacent to the Lady Chapel wall which contained 1,857 18th-c pipeclay wig-curlers, as well as a large quantity of post-medieval glass and pottery.

The site code BRT88 was later issued for potential work recording the crypt of the Lady Chapel, but in the event not used.

London Archaeol, 6, 1989, 48; *Medieval Archaeol*, 33, 1989, 181
Moore, A, 1988 'St Bartholomew's crypt', Finds Appraisal
Spence, C (ed), 1989 *Digging in the City: the annual review 1988* (DUA, MoL), 13
Wooldridge, K, 1988 'St Bartholomew the Great church Cloth Fair EC1', Archive Report

SKN87 (=CKL88)

J Ayre and R Harris
NGR: TQ 32545 80865
SMR: 043626–38; both site codes refer to the same site

Skinners' Hall kitchen, 8–9 Cloak Lane, EC4

In January–March 1988 excavations, sponsored by the Worshipful Company of Skinners, Reinhold plc and Ranelagh Developments Ltd, investigated two areas. In one of these, Skinners' Hall kitchen in the S part of the site, over 4m of stratigraphy survived. A watching brief was undertaken from September 1988 till the end of the year while the rest of the site was reduced.

The SKN87 code refers to the excavation inside Skinners' Hall kitchen, and CKL88 to the wider watching brief, but both sites are considered together in all post-excavation reports.

In the N trench, overlying the alluvial deposits of the Walbrook, which ran down the E edge of the site, were a number of Roman timber drains running E into the Walbrook. These were covered by more alluvial deposits which in turn were overlaid by an extensive yard surface. Patched and resurfaced numerous times, the surface sloped gradually down towards the Walbrook. It was constructed out of building debris and contained a large quantity of painted wall plaster. The other Roman feature on the site was a plain tessellated floor. The floor was covered by dark earth with a high content of building material including stamped roof tiles.

During the medieval period the area seems to have been divided into a number of properties. Numerous floors were excavated but few associated walls survived. This appears to be due to the continuity of property boundaries and the insertion of a large chalk gravel foundation in the late medieval period. The building phases were interspersed with phases of pits. Several were wicker lined and one appeared to have wooden sides and a 'lid'. In the E property the pits were larger and several contained industrial residues.

In the S trench the dark earth dumps were exposed but not excavated. They were truncated by a medieval building with a mortar floor to the E and external gravel yard surfaces and well to the W, property boundaries being defined by two large stone drains with yellow brick-vaulted roofs, one running N–S along the E side of the site, the other E–W through the middle of the site. The larger E drain was thought to have contained the enclosed course of the Walbrook; the other running into it to have contained a previously unrecorded tributary. A building to the S, also with external surfaces, and a well to the W, were seen in the watching brief.

In the post-medieval period the N building was replaced with gardens (probably shown on the Agas map c 1559) and large brick-lined cesspits. A brick building reused the foundations to the S but only a large tile hearth and part of a flagstone floor were recorded. After the Great Fire the same foundations were reused for the new buildings, but the hearth was filled in as were the pits to the W. Cesspits continued to be dug in this area, producing a large variety of environmental remains. The garden area was re-established (as shown on Ogilby and Morgan's map of 1676) and a small part of a curved garden wall and path were recorded.

The finds assemblage from this site is dominated by building materials, which include 19 examples of Roman *tegulae* with a civilian form of stamp. Abundant quantities of painted wall plaster were recovered from a confined area of the site. Medieval finds were sparser but include a chalk toy 'house' recovered from a rubbish pit. The cesspits of Skinners' Hall kitchen were filled with 17th-c ceramics, bottle glass and an exotic array of faunal remains, including duck, hare, eel and wild bird.

London Archaeol, 6, 1989, 47; *Britannia,* 20, 1989, 307; *Medieval Archaeol,* 33, 1989, 181
Ayre, J, 1989 'Excavations at 9 Cloak Lane and Skinners' Hall kitchen', Archive Report

Cannon Street Station south, Upper Thames Street (Cousin Lane), EC4

UTA87

R Bluer, F Meddens and
A Stephenson
NGR: TQ 32570 80730
SMR: 041614–19

Excavations were funded by Speyhawk. The earliest features found, to the N, were a 30m length of late Roman timber revetment running E–W, followed by a sequence of Saxon banks of clay, rafts of brushwood and stone rubble, with pits and hearths to the N. To the NW, controlled excavation revealed a masonry building 10.3m wide, extending S from the N end of the site for at least 17m. The walls, built of ragstone on chalk and gravel foundations, survived up to 1.4m in height above the level of the floor, the latter mostly of crushed chalk or mortar, frequently renewed. The building was a single-aisled hall, the ground floor of which was probably used for storage: architectural details of two square pier bases *in situ* and associated stones reused in a later context suggest a late 12th-c date.

This building is identified as the Guildhall of the merchants of Cologne, who are documented in London in 1175. Further chalk foundations indicated that the Guildhall was enlarged towards the river by at least 31m, probably c 1300, and that other buildings were constructed to the E, presumably the houses, shops and storerooms of the traders of the Hanseatic League who acquired the site in 1475, when it was known as the Steelyard. This precinct extended to a late medieval riverwall found as far S as the present river frontage. Later deposits were truncated by post-medieval cellaring partly reusing earlier masonry, and by construction of the railway viaduct in 1865. The latter included an inclined cab road running between the level of the street and the platforms, which was photographically recorded by EH before demolition.

Sparse evidence of Roman activity is provided by a penannular brooch, tweezers, a finger-ring and several coins. Medieval objects include a bone skate, a buckle and a Saxo-Norman decorative bone dress-pin and there are also good collections of post-medieval clay tobacco pipes and decorated floor tiles. The finds assemblage from this site is dominated by a collection of 156 moulded stones of medieval and later date.

London Archaeol, 6, 1990, 161; *Britannia*, 22, 1991, 270; *Medieval Archaeol*, 34, 1990, 176–7

Bluer, D, 1997 'The medieval German towns and the Hanseatic League', *Medieval Life*, No. 7, 14–18

Groves, J, 1988 'The Roman pottery from Cannon Street Station (UTA87)', Archive Report

Hunting, P, nd [1990] *Archaeology and development* (Speyhawk and MoL), 14–21

Robinson, J, 1989 'Cannon Street Station (south side) post-Roman pottery (UTA87)', Appraisal Report

Spence, C, & Grew, F (eds), 1990 *The annual review 1989* (DUA, MoL), 22–3

WOC87

A Westman
NGR: TQ 31440 81200
SMR: 043904

Ye Olde Cheshire Cheese, Wine Office Court, 145 Fleet Street, EC4

An archaeological examination of a cellar adjoining the Old Cheshire Cheese public house, Wine Office Court, was made in December 1987 for the proprietors, Samuel Smith Brewery. The brick cellar, built with cast-iron columns of early 19th-c type supporting iron beams and shallow brick ceiling vaults, was added to the E of existing 18th-c cellars and standing building, now occupied by the public house. Original entrances to the cellar were from the W and S; the latter, possibly leading to the ground floor, was later blocked and another doorway was inserted in the N wall, giving access to further cellars.

London Archaeol, 5, 1988, 384

Westman, A, 1988 'Archaeological examination of a cellar at the Old Cheshire Cheese public house, Wine Office Court, 145 Fleet Street, EC4 (WOC87)', Archive Report

YHA87

Sarah Gibson
NGR: TQ 31900 81080
SMR: 04130808

Youth Hostel, 36–38 Carter Lane, EC4

During refurbishment of a standing building, chalk foundations were recorded, possibly part of the medieval deanery of St Paul's Cathedral. Black dumps were also recorded.

London Archaeol, 6, 1991, 273; *Medieval Archaeol*, 35, 1991, 149

AGE88

P Travis
NGR: TQ 32090 81680
SMR: 044560

158–170 Aldersgate, EC1

On the W side of the site there was evidence of structural cut features which may have related to one of the large post-medieval mansions which are documented as lying close to the site. The rest of the site was truncated.

Travis, P, nd, '158–170 Aldersgate Street', Testpit Report

9–10 Angel Court, EC2

ANT88

L Dyson
NGR: TQ 32780 81330
SMR: 043535–7

A watching brief, funded by Prudential Assurance, took place between September and November 1988. Three sections were recorded, up to 7m long. Natural deposits were not recorded in detail because of the inaccessibility of the sections.

Sections 1 and 2 showed a similar sequence of alternating flood deposits and rubbish dumps. The dumps, which yielded a small number of Roman potsherds, were probably laid to combat flooding from the Walbrook stream which flowed immediately to the N. The remains of a timber structure, possibly part of a channel revetment or hut foundation, were recorded in Section 3. A dendrochronological date of AD191 was obtained from one of the vertical piles.

London Archaeol, 6, 1989, 46; *Britannia*, 20, 1989, 307
Dyson, E, 1988 'Watching brief at 9–10 Angel Court EC2 (ANT88)', Archive Report
Tyers, I, 1988 'Dendrochronological spot dates (SPT/18/88)', Archive Report

13–14a Austin Friars, EC2

AUF88

L Dyson
NGR: TQ 32930 81390
SMR: 043538–41

A series of sections was recorded in pile-probing trenches during July and August 1988. The work was funded by City Merchant Holdings Ltd and Friends Provident. The site lies about 15m E of an upper Walbrook tributary. In the SW of the site the W-sloping natural brickearth surface was overlaid by a series of gravel and rubbish dumps. These were probably intended to raise the ground level, and were no earlier than late 1st c in date. In the NE of the site natural brickearth was truncated by a number of pits or ditches. Subsequently, a phase of building construction was indicated by a brickearth floor.

Destruction dumps overlying the floor surface contained potsherds from the late 1st/mid-2nd c, and were sealed by an external surface. Substantial site-wide dumps were deposited or accumulation occurred during the late Roman or medieval periods.

London Archaeol, 6, 1989, 46; *Medieval Archaeol*, 33, 1989, 180
Dyson, E, 1988 'Watching brief at 13–14a Austin Friars EC2 (AUF88)', Archive Report

55 Basinghall Street, EC2

BAS88

N Hall
NGR: TQ 32480 81520
SMR: 04003330, 041487–9

Excavations here were funded by Wates City of London Properties plc. Natural strata consisted of brickearth and gravels. The site was located partly on the line of the E wall of the Cripplegate fort. The defensive ditch around the fort wall was located, with traces of a timber structure on the berm to the W. The wall was robbed and the backfilled ditch was sealed by floor surfaces and walls of late Roman date, later robbed in turn. These features, and natural deposits in other areas, were truncated successively by medieval refuse and cesspits, medieval and post-medieval cellars and Second World War bomb craters.

London Archaeol, 6, 1990, 160; *Britannia*, 22, 1991, 267; *Medieval Archaeol*, 34, 1990, 176
Groves, J, 1989 '55 Basinghall Street Roman pottery appraisal report (BAS88)', Pottery Appraisal
Hall, N, 1989 'Excavations at 55 Basinghall Street EC2 (BAS88)', Archive Report
Robinson, J, 1989 '55 Basinghall Street post-Roman pottery appraisal report (BAS88)', Pottery Appraisal

BIP88

M Watts
NGR: TQ 33110 81340
SMR: 041587–93

41–63 Bishopsgate, EC2

The earliest activity appeared as stained surfaces and pits, the latter containing ash, charcoal, a burnt timber and a complete pottery vessel dated to the Late Bronze Age–Early Iron Age. These were sealed by redeposited brickearth containing struck flints and pottery fragments of similar date.

Structural remains of the Roman period comprised, in the N half of the site, a beam slot, post-hole and stake-holes. To the W quarry pits for brickearth were backfilled with Roman building materials, and other pits contained cess and rubbish. Pits of definitely medieval date were located only to the W, implying different land use to the E, presumably the presence of buildings fronting onto Bishopsgate. Modern basements and foundations truncated all other evidence.

Most finds from the site are of Roman date, including fragments of glass bottles, bowls, flagons and flasks, as well as a counter and a stirring rod.

London Archaeol, 6, 1990, 160–1; Britannia, 22, 1991, 267
Watts, M, 1990 'Excavations at 41–63 Bishopsgate (BIP88)', Archive Report, draft

BOU88

B McCann
NGR: TQ 31370 81110
SMR: 044561–2

6–8 Bouverie Street, EC4

In October 1988 a site code was issued for this site and a visit made to it. A note in the site file describes five underpinning holes which had been excavated, '2 in the N and 3 on the S'. The holes had all reached the level of grey clay which was being removed. Shoring was being inserted so no sections were visible. Probable natural sands and gravels with bands of grey clay were seen in the N, approximately 0.5–0.7m below basement level. They were approximately 1m thick and overlay London Clay. In the S, redeposited gravels appeared to overlie black alluvial deposits which gave way to London Clay. A cut feature, possibly a medieval pit, was observed in one testpit, at least 0.5m deep. There was no sign of any evidence for the cemetery of the Whitefriars which occupied the site.

BPA88

K Wooldridge
NGR: TQ 33350 81740
SMR: 044752–6

Bishopsgate, junction with Brushfield Street, EC2

Recorded in two sections in a hole in the road, natural gravels were overlain by humic, waterlaid clay cut by the construction of a masonry foundation which comprised chalk and Reigate stone blocks. Above a silty deposit sealing the masonry was a horizontal timber which may have been associated with the masonry foundation. Silts and waterlaid clays overlay the timber and were sealed by a layer of burnt brickearth and mortar fragments. This was cut by a pit, its fill truncated by two large post-medieval drain trenches, and sealed by concrete. These features are undated; they could have been Roman or, if Bishopsgate was narrower in medieval times, medieval.

Wooldridge, K, 1988 'Watching brief at junction of Brushfield Street and Bishopsgate, London EC2 (BPA88)', Archive Report

Opposite 80 Lombard Street, EC3

BRD88

P Rowsome
NGR: TQ 32740 81070
SMR: 043759–62

A large quarry pit of 1st-c date cut into the natural gravels. It was followed by widespread external dumping of 1st- and 2nd-c date, after which a masonry building, including a tessellated pavement, was constructed, probably in the 2nd c. The building was of a similar alignment to the Roman street known to lie to the S of the site. Part of a tile and *opus signinum* structure to the E may have been an element of a hypocaust associated with the building. Extensive robbing of the building eventually took place and a gap then occurred in the sequence until the construction of a brick and stone built cellared building in the S of the site, probably in the 18th c. It fronted the S side of Lombard Street prior to the construction of King William Street in the 1830s. A number of drains and sewers, followed by cellar backfilling, indicated the disuse of the cellar in the 19th c. The site lay immediately W of LOM88.

St Bartholomew's Crypt, Cloth Fair, EC1

BRT88: see SBG87

28 and 30 Bush Lane, 2 Suffolk Lane, EC4

BSL88

P Travis
NGR: TQ 32680 80845
SMR: 041993–7, 0221127

Excavations were conducted in the basements of separate standing buildings at 28 and 30 Bush Lane from January to June 1990, before demolition. Testpits in the basement and the superstructure of a third building at 2 Suffolk Lane, to the E, were also recorded, until November 1990, during refurbishment. The site is part of a Scheduled Ancient Monument, the presumed Roman governor's palace. No. 2 Suffolk Lane is a Listed Building. Work took place by arrangement with MEPC Developments Ltd.

Intrusions survived cut into natural brickearth and gravel. Substantial Roman mortared ragstone foundations running W and S probably represented walls retaining terraces up slope, at least at the N (where extensive Roman buildings were recorded in 1988–9; see EAG87 above). A large tile built channel curving SE and part of a possible basin lined with *opus signinum* suggest elaborate drainage, subsequently abandoned. Later intrusive features included a N–S medieval chalk foundation and to the W a post-medieval brick-lined well, cesspit and a probable ice-house. Medieval moulded stones were reused, incorporated in the cellar walls of the 18th-c building at 30 Bush Lane and forming windows, later superseded, in a brick cellar at 2 Suffolk Lane.

The earliest elements of the standing building at 2 Suffolk Lane were parts of separate post-Great Fire buildings, later combined and substantially rebuilt. Floors, a staircase, door and window cases, panelling and fine, decorative plasterwork, dated to the early or mid-18th c, survived from this rebuild. The S half of this building was then altered to serve as a warehouse, and cast-iron columns of early 19th-c type were inserted. Later in the 19th c the entire building was refurbished as offices. Subsequent fire damage led to renewal of the roof and partial refacing of the walls.

London Archaeol, 6, 1991, 272–3; 6, 1992, 390; Britannia, 22, 1991, 270; Post-Medieval Archaeol, 25, 1991, 138

BUN88

Stuart Gibson and
C Mamwell
NGR: TQ 33330 81390
SMR: 041909, 041941

Bunge House, 53–71 St Mary Axe, EC3

Pre-demolition excavations and a watching brief in 1988 were funded by Bunge and Co. The line of the city wall, a Scheduled Ancient Monument, crossed the site from NW to SE. A probable Roman ditch, heavily truncated, was traced in front of this line. This was succeeded by a medieval ditch, on the flat base of which animal hoof prints were detected. This ditch was recut, and later a post-medieval brick-lined drain inserted. All other remains, of the upstanding defences or of the associated medieval church of St Augustine Papey, demolished in the 16th c, were presumably destroyed when Bunge House was built in 1926.

London Archaeol, 6, 1990, 166; Britannia, 22, 1991, 265; Medieval Archaeol, 34, 1990, 179
Hunting, P, nd [1990] Archaeology and development (Speyhawk and MoL), 59–60
Mamwell, C, 1989 '63–71 St Mary Axe Bunge House EC3', Archive Report

CEM88

A Mackinder
NGR: TQ 32660 81520
SMR: 043644–9

80 Coleman Street, EC2

In June–July 1988 partial demolition allowed a seven-week excavation, funded by City Holdings Ltd. This revealed two parallel E–W Roman ditches, which were backfilled with domestic rubbish and sealed by a dump containing evidence of burning. There were also traces of a brickearth building that was disturbed by extensive pits to the S. In the medieval period, there was another E–W ditch, partly wood lined, and a pit containing slag.

London Archaeol, 6, 1989, 48; Medieval Archaeol, 33, 1989, 181
Brehm, B, nd, '80 Coleman Street', Finds Appraisal
Groves, J, 1988 'The Roman pottery from 80 Coleman St (CEM88)', Archive Report
Holden, T, 1990 'Environmental appraisal report (ASS/06/90)', Archive Report
Mackinder, A T, 1989 '80 Coleman Street EC2 (CEM88)', Archive Report

CKL88: see SKN87

Skinner's Hall Kitchen, 8–9 Cloak Lane, EC4

CNN88

N Shepherd
NGR: TQ 32765 80855
SMR: 043594–7

108 Cannon Street, EC4

Between June and October 1988 a controlled watching brief funded by Speyhawk Mount Row Ltd took place after demolition.

Two main areas were investigated and natural was found to be truncated. Apart from a fragment of a possible surface only cut features survived. Gravel quarries and refuse pits dating to the 12th and 13th c were observed, probably representing an open area to the S of buildings fronting onto Cannon Street. The only evidence for these buildings was a chalk and ragstone lined cellar or cesspit, demolished some time after 1550.

London Archaeol, 6, 1989, 47–8; Medieval Archaeol, 33, 1989, 180
Hunting, P, nd [1990] Archaeology and development (Speyhawk and MoL), 59–60
Shepherd, N, 1988 'Watching brief at 108 Cannon Street (CNN88)', Archive Report

Cotts House, 27–29 Camomile Street, EC3

COT88

A Mackinder
NGR: TQ 33310 81410
SMR: 041934

In February–March 1988 six trenches were excavated within a standing building; the work was funded by Prudential Assurance. A NW–SE Roman ditch at least 25m long and 12 Roman inhumations lay outside the projected line of the city wall. Deposits backfilling the medieval city ditch were recorded. A post-medieval brick well 3.5m deep was also excavated. Finds from this site include a small amount of late medieval bone beadmaking waste and a medieval copper disc mount.

See also GM28, excavations on this site in 1958.

London Archaeol, 6, 1989, 46; Britannia, 20, 1989, 308
Groves, J, 1990 '27–29 Camomile Street', Roman Pottery Appraisal
Mackinder, A, 1989 '27–29 Camomile St EC3 archive report (COT88)', Archive Report
Robinson, J, 1989 '27–29 Camomile Street', Post-Roman Pottery Appraisal

Dominant House, 85 Queen Victoria Street, EC4

DMT88

N Hammond, P Rowsome
and K Wooldridge
NGR: TQ 32230 80890
SMR: 040623, 041801–8

This site comprised the W half of a Scheduled Ancient Monument, the Huggin Hill baths (partly excavated in 1964 and 1969; GM240 above), and an area further to the W. Trial excavations took place in 1988 (DMT88) and Scheduled Monument Consent entailed major excavations, funded by Hammersons plc, in 1989. An agreement was subsequently reached to preserve most of the Roman structural remains that had been found on the site. These are now beneath the new building on the site, but are not accessible; they were covered with suitable material and built over.

To the N, truncated natural gravel and, to the S, river-scoured natural gravel overlaid by natural clay, reflected a steep slope down to the Thames. The earliest activity recorded was terracing of this slope in the 1st c. A lower terrace formed the construction level for a large masonry building of early–mid-Flavian date, thought to have been the main public baths of the city. Oak piles supported foundations of Kentish ragstone and concrete and, internally, a thick ragstone and concrete raft. The superstructure of the building, much of it built of tile, and retaining walls to N and W, survived up to a height of 3m.

The building (Fig 50) contained a suite of large rooms originally extending further to the E, along the river. To the W, two rooms heated by an interconnected hypocaust and containing fragments of a polychrome mosaic floor are identified provisionally as a double-apsed caldarium and a tepidarium. To the E, two unheated rooms, probably frigidaria, contained internal corner buttresses or pier bases and mosaic floors. Substantial masonry culverts and drains through the foundations carried off ground water.

Fig 50 DMT88: the pilae and walls of the Roman bath-house from the S, within the standing building of 1964. This monument is now conserved by burial under the new building, and is not accessible.

Subsequently many modifications were made internally, a timber drain was inserted around the building to the W and, in the early 2nd c, another large double-apsed heated room was added. The terraced gravels to the W remained open ground; there was no sign of a waterfront revetment.

The baths were dismantled in the late 2nd c, valuable materials being salvaged, and evidence for glass- and metalworking suggests that industrial use was then made of the ruins. Clay and timber domestic buildings were constructed during the 3rd c, incorporating surviving masonry. Two large ditches were cut through the ruins, draining to the S. Later features included a sunken building of 10th–11th-c date, chalk foundations of other medieval buildings and, to the E, the tile-floored cellars of two 17th-c brick buildings containing evidence of fire destruction.

The site produced large quantities of Roman building material including several complete roof tiles. Some tile fragments bear a stamp, PPBRLON or PPRBR, pertaining to the Procurator of the Province of Britain and may have been intended for use in an official building. Part of a Purbeck marble slab from the site is inscribed '...]MAX...]NIA' and may have formed part of a dedicatory inscription. One of the drains consisted of 19 sections of ceramic drainpipe still *in situ*. Many fragments of Roman painted wall plaster were uncovered, some with elaborate and colourful designs.

Part of a late Roman or Saxon casket was found. The original wooden box had decayed but its decorative bone mounts survived intact. The casket appears to have been empty when buried. Many ceramic lamps were found including one in the form of the theatre mask of a slave, Flavian in date and probably made in Italy, and three late 1st- or 2nd-c Verulamium mica-dusted lamps, the only examples of such lamps known from London. Another unusual find is a limestone mould which would have been used in the production of small metal dishes. Roman glass finds include fragments of some high-quality vessels and a spindle-whorl.

London Archaeol, 6, 1990, 165–6; *Britannia,* 21, 1990, 342–4; 22, 1991, 269–70; *Medieval Archaeol,* 34, 1990, 179

Groves, J, 1990 'Dominant House', Roman Pottery Appraisal

Hammond, N, Rowsome, P, & Wooldridge, J, 1991 'Excavations at 85 Queen Victoria Street (Dominant House) (DTM88)', Archive Report, draft

Robinson, J, 1990 'Dominant House', Post-Roman Pottery Appraisal

Shea, M, 1989 '85 Queen Victoria Street/Dominant House EC4 (trial excavations)', Archive Report

Spence, C, & Grew, F (eds), 1990 *The annual review 1989* (DUA, MoL), 10–11

Tyers, I, 1988 'Dendrochronological spot date report: interim report (SPT/08/88)', Archive Report

DUH88

M Hinman
NGR: TQ 33190 80715
SMR: 044563

23–26 St Dunstan's Hill, EC3

Natural gravels had been truncated during the construction of the modern building and only undatable pits survived.

Hinman, M, 1989 'Excavations at 23–26 St Dunstan's Hill EC3 (DUH88)', Archive Report

EAS88

M Shea
NGR: TQ 33040 80800
SMR: 043692–6

14–18 Eastcheap, EC3

During mid-June–early July 1988 a week of excavations and two weeks of watching brief were sponsored by Peachey Development plc. The site, where the medieval church of St Andrew Hubbard (first mentioned in 1202) was located before the Great Fire, was mostly double-basemented and only the SE sector of the site was excavated. Natural gravels and brickearth were overlaid by an apparently site-wide horizon of redeposited brickearth. The surviving archaeology consisted mainly of intrusive features: wall foundations, pits and a chalk-lined well. The only surviving horizontal archaeology of any note were gravel metallings resting on top of the redeposited brickearth, but these were truncated on all four sides. The metallings could conceivably be the faint remains of a road or, more likely, a series of gravel paths. Only inconclusive evidence was provided therefore for a Roman road continuing eastwards from Cannon Street.

London Archaeol, 6, 1989, 49; *Britannia,* 20, 1989, 306

Shea, M, 1990 'Excavations at 14–18 Eastcheap (EAS88)', Archive Report

30–40 Eastcheap, 37–39 St Mary at Hill, EC3

ECH88

M Inzani
NGR: TQ 33130 80780
SMR: 042514–20

Excavations were conducted in the basement of a standing building from October to December 1989, funded by Norwich Union Insurance Group.

Natural brickearth was cut by beam slots for a Roman timber-framed building containing at least eight small rooms, aligned to a presumed E–W road to the S. After this building was dismantled, cesspits and rubbish pits were dug. Later strata were truncated and only intrusive features survived, including a medieval chalk-lined well repaired in brick and finally backfilled in the 17th c, and three post-medieval brick-lined cesspits and a possible ice-house. The chalk walls of medieval cellars, refaced in brick, also partly survived encased in the walls of the existing basement.

London Archaeol, 6, 1991, 273; Medieval Archaeol, 35, 1991, 149; Post-Medieval Archaeol, 25, 1991, 138
Inzani, M, 1990 'Excavations at 30–40 Eastcheap and 37–39 St Mary at Hill (ECH88)', Archive Report

Liverpool House, 15–17 Eldon Street, EC2

ELD88

P Potter
NGR: TQ 32980 81650
SMR: 041655–62

Excavations here were funded by Norwich Union Pensions Management Ltd. Natural gravels sloped steeply down from N to S. In the Roman period quarrying took place in the N The site was then levelled up in order to lessen the gradient of the ground and to consolidate it for the construction of an E–W road. The N part of the site became a burial ground, part of the extramural cemetery in this area; one of the burials is dated to the 2nd c. A timber-lined well was found in the S.

The burials were sealed by a horizon of disturbed soil, probably caused by Walbrook river action. Three E–W drainage ditches then crossed the centre and S parts of the site. They were filled and sealed by thick marsh deposits. A possible tanning pit succeeded the marsh, medieval or post-medieval in date. Victorian drains completed the sequence.

London Archaeol, 6, 1990, 163; Britannia, 22, 1991, 271
Potter, P, 1989 '15–17 Eldon Street/Liverpool House EC2', Archive Report

12–15 Finsbury Circus, EC2

FIB88

P Askew
NGR: TQ 32880 81680
SMR: 043716–22

Excavation funded by MEPC Developments Ltd took place here between June and August 1988. Large-scale intrusive activity on the site, identified as the foundations of the London Institution built in 1817, confined the areas of excavation to two trenches, designated A and B respectively: a N–S aligned trench measuring 11m x 2m on the E side, and one aligned E–W measuring 7m x 2m to the SW of the former.

Natural gravel was located. The earliest activity was found in Area A and was represented by a flexed inhumation (on its side with its knees up) aligned E–W with the head to the W, and a possible associated superstructure which was demolished prior to the construction of an E–W aligned cobbled road in the early 2nd c. Activity following the disuse of the road was indicated by the presence of redeposited brickearth with a series of six burials, four of which were aligned E–W, and two cremation pits cutting through it. Two of the burials contained whole pots, one a Black-burnished ware, as yet undated, and the other a colour-coated ware from Cologne provisionally dated to the late 2nd/early 3rd c. Evidence of a truncation horizon, postdating the cemetery, was indicated by the shallow depth of the graves and the absence of the brickearth in all but the N quarter of the trench, and was also represented by the construction of a drainage channel filled with marsh deposits sealing the Roman stratigraphy.

Similar activity in this later period was recorded in Area B with the presence of a NW–SE aligned channel also containing marsh deposits. No evidence of any earlier Roman activity was identified; although disarticulated human remains, probably of Roman date, were found at the bottom of the channel, they were presumably residual.

Sealing the marsh was a series of later medieval dumps approximately 1.4m in depth in both areas on the site. In Area A an E–W aligned ditch 1.4m deep cut through the dumps which contained backfill dating to the 17th c.

London Archaeol, 6, 1989, 49; *Medieval Archaeol,* 33, 1989, 182

Askew, P, 1989 'Excavations at 12–15 Finsbury Circus EC2 (FIB88)', Archive Report

Crowley, N, nd, '12–15 Finsbury Circus', Building Materials Appraisal

Ford, W, 1990 'An assessment of environmental material (ASS/02/90)', Archive Report

Groves, J, 1990 '12–15 Finsbury Circus', Roman Pottery Appraisal

Price, P, 1990 '12–15 Finsbury Circus', Finds Appraisal

FNC88

D Dunlop
NGR: TQ 33510 81080
SMR: 043697–704

88–93 Fenchurch Street, 5–7 Carlisle Avenue, EC3

Excavation was undertaken in two phases between May and October 1988, the main trenches being excavated before demolition, with two more trenches excavated afterwards; funding being provided by P & O Developments Ltd.

Natural deposits of sand and gravel overlaid by brickearth were located. A sequence of 1st-c clay and timber buildings was recorded in the N of the site, with a subsequent destruction level. This area had then been rebuilt in the late 2nd c, with a more substantial building and adjacent courtyard area, the courtyard having a metalled surface. Evidence of Roman light industrial activity was apparent in the S trenches, where floor surfaces were covered by ash, slag, and hearth rake-out. Between these areas lay a brickearth quarry pit and a Roman cesspit. After the destruction of the later Roman structures widespread dumping had taken place over the area, which had in some places been truncated by late medieval pits. A post-medieval cellar of chalk blocks, and a chalk well which had been lined with tiles, are thought to belong to the Saracen's Head, an inn dating from the 18th c. Widespread truncation had taken place over the site due to modern groundbeams, drainage pipes and other activities.

London Archaeol, 6, 1989, 49; *Britannia,* 20, 1989, 306

Groves, J, 1988 'The Roman pottery from 88–93 Fenchurch Street and Saracen's Head house (FNC88)', Archive Report

Murray, J, 1990 'Assessment of the environmental sample from 88–89 Fenchurch Street (ASS/03/90)', Archive Report

Riddler, I, 1989 '88–93 Fenchurch Street', Finds Appraisal

Robinson, J, 1989 '88–93 Fenchurch Street & Saracen's Head house post-Roman pottery (FNC88)', Appraisal Report

FRI88

B Watson
NGR: TQ 31810 81060
SMR: 04119424, 041631–2

10 Friar Street, 69 Carter Lane, EC4

Excavations here were funded by MEPC Developments Ltd. The earliest feature identified was an unlined well of 12th-c date and several gravel pits. Parts of the Dominican priory of Blackfriars, established c 1276, were known to have occupied the site. To the N, these included the E end of the choir of the priory church, but little of the walls of the choir remained as they appear to have been replaced by existing basement walls on the N and E edges of the site. Inside the choir, five burials and two brick burial vaults were found, the latter emptied and then used for rubbish disposal some time after the dissolution of the priory in 1538. To the S, the prior's lodging and a garden are documented. These were represented by stone foundations and an external garderobe pit, the former surrounding a floor of delftware tiles and last used as a coal cellar before demolition in the late 17th or 18th c.

The party wall along the S edge of the site incorporated stone foundations of the external wall of an undercroft (recorded further to the S in 1900, located below the provincial's hall and the S dorter). These foundations were buttressed to the N; to the W upstanding masonry contained a large window of c 14th-c date, subsequently blocked, which will be preserved and displayed in the new development. Along the W edge of the site, to the S, another substantial medieval foundation was recorded: probably the E wall of the chapter house.

Most of the finds are post-medieval in date. Copper-alloy objects include 11 coins and a variety of domestic articles. An iron Jew's harp was recovered, as well as two fragmentary ivory double-sided combs and some textile. A good selection of glass vessels, in turquoise and green as well as clear glass, includes an almost complete colourless wine glass. A gold coin of George III was recovered. The pottery includes several whole vessels, among which is a Westerwald panel jug depicting the seven electors of the Holy Roman Empire, with the date 1603, and a Frechen Bellarmine with the arms of Amsterdam on the medallion.

London Archaeol, 6, 1990, 162; Medieval Archaeol, 34, 1990, 177
Spence, C, & Grew, F (eds), 1990 The annual review 1989 (DUA, MoL), 16–17
Watson, B, 1988 'Testpit survey prior to excavation and development of 10 Friar Street, 69 Carter Lane EC4 (FRI88)', Evaluation
   Report

52 Gresham Street, 14 Ironmonger Lane, EC2

GAM88

A Mackinder
NGR: TQ 32530 81280
SMR: 041680–8

Excavations and recording of a standing building were funded by City Holdings Ltd. The earliest feature was a quarry pit cut into natural sands and gravels, backfilled in the late 1st c. Dumps and pits were sealed by the masonry wall and floors of a late Roman building. This was on the same alignment (NNE–SSW) as walls recorded in 1949 immediately to the S, at 11 Ironmonger Lane (see GM219 above). Further dumps, cut by a N–S 11th-c ditch, pits and a possible well, were followed by the chalk and gravel foundations of an 11th–13th-c building. In places, the brick walls of the standing building directly rested on these earlier foundations. The latter building was substantially of late 17th-c post-Great Fire construction, refaced and refenestrated in the 20th c apparently to reinstate its original appearance; 17th-c features such as floors, party walls and chimneys survived, and these were recorded before demolition.

Roman finds of interest include some crucibles and stamped samian pottery, ten copper-alloy coins, a copper-alloy brooch and a green glass bead. A medieval decorated bone counter and a fragment of a post-medieval opaque glass lamp were also found.

London Archaeol, 6, 1990, 163–4; Britannia, 22, 1991, 267; Medieval Archaeol, 34, 1990, 178
Giorgi, J, 1990 'Environmental assessment (ASS/04/90)', Archive Report
Groves, J, 1989 '52 Gresham Street Roman pottery appraisal report (GAM88)', Pottery Appraisal
Mackinder, A T, 1990 'Excavations at 52 Gresham Street/14 Ironmonger Lane (GAM88)', Archive Report

21–26 Garlick Hill, EC4

GRL88

C Goode
NGR: TQ 32380 80900
SMR: 041720–32

This site was watched at the same time as work on the adjacent site of 32–35 Queen Street (QUE88), and combined with it in post-excavation. See QUE88 below for summary and most reports.

Tyers, I, 1988 'Dendrochronological spot dates (SPT21/88)', Archive Report

GUY88

C Copper and G Porter
NGR: TQ 32480 81350
SMR: 04128902, 041689–94

Guildhall Yard, EC2

Excavations funded by the Corporation of London were sited immediately to the W of the previous excavations (GAG87), underneath the Yard, which remained in use. Excavations proceeded by tunnelling sideways from E to W to a level determined by the headroom required.

The earliest evidence recovered was of 12th- and 13th-c dumping. After this, successive kilns for bronze-smelting were constructed of roughly coursed chalk walls capped with brickearth and tiles. Fragments of buckle-moulds and some bronze buckles still *in situ* were found in association with these kilns. This evidence for industrial activity was truncated by foundations for medieval buildings to the W and E, the latter documented as the 14th-c Guildhall Chapel and, to the S of that, Blackwell Hall. To the W only ragstone and chalk wall foundations survived, and little associated occupation. In the central area, successive gravel metallings and chalk bedding layers for surfaces, dated from the late 14th c to the Great Fire of 1666, represented the Yard itself, the approach road to Guildhall. Fire debris was then dumped thickly over the site, presumably levelling up for further surfaces, but these were truncated by the concrete slab and overlying existing surface of the Yard, laid in 1973. Earlier features were also truncated by intrusive 18th- and 19th-c sewers, partly tunnelled from N to S.

The method of excavation produced few finds, but among these were decorated medieval and post-medieval floor tiles, including several 14th-c Penn tiles. As well as the ceramic buckle-mould, other finds of note are several copper-alloy coins, a copper-alloy needle and a fragment of medieval painted window glass.

London Archaeol, 6, 1990, 164; see GAG87 above for period journal summaries
Copper, C, & Porter, G, 1990 'Excavations at Guildhall Yard East (Phase 2: GUY88)', Archive Report, draft

HAR88

A Mackinder
NGR: TQ 33150 80685
SMR: 043598–601

British Telecom shaft, Harp Lane (south end), EC3

From January to August 1988 contractors cut a series of tunnels for British Telecom under Lower Thames Street. One tunnel 26m long from Harp Lane S to Lower Thames Street revealed an E–W clay-bank 3.3m wide within timber planks and a series of dump deposits. Another tunnel to the W along the S edge of Lower Thames Street followed the course of an E–W brick sewer, and exposed a chalk-built cellar. No finds were recovered and dating is problematic.

London Archaeol, 6, 1989, 50

HON88

D Shotliff
NGR: TQ 33440 81380
SMR: 044757–9

123–125 Houndsditch, 22–26 Cutler Street, 7–8 Exchange Buildings, EC3 & E1

Natural brickearth survived in the testpits in the S part of the site where it was cut by pits or ditches, with made-ground above or truncated by the basement slab. In the N part of the site natural gravels were overlain by redeposited brickearth, possibly a result of quarrying, or by thick deposits of agricultural or garden soil. Disarticulated human bone was also recovered.

The site was later excavated: see CCT90 below.

168–170 Bishopsgate, 14–15 New Street, EC2

Excavations here were funded by MEPC Developments Ltd. Natural sand and gravel, overlaid by brickearth, were cut by a series of intercutting pits dating from the Roman period onwards, including pits for quarrying brickearth, and for cess and rubbish disposal. No burials were found. A small flint and ragstone N–S foundation, brick drains and brick-lined cesspits were probably part of medieval and post-medieval buildings fronting onto Bishopsgate.

London Archaeol, 6, 1990, 161
Mamwell, C, 1989 '166–170 Bishopsgate/14–15 New Street EC2', Archive Report

ISH88

C Mamwell
NGR: TQ 33300 81570
SMR: 041602–7

80–84 Leadenhall Street, EC3

From February to April 1988, an excavation funded by Prudential Portfolio Managers Ltd took place. The site lies within the precincts of Holy Trinity Priory and is adjacent to St Katherine Cree church, which escaped the Great Fire of 1666.

Massive intrusion by the modern building broadly divided the site into two areas. Excavations in the area to the E recorded natural brickearth. After extensive levelling there followed a period of intense Roman activity featuring two buildings: the earlier, of clay and timber construction, was aligned NE–SW, and was seen to have undergone several phases of reconstruction and repair although adhering to the same layout, and perhaps use, throughout. It was subsequently replaced by a masonry building, represented by a partly robbed-out chalk wall and associated exterior surfaces.

In the area to the W beside St Katherine Cree, another Roman sequence was recorded. Here rather less substantial remains of a masonry building were found; they included an *opus signinum* floor and successive occupation layers. This area was largely truncated by pits, above which a heavily scorched brickearth structure or building was discovered; evidently burnt *in situ*, it was followed by immediate collapse, part of which included the remains of a plaster wall or ceiling. Further collapse ensued during a period of inactivity and disuse.

Also discovered were two adjoining Roman roads and their respective ditches. One ran E–W just N of Leadenhall Street, with a ditch to the S where, besides periodic patching and repairs, two distinct phases of construction could be seen. The other ran NE–SW with a timber-lined drain to its W, to which the clay and timber building was aligned.

Much of the site was sealed by a deposit of dark earth. This was truncated in the E by an early medieval cellar, and by a rectangular timber-lined pit. In the area to the W, a ragstone and chalk foundation was almost certainly associated with the nearby church. Two phases of simple timber coffin burials were also recorded.

Finally, a large, rather later building was recorded, comprising a row of structural columns, running N–S and set at precise intervals apart, from which two walls ran to the E. An entire brick cellar was also discovered but not recorded because of hazardous conditions. There were few finds of note from this site, with the exception of a Roman shale bracelet, a medieval iron horseshoe and a copper-alloy buckle.

London Archaeol, 6, 1989, 50–1; *Britannia*, 20, 1989, 306; *Medieval Archaeol*, 33, 1989, 182
Ryan, M, 1990 'Excavations at 80–84 Leadenhall Street (LAH88)', Archive Report

LAH88

M Ryan
NGR: TQ 33420 81140
SMR: 043747–57

Albion House, 34–35 Leadenhall Street, 4 Billiter Street, EC3

Excavations here were funded by Commercial Properties Ltd. Roman activity began with possible quarries for gravel and brickearth. These were followed by at least six separate or successive buildings constructed to the N and S. The earliest were timber structures, partly sunken. Building debris indicated that some of the later buildings may have been of high quality, with decorated walls and tessellated floors.

LDL88

A Thomas
NGR: TQ 33270 81110
SMR: 041580–6

To the N, the latest Roman building, constructed in masonry and tile, included a large room aligned NW–SE with a buttressed apsidal end wall.

To the E, chalk foundations may have represented a medieval cellared building. Truncating these foundations and running across the site was a series of large, deep pits, irregularly shaped except for a flat base, in association with much smaller pits or hearths, and working surfaces. All these pits were backfilled with fragments of bell-mould and with building rubble. Documentary evidence confirms that bell-foundries operated here and nearby in the 14th and 15th c.

Among the objects recovered from the site were a Roman bone die and fragments from several facet-cut glass beakers. A complete aryballos was also recovered, with copper-alloy rings still surviving in its handles. Medieval finds include several complete Rouen-style baluster jugs which had been deposited in a barrel-well, and large quantities of ceramic bell-mould.

For previous excavations on this site in 1953, see GM92 above.

London Archaeol, 6, 1990, 160; *Britannia*, 22, 1991, 268; *Medieval Archaeol*, 34, 1990, 176
Churchill, N, & Hinman, M, 1988 'Testpit survey at 34–35 Leadenhall Street, 4 Billiter Street (LDL88)', Archive Report

LHY88

P Rowsome and R Malt
NGR: TQ 32670 81270
SMR: 042812–15

Docklands Light Railway works in Lothbury, near Moorgate, EC2

Excavations took place as part of surface works for the Docklands Light Railway extension to Bank. The work was funded by Olympia and York and facilitated by DLR Ltd.

The original ground surface overlying natural sands and gravels was truncated or terraced. Late 1st-c pits were followed by evidence for a timber-framed building of early 2nd-c date. This was superseded in the mid-2nd c by a large building constructed in mortared ragstone and tile, which included a hypocausted room measuring about 5m square. This hypocaust was H-shaped in plan, the main central channel running from a furnace in an adjoining room to the W. Branch channels led N and S to box flue tiles set in the walls. An isolated box flue in the S wall, unused and not continuing above the level of the tessellated floor, suggests that the heating system was rearranged during construction.

In the late 3rd c this hypocaust was infilled and replaced by another with *pilae* supporting a new tessellated floor at a higher level. The furnace to the W was relocated, presumably to the N or E, and the room to the W was then connected to the new heating system by underfloor flues piercing the dividing masonry wall. With further modifications the building survived into the 4th c. The absence of much debris in its ruins suggests that the superstructure was deliberately dismantled before accumulation of dark earth. The dark earth was followed by a small post and sill building, dated to the mid-11th–mid-12th c. It was sealed by a sequence of road-metallings which formed part of Lothbury; one of the earlier metallings is dated to 1280–1350. The sequence was truncated in the 19th c by the construction of public toilets.

London Archaeol, 6, 1990, 164–5; 6, 1992, 388; *Britannia*, 20, 1989, 306; 22, 1991, 266; 23, 1992, 292
Groves, J, 1991 'DLR Lothbury', Roman Pottery Appraisal
Holden, T, 1991 'Environmental appraisal report LHY88 (ASS/09/91)', Archive Report
Keily, J, 1991 'DLR Lothbury Phase 2', Building Materials Appraisal
Keily, J, 1992 'DLR Lothbury', [overall] Building Materials Assessment
Malt, R, 1988 'Excavations in Lothbury EC2 near Moorgate Princes Street (LHY88)', Archive Report
Moore, A, & Harrison, J, 1988 'Finds appraisal for Docklands Light Railway shaft at Lothbury (LHY88)', Finds Appraisal
Spence, C (ed), 1989 *Digging in the City: the annual review 1988* (DUA, MoL), 22–3

LLA88

A Mackinder
NGR: TQ 31935 81748
SMR: 043764

60–61 Long Lane, EC1

In February 1988 refurbishment of a 19th-c building revealed a subdivided chalk and brick cellar 3.2m x 1.8m. This was backfilled in the late 18th c; the backfill included human bones, perhaps deriving from disturbance of burials originally associated with the nearby church of St Bartholomew the Great.

London Archaeol, 6, 1989, 52
Mackinder, T, 1988 'Watching brief at 60–61 Long Lane EC1 (LLA88)', Archive Report

Docklands Light Railway shaft, Lombard Street (near Pope's Head Alley), EC3

LOM88

M Burch
NGR: TQ 32770 81050
SMR: 044760 8

Excavations (immediately W of the DOC87 site) were funded by Olympia and York (Canary Wharf Development Company Ltd) and facilitated by Docklands Light Railway. Natural gravels were cut by small quarry pits and other features. These were sealed by dumps, the surface of which was cut by a number of stake-holes representing a structure, possibly on a NE–SW alignment. Subsequent truncation had removed any evidence of occupation associated with the structure. A large gravel quarry in the NE of the site may have continued into this period; it was backfilled with fire debris and then this and the structure were covered by make-up. Pitting and another general truncation horizon were overlaid by redeposited fire debris before dark earth was deposited and then cut by a substantial trench-poured masonry foundation, aligned ESE–WNW. No contemporary ground surface survived and its upper surface was truncated before being overlaid by deposits very similar to the earlier dark earth. These were sealed by cobbled surfaces, probably associated with an early phase of Lombard Street. A large brick sewer dated to 1785 (Ralph Merrifield, *The Roman city of London,* 1965, Gazetteer 198) cut through the road surfaces.

52–63 London Wall, 20–56 Copthall Avenue, EC2

LOW88

D Lees and A Woodger
NGR: TQ 32820 81470
SMR: 041636–49

Excavations here were funded by Scottish Widows. Natural sands and gravels were resorted along the line of a Walbrook tributary which flowed SW across the SE corner of the site. The earliest activity was Roman land reclamation along this channel. A series of industrial pits and drainage gullies were located along the W bank and the channel itself contained abundant leather waste and 20–30 human skulls. A road constructed of rammed gravel ran NNE–SSW, roughly through the middle of the site. Between this road and the Walbrook tributary, brickearth and timber buildings were built in at least two phases, possibly in the mid-2nd c. A timber-lined well, dated no earlier than AD130, was constructed between these buildings and the channel.

A second gravel road running ESE–WNW was recorded to the E. This road was partially silted over and stones from a monumental building were laid in a linear arrangement on its surface, probably to form a drain. In the NW corner of the site lay two more Roman buildings, one to the W constructed of brickearth sills and timber uprights and the other to the E built of wattle and daub. In an external yard associated with the latter building was a tile and mortar plinth, possibly for a statue. Marsh deposits accumulated after the disuse of these buildings. The only surviving later feature was a ditch running E–W cut into these marsh deposits, representing an attempt to re-establish drainage in the area in the 11th c. All later strata were truncated by 19th-c basements.

Among the varied finds, a good pottery assemblage is predominantly 2nd c in date. A fragmentary bowl, probably London ware, has strips of tin foil applied to the rim sherds. Such metal decoration on this type of pottery is hitherto unknown in Britain. Another unusual ceramic find is a Koan amphora with a painted inscription in Greek, a name in the genitive case, translated as 'Theoumrou' or 'Theouerou'. Other unusual finds include two leatherworking implements, consisting of an iron awl with leather thongs wound around the head and, among many good leather finds, a whole leather shoe with hobnails. Other organic objects recovered include a complete wooden spindle, a boxwood ladle head, a fragmentary wooden bowl, half an ivory bracelet with incised decoration and several bone pins, one of which has an animal hoof head. Among the metal finds are a complete pair of copper-alloy bevelled tweezers, a fragmentary seal box and more than 20 coins, most of which are copper alloy but one, overlaid with silver, is identified as a forged denarius.

The new building is known as 60 London Wall.

London Archaeol, 6, 1990, 162–3; *Britannia,* 22, 1991, 265–6; *Medieval Archaeol,* 34, 1990, 177

Groves, J, 1990 '52–62 London Wall', Roman Pottery Appraisal

Lees, D, & Woodger, A, 1990a '52–62 London Wall, 20–56 Copthall Avenue, EC2', Archive Report

Lees, D, & Woodger, A, 1990b *The archaeology and history of 60 London Wall,* MoL (with Scottish Widows)

Lees, D, Woodger, A, & Orton, C, 1989 'Excavations in the Walbrook Valley', *London Archaeol,* 6, 115–19

Nayling, N, 1989 'Dendrochronological spot date report: interim report (SPT/07/89)'

Nayling, N, 1990 'Dendrochronological report (02/90)', Archive Report

Orton, C, 1996 'Dem dry bones', in Bird, J, Hassall, M, & Sheldon, H (eds), *Interpreting Roman London: papers in memory of Hugh Chapman,* 199–208 [comparative statistical study of animal bones]

Pipe, A, 1991 'The animal bones from LOW88 (selected contexts)', Archive Report

Pringle, S, 1990 '52–62 London Wall', Building Materials Appraisal

Robinson, J, 1990 '52–62 London Wall', Post-Roman Pottery Appraisal

LSO88

D Hart
NGR: TQ 32350 81370
SMR: 043723–30

Leith House, 47–57 Gresham Street, EC2

Six trenches were excavated between April and July 1988 in advance of demolition; work was funded by Land Securities Properties Ltd.

The earliest use of the site was represented by the brickearth sill of a timber building and two parallel, steep-sided ditches. All of these early features shared the same E–W alignment. Also belonging to the earliest use of the site was a large quarry pit. After this a large part of the site was levelled by the dumping of redeposited brickearth, in the late 1st or early 2nd c. Directly succeeding the levelling were a metalled trackway, two shallow ditches and a stone-walled building, all sharing the same alignment as the earlier linear features. A cellar, or half cellar, with an *in situ* tile floor was then constructed, possibly much later.

Definite medieval occupation of the site was represented by a series of rubbish pits (10th–12th c) and a series of cellar floors (11th–13th c). Remaining strata were truncated horizontally by the basement slab of the standing building.

The majority of finds from this site are of Roman date and include 12 crucibles, mostly in Verulamium Region White ware, a ligula and several fragments of quernstones.

London Archaeol, 6, 1989, 49–50; *Britannia,* 20, 1989, 307; *Medieval Archaeol,* 33, 1989, 182

Edmondson, R, 1990 '47–57 Gresham Street', Finds Appraisal

Hart, D, 1988 'Excavations at Leith House 47–57 Gresham Street EC2 (LSO88)', Archive Report

LYD88

B Bishop, M Burch, J Hill and A Stephenson
NGR: TQ 32600 80830
SMR: 041620–5

Cannon Street Station north, Upper Thames Street (Dowgate Hill), EC4

Excavations funded by Speyhawk plc took place in the two bays of the railway viaduct immediately N of Upper Thames Street, on the site of part of the presumed Roman governor's palace, a Scheduled Ancient Monument.

Natural sands and silts on the E bank of the mouth of the Walbrook were enclosed behind a timber revetment; the infilled ground was terraced by substantial masonry retaining walls running N, parallel to the Walbrook, and E, parallel to the presumed Thames waterfront lying outside the site to the S. The S face of the latter wall was buttressed, probably with both curved and squared tile-built projections. A series of culverts and drains incorporated in these walls and the Walbrook revetment carried off surface water. The provisional date of these structures is Flavian, and they relate presumably to the palatial structures to the E (recorded in 1966–72) and N (observed in 1865).

These structures were superseded by more land reclamation in the late 2nd/early 3rd c, when a new revetment was constructed a further 25m to the W, on the Walbrook, and presumably also to the S, on the Thames (see Cannon Street Station south, UTA87 above). A large quantity of building rubble was used for infill, and a masonry building was constructed extending to the S and W. The foundations of this building included oak piles, many of which were reused house timbers of 1st-c date. One room contained a hypocaust and an *opus signinum* floor, and another contained a tessellated floor. Separate tiles and masonry walls indicated more buildings lying to the N. The Roman sequence was sealed to the E by a series of intercutting pits, sealed in turn by a stone-walled cellar, in which a new floor was inserted in the 18th c. Strata elsewhere were truncated by construction of the railway viaduct in 1865.

The site produced an important assemblage of finds, mostly of Roman date. They include a copper-alloy bell and a brooch, finger-rings, lock fittings and toilet implements. On-site metal-detecting enabled 367 Roman coins and other metal items to be recovered. Iron objects include a saw and two styli and there were also fragments from three shale bracelets, and an intaglio. Later finds include 87 moulded stones and, among post-medieval finds, glass phials and a bone syringe.

An earlier small excavation on this site took place in 1959, uncovering Roman beams: see GM175 above.

London Archaeol, 6, 1990, 161–2; *Britannia*, 22, 1991, 270

Groves, J, 1990 'Lloyd's Buildings, Cannon Street Station (LYD88)', Roman Pottery Appraisal

Hillam, J, 1989 'Dendrochronology spot date report (SPT/12/89)', Archive Report

Hunting, P, nd [1990] *Archaeology and development* (Speyhawk and MoL), 14–22

Murray, J, 1989 'Environmental assessment of the samples (ASS/01/89)', Archive Report

Robinson, J, 1990 'Lloyd's Buildings, Cannon Street Station (LYD88)', Post-Roman Pottery Appraisal

Schofield, J, 1995 *Medieval London houses*, 179–80 [The Erber, on or close to the site]

Spence, C, & Grew, F (eds), 1990 *The annual review 1989* (DUA, MoL), 20–1

Dunster Court, 21–38 Mincing Lane, 85 Great Tower Street, 12–18 Mark Lane, EC3

MCT88

B Watson
NGR: TQ 33270 80840
SMR: 041714–15

A watching brief was funded by Prudential Portfolio Managers Ltd. Among the intrusive features recorded were two chalk-lined wells. One well constructed in the 13th or 14th c was backfilled with cess and organic refuse, among which was a whalebone or walrus ivory book cover with incised decoration showing a griffin or winged lion, of 12th- or 13th-c date. The other well, probably constructed in the 15th or 16th c, was backfilled in the 17th or 18th c with hearth rake-out or fire debris.

London Archaeol, 6, 1990, 165

Watson, B, 1989 'Mincing Lane EC3 watching brief (MCT88): interim report', Archive Report

6–9 Middle Street, 24–26 Newbury Street, EC1

MDE88

D Lakin
NGR: TQ 32030 81770
SMR: 044769

The natural brickearth was truncated by construction of the modern basement, though a number of post-medieval cut features survived.

MOH88

D Shotliff
NGR: TQ 32740 81730
SMR: 041716–19

Moorgate Hall, 143–171 Moorgate, EC2

Excavations here were funded by Land Securities (Management) Ltd. The natural brickearth sloped down from N to S. Among a small number of Roman cut features was a single inhumation. In spite of the inhumation the site did not appear to be part of a Roman extramural cemetery. The Roman ground surface was sealed by organic waterlaid deposits which probably accumulated over several c and may represent the marsh known to have existed in this area of the City.

Eventually a series of E–W ditches were cut, probably associated with efforts to drain the land. This was followed, in the S of the site, by the extensive dumping of domestic and industrial rubbish and, in the N of the site, by the formation of a natural soil. This was later truncated and further dumping was carried out. The construction of Moorgate Hall in 1915 destroyed any later deposits.

Evidence for extramural Roman activity was not extensive. A single intact burial was found at the N end of the site and elsewhere large quantities of disarticulated human bone suggested that other burials had existed in the area. A fragment of a copper-alloy mirror, probably made in N Italy in the 1st c, may have come from one of these disturbed burials. The remains of the medieval Moorfields marsh appeared as a series of waterlaid clays and silts. Cut through these deposits were several large ditches running E–W, probably to drain the marsh. These ditches silted up naturally but were recut in places to prolong their usefulness. Partly contemporary with and partly succeeding the drainage ditches were extensive dumps rich in animal bone, leather waste and pottery. This domestic refuse was presumably carted out of the city and tipped into open areas at the side of the road as a kind of landfill. All later strata were truncated by modern basements and foundations.

London Archaeol, 6, 1990, 165; *Britannia,* 22, 1991, 271; *Medieval Archaeol,* 34, 1990, 179
Shotliff, D, 1990 'Excavations at 143–171 Moorgate (Moorgate Hall), EC2 (MOH88)', Archive Report

MSE88

S Jones
NGR: TQ 33450 81590
SMR: 044564–70

109–115 Middlesex Street, E1

Natural and redeposited brickearth were cut by a series of Roman quarry pits, two of which predated an E–W ditch. Possibly postdating the ditch were four or five graves which were cut into the natural gravel and represented part of the Roman extramural cemetery, probably from the 2nd c. Both the ditch and the cemetery were disused at the same time before another, less substantial, E–W ditch was dug in the mid-3rd c; quarrying may also have continued up to this time. The site then appears to have been abandoned until the late medieval period when an E–W drainage ditch was cut. Thereafter post-medieval activity was represented by a barrel-lined well, two horncore-lined pits and a brick-lined soak-away.

Groves, J, 1988 'The Roman pottery from 109–115 Middlesex Street (MSE88)', Archive Report
Jones, S, 1989 '109–115 Middlesex Street E1', Archive Report
Riddler, I, 1990 '109–115 Middlesex Street', Finds Appraisal

MYA88

M Hinman
NGR: TQ 33320 81320
SMR: 044571–7

46 St Mary Axe, EC3

Quarry pits, backfilled before c AD250, were the earliest recorded features. Systematic dumping and levelling took place until the 4th c; the site then remained open ground until the 14th c when dumping occurred, followed by cultivation, probably in a medieval garden plot. A post-medieval cellar, represented by several floor surfaces, wells and a brick-lined coal store, succeeded this.

Hinman, M, 1989 '46 St Mary Axe EC3', Archive Report, draft

18–25 Old Bailey, 10–18 Bishop's Court, 29–37 Fleet Lane, EC4

OBA88

A Bayliss
NGR: TQ 31720 81340
SMR: 043785–91

In addition to pre- and post-excavation watching briefs, excavations were undertaken between March and June 1988, funded by P & O Developments Ltd. Most of the site had been severely truncated by the basements of the standing buildings, although horizontal stratigraphy did survive under the cobbling of Elliot's Court.

The gravel terrace on the site sloped down to the S and W. Some levelling activity preceded the construction of several kilns in the Roman period. The structure of only one of these survived: no wasters were recovered, but the character of the kiln would suggest that it had been used for the manufacture of fine pottery. Demolition debris observed in the watching brief suggests that there were at least six other such features on the site.

These kilns were replaced by a large octagonal building, 16m in diameter, which was associated with large-scale terracing. This building was probably surrounded by an ambulatory 3.75m wide. The whole building would then have enclosed an area of 520sq m. It had been completely robbed but red-painted wall plaster, ragstone and *opus signinum* probably featured in its construction. This building has been tentatively interpreted as a Romano-Celtic temple.

The robbing was followed by the construction of a large masonry building of at least nine rooms. This building was rebuilt at least once, and at a later date a hypocaust was added. A coin of 335–41 dates the demolition and robbing of the building to the mid-4th c or later; its function is unclear.

Then 0.8m of dark earth accumulated on the site. Several pits cutting into this deposit, including a timber-lined well of Saxo-Norman date, attest to occupation of the site before the construction of a number of chalk buildings, probably in the 13th c. These buildings were aligned to the present street frontages. Later occupation was represented by several cut features.

London Archaeol, 6, 1989, 52; *Britannia*, 20, 1989, 308; *Medieval Archaeol*, 33, 1989, 183
Bayliss, A, 1988 'Excavations and watching brief at 19–25 Old Bailey EC4 (OBA88)', Archive Report
Fabrizi M, nd, 'Finds appraisal', Archive Report
Holden, T, 1990 'Environmental appraisal report (ASS/07/90)', Archive Report
Spence, C (ed), 1989 *Digging in the City: the annual review 1988* (DUA, MoL), 16–17
Tyers, I, 1988 'Dendrochronological spot dates', Archive Report

158–164 Bishopsgate, EC2

OPS88

J Oetgen and S Poole
NGR: TQ 33300 81540
SMR: 041594–601

Excavations and standing building recording were funded by Friends Provident. Natural gravels were cut in the early Roman period by large quarry pits. Gravel surfaces, perhaps tracks connecting with the Roman road immediately to the W, were also recorded. The quarry pits were backfilled, perhaps by the 2nd c, and thick deposits of dark soil resembling dark earth accumulated across the site, indicating horticulture. No human burials were found.

A long series of pits was cut into the dark soil in the medieval period and later. This area remained open until at least the 17th c. Two horncore-lined pits may have had an industrial use. To the SW, cess- and domestic refuse pits suggested occupation nearby, probably along Bishopsgate. Two dog skeletons were recovered from one of the pits.

A brick wall of probable 16th-c date was recorded along the S edge of the site and is identified from documentary sources as originally part of a building known as 'Fisher's Folly'. It featured reused 13th-c moulded stones as mullions in windows at half-cellar level. Other medieval and post-medieval structures, mainly chalk and brick cellar and cesspit walls, were truncated by 19th-c levelling of the site and construction of warehouses and the fire station. The fire station is a Listed Building and has been retained in the redevelopment.

Finds of note from the site include a medieval double-sided wooden comb and a complete London-ware conical drinking vessel. A complete Frechen jug of 1550–75 was also recovered, as well as a broad-rimmed pewter saucer bearing the initials 'TC'. These initials are thought to refer to the owner rather than the maker.

London Archaeol, 6, 1990, 161; *Britannia,* 22, 1991, 271–2; *Medieval Archaeol,* 34, 1990, 176
Groves, J, 1989 '158–164 Bishopsgate', Roman Pottery Appraisal
Keily, J, 1989 '158–164 Bishopsgate', Building Materials Appraisal, draft
Pitt, F, nd, '158–164 Bishopsgate', Finds Appraisal
Robinson, J, 1989 '158/164 Bishopsgate post-Roman pottery appraisal report (OPS88)', Post-Roman Pottery Appraisal
Schofield, J, 1995 *Medieval London houses,* 163 [Fisher's Folly]

ORM88

J Youle
NGR: TQ 32340 80960
SMR: 041741–50

Ormond House, 62–63 Queen Victoria Street, EC4

An excavation, funded by MEPC Developments Ltd, took place in February and March 1989.

Natural gravels were cut by a series of Roman quarry and rubbish pits. These were infilled and sealed by brickearth and gravel dumps prior to the laying of an external gravel surface, which may have been part of an E–W road. All surviving Roman deposits are dated to the late 1st c. These deposits were cut by a number of intercutting cess-, rubbish and storage pits dated to the 9th–14th c. One 12th–13th-c cesspit was wattle lined, with a surrounding privacy screen. This sequence was cut by later medieval chalk and ragstone foundations, which may have formed part of a building fronting onto Garlick Hill to the E. An early 18th-c brick cellar, disused and infilled by 1800, probably belonged to one of a number of properties also fronting onto Garlick Hill, and a contemporary brick-lined well was probably located in an open space documented immediately to the W. Strata beneath Ormond House were heavily truncated by its construction in the 1960s, although survival was better to the E, where deposits had been less deeply truncated by 19th-c coal cellars.

London Archaeol, 6, 1990, 165; *Medieval Archaeol,* 34, 1990, 179
Crowley, N, 1990 'Ormond House', Building Materials Appraisal
Groves, J, 1989 'Ormond House', Roman Pottery Appraisal
Robinson, J, 1989 'Ormond House', Post-Roman Pottery Appraisal
Webb, M, nd, 'Ormond House, 63 Queen Victoria Street', Finds Appraisal
Youle, J, 1989 '63 Cannon Street/62–63 Queen Victoria Street (Ormond House) EC4', Archive Report

PTD88

Sarah Gibson
NGR: TQ 32530 81350
SMR: 044770–1

72–73 Basinghall Street, EC2

Earliest recorded deposits appear to have been dark earth; these were truncated by the modern basement slab. In two of the testpits lengths of ragstone masonry were revealed and may have been contemporary with pre-15th-c foundations recorded to the W at GAG87.

Gibson, S, 1988 'Portland House, 72 Basinghall Street', Testpit Report

Pilgrim Street, EC4

PWB88

J Heathcote and W McCann
NGR: TQ 31680 81050
SMR: 040420

As part of the Blackfriars–Holborn Viaduct development, Rosehaugh Stanhope funded the excavation of an E–W trench, 18m x 5m, running down the roadway in Pilgrim Street between Ludgate Broadway and Waithman Street.

The central area of the trench was severely truncated by numerous service ducts and a live sewer lying 3.5m below the present road surface. On the N side substantial remains of the medieval city wall were located. Running the full length of the trench it survived to a height of 2.8m above foundation level. Built between 1283 and 1320, this wall enclosed the Blackfriars precinct within the city limits.

Only the S face of the wall was observed and this showed three distinct phases of construction. The predominant materials used were squared blocks of Kentish ragstone, regularly coursed, with some tile, flint, Reigate stone and chalk blocks. A number of offsets were observed which were not continuous along the length of the wall but were arranged step-wise in order to cope with the substantial natural slope in the ground surface on this W side of Ludgate Hill.

Towards the E end of the excavated length, the entrance to a bastion which stood on the N face of the wall was located. The entrance was 1.2m wide and allowed the width of the wall at this point to be determined as 3m, although the foundations could not be fully excavated. The S side of the trench contained the remains of the 18th-c frontage of Stonecutter's Alley. Due to the presence of live services it was impossible to fully excavate this but a series of irregular brick foundations, including a threshold, was observed. The most conspicuous finds assemblage from the site consisted of a quantity of mica schist waste, of early medieval date, derived from the cutting of imported raw material into hone-stones.

A further trial pit was observed by MoLAS in 1993, on the N side of Pilgrim Street. This located the foundations for the central tower on the medieval extension of the city wall S of Pilgrim Street, and further evidence of a suspected outer medieval ditch parallel to the Roman city wall; it went out of use between 1250 and 1280.

For observations in the street in 1925–6, see GM138 above.

London Archaeol, 6, 1989, 53; 7, 1993, 200
Ede, J, 1989a 'Environmental assessment', Archive Report
Ede, J, 1989b 'Seed assessment', Archive Report
Groves, J, 1990 'Ludgate Hill car parks (PWB88)', Roman Pottery Appraisal
McCann, B (ed), 1993 'Fleet Valley project (VAL88, PWB88)', Archive Report
Nayling, N, 1989 'Dendrochronological spot dates', Archive Report

32–35 Queen Street, 6A Great St Thomas Apostle, EC4

QUE88

C Goode
NGR: TQ 32410 80910
SMR: 041720–30

Excavations and a watching brief at 32–35 Queen Street from June to August 1988 were conducted concurrently with a watching brief at 21–26 Garlick Hill, immediately to the W (GRL88), and these sites are interpreted together. The excavations, funded by Legal and General, were in two phases, taking in the rear of 6A Great St Thomas Apostle, to the N, when this was added to the area of the development. The work in the site to the W was funded by Capital and Counties.

Natural brickearth was overlaid, to the E, by grey silt containing a prehistoric flint flake. Ragstone foundations of a Roman building were excavated to the E and a timber-lined well was recorded to the W. These were sealed by levelling-up dumps into which a large drainage ditch, running S, and a timber-lined pit were cut. Intrusive medieval features included a clay and timber lined drain to the N, dated to the mid-11th–mid-13th c, a circular chalk-lined cesspit, backfilled in the 16th or 17th c, and chalk foundations associated with a cellar floor to the N. This floor comprised reused decorated glazed 14th–15th-c tiles, surrounding reused plain-glazed 16th-c tiles. At the S and W edges of the site, chalk and brick medieval and post-medieval cellar walls survived, incorporated in existing party walls. To the W, the cobbled surface of Garlick Hill was recorded, dated to the 17th c, later raised to its existing level.

London Archaeol, 6, 1990, 165; *Britannia,* 22, 1991, 267
Goode, C, 1988 'Excavations at 32–35 Queen Street, 21–26 Garlick Hill (QUE88 and GRL88)', Archive Report

SAY88

N Elsden and V Ridgeway
NGR: TQ 33250 81300
SMR: 04182802,
04188414–17, 042698–705

25–51 St Mary Axe, 9 St Helen's Place, EC3

Excavations funded by Spaxe Properties Ltd were conducted in several phases both before and after demolition, between July 1989 and August 1990.

Natural sand and gravels capped by brickearth were quarried in the earliest activity on the site, beginning in and perhaps confined to the Roman period. The quarries were infilled and overlaid by dumps containing a large quantity of Roman painted wall plaster. These dumps were truncated by early medieval pits for disposal of domestic rubbish and cess.

The priory of St Helen was founded to the W of the site, in the 13th c. The chalk core of a wall and substantial foundations running N–S across the site, on the documented line of the priory boundary, were presumably the remains of its precinct wall, surviving embedded in later walls. Within the precinct were deposits of garden soil, cut by rubbish pits. There were also chalk-lined cellars of two buildings, either contemporary with the priory or belonging to the period immediately after its dissolution. The walls of one cellar, to the S, were faced with squared blocks, about half of them scratched with Roman numerals, probably masons' batchmarks. Brick-lined slots surviving in two corners probably held beams for a floor, stairs or some other structure. A ditch ran parallel to the priory boundary and there were extensive dumps of waste possibly from an industrial process such as bell-founding. To the E, outside the precinct, foundations of rammed chalk and gravel probably represented pier bases in the church of St Mary Axe, documented from the 12th c and converted to secular use in the 16th c. To its S, the associated graveyard was marked by nine burials; there were also two pits containing about 150 skeletons, without skulls, probably reinterred in the course of mid-20th-c redevelopment. Post-medieval brick cesspits, cellar walls and a well were also recorded.

The Roman painted wall plaster in the dumped deposits was of fine quality with a wide variety of colours, most still in good condition. Designs partly pieced together include a column, roundels and other architectural motifs. Later deposits from within a 14th-c pit were sieved, yielding much scrap from the manufacture of fancy knife handles; these had bone scales inlaid with jet and amber, and sheet copper-alloy and iron endcaps and shoulder bolsters. Only one knife of comparable form has been excavated hitherto in London.

London Archaeol, 6, 1991, 277; *Britannia*, 22, 1991, 267–8; *Medieval Archaeol*, 35, 1991, 152
Elsden, N, 1990 'Excavations at 9 St Helen's Place and 25–51 St Mary Axe, EC3 (SAY88)', Archive Report
Elsden, N, & Hamilton, N, 1989 'Testpit survey at 25–51 St Mary Axe and 9 St Helen's Place, EC3 (SAY88)', Archive Report

SEA88

Sarah Gibson
NGR: TQ 33380 80780
SMR: 041751–7

2 Seething Lane, EC3

Excavations after demolition between July and October 1988 were funded by British Land plc. A series of parallel Roman ditch segments may represent enclosures for animals, a function suggested by previous excavations in this area. Two medieval ragstone-built cellars were excavated, one of which had been used finally as a cesspit. Several post-medieval buildings were located, with accompanying external areas containing rubbish pits and a brick-built soak-away.

The earliest finds are six prehistoric flints, including scraping and cutting tools. Roman finds include a rare piece of 1st-c marbled glass. Post-Roman finds include a Late Saxon single-sided antler comb, 16 Penn floor tiles and fragments of an imported prunted beaker. A post-medieval glass beaker of 16th- or early 17th-c date is a further import, from the Low Countries or the Rhineland.

London Archaeol, 6, 1990, 166; *Britannia*, 22, 1991, 269; *Medieval Archaeol*, 34, 1990, 179
Gibson, Sarah, 1989 '2 Seething Lane EC3', Archive Report
Groves, J, 1988 'The Roman pottery from 2 Seething Lane (SEA88)', Archive Report

Salisbury House, 8 Salisbury Square, EC4

SHO88

J Stevenson
NGR: TQ 31500 81050
SMR: 044578

Most of the site had been truncated and all that survived was in the NE corner of the site: a (truncated) Victorian well which seems to have been infilled in the 1950s.

Stevenson, J, 1988 'Watching brief at Salisbury House, 8 Salisbury Square (SHO88)', Archive Report

St Mary at Hill church, St Mary at Hill, EC3

SMY88

B Watson
NGR: TQ 33080 80760
SMR: 041809–10, 042836–40

The roof and parts of the interior of this standing building were badly damaged by fire in May 1988. Immediately afterwards, photographic and photogrammetric recording (the latter by the York Institute for Advanced Architectural Studies) was sponsored by EH. In October and November 1988, with a view to restoration of the church (a Listed Building), boreholes and testpits were recorded by the MoL and fire debris was examined and roof remains were surveyed *in situ* by EH. Further recording work in 1991 was funded by the Diocese of London

Up to 3m of archaeological strata under the church showed evidence of intercutting pits, probably of Roman date, followed by medieval and post-medieval burials. In the SE corner of the church a brick-roofed burial vault was discovered, faced with reused Caen and Reigate stone. This vault was probably contemporary with the post-Great Fire rebuilding of the church by Wren, the stone deriving from the existing medieval church. The vault was emptied and sealed apparently in the late 19th c. The roof survey, and the sorting of the ceiling plaster recovered from the Fire, have allowed a reconstruction (by R Lea, FH) of the vaulted roof, built 1826–7, and a lantern and clerestory windows added in 1848–9, all to designs by James Savage.

London Archaeol, 6, 1990, 166; 6, 1992, 391; *Britannia,* 22, 1991, 269; 23, 1992, 292; *Post-Medieval Archaeol,* 26, 1992, 97–8
Jeffery, P, Lea, R, & Watson, B, 1992 'The architectural history of the church of St Mary at Hill in the City of London', *Trans London Middlesex Archaeol Soc,* 43, 193–200
Lea, R, 1989 'St Mary at Hill EC3', EH Report
Watson, B, 1989 'Report on the archaeological implications of a testpit report and borehole survey at St Mary at Hill, EC3 (SMY88)', Archive Report

Cayzer House, 2–4 St Mary Axe, EC3

SXE88

V Ridgeway
NGR: TQ 33260 81200
SMR: 043842–7

Between July and September 1988 excavations, funded by Bricomin Properties Ltd, were carried out in the basement of the standing building, before demolition.

The basement had truncated deposits to a depth below which only features cut into natural brickearth survived. Towards the E of the site two large, deep timber-lined features were found, possibly storage tanks, dating to the early Roman period. The largest of these in the N, at least 4m square and 3m deep, appears to have collapsed and been systematically backfilled with brickearth dumps. Overlying this, surviving due to slumping into the feature, was a series of clay and timber buildings. Subsequently a more substantial later Roman building was constructed with ragstone foundations, robbed out during the medieval period. Contemporary ground level did not survive.

The area was heavily truncated during the medieval period by a series of pits of varying dimensions. No evidence of structures of this period was found, but the alignment of cesspits offers possible evidence of property boundaries. Substantial chalk ragstone foundations of a N–S wall and pier base, provisionally dated to the early post-medieval period, were recorded. Slightly to the W, and presumably associated with the foundations, was a chalk-lined basement of similar date. This contained six successive floors, mainly of chalk and mortar. The final floor was constructed of brick and tile, incorporating Flemish green and yellow glazed tiles and a brick hearth. All structures on site respected the same alignment, suggesting continuity of the street plan through to the modern period.

The majority of finds from this site were of Roman date. They include a quantity of painted wall plaster with mock architectural motifs, and part of a 1st-c beaker in colourless glass, several bone pins and counters. A number of complete and near-complete jugs in Kingston ware came from medieval pits, and fragments of bell-mould were also present.

London Archaeol, 6, 1989, 53; Britannia, 20, 1989, 306; Medieval Archaeol, 33, 1989, 183

Davies, B, 1993 'Inter-site studies', in Milne, G, & Wardle, A, 'Early Roman development at Leadenhall Court, London and related research', Trans London Middlesex Archaeol Soc, 44, 135–50

Groves, J, 1989 '2–4 St Mary Axe Roman pottery (SXE88)', Pottery Appraisal

Ridgeway, V, 1989 'Excavations at Cayzer House, 2–4 St Mary Axe (SXE88)', Archive Report

Robinson, J, 1989 '2–4 St Mary Axe post-Roman pottery (SXE88)', Pottery Appraisal

Sidell, J, 1990 'Environmental assessment (ASS/08/90)', Archive Report

TEX88

M Colquhoun, C Milne,
G Milne, J Stevenson and
K Tyler
NGR: TQ 32455 80750
SMR: 041758–68

Thames Exchange, 78 Upper Thames Street and Bull Wharf Lane, EC4

An excavation and watching brief on a complex sequence of Thames-side land reclamation was undertaken between February 1988 and September 1989, funded by Kumagai Gumi UK Ltd.

The earliest waterfront structure recorded was a 35m length of 3rd-c Roman timber quay running E–W at the extreme N end of the site. This structure was robbed in antiquity and left to silt up. Built on the foreshore and sealing the disuse of the quay was a series of Saxon embankments raising the ground by up to 2m. These were of various types: post and plank revetments, vertically set staves, and clay-banks consolidated with timbers as hardcore and wattle fences. Incorporated in some of these structures were remains of several boats, including clinker planking, a keel, ribs and a large mast partner. From the beginning of the Saxon sequence the waterfronts respected the N–S line of an inlet,

located in the centre of the site, which developed into a property division later to be known as Three Cranes Lane. At least two other N–S property divisions were located and proved to be of Saxon origin. In the early medieval period the waterfront was advanced by successive earthen banks having cobbled ramps leading down onto the foreshore.

By the 12th c the transition had been made to large, complex, prefabricated revetments, which survived up to 2m in height. These front- and back-braced post and plank structures were initially earth-fast but later incorporated base-plates as carpentry techniques improved (Fig 51). A notable example was a framed scissor-braced jetty with assembly marks, dated to the early 13th c. Major property divisions developed, influencing both the waterfront and associated buildings. Some traces of Early Saxon buildings were recorded. A large 12th-c warehouse with foundations of split beech logs and massive oak baulks was found to the E, and was replaced by more extensive buildings with chalk and ragstone foundations up to 1.5m deep. At the extreme S of the site the base frame of Three Cranes Stairs was located, a major ferry terminal documented in the medieval period, continuing in use until Southwark Bridge was completed in 1819.

Fig 51 TEX88: 12th-c revetments stood as high as a person on this site (Upper Thames Street and Bull Wharf Lane), as on others. The accumulation of river silts against each revetment (left) gives much information about river levels, and the silts can be sampled to study ancient levels of pollution and tidal regimes.

With the help of the Thames Mudlarks a large quantity of metalwork was recovered from the site, in addition to worked bone and other organic artefacts. Roman finds include a boxwood scoop with a negroid head, a golden necklace decorated with glass beads, bone hairpins and an amber intaglio, together with a large amount of Roman pottery from the foreshore deposits. Late Saxon finds include a lead ring decorated with Anglo-Saxon runes, a copper equal-arm brooch, other lead brooches and some coiled wire beads. There were also bone awls, needles and a comb. A large collection of Saxon quernstones, imported as a partially worked stock from the Eifel Mountains, was recovered from the site. In addition a set of wooden pan-pipes was recovered from a Saxon context.

London's trading connections in the medieval period are revealed by weights and balances, French and German pottery imports, many foreign coins, two pewter spoons with Russian parallels and pilgrim badges of continental origin. Other badges include some from Thomas Becket's shrine, including a church-shaped ampulla. A pewter peacock and a fox staff head were also recovered. Industrial activity is attested by a stone metalworking mould and partially manufactured buckles. Other items include knives, hones, tweezers and leather scabbards and shoes. A post-medieval waterlogged pit contained several wooden bowls, two brooms, packing boxes, a pannier and a child's ball and skittle, together with Spanish, German and English domestic pottery. There were also some industrial ceramics used in sugar refining.

London Archaeol, 6, 1990, 166–7; Medieval Archaeol, 34, 1990, 179–80

Freshwater, T, 1996 'A lava quern workshop in Late Saxon London', London Archaeol, 8, 39–45

Milne, G, 1992 Timber building techniques in London, c 900–1400, London Middlesex Archaeol Soc Spec Pap 15 [joints and carpentry]

Milne, G, & Goodburn, D, 1990 'The early medieval port of London', Antiquity, 64, 629–36

Nayling, N, 1989 'Dendrochronological spot date report: interim report (SPT/09/89)'

Nayling, N, 1990 'Thames Exchange dendrochronology interim report', Archive Report

Parkhouse, J, 1990 'An assemblage of lava quernstones from the Thames Exchange site', Archive Report

Parry, J, 1994 'The Roman quay at Thames Exchange London', London Archaeol, 7, 263–7

Rutledge, T, 1994 'A 12th-century building on the London waterfront', London Archaeol, 7, 178–83

Sewart, R, nd, 'An assessment of the Albert Basin spoil-searching project', Assessment Report

Spence, C, & Grew, F (eds), 1990 The annual review 1989 (DUA, MoL), 26–7

Spencer, B, in prep. Pilgrim souvenirs and secular badges, Medieval finds from excavations in London 7

Stevenson, J, & Colquhoun, M, 1991 'Excavations at Thames Exchange', Archive Report, interim

Tyers, I, 1988 'Dendrochronological spot date report: interim report (SPT/12/88)', Archive Report

Tyers, I, 1989 'Dendrochronological spot date report: interim report (SPT/01/89)'

Trinity House, Savage Gardens, EC3

TRY88

K Wooldridge
NGR: TQ 33520 80800
SMR: 044579

Testpits and a lift-shaft were examined. Natural was not reached. The lowest deposit was possibly Roman in date and was truncated by modern foundations, drains and make-up.

Wooldridge, K, 1988 'Trinity House, Savage Gardens', Testpit Report

Fleet Valley between Blackfriars and Holborn Viaduct stations, EC4

VAL88

M Adams, P Askew, A Bayliss, S Bedford, J Chinca, S Davies, T Dawson, T Ellis, N Elsden, S Gibson, C Goode, R Greatorex, F Hammer, J Heathcote, W McCann, M McKenzie, G Oulton, A Swingler and N Truckle
NGR: TQ 31670 80920 — actually (S) TQ 31670 80920 — (N) TQ 31710 81480
SMR: 040417–18, 040420, 041663–70, 042526–35, 044047–52

A series of excavations, before and during this extensive redevelopment along the E side of the lower valley of the River Fleet, began in 1988 and ended in January 1992. Work was funded by Rosehaugh Stanhope Developments plc.

Natural topography and prehistory

Two small eyots lying alongside the E bank of the prehistoric Fleet river were discovered. The downstream eyot extended from the N side of modern Ludgate Circus to Apothecary Street and was approximately pear shaped with a maximum width of approximately 36m on its N side. The upstream eyot lay between modern Fleet Lane and a little to the S of Old Seacoal Lane. This was more symmetrical in shape than the downstream eyot being approximately 64m long and 52m wide. There was evidence of deep natural scouring in the channel between this eyot and the riverbank. This may have been associated with a natural stream which joined the Fleet at the NE corner of the channel. Both eyots were to be exploited in the historic periods.

There was very little which could be safely attributed to the prehistoric period. The skeletal remains of an infant which were recovered from the channel to the S of the upstream eyot did appear to be pre-Roman.

Roman

This area of Londinium was exploited at an early date by the Romans. The downstream eyot was used to import wheat around AD70. A substantial jetty and warehouse were constructed on the downstream eyot for this purpose. The upstream eyot was used for the processing of the imported wheat and the remains of a substantial tide mill were found here during the excavations. Both eyots were abandoned sometime towards the end of the 2nd c. This coincides with a tidal regression in the lower Thames which may have made the eyots unusable. The upstream eyot was not again used by the Romans. The downstream eyot, on the other hand, was used to help span a bridge across the Fleet. The remains of a substantial ragstone and tile structure were excavated on the N side of Ludgate Circus. The dating evidence suggests that this feature was contemporary with the construction of the city wall c 200.

The road down Ludgate Hill is earlier than this, probably being first laid in the latter half of the 1st c when it had a gradient of 1:20. This was subsequently reduced to 1:10 when the wall and bridge were constructed. There was no evidence of an earlier bridge across the Fleet, but as it was not possible to investigate the S side of Ludgate Circus the possibility cannot be categorically ruled out. The alignment of the later Roman road on Ludgate Hill together with its width strongly suggests that the Roman gate was a double gate, with only the southern carriageway being used in the medieval period.

Evidence of industrial activity was located on the Hill above the Fleet close to the present site of the Old Bailey and immediately to the S of the road to Newgate. The hillside was extensively terraced between AD40 and 100. Sometime before 120 a series of glassmaking kilns were constructed and these survived until the construction of the city wall c 200. Following their destruction a very large octagonal temple was constructed. With a total area of 520sq m, this is the largest yet found in Britain. A pit, situated adjacent to the outer wall-line of the temple, contained a human skull, which was possibly a foundation deposit for the temple. The main structure was constructed in masonry with *opus signinum* floors and a tiled roof. A significant quantity of wall plaster painted red with a border of white and green was recovered from one of the robber trenches associated with the destruction of the main building. There also appears to have been an ancillary building. The temple was completely destroyed, possibly by fire, c 270 and replaced by a large multi-roomed building with ragstone walls and *opus signinum* floors. The full extent of this building could not be determined as much of it lay beyond the limits of excavation. It appears to have been rebuilt or substantially altered at least four times. It may also have had a courtyard to the E. One unusual glass tessera hints at the existence of a high-quality mosaic. The building survived to at least 335.

Saxon

Between the end of the Roman period and the middle of the 11th c the area between the city walls and the Fleet river was apparently abandoned and it is not until the Late Saxon period that any evidence of activity was recorded: an unusual burial group on the foreshore at the confluence of the Fleet and Thames. The burials were not regular and given the partially disarticulated state of the individual skeletons, it is possible, although not proven, that the group had been decapitated and/or dismembered before burial. A preliminary scan of the skeletal material suggests that this may have been a family group. Deliberately placed pieces of ragstone were also associated with some of these burials. In one case the stone was placed in the position of the missing skull.

Saxo-Norman

The first of a series of shallow post-Roman resurfacing of the road out of Ludgate date from this period. A new timber bridge was built across the Fleet probably immediately before or immediately after the Norman conquest. It was founded on piles driven into the N end of the downstream eyot and stabilised with consolidation dumps. Longitudinal beams carried a walkway of transverse planks and there was evidence that the bridge had been burnt at some stage in its life with the more badly burnt timbers being subsequently repaired.

The Fleet prison

The first Fleet prison was constructed on the upstream eyot *c* 1180 and took the form of a square tower with polygonal turrets on all four corners. The channel around the eyot acted as a natural moat until the period 1230–61 when an artificial moat and a ragstone perimeter wall around the entire eyot were constructed. Between 1270 and 1400 the moat was dredged on a number of occasions. Often the dredged material was dumped inside the compound and used as make-up in some of the areas of the compound still prone to subsidence. The small strip of land immediately outside the perimeter wall was frequently encroached upon, notably for the construction of cesspits. Major rebuilding took place in the 16th c with a new prison building being added at the S end of the eyot. An annexe to this building served as a toilet block with timber seats arranged around three sides and a well-constructed drainage system beneath the paved floor. Occupation continued, with the moat finally being reduced to a bricked-over drain towards the end of the 16th c. Some industrial activity took place, notably pinmaking, in the properties which now encroached up to the perimeter wall itself. The prison suffered substantial damages in the Great Fire of 1666 which was followed by a substantial rebuilding programme. The original tower and later building were demolished and a brick and timber building erected on a completely new alignment. The perimeter wall was rebuilt in brick and it is likely that the western side of the compound was extended out to the newly constructed Fleet Canal at this period also.

The prison was again destroyed by fire in 1720 and rebuilt on the same alignment (Fig 52). It was again rebuilt in 1770 following another fire. The new building was much more substantial and followed the alignment established after the Great Fire. This building suffered some damage during the Gordon Riots in 1780 following which repairs were carried out. These included the doubling of the thickness of the perimeter wall by adding buttressed brickwork to the inside face. With the arrival of the railways the face of this part of London changed utterly. An Act for the demolition of the prison was passed in May 1842 and demolition took place in 1845. The railway viaduct which finally connected Blackfriars Station and Holborn Viaduct was built in stages between 1864 and 1876.

The Templars and the Blackfriars

The Knights Templar were granted the land S of Ludgate by Henry II in 1159. The excavations revealed that they immediately set in train a vigorous programme of reclamation around the downstream eyot. Problems were encountered around the S tip of the eyot and it was not until the end of the 12th c that the reclaimed land was fully consolidated. Further S, at the confluence with the Thames, similar reclamation activity took place, pushing reclaimed land to the S and SW. The western area was used to construct the tide mill which was a source of many complaints during the 13th c. A masonry tank with two culverts was probably associated with the maintenance of waterlevels in the millpond.

The remains of tenements established by the Templars were also recorded along the S side of Ludgate Hill and further to the S on both sides of the medieval Blackfriars Lane. One of the three buildings on the Ludgate Hill frontage was constructed at the turn of the 12th/13th c and survived in one form or another until the fire bombs on the night of 22 December 1942. The first step of a spiral staircase from the earliest building survived *in situ*. This was made from Reigate stone and was of the single block type which went out of use *c* 1200. Reigate stone was also used to provide an ornamental doorway to another building to the S of the first. An open area between the two properties contained a large barrel-lined well and a small lean-to which housed a three-seater toilet carved from oak.

Evidence of industrial activity, possibly a smithy, was associated with the tenements further S and lying to the E of the tide mill. A small alley between two of these tenements would later define the pre-19th-c Blackfriars Lane (Water Lane). Following the suppression of the Templars in 1314, a large parcel of their land was included in the grant to the Blackfriars who were to give their name to their area.

The excavations were confined to the western limits of the friary which appeared to have been used as gardens, but some light industrial activity did continue to the S. The major feature from this period found in the excavations was the extension of the city wall, built at the end of the 13th c to enclose the Blackfriars precinct. More than 80m of this structure were recorded along modern Pilgrim Street and New Bridge Street. Survival was good to excellent, with a foundation width of 3m and an overall height of 3.5m in places being found.

A large part of the NW area of the precinct appears to have suffered substantial problems from flooding for some time after the wall was constructed, with only the higher ground close to Blackfriars Lane being usable. There were also delays in completing the section of wall from Pilgrim Street S to the Thames and these appear to be a direct result of the obstruction caused by the Templars' mill and its associated millpond. The kink which can be seen today in the Fleet sewer is present also in the N–S stretch of the wall. It is now thought that this is a direct result of the difficult topography which occurs at the S end of the downstream eyot. A massive raft of crushed chalk, ragstone and hard mortar was constructed to carry the wall at this point.

The wall survived with numerous repairs until the massive reconstruction of the area following the Great Fire in 1666. This included the construction of the Fleet Canal between Blackfriars and Holborn. The excavations recorded the foundations and cellars of the warehouses which lined the E bank of the canal. The subsequent developments and building works on the E bank which accompanied the abandonment and covering of the canal when Blackfriars Bridge was constructed were recorded in detail in the excavations.

Fig 52 An inscribed pewter mug from the bar inside the 18th-century Fleet prison.

Much reused or discarded timber and stone were recovered during the excavations. They included staves, heads and hoops from about 40 casks, primary evidence for medieval cooperage, and about 500 moulded stones, ranging in date and type from a 12th-c window arch to 19th-c artificial stone from the original railway station at Ludgate Hill. During the redevelopment the railway line was repositioned to run under Ludgate Hill and the previous railway bridge over this street was demolished. Part of the E–W stretch of the medieval extension of the city wall was demolished but the longer stretch running N–S is to be preserved in the basement of new buildings.

The sites also produced a notable quantity of late medieval and post-medieval objects, recovery of which was enhanced by wet-sieving and by metal-detecting of deposits. The former technique was used, in particular, to retrieve the contents of an early 17th-c brick-lined drain. Finds recovered elsewhere include bone objects such as combs and thread-pickers of Late Saxon date, several pilgrim badges, much waste from the production of hone-stones, a complete Kingston ware jug of previously unrecorded form and several post-medieval medical implements.

London Archaeol, 6, 1989, 53; 6, 1990, 163; 6, 1991, 273–4; 7, 1993, 49; *Medieval Archaeol,* 33, 1989, 183; 34, 1990, 177–8; 1991, 149–50; *Post-Medieval Archaeol,* 25, 1991, 138

There are many specialist archive reports, notes and tables comprising the Fleet Valley Project research archive. They are ordered and accessible but usually not grouped into conventional reports. The MoL archive contains an index of the Fleet Valley archive computer files; for a general summary, see McCann 1993d. The reports dealing with environmental archaeology are given here.

Bates, M, 1990 'Sedimentological report', Archive Report (Geoarchaeological Service Facility)

Conheeney, J, 1993 'Scan of human bone from Fleet Valley (VAL88) (HUM/01/93)', Archive Report

Gerber-Parfitt, S, nd, 'Environmental appraisal', Archive Report

Hibberd, H, 1992a 'Dendrochronological spot date report: interim report (SPT/07/92)', Archive Report

Hibberd, H, 1992b 'Fleet Valley: extended dendrochronological spot date report (SPT/05/92)', Archive Report

Locker, A, 1994 'The fish bones from the Fleet Valley', Archive Report

McCann, B (ed), 1993a 'Animal bone interim report (BON/13/93)'

McCann, B (ed), 1993b 'Fleet Valley interim report (environmental) (ENV/REP/01/93)'

McCann, B (ed), 1993c 'Fleet Valley Project (VAL88, PWB88)', Archive Report

McCann, B, 1993d 'Fleet Valley Project', Post-excavation Assessment

McCann, B, & Orton, C, 1989 'The Fleet Valley Project', *London Archaeol*, 6, 102–7

Nayling, N, 1989 'Dendrochronological spot dates (SPT11/89)', Archive Report

Nayling, N, 1990 'Dendrochronological report (FV01/90)', Archive Report

Pipe, A, 1992 'Assessment of the animal bone from Fleet Valley (BON/12/92)', Archive Report

Spence, C (ed), 1989 *Digging in the City: the annual review 1988* (DUA, MoL), 18–19

Spence, C, & Grew, F (eds), 1990 *The annual review 1989* (DUA, MoL), 12–13

Spencer, B, in prep. *Pilgrim souvenirs and secular badges*, Medieval finds from excavations in London 7

5a–10 Wardrobe Place, 146a Wardrobe Chambers, EC4

WAP88

J Youle and C Mamwell
NGR: TQ 31890 81020
SMR: 04119802, 041781–2,
042719–22

The natural brickearth was cut by a large Roman quarry pit and the E edge of a stream channel (the 'western stream' of Roman London, flowing from the Paternoster Square area to the Thames, identified on various sites), the profile of which showed a very steep edge and a flat base. Stream deposits located on the adjacent site of Wardrobe Place imply a minimum width of 14m for the channel. Medieval material within the waterlaid deposits indicates that it was still in existence during this period. The rest of the site revealed several large 17th–19th-c brick-lined cesspits, one of which was abutted by a contemporary unmortared brick well or circular structure.

London Archaeol, 6, 1990, 167; 6, 1991, 278; *Britannia*, 22, 1991, 267; *Medieval Archaeol*, 34, 1990, 180

Heathcote, J, Richards, G, & Watson, B, 1988 'Wardrobe Place', Testpit Report

Mamwell, C, 1990a 'Excavations at Wardrobe Place (WAP88)', Archive Report

Mamwell, C, 1990b 'Interim report on archaeological excavations at Wardrobe Place, EC4', Archive Report

Wren House, 13–23 Carter Lane, EC4

WHO88

C Mamwell and B Bishop
NGR: TQ 32025 81030
SMR: 041626–30

Trial excavations funded by Warnford Investments plc were conducted in the basements of two standing buildings to the N and E of recent excavations and watching brief observations. Quarry pits for brickearth were identified and the form of the 'western stream' of the Roman city clarified at this part of its course. The latter channel was steeply incised on its E side to a relative depth of at least 4m; it had a flat base and was at least 14m wide. The waterlaid silts filling the channel contained pottery of early medieval date, indicating that it remained open until then. Later intrusive features included post-medieval brick-lined cesspits and an adjacent well.

London Archaeol, 6, 1990, 162; *Britannia*, 22, 1991, 267

Bishop, B, 1989 'Excavations at 13–23 Carter Lane/Wren House EC4', Archive Report

1–7 Whittington Avenue, EC3

WIV88

G Brown and B Pye
NGR: TQ 33100 81090
SMR: 041784–800

Excavations and a watching brief between June 1988 and September 1989 were funded by the developer, the Corporation of London.

At the beginning of the sequence, the naturally sloping ground surface was raised with dumps of brickearth by about 0.3–0.4m. A road was constructed of rammed gravel and sand, about 5m wide, running N–S and lined with clay and timber buildings. These were burnt down, perhaps in the Boudican revolt of AD60–1. The two sides of the road then developed separately. To the W, cultivation was followed by use as a rubbish tip, while to the E, buildings of high quality were constructed, with flint foundations and tile sleeper walls.

A major redevelopment occurred in the late 1st or early 2nd c with the construction of the forum–basilica complex and associated new roads. The existing N–S road was widened to about 9m and another road was constructed to the N, crossing at a right angle. Timber-lined drains were laid to the E of the former road and to the S of the latter road. Wooden pipes about 1.2m long joined together with iron collars were laid within the road gravels, supplying water to both public and private buildings. To the SW of the road junction the ground was raised and the basilica constructed on substantial ragstone and mortar foundations. The floors inside this major public building (the largest in Roman Britain) were of poor-quality mortar and even brickearth. After a fire in the mid-2nd c, the basilica was renovated and a portico added to the E, with a floor of tiles laid in a herringbone pattern (*opus spicatum*). By the mid-3rd c the portico was dismantled, although the rest of the basilica continued in use.

To the E of the N–S road were two large buildings, probably sharing a party wall. The N building, part of which was probably a shop, had stone foundations and both buildings had tessellated floors, hot air flues and walls decorated with painted plaster. These buildings appear to have fallen into disuse by the 3rd c. They were overlaid by destruction debris and dark earth.

Insertion of a late 19th-c basement destroyed most of the later strata, but intrusive features survived. An early medieval well was cut through the basilican foundations, which were subsequently robbed out. Various foundations survived from the later medieval period, some probably related to documented buildings, Green Yard Inn and the chapel of Leadenhall; others formed two chalk-lined cellars. To the NE of the site, a party wall incorporated masonry of c 14th-c date. This included chequerwork decoration of alternating chalk blocks and flints.

Finds of note include a Roman copper-alloy handle decorated with swan's head terminals and a glass Medusa or Maenad medallion from a jug. Roman glass was prolific and included well-stratified 1st-c groups. Roman building materials were present in substantial quantities. In addition to the well-made tessellated and herringbone floors, lengths of quarter-round plaster moulding occurred at floor and wall junctions. Large amounts of roof mortar were also preserved and marble fragments from a drain-lining were reconstructed as a near-complete decorative wall panel.

London Archaeol, 6, 1990, 167; *Britannia,* 22, 1991, 268; *Medieval Archaeol,* 34, 1990, 180

Brown, G, & Macphail, R, 1991 'First-century horticultural activities close to the municipal boundaries of Londinium: archaeology and soil micromorphological evidence (SED/01/91)', Archive Report

Brown, G, & Pye, B, nd, 'WIV88 Areas A, C, E & F', Archive Report

Brown, G, & Pye, B, 1992 'Whittington Avenue excavations: a summary', in Milne, G (ed), *From Roman basilica to medieval market: archaeology in action in the City of London,* 135–7

Davies, B, 1993 'Inter-site studies', in Milne, G, & Wardle, A, 'Early Roman development at Leadenhall Court, London and related research', *Trans London Middlesex Archaeol Soc,* 44, 135–50

Pringle, S, 1990 'Whittington Avenue', Building Materials Appraisal, draft

Robinson, J, 1990 'Whittington Avenue', Post-Roman Pottery Appraisal

Spence, C, & Grew, F (eds), 1990 *The annual review 1989* (DUA, MoL), 28–9

ALN89

C Goode
NGR: TQ 33430 81690
SMR: 041980–2

26–30 Artillery Lane, E1

Four testpits were recorded in the basement of a standing building in January 1989, by arrangement with Sheppard Robson, architects, for archaeological assessment of the site. Natural gravels and brickearth were truncated, in one of the testpits, by a cut feature containing post-medieval building debris. This was truncated in turn by a cesspit floored with stone flags and lined with yellow frogged bricks. There was no sign of Roman burials, which might have been expected on this extramural site.

London Archaeol, 6, 1991, 272

Goode, C, 1989 '26–30 Artillery Lane (ALN89)', Testpit Report

4–10 Artillery Lane, E1

ARY89

J Drummond-Murray
NGR: TQ 33370 81680
SMR: 041979

A watching brief funded by Provident Life Association Ltd took place between April and June 1990 to monitor groundworks. The site lies in the area of a Roman extramural cemetery and evidence of burials was expected. In the event, all strata had already been removed by truncation, and post-medieval landfill directly overlay natural gravels.

London Archaeol, 6, 1991, 272
Murray, J, 1989 'Environmental assessment of the samples (ASS/01/89)', Archive Report

Atlantic House, 45–50 Holborn Viaduct, EC1

ATL89

P Durnford
NGR: TQ 31530 81580
SMR: 042587–92

Testpits were recorded in the basement and sub-basements of a standing building between October 1989 and February 1990, for archaeological assessment of the site, funded by Prudential Portfolio Managers Ltd. Along the E side of the site, lying on the W bank of the River Fleet, remains of a possible medieval timber revetment were set in natural river gravels and silt. To the extreme S, mortared chalk, rag and Reigate stone may have been a foundation for the documented medieval bridge carrying Holborn (the road) over the Fleet. Thick organic dumps elsewhere were cut by medieval pits, one wicker lined, and post-medieval brick foundations and drains.

London Archaeol, 6, 1991, 275; *Medieval Archaeol,* 35, 1991, 151
Durnford, P, 1989 'Atlantic House, 45–50 Holborn Viaduct (ATL89)', Testpit Report

298–306 Bishopsgate, EC2

BOG89

N Roycroft
NGR: TQ 33390 81900
SMR: 041986–91,
08093413–14

Work on this site has been combined in post-excavation with work on the nearby site of 274–280 Bishopsgate (PSO90): see PSO90 below for summary and reports.

British Telecom shaft, Bishopsgate and Wormwood Street, EC2

BTB89

D Sankey
NGR: TQ 33230
81490–33198 81430
SMR: 041908, 041929–31,
041983

Investigations between November 1989 and April 1990 in a British Telecom tunnel running N from the site of Bishopsgate, a Scheduled Ancient Monument, revealed a foundation of flints and brickearth trench-built in natural brickearth, perhaps for a monument on the boundary of the Roman city, preceding the city wall. Adjoining this were later foundations of Kentish rag and clay, with mortared ragstones facing N, presumably representing the Roman gate. Further to the N a wide, flat-bottomed ditch is interpreted as a medieval recutting of the defensive ditch, no earlier ditch surviving. Subsequently a chalk-built arched foundation crossed this ditch, cutting waterlaid sediments within it.

London Archaeol, 6, 1991, 272; *Britannia,* 22, 1991, 265

CED89

T Thomas
NGR: TQ 32440 81140
SMR: 042766–78

64–66 Cheapside, EC4

Excavations funded by Sun Alliance Property Construction Ltd took place post-demolition from April to June 1991 in the S half of the site, concurrently with contractors' groundworks. Sections exposed in underpinning holes and by deeper groundworks were recorded in a watching brief which continued until September 1991.

Alluvial silts overlying natural sands and gravels marked a tributary of the Walbrook flowing SE. To the W, at least, this ground was consolidated with timber piles and brickearth dumps, probably in the 1st c, in advance of construction. To the W Roman buildings partly survived severe later truncation and presumably fronted onto a street to the N, the Roman precursor of Cheapside. The S edge of this street was located running E–W, with a roadside ditch. To the SE buildings were traced on either side of a narrow alley aligned to the street. These buildings had foundations of mortared ragstone, brick and tile, brickearth floors or floor make-ups, a tiled hearth and internal walls faced with painted plaster and with a quarter-round moulding at the base. To the SW two adjacent rooms of a different building were floored with *opus signinum*, divided by a timber partition wall.

These buildings burnt down, probably early in the 2nd c, and a thick dump of burnt building debris covered the site, cut in turn by post-holes or possibly tree holes. The latter were eventually infilled with dark earth, which also sealed the road surface to the N. Formation of dark earth was apparently interrupted by a phase of pits.

All later features were intrusive. Mortared chalk and gravel foundations on timber piles marked a medieval strip building running N, fronting onto Cheapside. There were at least two cellars in this building and the lowest courses of a cellar wall survived, with a mortared rubble core faced in ragstone. To the S a later building with differently mortared ragstone and chalk foundations ran SW, probably fronting onto Bow Lane. This had cellars with walls faced in squared chalk, a tiled floor and a corner hearth. These cellars were subdivided and extended before eventually being backfilled with rubbish or used as cesspits. One of the latter yielded well-preserved plant and animal remains. Some medieval foundations were incorporated in later buildings but brick foundations on a different plan indicated a separate building, probably post-Great Fire. A single basement to the S and double basement in the N half of the site completed the sequence.

London Archaeol, 6, 1992, 389; *Medieval Archaeol*, 36, 1991, 229
Groves, J, 1992 '64–66 Cheapside', Roman Pottery Appraisal
Holden, T, 1991 'Environmental assessment report (ASS/07/91)', Archive Report
Keily, J, 1992 '64–66 Cheapside', Building Materials Appraisal
Sidell, J, 1992 'The animal bones from 64–66 Cheapside (CED89) (BON/11/92)', Archive Report
Thomas, T, 1991 'Excavations at 64–66 Cheapside', Archive Report, interim

CIS89

K Wooldridge
NGR: TQ 31990 81370
SMR: 221052

Christchurch Greyfriars, Newgate Street, EC1

Floor levels and two underlying brick vaults of the Wren post-Great Fire church were located during landscaping work by the Corporation of London.

For earlier work on this site see GF73, CHR76 and CCN80 above.

London Archaeol, 6, 1991, 273; *Post-Medieval Archaeol*, 25, 1991, 116
Wooldridge, K, 1989 'Christchurch Greyfriars Newgate Street EC1', Archive Report

CLY89

B Watson
NGR: TQ 31760 81094
SMR: 040429

76 Carter Lane, 9 Ludgate Broadway, EC4

Four testpits were observed. The evidence suggested strata of the infilled ditch in front of the pre-1275 city wall in this area. A borehole at 9 Ludgate Broadway confirmed the existence of about 5.4m of infilled medieval city ditch surviving below the basement of the present building. No further archaeological work was undertaken as the development did not proceed.

Watson, B, 1989 '76 Carter Lane, 9 Ludgate Broadway', Testpit Report

Coleman Street (outside Armourers' Hall), EC2

Sewerworks revealed an apparently waterlaid deposit, possibly a flood deposit from a nearby Walbrook tributary, and timber stakes which may have derived from a revetment.

Mackinder, A, 1989 'Coleman Street (COE89)', Watching Brief Report

COE89

A Mackinder
NGR: TQ 32650 81530
SMR: 044580–1

8–11 Crescent, EC3

Excavations here were funded by Arundell House (City) Ltd. The foundations of the Roman city wall were cut into natural gravels; the outer face survived to a height of 3.5m above these foundations. To the E, no trace of an original ditch survived, but timber piles and, directly abutting the wall face, mortared ragstone and chalk were revealed. These are interpreted as the foundations of a bastion (2A) added to the wall in the late Roman period, presumably obliterating any earlier ditch; it confirms the regular spacing of such bastions in this sector.

Early in the medieval period the area in front of the wall was reduced and the bastion was dismantled; then the area was levelled up with dumps containing Roman building debris derived from the wall or the bastion. The wall itself was rebuilt above the existing Roman face and core, surviving to a level just below the presumed crenellations. Further to the E, possible medieval ditch cuts were traced. Later, gravel was dumped against the wall face.

Elsewhere post-medieval features included part of a horncore-lined pit or ditch, and ditch- or pitfills containing slag. Building rubble was then dumped extensively to prepare the ground for the brick foundations and drains of buildings in a documented late 18th-c development, of which Crescent was a part, designed by George Dance the younger. The bastion foundations and standing wall have been left *in situ*.

Finds from this site centre on the post-medieval period and include an ivory comb, a copper-alloy candlestick and a ceramic button with a representation of a crowned female figure, possibly the 'Queen of Africa'.

London Archaeol, 6, 1990, 163; *Britannia,* 22, 1991, 265; *Medieval Archaeol,* 34, 1990, 177
Robinson, J, 1989 '8–11 Crescent', Post-Roman Pottery Appraisal
Sermon, R, 1989 '8–11 Crescent', Archive Report, draft

CRT89

R Sermon
NGR: TQ 33610 00813
SMR: 041650–3

7–11 Bishopsgate, EC2

The remains of Roman floors and building debris, substantial medieval chalk walls and post-medieval brick walls were recorded in testpits.

This site was excavated by MoLAS in 1995–6; for details consult MoLAS archive (ETA89).

Anon, 1989 '7–11 Bishopsgate', Testpit Report

ETA89

S McCudden and O Belle
NGR: TQ 33020 81190
SMR: 044315–21

2 Fore Street, EC2

Four testpits were examined, most of which showed natural brickearth or gravels. One of the testpits indicated ditchfill above the gravel.

FRS89

Sarah Gibson
NGR: TQ 32510 81630
SMR: 044586

FUL89

J Henderson and R Sermon
NGR: TQ 31210 81490
SMR: 042536–8

32 Furnival Street, EC4

Testpits were recorded in April and May 1989 and a watching brief was carried out from July to October 1990, funded by J V Developments Ltd. Evidence for quarrying of gravel underlying natural brickearth was probably of Roman date. These quarry pits, backfilled with brickearth, were truncated by the brick foundations, walls and stone floor flags of 17th- or 18th-c cellars. The latest building, probably of early 19th-c date, was recorded before demolition. This comprised a cellar and three floors with timber floor frames, stud partition walls and roof, within a brick shell.

London Archaeol, 6, 1991, 274; *Britannia,* 22, 1991, 271
Henderson, J, & Sermon, R, nd, '32 Furnival Street', Testpit Report

GDS89

B Watson
NGR: TQ 32210 81360
SMR: 044587

Goldsmiths' Hall, Foster Lane, EC2

During January 1989 a watching brief was carried out to monitor the digging of one testpit and the drilling of one borehole in the SW corner of the basement of Goldsmiths' Hall. Cut into the natural brickearth was a truncated pit or ditch probably of Roman date.

Watson, B, 1989 'Report on the archaeological implications of a borehole and testpit survey at Goldsmiths' Hall, Foster Lane, EC2'

GTA89

M Hinman
NGR: TQ 32400 80955
SMR: 042556–62

13–14 Great St Thomas Apostle, EC4

Excavations funded by Poly Property Ltd took place between November 1989 and February 1990, after demolition.

Natural brickearth was overlaid by redeposited brickearth and two successive Roman clay and timber buildings were constructed. Both buildings burnt down. No further horizontal strata survived subsequent truncation. To the E were intrusive Saxo-Norman rubbish pits and to the W foundation and cellars of a large medieval building. The cellars were entered by stone stairs, the lowest steps of which, with part of an adjacent stone door jamb, were still *in situ.* A large chalk-lined cesspit was inserted to the N, backfilled in the 17th c, and brick cellar floors were inserted elsewhere.

The party wall along the W side of the site at basement level, forming three blind arches, was of post-Great Fire construction, reusing a variety of building materials. These included several moulded stones perhaps deriving from the nearby church of St Thomas Apostle, destroyed in the Great Fire and not rebuilt.

The most notable find is a Middle or Late Saxon hipped bone pin with an expanded head and with cruciform and ring and dot decoration.

London Archaeol, 6, 1991, 274; *Britannia,* 22, 1991, 267; *Medieval Archaeol,* 35, 1991, 150
Hinman, M, 1989 '13–14 Great St Thomas Apostle', Testpit Report

Pinners' Hall, Great Winchester Street, 8 Austin Friars Square, 105–108 Old Broad Street, EC2

GWS89

C Rosborough
NGR: TQ 32980 81390
SMR: 041489, 042563–75

Post-demolition excavations, funded by the Merchant Navy Officers Pension Fund, were conducted between May and July 1990, followed by a watching brief.

The earliest evidence of activity, cutting natural gravels and brickearth, was a U-shaped ditch or gully running E–W across the site, to the N, and a well, to the S, both of early Roman date. Widespread gravel-quarrying ensued. The quarry pits were backfilled and the ground consolidated, presumably in preparation for possible construction, all further evidence of which was truncated.

In the early medieval period, the site was open ground containing rubbish and cesspits, and three barrel-lined wells. It lay within the documented precincts of the Augustinian friary of Austin Friars, founded in the 13th c. Short lengths of masonry foundations, in several phases, were exposed and about 200 fragments of moulded stone, including column bases and window tracery, were recovered from destruction debris or found reused in later foundations. Few later features survived severe modern truncation.

Finds from the site include a good assemblage of mid-1st-c pottery, the earliest such assemblage found in the City of London, a complete Roman millstone from a watermill, medieval crucibles and bone skates, and a post-medieval crucible for glassmaking, with glass slag.

London Archaeol, 6, 1991, 274; *Britannia,* 22, 1991, 266; *Medieval Archaeol,* 35, 1991, 150; *Post-Medieval Archaeol,* 25, 1991, 138
Davies, B, 1990 'Great Winchester Street (GWS89)', Roman Pottery Appraisal
Robinson, J, 1990 'Pinners' Hall (GWS89)', Post-Roman Pottery Appraisal
Rosborough, C, 1990 'Excavations at Pinners' Hall (GWS89)', Interim Report

58–60 Houndsditch, EC3

HSD89

C Mamwell
NGR: TQ 33320 81400
SMR: 041935–6

Excavations here were funded by Speyhawk plc. The Roman city wall was exposed running along the SW edge of the site: the stones of the outer face were cut away by later cellaring, leaving only the core. The surviving portion was 5m long and 4m high and is to be preserved. The visible foundations of the wall indicated contemporary ground level. Although badly truncated, the associated defensive ditch, V-shaped in profile, clearly ran NW–SE in front of and parallel to the wall. The base of this ditch implied an original minimum depth relative to ground level of 2m. Eight burials, directly in front of the wall or partly in the backfilled ditch and probably of late Roman date, comprised seven adults and one child: their bodies were extended and aligned in different directions. The medieval city defences were represented by the ditch, at least 18m wide and, despite being badly truncated, one and possibly two recuts were distinguished. The ditchfills contained several complete dog skeletons.

London Archaeol, 6, 1990, 164; *Medieval Archaeol,* 34, 1990, 178
Mamwell, C, 1989 'Excavations at 58–60 Houndsditch EC3', Archive Report

Innholders' Hall, 29–30 College Street, EC4

IHA89

Sarah Gibson
NGR: TQ 32535 80830
SMR: 041634, 0200608

Excavations here were funded by the Worshipful Company of Innholders. The earliest evidence of activity is dated to the late Roman period and consists of dumps and a timber drain on the E bank of the Walbrook river. These probably represent land stabilisation or reclamation.

A medieval pile-based chalk foundation and chalk and ragstone walls may have related to an early Innholders' Hall, or to buildings predating it. Some of the larger roof timbers in the existing hall were evidently reused and were also charred: they may have been salvaged from the original hall for reuse after the Great Fire.

London Archaeol, 6, 1990, 162; *Britannia,* 22, 1991, 267; *Medieval Archaeol,* 34, 1990, 177
Gibson, Sarah, 1989 'Innholders' Hall 29–30 College Street EC4', Archive Report
Nayling, N, & Tyers, I, 1989 'Dendrochronogical spot date report: interim report (SPT/08/89)'

LEN89

J Youle
NGR: TQ 33110 81150
SMR: 042603–14

145–146 Leadenhall Street, EC3

A post-demolition excavation was carried out between October and December 1989, funded by Pension Funds Securities Ltd.

Natural gravels and brickearth were cut by early Roman quarry pits, associated with stake-holes possibly forming a small structure. The pits were backfilled and the site levelled in preparation for construction of a timber-framed building with brickearth walling and floors. This contained at least three rooms and adjoined a yard to the N. The walls were reinforced in a phase of repair before the building was demolished, and quarry and rubbish pits opened. In the early 2nd c two new clay and timber buildings were erected. Hearths, rake-out debris and iron slag in the building to the N suggest that it was a smithy. A pit in an open area to the S contained two human skulls. Later Roman features included, to the S, a tile-lined drain leading to a complete amphora set into the ground, perhaps for collecting rain water, and to the N a clay and tile lined kiln or oven. No other features survived severe later truncation except intrusive medieval wells and rubbish and cesspits.

Deposits of all periods were extensively sampled for environmental evidence. Finds from the site are mostly of Roman date and include fragments of painted wall plaster, decorated oil lamps, copper-alloy brooches and fragments of shale bowls and platters. The most notable object is a Roman copper-alloy saucepan, surviving in poor condition; complete saucepans are rarely found in Britain.

London Archaeol, 6, 1991, 275; *Britannia,* 22, 1991, 268
Anon, nd, 'Additional information on the environmental samples', Environmental Note
Youle, J, 1990 'Excavations at 145–146 Leadenhall Street (LEN89)', Archive Report

LHN89

C Goode and S Jones
NGR: TQ 33440 81130
SMR: 04169201006,
042596–602

78–79 Leadenhall Street, EC3

Excavation took place in several phases between January and April 1990, after demolition. Work was sponsored by P & O Developments Ltd.

The earliest evidence of human activity was a linear cut running roughly NW–SE, cut into natural brickearth. Brickearth was then dumped across the site, compensating for the natural slope. Subsequent stake-holes and post-holes, possible structural slots, and accumulated layers of burning and redeposited burnt debris, interspersed with occasional resurfacing of clean brickearth are interpreted as external and of Roman date. An isolated clay and timber wall running roughly NW–SE was destroyed by fire; any associated floor surfaces were probably removed by later truncation. An isolated patch of rammed gravel to the W is assumed to be a continuation of the Roman street found in previous excavations to the SW (see 80–84 Leadenhall Street, LAH88 above).

To the S, ragstone foundations aligned NW–SE were succeeded by chalk foundations on the same alignment; no construction horizons or floors survived. A total of 59 burials, concentrated mostly to the W, partly overlay the latter foundations. These burials, associated with the church of St Katherine Cree to the W and with Holy Trinity Priory to the N, were truncated by the latest, modern features on the site.

Finds of note include a Late Saxon composite bone comb and case from a pit predating the burials, the second of its kind to be found in London, a Late Saxon glass linen smoother and an Anglo-Norman bone skate.

London Archaeol, 6, 1991, 275; *Britannia,* 22, 1991, 268; *Medieval Archaeol,* 35, 1991, 151
Goode, C, & Jones, S, 1990 'Excavations at 78–79 Leadenhall Street (LHN89)', Archive Report, interim
Sankey, D, 1989 '78–79 Leadenhall Street', Testpit Report

LWB89

D Sankey
NGR: TQ 32940 81500
SMR: 044772

London Wall, junction with Blomfield Street, EC2

Undated waterlaid sediments of a Walbrook channel were recorded in a British Telecom shaft.

Mansion House Underground Station, 38 Cannon Street, EC4

MHS89

K Heard
NGR: TQ 32340 80960
SMR: 042674–80

A watching brief was conducted by arrangement with MEPC Developments Ltd in February–March 1990 during rebuilding of the underground station and after demolition of a building immediately to the W where excavations took place in 1989 (see ORM88 above).

Natural brickearth overlying gravels survived to the N, where disturbed soil horizons possibly indicated Roman agriculture. Elsewhere, natural strata were truncated by Roman quarry and rubbish pits, backfilled with brickearth and burnt building debris. Later intrusive features included trench-built chalk and gravel foundations, and cess- and rubbish pits, which were probably medieval, and a brick and ragstone structure that was probably post-medieval.

For earlier observations on the site of the underground station, in 1960, see GM178 above.

London Archaeol, 6, 1991, 276; Britannia, 22, 1991, 267
Heard, K, 1990 'Excavations at Mansion House Station, 38 Cannon Street (MHS89)', Archive Report

Colchester House, Savage Gardens, Pepys Street; Woodruffe House, Cooper's Row, EC3

PEP89

D Sankey
NGR: TQ 33520 80830
SMR: 042833–5, 044065–72

Excavations here were funded by Trinity House. Natural gravel and brickearth were cut by 1st- and 2nd-c features and by structural elements of buildings; in the SE of the site a gravel surface and associated ditch may have been a road. Above these a soil had formed which subsumed occupation and demolition remains associated with the buildings and which also included quantities of painted plaster. Glass waste, and the base of a substantial hearth which cut through the soil, may be evidence for Roman glassmaking. The hearth was truncated by general terracing associated with the construction of a 3rd-c building. It had a wide external wall and several square pier bases founded on timber piles capped with flint and chalk and topped with concrete. One area of *opus signinum* flooring survived. This building was overlaid by dark earth which may have formed the gardens of the Crutched Friars. It was cut by pits, a well or soak-away and robbing trenches for the 3rd c building. Also located were 17th- or 18th-c cellar foundations and floors and a late 17th-c ice-house which was backfilled in the 18th c with wine bottles, unused clay pipes and some Chinese and European imitation porcelain.

For observations during road widening of Savage Gardens in 1951, which are also catalogued 'Colchester House', see GM23 above.

London Archaeol, 6, 1992, 391; 7, 1993, 50; Britannia, 25, 1994, 281; Post-Medieval Archaeol, 27, 1993, 230
Mcphail, R, 1983 'Research design for micromorphological studies'
Sidell, J, 1993 'Animal bone assessment (BON/12/93)', Archive Report
Sidell, J, in prep. 'Dark earth and obscured stratigraphy', Assoc for Environmental Archaeol 1993 Annual Conf at Durham University proceedings

40 Queen Street, 1 Skinner's Lane, EC4

QSK89

T Mackinder
NGR: TQ 32415 80854
SMR: 041731–40, 020069401

Excavations here were funded by Ortem Development Ltd. The earliest features were three wooden drains and a post and plank revetment on the probable line of a Roman waterfront. These were succeeded by a large Roman masonry building having at least four rooms with worn brickearth and chalk floors and another room with a plain concrete floor. Disuse of this building was marked by a large amount of demolition debris filling it.

Later dumps were cut by several pits, wall foundations and, to the N, early 17th-c chalk-lined cesspits and the remains of post-Great Fire cellars. The latest features were a brick soak-away, a cesspit and a brick burial crypt, emptied and backfilled, associated with the church of St James Garlickhithe immediately to the W.

London Archaeol, 6, 1990, 165
Mackinder, T, 1990 'Excavations at 40 Queen Street, 1 Skinner's Lane (QSK89)', Archive Report

REC89

J Mills
NGR: TQ 32743 80787
SMR: 04093006, 042593–4

Rectory House, 7a Laurence Pountney Hill, 9 Laurence Pountney Lane, EC4

Testpits were recorded in the basement of a standing building, during refurbishment. This building is of late 17th-c date and listed as of special architectural or historic interest. The work was carried out intermittently in 1989 and early 1990, by arrangement with Seifert Ltd, architects.

Natural strata were not reached. The earliest features identified were two ragstone wall foundations running N–S, possibly related to the presumed Roman governor's palace to the W. This masonry was later incorporated in medieval chalk foundations, mostly running E–W. Post-medieval deposits and a brick-lined culvert, to the W, probably predated the existing building.

London Archaeol, 6, 1991, 275; *Britannia*, 22, 1991, 270
Mills, J, 1990 'Rectory House, 7a Laurence Pountney Hill, 9 Laurence Pountney Lane', Site Assessment Report

TCP89

B Watson
NGR: TQ 31290 81000
SMR: 041706–7

King's Bench Walk, Inner Temple, EC4

A shaft 3.9m deep was excavated for new cabling, and a watching brief funded by British Telecom. London Clay was cut by two successive features, possibly clay pits originally on the Thames foreshore. Both were backfilled with waterlogged silt and peat. The backfill of the later feature is dated to the 12th c and may coincide with documented occupation of the site by the Knights Templar. Both features were overlaid by thick dumps of post-medieval rubble and soil.

London Archaeol, 6, 1990, 164; *Medieval Archaeol*, 34, 1990, 178
Watson, B, 1989 'Watching brief at King's Bench Walk, Inner Temple', Archive Report

THM89

N Elsden and D Lawrence
NGR: TQ 32400 80930
SMR: 042553–5

1–7 Great St Thomas Apostle, 29–30 Queen Street, EC4

Excavations funded by London Underground Ltd, formerly London Regional Transport, took place in the basement of a standing building in April 1990 before demolition.

A line of stakes running N–S in natural brickearth was sealed by thick dumps of brickearth containing burnt building debris. Large pits were then opened for rubbish and human waste, and fragmentary slots suggest that a timber-framed building may have been erected, also aligned N–S. All post-Roman strata were truncated by modern foundations, the basement and the underground railway.

Notable finds from the dumps include a complete copper-alloy hinged ruler and a glass gaming counter.

London Archaeol, 6, 1991, 274; *Britannia*, 22, 1991, 267
Elsden, N, 1991 '1–7 Great St Thomas Apostle, 29–30 Queen Street, EC4', Watching Brief Report
Lawrence, D, 1990 '1–3 Great St Thomas Apostle, EC4', Archive Report

1–4 Great Tower Street, EC3

TWR89

C Rosborough
NGR: TQ 33170 80765
SMR: 011671–8

Excavations here were funded by Harrisons & Crosfield plc. Natural gravels capped by brickearth were cut, to the N, by the foundations of a clay and timber building aligned E–W, dated to the late 1st/early 2nd c. This in turn was superseded by late Roman quarry and rubbish pits and a N–S ditch; elsewhere there were other Roman rubbish pits and cesspits and an E–W ditch. Surviving later features included four medieval chalk-lined cesspits and other pits, and post-medieval brick-lined wells and cellars, relating to buildings fronting onto Great Tower Street and Idol Lane, to the N and W respectively. Other strata were truncated by construction of the existing building in 1905.

Roman finds from the site include large quantities of painted wall plaster and fragments of vessel glass. The largest of the chalk-lined cesspits was filled with an impressive group of ceramic vessels and glassware, among which were four Siegburg jugs and a later Roman vessel, as well as a variety of tin-glazed wares. Two important glass vessels were also retrieved from this feature. A late medieval Italian beaker has extensive gilding and enamel decoration, which surrounds a colloquial inscription (Fig 53); and a colourless stemmed cup with blue and white trails is of a type for which no accurate dating had hitherto been possible.

London Archaeol, 8, 1990, 163; *Britannia*, 22, 1991, 269; *Medieval Archaeol*, 34, 1990, 178

Robinson, J, 1990 '1–4 Great Tower Street', Post-Roman Pottery Appraisal

Rosborough, C, 1989 'Excavations at 1–4 Great Tower Street (TWR89)', Archive Report, draft and synthesis

Spence, C, & Grew, F (eds), 1990 *The annual review 1989* (DUA, MoL), 18–19

Fig 53 TWR89: this gilded and enamelled glass beaker from Great Tower Street was probably made in Venice at the end of the 15th c.

Vintry House (Vintners' Place) (watching brief), 68–69 Upper Thames Street, EC4

VHA89

R Brown
NGR: TQ 32370 80750
SMR: 04177704, 042710–18, 042854–64

This site code was given to the watching brief on the Vintners' Hall / Vintners' Place site, VRY89. See the VRY summary below for the main findings. This code is retained for any reports dealing solely with the watching brief.

London Archaeol, 6, 1990, 167; 6, 1991, 277–8; 6, 1992, 391–2; *Medieval Archaeol*, 34, 1990, 180; 35, 1991, 153; 36, 1992, 230

Barham, A, 1990 'Report on the sedimentological characteristics of monolith samples from the basal stratigraphy (90/03)', Archive Report (Geoarchaeological Service Facility)

Blackmore, L, nd, 'Medieval and later pottery from Vintners' Place', Appraisal

Drinkall, R, & Stevenson, J, 1996 'Weighing it all up', *London Archaeol*, 8, 3–9 [Roman–late medieval weights]

Edwards, J, 1989 'Medieval pottery', Appraisal [with separate notes on 'V' groups recovered from spoil after transport to landfill sites]

Nayling, N, 1990 'Dendrochronological spot dates: interim report (SPT/07/90)', Archive Report

VRY89

R Brown
NGR: TQ 32370 80810
SMR: 04177704, 042710–18,
042854–64

Vintry House (Vintners' Place), 68–69 Upper Thames Street, EC4

Roman and Early Saxon deposits were overlaid by naturally laid alluvial mud, indicating a rapid rise in sea level. This was followed by a sequence of buildings, dated to the 10th–early 11th c, with walls and roofs supported by posts. Wattle stakes marked internal partitions or structures; one building had at least six successive floors, one made of planks and others marked by brushwood and compacted silt; and timber edging to a tile hearth was repaired at least once. Outside the buildings were wattle fences; waterlaid sand and gravel against the S face of one of these showed that it had acted as a riverside revetment.

At least six further revetments were recorded, dated by their carpentry from the 12th to the 16th c, indicating progressive reclamation and migration of the waterfront to the S. Carpentry techniques include a form of scarf joint not recorded before in London and a back-braced edge-trenched mortice and tenon joint dove-tailed in three directions. The latest revetment, a chalk and Kentish rag wall founded on an elm timber raft, was on the line of the existing riverside wall. To the N chalk foundations, including some built on split beech timber rafts, indicated buildings on the reclaimed land.

To the S of the existing Vintners' Hall was a set of tile hearths, separated by low tile walls and extended and repaired, reusing roof tiles on edge, at least three times. These were probably part of the kitchens of the original hall, in use until the Great Fire of 1666 when the hall was destroyed. Other strata were removed by modern basementing and foundations.

Spoil from the pile holes on the site was metal-detected with the help of members of the Society of Thames Mudlarks, producing a very large assemblage of well-preserved early and late medieval ceramic and inorganic finds. In addition to large quantities of dress fittings, coins, trade seals and waste products of metalworking, numerous badges were found commemorating pilgrimage and denoting personal allegiance. Notable in the latter category is a small pewter hart and tree badge used by Richard II and his followers, the first example found in London. Deposits in the cofferdam in the river produced a large pewter plate with the letter V on it possibly signifying its use by the Vintners' Company. Other finds from the cofferdam include an elaborate pewter crucifix badge of late 14th–15th-c date, a 15th-c Talbot badge of allegiance to the earls of Shrewsbury and a small lead ingot with the mark of the Plumbers' Company, paralleled by one found at Nonsuch Palace, Surrey. A wattle-lined cesspit at the N end of the site contained two almost complete wooden bowls, a large boxwood comb and Spanish and German pottery of late medieval date.

The watching brief on this site was given the code VHA89.

London Archaeol, 6, 1990, 167; 6, 1991, 277–8; 6, 1992, 391–2; *Britannia*, 22, 1991, 270; *Medieval Archaeol*, 34, 1990, 180; 35, 1991, 153; 36, 1992, 230

Blackmore, L, 1991 'An appraisal note on the post-Roman "V" numbered pottery from VRY89', Appraisal

Blackmore, L, ?1991 'The medieval and later pottery from Vintners Place — VHA89', Appraisal

Edwards, J, 1991 'An appraisal note on the "V" numbered pottery from VRY89', Appraisal

Goodburn, D, 1992 'Fragments of a 10th-century timber arcade from Vintners' Place on the London waterfront', *Medieval Archaeol*, 37, 78–92

Hibberd, H, 1992 'Dendrochronological extended spot date report (SPT/02/92)', Dendrochronology Report

Holden, T, nd, 'Environmental appraisal report (VRY89 Phase I) (ASS/03/91)', Archive Report

Holden, T, 1991 'Environmental appraisal report for Vintry House (VRY89 Phase II)'

Holden, T, 1992 'Areas of special interest relating to the post-excavation on Vintry (VRY89)', Environmental Note

Pipe, A, 1989 'A short note on 19th-/20th-century animal bones from Vintry House, 68 Upper Thames Street, EC4', Archive Report

Schofield, J, 1995 *Medieval London houses*, 215

Spencer, B, in prep. *Pilgrim souvenirs and secular badges*, Medieval finds from excavations in London 7

Tyers, I, 1991 'Dendrochronological spot dates: interim report (SPT/06/91)', Archive Report

WES89

B Langton
NGR: TQ 31810 81530
SMR: 042723–35

24–30 West Smithfield, 18–20 Cock Lane, 1–4 Giltspur Street, EC1

Excavations were carried out in the single basements of standing buildings at 1–4 Giltspur Street and 18 Cock Lane, in May and June 1989. After demolition of these buildings further excavation took place both there and in an unbasemented area to the N and W, next to 24–30 West Smithfield from September to December 1989, followed by a watching brief. This work was by arrangement with Vestey Estates Ltd, formerly Commercial Properties Ltd.

Natural sand and gravels were cut by pits, one of which contained Late Bronze Age pottery. In the early Roman period pits were dug to quarry gravel. These were then backfilled with rubbish or left to silt up. Later the site was partly levelled up with brickearth, pits were dug and hearths were used, perhaps for an industrial purpose. These features were truncated by a series of at least 127 burials, forming part of an extensive late Roman cemetery. These burials, including 14 chalk burials, were aligned variously, but generally N–S or E–W. The density of burials was variably localised, some phases of graves coinciding with pits and rubbish disposal and one small area remaining free both of graves and pits. The cemetery deposits were cut by intrusive medieval rubbish or sand-lined pits, chalk foundations and gravelled surfaces, cut in turn by post-medieval brick cellar floors, drains and wall foundations.

The Late Bronze Age pottery is a substantial bucket urn of post-Deverel-Rimbury type. It is unusual to find a complete vessel of this kind in the City. One of the Roman burials, of a child, contained ten bracelets of shale, copper and bone, as well as a silver earring and a glass bead necklace. Another grave contained five copper-alloy bracelets, a silver earring and an intact Nene Valley ware colour-coated beaker. A jet necklace of more than 220 beads in segmented, faceted and other shapes was found with another burial. Two burials were accompanied by decorated bone combs, one of which is a rare form: a double-sided comb made of composite materials, dated to the 4th c. One of these combs was situated behind the skull and was presumably a hair comb *in situ*. A copper-alloy ring was found on the finger of another skeleton. One body was buried with a wooden box containing jewellery and cosmetic equipment.

Among other finds were an iron barrel-lock, key and chain, in a medieval pit, and a bone syringe, copper-alloy candle snuffers and a large 17th–early 18th-c Staffordshire slipware dish.

London Archaeol, 6, 1991, 277; *Britannia,* 22, 1991, 271

Baynard's Castle, [new] City of London Boys' School, EC4

BEX90

Sarah Gibson and D Shotliff
NGR: TQ 31930 80830
SMR: 042737

Insertion of drain runs and manholes on the site of the SE corner of Baynard's Castle uncovered only post-medieval backfill and make-up, leaving the fabric of the monument undisturbed. The watching brief took place by arrangement with the Corporation of London. This was also the site of the BYD81 excavations.

London Archaeol, 6, 1992, 388

Broadgate, phases 12–13: Norton Folgate and Primrose Street, EC2

BGA90

L Dunwoodie
NGR: TQ 33380 81990
SMR: 044588

Five testpits were examined. Pits had been dug into natural brickearth; but there was no dating evidence.

Dunwoodie, L, 1990 'Broadgate phases 12–13', Site Assessment

Brook's Wharf, 48 Upper Thames Street, EC4

BHD90

C Rosborough
NGR: TQ 32220 80800
SMR: 044589

Eight testpits were monitored. Land reclamation deposits probably of medieval date were recorded.

Rosborough, C, 1990 'Brooks Wharf', Archaeological Evaluation

BRO90

L Dyson
NGR: TQ 33060 31490
SMR: 042824–9

Boston House, 90–94 Old Broad Street, 63–64 New Broad Street, EC2

The Roman city wall was known to have crossed the S part of the site but any traces of this were completely removed during the construction of later buildings. Truncated remains of the V-shaped city ditch dated to the 3rd c were recovered about 5.5m out from the line of the wall. In the W part of the site the backfill of the ditch contained two disarticulated skeletons; a further burial was laid out parallel to the line of the Roman wall. This may have been disturbed during the construction of Boston House and reburied near its original find spot.

A shallow ditch at the N end of the site may be the medieval city ditch. A later, flat-bottomed ditch probably of the late medieval or Tudor period ran across the site, truncating both the Roman and medieval ditches. The latest ditch was backfilled with dumps containing quantities of whole and broken pots. The area was backfilled in the 17th c; this backfill contained quantities of glass which may have been from the manufacturing complex nearby in Austin Friars.

London Archaeol, 6, 1992, 390–1; *Britannia,* 23, 1992, 291; *Medieval Archaeol,* 36, 1992, 229; *Post-Medieval Archaeol,* 26, 1992, 109
Dyson, L, 1992 'Excavations at 90–94 Old Broad Street, EC2 (BRO90)', Archive Report
Heard, K, 1991 'Clay pipes from Broad Street', Archive Report
Holden, T, 1991a 'Environmental Appraisal Report (ASS/07/91)', Archive Report
Holden, T, 1991b 'The botanical remains from BRO90', Archive Report
Locker, A, 1992 'Fish identifications (FIS/08/92)', Archive Report
Pearce, J, 1992 'The pottery from BRO90', Archive Report
Pearce, J, in prep. *Redwares,* Post-medieval pottery from London 2
Pipe, A, 1992a 'The animal bones (by group) from 90–94 Old Broad Street', Archive Report
Pipe, A, 1992b 'The animal bones (by phase) from 90–94 Old Broad Street', Archive Report
Shepherd, J, 1992 'The glass from BRO90, with technical analyses by C Mortimer (AML)', Archive Report
Taylor, C, 1991 'Documentary survey for BRO90', Archive Report

BSS90

Sarah Gibson
NGR: TQ 32410 81250
SMR: 044105–6, 044599

Blossoms Inn, 3–6 Trump Street, 20–27 Lawrence Lane, 2–4 Russia Row, EC2

Three testpits were excavated, two of which revealed extensive Roman deposits. In one, an E–W ragstone wall, almost certainly Roman, survived to a height of 1.35m. In the other, waterlaid deposits, which may have been associated with a tributary of the Walbrook stream, were recorded. They were overlaid by a Roman road surface.

The site was observed by MoLAS in 1994; see MoLAS archive for details.

Gibson, Sarah, 1990 'Blossoms Inn (BSS90)', Site Evaluation, draft

BUF90

D Lees and J Ayre
NGR: TQ 31760 81070
SMR: 044197–9, 044322–9

Bull Wharf, 16–19 Queenhithe, 66–67 Upper Thames Street, EC4

This investigation was begun in 1990 but largely undertaken by MoLAS from the beginning of 1992 until 1996. The work up to the end of 1993 is described here.

Excavations were undertaken in the S half of Bull Wharf Lane as part of the large waterfront redevelopment commenced to the NE in 1990–1 (see UPT90 below), next to the medieval inlet of Queenhithe (a Scheduled Ancient Monument). The earliest structure found was a N–S earth-fast post and plank revetment which marked the E edge of Queenhithe dock; it is dated by dendrochronology to 1146. To its S and W were the remains of the posts of a robbed revetment which indicated that the E edge of Queenhithe was moved about 3m to the W. This reclamation can be dated to between 1146 and 1151. Further to the S, groups of timber wedges, set into the foreshore to secure the angled front-braces of a timber waterfront, indicated the robbed remains of an E–W revetment. Recorded at the S end of the trench were four substantial posts over 3m in height and a number of planks forming an E–W revetment dated to 1181. This was a continuation of a structure first noted during the previous redevelopment of Bull Wharf in 1979 (BLL79 above). Its position and form indicate that the E edge of Queenhithe had again migrated to the W (Fig 54).

The revetment sequence was sealed by dumped make-up deposits and road surfaces. The earliest road surface was well preserved, over 10m in length and edged with reused timbers as kerbs. The latest surfaces were associated with arched chalk foundations with Reigate stone walls and tile floors of riverside buildings from the 13th to the 17th c. They often respected earlier revetment alignments, indicating a continuity of property boundaries. One particular rubble and mortar foundation contained over 30 dressed Reigate stones, some with recognisable architectural features.

Excavation by MoLAS continued in 1994, but is not summarised here.

Fig 54 BUF90: one of the latest waterfront excavations to be reported in this Guide. *The site at Bull Wharf was significant for its contribution to the chronology of waterfronts of the 12th c immediately E of Queenhithe.*

London Archaeol, 7, 1994, 199; *Britannia,* 23, 1992, 292; *Medieval Archaeol,* 36, 1992, 228–9

Boswijk, G, & Tyers, I, 1996 'Dendrochronological spot dates for 268 timbers from nine London sites (1994–5): (DEN/02/96)', Dendrochronology Report

Conheeney, J, 1996 'The second foreshore burial from Bull Wharf (BUF90 context 3229)'

Davis, A, 1993 'Bull Wharf Phase I: assessment of the soil samples (ENV/ASS/12/93)', Archive Report

Giorgi, J, 1996 'An assessment of the plant remains from Bull Wharf/ Upper Thames Street (BUF90/UPT90): BOT/ASS/10/96', Archive Report

Holden, T, nd, 'Environmental evidence (Phase 1)', Archive Report

Holden, T, & Gerber-Parfitt, S, 1992 'Environmental sampling, processing and some preliminary results from Bull Wharf', *London Archaeol,* 6, 427–34

Rielly, K, 1996 'Assessment of the animal bones from Bull Wharf Lane and Upper Thames Street (BUF90 and UPT90) (BON/ASS/08/96)', Archive Report

Tyers, I, & Boswijk, G, 1996 'Dendrochronological spot dates for timbers from Bull Wharf (BUF90) & Regis House (KWS94) (DEN/01/96)', Dendrochronology Report

Wilkinson, K, 1995 'Design for an assessment of sedimentological samples from Bull Wharf (BUF90) (SED/02/95)', Archive Report

Wilkinson, K, 1996 'An assessment of the fluvial sedimentary stratigraphy at Bull Wharf, EC4 (SED/11/96)', Archive Report

1 Carter Court, 77–79 Carter Lane, EC4

CAE90

D Shotliff and B Watson
NGR: TQ 31765 81075
SMR: 041194, 041998–9

A watching brief was carried out between August and November 1990, by arrangement with John Mather and Partners, architects, during the excavation of a new light well in Carter Court and lowering of an adjacent basement floor. Nos 79 and 81 Carter Lane are both partly timber framed, probably dating from the late 17th c, and are listed.

Internal groundworks revealed a ragstone foundation running E–W, about 1.5m wide, interpreted as part of the N wall of the nave of the late 13th-c church of the friary of Blackfriars. A freestanding ragstone foundation to the S, matched by a possible buttress on the N side of the wall, may represent part of a pier base for the nave arcade. Further to the S, excavation to a depth of 1.8m revealed post-medieval dumps containing human bones, probably from disturbance of burials within the church. A late 16th–17th-c brick-built cesspit abutted the S face of the wall of the church.

London Archaeol, 6, 1991, 273; *Medieval Archaeol,* 35, 1991, 149

Watson, B, nd, '1 Carter Court (CAE90)', Summary Report

8 Crosby Square, 4 Great St Helens, EC3

CBY90

Sarah Gibson
NGR: TQ 33140 81250
SMR: 044773

Testpits found natural gravels truncated by the footings or slab of the standing building.

CCT90

R Sermon
NGR: TQ 33450 81390
SMR: 042507–13

20–26 Cutler Street, 123–125 Houndsditch, 5–8 Clothier Street, E1

Excavations and a watching brief were undertaken from January to March 1990, after demolition. Work was funded by Greycoat Construction Ltd.

Natural gravels capped by brickearth were cut by early Roman quarry pits, into which at least one Roman mortar burial was inserted. Evidence survived of widespread medieval pits, for disposal of rubbish and cess as well as for gravel extraction. Many pits contained quantities of human bone, including a trepanned skull, presumably from disturbance of pre-existing burials. In one case an attempt seems to have been made to reinter bones on an E–W alignment. The sequence was completed by two post-medieval brick-lined wells and by pits containing domestic refuse, slag, burnt brick and crucible or mould fragments.

For testpits observed on the site in 1988, see HON88 above.

London Archaeol, 6, 1991, 273; *Britannia,* 22, 1991, 272; *Medieval Archaeol,* 35, 1991, 149
Anon, 1989 '123–125 Houndsditch and 5–8 Exchange Buildings', Testpit Report
Sermon, R, 1990 'Excavations at 20–26 Cutler Street (CCT90)', Archive Report, part

CID90

J Hill and A Woodger
NGR: TQ 32490 81120
SMR: 042779–99

72–80 Cheapside, 83–93 Queen Street, 12 Pancras Lane, EC2 & EC4

Excavations were carried out after demolition between July and December 1991, followed by a watching brief. The work was sponsored by Wates (City) Ltd.

Natural gravels capped by brickearth sloped gently down to the S. Although the subsoil was quite wet there was no sign of the stream which had been expected flowing SE to join the Walbrook. The first activity recorded was construction of a Roman road, about 9m wide, the known Roman precursor of Cheapside crossing the site from E to W. A pit, cutting into the brickearth make-up for this road and sealed by the earliest metalling of rammed gravel, contained part of a bone sword-grip. To the S of the road and running parallel to it a V-shaped ditch was dug with an 'ankle breaker' profile at its base. Also to the S, brickearth was quarried, a circular wattle structure was built, about 4m in diameter, and organic refuse, including woodworking debris, was dumped extensively. N of the road a timber-lined cesspit was dug.

Clay and timber buildings were then constructed along both sides of the road. Within a relatively short time all were burnt in what is identified tentatively as the Boudican fire of AD60–1. In the burnt debris to the S were large quantities of charred grain: barley and both spelt and emmer wheat. The relatively clean appearance of this grain and the inclusion of several fragments of stone querns suggest the presence of a mill. After levelling of the debris these buildings were replaced, probably quickly as the debris was unweathered. A succession of similar clay and timber buildings, respecting the same property lines, continued into the 3rd c.

There was virtually no deposit of dark earth and when the site was next definitely occupied, in the 10th c, the latest Roman metalled road surface was still at ground level. To the S and N of the road, respectively, two successive buildings and a single building were constructed using the former road surface in between as perhaps a yard or alleyway. The later building to the S and that to the N had sunken floors and their walls surviving below ground level comprised earth-fast posts retaining planks on edge. These buildings measured about 4m x 3m and about 2m x 4m respectively. Midden deposits containing large amounts of iron smithing slag accumulated thickly on the floor of the N building. This was then refloored using barrel fragments. The floor of a possible surface-laid building was also recorded N of the sunken buildings near the Cheapside frontage. After dumping and levelling up, pits were dug to the S and a chalk-lined cellar was inserted to the N, dated to the 11th–12th c. A yard to the S of the cellar was cut by several rubbish pits and wattle-lined cesspits. These cesspits contained large quantities of plum, sloe and cherry stones, grape pips and cereal bran, giving a good picture of local diet. In the S of the site, 11th-c pits preceded the insertion of beechwood foundation piles with a felling date of 1090–1 (an absolute date from bark and several crossmatched timbers).

By the 14th c, a large chalk-lined cesspit was built in a corner of the yard and the cellar became disused. The absence of intrusions further to the N indicates the presence there of medieval buildings, presumably fronting onto Cheapside, running along the N side of the site. The only post-medieval features were a brick-lined pit and recent basements, suggesting considerable late medieval or post-medieval levelling up of the ground, or a change of use of the site.

Site conditions ensured very good survival of a large quantity of Roman metalwork. Several fine complete copper-alloy brooches were recovered among which is a British Aesica type, the first example to be found in London. Another enamelled brooch would have had a manicure set suspended from it. Other enamelled objects include seal boxes and studs. Two copper-alloy phalli were found that may originally have been mounted on leather, while a third example is probably from a figurine. Other Roman finds of note include part of a ceramic figurine depicting a mother goddess suckling a child, lamps bearing theatrical masks and a Cupid, and a bone die shaped so that, when cast, it favours six and one.

Saxon and medieval finds include several lead brooches, one of which is similar to examples in the Cheapside hoard of 11th-c pewter jewellery, a bone trial piece and a leather whip with a wooden handle. The infill of the chalk-lined cesspit included a lead ampulla depicting St Thomas Becket, the first to be excavated in London away from the Thames waterfront.

London Archaeol, 6, 1992, 389–90; Britannia, 23, 1992, 292; Medieval Archaeol, 36, 1992, 229
Askew, P, 1990 '74–75 Cheapside, EC2', Test Pit Survey
Hill, J, & Woodger, A, 1992 '72–75 Cheapside, 82–90 Queen Street, EC2', Archive Report
Holden, T, 1992 'Environmental assessment (ASS03/92)', Archive Report
Nixon, T, 1991 '72–75 Cheapside, 82–90 Queen Street, EC2', Project Design
Shotliff, D, 1990 '72–75 Cheapside', Archaeological Evaluation
Tyers, I, 1992 'Priority spot date report (SPT/06/92)', Archive Report
Woodger, A, 1992 '72–75 Cheapside, 82–90 Queen Street, EC2', Watching Brief Report
Woodger, A, 1993 '72–75 Cheapside, 82–90 Queen Street, EC2', Assessment of the Saxon Sequence

75–77 Cornhill, EC3

COH90

Sarah Gibson and D Dunlop
NGR: TQ 32940 81140
SMR: 044201–3

In nos 75–77 natural gravels and brickearth were truncated by the double basement slab. In the S and E of the site, in no. 74, a large NE–SW ragstone wall was exposed immediately beneath the single basement slab; it is probably an internal partition wall dividing the N range of the Roman basilica and forum, very close to its NW corner. Beside the wall was Roman demolition material which also occurred in another testpit where it sealed Roman occupation layers, probably within the basilica. Also recorded was a linear cut interpreted as a robbed foundation cut for an E–W wall within the basilica which, if projected, would join with the E side of the W portico.

A watching brief in 1992 was undertaken to monitor the demolition of the standing building but in the event the S and SE of the site, where the basilica survived, was not affected.

This site was also excavated by MoLAS in 1995: site code COI95.

Drummond-Murray, J, & Macdonald, S, 1990 '74 Cornhill, archaeological assessment of engineers' testpits', Testpit Report
Dunlop, D, & Macdonald, S, 1990 '74–77 Cornhill, archaeological assessment of engineers' testpits', Testpit Report
Gibson, Sarah, 1992 '74–77 Cornhill, EC3, an archaeological investigation', Watching Brief Report

Cripplegate House, Golden Lane, EC1

CPG90

Sarah Gibson
NGR: TQ 32290 81340
SMR: 042539–40

Roman quarry pits and medieval rubbish pits were recorded during ground reduction, work being funded by Golden Lane Properties Ltd.

London Archaeol, 6, 1991, 274; Britannia, 22, 1991, 271; Medieval Archaeol, 35, 1991, 150
Gibson, Sarah, 1990 'Cripplegate House', Archive Report, draft
Thomas, T, nd, 'Golden Lane', Testpit Survey

CTL90

R Sermon and Sarah Gibson
NGR: TQ 31860 81340
SMR: 042865–6

Cutlers' Hall, 4 Warwick Lane, EC4

One testpit recorded post-medieval dumping.

London Archaeol, 6, 1992, 392
Sermon, R, 1990 'Cutlers' Hall (CTL90)', Site Assessment

FAO90

A Miles
NGR: TQ 31560 81320
SMR: 044024–8

75–82 Farringdon Street, EC4

Excavation here was funded by National Provident Institution. River-lain clay above natural river gravels was cut by a single 13th–14th-c pit. Crossing the site from NW–SE was a vaulted brick drain which predated a cellared building of *c* 1650. Within the building were two brick-lined cesspits and the remains of floor surfaces and internal walls. The building was demolished between 1720 and 1750. To the NE were traces of a wooden structure dated to the mid-16th–mid-17th c. In 1610 a burial ground was opened on the site; 606 burials, dating to between 1770 and 1849, were recovered during the excavations. Most of the burials were in wooden (elm) coffins, stacked up to eight deep, which in turn formed nine intercutting N–S rows across the site, in at least two phases. At the W end of the site a brick burial vault, truncating the earlier cellared building, contained 47 burials in coffins and a further 75 individuals that had been pushed to the far end of the vault to create space.

London Archaeol, 7, 1993, 48; *Medieval Archaeol,* 37, 1993, 259; *Post-Medieval Archaeol,* 27, 1993, 229
Anon, nd, 'Assessment of finds', Finds Report
Bates, M, 1991 'Preliminary stratigraphic assessment', Assessment Report
Conheeney, J, 1992 'Assessment of human bone (HUM/01/92)', Archive Report
O'Connor-Thompson, S, & Harding, C, 1990 'Overview assessment of archaeological resources', Assessment Report
Vaughan, D, nd, 'Charred remains', Archive Report
Wooldridge, K, 1991 'Evaluation and assessment of archaeological resources for the proposed development at 75–82 Farringdon Street, 20–30 Shoe Lane', Assessment Report
Wooldridge, K, 1992 'FAO90', Research Design

FRN90

J Henderson and R Sermon
NGR: TQ 31220 81490
SMR: 042538

32 Furnival Street, EC4

A building, probably of early 19th-c date, was recorded before demolition. It comprised a cellar, three floors with timber floor frames and stud partition walls, within a brick shell, and roof.

Post-Medieval Archaeol, 25, 1991, 138

FUS90

J Henderson
NGR: TQ 31210 81510
SMR: 044593

34–35 Furnival Street, EC4

Four testpits found mostly sand and gravel; there were some pits, probably medieval.

Henderson, J, 1990 '34–35 Furnival Street (FUS90)', Site Assessment

2–4 Gough Square, EC4

GOG90

R Sermon
NGR: TQ 31380 81270
SMR: 042800

Groundworks during refurbishment were monitored in an intermittent watching brief in 1990 and 1991, sponsored by Provident Mutual. Only the bases of post-medieval rubbish pits intruding into natural gravels had survived severe horizontal truncation.

London Archaeol, 6, 1992, 390
Sermon, R, 1990 '2–4 Gough Square (GOG90)', Site Assessment

50 Gresham Street, EC2

GRM90

D De Rosa
NGR: TQ 32340 81380
SMR: 042577–85

Excavations were carried out in the basement of a standing building in March 1990, funded by the Corporation of London.

The surface of natural brickearth was covered by an area of burning. This was cut by domestic rubbish pits, which were followed in turn by dumps, pits and a metalled surface, all suggesting continuously open ground. A layer of demolition debris was superseded by dark earth. This was cut by two sets of pits, one possibly late Roman, the other medieval, including a wood- or wicker-lined cesspit. A later wall built of chalk blocks may have formed part of a medieval cellar or cesspit. This and other deposits were truncated by the foundations and basement of the latest building.

London Archaeol, 6, 1991, 274–5; *Britannia,* 22, 1991, 267; *Medieval Archaeol,* 35, 1991, 150–1
De Rosa, D, 1990 'Excavations at 50 Gresham Street (GRM90)', Archive Report

Opposite 1 Gutter Lane, sewer trench, EC2

GTR90

Sarah Gibson
NGR: TQ 32250 81240
SMR: 044594

Tunnelling for a sewer linkage was monitored. Deposits about 1m deep from basement level were recorded, the best section showing destruction debris, including scorched brickearth, followed by brickearth make-up for a clay floor.

Hand and Shears public house, 1 Middle Street, EC1

HAS90

T Mackinder
NGR: TQ 32050 81758
SMR: 0412400I009, 42688

A watching brief during underpinning and refurbishment of a standing building revealed evidence of a wall running NE–SW, possibly medieval and subsequently robbed, and a burial, probably associated with the priory or, later, the parish church of St Bartholomew the Great, to the W. The existing brick and timber-framed building, mainly 19th c in date, incorporated older, reused timbers, and had been underpinned previously. Work was undertaken by arrangement with Neil Kirsop and Co, surveyors.

London Archaeol, 6, 1991, 276; *Medieval Archaeol,* 35, 1991, 151; *Post-Medieval Archaeol,* 25, 1991, 139

20–21 Lime Street, 8–11 Ship Tavern Passage, EC3

LIE90

D Shotliff
NGR: TQ 33070 80985
SMR: 044774

Six testpits and two boreholes showed over 2m of Roman strata.

Shotliff, D, 1990 '20–21 Lime Street (LIE90)', Site Assessment

LOA90

Sarah Gibson
NGR: TQ 32980 81030
SMR: 042801–3, 044043–6

54 Lombard Street, 15–16 Gracechurch Street, EC3

An evaluation funded by Fleetway Construction was conducted in April and May 1991. Most of the site was totally truncated by triple basements (see earlier excavations on this site in 1933 and 1939–40: GM101, GM102 above) but parts of the Roman forum and basilica, a Scheduled Ancient Monument, survived to the NE. Masonry foundations of the W wall and portico of the 1st-c forum–basilica were recorded, running further to the N than could be recorded in the 1930s and 1950s. The remains of the portico are to be retained *in situ* in the new development. All associated horizontal strata had been truncated, but intrusive early medieval rubbish pits and a medieval chalk-lined cesspit survived.

The backfill of the cesspit, dated to the 16th c, included remains of insects such as grain weevils, as well as species that would have lived in the cess deposits, and remains of grape, fig, cereals and pepper. These indicate an enclosed pit with few external contaminants, and suggest a rich, high-status diet. Finds include a medieval bone skate and a complete post-medieval copper-alloy candlestick.

London Archaeol, 6, 1992, 390; 7, 1993, 49
Gibson, Sarah, 1990 'Excavations at 15–16 Gracechurch Street (LOA90)', Archive Report
Holden, T, 1991 'Environmental appraisal (ASS/05/91)', Archive Report
Holden, T, 1992 'Plant remains from a cesspit on 54 Lombard Street (BOT/REP/02/92)', Archive Report
Smith, D, 1992 'An insect fauna (INS/02/92)', Archive Report

ORN90

Sarah Gibson
NGR: TQ 32760 81110
SMR: 042506

Opposite 1 Cornhill, EC3

A Roman bowl and an amphora were recovered from deposits that were probably intrusive within natural strata, in a shaft dug by contractors for London Underground Ltd.

London Archaeol, 6, 1991, 273

PAT90

Sarah Gibson
NGR: TQ 31950 81250
SMR: 044775

Paternoster Square, EC4

Testpits and boreholes were examined, most of which revealed modern debris, though natural brickearth survived in a testpit in Panyer Alley / 45 Newgate Street (in the pre-1960s configuration of buildings), with a possible Roman building above.

For observations in the 1960s, see GM136 above.

PEM90

J Heathcote
NGR: TQ 31340 81250
SMR: 042689–91

1–3 Pemberton Row, EC4

A medieval ditch, garden soil and post-medieval rubbish pits were recorded during underpinning works.

London Archaeol, 6, 1991, 276; *Medieval Archaeol*, 35, 1991, 151
Heathcote, J, 1990 '1–3 Pemberton Row', Archive Report

274–280 Bishopsgate (PSO90) and 298–306 Bishopsgate (BOG89), EC2

PSO90 (and BOG89)

N Roycroft
NGR: TQ 33400 81850
SMR: 041984–5, 08093412

A large redevelopment on the E side of Bishopsgate was resumed and excavations, funded by Spitalfields Developments Ltd, were carried out between February and April 1990, after demolition. These excavations were at nos 274–280 and 298–306, to the S and N respectively of areas excavated in 1987–8, at 284–294 Bishopsgate (BOS87 above).

To the S nearly all strata were truncated to the level of natural gravels, in which at least 11 large circular features containing mixed brickearth and gravel are attributed to natural periglacial cryoturbation. They ran roughly NE–SW, along a possible spring-line at the S edge of a brickearth capping to the gravels. To the N this brickearth was truncated by a very large Roman quarry pit. This had filled with water, which was then deliberately ponded. Later, thick marsh deposits accumulated. Smaller quarry pits to the S were infilled in the Roman period.

Parallel N–S ditches (also detected in 1987–8) indicated medieval drainage. To the N, a large tank or cistern was dug with a gravel base and timber-revetted sides; this was fed from the S and an outlet channel ran off to the N. This tank silted up and was then redug and slightly repositioned at least twice before being abandoned. It may have supplied clean water to the Hospital and Priory of St Mary without Bishopsgate, known to have been founded a short distance to the N, initially in the late 12th c and refounded in the mid-13th c. Similarly, a series of four burials to the extreme N were probably associated with this hospital (see also excavations at 1–2 Norton Folgate, *London Archaeol*, 5, 1986, 164, and at 4–12 Norton Folgate, and at 4, 15 and 38 Spital Square, *London Archaeol*, 6, 1989, 79–80).

These burials and the tank were sealed by the foundations, cellars and stone-lined cesspit of a substantial late medieval or 16th-c building, fronting onto a N–S road directly to its E and, presumably, onto Bishopsgate to the W. This building, and other brick buildings to the S, survived until construction of the latest buildings on the site in the late 19th–20th c. Further to the S, remains of a timber-lined well, cess- and rubbish pits and a brick-lined soak-away indicated medieval and later buildings, presumably also fronting onto Bishopsgate.

Among finds recovered was a spout from a 13th–14th-c Kingston ware jug, in the shape of a dog's head.

London Archaeol, 6, 1991, 272; *Britannia*, 22, 1991, 272; 23, 1992, 191; *Medieval Archaeol*, 35, 1991, 149; *Post-Medieval Archaeol*, 25, 1991, 137
Roycroft, N, 1990 'Excavations at 274–280 and 298–306 Bishopsgate (PSO90, BOG89)', Archive Report

St Peter Cornhill church, Cornhill, EC3

PTE90

J Ayre
NGR: TQ 33400 81850
SMR: 043499–501

A watching brief was conducted during insertion of groundbeams and renovation of the floor of the nave of the church of St Peter Cornhill, in August and September 1990, funded by the Proclamation Trust. Strata were removed to a maximum depth of 1m, revealing column bases of the nave arcade, consisting of reused stone. A brick burial vault, memorial stones, lead coffins, coffin fragments and disarticulated human bone were also recorded. The burial vault was cleared in the 19th c, probably before refurbishment in 1889, when a mosaic tile floor was laid and pews were installed.

London Archaeol, 6, 1991, 277; *Post-Medieval Archaeol*, 25, 1991, 116
Ayre, J, 1990 'Excavations at St Peter Cornhill', Archive Report

55–58 Gracechurch Street and Brabant House, St Benet's Place, EC3

RAC90

G Martin
NGR: TQ 32980 80850
SMR: 042541–51

Excavations funded by Land Securities Properties Ltd took place from July to September 1990, after demolition.

The earliest feature, cut into natural brickearth, was a pit containing Late Bronze Age pottery. Traces of early Roman occupation, consisting of parallel gullies running N–S, were followed by a substantial building to the E. Part of this comprised foundations of unmortared Kentish ragstone in rows up to 1m apart, infilled with flints, topped by rammed clay and sand and then a thick *opus signinum* floor.

Possible imprints of *pilae* in this floor surface suggest the existence of a hypocaust. To the S and W were less substantial floors of mortar and brickearth. Later a very large pit, at least 15m in diameter and 6m deep, was dug to the S; the function of this pit, backfilled in the early 2nd c, was unclear. To the W were stake-holes, slots, two wells and a series of intercutting pits. Among later features only intrusive medieval pits, a chalk-lined cesspit and post-medieval brick-lined wells or soak-aways survived modern truncation.

Several complete pottery vessels were recovered, including Roman decorated hunting cups, and a mid-10th–mid-13th-c red-painted ware spouted pitcher with finger prints on the inside.

London Archaeol, 6, 1991, 274; *Britannia*, 22, 1991, 269; *Medieval Archaeol*, 35, 1991, 150
Bates, M, 1990 'Gracechurch Street (RAC90): field report and sedimentological assessment (SED/02/90)', Archive Report

RON90

D Hart
NGR: TQ 33350 80780
SMR: 042681–7

Corn Exchange, 51–60 Mark Lane, and Cereal House, 58 Mark Lane, EC3

Excavations were conducted in April–May 1990 within the single basement of a standing building at 58 Mark Lane. A watching brief continued on the rest of the development, to the E and S at 51–60 Mark Lane, which was double-basemented. Work was funded by British Land Company plc.

The site straddles a small valley running from NE to SW. A ditch crossed this, perhaps to enclose animals. Later a Roman timber-framed building and a timber-lined well were built. They went out of use and rubbish pits were dug in what was then open ground. Surviving medieval features included rubbish pits and a large chalk-lined cesspit. These were succeeded by brick foundations, identified with the Corn Exchange, documented here from the 18th c and several times rebuilt.

London Archaeol, 6, 1991, 276; *Britannia*, 22, 1991, 269; *Medieval Archaeol*, 35, 1991, 151; *Post-Medieval Archaeol*, 25, 1991, 139
Bates, M, 1990 'Corn Exchange (RON90): field report and sedimentological assessment (SED/01/90)', Archive Report
Hart, D, 1990 'Excavations at the Corn Exchange, 51–60 Mark Lane, and Cereal House, 58 Mark Lane (RON90)', Archive Report

SAK90

S Macdonald
NGR: TQ 33145 80960
SMR: 042521–5

Sackville House, 143–149 Fenchurch Street, 17–20 Cullum Street, EC3

Testpit sections were recorded in June 1990 and a small area was excavated in the basement of a standing building, before refurbishment and installation of a lift-shaft. This work was funded by Nico Construction Ltd and took place by arrangement with Sedgwick Group Properties and Services Ltd.

Natural brickearth was levelled up with dumped brickearth in the Roman period in preparation for the construction of at least one building, evidenced only by floors. Three phases of flooring, the last being a black and white tessellated floor, ended in destruction by fire. The destruction debris was levelled and posts were inserted in what was probably then open ground. These features and later intrusive medieval pits were truncated by the brick foundations, partition walls and the cobbled floors of a post-medieval cellar.

London Archaeol, 6, 1991, 273
Macdonald, S, 1990 'Excavations at 143–149 Fenchurch Street, 17–20 Cullum Street (SAK90)', Archive Report

34–35 Great St Helens, EC3

SHL90

D Lakin
NGR: TQ 33160 81300
SMR: 044029–33

Excavation here was funded by Cadbury Schweppes Ltd. Earliest activity was represented by the construction of a large masonry building in the Roman period, aligned on Bishopsgate street to the W. It had substantial external rubble walls and *opus signinum* floors which were worn and patched. This building was eventually destroyed by fire, demolished and the site left vacant until a smaller but equally substantial building was erected. After the demise of this building dark earth built up over the site. A third, pile-founded building was then constructed, aligned on Bishopsgate. Subsequently, a cemetery, associated with the adjacent parish church of St Helen's, was established which entirely reworked the dark earth horizon. The cemetery and the robbed remains of the pile-founded building were then superseded by a series of probably short-lived buildings with open areas. Hereafter, the establishment on the site of the outer courtyard of the adjacent nunnery (founded in 1212) largely dictated the alignment of subsequent buildings to the nunnery church to the E. Brick additions to some of the nunnery buildings suggest that in the post-Dissolution period the buildings of the outer court remained in use for a considerable time, with only minor modifications; only later, in the post-medieval period, were the remaining medieval elements swept away and a different pattern imposed on the site.

London Archaeol, 7, 1993, 48; Medieval Archaeol, 37, 1993, 259
Pearson, E, & Sidell, J, 1992 'Environmental assessment (ASS/05/92)', Archive Report
Sidell, J, 1992 'Assessment of animal bone (BON/06/92)', Archive Report

British Telecom tunnel, Old Broad Street, EC2

SOB90

D Sankey and A Westman
NGR: TQ 33025
81366–32990 81223
SMR: 042817–23

The remains of three Roman buildings, a Roman road and a medieval building were recorded in a tunnel together with evidence of associated external activity. A collection of Victorian pottery and handmade glass vessels for mixing chemicals was also recovered; one of the pots being marked with the address 53 Threadneedle Street. The archive contains notes on the glass and pottery.

Tallow Chandlers' Hall, 4 Dowgate Hill, EC4

TAH90

J Drummond-Murray
NGR: TQ 32550 80880
SMR: 042706–8

Insertion of new drain runs and floor slab in the basement of Tallow Chandlers' Hall, a post-Great Fire building and a Scheduled Ancient Monument, entailed a watching brief in July 1990, in accordance with Scheduled Monument Consent. This was funded by the Worshipful Company of Tallow Chandlers.

A masonry foundation at least 1.5m wide, running N–S, is interpreted as representing a Roman wall on the W bank. Dumps in the Walbrook Valley were cut by masonry foundations for an internal partition wall running E–W, associated with a beaten clay floor, probably part of the kitchen under the original medieval hall. This was sealed by demolition debris derived from destruction of the hall in the Great Fire. Oak sill-beams, oak joists and pine studs, with lath and plaster, survived from the rebuild of the hall, behind modern refacing in the existing basement.

The site produced a 13th–14th-c floor tile of unknown source, decorated with a unique geometrical pattern.

London Archaeol, 6, 1991, 277; Britannia, 22, 1991, 266–7; Medieval Archaeol, 35, 1991, 152–3; Post-Medieval Archaeol, 25, 1991, 138
Drummond-Murray, J, 1990 'Excavations at Tallow Chandlers' Hall (TAH90)', Archive Report

TED90

D Sankey and D Shotliff
NGR: TQ 32900 81200
SMR: 042709

Opposite 1 Threadneedle Street, EC2

Remains of a Roman building with masonry wall foundations and tile and *opus signinum* floors were recorded in a tunnel under the existing street.

London Archaeol, 6, 1991, 277; *Britannia*, 23, 1992, 292
Sankey, D, 1990 'Observations in tunnel, Threadneedle Street (TED90)', Archive Report

TIM90

J Ayre, Sarah Gibson and
D Malt
NGR: TQ 32235 80800
SMR: 042586

High Timber Street and Stew Lane, EC4

Medieval foreshore deposits were recorded, at Ordnance Datum (mean sea level), during construction of new sewer connections.

London Archaeol, 6, 1991, 275; *Medieval Archaeol*, 35, 1991, 151

UPT90

J Ayre
NGR: TQ 32340 80830
SMR: 042747–65

Bull Wharf Lane, 66–67 Upper Thames Street, EC4

Excavations were conducted after demolition from January to May 1991 in the first phase of an intended large waterfront redevelopment at Queenhithe. Work was funded by Beaver House.

On the N side of the site a foreshore was found on which was constructed a timber quay running E–W. Dated by dendrochronology to the early 3rd c and identified as the Late Roman Quay, this comprised very large squared oak timbers laid in horizontal courses, all but the lowest course of which had been subsequently removed or displaced. The remaining course was sealed by naturally deposited river silts, about 1m thick, overlaid in turn by foreshore gravels.

To the W a woman's body encased in bark, reeds and moss was laid out on these gravels. This burial, comparable to certain Viking burials in Scandinavia, was removed *en bloc* for micro-excavation off site. Stakes and withies were then laid out on the foreshore forming fences and groynes. Attempts were made to stabilise the waterfront and reclaim land by mounding up the ground behind low revetments composed of reused fragments of boat and building timbers, held in place by stakes, but these materials were partly washed away or dismantled. Further revetments were then built more extensively and successfully, reusing large timbers from the Late Roman Quay laid as footings. One revetment, running to the E, incorporated bundled brushwood and wattle, and was later repaired. The other, running to the W, included timbers and large cobbles, and was later replaced entirely. Part of the latter revetment included a reused timber panel with a small triangular window opening.

To the N, behind these revetments and in association with them, was a complex sequence of buildings and occupation surfaces, dated by dendrochronology to the 10th and 11th c. The first, wattle-built structures, to the E, were not aligned with the waterfront, but all subsequent buildings were. They ran N in three distinct blocks, presumably respecting property boundaries. These buildings were constructed using large timber posts set on rough rubble foundation platforms, or with large earth-fast posts and substantial sill-beams. Evidence was found of a joisted timber floor in one of the buildings to the E. Most floors were of beaten earth or clay, incorporating occupational debris such as wood shavings, and there were numerous shallow hearths, especially a series in the central block. Food debris and other organic remains were well preserved in and around these buildings. To the W successive floors and make-up layers provided the main structural evidence, situated at first only to the N with gravel surfaces to the S.

Later these surfaces formed an alley between buildings to N and S, and later still were entirely built over. Along the W side of the site successive structural divisions (observed during installation of a temporary retaining wall) indicated a frontage on the line of modern Bull Wharf Lane. Many elements of these timber buildings were well preserved: oak thresholds and ash door posts flanked outside by bushes or small trees, internal roof supports and partition walls, buttress timbers for external walls, a variety of jointing and reused timbers such as barrel heads and staves.

This sequence of buildings was sealed by natural silts, probably a flood deposit. To the S, in front of the existing revetments, a raft of rough timbers indicated continuing reclamation. The waterfront to which this related lay further to the S, beyond the site, where it had been destroyed during redevelopment of Bull Wharf in 1979 (see BLL79 above) and was continuous with that recorded directly to the E, at Vintners' Place (VHA89). Only later intrusive features survived eventual horizontal truncation. Foundations of chalk rubble and mortared chalk dated to the 12th c were inserted running N, respecting the previous three principal property lines. Other features included a stone-lined tanning pit and post-medieval brick-lined wells, a cistern, cellars, drains and cesspits, some bearing signs of burning, perhaps in the Great Fire of 1666.

The revetment dumps produced an impressive collection of Saxon leather turnshoes with thonged-on soles. Several are nearly complete and many show evidence of repair.

For subsequent excavation on this site, see BUF90 above.

London Archaeol, 6, 1991, 388–90; *Britannia*, 23, 1992, 292

Boswijk, G, & Tyers, I, 1996 'Dendrochronological spot dates for 268 timbers from nine London sites (1994–5): (DEN/02/96)', Dendrochronology Report

Giorgi, J, 1996 'An assessment of the plant remains from Bull Wharf/ Upper Thames Street (BUF90/UPT90): BOT/ASS/10/96', Archive Report

Holden, T, 1991 'Environmental appraisal for 67 Upper Thames Street UPT90 (ASS/06/91)', Archive Report

MacLaughlin, S, & Scheuer, L, 1992 'Human bone report on individual from UPT90 (HUM/08/92)', Archive Report

Nayling, N, 1991a 'Dendrochronological spot date report: interim report (SPT/02/91)'

Nayling, N, 1991b 'Dendrochronological spot date report: interim report (SPT/04/91)', Archive Report

Rielly, K, 1996 'Assessment of the animal bones from Bull Wharf Lane and Upper Thames Street (BUF90 and UPT90) (BON/ASS/08/96)', Archive Report

Tyers, I, 1991 'Dendrochronological spot date: Frisian boat — interim report (SPT/07/91)', Archive Report

6 Broad Street Place, EC2

BSP91

Sarah Gibson and J Hill
NGR: TQ 32990 81660
SMR: 042746

An excavation and watching brief funded by Norwich Union Pensions took place in July 1991 during contractors' groundworks, after the contractors had discovered evidence of ancient burials. One complete burial was recorded and further evidence was found for others, all probably part of a Roman cemetery known to have existed in the area.

London Archaeol, 6, 1991, 388

Bishopsgate, pedestrian subway near Liverpool Street Station, EC2

BSY91

D Bluer
NGR: TQ 33280 81590
SMR: 042738–45

A watching brief was maintained during excavations for a subway running E–W under Bishopsgate in August and in November–December 1991, work being funded by the Corporation of London.

Natural gravels and brickearth were quarried early in the Roman period, to the E, well away from the presumed line of a known N–S Roman road, Ermine Street, beyond the site to the W. No trace of this road was seen, but a cremation was excavated, contained within an Alice Holt Surrey ware jar, indicating the known roadside cemetery. To the W a well shaft was located, backfilled possibly in the 2nd c. To the E dumps of medieval roof tiles were sealed by gravel metalling, confirming the medieval realignment of Ermine Street (on a line followed by the modern road, or perhaps a little to the E of it). Rubbish pits and a well of medieval date, post-medieval cellars and the existing road and services completed the sequence. A notable find of Roman date is a copper-alloy horse fitting.

London Archaeol, 6, 1991, 388; *Medieval Archaeol*, 36, 1992, 228

COC91

Sarah Gibson
NGR: TQ 31710 81030
SMR: 044776

35–37 Cock Lane, EC1

Engineers' testpits and one borehole were examined. Natural gravels were generally truncated but some medieval chalk footings survived in one of the testpits.

CTW91

G Porter and D Sankey
NGR: TQ 31850 81220
SMR: 040481

City wall at Barbican Waterside and next to Bastion House, London Wall, EC2

Roman, medieval and post-medieval work of Bastions 12 and 14 and a straight stretch of wall W of Cripplegate were identified and recorded for the Corporation of London, including Roman fabric newly identified in the last stretch (numbered W40A, in accordance with the gazetteer of Roman sites in R Merrifield's *The Roman city of London*, 1965). This Roman fabric is interpreted as part of the N wall of the fort, ascribed to the early 2nd c, and possible modifications to its outer face, perhaps when this wall was incorporated in the defensive wall around the city in c AD200, but no thickening on the inner face of the fort wall was evident. The base of B12 and most of B11A, which project into an ornamental lake, were apparently wholly rebuilt during landscaping in the late 1960s and early 1970s for the Barbican development.

Britannia, 25, 1994, 281

DEN91

K Heard
NGR: TQ 33290 81150
SMR: 042804–11

104–106 Leadenhall Street, EC3

Excavations took place post-demolition from June to August 1991, funded by Refuge Assurance plc.

Natural brickearth overlying gravel survived mostly in the S half of the site, where the earliest signs of human activity were shallow scoops and layers containing burnt and worked flint and Bronze Age pottery. Roman pits, a timber-lined well and possible emptied beam slots contained a mixture of rubbish and building debris, deriving probably from later Roman buildings not otherwise represented. In the N half of the site large medieval rubbish pits and cesspits truncated all pre-existing strata. Several post-medieval brick-lined pits were inserted, and one stone-lined cellar or cesspit was backfilled with large quantities of elderberry seeds and bovine metapodials.

Notable finds include a Roman copper-alloy phallic mount of a type otherwise unknown in London, a complete face jug of Raeren-Aachen stoneware of early 16th-c date and two very rare examples of late medieval–early post-medieval decorated ridge tiles.

London Archaeol, 6, 1992, 390; *Britannia*, 23, 1992, 292
Heard, K, 1992a 'Excavations at 104–106 Leadenhall Street (DEN91)', Archive Report
Heard, K, 1992b '104–106 Leadenhall Street', Finds Appraisal
Holden, T, 1991 'Environmental appraisal (ASS/08/91)', Archive Report
Jenner, A, 1991 '104–106 Leadenhall Street', Post-Roman Pottery Appraisal
Symonds, R, 1991 '104–106 Leadenhall Street', Roman Pottery Appraisal

ETL91

Sarah Gibson and D Sankey
NGR: TQ 32880 80800
SMR: 044777–8

Equitable House, 47–51 King William Street, EC4

Three testpits were monitored in 1991. In the S of the site a possible Roman masonry wall was located; in the N of the site a post-medieval well cut into the natural. The site was later excavated by MoLAS, using the same site code.

St James Garlickhithe church, Garlick Hill, EC4

A burial vault on the NE side of the church and five lead coffins within were recorded. The work was funded by the parish.

This code also includes a photographic survey of the church when it was hit by the fall of a construction crane in 1989. Though the roof and floor were damaged, no other archaeological recording was necessary.

London Archaeol, 6, 1992, 391; 7, 1993, 49; *Post-Medieval Archaeol,* 26, 1992, 98; 27, 1993, 206
Miles, A, 1993 'St James Garlickhithe', Watching Brief Report

JAS91

A Miles
NGR: TQ 32390 80855
SMR: 042882

1 and 5–6 Amen Court, EC4

Limited recording took place from August to October 1991 during refurbishment of a Listed standing building, 1 Amen Court. The work was funded by the Dean and Chapter of St Paul's Cathedral. Pitfills and garden soil were cut by mortared chalk foundations, at cellar level. These foundations were truncated by the existing building, the furthest to the E in a terrace of three houses documented as having been constructed in the 1670s for canons residentiary of St Paul's. This house formed a brick shell with timber-framed floors and roof and some timber-framed internal walls. Evidence was found suggesting later rearrangement of a service staircase beside a central light well, rebuilding of cellars under the street, and the addition of the uppermost floor, or perhaps merely its enlargement. Minor internal alterations included refacing a wall with timber panelling and covering up 18th-c wallpaper depicting a pastoral scene. A watching brief in the basement revealed a garden-like soil, or possibly a pitfill.

A watching brief within 5–6 Amen Court revealed nothing.

London Archaeol, 6, 1992, 388; *Post-Medieval Archaeol,* 26, 1992, 97
Brigham, T, 1994 '1 Amen Court, London EC4: survey of a standing building', MoLAS Report

MEN91

Sarah Gibson, D Lakin and A Westman
NGR: TQ 31850 81220
SMR: 042867–9

Niblett Hall, King's Bench Walk, Inner Temple, EC4

Recording here was funded by the Honourable Society of the Inner Temple. Three Roman burials were recorded, truncated by Roman or Saxon pits. An 18th-/19th-c cellar may have been part of Serjeants' Inn, Fleet Street, which lay N of the site.

Britannia, 25, 1994, 282; *Medieval Archaeol,* 37, 1993, 260; *Post-Medieval Archaeol,* 27, 1993, 229

NIB91

P Askew
NGR: TQ 31330 81070
SMR: 044036–40 (recorded under MoLAS site KBK92)

119–122 Old Broad Street, EC2

Natural gravels sloped down to the W and in one of three underpinning holes were overlaid by a large dump or pitfill. In another they had been truncated and covered by a silt with a possible waterlaid deposit above.

London Archaeol, 6, 1992, 391

OBS91

Sarah Gibson
NGR: TQ 32960 81320
SMR: 042830–1

PUM91

N Elsden
NGR: TQ 31180 81030
SMR: 044627

5–6 Pump Court, EC4

Six testpits were observed. Modern layers and pits had cut into natural gravels.

Elsden, N, 1991 '5–6 Pump Court (PUM91)', Site Evaluation (MoLAS)

SEN91

Sarah Gibson
NGR: TQ 33505 80884
SMR: 044287–9

25–26 Savage Gardens, EC3

Testpits were observed. Spongy wet dumps, possibly the infill of a stream valley, were succeeded by medieval walls which might be part of the buildings of the Crutched Friars.

Gibson, Sarah, 1991 '25 Savage Gardens', Site Assessment

SMT91

L Howe
NGR: TQ 31910 81680
SMR: 044609

57a–59 West Smithfield, EC1

This site lies in the NW corner of the precinct of St Bartholomew's Priory. The site was truncated down to the natural gravels though one of three testpits examined showed a deep cut feature (undated).

Howe, L, 1991 '58–59 West Smithfield', Site Assessment

TEE91

Sarah Gibson
NGR: TQ 32960 81250
SMR: 042943–64, 044075–6

41–53 Threadneedle Street, 1–17 Old Broad Street, EC2

An evaluation here was funded by National Westminster Estates plc. In the SE corner of the site cut features and redeposited brickearth slabs probably of Roman date were recorded above natural. Pits probably of medieval date and post-medieval structures were also recorded.

London Archaeol, 7, 1993, 50; *Britannia,* 25, 1994, 282
Gibson, Sarah, 1991 '41–53 Threadneedle Street (TEE91)', Site Evaluation

WOL91

Sarah Gibson and Stuart Gibson
NGR: TQ 33440 80500
SMR: 082571

Devlin Tower, Tower of London, EC3

The removal of a 17th-c cannon barrel, formerly in use as a bollard, was monitored.

London Archaeol, 6, 1992, 391; *Post-Medieval Archaeol,* 26, 1992, 109

MAPS

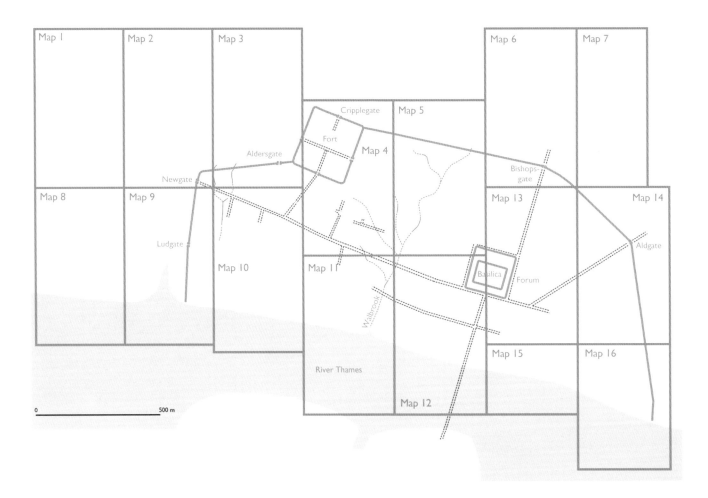

The sites are located on a base of the Ordnance Survey 1:1250 map of 1989 (reproduced from Ordnance Survey mapping with the permission of The Controller of Her Majesty's Stationery Office © Crown Copyright Licence no. MC 88194M). The main features of Roman London are added to the map.

△ Guildhall Museum sites (1907–73)

▽ Department of Urban Archaeology sites (1973–91)

Map I

Map 2

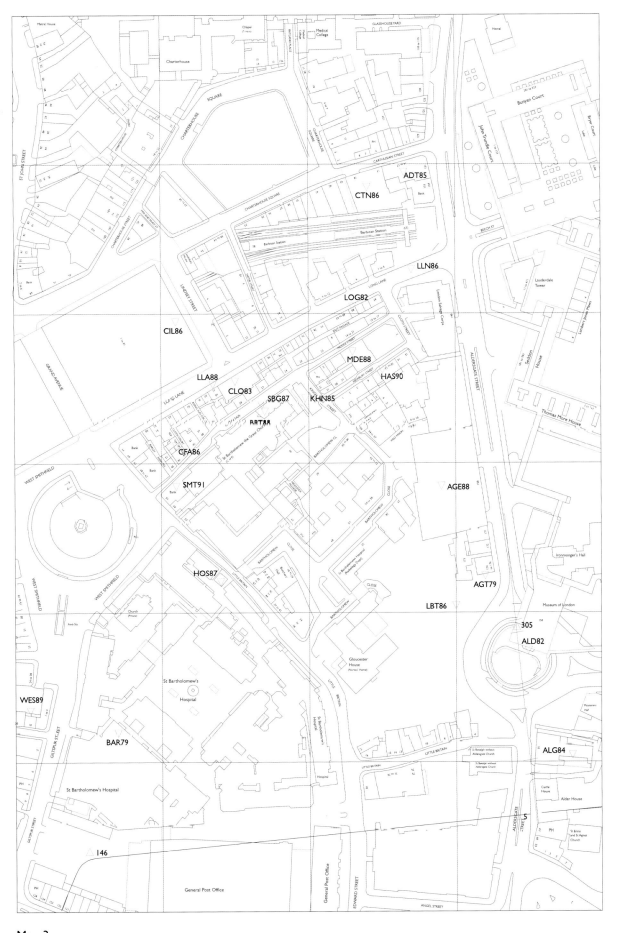

Map 3

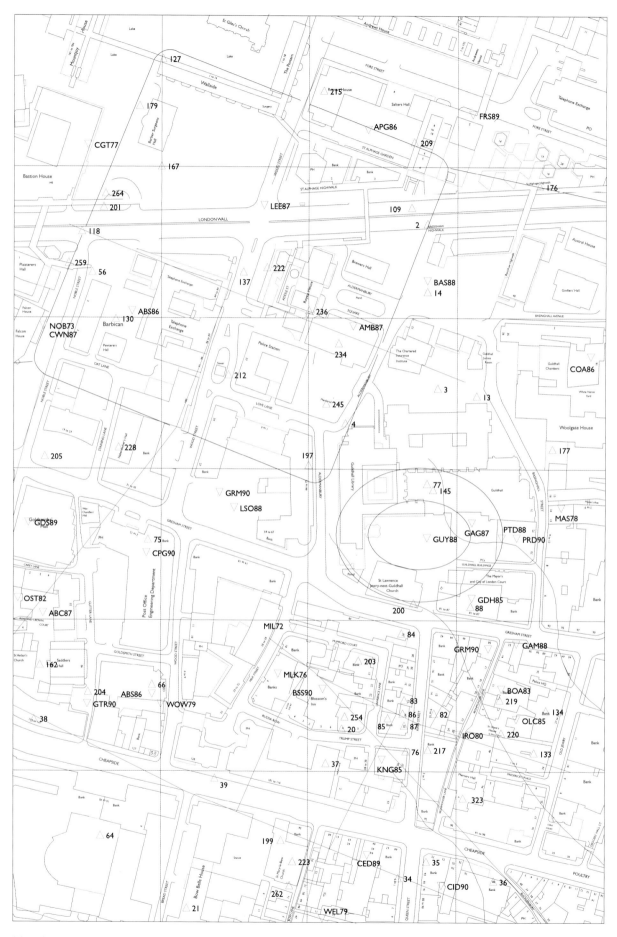

Map 4

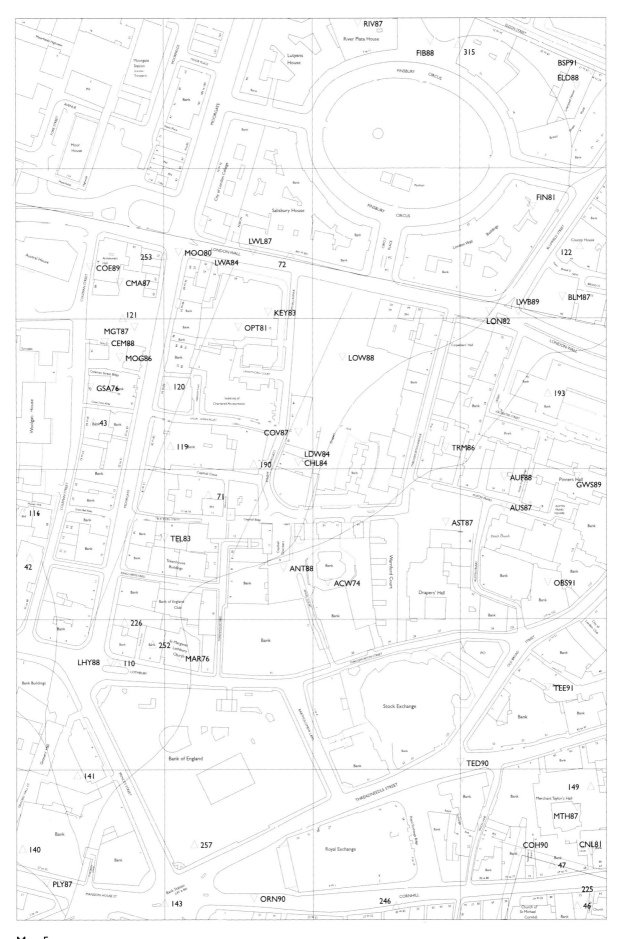

Map 5

Map 6

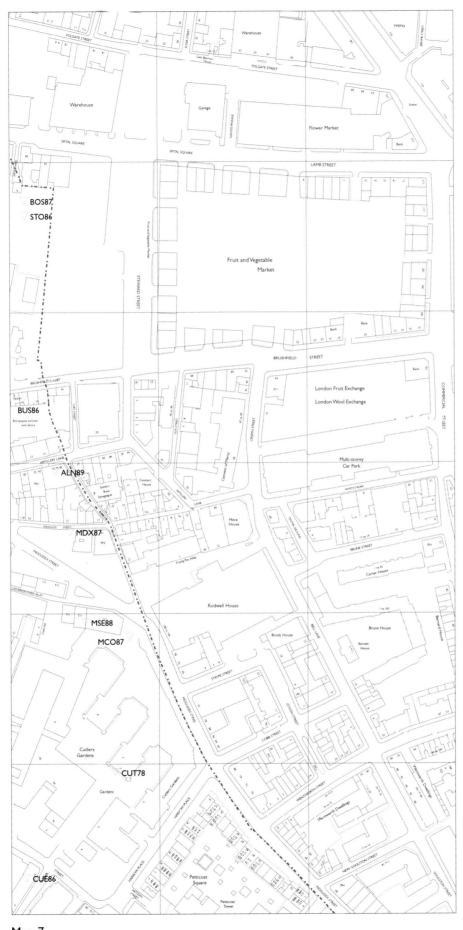

Map 7

Map 8

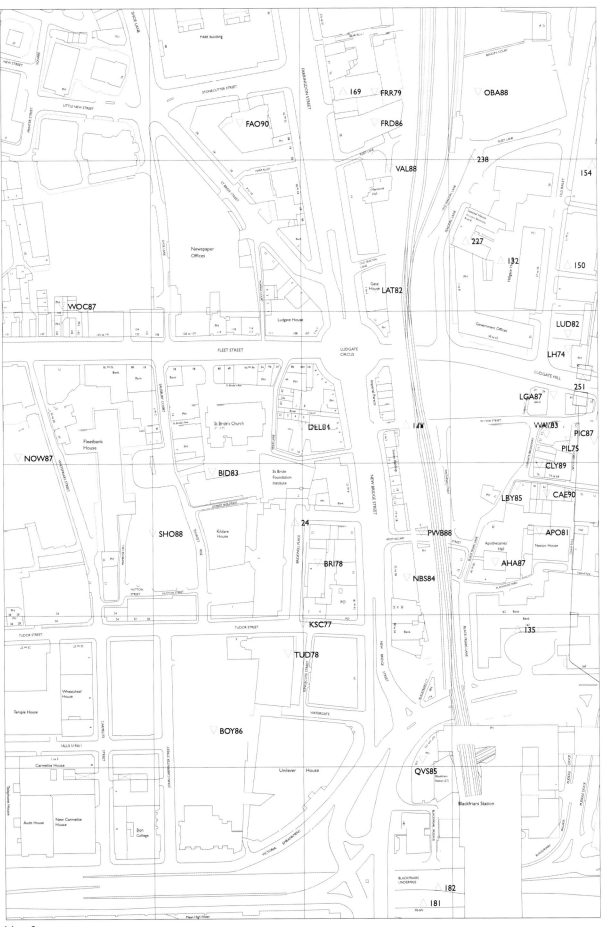

Map 9

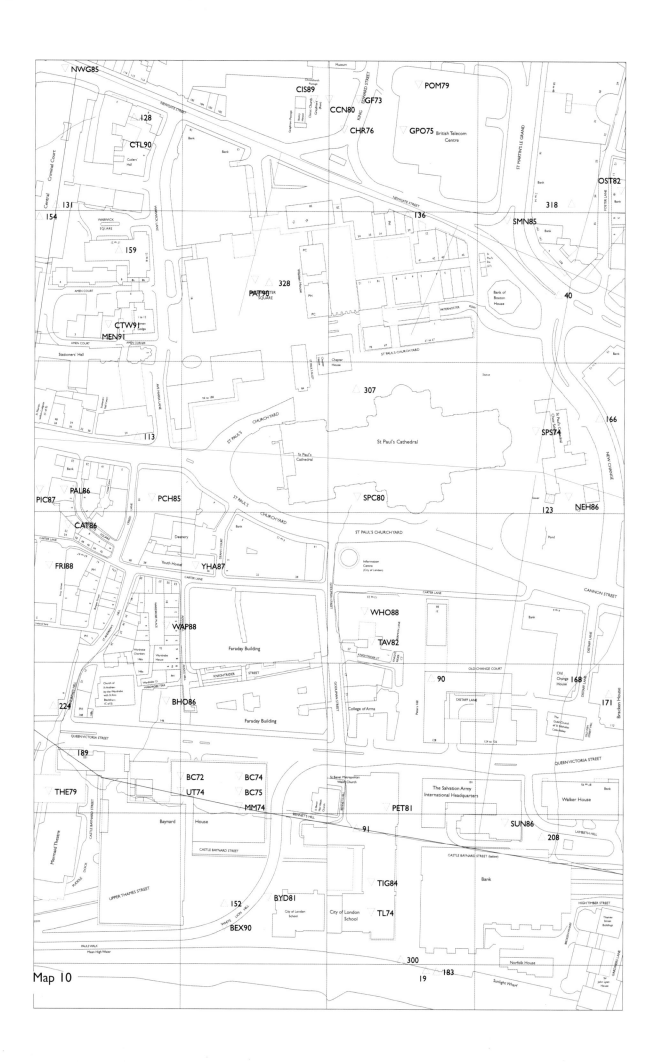

Map 10

Map 11

Map 12

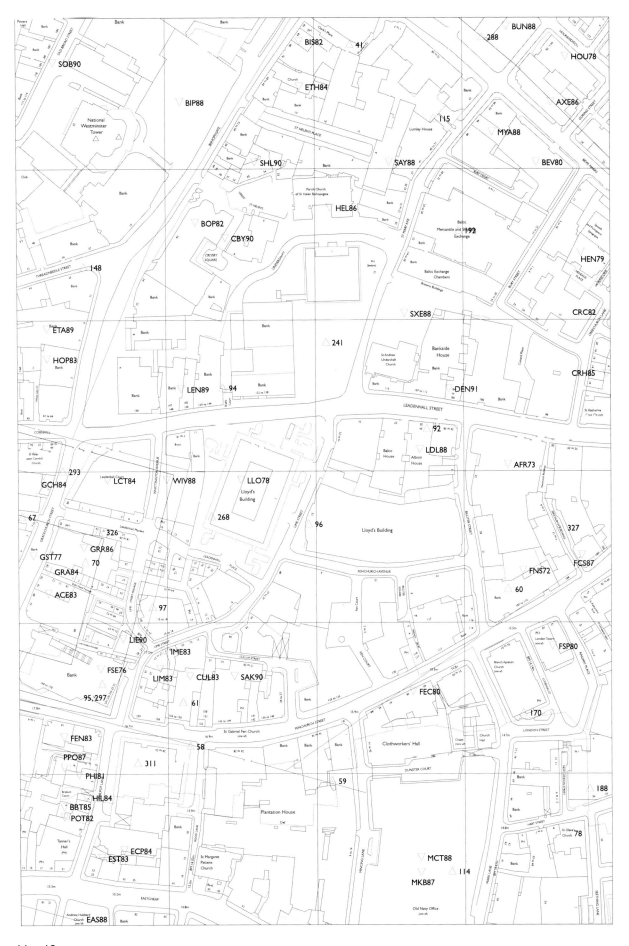

Map 13

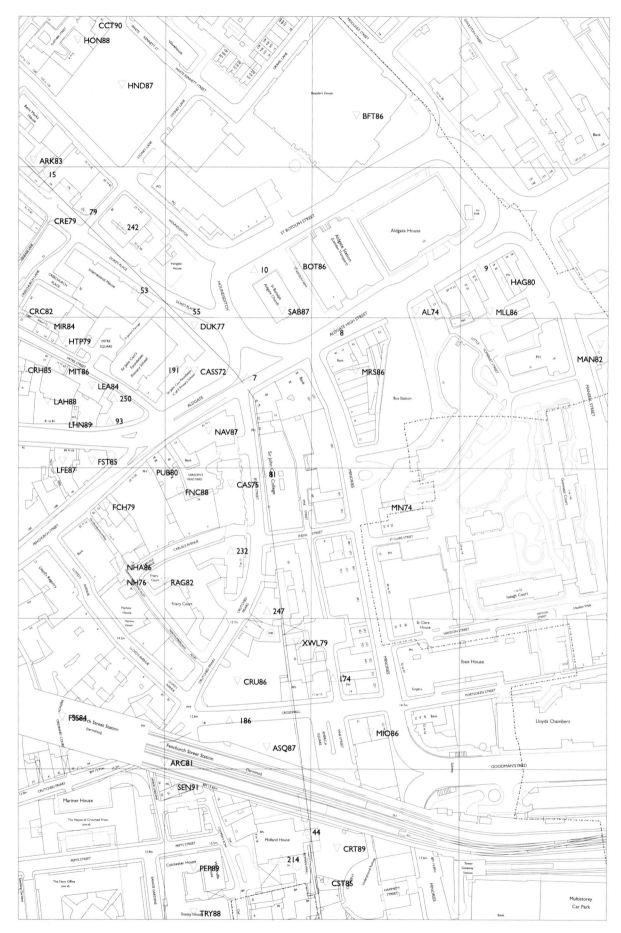

Map 14

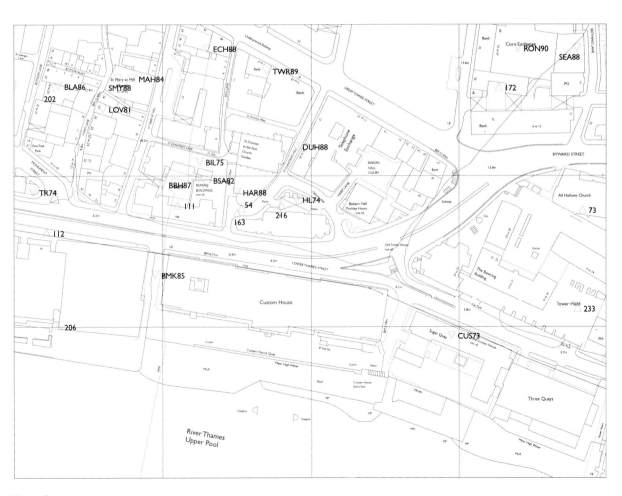

ECH88

TWR89

St Mary at Hill MAH84

BLA86 SMY88

202 LOV81

One Tree
Park

MOUNT STREET

TR74

112

BMK85

Custom House

206

DUH88

BIL75

BBH87 BSA82

HAR88

111 54 HL74

163 216

ROMAN
BUILDINGS
(site of)

GREAT TOWER STREET

Telephone
Exchange

BAKERS
HALL
COURT

Bakers Hall
Thackley House
(site of)

Old Trinity House
(site of)

LOWER THAMES STREET

Custom House Quay

Mean High Water

Crane

Crane Posts

Sugar Quay CUS73
Custom House
(site of)

Custom House
Stairs East

River Thames
Upper Pool

Corn Exchange RON90

SEA88

172

PO

Bank

BYWARD STREET

All Hallows Church

73

The Bowring
Building

Statue

Tower Place 233

PH

Three Quays

Map 15

Map 16

INDEX

Compiled by J D Lee

Page numbers in *italics* after the names of people are references to sites supervised by them.

This index is preceded by a list of site codes for sites of 1972 and later in alphabetic order.

333